Aspects of Housing Law

Jill Morgan

Routledge·Cavendish
Taylor & Francis Group
LONDON AND NEW YORK

First published 2007 by Routledge-Cavendish
2 Park Square, Milton Park, Abingdon, OX14 4RN, UK

Simultaneously published in the USA and Canada
by Routledge-Cavendish
270 Madison Avenue, New York, NY 10016

Routledge-Cavendish is an imprint of the Taylor & Francis Group, an informa business

© 2007 Jill Morgan

Typeset in Sabon by Exeter Premedia Services Private Ltd, Chennai, India
Printed and bound in Great Britain by TJ International Ltd, Padstow, Cornwall

British Library Cataloguing in Publication Data
A catalogue record for this book is available from the British Library

Library of Congress Cataloging in Publication Data
Morgan, Jill.
Aspects of housing law / Jill Morgan.
   p. cm.
ISBN–13: 978–1–84568–014–5 (pbk. : alk. paper)
ISBN–10: 1–84568–014–6
1. Housing—Law and legislation—Great Britian. 2. Rental
housing—Law and legislation—Great Britian. 3. Landlord and tenant—
Great Britain. 4. Rent control—Law and legislation—Great Britain.
I. Title
   KD1179. M67 2007
   344.41'063635—dc22   2007003818

ISBN 10: 1–84568–014–6
ISBN 13: 978–1–84568–014–5

To my parents, John and Pat Christie

Contents

Preface

The origins of this book lie in an earlier work published by the Blackstone Press in 1998. Since then housing law has continued to develop apace: there have been a number of important cases and several pieces of major legislation, most notably the Human Rights Act 1998, the Homelessness Act 2002, the Anti-social Behaviour Act 2003 and the Housing Act 2004. It has proved almost impossible to keep up with the policy documents and guidance emanating from whichever government department has been responsible for housing at any one time (currently the Department for Communities and Local Government). Some fascinating work has been carried out by the Law Commission which has proposed a radical overhaul of the legal bases on which non-owners occupy their homes. If its Renting Homes Bill ever finds its way onto the statute book, any future edition of this book will be very different indeed.

Aspects of Housing Law is structured quite differently from its predecessor. Part I contains an overview of the four housing tenures. Part II, entitled 'General Concerns', deals with some of the universal issues which affect occupiers: how is the property to be paid for and can the rent be changed or challenged? Who is responsible for repair and maintenance? Can other members of the household carry on living in the property if the original tenant dies? What will happen in the event of homelessness? Parts III and IV cover private renting and social housing respectively.

It has taken far longer to write this book that I anticipated. My thanks are due first and foremost to my husband and colleague, Mark Stallworthy, for his words of wisdom, good humour and wonderful cooking, all of which sustained me while I was writing. Thanks (and apologies too) to Ellie who patiently tolerated a mother who was often present in body but absent in mind. Finally, I should like to thank the staff at Routledge-Cavendish for being so patient.

Jill Morgan
January 2007

Table of cases

Table of statutes

Table of statutory instruments

Part 1

An overview of housing tenure

Chapter 1

An introduction to housing policy and housing law

The functions of housing policy

Housing policy has best been described as consisting of 'measures designed to modify the quality, quantity, price and ownership and control of housing' (Malpass and Murie, 1999: 7). The ways in which policy is put into practice are inevitably matters of political concern. The main objective of housing policy is generally considered to be the provision of 'sufficient affordable housing so that every household enjoys real choice between housing options, each of which offers good physical standards, security of possession, an attractive neighbourhood, convenient location and all at a price or rent that the household can afford' (Merrett, 1992: 48). It is clear, however, that housing policy need not be designed to *improve* security or affordability or housing conditions and that governments sometimes deliberately withhold investment in housing for the benefit of other services such as health and education (Donnison and Ungerson, 1982: 13) or to maintain or reduce levels in the taxation of income.

It is important therefore to recognise that housing does not exist in a vacuum but is affected by – and may be subservient to – other policy areas such as economic policy and personal taxation, the labour market, social security, and social exclusion. Moreover, despite the different political persuasions of successive governments, there is evident a certain commonality and continuity in the rhetoric of their housing policy, its key themes and much of its substance (Cowan and Marsh, 2001: 261). Central government formulates policy and, through legislation, can provide the powers and the financial means for its implementation. However, within the context of housing, the major responsibility for translating policy into action is borne by local authorities, housing associations, building societies, builders, private landlords and others which, as decision- and sometimes policy-making bodies in their own right, are likely to modify central government policy at local level. As a result, 'the impact of new policies is rarely as dramatic as either their advocates hope for or their critics fear' (Donnison and Ungerson, 1982: 161). In addition, the legislation passed to give effect to housing policy will be interpreted and further refined by the courts (which may also point the way for the reform of housing law and a consequent rethinking of housing policy). Over the years, therefore, by a process akin to 'Chinese whispers', an effect quite different from that anticipated by policy-makers and the promoters of the legislation may be produced.

The determinants of housing policy and law

Housing policy (and, therefore, housing law) depends on how housing itself is viewed. At one extreme it can be regarded as a commodity subject to the laws of the market place. As such it will be supplied if and when the supplier anticipates the probability of securing a reasonable return and it will be bought by those able and willing to pay the price which will yield that return. Accordingly, it is given no special treatment to differentiate it from any other commodity; state intervention is limited to 'general regulation guaranteeing the right of ownership and ... freedom of exchange in a capitalistic economy' (Bengtsson, 2001: 262) and no provision is made to give landlords and tenants or lenders and borrowers any rights or obligations over and above those which are contractually agreed (Donnison and Ungerson, 1982: 1). Such a state of affairs has not existed in England and Wales since the middle of the nineteenth century, in recognition of the fact that although housing is indeed something which can be bought and sold, it possesses a number of features which distinguish it from other commodities. First, the housing market differs from other markets insofar as houses and households can move between the ownership market (in which the houses themselves are bought and sold) and the rental market (where only the use of house room is bought and sold). Secondly, the multiplicity of interests which can exist in land is unparalleled compared with other commodities (see Gray and Gray, 2005: 1.13–1.189) and can give rise to complicated property relations. Thirdly, although the law regards the ownership of land as extending up to the heavens and down to the depths of the earth,[1] land is of course non-renewable and there are no new frontiers to explore. Fourthly, because a house is fixed in one place, a person who buys or rents housing is also buying or renting accessibility to employment opportunities, city centre services, the countryside, and so on (Holmans, 1987: 5, 6). Fifthly, houses take a comparatively long time to build, are expensive to produce and, unlike other commodities, they cannot be imported from abroad, even if they can be produced more cheaply overseas (Ivatts, 1988: 198). Sixthly, their durability means that houses retain their value over many years and in real terms their value may actually grow. The heterogeneous nature of housing means that one unit cannot easily be substituted by another (Bengtsson, 2001: 258). Finally, and most importantly, housing

---

1   For an explanation of what this entails, see Gray and Gray (2005: 1.13 *et seq*).

serves one of the most basic human needs. Whether taken separately or together, these factors mean that housing warrants special treatment and its provision should not be left simply to the vagaries of an unregulated market because it would not then be available to all citizens at an acceptable price and quality or with an adequate degree of security (ibid.).

A modified market model has underpinned British social policy for most of the past century under both Labour and Conservative governments, although it has been particularly marked since 1979. Market competition rather than state action has been promoted as the most effective mechanism by which resources can be most efficiently distributed and choice exercised. Adherents of the market model expect people to be self-reliant or, if necessary, to rely on the market, their families, and the generosity and support of other members of their communities, rather than the state. The prevailing liberal economic view has been that the state should confine itself to protecting private property and wealth, enabling people to fend for themselves and creating conditions which help the market to run smoothly. As Bengtsson points out, 'housing policies in most Western countries are best perceived as *the state providing correctives to the housing market*' with housing being regarded as 'an individual good which, as far as possible, should be distributed in accordance with individual consumer preferences' (Bengtsson, 2001: 257). Voluntary contracts formulated within the market – between buyer and seller, between landlord and tenant, and so forth – serve as the main mechanism for distributing housing, while state intervention takes the form of correctives defining the economic and institutional setting of those contracts (Oxley and Smith, 1996: 2–3). Because housing provides opportunities for profit-making and wealth creation, and a system of private property rights lies at the core of capitalist societies, state intervention in housing tends to be regarded as something which should be imposed only in exceptional circumstances when market provision proves defective and then only for particular groups. Direct state support is acknowledged as necessary therefore for the elderly, disabled or very poor, who lack the capacity to compete effectively in a market system but, even then, there is pressure to keep it to a minimum. Such a market philosophy identifies private property with individual freedom and has an overriding aim of minimising public spending in favour of low rates of taxation and the stimulation of enterprise and effort. State incursions on grounds of social protection and equality are viewed with suspicion (see Friedman, 1962). The growth of a large market sector in housing is widely recognised as a reason for depicting housing as part of the welfare state. If so, it occupies a distinct position therein,[2] one which since the late 1970s has been changing in ways which imply a retreat

2   Housing has been described, for example, as the 'wobbly pillar under the welfare state' (Torgerson, 1987: 116) and 'a stillborn social service lodged within a capitalist dynamic of property relations' (Cole and Furbey, 1994: 6).

from other, more entrenched, services which comprise the welfare state. Now, because council housing has come to be seen as the tenure of last resort, it is considered inferior to housing provided by the market. Until recently, a contrast could therefore be drawn with the National Health Service (NHS) and state education which – because they are used by the bulk of the population (even those who can afford to pay for private medical provision, and to send their children to fee-paying schools) – enjoy a level of political (and popular) support that ensures a relatively higher quality service than would be the case if they were used only by the poor. In certain respects, however, housing – no longer to be considered as a major public service – is emerging as a model for the reduction of public spending and the wider restructuring of public services with its emphasis on 'markets, choice, individual responsibility and a strong regulatory role for the centre' (Malpass, 2004: 224). Thus, the past 15 years have witnessed the development of the internal market within the NHS, the introduction of trust status for hospitals and devolved decision-making in schools. Such developments, including what we shall see is arguably the 'privatisation' of council housing, have not, however, meant a withdrawal of the state. Indeed, they have been made possible only by extensive legislative intervention from the centre.

In contrast with the above picture, those broadly on the political left, who subscribe to the social democratic model, take the view that homelessness, overcrowding, disrepair and so on stem from the fundamental inability of the market to produce enough satisfactory housing, especially for the poorer sections of society (Clapham *et al.*, 1990: 28–31). It is argued that 'in all countries of advanced capitalism ... state housing has been introduced after conditions in the private sector have reached the level of human degradation' (Karnavou, 1981: 50–53, 52). Because of the inequalities inherent in, and engendered by, market society, state intervention is regarded as necessary to ensure that there is 'an adequate supply of suitable accommodation at a price which the poorest can afford' (Malpass and Murie, 1999: 4). The provision of housing is thus regarded as a social service, the state deciding how much to supply and how it is allocated. Moreover, the choice offered by the market is viewed as illusory. It may work 'rather more satisfactorily for the better off' but 'tends to establish a close link between poverty and poor housing' (ibid.).

It has been observed that 'discussions on housing policy generally either ignore ... [the] law or regard it as a passive instrument for policy implementation' (Goodchild, 2001: 75). Indeed, there may be conjecture as to whether 'housing law' is in the strictest sense a distinctive area of the law at all, or merely a convenient umbrella term for elements of contract law, landlord and tenant law, tort law and public law as they relate to housing. While the grouping together of legal principles in a certain way may be informative, it will not necessarily reflect any 'penetrating analytical insight into the materials so arranged' or of 'any coherent project that the law self-consciously pursues' (Coyle and Morrow, 2004: 1). The question therefore is whether housing law possesses the 'doctrinal coherence' or 'philosophical underpinning' to exist as an established, free-standing body of law (ibid.). Certainly, housing policy and law have developed in a piecemeal fashion (rather than in terms of dominant motivation and ideologies), moulded by a gradual acceptance that some interference with the free market is necessary. However, although 'the present legislative position has been reached more through a series of political responses to particular social pressures than the acceptance of any statement of principle ... this does not mean ... that the present position cannot be justified in principle' (Law Commission, 2002a: 1.20).

There is much to be said for the application to housing law of the three ideologies identified by McAuslan as competing against each other in the context of planning law. The first – the traditional common law approach to the rule of law – holds that the law exists for the purpose of protecting private property and its institutions. Its roots can be found in the principles developed by the courts in the late nineteenth and early twentieth centuries to provide protection for urban landowners against government action to improve the terrible living conditions of the new urban working classes. McAuslan explains that because, well into the nineteenth century, the lawful exercise of political power was inextricably linked with the possession and ownership of land, the protection of private property also involved a defence of the constitutional order. Moreover, 'it was the property owners who used the courts and it was in the resolution of their disputes that the common law was formed' (McAuslan, 1980: 3). In contrast to nuisance law and the law on easements and restrictive covenants, housing law (much of which originates in statute) has not grown organically 'through the courts' response to changing social conditions' and can be vulnerable to interpretation in such ways as interfere as little as possible with the interests of the land-owner.

The basis of the second ideology – the orthodox public administration approach – is that the law exists and should be used to advance the public interest, if necessary against 'the selfish interests of the private landowner' (McAuslan, 1980: 4). It manifests itself in laws which confer extensive powers on administrators to do as they see fit. Traditionally they either provided no redress or appeal or redress within the administrative system only, e.g. an appeal from a lower administrator to a higher one, the presumption being that public officials act in good faith and 'in the final analysis [are] accountable to Parliament for their actions and policies' (ibid). The housing legislation which proliferated throughout the twentieth century was largely motivated by and constructed in accordance with the public interest ideology but the courts have constantly oscillated between 'their desire to reassert the rights of private property against the all-pervading bureaucracy and their sense of obligation to uphold the lawfully constituted authority of government' (ibid.: 5). Moreover, so far as housing law is concerned, particularly that which concerns the control and allocation of council housing (including the law on homelessness), the presumption that 'public officials act in good faith' has often operated to the detriment of applicants, with the courts being reluctant to interfere with the decisions which local authorities have reached.

The third ideology – the radical or populist approach – envisages the law as a vehicle for the advancement of public participation in the housing system, 'not by virtue of the ownership of property but by virtue of the more abstract principles of democracy and justice' (McAuslan, 1980: 5). It involves greater attention being paid to 'social, community and ecological factors in decision-making and less attention paid to economic and technological factors which assume or are geared to reproducing the same kind of society that exists at present' (ibid.: 6). So far, there are few such examples in housing law (despite the attempts during the 1980s and 1990s to achieve tenant empowerment). Yet it may be that the Law Commission's proposals as regards the simplification and reform of the law relating to existing forms of housing tenancies may pave the way for a radical rethinking of the basis on which housing is occupied, given its attempt to move away from the property-based perspective of the landlord and tenant/occupier relationship.

Housing law, house and home

A 'consumer perspective' of rented housing (or, at least its legal regulation) lies at the heart of the Law Commission's proposals. This involves the conceptualisation of housing law as a branch of consumer law with the contract as the key component of the landlord-occupier relationship. While such an approach would appear to signal a return to the pre Rent Acts position and to leave occupiers vulnerable to exploitation by landlords, the Commission emphasises that the terms of the contract will be mediated by provisions on unfair terms. Thus all landlords and occupiers will have a written statement of their contract, setting out their rights and obligations, including those provided for by the Rented Homes Bill (Law Commission, 2006). The intention is to make a break with past 'legislative strategy' that has involved landlords and tenants entering into contractual arrangements which are then substantially ignored 'as details in the agreement are overridden by statute' (Law Commission, 2002a: 1.33). The development of legislation over the last 30 years to ensure the fairness of the terms on which consumers contract means that there can now be 'a much clearer focus on ensuring that the terms on which homes are rented are fair from the outset, rather than suspecting that they may be unfair and creating statutory provisions to enable them to be ignored' (ibid.).

There are a number of jurisdictions (notably Canada, Australia, and New Zealand) in which the courts have been prepared to apply contract rules to leases, albeit within a property paradigm, and the question of whether – and, if so, to what extent – the landlord and tenant relationship should be confined to property law principles has been the subject of extensive debate for a number of years. However, consumer-based arguments have failed to bear much fruit in the context of housing law. Thus, in *Dunn v Bradford Metropolitan District Council* [2003] HLR 15, in holding that s. 13 of the Supply of Goods and Services Act 1982 did not place a duty on a local authority to carry out repairs which it was not contractually obliged to do, Chadwick LJ said that:

> in recognising the tenant's right to occupy the premises, the landlord is doing no more than giving effect to [the] grant; the landlord is not carrying out a service … but is simply respecting existing property rights. Even if it can be said that in granting tenancies in respect of its housing stock, a local authority is carrying out a service … that service ends when the tenancy is granted. Thereafter the landlord's obligations are found in the terms of the tenancy.
>
> (At para. 52.)

More recently, however, the Court of Appeal confirmed in *London Borough of Newham v Khatun* [2005] QB 37 that the Unfair Terms in Consumer Contracts Regulations 1999 (which implement EU Directive 93/13/EEC) apply to contracts dealing with interests in or rights of occupation over land (including tenancy agreements) and that local authorities must conform with Regulations with regard to the standard terms upon which they let accommodation (even where they are under a statutory duty to supply it). The Court of Appeal held that when acting in a business capacity (e.g. as landlords), local authorities are 'sellers' or 'suppliers' of the relevant consumer item (namely accommodation) and tenants are 'consumers' (even where they are in receipt of benefit). Laws LJ recognised that some tenants or prospective tenants are especially vulnerable people and for most consumers the acquisition of a home is a key event in their lives. While acknowledging that transfers of houses are most often effected between consumers rather than between a consumer and a trader, he noted that it is common for tenancies to be granted by landlords who are in business. He was unable therefore to perceive any rationale for the exclusion of land transactions from the legislation's scope. The decision would appear therefore to signal an important step forward as regards the assimilation of consumerist principles within the landlord and tenant relationship or (as the Law Commission would have it), the 'landlord and occupier' relationship.

It has been suggested that the term 'housing' law was initially chosen for convenience sake, focusing at first on the 'external' rights of those who were already housed against another person or an organisation and only recently on the importance of 'home' (Cowan, 1999: 22–3). Throughout its development, however, housing law can be said gradually to have embraced more and more of what is generally regarded as constituting a home: physical structure, territory, a centre for self-identity, and a social and cultural phenomenon (Fox, 2002: 590). The physical structure (which in legal terms can be translated into the socio-economic right to adequate housing) involves the provision of material shelter: a place which is 'dry and warm and in reasonable repair' (Archbishop of Canterbury's Commission on Urban Priority Areas, 1985: 230) and which offers protection against the elements, and intrusions from nature and from other people (Buyse, 2006: 294). Although it can be or become a place of danger (because of domestic violence or sexual or other abuse), the 'territorial' aspect of home provides 'the spatial framework for the occupier's life' and, by fostering 'a sense of belonging, rootedness and community' (Fox, 2002: 593), can promote emotional and social well-being. A sufficient degree of privacy is needed in order to provide 'a place where people can grow, make choices, become more whole people' (Archbishop of Canterbury's Commission on Urban Priority Areas, 1985: 230). Home as a centre for self-identity – which relies upon a level of confidence about being able to stay in one place – gives a person an opportunity to express ideas and values, and acts also an indicator of personal status. Its role as a 'social and cultural phenomenon' serves as the setting for relationships with family and friends.

The needs served by housing are complex and constantly changing as cultural and living standards evolve and households grow and disperse (Donnison and Ungerson, 1982: 11). Further, it is difficult to regard people as being 'fully included in society and ... able to enjoy their citizenship rights' unless they have adequate housing (Pawson and Kintrea, 2002: 646). Such concerns may explain the 'renewed policy focus' and 'arousal of academic interest in homelessness as a blatant source of exclusion' (ibid.) – and why, therefore, a book on housing law can and should include coverage of the law as it relates to homelessness.

From a legal perspective, the meaning of the term 'home' has been the subject of significant judicial consideration in recent years, with the infusion into English law, via the Human Rights Act 1998, of the rights contained in the European Convention on Human Rights (ECHR). Of most obvious significance in the housing context is Art. 8(1) which provides everyone with 'the right to respect for his private and family life, his home and his correspondence'. Compared to most other Convention rights, the right to respect for the home has been the subject of relatively few applications to Strasbourg. The first specific case on what constituted a 'home' for the purposes of Art. 8 was *Gillow v United Kingdom* (1986) 11 EHRR 335. Here, the applicants built a house in Guernsey which they occupied for five years until they moved abroad to work. When they returned, 18 years later, they were refused permission to occupy the house under Guernsey's licensing system and were subsequently prosecuted for unlawful occupation. The European Court of Human Rights (ECtHR) held that they had no home elsewhere in the UK and – despite their absence – had retained 'sufficient continuing links' with the house (because of their prior occupation, the fact that they owned the house, had kept their furniture in it and intended to live there permanently after their return) for it to be considered their 'home' for the purposes of Art. 8. The test of 'sufficient and continuing links' was applied and expanded upon in *Buckley v United Kingdom* (1997) 23 EHRR 101, para. 63 in which the ECtHR made it clear that 'home' within the meaning of Art. 8 is an 'autonomous concept' which does not depend on classification under domestic law (thus rendering irrelevant in this context the English law notions of tenancy, licence or trespass) and is 'not limited to those which are lawfully occupied or which have been lawfully established'. In *Harrow London Borough Council v Qazi* [2004] 1 AC 983, Lord Bingham said that the Convention's use of the expression 'home' appeared to invite a 'down-to-earth and pragmatic consideration' as to whether the place in question was where a person 'lives and to which he returns and which forms the centre of his existence' (*Uratemp Ventures v Collins* [2002] 1 AC 310, para. 31). In *O'Rourke v United Kingdom* (Application No 39022/97 (unreported) 26 June 2001) the ECtHR expressed 'significant doubts' as to whether a person's links with a hotel room which he had occupied for just over a month were sufficient and continuous enough to make it his 'home' at the time of his eviction.

While the lawfulness (or otherwise) of the occupation is not an issue in determining whether there is a 'home' for the purposes of Art. 8(1), it will be relevant in relation to Art. 8(2) by which an interference with the primary right may be justifiable because it is 'in accordance with the law and ... necessary in a democratic society ... for the protection of the rights and freedoms of others'. In assessing the necessity of any interference, a balance has to be struck between the interests of the community and those of the individual.

In *Harrow London Borough Council v Qazi* [2004] 1 AC 983, the House of Lords took the view that Art. 8 'was intended to deal with the arbitrary intrusion by the State or public authorities into a citizen's home life' and not 'to operate as an amendment or improvement of whatever social housing legislation the signatory state had chosen to enact' (para. 89). It has been so used, however, both by the ECtHR (see e.g. *Larkos v Cyprus* (2000) 30 EHRR 59) and by the House of Lords itself (see e.g. *Ghaidan v Godin-Mendoza* [2004] 2 AC 557) and to assume that the intended scope of the Convention crystallised at the time of its inception overlooks its character as an inherently 'living instrument which ... must be interpreted in the light of present day conditions' (*Tyrer v United Kingdom* (1978) 2 EHRR 1, para. 31). It is clear however that Art. 8 does not give a right to be provided with a home (*Chapman v United Kingdom* (2001) 33 EHRR 399) nor does it guarantee to have one's housing problems solved by the authorities (*Marzari v Italy* (1999) 28 EHRR 175).

Housing tenure in England and Wales

There are four main types of tenure in Great Britain: owner-occupation, council renting, housing association renting and private renting, and Table 1.1

Table 1.1 Housing tenure in England and Wales

	Rented from private landlords (%)	Rented from local authorities and new towns (%)	Rented from housing associations (%)	Owner-occupied (%)
1914	90	negligible		10
1953	50	18		32
1971	20	28	1	
1981	11	30	2	57
1991	9	20	3	68
2005	12	11	7	71

shows how their fortunes have waxed and waned over the past century. It will be observed that the most dramatic changes have occurred with the decline of the private rented sector and the growth of owner-occupation. It has been argued that private renting was a mode of provision which was appropriate in the nineteenth century when the new urban working class earned low wages and had little opportunity to save. Renting thus enabled them to obtain access to an essential commodity which they could not afford to buy outright. The decline of the private rented sector is said to reflect its economic obsolescence, with home ownership being a more appropriate form of housing provision in the context of twentieth (and twenty-first) century capitalism, given the substantial and sustained growth in the real income of the working population (Malpass and Murie, 1999: 11–12). It is quite true that the expansion of home ownership has been possible only because of an increase in real incomes. But that is only part of the story. As is explained in Chapter 3, the move to home ownership could not have occurred without the ready availability of mortgage finance, the capacity to sustain a mortgage depending on greater stability in employment than that enjoyed by a large part of the working population in the nineteenth century. Furthermore, the growth in owner-occupation as an alternative to private renting was politically determined and, to a large extent, made possible by financial incentives such as favourable tax treatment.

Tenure gives an indication of the terms on which households occupy their homes, but each one is far more complex than the labels imply. Owner-occupation will be a very different experience for someone who has recently taken out a large mortgage to buy a converted flat in a run-down inner city area, compared with a person who owns outright an executive detached residence in the provinces. In addition, the boundaries between the tenures are sometimes blurred, e.g. long leases. Moreover, a major misconception about housing in Great Britain is that the private sector depends wholly on the market, while the public sector depends wholly on state intervention. In fact, both private and public sectors receive state support and use private institutions to meet their needs. Public housing is really only publicly managed; it is not financed out of taxation but from loans – usually borrowed for long periods at fixed rates of interest – from a variety of sources: financial institutions, the government's Public Works Loan Board, companies and individuals. While local authorities have acted as developers to produce public housing, most local authority dwellings were in fact 'built by private contractors, with privately produced materials on land bought from private owners with capital borrowed from private financial institutions' (Malpass and Murie, 1999: 6). Housing associations are also increasingly involved in building for sale. In the private sector, rents are effectively underwritten by housing benefit in many cases and support has been given to owner-occupation by the tax system. Indeed, since 1945, there have been substantial areas of broad inter-party consensus. Between the 1950s and the early 1970s, both Conservative and Labour governments extended owner-occupation and council housing. In the early 1950s, the Conservatives even facilitated the construction of more council dwellings than owner-occupied houses, whilst under Labour in the mid-1960s and late 1970s more private sector houses were started than council properties. Until 1979, both parties agreed that council housing should be a 'general needs' tenure. Since then, however, public investment has fallen dramatically, the building of council houses has all but completely dried up, and the prevailing policy – shared by both Conservative and Labour governments alike – has been the promotion of owner-occupation.

Legislators have tended to treat each tenure separately 'as if each was an independent entity unaffected by and unaffecting events and processes in other tenures' (Doling and Davies, 1984: 7) and, for the sake of clarity and convenience, this book is to some extent guilty of the same offence. However, it is important to recognise that changes in one part of the housing system can affect the others. The plea has been made that government should make a break with the 'tenure fetishism' of the past and that all tenures should be regarded as 'legitimate vehicles in eradicating housing poverty' (Merrett, 1992: 48).

Social trends

The realignment in housing tenure has occurred in the context of important social trends and it has become clear that reliance on market-oriented policies is seriously limited, given the pattern of housing needs, general levels of income and demographic factors – notably the rate at which new households are being formed. In England, household formation has been estimated at 179,000 per annum, yet in 2002 only 134,000 extra homes were built (see Barker, 2004: 1.16–17). The number of households in Great Britain has increased significantly over recent decades, partly because households now contain fewer people. The average household size fell from 2.9 in 1971 to 2.4 in 2003 and there has been a particularly large increase in the number of people living alone (29 per cent in 2003, compared with 18 per cent in 1971). While, over the same period, the population has increased by 6 per cent, the number of households has increased by 31 per cent (National Statistics, 2004: 25–27).

These changes in the size and number of households can be attributed to a number of factors. They include increased longevity, together with a desire among older people to continue to live independently rather than with relatives or in institutions, a decline in the birth rate, and a move on the part of many younger people to establish separate households either as single people or with other unrelated adults (the decision to marry being made later in life – or not at all) (Marsh, 1998: 2). The picture is further complicated by the rise in divorce rates and an increased incidence of relationship breakdown among cohabiting couples. There has been a decrease however in the proportion of households containing the traditional family unit and an increase in the proportion of one-parent families. Today, fewer than 40 per cent of households fit the model of the conventional nuclear family and yet it is arguable that housing policy has only just begun to come to terms with the shift in the foundations of British family life which these figures represent.

In sum, government projections for England for a 20-year period to 2016 suggest expectation of an increase of in excess of four million households requiring to be housed. This represents an increase of around 23 per cent (DoE, 1996a). The main reason for the increase is a demographic one, not accounted for by population alone. An increase in population of around 7 per cent, or 3.4 million, is expected for the quarter-century 1996–2021, whilst over that same period the number of households is anticipated to grow from a figure of around 20 million to over 24 million (DETR, 2000b: 2.3).

Despite the growing number of new households the supply of new housing has fallen with house building for all tenures at its lowest peacetime level for decades (DCLG, 2007a: Table 201). There are two primary reasons for this: first, council housing is no longer being built (and building by housing associations is not making up for the deficit); and, secondly, private sector building is producing a supply side shortfall, which it is argued is largely a consequence of development planning controls imposed by the state (Barker, 2006: Ch. 1).

The geographically uneven pattern of economic growth means that a greater proportion of the additional households are to be found in the south than in the north. Between 1996 and 2001 the average annual increase in households in England was almost 200,000, but this comprised a growth of 136,000 households in London, the south east, the south west and the east of England, compared to only 64,000 in all the other six regions together (Stewart, 2002). However, more new homes have been built in the north of

England than extra households formed. Problems of low demand and even abandonment in the least popular areas have followed. A result has been greater social polarization, with many poorer people trapped on housing estates in the most deprived urban areas. By contrast, in southern England the number of extra homes has fallen significantly short of the increase in households. The deficit has been by far the largest in London.

The housing shortage has coincided with significant changes in employment. Although the UK has recently experienced the lowest unemployment for a quarter of a century and now compares favourably with other large economies, one of the key legacies of the last 25 years has been the polarisation between dual earner households and no earner households (Stephens *et al.*, 2005: 2.17). Indeed, the government accepts that since the 1980s, the UK 'has seen a rise in income inequality almost unique among developed countries' (UK Government, 1999: 7.13). Over the same period, there has been a redistribution of work opportunities from men to women, but also from the unskilled and less educated to those possessing educational and professional qualifications. Long-term economic decline, together with the impact of industrial obsolescence and new technology, has combined to produce a larger pool of people who are permanently or semi-permanently unemployed. These 'marginalised poor' can be found in all tenures but tend to be concentrated in social housing whose occupants 'possess disproportionately the characteristics (such as low skill levels and poor health) that make them vulnerable to worklessness' (Stephens *et al.*, 2005: 2.18). In 2003/4, two-thirds of local authority and housing association households recorded no earning member (Wilcox, 2005: Table 34). The increase in the 'equity divide' has led to greater distance between the 'haves' and the 'have nots'. Between 1970 and 2001, the value of the net equity of personally owned housing increased from £36 billion to £1,525 billion. After allowing for inflation, the index of the real growth of gross assets in personally owned housing rose from 62.6 in 1970, to 100 in 1980 and to 329 in 2000 (Burrows, 2003).

The reduction in the number of homes which has been built for rent over the past 25 years by social landlords has produced longer waiting lists for social housing and more 'hidden homelessness'. Most significant perhaps, has been the huge growth in the number of homeless households in temporary accommodation in Great Britain, from fewer than 5,000 in 1980, to around 60,000 in 1995 and to a record number of more 135,000 in 2004 (Wilcox, 2005: Tables 90, 91a, 91b). Homelessness figures showed a 20 per cent increase between 1997 and 2003. The fall in the number of new lettings available to local authorities (either directly or through nominations to housing associations), lower output from the Housing Corporation programme, loss of council stock through the right to buy, and fewer moves out of the public sector because of increasing house prices, have all contributed to the problem of homelessness, which is particularly acute in London (where almost half of the households in temporary accommodation – around 67,000 – are to be found) and the south east of England.

Chapter 2

Homelessness: definitions, causes and historical context

Introduction

Although there is, in crude terms, a surplus of housing in England,[1] much of it is situated in areas where there is no work, and many properties stand empty because they are either dilapidated or in serious disrepair. Others await incoming tenants or purchasers, or are second homes. However, despite this housing surplus, there is nevertheless a serious housing shortage, which is particularly pronounced in London and the south east of England. In 2004–5 there were 90,000 fewer housing completions in the UK than in 1975. Thus, in 2004–5, 183,933 new homes in the private sector (i.e. for owner occupation) were completed, compared with 22,716 new housing association homes and 131 local authority homes (DCLG, 2007b: Table 201). In 1975, the figures were 129,883, 14,693 and 150,752 respectively (DoE, 1986: Table 6.1). It has been estimated that an annual increase in supply of 70,000 private homes is required to reduce the trend in real house prices to 1.8 per cent and 17,000 social homes to meet the needs arising from the continued increase in the number of households (Barker, 2004: 1.41). Even if plans were to be put in place immediately to make good the shortfall, it would take many years to achieve the desired outcome, owing to strict planning regulations, lack of suitable and available land, the time involved in completing the construction work, and insufficient skilled workers.

In the meantime, Part 4 of the Housing Act 2004 empowers local authorities to make empty dwelling management orders (EDMOs) in order to take over the management of long-term empty properties and to bring them back into occupation. There are two forms of order: interim and final. Crucially, whereas an interim order only allows the authority to let out the dwelling with the proprietor's consent, a final order allows it to let it out without

---

1   According to the 2001 Census, the total number of empty homes (or 'vacant dwellings') in all tenures in England stood at 977,000 (3.7 per cent of the total stock). Even in the economically powerful London and south east sub-region, there are estimated to be 70,000 private empty houses: see Kennedy, M., *The Guardian*, 27 November 2003.

such consent. Before making an interim EDMO, the authority must obtain the authorisation of the residential property tribunal (s. 134). The authority must have made reasonable efforts to notify proprietors that it is considering making an order and to ascertain what steps (if any) they are taking (or propose to take) to secure that their dwellings are occupied.

The first part of this chapter explores different perceptions of homelessness and the extent of the homelessness problem. It then takes a long-term view, tracing the slow development of state intervention in homelessness, from the early days of the Poor Law through to the Homelessness Act 2002.

Definitions of homelessness

Housing can be viewed as a continuum with outright, mortgage-free ownership at one end and sleeping rough at the other. In between is a large grey area which includes hostels, residential hotels, staying with friends and relatives, licences and insecure tenancies in the private rented sector, accommodation provided by employers, protected and assured tenancies, mortgaged accommodation, and tenancies granted by housing associations and local authorities. The definition of homelessness that is chosen (i.e. where the line of homelessness is drawn on this continuum), has implications for housing policy and provision. Obviously the further it is drawn from the 'rooflessness' end of the continuum, the larger the problem appears to be (Watson, 1986: 9, 13).

Homelessness is a socially determined and relative concept, definitions of which change with the passage of time and depend on, e.g. the availability of housing generally and the quality of that housing. Mention has already been made in Chapter 1 of the different approaches taken to housing by those who advocate a market-oriented approach towards welfare provision and those who favour the social democratic model. As regards homelessness, the former may incline to 'favour an absolute definition that ends towards rooflessness' (Clapham, 1990: 115). The latter 'extend the concept further along the continuum to embrace a more relative definition in which homelessness begins once the social rights associated with shelter are infringed upon' and might regard as homeless, for example, a woman living in an unsatisfactory relationship who wants to leave her home but cannot afford to do so, or a person living in housing that is in a poor state of repair or lacks certain basic amenities (ibid.). The statutory definition of homeless (now contained in s. 175 of the Housing Act 1996) was originally to be found towards the narrower end of the spectrum although it did provide that a person would be homeless if he or she had accommodation but it was probable that occupation of that accommodation would lead to domestic violence or threats of violence. The definition was further extended as a result of the House of Lords decision in *R v Hillingdon London Borough Council ex p Pulhofer* [1986] AC 484 so that regard may now be had to whether it is reasonable for the applicant to continue to occupy existing accommodation (see Chapter 10). There is, therefore, no universally accepted definition of homelessness, but the recognised definitions have been identified as follows (Robson and Poustie, 1996: 10–16).

Rooflessness

This, the narrowest definition – which equates homelessness with sleeping rough – was the definition accepted by government until the early 1970s (Robson and Poustie, 1996: 11). A proposal to restore this narrow definition in the Housing Act 1996 (see DoE, 1994: 5, 8) was dropped at Committee Stage. The single homeless and childless couples are most likely to be roofless, as households with children are generally able to secure accommodation of some sort, even though it may be unsatisfactory.

Houselessness

This definition includes not only those who sleep rough but also those who occupy:

- emergency accommodation; or
- accommodation which is not strictly of an emergency nature but offers little more than a bed;
- accommodation which (for a limited period) provides special support; and
- other forms of short stay accommodation such as night shelters, local authority reception centres, model lodging houses, working men's hostels, alcoholic recovery units.

Pressure groups such as MIND have argued that the definition of 'homelessness' should include people who are admitted to mental hospitals and other long-term institutions simply because they have nowhere else to go. Such people may find themselves on a 'circuit of homelessness' which also embraces prisons, sleeping rough and night shelters. The policy of care in the community of the mentally ill (especially since the passing of the National Health Service and Community Care Act 1990) has shifted the problem: people are no longer detained in hospital and some may be 'discharged to unsupported families or left to fend for themselves ... Homelessness or prison have become the unacceptable outcomes for growing numbers of discharged people' (Braisby et al., 1988: 5). Even where housing authorities accept former psychiatric patients for re-housing, the lack of follow-up support and the consequent inability to cope may lead to their either being evicted as difficult tenants, or abandoning their tenancies of their own accord.

Insecure accommodation

This definition includes those with no or limited security of tenure, e.g. occupying squats, 'holiday' or out of season lets, or tied accommodation, living with relatives, sharing with the landlord, residing in lodgings or under licences or non-exclusive occupation agreements (see Chapters 12 and 13).

Intolerable housing conditions

For some time, Shelter has argued that the definition of homelessness should include people who live in overcrowded accommodation or accommodation which is unsatisfactory in that it lacks basic amenities such as a hot water supply, fixed bath or inside WC, or is unacceptably damp (Bailey and Ruddock, 1972: 9). This definition acknowledges the importance of a 'home' in providing accommodation of a decent standard. To some extent it is recognised by s. 175(3) of the Housing Act 1996 which provides that 'a person shall not be treated as having accommodation unless it is accommodation which it would be reasonable for him to continue to occupy'. The physical conditions of the property which an applicant for housing has vacated may also be taken into account in deciding whether s/he left it intentionally. Further, s. 167(2)(a) of the Act obliges local authorities to give reasonable preference in the allocation of accommodation to 'people occupying insanitary or overcrowded housing or otherwise living in unsatisfactory housing conditions'. However, a household will not automatically be regarded as 'homeless' simply because it occupies unsatisfactory accommodation. In 1991, some 1.5 million dwellings in England (7.6 per cent of the total housing stock) were found to be unfit for human habitation (DoE, 1993). Even though, by 2001, the number had fallen to 885,000, i.e. 4.2 per cent of the total stock (Wilcox, 2005: Table 23b), the extension of the official definition of homelessness to people falling in this category would impose an intolerable burden on local authorities.

Causes of homelessness

As indicated by Table 2.1, the reasons officially given for homelessness have been fairly consistent. It should be noted, however, that the immediate cause of homelessness tends to mask the fact that it is actually the result of complex processes operating at different levels. Since 1979, government reliance on market-oriented policies, including the virtual cessation of council-house building and the introduction of the right to buy scheme, has resulted in a critical shortage of decent, affordable accommodation, a situation which is progressively worsening, especially given the rate at which new households are being formed (see Barker, 2004). Changes in the legal regulation of the private rented sector since 1988 mean that those living within it are most

Table 2.1 Reasons for homelessness in England

	1989	1994	1999	2004
Parent(s), relative(s) or friends no longer able/willing to accommodate	43	34	28	38
Breakdown of relationship with partner	17	20	24	20
Loss of private dwelling, including tied accommodation	16	19	22	18
Mortgage arrears	6	8	5	2
Rent arrears	5	2	3	2
Other	13	16	19	20

Source: Adapted from ODPM, Homelessness statistics.

likely to have assured shorthold tenancies which carry virtually no security of tenure, with homelessness being a possible outcome when those tenancies come to an end. Factors such as low wages, unemployment, changing patterns of work, and cuts in entitlement to welfare benefits not only make it increasingly difficult to obtain and to maintain housing, but also interact to create preconditions of homelessness. Social and health factors (including mental illness, drug misuse and alcohol problems), life-cycle and personal crises (including relationship breakdown and debt) cause some people to be more vulnerable to those preconditions.

Who are the homeless?

Some MPs who contributed to the debates on the Housing (Homeless Persons) Bill viewed the homeless as queue-jumpers, feckless or nomadic Scots and Irish. Men are more likely than women to be long-term homeless and many single homeless also suffer from physical or mental disabilities and drug or alcohol problems. Rough sleepers often come from poor or disadvantaged backgrounds, and have spent part of their childhood in care. They may have experienced sexual abuse, domestic violence, bereavement or family or relationship breakdown (Fitzpatrick and Kennedy, 2001: 557). Otherwise, homelessness is experienced by people from all walks of life.

A mythology has developed that homelessness is caused by the irresponsible behaviour of homeless people themselves. Charges are made that young people flock to London and the south-east of England from other parts of the country, encouraged by 'overliberal' housing and social security policies, families deliberately make themselves homeless so that they can jump the social housing queue, and teenage girls get themselves pregnant in order to obtain council housing. The real causes of homelessness are masked by these 'pejorative stereotypes and myths' which stigmatise homeless people and dismiss them as undeserving and sees more responsible behaviour is both as 'a prevention and a cure' for homelessness (Greve, 1991: 30).

Home ownership has spread more widely among income groups, but to the detriment of people who are single and separating, especially women (Gilroy, 1994), and a disproportionate number of the statutorily homeless in England are female lone parents (38 per cent). The statutory provisions on priority need (see Chapter 10) have traditionally meant that 'pregnancy and parenthood' are 'privileged' but the way in which local authorities define housing need means that two-parent families are more likely to obtain accommodation via the waiting list while one-parent families are 'driven into homelessness' (Pascall and Morley, 1996: 196–7). The Conservative government seized upon the phenomenon of young single mothers entering social housing in the later part of 1993 as part of its Back to Basics campaign. The fundamental change in policy towards the homeless latched on to the 'moral panic' generated by this campaign and led eventually to the Housing Act 1996 (Cowan and Fionda, 1994: 613).

The extent of the homelessness problem

Since the Housing (Homeless Persons) Act 1977 was passed, the number of households accepted for rehousing by local authorities increased each year until 1993.

The statistics show only those who are accepted by local authorities as 'statutorily homeless' under the homelessness legislation. Yet there are a great many people who are not rehoused by local authorities, either because they do not bother to apply in the first place or, if they do, because they do not fall into one of the priority need groups. Homeless single (non-elderly) people and childless couples are not usually provided with accommodation under the legislation. These 'able-bodied' households are expected to be able to fend for themselves in the market place (Clapham, 1990: 137). The precise number of households affected by this so-called 'access crisis' is unknown.

Table 2.2 Local authority homeless acceptances

Year	England	Wales	Scotland	Great Britain
1980	62,920	5,446	7,976	76,342
1985	93,980	5,371	11,972	111,323
1990	145,800	9,963	15,813	163,809
1995	122,410	9,001	16,900	148,311
2000	120,200	4,666		
2004	141,400	10,992		

Sources: ODPM, Scottish Executive, National Assembly for Wales.

There are also the 'hidden homeless' who occupy inadequate or overcrowded accommodation.

In 2004, the proportion of those households statutorily rehoused but placed in temporary accommodation rose for the eighth year running to 101,000, 60 per cent of whom were in London. The three main types of temporary accommodation are bed and breakfast, hostels and private sector leasing (PSL). PSL is a scheme under which housing is leased by local authorities from private landlords under short, fixed term leases (for a maximum of three years) and the authorities then sub-let it to homeless households on a non-secure basis. A second type of PSL is the Housing Associations as Managing Agents (HAMA) scheme, under which housing associations lease properties from private owners for reletting to local authorities for the accommodation of homeless households. PSL was pioneered as an alternative form of temporary housing in the 1970s by a handful of councils such as Eastbourne, and the London boroughs began to make substantial use of it in the late 1980s. While PSL may well have provided a high standard of accommodation a few years ago, it is likely that its recent rapidly increased usage has led to a lower standard of property being leased.

The use of bed and breakfast as temporary accommodation for families has been widely criticised as being detrimental to health, safety, general well-being and the children's education. It is also expensive. In March 2002 the government set a target to end the use of bed and breakfast hotels for families with children, except in emergencies, and even then for no more than six weeks. Since then the number of families with children living in bed and breakfast has dropped from 6,700 to 1,680 (as at the end of December 2003), of whom 55 per cent had been resident for more than six weeks. The Homelessness (Suitability of Accommodation) (England) Order 2003, which came into force on 1 April 2004, applies to applicants with 'family commitments' who are pregnant or with whom a pregnant woman or dependent children reside or might reasonably be expected to reside. It provides that, where accommodation is made available for occupation in discharge of certain of a local authority's duties under the homelessness legislation, bed and breakfast accommodation is not to be regarded as suitable unless (a) only bed and breakfast accommodation is available for occupation; and (b) the applicant occupies it for a period, or a total of periods, which does not exceed six weeks.

The historical context

The Poor Law

State intervention to assist the poor, including the homeless, originated in the sixteenth century. First, begging was authorised, then gifts for the succour of the needy were encouraged and then, in 1563, parishes were allowed to introduce a weekly tax for the same purpose. The Elizabethan Poor Law, administered by JPs, Overseers of the Poor, and vestry officials, established a dual structure of poor relief: domiciliary (or 'outdoor') relief for families who continued to live in the community, and institutional care (Glastonbury, 1971: 27). The poor fell into two groups: the 'impotent' poor, such as the very old, the very young, the sick, the crippled, the blind and the insane, who were in no position to maintain themselves, and the 'able-bodied' poor who had no work (Longmate, 1974: 14). Whether or not help would be forth-coming depended on whether the poor or homeless person was a local citizen with a right to settle in the district (Donnison, 1982: 264). Each parish had a duty under the Poor Law to maintain its own aged and infirm and to provide the able-bodied with means of making a livelihood, if necessary main-taining them in the workhouse (Gaudie, 1974: 33). Those who had no right to settle in the district could be punished or ejected under the Vagrancy Acts. Both central and local authorities regarded vagrants as 'the lowest of the undeserving poor' (Wood, 1991: 127) and successive statutes, from 1531 onwards, empowered parish officials to deal with them by, e.g. having them tied to the tail of a cart and whipped 'until the blood streams from their bodies' (see *Ledwith v Roberts* [1937] 1 KB 232, 271–6). These statutes were strictly applied as increased poverty and a growing popu-lation made the Poor Law system unworkable 'or rather, made it so much resented by those on whom fell the burden of paying the poor-rates, that they were unwilling to maintain it efficiently or interpret it charitably' (Gauldie, 1974: 33).

The Poor Law Amendment Act 1834 took the administration of the Poor Law out of the hands of parish officials and passed it to a central authority. The Act aimed drastically to reduce outdoor relief by allowing help only to those willing to enter the workhouse. Supporting a family in its own home cost less than providing it with minimal standards of care in an institution, but it increased the demand for relief, and led to accusations that the system was being exploited by those who were in no real need of funds (Glastonbury, 1971: 28). In accordance with the principle of 'less eligibility', conditions in workhouses were deliberately made worse than those of the poorest labourer outside. It was believed that 'every penny bestowed that tends to render the condition of the pauper more eligible than that of the independent worker is a bounty on indolence and vice' (*Report of the Royal Commission on the Poor Laws*, quoted in Wood, 1991: 68). Such punitive measures were designed to separate the indigent from the working poor. The workhouse system was intended to encourage self-help. While those who were genuinely desperate would enter the workhouse rather than starve, 'those who were not in such straits would prefer to remain independent and thus avoid contracting the morally wasting disease of pauperism' (Rose, 1971: 8). The workhouse became known as a 'refuge for undesir-ables' and being an inmate carried a considerable stigma. The attempt to put the 1834 Act into operation and 'the fear of the workhouse ... was an important step in driving the country poor into the towns, there to increase the overcrowding, the unemployment and the disease of fast-growing town populations' (Gauldie, 1974: 68).

Under the new Poor Law, the punishment of vagrants took a different form from that previously inflicted upon them. They were put in the casual wards – the dirtiest accommodation which often lacked even the most basic facilities. Such meagre assistance as there was – bare boards and a diet of bread and gruel – had to been earned, e.g. by breaking stones, grinding corn or picking oakum. Only when they had completed their appointed tasks were they to be released to search for work elsewhere. A casual had to move on after two nights to another ward, often a considerable distance away.

While the harsh and unattractive conditions were intended to act as a deterrent, the workhouse did provide shelter, clothing, regular food and companionship. The census of 1911 recorded a population of 258,000 people in the Poor Law institutions of England and Wales. These included 25 per cent of all single men and 5 per cent all single women aged 65 or over (Donnison and Ungerson, 1982: 264). This widespread reliance on the work-house is not surprising, given the social conditions prevailing at the time. Only very limited welfare provision existed for older people, the unemployed, sick and disabled. The labour market was subject to marked seasonal and cyclical fluctuations. The bulk of the population lived in the private rented sector and it was common for tenants to be evicted for non-payment of rent (Wohl, 1977). The first public sector house-building schemes in Britain were deliberately not directed towards the needs of the poor and the home-less. They aimed instead to provide housing for the families of industrious artisans who would be able to afford the, generally unrebated, rents charged for the accommodation (see Chapter 4). The concept of a 'comprehensive' housing service emerged only at a much later stage and was only being actively propagated by the time of the Cullingworth Report in the late 1960s (Raynsford, 1986: 39). The introduction of unemployment benefit under the National Insurance Scheme in 1911 removed the 'able-bodied poor' from the ambit of the Poor Law, which nonetheless lingered on until the passing of the National Assistance Act 1948. It would appear that 'the housing prob-lems of the general population were so severe that homelessness was rarely discussed as a distinct housing issue' (Anderson, 2004: 371). Rather, it was regarded as a consequence of poverty and the term 'destitution' was used instead.

Despite its official demise, however, the Poor Law regime has had a last-ing influence on homelessness law and policy. The two principles of local connection and less eligibility have been carried over, and the attitude of many councils to the homeless has been described as 'ambiguous and, at times, distinctly punitive' (Clapham, 1990: 114).

The National Assistance Act 1948

The National Assistance Act 1948 – an Act shaped by 'post-war optimism' – was a significant development in state provision for the homeless which 'heralded the dawn of a more humane approach to the problems of vagrancy and homelessness' (Robson and Poustie, 1996: 37). It was a time when 'full employment, the new free health services and more generous social security payments were enabling more and more people to maintain independent households, and more and more of their houses were built and subsidized by local authorities' (Donnison and Ungerson, 1982: 264). These developments combined, however, to obscure the problem of homelessness; the expansion of the welfare state operating within the context of a strong economy meant that housing shortages tended to be interpreted as short-term problems which could largely be solved through broader housing programmes.

The 1948 Act abolished the Poor Law. Most remaining casual wards were closed, although the National Assistance Board retained some as short-stay reception centres in order to meet its obligation under the Act to provide shelter for those without 'a settled way of living'. The Act further obliged the National Assistance Board and local authority welfare departments (now social services departments) to provide permanent residential care for the people 'who by reason of age, infirmity or any other circumstances are in need of care and attention which is not otherwise available to them' (s. 21(1)(a)) and temporary accommodation for 'persons who are in urgent need thereof, being need arising in circumstances which could not reasonably have been foreseen or in other such circumstances as the authority may in any case determine' (s. 21(1)(b)). The Ministry of Health circular 87/48 made it clear that the latter provision was not intended to deal with the 'inadequately housed' but to assist people made homeless through an emergency such as flood, fire and (significantly) eviction.

In the immediate post-war period, there was, not surprisingly, an overall shortage of properties fit for residential occupation. Hundreds of thousands of houses had been destroyed or made uninhabitable by bomb damage, and new house building had been at a virtual standstill throughout the war. The first post-war Labour government initiated a major building programme and from 1945 to 1948 local authority completions increased from 2,000 units to 190,000 (Merrett, 1979: 239). At the time the 1948 Act was passed, homelessness was seen as a diminishing and residual problem. It was assumed that households accommodated under s. 21(1)(b) would soon be able to make alternative arrangements, and there was a failure to recognise that most households were homeless as a result of eviction, rather than as the result of flood, fire or some other emergency. After a brief 'honeymoon period' during which evicted families were accepted much as the bombed-out families had been, local authorities resorted to Poor Law practice. For at least 15 years after the passing of the 1948 Act, the old workhouses were used as hostels to accommodate families, supplemented by temporary structures erected during the war and, increasingly, inadequate hostel and bed and breakfast accommodation. The standard of accommodation provided, in terms of privacy, basic comfort and facilities for cooking and washing, was poor. Stays of any length of time were thus discouraged by policies of 'deterrence' and 'less eligibility' reminiscent of the Poor Law (Glastonbury, 1971: 40; Burke, 1981: 65).

The 1948 Act gave local authorities much discretion in interpreting the legislation. It gave no guidance as to the meaning of 'temporary', 'urgent need' and 'reasonably foreseeable' and, in consequence, there were considerable variations in the ways in which different councils met their obligations. Requiring the need for assistance to be unforeseen meant that the concept of need was generally qualified by the notion of 'intentionality', a notion which has been carried through into the current homelessness legislation. It implied that those who anticipated possible homelessness but took no steps to avoid it would not deserve assistance. A circular in 1966 stated that any distinction between foreseeable and unforeseeable homelessness was 'artificial' (see Berry, 1974) but when the extent of the duty was under s. 21(1)(b) was tested in *London Borough of Southwark v Williams* [1971] All ER 175, the Court of Appeal held that a family which had moved to London could have foreseen that it would have become homeless and was not entitled, therefore, to temporary accommodation. The court decided that, in any event, individuals could not pursue any remedy under the Act, apart from one already provided for in the legislation, i.e. the default powers given to the Minister by s. 36(1).

Placing the responsibility to accommodate homeless households on welfare, rather than housing, departments placed an intolerable strain on the little accommodation they were able to offer. Faced with a problem with which they were ill-equipped to deal, many authorities interpreted 'urgent need' to apply exclusively to homeless families, or more precisely the mother and children of homeless families, rather than to homeless persons in general. As a result, families were split up (Glastonbury, 1971: 17), and the children sometimes taken into care. A report by Shelter Housing Aid Centre (SHAC) in 1974 showed that most London boroughs would not accept responsibility for pregnant applicants before the pregnancy had reached seven months, and that a few of them refused to do so until the woman had given birth (Raynsford, 1986: 46). Generally, housing departments were unwilling to house homeless people, as they were seen as undeserving and irresponsible and it was considered contrary to waiting list principles. People who lost their homes as the result of an emergency were clearly acknowledged as both homeless and in need of support. Those who did so in non-emergency circumstances were generally assessed according to the extent of their responsibility for the loss. The decision on blameworthiness was an arbitrary one, and different officers and different local authorities might reach different conclusions (Glastonbury, 1971: 17).

As a result, geography played a significant part in determining a homeless household's chances of receiving assistance. Co-operation between welfare and housing departments (where they existed) was poor.

The 1948 Act placed the wrong powers in the wrong hands. Instead of imposing duties on the Ministry of Housing and local housing departments to provide permanent housing for large numbers, it imposed obligations on the Ministry of Health and the county welfare departments to provide temporary shelter for small numbers (Donnison and Ungerson, 1982: 271). The result was a serious policy vacuum at central government level, explicable in part by the prejudices which still attached to the homeless but, probably more importantly, to the perceived conflict of interest between the homeless and those on the council house waiting lists, who were assumed to be competing against each other for the limited supply of council letting (Raynsford, 1986).

The housing boom in the 1950s, coupled with the relaxation of rent controls in the private rented sector, led to an increase in the supply of housing. A consequent fall in the number of persons admitted to local authority temporary accommodation obscured the fact that the housing needs of many people remained unmet. Public housing policy favoured and reinforced nuclear family households. Local authorities focused on the construction of three-bedroomed family dwellings, a policy which continued throughout Labour's term of office, and under the Conservatives until 1953 (Watson, 1986: 49). Those most likely to be neglected were:

> returning servicemen, immigrants and other mobile people who had not spent long enough in any one place to get onto the waiting-lists or to the head of the queue, unmarried mothers and fugitive wives who were expected to stay with their relatives or fend for themselves, and single and childless people who had little chance or being rehoused unless their homes were pulled down in clearance programmes. Most of these found somewhere to live but some could not.
>
> (Donnison and Ungerson, 1982: 265.)

The late 1950s witnessed an unexpected rise in the numbers of families rehoused by the welfare authorities in temporary accommodation. The relaxation of controls by the Rent Act 1957, the rapid growth in sales of what had been rented housing for owner-occupation, the reduction in council house building for general needs, the greater confidence with which people threatened with homelessness demanded help from local authorities, all played a part. Most people who sought help with housing were not victims of an emergency, but of the housing shortage. They needed permanent homes which welfare departments, with no permanent housing stock, were unable to provide. However, homelessness was a subject 'on which government expressed concern, commissioned research, set up working parties and issued guidance and advisory circulars, but did not legislate' (Raynsford, 1986).

Homes were also lost through the renewed expansion of slum-clearance programmes and road building schemes. The evictions and harassment which followed the Rent Act 1957 first drew public attention to the homeless, and subsequently to the condition of homeless family accommodation (Burke, 1981: 65–6). 'Cathy Come Home', a TV drama documentary which gave a moving portrayal of a homeless family's despair and eventual disintegration, touched the public imagination and turned homelessness into a media issue. Towards the end of its life, s. 21(1)(b) was described as offering 'last-ditch support for families who have not been effectively covered by housing provisions and the growing body of preventive services' (Glastonbury, 1971: 15).

Homelessness continued to grow through the 1960s into the 1970s. In 1966 there were 2,558 households in temporary accommodation, by 1970 there were 4,926 and by 1976 there were 10,270. The decline of the private rented sector through the transfer of investment from residential properties to commercial development or selling for owner-occupation, illegal evictions, the growth of public-sector activity in slum clearance and redevelopment, and the continued rise in the cost of renting or buying were all contributing factors (Burke, 1981: 66). A sharp increase in the value of housing land and construction costs occurred in the early 1970s (Merrett, 1979: 263). Cuts in public expenditure led to cuts in the construction of council housing. Council house 'starts' were at a lower level in 1970 than at any time since 1962. Local authorities made increasing use of bed and breakfast accommodation to house homeless families.

Throughout the 1960s and early 1970s, the case for reform mounted. Two particularly important and, ultimately, influential studies were Glastonbury's investigation of homelessness in South West England and South Wales (Glastonbury, 1971) and Greve's on homelessness in London (Greve et al., 1971) both of which provided extensive documentary evidence of the inadequacies of the 1948 Act. Around the same time, a number of important committees demanded a radical reappraisal of government policy towards the homeless, all emphasising homelessness as a housing problem rather than a welfare one and recommending the transfer of statutory responsibility from social services to housing departments.[2] Another recommendation was that housing departments should be made responsible for securing permanent accommodation to preserve families and prevent children being taken into care. In 1974/5, 2,800 children in England and Wales were placed in care solely because of homelessness (Richards, 1992: 130).

---

2   These were the Seebohm Report (1968) *Report of the Committee on Local Authority and Allied Personal Social Services*, London: HMSO; the Cullingworth Report (CHAC) (1969); the Finer Report (1974) *Report of the Committee on One Parent Families*, London: HMSO; and, in Scotland, the Morris Report (1975) *Housing and Social Work: A Joint Approach*, Edinburgh: HMSO.

As the private rented sector continued to decline, the supply of immediate access housing dried up and the 1970s witnessed a marked growth in the number of households provided with temporary accommodation by local authorities in England and Wales. The lack of co-operation between welfare and housing departments was exacerbated by local government reforms in 1972 which gave the responsibility for personal social services to county councils and metropolitan district councils, and housing to district councils. Yet, despite evidence that the 1948 Act was not working and homelessness was in fact increasing, s. 195 of the Local Government Act 1972 reduced the duty to provide temporary accommodation to a discretionary power, with effect from April 1974. This prompted Shelter, the Catholic Housing Aid Society, the Campaign for Homeless and Rootless, SHAC and the Child Poverty Action Group, to form the Joint Charities Group (JCG) with the aim of amending the Local Government Bill 1974 so as to restore the statutory duty. Although they were unsuccessful, their campaign roused considerable sympathy from MPs on all sides of the house and the Secretary of State for Social Services was obliged to issue a joint DoE/DHSS Circular 18/74 which took effect at the same time as local government reorganisation. This circular formed the blueprint for the Housing (Homeless Persons) Bill and the Code of Guidance. It acknowledged that homelessness was an 'extreme form of housing need' and recommended that housing authorities take over homelessness duties from social services. It also introduced the concept of priority groups, advocating that where the housing situation was particularly difficult, authorities should give priority to families with dependent children, and to single people who were homeless through emergency, or vulnerable because of old age, disability, pregnancy or other special reasons. On 1 February 1974, however, the Secretary of State issued a further local authority circular which re-imposed the duty on social service authorities to provide temporary accommodation. Chaos ensued, the existence of some sort of duty on social services authorities encouraging some housing authorities to ignore the exhortations of Circular 18/74 (Hughes and Lowe, 1995: 240).

A Labour government was returned in the general election of February 1974 but, despite its pre-election pledges, homelessness legislation was not high on its list of priorities. The following year it produced a consultation paper which indicated a clear reluctance to legislate. A survey carried out by the Department of the Environment into the implementation of Circular 18/74 revealed that by April 1975 most authorities had failed to adopt the priority group criteria and only a third of housing departments had accepted sole responsibility for the homeless. In some areas, neither housing nor social services would accept responsibility, with the result that families were shunted backwards and forwards. Even in the early 1970s it was still not unknown for homeless families to be transported across local authority boundaries, and 'dumped' in another 'parish' (Raynsford, 1986: 36).

Homelessness was a growing political embarrassment and, by late October 1975, the government had conceded that legislation was necessary after all. In 1976, English authorities accepted as homeless around 33,700 households – more than double the number in 1971. Faced with pressure from all sides for reform, it was clear that Circular 18/74 would only be implemented if it had the force of the law and, in the spring of 1976, the Department of the Environment began separate but parallel consultation meetings with the local authority associations and the JCG to consider proposals for legislation. The government's lack of commitment to the legislation became apparent when it dropped the Homeless Persons Bill from the 1976 Queen's Speech, ostensibly because of insufficient parliamentary time. Stephen Ross, Liberal MP for the Isle of Wight, introduced it into the House of Commons as a private member's Bill (actually the Department of the Environment's own draft), with government support.

The objective of the Bill in its original form was to give legislative power to Circular 18/74. It provided a statutory definition of homelessness and gave housing authorities duties to secure accommodation for people in priority need and to advise and assist others. It fell short, therefore, of the demands of the JCG which also wanted a statutory right of appeal, default powers for the Secretary of State, the extension of priority need to cover single people and a requirement that the accommodation provided be reasonably suitable for the person's needs. Moreover, the Act was passed at a time when a new complacency about housing policy was becoming apparent, the Housing Policy Review Green Paper presenting the housing problem as a localised and essentially residual problem which affected some areas and a limited number of disadvantaged groups, rather than one of national significance. From this perspective the need to provide immediate accommodation for a small number of 'deserving' homeless families could be acknowledged without recognising or taking responsibility for a wider problem of housing market or policy failure.

The Association of County Councils was largely in favour of the provisions contained in the Bill, but the Association of District Councils and the Association of Metropolitan Authorities were concerned about the cost of putting it into practice and the loss of local autonomy. They opposed a legal definition of homelessness, and a statutory right to housing, preferring a general duty on housing authorities to give homeless people advice and help to secure accommodation. Their vehement opposition to the proposed legislation led to a significant dilution of its potential effectiveness and a heavy reliance on entitlement criteria which 'reserved considerable interpretative discretion to the administering authority' (Loveland, 1992: 349).

Housing (Homeless Persons) Act 1977

The Housing (Homeless Persons) Act 1977 has been described as 'a landmark in British housing policy' (Richards, 1992: 129) and 'one of the last reforming measures of the social democratic consensus ... reflecting the belief – soon to be overturned by the Thatcher era – that public authorities should express social obligations' (Pascall and Morley, 1996: 190). It demonstrated that, even in a society 'increasingly dominated by corporate groups', 'plu-ralistic bargaining and democratic pressure' can be used to win 'significant concessions ... for the poor and the powerless', and it was 'an important advance towards securing citizenship rights in an area of social welfare in which ... private property [is] paramount' (Clapham, 1990: 120). It marked a significant turning point in the legislative response to homelessness by giving, for the first time, a statutory right to certain groups of homeless people to be rehoused.

However, the Act has also been criticised. The passage of the Bill through Parliament was obstructed by the local authority lobby which attacked it as a Scroungers' Charter, alleging that 'hoards of misplaced miscreants from the hinterlands of Britain and abroad ... would descend on seaside resorts and areas with major seaports, airport and rail termini clamouring to be housed' (Robson and Poustie, 1996: 44). Although the Labour government supported the Bill, its slim majority at Westminster forced it to concede to pressure from the local authorities. The Act thus became 'a series of obsta-cles to be successfully negotiated before the right to be rehoused could be claimed' (Robson and Watchman, 1981: 2). It was transformed from a rights-based measure to a discretionary one, representing a compromise between 'the needs of the most vulnerable and the prejudices of an uninformed legislature' which legitimised the restriction of help to local people, and discriminated between the 'deserving' and the 'undeserving' (Clapham, 1990: 120). Central government provided no additional funding to assist local authorities in meeting their new responsibilities. While they were generally able to discharge their duties to priority need applicants by placing them their own stock, they were only obliged to provide advice and assistance to homeless households who were not in priority need. As Anderson notes, 'the detail of the 1977 legislation thus preserved the centuries-old division between the more and less deserving poor and continued to allow consider-able local [government] discretion over the implementation of central [gov-ernment] policy' (Anderson, 2004: 374). In 1985 the 1977 Act was codified with the rest of the housing legislation and became Part III of the Housing Act 1985.

The Housing Act 1996

Another steep increase in the number of households applying to local authorities under the homelessness legislation occurred during the 1980s and early 1990s, peaking in 1992 (when 170,408 households in Great Britain were accepted as being statutorily homeless). At the same time, there were major changes in government housing policy. Subsidies for new council housing were cut, and there was a massive thrust towards home ownership. Neither housing associations nor the private rented sector could fill the gap.

The homelessness legislation was subjected to reviews in 1982 and 1989. No significant changes were proposed but some additional funding was made available, most of which was targeted on the renovation of empty homes and some on cash payments to help tenants into owner-occupation, thereby releasing properties for homeless people (DSS, 1990: 5). In late 1992 housing associations were given funds to provide extra housing to accommodate the homeless. Not surprisingly, however, the obligations to homeless applicants under the 1985 Act imposed a considerable strain on resources. In January 1994, the government published a Consultation Paper (DoE, 1994). Despite large-scale protests to the changes it proposed (see Shelter, 1994) the government's proposals found their way into the 1995 White Paper (DoE, 1995) but were subject to some modification before they reached the statute book in the form of the Housing Act 1996. The new legislation was arguably unnecessary, much of the agenda contained in the Consultation Paper having already been achieved by 'indefensibly restrictive judicial interpretations' (Loveland, 1996) of the existing legislation, including *R v London Borough of Brent ex p Awua* [1995] 2 WLR 215 (see Chapter 11). The homelessness provisions in Part III of the Housing Act 1985 were repealed and replaced with a new statutory code contained in Part VII of the 1996 Act but many of the old provisions were retained or re-enacted with only minor amendments.

Homelessness has been a key policy concern for the Labour government which has made further changes to the 1996 Act by the Homelessness Act 2002. Devolution was rapidly put into effect after New Labour was returned to power in 1997, with the creation of the Scottish Parliament, Welsh Assembly, Northern Ireland Assembly, and Greater London Assembly, all of which have some responsibility for housing strategy and the implementation of housing policy. Most notably, in the Homelessness etc (Scotland) Act 2003, the Scottish Parliament has taken the courageous steps of replacing the duty to investigate intentionality with a power to do so, phasing out priority need and suspending the local connection provisions.

Other homelessness legislation

The Housing Act 1996 is not the only piece of legislation which deals with homelessness and it operates alongside the National Assistance Act 1948, the Mental Health Act 1983, the Children Act 1989 and the Local Government Act 2000.

National Assistance Act 1948

Section 21(1)(a) of the National Assistance Act 1948 (as amended) empowers (and where the Secretary of State for Health directs, requires) local social services departments to provide 'residential accommodation for persons aged 18 or over who by reason of age, illness, disability or any other circumstances are in need of care and attention which is not available to them'. Although the person who seeks assistance must generally be ordinarily resident in the local authority's area, s. 21 acquired a renewed significance in the 1990s when it formed the basis of claims for accommodation made by asylum seekers who had not claimed asylum immediately upon their arrival in the UK and were thereby excluded from rights to public housing or welfare benefits (but see now s. 21(1A)). More recently it has featured in important cases concerning the Human Rights Act 1998 in which local authorities, having assessed people as being in need of care under s. 21, then arrange for the accommodation to be secured from a private provider such as a charity or housing association (see Chapter 4).

It is the need for care and attention, rather than the need for housing, which is the prerequisite for the application of s. 21(1)(a) and, although it is commonly associated with the provision of residential accommodation (such as a care home), care and attention can be provided in ordinary housing. 'A need for care and attention is not limited to physical and bodily functions [and] does not suggest care of an intrusive nature ... [but] can arise, for example, because someone is penniless, hungry or traumatised' (Bates, 2005: 23).

Mental Health Act 1983

Section 117 of the Mental Health Act 1983 imposes a duty on the primary care trust or health authority and the local social services authority to provide after-care services for any person who has previously been detained under s. 3 or admitted to a hospital under s. 37 or transferred to a hospital under ss. 47 or 48, and then released. Aftercare services can include housing and must be provided until the person concerned is no longer in need of them (see *R v Redcar and Cleveland Borough Council ex p Armstrong* [2002] 2 AC 1127).

Children Act 1989

Section 17(1) of the Children Act 1989 imposes a *general* duty on every local authority (a) to safeguard and promote the welfare of children within their area who are in need; and (b) so far as is consistent with that duty, to promote the upbringing of such children by their families, by providing a range and level of services appropriate to those children's needs. By s. 17(10) 'a child shall be taken to be in need if – (a) he is unlikely to achieve or maintain, or to have the opportunity of achieving or maintaining, a reasonable standard of health or development without the provision for him of services by a local authority under this Part; (b) his health or development is likely to be significantly impaired, or further impaired, without the provision for him of such services; or (c) he is disabled.' In practice, local authorities tend to use s. 17 in extreme cases in order to keep the family together and to save the children being taken into care, generally where there would be a finding of intentional homelessness under Part VII of the Housing Act 1996 (Bates, 2005).

More specifically, s. 20(1) of the Children Act 1989 requires social services authorities to provide accommodation for 'children in need' within their areas who appear to require accommodation because no one has parental responsibility for them, or they are lost or have been abandoned, or whoever has been caring from them (whether or not permanently and for whatever reason) is prevented from providing suitable accommodation and care. Section 20(3) obliges them to house children over the age of 16 whose welfare will otherwise be 'seriously prejudiced' and subs. (4) gives them a power to provide accommodation for any child (regardless of need) if it considers that to do so would safeguard or promote the child's welfare. In all cases, the local authority must, as far as is reasonably practicable, and consistent with the child's welfare, ascertain the child's wishes and give them due consideration (s. 20(6)). Under s. 27 of the 1989 Act, a local social services authority can ask a local housing authority to help in delivering services for children in need, and the housing authority must comply with such a request to the extent that it is compatible with its own statutory duties and other obligations, and does not unduly prejudice the discharge of any of its own functions. In *R v Northavon District Council ex p Smith* (1994) 26 HLR 659, the House of Lords held that s. 27 cannot be used to obtain permanent accommodation for an applicant and his or her children when a housing authority has already determined that the applicant was intentionally homeless. The 1989 Act imposes a duty of co-operation between the authorities, both of which must their best in carrying out their respective responsibilities for children and housing but judicial review is not the way to obtain co-operation.

The Children Act 1989 also requires social services departments to safeguard and promote the welfare of 16- and 17-year-old care leavers by providing with, or maintaining them in, suitable accommodation unless they are satisfied that their welfare does not require it (s. 23B(8)(b)). The authority responsible for meeting this duty is the one which last looked after the child, regardless of where the child is now living in England and Wales. If a relevant or eligible child presents him- or herself in the area of another local authority, the second authority should provide short-term assistance under s. 17 of the 1989 Act. The two authorities should then agree on how the young person should continue to be assisted, although the responsibility remains with the local authority which last looked after the young person. Local authorities are likely to make use of a range of options, such as supported lodgings, foyers, hostels, and specialist accommodation for young people with particular support needs (see Benjamin, 2002: 18–20) (in which cases licences are likely to be granted) as well as self-contained accommodation (in respect of which a tenancy may well exist).

Local Government Act 2000

Section 2(1) of the Local Government Act 2000 empowers local authorities to do anything which they consider is likely to achieve the promotion or improvement of the economic, social and environmental well-being of their area. Their powers – which can be exercised for the benefit of any residents in the area or any person situated outside it – include incurring expenditure, giving financial assistance, entering into arrangements or agreements, and providing goods, services or accommodation. However, despite the wide terms of s. 2, it has been of limited application, with most of the case law focusing on its relationship with the various prohibitions on assisting asylum seekers. In non-asylum situations, most applicants seem able to rely on s. 21 of the National Assistance Act 1948 or s. 17 of the Children Act 1989 as well as s. 2 and prefer their claims to be assessed under the former provisions (Bates, 2005). In *R (on the application of Badu) v Lambeth London Borough Council* [2006] 1 WLR 505, the applicant was unable to establish priority need under Part VII of the Housing Act 1996 because his child was subject to immigration control. The Court of Appeal held that a local authority is not obliged to use their powers under s. 17 of the 1989 Act or s. 2 of the 2000 Act to 'make up for their enforced discrimination' but may do so provided that it does not exercise those powers solely to circumvent restrictions.

Chapter 3

Owner-occupation

Introduction

As indicated in Chapter 1, the owner-occupied sector today provides accommodation for the majority of households in England and Wales. Even so, the level of home ownership in the United Kingdom[1] is lower than that in a number of other countries – including the Republic of Ireland, Italy, Spain and Greece – and there are also significant regional variations, with only 59 per cent of housing in London being owner-occupied, compared to 75 per cent in the south east and south west of England. As the sector has grown, so it has come to accommodate a wide variety of households with very different economic circumstances in very different types of dwellings, including the 900,000 houses and one million flats held on long leases (DETR, 1998).[2] In this chapter we shall consider the reasons for the dramatic growth of owner occupation during the second half of the twentieth century (and its consequent transformation from a tenure of privilege to the mass tenure) and explore some of the legal protections afforded to the many homeowners who finance the purchase and improvement of their properties by way of a mortgage.

The growth of home ownership

Access to finance

Two particularly important factors which contributed to the increase in owner occupation during the twentieth century were the rise in real incomes and the increased availability of mortgage finance. In the nineteenth and early twentieth centuries, working-class housing in England was normally let on weekly basis. Short lets enabled tenants to leave their accommodation at short notice and were particularly appropriate therefore in an industrial

---

1   The UK average of 70 per cent compares with 64 per cent in Scotland and 75 per cent in Northern Ireland.
2   For an explanation of the statutory protections afforded specifically to long leaseholders, see Wilkie *et al.* (2006: Ch. 17).

society in which much work was carried out on a casual basis. It has been estimated that, in mid-nineteenth century London, one in 10 families was connected with the casual labour market and a mere week's wages separated them, therefore, from complete destitution. A survey carried out in 1887 of the wages and living conditions of 30,000 men in various parts of London revealed that 89 per cent had been unemployed over the past few months (Wohl, 1977: 314–15). Very few people could expect a life of stable employment and, although casual labour was primarily associated with the unskilled and the semi-skilled, even white-collar occupations were affected. There was said to be 'a sizeable fringe of casual law clerks, who filled in time between one job and another, addressing envelopes and writing begging letters' (Stedman-Jones, 1976: 64). Private renting was, therefore, a mode of housing provision which was appropriate in the 1800s when the new urban working class (and many middle-class households) earned low wages, had little opportunity to save or to borrow, and could not afford to buy their housing outright.

After the First World War the casual labour market was replaced by more stable and better-paid employment. From the 1920s onwards, home ownership became a reality for an increasing (predominantly middle-class) proportion of the population, despite high unemployment which persisted until 1939. Interest rates were low, land, materials and labour were cheap, and building societies (which had accumulated an embarrassment of riches) made a concerted effort to attract borrowers. The Housing Act 1923 provided direct subsidies to builders for private construction and allowed local authorities to make loans to them for the same purpose. Planning legislation (such as it was) exerted little control over residential development, and mortgage repayments compared favourably with rents (Saunders, 1990: 23–5). After the Second World War, the rise in incomes of skilled manual workers allowed them increasingly to become owner-occupiers. The majority of unskilled households remained tenants, mainly of local authority housing.

The past 30 years or so have witnessed significant changes for many people in the nature of their employment. Running alongside the decline in full-time male work, especially in the traditional manufacturing and mining industries, has been a growth in flexible or 'atypical' employment, i.e. part-time, temporary and self-employment, very often carried out by women. Historically, this type of employment was concentrated on the weakest groups, being correlated to a significant extent with low pay and inferior working conditions. In recent years however temporary employment has spread into white-collar jobs which previously enjoyed long-term security, and there has been a sharp rise in the number of people who are self-employed – from 1,825,000 in 1977 to nearly 3,375,000 in 2006 (National Statistics, 2006: Table 3). Although small employers and self-employed households have the highest proportion of homes owned outright (Anderson, 2004: 42), they are also more highly indebted than other borrowers, typically because they have withdrawn equity from their homes in order to fund the 'establishment, expansion or crisis management of their businesses' (Ford, 1997: 18). As Lord Browne-Wilkinson pointed out in *Barclays Bank v O'Brien* [1994] 1 AC 180, 188 'the jointly owned [matrimonial] home has become a main source of security' where finance is needed 'for the business enterprises of one or other of the spouses'. Furthermore, the rapid development of self-employment and small businesses has been supported by the rise in value of residential properties. This means however that slumps in the housing market can result not only in repossessed homes but also in bankrupt businesses.

Fiscal and financial support

In the first half of the twentieth century, governments were largely indifferent to owner-occupation and were more concerned to revive the ailing private rented sector and to promote local authority housing. The 'desire' for home ownership can be seen as 'more of a response to a lack of choice than a reaction against renting' and significant growth began only after 1933 as private renting declined and local authority housing became generally restricted to the displaced families of slum clearance schemes (Balchin and Rhoden, 2002: 259). As owner-occupation became more popular and it was realised that no significant revitalisation of private renting was going to take place, government attention turned to the promotion of owner-occupation. Given that, 'the expectation of social rights to housing puts pressure on governments to provide them' (Stewart, 1996: 23), the encouragement of home-ownership offered a way of limiting the state's involvement with housing. By relocating responsibility to the market, housing provision would become a matter between individual consumers and suppliers and lenders and borrowers, and increase the number of households whose housing caused the government neither expense nor trouble (Holmans, 1987: 464).

While, during the 1950s and 1960s, Conservative and Labour governments vied with each other as to which could oversee the production of the greater number of council houses, by 1965 even the Labour Party had decided that the expansion of building for owner-occupation was 'normal', reflecting 'a long-term social advance which should gradually pervade every region' (MHLG, 1965: 8). The following two decades can be seen as the 'golden age' of home ownership during which – because of demographic and demand factors – the sector expanded rapidly, and properties appreciated in value. At the same time, the existence of generous tax reliefs, financial privileges and safety nets in the form of the social security system and good quality council housing meant that home owners were not fully exposed to risk (Murie, 1998: 96). The encouragement of owner-occupation may be seen as part of the process of 'rolling back the state', in some respects symptomatic, particularly since the late 1970s, of what has been described as the demotion of the individual from 'citizen' to 'consumer' (and one for whom rights protection and choice increasingly depend upon ability to pay) (Whitehead, 1998b: 183).

The promotion of owner-occupation was a policy supported by full employment. One significant way therefore in which governments could encourage and facilitate home ownership was by providing financial support through the tax system. The introduction of tax relief on mortgage interest in 1929 did not affect the majority of households, given that the bulk of the population was not liable to pay income tax. However, a continuing reduction in the starting point of income tax in real terms and the rise in real incomes boosted the number of borrowers who benefited from tax relief and, in the 1960s and 1970s, it became a particularly valuable tool in cutting the cost of house purchase for very many households (Holmans, 1987: 463). The fact that tax relief broadly increased in value with income and the size of the loan encouraged many households to trade up (Forrest and Murie, 1995: 63). From 1983, mortgage interest relief was paid direct to lenders by way of the Mortgage Interest Relief at Source (MIRAS) system, but having achieved its aim of creating a housing system dominated by home ownership, the government felt that significant fiscal incentives were no longer necessary (Whitehead, 1998a: 135). Over the following two decades therefore, the value of mortgage interest relief was whittled away: first to the basic rate of income tax, then to 20 per cent and, from 1995, to 15 per cent. From 1 April 1998 it was reduced to 10 per cent and was finally withdrawn in April 2000. At its peak in the mid-1970s, it was meeting about 38 per cent of a household's mortgage interest payments, but this had dropped to below 5 per cent towards the end of its lifetime (*The Independent*, 18 March 1998).

Fiscal support for owner-occupation was bolstered by the ending, in 1963, of Schedule A income tax for owner occupiers on imputed rental income (by a Conservative government) and the total exclusion of sole or main residences from liability to capital gains tax in 1965 (by a Labour government), measures which turned a basically neutral tax system into one which provided substantial fiscal support for owner-occupation and house purchase. More recently, New Labour may be said to have capitalised on the popularity of home ownership by progressively increasing stamp duty, the £3.6 billion levied in 2002/3 representing a 700 per cent increase in the revenue derived from the tax since 1985/6. The continuing rise in house prices coupled with the government's failure to raise allowances has also meant that there is an increasing number of estates on which inheritance tax is payable, although it remains a small percentage of all estates.

Welfare support

The 1960s and 1970s were decades of virtually full employment but the ability to raise finance by way of a mortgage depended on households having reasonably stable incomes which were sufficient to cover the required payments with only tax relief to assist them. It was not the tenure, therefore, for households 'with only low or intermittent earnings, or no earnings at all' (Holmans, 1987: 189). However, the greater weight placed on market-based solutions to individual housing needs coincided with widespread unemployment. Welfare support therefore assumed a particular significance in relation to less financially stable households. The provision of state assistance for home buyers, currently provided as part of the Income Support scheme, has existed since 1948. The importance of this safety net has grown as owner-occupation has spread across a wider income range, unemployment has risen and the flexible workforce has expanded. Entitlement to assistance under the Income Support for Mortgage Interest (ISMI) scheme is restricted to interest payments on loans taken out to acquire an interest in the dwelling occupied as the home (i.e. for the purpose of house purchase) or for the purpose of financing repairs or improvements which are undertaken in order to maintain 'the fitness of the dwelling for human habitation'. The fact that assistance is only provided for the interest payable on a loan means that no assistance will be given with the capital repayments if a claimant has entered into a repayment mortgage. In the case of an endowment mortgage, all of the payments (which are normally of interest only for the full term of the mortgage) will be met. However, the associated life assurance payments will not be covered. Payments are made on a standard rate of interest.

When ISMI was introduced, assistance during the first 16 weeks of a claim was limited to 50 per cent of the household's eligible mortgage interest liabilities, but the expansion and composition of home ownership, together with the economic recession, brought about a rapid growth in the numbers claiming ISMI in the late 1980s and early 1990s. The cost of ISMI support was also affected by rising house prices in the 1980s and the consequent increase in the size of mortgages, and increases in interest rates between 1988 and 1991. In August 1993, a limit on eligible mortgages of £150,000 was applied to new claims, and this was reduced in stages to £100,000 in April 1995. The reforms culminated in October 1995 with the Social Security (Income Support and Claims and Payment) Amendment Regulations 1995, the effect of which is that for loans taken out before 1 October 1995, no assistance is given for the first eight weeks of a claim, 50 per cent of the claimant's eligible interest payments are met in the next 18 weeks and the full amount of eligible interest thereafter. For loans taken out since 1 October 1995, no support is given for the first 39 weeks of a claim, after which the full amount of eligible interest is covered. The aim of the 1995 restrictions was further to privatise the housing system by encouraging home owners to arrange private insurance provision to cover their housing liabilities in the event of unemployment rather than to rely on state support, but take-up has been relatively low, with fewer than 40 per cent of homeowners having mortgage payment protection insurance cover (Ford *et al.*, 2004: Ch. 2).

Transfers from other tenures

The growth of the sector over the past century has also been achieved by transfers of existing dwellings from other tenures as well as by new building. Forty per cent of the net increase in owner-occupation in the inter-war period was attributable to sales by private landlords to sitting tenants, a trend which continued through into the 1960s, bottoming out in the 1980s, by which time the private rented sector had shrunk (through a combination of sales and slum clearance) to around 10 per cent of households (Lowe, 2004: 190). The last 40 years have also witnessed the emergence of a variety of schemes designed specifically to facilitate owner-occupation by drawing in properties from other tenures and broadening the social and economic base of the sector (Stewart, 1996: 19). The first such scheme was the Leasehold Reform Act 1967 which enables holders of long leases – now including companies and not just individuals, as was previously the case (*Hareford Ltd v Barnet London Borough Council* [2005] 28 EG 122)[3] – to purchase the freehold of their properties[4] or to extend their leases for a further 50 years. Given that the Act applies only to houses, it was – and is – of limited application. However, the Leasehold Reform, Housing and Urban Development Act 1993 – prompted perhaps by the Conservative Party's perception during the 1980s and 1990s of leasehold reform as 'a natural (and vote-winning) extension of its ideological commitment to home ownership' (Blandy and Robinson, 2001: 399) – gives long leaseholders of flats the right as a group to buy the freehold of the buildings in which their flats are situated by means of 'collective enfranchisement'. While these measures have allowed often more affluent households to become home owners, the expansion of owner-occupation has come increasingly to depend on its filtering down to households at the lower end of the income spectrum. A major source of supply in this respect has been the right to buy (RTB) which since 1980 has resulted in the transfer of over two million dwellings in the UK from local authority ownership into owner-occupation. Now, however, the virtual cessation in the construction of new local authority housing together with the diminution of the sector as a result of stock transfer (see Chapter 16) has resulted in fewer tenants having the RTB. Thus, as the balance between secure tenancies and assured tenancies shifts, so the RTB is replaced by the more complicated and restrictive arrangements which apply to the right to acquire conferred by the Housing Act

3   This is as a result of the Commonhold and Leasehold Reform Act 2002 which removed the requirement that the tenant had been resident in the property for the last three years or for an aggregate of three out of the past 10 years.
4   In *James v United Kingdom* (1986) 8 EHRR 123, the ECtHR ruled that the Leasehold Reform Act 1967 did not infringe Art. 1 of the First Protocol of the ECHR. It held that a taking of property in pursuance of legitimate social, economic or other policies may be 'in the public interest', even if the community at large has no direct use and enjoyment of the property taken.

1996 upon assured tenants of housing associations (Murie and Ferrari, 2003: 13).

Running alongside these statutory schemes have been a number of other initiatives. During the 1970s and 1980s, governments introduced savings schemes and tax incentives to make home ownership more affordable for low-income first-time buyers and provided grants to improve older and cheaper properties (Stewart, 1996: 19). Many of these schemes – which were administered by local authorities which could themselves lend money to potential purchasers considered to be too much of a risk for building societies – 'proved unattractive economically or just too complicated and did not lead to a significant increase in the number of owners' (ibid.). Today, the two main types of low-cost home ownership are shared ownership (where the occupier part rents the property from a housing association and mortgages the rest) and Homebuy (an equity loan scheme under which the occupier purchases 75 per cent of the property, and the remainder stays with the housing association, no rent being paid). Priority is given to existing tenants in social housing and those on the housing register, although others who are in housing need and nominated by local authorities may also be eligible. The occupier can change the share which is owned – either upwards or downwards – through a process known as 'staircasing'. Currently, about 3,000 units per year are provided on a shared ownership basis and 1,500 units per year by Homebuy. The Starter Home Initiative which was introduced in 2001 and its successor, the Key Worker Living Scheme, were both targeted at key workers (primarily those working in education and the health and police services) working in high cost areas to enable them to buy properties near their work. Again, take up has not been as successful as was hoped. However, while low-cost home ownership schemes have been relatively ineffectual in volume terms, in political terms 'they create an impression of policy action while imposing little cost on government funds' (Malpass, 2005: 148).

Although owner-occupation remains the favoured tenure choice with around 80 per cent of the population aspiring to become home owners within the next 10 years (Siebrits, 2005: 3), there comes a point at which 'filtering down touches an impenetrable barrier of low income' and home ownership is simply unaffordable, 'even with the support and encouragement of government schemes' (Lowe, 2004: 198). As Lowe points out, sales of private and public sector properties to sitting tenants can no longer be 'a major source of tenure transformation as they were through [much] of the twentieth century' (ibid.: 198). In short, 'the well-spring of rental housing which fed the rising tide of home ownership has all but dried up' (ibid.: 192).

The demographics of owner-occupation

Given that the combined resources of both partners to a relationship are often essential to enable the home to be bought at all, the growth of home ownership has been very much dependent on the changing economic and social status of women (Stewart, 1996: 27). Today, couples (whether married or unmarried) who buy homes together are likely to have the property conveyed or transferred into their joint names. For many years however – even where the woman (as was usually the case) had contributed or was contributing to the purchase price – legal title would be in the man's sole name. When therefore the husband (re)mortgaged the property (often to prop up his ailing business) and then failed to keep up the repayments, the wife would find herself having to defend possession proceedings. In *Northern Bank Ltd v Beattie* [1982] 18 NIJB 1, Murray J was moved to observe that:

> the phrase 'the eternal triangle' has taken on a new meaning ... Instead of the ... situation of old, the people involved are a husband-[borrower] of his matrimonial home, a bank lender of that home, and an estranged wife still living in the home.

However, until the House of Lords decision in *Williams & Glyn's Bank v Boland* [1981] AC 487 a wife's presence in the property did not signify that she might also have an interest in it. Where legal title was vested in one spouse alone, the other was not regarded as being in occupation on her own account but rather as 'a shadow of occupation of the owner' (*Bird v Syme Thompson* [1979] 1 WLR 440, 444). Since the lender would not be expected, therefore, to assume that the wife might have any interest of her own in the property, there was no need to bother with obtaining her consent to (or even notifying her of) any (re)mortgage.

Recognition of the wife's rights being evident via her presence in the property came with the House of Lords judgment in *Boland*, a decision which has been described as 'the triumph of social justice over commercial interests' in which 'family security was considered more important' and 'women's changed position within households' was recognised (Stewart, 1996: 35). As the result of *Boland*, where title to a property is registered in the name of one person, a beneficial co-owner who is in actual occupation (but has failed to protect her interest by entering it on the register of title) nonetheless has an overriding interest under the Land Registration Act 2002. This protects the interests of persons in actual occupation except where enquiry is made of them and they fail to disclose the interest when they could reasonably have been expected to do so or where their occupation would not have been obvious on a reasonably careful inspection of the land at the time of the disposition (Sch. 3, para. 2). The reasoning in *Boland* was applied in *Kingsnorth Trust v Tizard* [1986] 1 WLR 783, a case which concerned unregistered land so that the wife's interest was subject to the doctrine of notice. Following the decision in *Boland*, lending institutions encouraged borrowers to buy jointly so that they, the institutions, had the advantage of the statutory overreaching rules. Gradually, however, the principle of *Boland* has been eroded so that a wife who finds herself in the situation outlined above may be regarded as having impliedly consented to the re-mortgage even if she had no actual knowledge of it (*Equity and Law Home Loan v Prestidge* [1991] 1 WLR 137). There may also be problems where the wife (as joint legal owner) signs the mortgage documentation but only under duress (see *Royal Bank of Scotland v Etridge (No 2)* [2002] 2 AC 773).

Younger households are now more likely to defer house purchase and in the meantime to prefer the flexibility and easier mobility of associated with private sector renting. Doubtless this is partly due to property prices which in some part of the country are so high as to put them beyond the reach of many potential first-time buyers. At the same time, however, there has been a decline in the earnings of younger working people compared to those of older groups. Thus, for example over the last two decades male earnings for men aged 21 to 24 have fallen from 75 per cent to 65 per cent of the average for all working men, while the average for men aged between 25 and 29 has fallen from 95 per cent to 90 per cent (Wilcox, 2005: 59). This means that people who become home owners in their twenties, are likely to be experiencing high housing costs (i.e. substantial entry costs and high real levels of mortgage repayment) 'two decades or more before their earnings peak' (Ball and Harloe, 1998: 6). It has been predicted that the slowdown in the rate of entry by younger purchasers will ultimately depress the size of the sector (Lowe, 2004: 192).

At the same time however home owning is growing among over sixties as those who were mainly tenants die out and are replaced by middle-aged home owners who have paid off their mortgages, i.e. the beneficiaries of the 'golden age' of home ownership. Over the next decade or so, an ageing housing stock will be owned and occupied by an ageing cohort of elderly and very elderly home owners who are equity rich but income poor and becoming physically less able to carry out their own repair and maintenance work (Forrest and Leather, 1998: 38). The 'wealth' stored in their homes is a tempting target 'not only for repair and maintenance but also for other purposes including social care provision' especially given that 'the value of state pensions is declining and the costs of health care are increasing' and governments are keen to restrict or redirect public spending (ibid.: 38, 40).

Mortgages

The general social problems of the housing market so far as owner-occupation is concerned tend to be translated into the individual rights of borrowers. Most households in England and Wales cannot afford to buy a home outright and will need to finance the purchase by borrowing – usually by way of a mortgage.

In the nineteenth century the mortgage was primarily a form of private investment and most lenders were small-scale private individuals. Borrowers (who also tended to be individuals but were occasionally small businesses) usually already owned the property which was to act as the security and needed money only for a short time in order to meet a period of temporary indebtedness. Today, by contrast, individual borrowers are of people of average or below-average wealth who turn to institutional lenders – such as banks and building societies – to help them raise sufficient funds to finance the purchase of a home in which they intend to live. The repayments are calculated on the basis of there being a long-term financial relationship between these parties, and commitment to a mortgage can therefore become a central concern in a person's life. A mortgage will usually represent the largest single financial debt which a person ever incurs, providing the opportunity to acquire both a personal and/or family base and a major capital asset by means of what is essentially an instalment purchase spread over a period of, typically, 20 to 25 years. The availability of mortgage finance has a significant impact on borrowers' life chances, often permitting them a greater degree of geographical mobility. It may influence their marriage prospects and determine the timing of their marriages, the arrival of their children and the ultimate size of their families. Home ownership provides a means of storing and accumulating wealth and, given that 'a family may gain more from the housing market in a few years than would be possible in savings from a lifetime of earnings' (Pahl, 1975: 291), it may provide a source of capital to help in old age. Home ownership will affect a person's credit-worthiness, e.g. for buying goods on hire purchase, and during his or her working life may provide an asset against which (because of rising property values) further money can be borrowed. A small business person can use the family home as security for a bank loan to finance the business. However, the responsibility for a mortgage may tie borrowers to their current employment, thus acting as 'a silent disciplinary force within the workplace' (Gray and Gray, 2005: 15.2) and if borrowers fall into arrears, homelessness may be a possible consequence.

Lord Diplock once observed that 'we now live in a "real-property-owning", particularly a "real-property-mortgaged-to-a-building-society-owning" democracy"' (*Pettit v Pettit* [1970] AC 777) and until the late 1980s building societies were responsible for the majority of mortgage lending. The deregulation of the finance industry by the Financial Services Act 1985 (which allowed financial institutions other than building societies to offer mortgage finance) and the Building Societies Act 1986 (which increased the scope of services which building societies could provide and allowed them to demutualise and become banks) meant that mortgage loans became much more quickly and easily available, thereby enabling a wider range of households the opportunity of entering into home ownership. In this competitive environment, lenders were willing to offer higher percentage mortgages on the basis of more relaxed requirements regarding the borrower's status. There followed 'a pronounced shift from mortgage rationing towards lending on demand

and loans related to a high proportion of property value' with lenders competing for custom 'by being willing to lend more' (Malpass and Murie, 1999: 84). The deregulation of the finance industry and the increased availability of mortgage finance may also be perceived as providing 'a justification for the withdrawal of government support from the housing system', with greater choice and the regulatory efficiency of competition together ensuring that 'mortgages operated in a manner consistent with the demands of consumers' (Whitehead, 1998a: 132). Since the mid-1980s mortgage lending has been more openly competitive and there are thousands of mortgage products on the market (from around 155 lenders) including fixed and capped rate mortgages, and current account and off-set mortgages. Many borrowers now switch lenders on a regular basis, shopping around for the best terms, and the long-term relationship between lender and borrower upon which repayment of the loan is predicated is a thing of the past. There are also high rates of equity withdrawal as re-mortgaging owners increase their borrowing to fund non-housing expenditure.

A number of factors – deregulation, the greater availability of credit and the increased popularity of owner-occupation – combined to fuel the housing boom of the 1980s. The subsequent 'bust' was triggered by rising rates of interest and unemployment and less favourable tax treatment for borrowers. At the beginning of 1988, base rates stood at 8.5 per cent and unemployment appeared to be on a downward trend, but in April the government announced that in August per capita tax relief on mortgage interest would be replaced by a single relief per property. First-time buyers rushed to enter the market before the tax relief was withdrawn. At the same time inflation and interest rates were rising. By October 1988 the base rate had reached 15 per cent. Inevitably, high interest rates created problems for manufacturers and other employers, and unemployment began to climb again. It was precisely those borrowers who were most vulnerable to unemployment and rising interest rates who had extended themselves to enter the housing market. In the past, borrowers who could no longer meet their mortgage repayments would simply have traded down to a smaller property or moved out of owner-occupation altogether. In the early 1990s however many were unable to do so, as confidence and demand had declined to such an extent that house prices had fallen by as much as 20 per cent in many areas (Anderson, 2004: 16) and the removal of rent control in the private sector had resulted in much higher market rents for new tenancies. The number of repossessions peaked in 1991 at over 75,000.

The prolonged and serious slump in the property market in the early 1990s – the worst since the birth of the property-owning democracy in the 1920s, and resulting in record numbers of repossessions – 'severely challenged simplistic assumptions about security, affordability and wealth accumulation' (Malpass, 2005: 143). More recently, however, the owner-occupied sector is often described as having 'matured' in that its growth over the last few years has been relatively slow and the likely short-term consequences of recession are less extreme. First time buyers, who are generally most heavily exposed to debt, have accounted for a falling proportion of total borrowers. Their average age is also higher. As more purchasers are able to put down a larger deposit, the number of households borrowing more than 100 per cent is now fairly low and concentrated more in the cheaper areas (Stephens *et al.*, 2005: 3.5). Nonetheless, the current, relatively low, level of repossessions is set against a benign background of low interest rates. Prospective home owners are now able to borrow up to five times their gross income and it would take an increase in interest rates of only a few percentage points and a relatively modest downturn in the property market to plunge many borrowers into negative equity while having to meet high – sometimes unaffordable – payments.

Protection for the lender

Where borrowers fail to discharge their obligations, two separate sets of rights – one proprietary and the other personal – are available to lenders. The former – which may be enforced against the property to realise its value – include the lender's right to possession and, provided that certain conditions are satisfied, the power to sell the repossessed property (Law of Property Act 1925, ss. 101 and 103). The second set of rights is personal to the borrower and arises out of the borrower's contractual obligation to pay. Given that prudent lenders will limit the loan to a sum which is significantly less than the property's market value, there is usually no problem; the advance will be adequately secured (and, in a rising market, ultimately well secured). Where borrowers are unable to meet their payments, lenders will usually try to accommodate the borrower's personal difficulties by, for example, extending the repayment period or allowing a payment holiday. Only if such rescue measures fail, will lenders turn to their proprietary rights, obtain possession of the property, sell it for the best price that can reasonably be obtained,[5] pay off the loan and interest together with the expenses of sale, and account to the borrower for any surplus. While the lender's proprietary and personal remedies may be pursued either concurrently or successively, the personal remedy usually only becomes of significance if the sale proceeds are insufficient to pay off the amount due and the borrower faces a 'shortfall debt'. Interest will generally continue to be charged on the loan until it is repaid in full. The lender can sue on the personal covenant to repay the principal sum – or any shortfall – at any date after the legal date for redemption and may sue for interest in arrears at any time. At the end of the 1980s many

---

5 Building societies are required to secure 'the best price which can reasonably be obtained (Building Societies Act 1986, s. 13 and Sch. 4). Other lenders should seek to obtain the 'true market value' (*Cuckmere Brick Co. Ltd v Mutual Finance Ltd* [1971] Ch 949).

thousands of borrowers found themselves unable to meet their mortgage commitments. Some simply handed in their keys, in the mistaken belief that their liability was thereby ended. Others were eventually dispossessed by court order, their homes later sold (often at auction) at the base of a weak market. While the majority of these debts have long since been written off, a significant number have since been assigned to debt recovery companies and hundreds of people still face proceedings for recovery of shortfall debts, some the result of failed mortgages taken out over 15 years ago (Dabbs, 2004; Prime, 2005).

Normally the lender will go into possession of the mortgaged property only as a prelude to exercising its power of sale (so that the property can be sold with vacant possession and a higher price obtained). Because it is a right rather than a remedy, the lender can in theory take possession at any time after the mortgage is created. As Harman J stated in *Four Maids Ltd v Dudley Marshall Properties Ltd* [1957] Ch 317, 320:

> The right of the [lender] to possession ... has nothing to do with default on the part of the [borrower]. The [lender] may go into possession before the ink is dry on the mortgage unless there is something in the contract, express or by implication, whereby he has contracted himself out of that right.

In practice however the mortgage agreement will expressly limit the lender's exercise of the right to cases of actual default by the borrower. Sometimes borrowers who have fallen into arrears and have little or no prospect of repaying them will simply vacate the property without warning the lender. Alternatively, they may reach an agreement with the lender to hand over the property without the need to obtain a court order. The borrower may be asked to sign a voluntary possession declaration to confirm the agreement, which will make it clear that the interest on the loan together will continue to accrue until the property is sold. Unless the borrower moves out voluntarily, the lender who physically re-enters the mortgaged property may run the risk of criminal liability under s. 6 of the Criminal Law Act 1977. This makes it an offence for a person without lawful authority (such as a bailiff executing a warrant of possession) to use or threaten violence for the purpose of securing entry to premises upon which, to his knowledge, someone is present who is opposed to the entry. In consequence, where residential premises are concerned, the lender will invariably obtain a court order before taking possession rather than attempting peaceable re-entry.

At common law the court has a very limited jurisdiction to grant relief to borrowers who have fallen behind with their mortgage repayments. It can adjourn the application for a short time (normally for no longer than 28 days) 'to afford to the [borrower] a chance of paying off the [lender] in full or otherwise satisfying him' if there is a reasonable prospect of either of these events occurring (*Birmingham Citizens Permanent Building Society v Caunt* [1962] Ch 883). So as to mitigate the harshness of the common law and to give borrowers the same kind of legal protection as is afforded to residential tenants (Payne, 1969: para. 1386), s. 36 of the Administration of Justice Act 1970 provides that in an action by a lender for possession of a dwelling-house, the court may suspend for such period as it thinks reasonable a possession order granted against a borrower it appears that the borrower is likely to be able to pay the sums due within a reasonable period, or to remedy any default. Further, by s. 8 of the Administration of Justice Act 1973, the court may treat the sum due under the mortgage as being only the arrears of the instalments or interest, notwithstanding that the terms and conditions of the mortgage require the whole loan to become payable immediately on default. The purpose of making an order under s. 36 is to enable borrowers who have fallen into arrears to resume their payments and to pay off the arrears with a view to the ultimate redemption of the mortgage by instalments in the ordinary way (*National & Provincial Building Society v Ahmed* [1995] 2 EGLR 127). However, the Court of Appeal has held that s. 36 does not impliedly impose a requirement of a prior court order before a lender can take possession of a dwelling-house (*Ropaigealach v Barclays Bank plc* [2000] 1 QB 263). The lender may therefore take possession peaceably provided that the property is unoccupied. Thus, although s. 36 protects borrowers against eviction by court process, it leaves them open to eviction by self-help, presumably even where a court has previously refused to grant the lender immediate possession (Clarke, 1983: 296).

Prior to the decision in *Cheltenham and Gloucester Building Society v Norgan* [1996] 1 WLR 343, most district judges construed a 'reasonable period' as being two to four years. In *Norgan* however the Court of Appeal held that the logic and spirit of the legislation required that the court should take as its starting point the full term of the mortgage and consider whether it would be possible to maintain pay-off of the arrears by instalments over that period. Such an approach would necessitate a more detailed analysis than had hitherto been customary, so that borrowers might be required to supply detailed budgets as to income and expenditure. The decision in *Norgan* allows the court to delay possession so long as it is satisfied that the lender will receive substantially what it bargained for, albeit at a later date. The problem is, of course, that for many borrowers this is simply not possible. Once they have fallen behind with their payments, the amount which they owe starts quickly to escalate. The arrears themselves attract further interest, and lenders will usually add to the debt the often unnecessarily high charges they make for telephone calls, letters etc to the borrower. Not surprisingly therefore it seems that, despite the decision in *Norgan*, district judges still tend to suspend the order for only a few years, believing that 'a shorter period than that of the remaining term of the mortgage is in the best interests of the [borrower]' (Whitehead, 1998b: 196).

In most cases borrowers try to satisfy the court that the arrears will be paid within a reasonable period by giving evidence about their income and expenditure. However, where their income is not sufficient to repay arrears (as well as covering the current repayments) they may seek time in which to sell the property so that the outstanding balance (including the arrears) can be repaid. Where the security is not at risk the court will usually adjourn or make a postponed order to allow the borrowers themselves to arrange a sale as it is generally accepted that borrowers occupying premises achieve a better price on sale than lenders through forced sales (see *Target Home Loans v Clothier* [1994] 1 All ER 439). If the lender does not agree to the borrower selling the property, the borrower may apply for an order for sale under s. 91(2) of the Law of Property Act 1925 which permits the court at the request of the lender or borrower to order a sale of the mortgaged property on such terms as it thinks fit even if this goes against the wishes of the other party. Normally a sale will only be ordered if it is likely to produce enough to clear the entire mortgage debt. However, in *Palk v Mortgage Services Funding plc* [1993] 2 All ER 481, the Court of Appeal held – for the first time – that s. 91(2) gives the court a discretion to order a sale even where this would result in a shortfall (although this could apparently be met from the borrower's personal resources). More surprisingly, in *Polonski v Lloyd's Bank Mortgages Ltd, The Times,* 6 May 1997, it was held that, in exercising its discretion, the court is not limited to considering financial matters but can also take into account social considerations. Here, the court decided that it could not be just to require the borrower to stay (even though she would not be in any position within the foreseeable future to pay the shortfall) when she had shown good reasons for wanting to move to a better area and nothing in her past conduct showed that she had acted in anything other than a financially responsible manner. This surprising decision may, in future, incline lenders to seek possession as soon as the borrower defaults in cases of negative equity.

Protection for the borrower

The terms and conditions on which the loan is made are very much a matter of contract, the legal assumption being that the parties are of equal bargaining strength. Although, as we have seen, the law imposes some constraints upon lenders, there has been a tendency to rely on self-regulation by the mortgage industry. Members of the Council of Mortgage Lenders (CML) – which represent over 98 per cent of the residential mortgage market – have over £750 billion mortgage balances outstanding on nearly 11.5 million owner-occupied homes (Anderson, 2004: 7). It is clear therefore that the increased dependence on mortgage provision has turned lenders into the 'gatekeepers' of the owner occupied sector, determining who will enter and be allowed to remain in it (Whitehead, 1998a: 126–7).

In the early days of mortgages, lenders could take advantage of their superior bargaining position by trying to exact further profit by purporting to limit, postpone or exclude the borrower's right to redeem, either completely or substantially. As Lord Henley famously stated in *Vernon v Bethell* (1762) 28 ER 838, 839 'necessitous men are not, truly speaking, free men, but, to answer a present exigency, will submit to any terms that the crafty may impose upon them'. In the nineteenth and early twentieth centuries a number of important cases gave rise to the development of an equitable jurisdiction to strike out any terms of a mortgage which operated in an oppressive or unconscionable manner and were inconsistent therefore with its nature as a security interest and to rewrite the mortgage bargain. The courts' sympathy towards borrowers was no doubt influenced by the fact that the party in the weaker position was a landowner (as were most of the judiciary) while the stronger party was a moneylender or financier (Clarke and Kohler, 2005: 669). Such concern has now been incorporated in legislation directed specifically at the lower end of the mortgage market – often the only source of mortgage finance for some particularly vulnerable people.

The secured lending market in the UK comprises three main sectors. As Dyson LJ explained in *Broadwick Financial Services v Spence* [2002] EWCA Civ 35, the primary lenders are the banks and building societies which generally lend at the lowest rates of interest and will normally only grant second mortgages by way of a further advance to existing customers. The secondary lenders, which have generally lent at rates in the APR range of 19 to 29 per cent for second mortgages, have more lenient lending criteria than primary lenders, and will often accept applications which primary lenders have rejected. The third sector consists of 'tertiary or non-status lenders' who generally lend to people who cannot obtain finance from primary or secondary lenders. This is because they have either an 'impaired' credit rating (as a result of, e.g. outstanding country court judgments or arrears) or a 'low' credit rating (because of, e.g. a poor employment history or because their income through self-employment is irregular or difficult to verify) or because they lack the 'supporting documentation necessary to obtain a loan from a high street lender' (DGFT, 1997: 3). The fact that they may be 'less knowledgeable or experienced in financial matters than a generality of customers' means that, on the whole, they are 'more vulnerable' (ibid.: 2). Usually such borrowers have 'already exhausted the patience of institutional lenders in connection with existing loans and [are] on the verge of bankruptcy or repossession', their only remaining hope of averting disaster lying in a further loan or re-mortgaging arrangement with a 'sub-prime' lender (Gray and Gray, 2004: 15.64).

To protect such borrowers, the Consumer Credit Act 1974 establishes a comprehensive code which regulates the supply of credit to an individual. It includes provisions on advertising and canvassing, the licensing of credit and hire businesses, all aspects of the agreement and judicial control over its enforcement. To come within the Act a mortgage must constitute a regulated consumer agreement, i.e. a consumer credit agreement by which a creditor provides a debtor with credit of any amount (s. 8(1)). There are, however, exempt agreements, of which the most important are loans made by a building society or local authority for the purchase of land or the provision of dwellings on any land (s. 16(1)). Banks are not exempt. If the formalities prescribed by the Act are not complied with, s. 65 provides that an agreement which is 'improperly executed' can be enforced against the debtor only by order of the court. Formerly, even a relatively minor error on the face of an agreement as to the amount of credit provided by the lender could render the agreement completely unenforceable. Having particular regard to the 'social mischief' implicit in the exploitation of vulnerable or unsophisticated borrowers, the House of Lords declined in *Wilson v First County Trust Ltd* [2001] QB 407 to hold such a drastic penalty for the lender to be incompatible with Art. 6 and Art. 1 of the First Protocol. Indeed, said Lord Nichols of Birkenhead it was entirely open to Parliament to decide that, 'severe though this sanction may be, it is an appropriate way of protecting consumers as a matter of social policy' (para. 75). However, as a result of amendments introduced by the Consumer Credit Act 2006, errors in an agreement will no longer mean that the agreement is irredeemably unenforceable and a court will always have the power to grant an enforcement order under s. 127(1) of the 1974 Act.

In theory, the most far-reaching provision in the 1974 Act for the protection of the borrower was the power given to the court to 're-open' a credit agreement if the credit bargain was extortionate (ss. 137–140). This power extended to all credit agreements made by individuals. A credit bargain was extortionate if the payments to be made under it were 'grossly exorbitant' or if it 'otherwise grossly contravene[d] the ordinary principles of fair dealing' (s. 138(1)). The court was required to take into account interest rates prevailing when the bargain was made, factors in relation to the debtor (such as his age, experience and business capacity, and the degree to which he was under financial pressure when he made the bargain) and the degree of risk accepted by the creditor. If it found that the credit agreement was indeed extortionate, it had wide discretion 'to do justice between the parties' (s. 137(1)). However, it was difficult to find cases in which the courts regarded an interest rate as being sufficiently excessive to render a credit bargain extortionate. For example, in *Woodstead Finance Ltd v Petrou* [1986] FLR 158, the defendant charged her home to stave off her husband's bankruptcy. The court held the interest rate of 42 per cent to be 'very harsh' but did not find it to be extortionate because of the husband's 'appalling record of payments'. Another of the Act's failings was that it allowed the court to re-open only the terms originally agreed by the parties and not interest rates later varied in accordance with the agreement (*Paragon Finance plc v Nash* [2002] 1 WLR 685).

In 1991, the Director-General of Fair Trading identified certain abuses affecting non-status borrowers in the secured lending market, and expressed the opinion that the extortionate credit bargain provisions of the Act had not dealt effectively with the problems to which they were addressed. He recommended that the government should introduce legislation to recast the relevant provisions of the 1974 Act so as to make them work as originally intended (DGFT, 1991: 1.9). Now, when the relevant provisions of the Consumer Credit Act 2006 come into force, s. 140 of the 2004 Act will empower the court to make an order if it determines that the relationship between the creditor and the debtor is unfair to the debtor as regards:

(a) any of the terms of the agreement or of any related agreement;
(b) the way in which the creditor has exercised or enforced any of [the creditor's] rights under the agreement or any related agreement; or
(c) any other thing done (or not done) by, or on behalf of the creditor (either before or after the making of such agreements).

By s. 140A(2), the court shall have regard to all matters it considers relevant (including matters relating to the creditor and the debtor) and it will not be surprising if the application of the 'unfair relationships' provisions have the same outcome as those relating to extortionate credit bargains. It appears that the more 'desperate and vulnerable' the borrower, the more justified is the imposition of a high interest rate, and the less able are the courts to intervene' (Gray and Gray, 2005: 15.64).

Another source of protection for borrowers is the Financial Services and Markets Act 2000 which applies to 'regulated mortgage contracts' entered into on or after 31 October 2004 and requires a firm engaged in mortgage lending or administration to be authorised by the Financial Services Authority and to 'pay due regard to the interests of its customers and treat them fairly' (FSA, 2003: 2.31). A 'regulated mortgage contract' is one under which a loan to an individual or to trustees is secured by a first legal mortgage on land located in the UK and at least 40 per cent of that land is used, or intended to be used, as or in connection with a dwelling by the borrower or (in the case of credit provided to trustees) by a trust beneficiary or some 'related person' (i.e. a member of the immediate family). Although 'the level of charges under a regulated mortgage contract is not typically a matter for regulation', firms are obliged to ensure that it does not impose, and cannot be used to impose, 'excessive charges upon a customer' (ibid.: 12.5). In determining whether a charge is excessive, a firm should consider 'charges for similar products or services on the market, the degree to which the imposed charges are an 'abuse of the trust that the customer has placed in the firm', and the nature and extent of the disclosure of the charges to the customer.

Further – albeit limited – statutory regulation for many borrowers is provided by the Unfair Terms in Consumer Contracts Regulations 1999 which render unenforceable any 'unfair term', i.e. any term which 'contrary to the requirement of good faith causes a significant imbalance in the parties' rights and obligations arising under the contract, to the detriment of the consumer'. Although not directly applicable in determining the 'fairness' of the interest rate fixed by a credit agreement, the Regulations apply to security interests and may prove to have some impact on standard form mortgage terms (see *Director General of Fair Trading v First National Bank plc* [2002] AC 481).

Chapter 4

The development of social housing

Introduction

The United Kingdom is unusual in that most of its social housing is owned and managed by local authorities rather than by the voluntary sector. Since 1988, however, housing associations have been thrust into the limelight as the main providers of new not-for-profit housing and they have also taken over a significant amount of housing which was previously in local authority ownership. The term 'social housing' began in the 1990s to be applied to rented housing in both tenures with the aim of asserting 'both a distinctiveness and commonality of purpose' within this context of 'a rapidly demunicipalising not-for-profit rented sector' (Cowan and Marsh, 2004: 23). Nevertheless, in so far as the state helps finance its construction and contributes to its income (through housing benefit), social housing in the UK remains 'overwhelmingly a matter of state provision' (Law Commission, 2002a: 6, n. 17).

This chapter considers the origins and development of the council housing sector (which, despite its decline, is still large in comparison with other countries) and concludes with an examination of the voluntary housing sector.

From the nineteenth century to the First World War

The nineteenth century was a period of dynamic change in Great Britain. Between 1801 and 1841 the population rose from nine million to 16 million and by 1901 it was twice as large again (Merrett, 1979: 3). Growth was concentrated in the towns and cities where opportunities for employment existed. Industrial pollution, inadequate drainage and sanitation, a shortage of decent housing and consequent overcrowding combined to produce appalling living conditions. In 1844, Engels vividly described parts of Manchester in which each house was 'packed close behind its neighbour ... all black, smoky, crumbling, ancient, with broken panes and window frames' and where, at the entrance to one courtyard, stood 'a privy without a door, so dirty that the inhabitants can pass into and out of the court only by passing through foul pools of stagnant urine and excrement' (Engels, 1958: 58–60). Nearby tanneries filled the neighbourhood with 'the stench of animal putrefaction' while 'the contents of all the neighbouring sewers and privies' found their way into the river into which was also discharged effluent from the 'tanneries, bone mills and gasworks' (ibid.). Continuing industrial development increased housing demand but also reduced the existing supply. The new railway system cut a swathe through residential areas into city centres, and the space produced by slum clearance was often filled, not with new homes, but with warehouses, offices, grand new thoroughfares and the civic monuments to commercial success exemplified by law courts and town halls (Wohl, 1977: 26–7; Merrett, 1979: 12; Forrest and Murie, 1991: 18).

The disease caused by overcrowded and insanitary conditions adversely affected labour productivity and profits while the dissatisfaction they engendered led to fears of civil unrest. One response lay in public health legislation and the regulation of new buildings (Merrett, 1979: 6, 9). The Public Health Act 1875 empowered local authorities to make by-laws setting out basic requirements regarding housing standards and amenities, thus preventing the construction of new slums but leaving existing ones untouched.

The Artisans and Labourers' Dwellings Act 1868 (the Torrens Act) gave local authorities the power to close or demolish *individual* unfit dwellings while the Artisans and Labourers' Dwellings Improvement Act 1875 (the Cross Act) enabled them to demolish and clear *areas* of unfit housing. The 1875 Act also, and significantly, imposed an obligation upon local authorities to rehouse on site those households which had been displaced during the clearance. Any housing built in pursuance of this obligation was to be sold within 10 years of its completion. However, councils built very little housing themselves under the Act, preferring to sell the sites to charitable housing trusts endowed by wealthy philanthropists such as Guinness and Peabody, or to 'model dwelling companies' such as the Improved Industrial Dwellings Company. These bodies aimed to provide affordable working-class housing with a regular water supply, adequate sewage disposal and proper ventilation, while ensuring a limited return to investors of about 5 per cent. Often, however, their rents were beyond the reach of the displaced tenants.

The Royal Commission on the Housing of the Working Classes (1884–5) found that overcrowding was on the increase in nearly all the areas of London it surveyed. It emphasised that overcrowding was a housing problem caused by high rents and the need for people to live near their work. It was not a sanitary problem which could be resolved merely by public health measures. Nor was it the fault of the feckless and undeserving poor since it affected even better paid artisans. It was the 'stye that made the pig', and not the other way round.

The Housing of the Working Classes Act 1890 brought together the Torrens and Cross Acts but also enabled local authorities to redevelop a site themselves if no other agency came forward (Part I), and to build, renovate and improve 'working class lodging houses' (Part III). It was 'a qualitative turning point' and a 'quantitative watershed' in the history of British public housing (Merrett, 1979: 26) in that it permitted public housing to be built independently of clearance operations. Yet the fact that housing built under these schemes was expected to be self-financing meant that only a few authorities used their Part III powers. In consequence, the model dwelling companies retained their role as the main providers of social housing and 'the market model, largely unconstrained by the redistributive influence of the state, dominated housing policy' (ibid.).

The Liberal government which assumed office in 1906 initiated a number of measures which paved the way for the construction of the welfare state but, so far as public housing was concerned, its only contribution was the Housing and Town Planning Act 1909 which brought to an end the requirement that dwellings built under the 1875 and 1890 Acts should be sold after 10 years. By 1914, local authorities owned about 24,000 dwellings (well under half a per cent of the entire housing stock at the time).

The inter-war years

No recognisable housing policy existed before 1914. Between the wars, it consisted of two main elements: rent control in the private sector and the development of the public sector, the latter emerging initially as a tenure which served mainly clerks and small tradesmen, skilled and semi-skilled workers with above average wages, average sized families and secure jobs. Towards the end of the 1920s, however, attention turned to the accommodation of people displaced by slum clearance. The Conservatives supported private enterprise and regarded state intervention merely as a temporary expedient whilst Labour envisaged a permanent role for public housing but was hindered by a lack of political power and economic resources. Even so, nearly four million new houses were built between 1919 and 1939: 1,112,000 by local authorities and 2,886,000 by private enterprise of which 430,000 were subsidised (Burnett, 1978: 242). Most of the privately built properties were sold to owner-occupiers but as many as 900,000 were added to the private rented sector (Malpass and Murie, 1999: 38). Housing standards were higher than those which had prevailed in the nineteenth century.

Council housing began in earnest soon after the First World War. The low level of building both before and during the war, together with a huge increase in household numbers, resulted in many men returning to housing conditions which were worse than those they had left. Often they had to move in with relatives, to occupy one or two rooms in houses shared with several other families, or to live in various 'temporary dwellings', including wooden shacks, caravans and railway carriages with no sanitary facilities (Burnett, 1978: 217). In November 1918, Lloyd George declared that 'Slums are not fit homes for the men who have won this war'.

The First World War brought about a major social shake-up, challenging long-established class divisions and highlighting a growing dissatisfaction with pre-war standards of working-class life in general and of housing in particular (Bowley, 1945: 3, 4). The Russian Revolution had only recently taken place and the British labour movement had become much stronger during the war with the growth of the trade unions. 'The money we propose to spend on housing is an insurance against Bolshevism and revolution' pronounced Lord Astor, Parliamentary Secretary to the Local Government Board, although he was mindful too of the moral and social casualties inflicted by bad housing and 'the awful havoc upon the morality of young girls wrought by overcrowding' (HC Deb (1919) vol. 114, col. 1956). Suddenly, housing became a national and party political issue, rather than one in which only isolated groups of social reformers were interested.

The Housing and Planning Act 1919

A coalition government of Liberals and Conservatives, led by Lloyd George, took office in November 1919. The Housing and Planning Act 1919 (the Addison Act) gave local authorities a new, significant role in the provision of housing, requiring them to survey the housing needs of their districts and to make and carry out plans to provide the houses which were needed. Ministerial approval was required before the plans were put into practice and for the rents at which the houses were to be let.

The government intended that half a million dwellings should be built over three years. Local authority co-operation was secured by limiting their liability to a penny rate, with the Exchequer meeting the difference between the income from rents and the cost of providing houses. In effect, therefore, the state assumed financial responsibility for the provision of working class houses, the 1919 Act setting up a framework for the production, financing, and management of council housing which was to last until the end of the 1960s. Despite the ostensible autonomy of authorities, the subsidy allowed central government considerable influence in deciding how much and what sort of housing they should provide (typically general needs or slum clearance).

With hindsight, the Addison Act can be seen as having dramatically improved standards of working class housing and living. Hundreds of thousands of people were moved from crowded inner-city areas to new residential districts on the outskirts and, in some cases, to completely new planned communities far from their former homes. The working classes were thus absorbed into the process of suburbanisation which the middle classes had followed since at least the middle of the nineteenth century. A geographical separation was achieved between home and work. By 1921, when all new approvals were stopped, the 214,000 houses for which approval had been given fell far short of the 500,000 target and the scheme was abandoned because of its cost.

The Housing Act 1923

When he introduced the Housing Bill in the House of Commons, Neville Chamberlain, then Minister of Health in the new Conservative government, expressed the hope that future state intervention would be unnecessary, and that the building industry would return to its pre-war economic basis. In reply to questions about the housing problems of newly-married couples, he observed that 'they should be so happy that they can enjoy living even in one room' (Burnett, 1978: 222).

The policy of encouraging local authorities to become major providers of working-class housing was reversed. The Housing Act 1923 (the Chamberlain Act) aimed to encourage speculative building of working-class houses for sale or rental, and to limit local authority activity. Local authorities were permitted to build only if they could convince the Minister that private provision would not suffice. The Treasury would provide a subsidy for any house built, whether by private enterprise or by local authorities, which satisfied certain conditions as to size, etc. No contribution from the rates was required. Between 1923 and 1929 (the year in which the subsidy was extended), 363,000 houses were built by private enterprise and only 75,000 by local authorities. The subsidy undoubtedly played some part in stimulating private house-building, but of more consequence were falling building costs and an expansion of home ownership made possible by easier mortgages.

Housing (Financial Provisions) Act 1924

The first Labour government came to power in 1924, but for only nine months. Wheatley was the new Minister of Health. The primary purpose of the Housing (Financial Provisions) Act 1924 (the Wheatley Act) was to make local authorities part of the permanent machinery for the provision of working-class housing. A long-term housing programme was put in place and their powers to construct houses without first having to prove that they could not be provided by private enterprise were restored.

A new Treasury subsidy was made available for houses built by local authorities which complied with certain standards as to size, etc. The amount needed to keep average rents on a par with controlled rents in the private sector determined a mandatory rate contribution. The Wheatley Act is generally regarded as the most successful of the inter-war housing measures, its subsidies continuing in place under the new Conservative administration until 1933 by which time it had produced a total of 508,000 houses, all but 15,000 provided by local authorities. Even so, council housing remained unaffordable for unemployed people (who numbered three million by 1931) and those on low pay or in insecure employment who continued to live in old privately-rented property, much of which was deteriorating into slums (Burnett, 1978: 234).

The Housing Act 1930

A Labour government was returned to office in 1929 with Greenwood as Minister of Health. The Housing Act 1930 (the Greenwood Act) was passed in the depths of the economic depression to deal with 'the worst housed sections of the community for whom the ordinary subsidy was of no use' (Bowley, 1945: 45). It obliged local authorities to draw up plans for, and to rehouse those who were displaced by, slum clearance. They were required to set 'reasonable' rents and allowed to put in place rent rebate schemes, with better off tenants effectively subsidising the lower rents paid by poor tenants (Malpass and Murie, 1999: 50). The Exchequer subsidy was based on the numbers of people displaced and rehoused. Unsurprisingly, the per capita subsidy and the need to keep rents affordable for poorer families, resulted in smaller, lower-standard houses, incidentally reducing the appeal of council housing to people who could afford accommodation in the private sector (ibid.: 38). A special subsidy was made available for flats and, although it formed only a small part of the housing built during the inter-war years, multi-storey living began to be accepted less grudgingly as a normal type of city housing (Bowley, 1945: 241).

From the Addison Act until 1935, the rents were calculated as each scheme was completed, taking into account annual costs (loan charges, repairs and management), and any Exchequer subsidy or contributions from the rate fund. Each scheme was kept separate, and each account had to balance. Significantly different rents might be payable therefore for identical houses, depending on the scheme under which they had been built. The Housing Act 1935 required each authority to maintain a single housing revenue account for its entire stock. Subsidies and rate fund contributions were deducted from total outgoings, and the difference determined rental income. Eventually, this 'rent-pooling' enabled the local authorities to transfer the subsidies on older, cheaper properties to more modern ones which had cost much more to build. Initially, however, the object of the single account was to facilitate rebates: the subsidies which were brought together could fund rebates to poorer tenants, while the rest paid full, economic rents. Local resistance to rebate schemes persisted, however, and by 1939 only a few authorities were operating them (Merrett, 1979: 58; Malpass and Murie, 1999: 51; Aughton and Malpass, 1994: 27).

1945 to 1964

Housing policy from 1945 to 1964 bore a marked resemblance to policy between the wars. In the first decade after each world war, attention was focused on reducing the severe housing shortage. Despite the disruption to the economy, the quality of new local authority housing was at its highest. When the immediate problem had been dealt with, the question of slum clearance re-emerged and the quality of new public sector housing fell.

Local authorities were edged out of general needs housing, and the private sector moved in (Malpass and Murie, 1999: 55).

Labour won the general election in July 1945. Not surprisingly, the air raids of the Second World War had wreaked havoc with the housing stock in many parts of Britain. Some 450,000 dwellings had been destroyed or made uninhabitable, and an estimated three million damaged to a lesser extent (Malpass and Murie, 1999: 52). Although new building had been at a virtual standstill during the war, the population had increased by about one million. In the short-term, temporary housing was produced (often in the form of prefabricated dwellings) and severely damaged dwellings were repaired. Local authorities and private builders rebuilt houses destroyed by bombing, existing premises (including houses and war-time hostels built for factory workers) were converted and adapted, empty properties were requisitioned, and use was made of service camps which had been built during the war (Merrett, 1979: 238–9).

The new government possessed the will but not the means to promote new homes. Industry, nationalisation and the welfare state programmes were also strong contenders for state support, and the housebuilding programme fell prey to the balance of trade deficit in the mid-1940s which led to cuts in public spending (Burnett, 1979: 277). The Housing Act 1949 removed the previous limitation, whereby councils could only provide housing for 'the working classes', so that account could be taken of the housing conditions and needs of all members of the community. During the Labour government's period of office, over one million dwellings were built (over 80 per cent of them by local authorities) and they were generally of good quality. This represented the first large-scale investment in public housing since the Wheatley legislation, but the failure to meet the target of 240,000 per year was one of the reasons for the government's electoral defeat.

In October 1951, the Conservatives were returned to power and did not allow the grave balance of payment deficit of 1951–2 to stand in the way of their target of building 300,000 dwellings a year. In 1952 the Exchequer subsidy and the rate fund contribution were increased. In 1954, a record 348,000 new homes were built, but building and design standards were low, underlining the Conservatives' residualist attitude towards public housing.

In its 1953 White Paper, the government set out its strategy which, broadly, represented 'a return to the philosophy of Chamberlain and the "golden years" of the 1930s' (Merrett, 1979: 247). Output was to be stabilised at about 300,000 dwellings per year. The private sector was to be responsible for new general needs housing and the construction of houses for owner-occupation (the form of ownership regarded as 'the most satisfying to the individual and the most beneficial to the nation') was to be promoted by all possible means. Local authorities would make up the shortfall. Finally, large-scale housing renewal was to be stimulated.

A boom in the building industry in 1954 coincided with the ending of building licensing and a reduction in the subsidy for general needs housing. The subsidy was cut by a further 50 per cent by the Housing Subsidies Act 1956 and abolished altogether soon afterwards. Subsidies were retained, however, for the construction of one-bedroomed dwellings for the elderly, for slum clearance and for flats in blocks which exceeded a certain number of storeys. Many local authorities favoured blocks of flats in inner city slum clearance areas where space was limited and land was relatively expensive, even though 'the increased construction costs in high-rise building more than outweighed the savings in other costs' (Forrest and Murie, 1991: 26). So far as tenants were concerned, however, high-rise blocks of flats often destroyed communities and damaged family life.

In 1955, the government took a new approach to local authority rents, urging the adoption of 'realistic' rents, and the use of rent-rebate schemes to channel subsidy towards low-income households. The Housing Subsidies Act 1956 removed the obligation on local authorities to contribute to the Housing Revenue Account from the rate fund, regardless of their total rent income. This enabled them to raise rents generally (while providing rebates for the needy), and increase their total income (thereby reducing the need for a rate fund contribution). Realistic rents therefore meant higher rents for those who could afford to pay the full economic cost of their housing and lower rents for the poor. Subsidising better-off tenants was seen as a misuse of public money.

As regards general needs housing, the government pinned its hopes on private enterprise and on the Rent Act 1957 which was intended to introduce greater mobility into the housing market by partial deregulation in the private rented sector. By the end of the decade, however, it was clear that a new housing crisis was looming. The 1957 Act had failed to halt the decline of private renting, homelessness was growing and lower-paid workers, immigrant groups and the elderly often lived in very poor conditions. The early 1960s became, therefore, a period of 'policy reconsideration' (Merrett, 1979: 252).

The Housing Act 1961 reintroduced subsidies for general needs building and the rate of council-house construction began to recover. Both the Conservative government and the Labour opposition agreed that a very high level of house building was needed. In the event, the Conservative government fell from office in 1964 in a year of record housing output: 374,000, of which 156,000 were built by public authorities.

1964 to 1979

In its election manifesto, Labour had pledged to build 500,000 houses a year but it was forced to cut back on its building programme as part of the package of public spending cuts which followed the devaluation of the pound in

November 1967. Even so, approximately 1.8 million houses were built between 1965 and 1969, almost equally divided between the public and private sectors (Burnett, 1978: 278).

The 1965 White Paper marked a significant change of direction in Labour's attitude towards the relative roles of council housing and owner-occupation, presenting the expansion of building for owner-occupation as 'normal' and 'a long-term social advance which should gradually pervade every region'. Council housing was relegated to a residualist role, to be provided until Britain had overcome 'its huge social problem of slumdom and obsolescence, and met the need of the great cities for more houses let at moderate rents'. With the Housing Act 1969, the emphasis was switched to the private rehabilitation of older properties and local authorities were permitted to make more generous grants.

A Conservative government was elected in June 1970 with Edward Heath at the helm. In 1971 the White Paper, *Fair Deal for Housing*, advocated the establishment of a uniform system of fair rents for all private and public sector tenants. Ministers regarded council rents as being unacceptably low as a result of the machinations of Labour-controlled local councils and a subsidy system which operated across the board, instead of focusing on tenants who were in particular need. The 'fair rent' system in the private rented sector, introduced by the Rent Act 1965, had led to increases in rent levels and a gap was growing between private sector rents and those in the public sector. The Housing Finance Act 1972 introduced an entirely new rent and subsidy system, removing the autonomy which local authorities had enjoyed since 1923 in setting rents and granting rebates. Henceforth, council rents were to be brought into line – by staged increases – with fair rents. Authorities were obliged to set provisional fair rents but the final decision rested with an independent committee for each area. For the first time, the link between rents and the costs of providing council houses was broken. A new mandatory rent rebate system was introduced for council tenants on low incomes. A new Exchequer subsidy was introduced, based on the deficit on the housing revenue account after 'reckonable expenditure' on loan charges, repairs and maintenance had been sent against rental income.

These reforms 'aroused sharper controversy than at any time since councils first became involved with housing' (Aughton, 1994: 30) as it was clear that the move to fair rents would lead to substantial rent increases and to considerable savings as regards the subsidy from central government. As it was, the 1972 Act never had the opportunity to operate as planned because the Labour government which came to office in 1974 immediately froze council rents, as part of its counter-inflationary policy. The Housing Rents and Subsidies Act 1975 repealed the fair rent provisions for council housing and restored the freedom to set 'reasonable rents' based on historic costs. Once again local authorities were empowered to make rate fund contributions at their own discretion. The deficit subsidy was replaced with a new temporary subsidy related to the cost of new borrowing and this regime operated until it was replaced by the Housing Act 1980 (Aughton and Malpass, 1994: 30).

From 1979 to the present

Some major pieces of housing legislation were introduced under the leadership of Margaret Thatcher. Particularly notable were the Housing Act 1980 (which introduced the right to buy (RTB) for council tenants), the Housing Act 1985 (which facilitated the disposal by local authorities of their housing stock to the voluntary sector via large-scale voluntary stock transfers (LSVTs)), and the Housing Act 1988 (which, in relation to the public sector, introduced the housing action trust and tenants' choice provisions). The Local Government and Housing Act 1989 introduced a new financial regime. Formerly, capital expenditure (on the acquisition and development of land, building work, vehicles, plant and machinery, capital grants and advances) had been authorised by the annual Housing Investment Programme (HIP), and the allocation was normally backed by borrowing approval. Authorities could also use capital receipts (mainly from the sale of council houses under the RTB and from LSVTs), although only 20 per cent could be used for 'prescribed expenditure' (e.g. for new building) during the year in which the council received the money. Twenty per cent of any remaining receipts could be used the next year and so on. Over a period of years, therefore, this 'cascade' effect permitted virtually the whole amount to be spent. The 1989 Act permitted only 25 per cent of receipts to be spent on new developments and required at least 75 per cent to be used to repay debt, even though councils faced huge problems of repair and modernisation. It has been said that this made as much sense as a householder, faced with a leaking roof, using all his or her available cash to make a premature reduction on his or her mortgage (Aughton and Malpass, 1994: 39). The housing revenue account was 'ring-fenced' and authorities could not subsidise it out of other accounts. A requirement that rent increases should reflect differences in capital values led to significant increases in council rents designed perhaps to encourage more tenants to exercise the right to buy or to opt for another landlord. More importantly, the cost of housing benefit for council tenants was added to the expenditure side of the housing revenue account which meant that most fell into deficit and local authorities had to rely on central 'subsidies' to keep rents at reasonable levels. Any surplus had to be paid into the authority's general fund and could be spent on all local services or on reducing taxation.

Under the leadership of John Major, who succeeded Margaret Thatcher as Prime Minister, the measures set in process during the Thatcher years were continued (e.g. LSVTs) and extended (e.g. Compulsory Competitive Tendering). Significant changes were made to the allocation of council housing and the housing of homeless households and concern over anti-social behaviour among tenants became more prominent.

Since coming to power in May 1997, the Labour government has used delegated legislation to curb some of the worst excesses of the previous administration's legislation on allocations and homelessness. Although it released the estimated £5 billion of capital receipts from homes sold under the right to buy scheme, it failed to remove the restrictions which limit authorities' spending to 25 per cent of receipts. Production targets were a familiar feature of housing politics in the 1950s and 1960s but in the past three decades they have ceased to be a measure of 'ministerial virility', and have therefore disappeared completely (Malpass and Murie, 1999: 53). Since 1979 new local authority building has declined to its lowest peacetime level since 1921, and receipts from council house sales and stock transfer have enabled central government dramatically to reduce investment in housing. In 2001–2, although HIP and Approved Development Programme expenditure totalled £1,580 million, it was offset by set aside RTB receipts of £976 million and stock transfer receipts of £272 million. This meant that the Exchequer had to contribute just £332 million. General bricks-and-mortar subsidies (which benefit all council tenants) have been replaced by individual means-tested subsidy in the shape of housing benefit (itself subject to continuing restrictions and adjustments), and council rents have risen in real terms to a level greater than at any time since 1945. The role of council housing has become increasingly a residual, welfare one. The emphasis of housing policy, informed by taxation and public expenditure considerations and a desire to extend the role of the private sector, has shifted from having a single focus on expanding market provision to creating a restructured social rented sector outside public control in which housing associations play a major role.

Housing associations

What are housing associations?

The 1987 White Paper criticised the 'distant and bureaucratic' housing operations of local authorities in many big cities, and the insensitive design and bad management of some housing. Housing had been badly maintained, tenants alienated, and a wide range of social problems had emerged: an increase in crime and violence; the departure of many people for better opportunities elsewhere; the disappearance of local enterprise and employment; and the welfare dependency of whole communities. A 'more pluralist and more market oriented system' was advocated which would ensure that housing supply could respond more flexibly to demand, provide tenants with more choice and allow 'greater scope for private investment and more effective use of public sector money'. Provision of housing by local authorities as landlords should gradually be diminished and alternative forms of tenure and tenant choice should increase. The government felt that housing associations had a vitally important role to play in the revival of what it described as the 'independent' rented sector (DoE, 1987: 1.9, 1.11, 1.16, 4.3).

There are approximately 2,200 housing associations. In 1988, they owned just over 500,000 homes (Malpass, 2005: 291) but now they own or manage about two million. Collectively, they are sometimes referred to as the 'voluntary housing movement' but labelling them as a 'movement' obscures the fact that they come in a variety of shapes and sizes.[1] Several associations can trace their roots back to twelfth century almshouses, while some of the best known (such as the Peabody Trust) were endowed by wealthy employers or philanthropists in the nineteenth century.[2] Many others came into existence in the 1960s and 1970s as the result of government initiatives designed to encourage alternatives to owner-occupation and council housing, and to revive run-down inner city areas. More recently the structure and dynamics of the voluntary sector have been transformed by the many new organisations which have been created to allow for stock transfer (Malpass, 2005: 190).

Most housing associations are constituted as industrial and provident societies. Many others are registered as companies limited by guarantee, and the remainder are trusts, most of them charitable. Although housing associations take several – sometimes overlapping – forms, the one characteristic they have in common is that they are all non-profit-making bodies. (This does not prevent the association from making a surplus which is then reinvested for housing purposes.) The larger associations have paid staff with operational responsibility but ultimate responsibility for the work of each organisation rests with a committee or board of management made up of volunteers. The voluntary sector, in the form of housing associations, remains the smallest of the main tenure categories yet it has been described as 'the fastest growing and most dynamic part of the housing system at the present time' (Malpass, 2000: 3).

Over 1,800 housing associations are registered with the Housing Corporation as registered social landlords (RSLs).[3] The Housing Corporation

---

1   A housing association is 'a society, body of trustees or company which is established for the purpose of, or amongst whose objects or powers are included those of, providing, constructing, improving or managing, or facilitating or encouraging the construction or improvement of, housing accommodation' (Housing Associations Act 1985, s. 1(1)).

2   For a description of the historical evolution of the voluntary housing movement, see Alder and Handy (2003: 1–006–1–009).

3   A body may apply for registration with the Housing Corporation if it is a registered charity which is a housing association, a society which is registered under the Industrial and Provident Societies Act 1965 or a company registered under the Companies Act 1985 provided that the society or company is non-profit making and is established for the purpose of providing housing (Housing Act 1996, s. 2).

is a statutory body whose 15 board members are appointed by the Secretary of State for Communities and Local Government (see the Housing Associations Act 1985, Sch. 6). The Corporation was established under the Housing Act 1964 to promote and assist the development of new-style housing societies and old-style housing associations as a response to the nefarious activities of certain private landlords such as Rachman (see Chapter 15) but its role was considerably extended, in terms both of funding and regulatory powers, by the Housing Act 1974. A consequence of the 1974 Act was that housing associations – historically 'small, under-funded and therefore insignificant and marginal' – were brought nearer the centre of housing policy and given the resources they had lacked – although at the price of lost independence (Malpass, 2005: 115–16). Today, registration with the Housing Corporation or Housing for Wales is an essential prerequisite of eligibility for public funding, not only from central government (usually via the Corporation) but also from local authorities. Local authorities can fund RSLs directly (Housing Act 1996, s. 22) and may also assist non-registered housing associations by lending money or subscribing for shares (Housing Associations Act 1985, s. 58). When a new RSL registers with the Corporation, its principal object must be to provide social rental housing, which must account for at least 50 per cent of its activities. Other activities may include shared ownership schemes and the provision of non-social housing, e.g. keyworker housing, student accommodation, and letting properties on the open market. Recently RSLs have been permitted by the Social Landlords (Permissible Additional Purposes) (England) Order 2006 to build and manage gypsy and travellers' sites and to receive Social Housing Grant for that purpose.

Initially, although the Corporation made loans to help finance their activities, two-thirds of any finance had to be raised from the private sector – usually building societies (Harriott and Matthews, 1998: 7). However, the 1974 Act introduced a legislative and financial framework which existed until 1988. Particularly significant was the introduction of the Housing Association Grant (HAG – a lump sum provided by central government to housing associations registered with the Housing Corporation) to cover building and rehabilitation costs and thus assist in the renewal of General Improvement and Housing Action areas. A 'fair rent' (as defined by the Rent Act 1977) was determined for each dwelling by the rent officer. How much of the cost of any project was to be borne by way of a mortgage was determined by whatever amount could be repaid from the rental income after management and maintenance costs were taken into account. The HAG (which was calculated at the end of the project) accounted on average for about 85 to 90 per cent of the total scheme cost. Housing associations could develop projects safe in the knowledge that most of their borrowing would be underwritten by central government. This arrangement not only promoted growth but also allowed associations to build up substantial, and largely debt-free, assets. The period from 1974 to 1989 can be seen therefore as a 'pump priming exercise' in which associations were supported by public funds until they had reached a point where they could operate effectively in the capital markets and take over from local authorities as the providers of new social rented housing (Malpass, 2005: 198–9).

The Housing Act 1988 established a radical new system of housing association finance which 'plunges housing associations into a swirling sea of private finance, risk taking and competition' (Alder and Handy, 2003: 1–001). The HAG (renamed the Social Housing Grant – SHG – by the Housing Act 1996) is now set in advance as a predetermined amount and the rent level is adjusted to cover the balance to be met by loans from private lenders. The new regime was based on the premise that these 'market principles' would lead to 'greater efficiency' and make associations 'more independent and more responsible for the quality and effectiveness of their investment decisions and the competence of their management' (Alder and Handy, 2003: 9–001). On the one hand, the combination of grant funding and private finance has indeed been very successful, with the total amount of private finance raised by RSLs standing at £35.9 billion (*Public Finance*, 14 July 2006). Yet, while significant savings for the public purse have resulted, it is worth noting that ultimately, the funding of this increased investment has been helped by public money, given that 'the interest paid to commercial lenders by housing associations [is] financed by rental revenue streams which, although nominally, paid by the tenants, are often in practice reimbursed by the Government in the form of housing benefit' (Law Commission, 2002a: 42, n. 114).

During the 1990s, housing association rents rose as government subsidy fell from a peak of £2.2 billion in 1992 to a little over £600 million in 1998. Yet recent years have witnessed 'a reverse trend of increasing grant rates in order to ensure rents remain affordable and limit the cost of the housing benefit bill' (Alder and Handy, 2003: 9–001). In addition, the introduction of the rent restructuring framework – giving effect to the government's objective that rent setting in the social rented sector be brought onto a common system based on relative property values and local earnings levels (see Chapter 6) – means that by 2012 existing rent differentials between local authority and RSL stock should have disappeared.

The nature of housing associations

Until 1954, housing associations which provided accommodation within the relevant rateable value limits were subject to the security of tenure provisions of the Rent Acts, i.e. the same code to which private sector tenancies were subject. However, the 1977 Act removed from its protection tenancies granted by housing associations which were registered with the Housing Corporation. As a result, such tenancies were in the same position as local authority tenancies: security of tenure was essentially determined by the tenancy agreement and landlords were not required to prove any statutorily defined grounds in possession proceedings against their tenants. By contrast, tenants of housing associations which were *not* registered with the Housing Corporation were subject to the security of tenure provisions of the Rent Act 1977, and their rents were limited in the same way as private sector rents. The Housing Finance Act 1972 extended the 'fair rent' regime to some housing association tenancies which were not otherwise regulated (Law Commission, 2002a: 2.58–2.61). This was a particularly important development given that 'the level of subsidy provided to housing associations was then based – broadly – on the difference between the fair rent and the actual cost of running the dwelling (including the cost of servicing the loans which had provided the capital for the buildings)' (ibid.: 2.62).

Whilst therefore housing associations were traditionally regarded as part of the private rented sector (often providing housing for specific groups such as the elderly, ex-offenders, single homeless, mentally or physically disabled), they have come to play a significant role in the provision of social housing in the last quarter century. Thus, when the Housing Act 1980 created statutory security of tenure for local authority tenants, the same provisions were also applied to the tenants of registered housing associations and a limited number of others (see Chapter 18). So far as security of tenure was concerned, tenancies granted by housing associations which fell outside these two groups were still governed by the Rent Act. As regards rent regulation, however, the fair rent procedures of the Rent Act continued to apply to all housing associations (Law Commission, 2002a: 2.97). This meant that 'the tenants of most housing associations were treated on a par with the tenants of local authorities for the purpose of security of tenure, but on a par with private sector tenants for the purpose of rent regulation' (ibid.: 2.98).

Thus, from the viewpoints of finance, philosophy and tenant security, housing associations seemed, for a brief period in their history, to be closer to the public than the private sector, but they moved 'to centre stage' in the early 1990s (Langstaff, 1992: 46), the Housing Act 1988 having pushed them firmly out into 'the more dangerous waters of the open market, of the private sector' (Bridge, 1989: 77). The Act gave effect to the recommendation contained in the 1987 White Paper that, henceforth, all housing associations should grant assured and assured shorthold tenancies in the same way as the private rented sector. The aim was to give housing associations 'the essential freedom and flexibility in setting their rents to enable then to meet the requirements of private sector finance instead of relying on funding from public sources' (DoE, 1987: 4.6). Government may also have wanted to emphasise the dissimilarity between local authorities and housing associations, the use of assured tenancies providing 'symbolic confirmation that the housing association movement should not be seen as part of the public sector' (Mullen, 2001: 48).

When housing associations first began to grant assured tenancies, the Housing Corporation issued the 'Tenants' Guarantee', the object of which was to give assured tenants additional rights which were broadly similar to those contained in the Tenants' Charter. As such, the Guarantee conferred rights in respect of repairs, complaints procedures, rents, exchanges, taking in lodgers, the carrying out of improvements, and consultation. While, importantly, the Tenants' Charter was enshrined in statute (the Housing Act 1980), the rights provided by the Guarantee were incorporated into individual tenancy agreements and were enforceable therefore only on a contractual basis. Over the years, the documentation produced by the Corporation has become far less prescriptive in nature and it no longer includes a checklist of the legal rights enjoyed by residents in the way that the Guarantee once did. Now, the Corporation's Regulatory Code and Guidance simply advises that, for example, tenants should be offered 'the most secure form of tenancy possible compatible with the purpose of the housing and the sustainability of the community' (HC, 2005: 3.5.2).

The accountability of housing associations

The shift of responsibility for the provision of social housing from local authorities to housing associations (which is more fully explored in Chapter 16) raises important issues of both accountability and the forms of redress available to tenants (and prospective tenants) who are dissatisfied with decisions reached by their (prospective) landlords. The growing involvement of housing associations in the provision of housing means that they are necessarily making more decisions, and a growing number of their decisions are likely to be questioned (Belcher and Jackson, 1998: 112). Further, many housing associations are now finding themselves involved in care and support which were formerly the domain of statutory social services. Finally, problems ancillary to housing provision, e.g. anti-social behaviour, require landlords to engage in activities such as CCTV surveillance which have important wider social and legal implications.

We have seen that one of the principal players in the regulation of the majority of housing associations is the Housing Corporation. By registering with the Corporation, a housing association subjects itself to the Corporation's regulation and guidance, with further conditions and obligations being imposed on the receipt of funding (Alder and Handy, 2003: 2–105). The registration process and the registration criteria contained in s. 2 of the Housing Act 1996 circumscribe the functions and powers of housing associations, and increasingly detailed requirements regarding their behaviour (including their development activity, the rents which they set, the allocation of properties, and corporate governance structures and practices) has led to the observation that they have become 'hired agents of central government, operating as branch offices of the Corporation' (Langstaff, 1992: 43). The fact that RSLs have been chosen to deliver affordable housing means that they are 'constantly exposed to attempts to get them to follow the twists and turns of government by initiative, whether it be rent restructuring, choice based lettings, key worker housing or new methods of building procurement' (Malpass, 2005: 199). The role of the Corporation has been strengthened over recent years, reflecting the sizeable public subsidy which RSLs receive and also the contribution of private investment in the sector. Its powers in relation to an unsatisfactory RSL include the making of appointments to its governing body, the removal of employees or governing body members, and the withdrawal of funding (Housing Act 1996, Sch. 1). Where there is found to have been mismanagement in the administration of an RSL, the Corporation may even direct that its property be transferred to another RSL.[4] An inspectorate for local authority housing in England was set up within the Audit Commission by the Local Government Act 1999 and in April 2003 it took over the separate inspection system for RSLs which had been established by the Housing Corporation in 2002. There now exists therefore a unified inspection service for social housing – the Housing Inspectorate – which administers the Best Value scheme and subjects local authorities and RSLs to regular inspections to monitor local performance (see Chapter 16). The work of the Audit Commission and its various inspectorates can be seen as signifying 'a fundamental change in the notion of accountability in the UK' in that 'accountability has itself become managerialised and centralised' and 'performance indicators' (rather than 'votes gained and seats lost') become its new currency. Such a view assumes that 'political models of accountability no longer work (at least at the local level), that the electoral process no longer has an impact on local councils [and] ... that it does not really matter whether those entrusted with exercising local governance are elected or appointed' (Maile and Hoggett, 2001: 512).

If an individual tenant of an RSL has a grievance which cannot be resolved via the landlord's complaints process, an approach may be made to the Housing Corporation and, ultimately, the Independent Housing Ombudsman (Housing Act 1996, s. 51). An aggrieved tenant may also raise concerns with the association's committee or board of management which, as mentioned earlier, is ultimately responsible for the association's actions. However, the board's legal accountability depends upon private law fiduciary duties which are owed only to the association itself. The board's main concern is with standards of care and conflicts of interest 'and does not substitute for the supervisory jurisdiction of the courts' (Alder, 1997: 166).

---

4   See *R v The Housing Corporation ex p Clays Lane Housing Co-operative Ltd* [2005] 1 WLR 2229 in which there was held to have been no breach of Art. 1 of the First Protocol of the ECHR where the Housing Corporation decided that, following a finding of mismanagement, the association's land should transferred to a social landlord other than the one which the association preferred. The Court of Appeal held that where the decision is between two proffered alternatives, any deprivation under Art. 1 must be 'reasonably', rather than 'strictly' or 'absolutely', necessary. Proportionality requires a balancing exercise and a decision which is reasonably necessary but not obligatorily the least intrusive of human rights.

Clearly therefore the regulatory regimes to which housing associations and local authorities are subject have been markedly different, even though their activities of have much in common. Thus, because a local authority is subject to public law, the exercise of its housing functions (e.g. to allocate or terminate a tenancy) may be subject to challenge by way of judicial review on the grounds of unfairness and irrationality. By contrast, there have been few cases concerning the reviewability of decisions made by housing associations. It was held in *Peabody Housing Association Ltd v Green* (1978) 38 P & CR 644 that a housing association is not a public body and not subject therefore even to the substantive principles of judicial review because its powers over its tenants derive from the private law mechanisms of landlord. Funding from the Housing Corporation which the association was obliged to spend in a particular way did not turn its 'normal and essential activities' into the exercise of a statutory power. However, in *Boyle v Castlemilk East Housing Co-operative Ltd* 1998 SLT 56, the Scottish Outer House was prepared to review the refusal of a housing association to consider an application by one of its tenants for a home loss payment under the Land Compensation (Scotland) Act 1973, ostensibly ignoring the fact that the association might be regarded as a private body and its decisions not amenable to judicial review. More recently though, in *R v Servite Houses ex p Goldsmith* (2001) 33 HLR 35, it was held, somewhat reluctantly, that Servite (an RSL) was not amenable to judicial review even though, by housing the applicants in one of its purpose-built care homes, it was enabling the local authority (Wandsworth Borough Council) to discharge a statutory duty under the National Assistance Act 1948 to provide them with residential accommodation. Both applicants had allegedly been assured by Servite that they would be able to remain in the care home for the rest of their lives, and they argued that its closure – for financial reasons – constituted a breach of both Wandsworth's and Servite's public obligations. Had the assurances been given by Wandsworth itself, then the applicants would have been able to seek a public law remedy and, on the basis that the assurances raised a substantive legitimate expectation, the court would probably have required Wandsworth to honour them unless the court judged that there was an overriding public interest that the home be closed (*R v North and East Devon Health Authority ex p Coughlan* [2000] 2 WLR 622). Moses J held that in providing residential accommodation, Servite was not performing a public function and was not under any public law duty to the applicants.

The debate has recently shifted to the human rights arena.[5] A claim under the Human Rights Act 1998 may be brought directly only against a 'public authority'. Local authority tenants can, in appropriate circumstances, challenge their landlords under the Human Rights Act 1998, as can applicants for

---

5   For an extended discussion of this topic, see Morgan (2003).

housing who come through either the homelessness route (see Chapters 10 and 11) or the waiting list (see Chapter 17). Given that, unlike local authorities, housing associations are not obviously 'standard' public authorities, the question is whether they can be categorised as 'functional' public authorities (which carry out some public functions) or as organisations with no public functions and thus outside the Act. The distinction is important: a standard public authority must act in accordance with Convention rights in relation to all its activities, be they public or private but, by s. 6(5), a functional public authority is not acting unlawfully where the particular act challenged is 'of a private nature'. Because local authorities are standard public authorities, it follows that, as landlords of residential property, they may be under direct duties under Art. 8 to respect the rights to privacy and family life of their tenants (Oliver, 2000: 346). By contrast, a housing association may be a functional public authority but only in relation to those of its functions which can be classed as public as opposed to private acts.

Thus far, only one reported case has focused upon the status of a housing association for the purposes of the Human Rights Act 1998. In *Donoghue v Poplar Housing and Regeneration Community Association Ltd* [2001] 3 WLR 183, the local authority was under a statutory duty to accommodate the tenant while it carried out inquiries as to her status as a homeless person and any further duties which it might owe her. It subsequently transferred some of its stock, including the tenant's flat, to Poplar, a housing association which it had set up to take over a substantial proportion of its housing. Having completed its inquiries, the authority decided that the tenant was intentionally homeless, and Poplar served a notice to terminate her tenancy (which had metamorphosed upon the transfer from a weekly non-secure tenancy into an assured shorthold). The Court of Appeal dismissed the tenant's claim that the mandatory nature of the repossession process relating to assured shorthold tenancies (see Chapter 14) contravened her rights under Art. 8 but held that Poplar was a 'public authority' for the purposes of the Human Rights Act 1998.

The court set out a number of matters which it regarded as particularly important in determining Poplar's status. First, the transfer of the authority's housing stock to Poplar did not involve the transfer its primary public duties, Poplar merely acting as the means by which those duties were performed. Secondly, the provision of rented accommodation is not in itself a public function, regardless of the section of society for whom it is provided. Thirdly, an RSL's status as a charity or other non-profit-making body does not point to its being a public authority, even though it may well be motivated by what it perceives to be the public interest.[6] In addition, even if a body

---

6   It has been suggested that this view understates the significance of charitable status which 'requires a body to act only for designated public purposes by virtue of which it is given special legal and fiscal privileges' (Alder and Handy, 2001: 71).

performs an activity which would be considered to be public if performed by a public body, it may remain of a private nature for the purpose of ss. 6(3)(b) and 6(5).

In the end, recognising that this was a borderline case, the court held that Poplar was so closely assimilated to Tower Hamlets in relation to Ms Donoghue's tenancy that it should be regarded as a functional public authority. Five of Poplar's board members were also members of Tower Hamlets, and it was subject to the authority's guidance to the manner in which it acted towards Ms Donoghue. At the time of transfer, she was a sitting tenant of Poplar and it was intended that she would be treated no differently than if she had still been a tenant of Tower Hamlets. So long as she remained a tenant, Poplar therefore stood in relation to her in very much the position previously occupied by Tower Hamlets. The court stated categorically that this did not mean that Poplar was a public authority for all purposes, and made it clear that the position would not necessarily have been the same had Ms Donoghue been a secure tenant.

Having accepted that s. 6 requires 'a generous interpretation of who is a public authority', the Court of Appeal nonetheless took the view that the performance of an activity which otherwise a public body would be under a duty to perform could not mean that 'such performance is necessarily a public function'. A public authority can, and often does, use the services of a private body in order to perform its public duties, including the accommodation of homeless persons. As the court explained, if the provision of services by a private body on behalf of a public authority meant that the nature of the functions were inevitably public, then:

> a small hotel [which] provides bed and breakfast accommodation as a temporary measure, at the request of a housing authority ... under a duty to provide that accommodation ... would be performing public functions and required to comply with the HRA. That is not what the HRA intended ... Section 6(3) means that hybrid bodies ... are public authorities, but *not* in relation to acts which are of a private nature. The renting out of accommodation can certainly be of a private nature. The fact that through the act of renting by a private body a public authority may be fulfilling its public duty, does not automatically change into a public act what would otherwise be a private act.
>
> (At p. 199.)

In *R (on the application of Heather) v The Leonard Cheshire Foundation* [2002] 2 All ER 936 (the facts of which were, in material respects, identical to those of *Servite Homes*), the Court of Appeal held that the provision of residential accommodation to disabled people by a private charity, under contract with a local authority, was not the performance of a public function for the purposes of the Human Rights Act 1998. Section 6(1) would have applied had the local authority provided the accommodation itself, because standard public authorities are bound to respect Convention rights in all that they do, whether their acts are public or private. Citing and applying the court's reasoning in *Donoghue*, Lord Woolf accepted that a local authority is performing a public function not only if it provides accommodation itself but also if it makes arrangements for the accommodation to be provided by a third party. However, it does not follow that the third party is performing a public function when it provides accommodation to those to whom the authority owes a statutory duty under a statutorily authorised arrangement.

If this analysis is correct then it is difficult see why the nature of a function should change if it is performed in-house or contracted out (Craig, 2002). Oliver (2004), however, suggests that Lord Woolf's premise is mistaken. She argues that a local authority which provides accommodation (or some other service it is under a duty to secure) is not necessarily performing a public function or a function of a public nature. Rather it is performing a statutory duty and it does not follow that the activity it engages in is a function of a public nature. Her argument is attractive but leaves unanswered the question of what features mark out a function as a public as opposed to a private one.

Returning to *Donoghue*, by focusing on the body rather than its functions, the decision 'causes confusion' (Oliver, 2004: 337). It does however suggest that RSLs created specifically to receive LSVTs are more likely to be 'public authorities' for the purposes of the Human Rights Act 1998 with regard to some of their actions, and especially in relation to former local authority tenants. Beyond this it leaves several questions unanswered. For instance, might an existing association which has taken a stock transfer from a local authority be regarded as a public authority? If it were, would it be subject to the Human Rights Act 1998 as regards public functions carried out as regards those whose tenancies commence after the transfer or only those tenants transferred along with the stock? Would a traditional RSL which has not taken a stock transfer be a public authority in relation to its dealings with its tenants, or prospective tenants, or others, e.g. adjoining occupiers, affected by its (in)actions?

In *Leonard Cheshire*, Lord Woolf suggested that there might be a contractual solution: a resident might be able to require the local authority to enter into a contract with the provider which fully protected the resident's Art. 8 rights. Then not only could the local authority rely on the contract, but possibly the resident could do so also as a person for whose benefit the contract was made. Clearly there are practical problems with this approach. As Craig points out, 'the claimants in the cases under discussion would not necessarily know of the Convention rights at the time the contract was drawn up ... [and would not] feel able to require the local authority to contract with the private contractor on these terms'. It is unlikely, he says, that the local authority would choose to contract with the private party on terms which bound the latter to observe Convention rights because although it might gain 'in moral rectitude' by such action, 'it would lose financially through the increase in the contract price to be paid for the service' (Craig, 2002: 560).[7]

Other providers

Issues of accountability arise also in relation to non-RSL housing associations and, more particularly, commercial bodies which can now compete, alongside RSLs, for funds from the Housing Corporation to provide social housing. A proposal in the 1995 White Paper to allow profit-making companies to apply for funding from the Corporation was dropped during the parliamentary passage of the Housing Act 1996. It was subsequently revived, however, and s. 27A of the 1996 Act (inserted by s. 213 of the Housing Act 2004) extends the Corporation's grant-giving powers to bodies which are not registered as social landlords. Accordingly, since April 2006, the Housing Corporation's £200 million New Partnerships in Affordable Housing programme allows both non-RSL housing associations and commercial firms to be developers, landlords and managers.

The Corporation's model for the New Partnerships programme is similar to the traditional SHG system. Organisations bid to provide homes to agreed standards for a fixed level of grant. RSLs which take part in the programme receive 50 per cent of the grant at the start on site and 50 per cent on completion; non-RSLs will receive it all on completion. The payment method is relatively simple therefore compared, for example, with the output specifications and payment mechanisms required for PFI schemes. However, the Corporation does not have the same regulatory powers over non-RSLs as it does RSLs. On the basis that 'private companies are accountable to their shareholders' the Corporation states that it would be 'inappropriate and unrealistic to expect unregistered bodies to work within the same regulatory regime' which applies to housing associations (HC, 2004: 3.3). The Corporation has therefore devised a set of policies and procedures which 'draw from but do not exactly replicate, [the] existing regulatory framework' (ibid.). Minimum standards and output requirements will be contained in an enforceable contract with each bidder. For those non-RSLs which do not contract to pass ownership of homes to RSLs on completion, some form of legal security will be required to ensure that the grant conditions are met (e.g. that the homes are kept as affordable housing and maintained to the standards required). Parliament has been assured that tenants will have the same protection as RSL tenants in respect of legal rights and the terms and conditions of occupancy and that they will have recourse to the Independent Housing Ombudsman. After completion, there will be no financial sanction over the provider but a 'rent charge' registered on the title

---

7   For another criticism of the contract 'solution' see Donnelly (2005).

of the properties will allow the Corporation to reclaim grant if conditions are breached. In parallel, the Corporation is setting up a new Housing Management Accreditation Scheme which aims to ensure that affordable housing is only managed by approved managers, be they RSLs or other bodies. It was reported in March 2006 that just seven private companies were being granted funds under the National Affordable Housing Programme over the next two years (compared with 74 RSLs) and that a total of £66.8 million was going to the private sector – less than 2 per cent of the £3.9 billion on offer from the Housing Corporation in 2006/08 (*Public Finance*, 31 March 2006).

Chapter 5

The private rented sector: history and characteristics

Introduction

Labelling it as 'a' sector masks the fact that the private rented sector provides accommodation for a diverse array of households and is highly fragmented (Cowan and McDermot, 2006: 145). As well as charting the history of legislative intervention, this chapter explores the reasons for its decline and considers some of its characteristics, specifically the nature of landlordism, the different tenant groups and housing conditions.

Legislative history of the private rented sector

Private letting before 1915

By the time the first statutory rent controls directed specifically at the private sector were introduced by the Increase of Rent and Mortgage Interest (War Restrictions) Act 1915, the housing market had already been subject to legal regulation for some years. As the nineteenth century progressed, more and more local councils introduced by-laws designed to stamp out the consequences of poor quality and insanitary construction, and in 1875 the Public Health Act was passed, giving general powers to sanitary authorities to make by-laws which provided detailed control over building standards and layout.

As was explained in Chapter 3, working-class housing in England during the nineteenth and early twentieth centuries was let on a weekly basis. By the later nineteenth century long lets were confined to middle-class households (which did not need to move around frequently to be close to work) and to agricultural tenancies (Daunton, 1987: 20–1). Rents of residential properties rose continuously until 1914, accounting for an ever-increasing share of earnings. The lower the income, the higher the proportion devoted to rent. 'Flitting' was the most common form of rent evasion and in London, where furnished accommodation was fairly common among the poorer classes, absconding tenants had a habit of pawning or taking with them the landlord's furniture. The high rate of residential mobility was not confined to casual labourers, but extended to the skilled working-class in search of better accommodation (Englander, 1983: Ch. 1). Recovery of possession was a cumbersome process, involving a trial by jury at which the landlord was required to prove his title to the property in dispute. As a result the Small Tenements Recovery Act 1838 was passed. It provided that where a tenant of a small tenement (defined as premises rented for not more than £20 per annum) refused to vacate on expiry of notice to quit, the landlord should serve notice indicating an intention to apply to the justices to recover possession. If the tenant did not appear at the hearing or failed to show why possession should not be given, the justices could issue a warrant putting the matter in the hands of the constabulary. The reasons why the landlord wanted to terminate the tenancy were deemed irrelevant. Even so, a tenant who was in arrears would receive a week's notice, followed by a warrant of ejectment ordering departure within 21 days, and would therefore enjoy four weeks' rent-free occupation before the landlord secured possession (Daunton, 1987: 23).

The pre-war housing market faced serious problems. The rate of population growth had fallen, wages stagnated, and interest rates rose. Councils, faced with having to pay for improved sanitation, water supply, schools and so on, sought to defray the cost through the rating system, which in turn became an increasing burden on landlords. While a building boom at the turn of the century had created a surplus of houses, fewer houses than usual were built during the years leading up to 1914, and 'the war created the conditions which made rent control possible' (Englander, 1983: 193). Men volunteered for, or were drafted into, the armed forces, families moved to join relatives in other parts of the country and others went in search of well-paid work in munitions factories, thus aggravating already difficult housing conditions in many towns. In Barrow, for example, where Vickers had an engineering factory, the working population went up from 16,000 to 35,000 during the first three years of the war, and overcrowding reached the level of nine or ten people to a room (Orbach, 1977: 11). Demand for houses exceeded supply, especially in industrial towns and cities, and rents rose accordingly. Rent strikes began within weeks of the declaration of war and there was particular concern over the unrest among munitions workers, especially in Glasgow (Dickens, 1977: 341–51).

The Increase of Rent and Mortgage Interest (War Restrictions) Act 1915

Rent control was introduced by the Increase of Rent and Mortgage Interest (War Restrictions) Act 1915. Some commentators have viewed the Act as a 'class victory' for 'organised labour' which 'broke the stranglehold of the [bourgeois] rentiers ... over the development and reproduction of capital at the local level' (Damer, 1980: 102). Others have seen it as 'a sop to industrial militants', designed to interfere as little as possible with the interests of banking and industrial capital (Dickens, 1977: 350). On a more practical level perhaps, it was 'a short-term response to the exigencies of running a semi-controlled war economy' (Saunders, 1990: 22), the government being compelled to try to regulate the economy and, where necessary, 'to subordinate market forces to the efficient prosecution of the war' (Englander, 1983: 193).

The 1915 Act provided that the rents of all houses below a certain rateable value should be set at the amount which had existed on 3 August 1914 (i.e. the day before Great Britain declared war on Germany). So as to prevent the eviction of tenants who tried to enforce their rights – e.g. by complaining that their rents were above the legal limit – it also provided security of tenure, thereby setting out a basic framework for the regulation of the private rented sector – rent control and security of tenure – which continued until 1988. Most of the other protagonists involved in the First World War also introduced rent control, as they too were faced with housing shortages caused by a virtual halt to building and large-scale movements of population. However, they either removed rent controls after the 'post-war readjustments' (as in the US) or offered landlords compensation for loss of rental (as in France and Germany). Britain was unusual in that decontrol was slow and only partial, and no compensation was provided (Daunton, 1987: 28).

1919 to 1954: the pendulum of control and decontrol

As its name suggests, the 1915 Act was seen as a temporary measure, designed to deal with war-time difficulties, and its operation was restricted to the duration of the war and six months after. However, it was inevitable that with a post-war shortage of some 600,000 houses, decontrol would result in immediate rent increases. The Increase of Rent and Mortgage Interest (War Restrictions) Act 1919 permitted rent increases of 10 per cent (which did not come close to covering the wartime inflation) and doubled the rateable value limits of the houses brought under control, thus extending controls to 98 per cent of all residential tenancies. The extension of rateable value limits in 1920 made all but the largest houses subject to control. The Increase of Rent and Mortgage Interest (Restrictions) Act 1920 also provided for succession to the tenancy by the widow of a tenant who had died intestate or by a member of the tenant's family if the tenant had been a woman, or had been unmarried and intestate, thus adding a third element to the Rent Act regime: statutory succession. A fall in prices and interest rates led to the Rent and Mortgage Interest Restrictions Act 1923 under which sitting tenants remained subject to control but all new lettings were excluded.

Over the next 10 years there was a massive investment in public housing for general needs (see Chapter 4) and it could be argued that, except for the bottom end of the market, the housing shortage had been ended. The response of the Conservative government was the Rent and Mortgage Interest Restrictions

(Amendment) Act 1933, the purpose of which was to remove rent controls by stages on all but the lowest-value properties. Confidence was restored in the future of housing investment and once more landlords began to borrow against the security of future rental income. In 1934, 39,000 dwellings for rent were built for private landlords. This had risen to over 74,000 in 1938, by which time an estimated 2.75 million privately rented dwellings out of a total of 6.5 million were let on controlled tenancies (Holmans, 1987: 400).

The Rent and Mortgage Interest Restrictions Act 1939 – one of a number of Acts hurried through Parliament in preparation for the outbreak of war – brought the great majority of residential properties under control again. Rents were held at the level at which they had stood when the Act became law (1 September 1939). For about 60 per cent of the stock, that was the rent agreed between landlord and tenant; for the other 40 per cent it was the controlled rent. The security of tenure for controlled tenants was in substance the same as provided for by earlier legislation. Repossession was possible only by order of the court, and then only within narrowly defined parameters (e.g. non-payment of rent, wilful damage, allowing the property to be used for immoral purposes, or, for a dwelling occupied by virtue of employment, that the accommodation was needed for a new employee).

The Housing Repairs and Rents Act 1954 was the first major effort after the Second World War to encourage private enterprise to provide accommodation for letting. It entailed that all new housing built for letting, and properties converted to be let as housing, should fall outside Rent Act control. Limited increases in controlled rents were permitted on proof of recent repairs by the landlord. Otherwise they remained until 1957 at the levels set by the 1939 Act (by which time the value of money had fallen by a half).

The Rent Act 1957

A much more significant statute than its immediate predecessors was the Rent Act 1957 which, put simply, raised controlled rents to twice the gross rateable value as it stood in 1956. All houses with a rateable value of more than £40 in London and £30 elsewhere (approximately the top 10 per cent of the market) were subject to almost immediate decontrol. Tenants whose dwellings were decontrolled could not be evicted immediately, but were to be given at least six months' notice which could not expire within 15 months of the Act's commencement. A power to extend block decontrol to lower tranches of rateable values by statutory instrument was never used. Control also ceased to apply where there was a change of tenant.

It is important to realise that decontrol affected not only rents but also security of tenure. Ever since the 1915 Act, tenants' rights had been all or nothing. Controlled tenants had full security, including a right of succession for a widow or other member of the family living with the tenant. Tenants of lettings not subject to control had no statutory protection against eviction other than the right (introduced by the 1957 Act) to a minimum of four weeks' written notice. Previously they had been entitled to only one week's notice. In Inner London especially, where there was a shortage of accommodation, rents rose dramatically and some landlords, of whom Rachman was the most notorious, used heavy-handed tactics to 'persuade' controlled tenants to leave (see Chapter 15).

The Rent Act 1965

Most of the properties decontrolled by the 1957 Act were brought back into protection on a change of government by the Rent Act 1965. The 1965 Act overhauled the system, introducing 'regulated tenancies' and a new system of rent control involving the registration of fair rents via rent officers and rent assessment committees. This was a means of imposing individual rather than national restrictions. The onus was on the landlord or (more commonly) the tenant or both of them to apply to the rent officer for registration of a fair rent, which then became the maximum rent which the landlord could charge. For the first time, security of tenure existed independently of a controlled rent. The Act also extended the provisions for succession, establishing a right to a second transmission for the first successor's widow or a member of his or her family. The Rent Act 1968 consolidated all former Rent Acts.

Holmans has suggested that, with the benefit of hindsight, the security provided by the Rent Act 1965 was 20 years too late. Policies to reduce insecurity in health provision, education and welfare, had been put into legal effect between 1945 and 1950. The National Insurance scheme, for example, was revised and extended to ameliorate the financial consequences of wages lost through sickness, injury or unemployment. The creation of the National Health Service in 1948 reduced the risk posed to a household's finances by the cost of lengthy or complex medical and hospital treatment. The security afforded by the Rent Act 1965 can be seen therefore as bringing private rented housing into line with health provision and the general availability of welfare benefits (Holmans, 1987: 444–5).

The phasing out of controlled tenancies

The Housing Act 1969 provided for the transfer from controlled to regulated tenancies of dwellings in satisfactory repair and with all the basic amenities. Because controlled rents were fixed, they were falling further and further out of line with current values. It was in the landlord's interests, therefore, to let property under regulated rather than controlled tenancies. The 1969 Act gave landlords an incentive to improve their properties, while the Housing Finance Act 1972 provided for the staged transfer of the remainder, unless formally declared to be unfit for human habitation. Both the 1969 and 1972 Acts required a fair rent to be registered in order to transfer the tenancy to regulation and provided for resulting increase in rent to be phased over different periods depending on the circumstances. Since transfer from control to deregulation was likely to result in a steep increase in rents, private tenants were to be protected against financial hardship by the introduction of a mandatory scheme of means-tested rent allowances, equivalent to the rent rebates of local authority tenants.

Furnished lettings and resident landlords

None of the legislation so far mentioned applied to furnished lettings. On the assumption that a tenant taking this type of accommodation did not intend to stay there permanently, lesser protection was introduced by the Furnished Houses (Rent Control) Act 1946. Application could be made to a rent tribunal for a reasonable rent to be fixed and for the operation of a notice to quit to be deferred for up to six months. By the mid-1970s it was apparent that landlords were choosing to let property furnished, often poorly, so as to avoid regulation (see Chapter 13). The Rent Act 1974 ended the distinction between furnished and unfurnished lettings and also introduced a 'resident landlord' exemption designed to encourage owner-occupiers to let part of their homes without the tenant gaining full protection – a policy which persists in the current legislation. Tenants of resident landlords had 'restricted contracts' with broadly the same rights as previously enjoyed by tenants of furnished accommodation.

The Rent Act 1977

The 1977 Act (which is still in force) is a consolidating Act which brought together the 1968 and 1974 Acts. It seeks to protect tenants in four main ways. First (via the machinery of the fair rent scheme), it limits the maximum amount of rent a landlord can charge. Secondly, it confers security of tenure on tenants by (a) requiring the landlord to obtain a court order before actually regaining possession and then (b) limiting the grounds on which the landlord may obtain an order for possession. Thirdly, it prohibits the payment of 'premiums' (that is, capital sums in addition to rent, popularly referred to as 'key money') as a condition of the grant, continuance, renewal or assignment of a tenancy to which the Acts apply (see ss. 119–121, 123–128). Finally, it confers succession rights.

As demand for rented housing generally outstrips supply, the landlord is usually in the stronger bargaining position and it is this inequality which has led to government intervention in the landlord and tenant relationship, in particular to protect the tenant from rising rents and eviction. As Scarman LJ said in *Horford Investments Ltd v Lambert* [1976] Ch 39, 52:

> The policy of the Rent Acts was and is to protect the tenant in his home, whether the threat be to exhort a premium for the grant or renewal of his tenancy, to increase his rent, or to evict him ... The Rent Acts have

throughout their history constituted an interference with contract and property rights for a specific purpose – the redress of the balance of advantage enjoyed in a world of housing shortage by the landlord over those who have to rent their homes.

The 1980s to the present: revival of the private rented sector

The Housing Act 1980 abolished the remaining controlled tenancies (about 200,000) and introduced two new forms of letting: protected shorthold tenancies and assured tenancies. Protected shorthold tenancies were granted for a fixed term of between one and five years. During the fixed term, the tenant enjoyed the same security of tenure as a regulated tenant, but when the term expired, the landlord was under no obligation to renew the tenancy and the court was obliged to grant possession should the landlord apply for it. While these have been described as 'all the rage in [the 1980s] for landlords in the know' before their 'perils and pitfalls' had become apparent (Bridge, 1993: 238), the retention of the fair rent concept unsurprisingly placed a limit on their popularity.

Assured tenancies were designed to encourage new accommodation to be built by 'approved landlords' (such as pension funds, housing associations and building societies). Rents were free from Rent Act control, but lettings were subject to the business tenancy code of control contained in Part II of the Landlord and Tenant Act 1954. The tenant therefore had security for the contractual term and a right to a new lease at a market rent at the end of the term. The landlord could oppose the application for a new tenancy on a number of grounds set out in s. 30 of the 1954 Act: disrepair attributable to the tenant's default, persistent delay in paying rent, other substantial breaches of obligation under the tenancy, the provision of suitable alternative accommodation, and the landlord's intention to demolish or substantially to reconstruct the premises. The scheme brought little new property into the private rented sector and only a small minority of those who had applied for and received approval were financial institutions of the type which the scheme had been intended to attract (Kemp, 1993: 65). As regards holders of new restricted contracts (i.e. those created after 28 November 1980), the Housing Act 1980 abolished the automatic (albeit limited) security available to an occupier on whom notice to quit had been served. Instead it gave discretion to the court to postpone the execution of an order for possession for up to three months (Rent Act 1977, s. 106A).

After 1979 in particular, the government's housing policy focused on the encouragement of owner-occupation. The Conservative Party's election manifesto of 1987 continued to give pride of place to home ownership, but also promised a new package related to rented provision. A 'right to rent' would involve a fuller deregulation of private renting and a more substantial role for housing associations. In its 1987 White Paper, the government expressed the view that the decline of the private rented sector was attributable to the twin evils of rent control and security of tenure. It recognised, however, that the abolition of all controls, leaving determination of rent levels and the extent of security of tenure to be settled contractually between landlord and tenant with no statutory constraint, would not give sufficient protection to tenants' interests (DoE, 1987: 3.9).

The aims of the Housing Act 1988, as regards the private rented sector, are quite different from those of the Rent Acts. While the former concentrated on tenant protection, the 1988 Act was intended to regenerate a freer market in housing and to reverse the decline in the private rented sector. This was to be achieved by removing rent restrictions so that lettings would be at market rents, changing the security of tenure system (by extending the shorthold tenancy concept and introducing new mandatory grounds for possession), and limiting the circumstances in which succession would be possible on the tenant's death. Fears were expressed that the move to market rents would lead to a new wave of Rachmanism and that landlords would force out existing Rent Act tenants (paying a fair rent) in order to replace them with new market rent tenants. To meet these concerns the 1988 Act also strengthened the pre-existing laws on harassment and unlawful eviction. Rent Act regulated tenancies in existence at 15 January 1989 (the date on which the Housing Act 1988 came into force) continue but, subject to a few exceptions, no new regulated tenancies can be created.

During the 1990s, the expansion of home ownership remained one of the Conservative government's key policy objectives. Yet the importance of the private rented sector was also recognised in providing a home for the 'substantial minority of households – in particular the young, the mobile and those with low incomes – who need or prefer to rent' (DoE, 1990: 3). In its 1995 White Paper, the government stated its determination 'to sustain the revival in the private rented sector that deregulation has achieved' (DoE, 1995: 20). To this end, the Housing Act 1996 made the assured shorthold the default form of tenancy and also made changes to the grounds on which possession can be recovered when property is let on an assured tenancy (see Chapters 12 and 14).

Private renting is seen as a central plank in New Labour's housing policy, and the Labour government has made it clear that it will not re-introduce rent control, nor change the present structure of assured and assured shorthold tenancies which has made it easier for landlords to gain possession and which it sees as 'working well' (DETR, 2000a: 5.2). Instead, government concern – which in the 1990s was confined almost exclusively to the problems of anti-social behaviour in and around social housing – has more recently extended to embrace the private sector, resulting in new measures to introduce selective licensing (see below).

The decline of the private rented sector

The supply of private rented accommodation in the UK declined during most of the twentieth century, from about 90 per cent of the total housing stock in 1900 to 8.6 per cent in 1989. A combination of factors (which include deregulation of the sector, a growth in the number of households, the availability of housing benefit and an increase in the number of young people entering higher education) has brought about a revival of the sector and it now accounts for around 11 per cent of housing in England, 9.7 per cent in Wales, 9.2 per cent in Northern Ireland and 8 per cent in Scotland (Rhodes, 2006: 15). Out of a total of 26,194,000 dwellings in Britain, 2,762,000 are rented privately or with a job or business (DCLG, 2007a: Table 102). Few other developed countries have such a low proportion of private renting. Only the Netherlands has a lower share and Ireland's is roughly the same. However, like the Netherlands, the UK has a large social housing sector so it is not the case that it has a low share of rental housing overall. There are very few countries in which the private rented sector is larger than the owner-occupied one, and they are characterised by 'supply-side distortions' created by either extensive rent controls and/or significant tax breaks to landlords, enabling them to survive in a rent-controlled environment (Ball, 2004: 9).

'The long decline of private renting was the outcome of a complex set of factors, the relative importance of which varied over time. One of these factors has been the appeal of rented property as an investment. In the nineteenth century, prospective landlords could obtain a mortgage to cover about two-thirds of a property's purchase price. If interest rates increased, they passed on as much of the cost as possible by raising rents. Most landlords were small capitalists, content with a secure return on their investment, who could achieve an 8 per cent gross return from letting, a sum which compared favourably with other forms of investment (Balchin and Rhoden, 2002: 122). In the 1880s, 'rising local property taxes (following the extension of the franchise) and static wage levels (which limited the rents which tenants could afford to pay) combined to squeeze landlords' profits' (Saunders, 1990: 21). With the extension of limited liability in the late nineteenth century, investment in joint stock companies became a possibility for people of modest means, and the development of the stock exchange and building societies, the expansion of government and municipal stock, and increased investment opportunities overseas meant that investment in private rented property became a much less attractive proposition.

Rising standards in housing also played a part in the decline of the sector. Together with higher construction costs and rent control, they put a brake on the production of houses to rent after the First World War. The price of new houses quadrupled between 1914 and 1920, putting economic rents beyond the means of most potential tenants. The Housing and Town Planning Act 1919 enabled local authorities partly to make good the deficiency of supply by giving them powers to provide subsidised housing for the needs of the working class. The subsequent growth of local authority rental housing 'attracted many of the more affluent and reliable households among the pool of potential tenants' (Saunders, 1990: 25).

For a decade after the end of the First World War virtually no slum clearance took place. Until the housing shortage was reduced there was little sense in demolishing existing houses even though they were unsatisfactory. In 1930, however, local authorities were required to draw up plans for slum clearance, and displaced households were re-housed in accommodation built by local authorities. Again, after the Second World War slum clearance was held in abeyance, the main objective being the supply of dwellings. Between 1953, when the government announced its intention to recommence slum clearance, and 1981, over one million dwellings (one-fifth of the private rented housing stock) were simply demolished (Holmans, 1987: 432).

Slum clearance went hand in hand with housing rehabilitation. The Housing Act 1949 made discretionary improvement grants available. The amount payable was increased significantly by the Housing Act 1969 which also withdrew most of the restrictive conditions previously attached to the payment of grants (in particular a minimum length of time for which the owner must live in the house where grant-aided work has been done or let it to a tenant). The housing price boom of 1971–3 provided an additional incentive to landlords, who were unable to charge sufficiently high post-improvement rents to recoup their share of the cost of improvements, to sell their properties into owner-occupation. Ball recounts how, in the 1970s and 1980s, previously rented properties were bought and improved by owner occupiers – using 'highly tax efficient mortgage borrowing' and generous improvement grants. Unlike private landlords, who would have been subject to capital gains tax had they improved and then sold the properties, the 'resultant improved properties provided substantial tax-free gains for their new owners' (Ball, 2004: 10). The Housing Acts of 1961, 1964 and 1969 increased controls over houses in multiple occupation. Again, landlords sold vacated properties into owner-occupation and tenants turned to the public sector.

An important factor in the failure of the private rented sector has been the lack of political support given to private landlords. Since the nineteenth century, most private landlords have been small, lower middle class investors. A consequence of their association with 'the Dickensian slums and, more recently, Rachmanism' (Ginsburg, 1989: 58) is that they have often been regarded as a 'morally repugnant form of capitalist' unable to find 'a sympathetic ear in Westminster, Whitehall or Fleet Street'. Unlike other countries such as Sweden and the US, there has never been any political support in Great Britain for publicly subsidising the private landlord (Saunders, 1990: 22; Daunton, 1987: 30–9). Apart from improvement grants, the only subsidies provided to private landlords have been Exchequer grants payable on new housing built for letting under the Housing Act 1924. Subsidies and preferential tax treatment have put local authority tenants and owner-occupiers in a far better position than private landlords and tenants.

Conservative governments in the 1980s blamed statutory rent control and security of tenure for the decline of the private rented sector. Because of rent controls, the return to private sector landlords was inadequate to persuade them to stay in the market or to keep property in repair. People who might have been prepared to grant a temporary letting were also deterred by laws on security of tenure which made it often difficult and sometimes impossible to recover possession of their property when they wanted to (DoE, 1987: 1.3, 1.8). It should be borne in mind, however, that decontrol in the past has not spurred on an upturn in the number of houses made available for private renting. The responses of landlords to decontrol in 1933 and 1957 were many and varied: some did not raise rents at all; some did raise rents but only a little; and some raised them to such an extent that tenants fell into arrears, were evicted and the properties sold into owner-occupation. Any additional income was not necessarily spent on repair and maintenance. Above all, the private rented sector continued to decline (Doling and Davies, 1984).

Between 1914 and 1939 over one million privately rented houses (14 per cent of the total housing stock in 1914) were sold into owner-occupation, mostly to sitting tenants at substantial discounts. Running parallel to this, however, an annual average of over 66,000 dwellings were sold to private landlords. In the 1930s home ownership became a reality for an increasing proportion of the population: interest rates were low, land, materials and labour were cheap and building societies (which had expanded rapidly in the 1920s) went out to attract borrowers. Planning legislation exerted little control over residential development. To have made a profit, landlords would have had to charge rents which were uncompetitive with mortgage repayments (Saunders, 1990: 23–5). While in 1900, most of the 150,000 new homes completed in this country were built by private landlords, the number had dropped to 50,000 by 1913 (Holmes, 2006: 41) and, for most of the period since the Second World War, very few houses have been built for private renting.

It can be seen, therefore, that the decline of the private rented sector was largely 'a consequence of social progress and economic affluence' and should not be dismissed as an entirely negative phenomenon (Ball, 2004: 8). What is more, since the late 1980s, the sector has been expanding again. While looked at in percentage terms as a share of all housing, the growth has been quite small, it is far more dramatic when considered in the context of the number of households and people it accommodates. Between 1991 and 1992 the number of households living in private rented accommodation rose by 27 per cent and the number of people by 44 per cent (ibid.: 10). On the absolute growth measure, therefore, the recent expansion of the private rented sector has been substantial.

Characteristics of the private rented sector

Landlords

Private letting is a small-scale industry which is dominated by private individuals rather than companies. In this respect, therefore, it has changed very little and has not been subject to the trends towards concentration and centralisation witnessed in other areas of the economy (Best *et al.*, 1992: 17). In the early 1990s, individual landlords owned just over half of all privately rented properties. Sixty four per cent owned fewer than five lettings and 82 per cent fewer than 10. Forty nine per cent had acquired the property as an investment, 38 per cent had bought it to live in at some time, and 17 per had cent inherited. (Some respondents gave more than one answer.) Forty four per cent of partnership and company landlords owned fewer than 24 properties but 33 per cent owned more than 250. Sixty per cent had acquired the property for investment reasons; 30 per cent to house an employee (DoE, 1995: 21). A survey carried out in 1993/4 showed that landlords who were only in the sector because of the property slump owned about one in 10 private lettings (Crook *et al.*, 1995: 45). By 2001, the percentage of rental properties owned by individuals had risen to 65 per cent but only 7 per cent were owned by residential property companies (Rhodes and Bevan, 2003). The proportion of landlords who had purchased the property as an investment was 49 per cent (ODPM, 2001) and nearly all part-time landlords interviewed in 2002 and 2003 regarded their properties as a form of retirement planning (Rhodes and Bevan, 2003), regarding rental property as preferable to a traditional pension because it was more flexible and did not rely on stock-market performance.

In the early part of the twentieth century when private renting formed the principal source of housing, institutions such as insurance companies were major landlords. Between 1960 and 1980, spurred on by the shift towards owner-occupation and the emergence of other types of investment which could be used as a hedge against inflation, most corporate and institutional investors broke up and disposed of their rental portfolios, selling either to private landlords or into owner-occupation. At the same time, they invested billions of pounds in commercial property such as shops, offices and factories. During the 1980s and 1990s the Conservatives were keen to increase the involvement of corporate landlords in the residential lettings market, and to restore the role of financial institutions as major investors. By involving such bodies – rather than the small-scale sideline landlords who characterised current provision – their aim was to create a new 'structure of housing provision' which would not only make it possible to increase the scale of investment but would also facilitate a modernisation of the ownership of the sector, making it more professional and enhancing its reputation (Crook and Kemp, 2002: 742). There were two steps in this modernisation process: the Business Expansion Scheme (BES) and Housing Investment Trusts (HITs).

The BES was launched in 1983 to encourage small private investors to provide venture capital to unquoted companies. Tax relief on the whole of the initial investment (up to £40,000) could be claimed at the investor's top rate of tax. Thus, for a higher rate taxpayer, an investment of £40,000 would actually cost £24,000 after BES relief at the 40 per cent tax rate was taken into account. After 1986, there was no liability to capital gains tax on the disposal of qualifying shares, provided that the investor kept them for five years. The Finance Act 1988 extended the scheme to include companies which carried on the business of providing and maintaining properties to let by way of assured (not assured shorthold) tenancies under the Housing Act 1988. The companies could either build new properties or acquire existing ones which were not already let. Upper limits were placed on the value of each property (£125,000 in Greater London and £85,000 elsewhere). The initial response to the scheme was encouraging, £320 million being invested in 1988/9. Building societies and insurance companies became involved in the scheme, as did some local authorities – the Conservative-controlled Royal London Borough of Kensington & Chelsea initiating two BES share issues: one to promote housing for employees to encourage teaching staff to move into the area and the other to address the borough's broader housing needs (*The Independent*, 28 May 1992). As house prices fell in the late 1980s and early 1990s, investors' expectations of capital growth diminished and they became concerned about their ability to exit after five years. One way in which companies responded was by the introduction of 'contracted-exit' schemes, typically requiring the vendor (such as a university or housing association) to buy back the properties at the end of the qualifying period at an agreed price above that at which they had originally sold, thus providing shareholders with a profit. Another response was to exploit the slump in the property market by buying up unsold or repossessed houses. A report by the Joseph Rowntree Foundation in 1992 described as 'predators' the eight out of 72 new housing companies launched under the BES in 1990/1 tax year which had bought repossessed houses at auction or in bulk from builders who could not sell (*The Independent*, 10 August 1992).

During its lifetime, the BES raised about £2 billion for about 1,750 companies, 250 involving investment in residential property (*The Independent*, 12 March 1992). BES companies acquired about 81,000 dwellings but it is estimated that the scheme financed only 12,000 new units, the remainder simply being transferred into private renting from other tenures or from one segment of the private rented sector to another. Almost 40 per cent were university, 10 per cent housing association and around 25 per cent entrepreneurial company dwellings. Repossessed housing accounted for over 20,000 units (Crook *et al.*, 1995: 18–20). The scheme proved to be extremely costly to the Treasury (working out at about £20,000 per unit) and was described by the editor of BESt Investment, the industry newsletter, as 'a lousy use of taxpayer's money' (*The Independent*, 11 March 1992). The BES was ended on 31 December 1993 (Finance (No 2) Act 1992, s. 38) the reason given by the then Chancellor, Norman Lamont, being that it was too complex.

In the 1995 White Paper, the government observed that the lack of a suitable investment vehicle acted as an obstacle to more institutional investment in residential property. Most financial institutions, it was said, do not wish to take on the management obligations which direct ownership involves (DoE, 1995: 22). It proposed, therefore, that institutions should be given the opportunity to invest in HITs set up to own and manage residential property. This was put into effect by Sch. 30 to the Finance Act 1996. HITs were quoted on the stock exchange with a minimum size of £30 million. The same limits on purchase price as the BES applied, and the property had to be unlet or subject to a shorthold tenancy when it was acquired. As HIT property, it had to be let under an assured tenancy. HITs were exempt from capital gains tax and subject to a reduced rate of corporation tax (24 per cent instead of 33 per cent) on income derived from residential lettings. It became evident, however, that the financial institutions did not regard HITs as an attractive investment opportunity and although several attempts were made to set up HITs, none of them succeeded.

Despite the difficulties encountered so far in attracting institutional investment in the private rented sector, the current Labour government has expressed its desire to see the sector 'grow and 'prosper' and has stressed its commitment to fostering increased investment by major investors such as the pension funds (DETR, 2000a: 5.19–5.21). As Leather points out, 'the Green Paper devotes several pages to the issue of persuading reputable investors to expand the supply of private rented housing. This is a difficult section, not least because the term "reputable" implies that current investors (mainly . . . small landlords . . .) are less desirable' (Leather, 2001: 105). It is true that small-scale landlords (especially resident landlords) may have insufficient money, patience or legal awareness to deal with tenants who cannot or will not move. Their limited resources, expertise, and a desire to maximise their investment may also have repercussions as regards repairs and maintenance. By contrast, the difficulty and/or expense of removing a tenant may be a nuisance for commercial landlords, but usually they can either afford to put up with tenants or remove them via the legal process or by offering a financial inducement. There is certainly a feeling in government that increased involvement by company landlords would professionalise the sector and thereby raise standards even though there appears to be little empirical evidence as to whether one type of landlord is in any way superior to another (Ball, 2004: 28).

In March 2004 the government published a consultation paper (HM Treasury and Inland Revenue, 2004) to consider the introduction of Real Estate Investment Trusts (REITs) on the basis that such a reform (while of particular benefit to the commercial property market) 'would also aim to address the unresponsive supply of housing through greater institutional investment participation in the residential market' (HM Treasury and Inland Revenue, 2005: 1.2) and have the potential to improve the housing market 'through greater professionalism in the private rented sectors' (ibid.: 2.5). REITs (which are used in many countries, including the US and Australia) are closed-ended companies or trusts which, for investment purposes, hold, manage and maintain real estate which is let to tenants. For tax purposes, the REIT's property-letting business (which is separated from the activities which take place on the property) is ring-fenced. The fact that income derived from its ring-fenced activities (which accounts for at least 75 per cent of its business, measured by assets and total gross income) is exempt from corporation tax will, it is hoped, make it attractive to larger property companies. It is required to distribute at least 90 per cent of its ring-fenced income as dividends. The government legislated for a UK-REIT in Part 4 of the Finance Act 2006 but it remains to be seen whether the scheme is any more successful than the BES and HITs in attracting institutional investors into the private rented sector. The government acknowledges that most respondents to the consultation paper believed that UK-REITs could play a role in the private rented sector, though some noted that their effects on the development of the sector were likely to be 'modest'.

In the meantime, an industry-led initiative in the form of the buy-to-let scheme has succeeded in encouraging investment in rental property by private individuals. The scheme was launched in September 1996 by the Association of Residential Letting Agents and four mortgage lenders, lending money at an interest rate which was only slightly higher than the interest rate on mortgages for owner-occupied properties. Previously, commercial funding for rented property had carried a high interest-rate premium (Scanlon and Whitehead, 2005: 5). Since then the number of buy-to-let providers has grown significantly. Buy-to-let mortgages now account for about 7 per cent by value of the total stock of mortgages outstanding in the UK. There are currently 767,000 outstanding buy-to-let mortgages worth a total of £83.9 billion (*The Guardian*, 19 August 2006), and the buy-to-let phenomenon has proved to be one of the most significant contributors to Britain's economic growth in the past 15 years although, at the same time, it can be criticised for removing from the market the types of properties which would normally be attractive (and within the price range) of first-time buyers.

Tenants

Its geography, the variety of tenants it houses and the different types of statutory code (if any) to which they are subject means that when treated as a whole, the private rented sector 'is as much an artefact of statistical convenience as an expression of reality' (Ball, 2004: 17). A significant proportion of the private rented sector (15 per cent) is not generally accessible to the public as it comprises lettings (sometimes rent-free) to relatives or employees of the landlord, the latter including farm workers, people employed in the armed forces and by health and police authorities, and caretakers. Accommodation provided in connection with employment has fallen, however, with the decline in industries such as agriculture, mining and steel-making where tied tenancies were traditionally concentrated (Ball, 2004: 15). Furthermore, the private rented sector no longer caters for general housing needs in the way it once did although the 'housing biographies' of many households are now likely to include at least a short spell of renting from a private landlord (Rugg *et al.*, 2002: 290). Deregulation of the private rented sector and its recent expansion has resulted in the vast majority of new tenancies being let on a free market basis, resulting in a significantly higher turnover compared to 30 years ago when 'perhaps only three per cent of the housing stock was generally available to new entrants' (Stephens *et al.*, 2005: 1.17). With assured shorthold tenancies making up 63 per cent of all private sector tenancies (DCLG, 2007: Table S510), short-term lets of six months or a year are common and turnover is high: in 2004/5, 41 per cent of private sector tenants had moved into their present accommodation within the past 12 months (ibid.: Table S250). Well over half of all private tenants have a full-time paid job – slightly more than the average for all tenures but considerably more than double the proportion for social tenants (ibid.: Table S111). Private renting is often characterised therefore as the bottom rung on the housing ladder, 'where new entrants begin their climb to home ownership, with social housing representing a stopping off point in some cases' (Lowe, 2004: 220). It thus provides easy access and exit accommodation for young people leaving home for the first time (including students) and young professionals sharing property before entering owner-occupation. Forty-eight per cent of private tenants are aged under 35 (Rhodes, 2006: 44).

However, as well as being a first stage for young people leaving home and those saving for a deposit in order to access owner-occupation, it should also be remembered that some households who live in privately rented housing have 'gone down the ladder, from social housing (often by choice) and from owner-occupation (often by necessity)' (Lowe, 2004: 220). Those in the former category may have taken advantage of the opportunity presented by the greater availability of dwellings in the deregulated private sector to move away from unpopular housing estates, their higher housing costs being met in full or in part by an increased level of entitlement to housing benefit. In other cases, moves from the social sector have been prompted by local authority or housing association landlords securing possession orders for, e.g. rent arrears and anti-social behaviour (Wilcox, 2002: 34). So far as former owner-occupiers are concerned, households experiencing relationship breakdown or following mortgage repossession may use the private rented sector on a short-term or emergency basis. Yet, at the same time, the private rented sector is home to people who are unable to gain access to other tenures, i.e. who cannot afford owner-occupation and are not in priority categories for social housing, such as single people or childless couples. Indeed, around 719,000 tenants in the private rented sector rely on housing benefit to pay all or part of their rent (DWP, 2004: Table 3.1).

The private rented sector also accommodates households with a preference for private renting. This category includes older people who have been in the sector for several decades, often living in the same property, and who may never have considered any alternative. They are most likely to live in unfurnished properties (in houses rather than flats and with more space but fewer amenities), which are still subject to a form of rent control and legally guaranteed security of tenure. In the early 1990s, about 20 per cent of private sector tenants were aged 65 or older and 8 per cent had lived in the same house for 40 years or more, dating back to the time when private renting was much more common (DoE, 1995: 20). The percentage has since dropped to 11 per cent (DCLG, 2007: Table S418). The private rented sector is the most ethnically diverse tenure (Rhodes, 2006: 48–9). Ethnic minority households may choose to rent privately because of experiences of harassment on social housing estates and the limited availability of social housing properties of sufficient size (Rugg *et al.*, 2002: 291), and to live in areas occupied by other members of the same ethnic group.

Housing conditions in the private rented sector

The sector contains a small sub-sector of luxury properties situated mainly in London. Otherwise, in England, converted flats figure significantly in the private rented sector (16 per cent compared with only 4 per cent of housing as a whole). Terraced houses are found in this sector in about the same proportions as for all housing, while detached and semi-detached houses are less common. Reflecting the fact that most privately rented properties are located in the more central parts of towns and cities, the stock is considerably older than in other tenures, with 40 per cent being built before 1919 and almost 60 per cent before 1945 (Ball, 2004: 17).

The private rented sector is – and always has been – associated with some particularly poor housing conditions. Until the 1960s, the preferred solution to dealing with substandard stock was its compulsory acquisition at site value followed by demolition. However, as more older privately rented dwellings were sold into owner-occupation, acquisition became progressively more expensive, with owners demanding greater compensation and tenants opposing rehousing in unattractive non-traditional local authority accommodation, often in peripheral or overspill locations. In the late 1960s, the emphasis shifted to the renovation of older stock (Leather, 2001: 95). Now, although deregulation and the popularity of the buy-to-let scheme have introduced better quality properties into the sector, it still contains, age for age, dwellings which are in a worse state of repair than those in other tenures. In 2004, 42 per cent of all private tenants were living in non-decent accommodation, compared with 62 per cent in 1996 and 51 per cent in 2001 (ODPM, 2006a: Table 1). Over 400,000 private tenants (almost one-third of all private tenants) live in the worst housing which is dominated by pre-1919 housing and converted flats. Nearly three-quarters of those in such housing are on low incomes or workless.

The amount of rent which tenants pay is not necessarily reflected in the quality of their accommodation and there is evidence of 'a growing problem of poor quality private renting in deprived areas' (Stephens *et al.*, 2005: 1.17). Landlords may be unaware of problems with their properties, or budget only small (and insufficient) amounts for annual repair and maintenance. The annual costs of a significant minority of properties (7 per cent) exceed the rental income which suggests that some landlords subsidise their letting activities on a day-to-day basis, perhaps in the hope that they will eventually be compensated by rising capital values. Additionally, small-scale landlords face similar difficulties to home owners when it comes to diagnosing and remedying faults, and hiring and managing contractors. Ball, however, argues that the imposition of high minimum standards in housing may look good in housing condition surveys but it also leads to higher rents and less housing available overall. He maintains that 'low price-low quality outcomes' may suit some tenants who will soon move on again and help others afford a better home later on or enable them to move into a different locality where they can then look for something better (Ball, 2004: 48).

The current government acknowledges that low house prices in areas of low demand have resulted in an influx of '... unprofessional landlords [who] ... frequently show no interest in managing their properties properly, often letting to anti-social tenants who cause a range of problems ... [creating] misery for the local community and cause further destabilisation of these areas. ...' There is said to exist a 'small minority' of private landlords who 'set out to exploit their tenants and the community at large in flagrant disregard of the law'. Seeing their role as confined to collecting rent (which often takes the form of housing benefit paid directly to the landlord), 'they take no interest in either the condition of their property or the behaviour of their tenants' and have 'no incentives to enforce tenancy agreements or manage their property effectively' (DETR, 2000a: 5.4). In contrast to social tenants, private tenants are unlikely to be the subject of specific anti-social behaviour clauses in their tenancy agreements. Private landlords are said to be 'much less prepared to take action' against anti-social tenants so that 'victims living next to perpetrators in private rented or owner-occupier accommodation are less protected from anti-social behaviour than social tenants' (National Strategy for Neighbourhood Renewal, 2000: 95). The government maintains that there are 'areas of declining housing demand, particularly in parts of our northern cities, where the larger-scale operations of some unscrupulous landlords, often linked to housing benefit fraud, drug-dealing and prostitution, are destabilising local communities, creating a range of social and economic problems, and seriously hampering efforts at regeneration' (DETR, 2000a: 5.32).

Fear of 'choking off supply' has made governments wary of trying to improve privately rented stock by imposing higher regulatory standards (Stephens *et al.*, 2005: 1.71) and the current government has ruled out the possibility of subjecting the whole sector to a compulsory licensing scheme, in the belief that such a 'massive undertaking' would involve too much red tape for 'some perfectly respectable landlords' who would leave (DETR, 2000a: 5.31). Describing the private rented sector as having 'a far worse image than it deserves' (ibid.: 5.5), it considers that instead of 'heavy regulation', small-scale landlords need 'encouragement, support and education' which is best provided by 'local authorities, professional and voluntary organisations' (ibid.: 5.10). In order therefore to combat the effect of anti-social behaviour on communities, it has opted for a system of selective licensing.

Part 3 of the Housing Act 2004 gives local authorities the power to license all private landlords in a designated area. Before making a designation (which may relate to the whole of their area or part of it) the local authority must be satisfied that one of two general sets of conditions applies. The first is that the area is, or is likely to become, an area of low housing demand and the designation will, when combined with other measures, 'contribute to the social or economic conditions in the area' (Housing Act 2004, s. 80(3)). In deciding whether an area is, or is likely to become, an area of low housing demand a local housing authority must take into account (among other matters) (a) the value of residential premises in the area, in comparison to the value of similar premises in other areas which the authority consider to be comparable (whether in terms of types of housing, local amenities, availability of transport or otherwise); (b) the turnover of occupiers of residential premises; and (c) the number of residential premises which are available to buy or rent and the length of time for which they remain unoccupied.

The second set of general conditions is that (a) the area is experiencing a significant and persistent problem caused by anti-social behaviour; (b) some or all of the private sector landlords who have let premises in the area (whether under leases or licences) are failing to take action to combat the problem that it would be appropriate for them to take; and (c) making a designation will, when combined with other measures, lead to a reduction in, or the elimination of, the problem. A 'house' as defined in s. 99 means 'a building or part of a building occupied or intended to be occupied as a separate dwelling'. The selective licensing provisions will not apply where any part of the house is let on an exempt tenancy, e.g. one granted by an RSL.

A local housing authority cannot grant a licence unless it is satisfied that the licence holder is a fit and proper person and that the proposed management arrangements are acceptable. Controlling or managing a house which ought to be licensed but is not is, in the absence of a reasonable excuse, a criminal offence. Further, where no application for a licence or exemption from licensing has been made to the local housing authority, the landlord may not use the procedure under s. 21 of the Housing Act 1988 to recover possession at the end of an assured shorthold tenancy. If the local housing authority is not satisfied that it can grant a licence, it must refuse to do so and make an Interim Management Order. Before refusing to grant a licence it must give its reasons in advance and give the applicant 14 days in which to make representations. The applicant has a right to appeal if the refusal to grant a licence is then confirmed. A Part 3 licence must (and may) be subject to conditions and normally lasts for five years. Provisions also exist for the revocation and cessation of licences.

In 2003 the government launched its Communities Plan, setting out an action programme with the threefold aim of bringing all social housing up to a decent standard by 2010, improving the local environment of all communities, and improving conditions for vulnerable people in private housing (i.e. those in receipt of means-tested or disability-related benefits). A decent home is one which (a) does not contain a category 1 hazard (see Chapter 8); (b) is in a reasonable state of repair; (c) has reasonably modern facilities and services; and (d) provides a reasonable degree of thermal comfort. The vehicles by which the improvement of conditions for private sector tenants is to be achieved include more 'statutory protection' via mandatory licensing for Houses in Multiple Occupation (HMOs) and selective licensing of private landlords in low demand areas (ODPM, 2003: 1.14–117) together with the introduction of the Housing Health and Safety Rating System (HHSRS) which introduces a new approach to the assessment and regulation of housing conditions (see Chapter 8). This means that it will be left mainly to the market (supported by local authorities' general regulatory powers) to improve conditions in higher demand areas. If the standards which are set are 'too distinct' from what the market is prepared to pay for, it is possible that strict implementation will result either in the loss of poorer quality private rented housing or an increase in illegal lettings or both (Stephens *et al.*, 2005: 2.98).

Conclusion

The private rented sector can be seen to have enjoyed something of a chequered history, although a combination of factors – including the deregulation achieved by the Housing Acts of 1988 and 1996 – appear to have halted its decline. More positive images, both of private landlords and of private renting, are in greater evidence than they were two decades ago but the private rented sector is not now, as it was once and remains elsewhere in Europe, a source of accommodation for large numbers of middle income, middle class people who can afford to look after their own interests. Nonetheless, a healthy private rented sector is important and, in recognition of its flexibility, the part it plays in providing accommodation in those areas in which social rented housing is in short supply, and the fact that many people will need to use it at some stage in their lives, the government is keen to secure 'a larger, better-quality, better-managed private rented sector' (DETR, 2000a: 5.7).

Inevitably, the cost of deregulation has been higher rents (mediated by the availability of housing benefit at the bottom end of the market) and less security. However, the fact that many private sector tenants do not want to be housed on a long-term basis means that – although the potential for exploitation of tenants by landlords remains – 'there is less need for the State to guarantee long-term security of tenure' and a 'market framework' is perhaps more appropriate (Law Commission, 2002a: 1.23). Certainly, the Rent Acts – and the long-term security which they provide – have become less significant with the decline of the private rented sector. Indeed, by the early 1980s, Rent Act evasion and avoidance had become so common-place that there was conjecture as to whether the Acts had any practical relevance at all (Doling, 1983). The Housing Act 1988 hammered the final nail into their coffin by providing that (subject to a few exceptions) no new Rent Act tenancies could be granted on or after 15 January 1989. In 1994, they accounted for 14 per cent (310,000) of all private tenancies (Green *et al.*, 1996: 55) and now comprise a mere 5 per cent (126,000) (DCLG, 2007b: Table S510). Nevertheless, even though relatively few of them are still in existence, the Rent Act 1977 is considered in some detail in this chapter as well as in a number of later ones, not only because of the similarity of many of its provisions with those of the Housing Acts of 1985 and 1988, but also because it represents what can be seen – at least in theory – as the apogee of tenant protection.

Part II

General concerns

Chapter 6

The regulation of rents

Introduction

In the private sector, legislation was passed as early as 1915 to impose a freeze on rents following their rapid escalation (and the civil unrest which ensued) brought about by wartime conditions. In the mid-1960s, control of private rents operated through the fair rent scheme. Now, the fact that lettings under the Housing Act 1988 are at market rents has not only led to tenants having to pay appreciably higher amounts but has also had a significant impact on housing benefit. In the RSL sector (most of whose tenants, it will be remembered, are also subject to the Housing Act 1988) the reduction of capital grants for new construction has necessitated greater reliance upon private loans, and for rents to be set at a level which will sustain them. So far as local authority housing is concerned, general 'bricks and mortar' subsidies which aimed 'to assist authorities in meeting the costs of long-term loans taken out to finance construction' (Walker, 1998: 158) have been gradually withdrawn since 1980 and replaced by a reliance on housing benefit to assist low-income households. The influence of central government on rents is therefore well-established (Cowan and Marsh, 2001: 269).

This chapter explores the different mechanisms for the setting of rents in the private and social housing sectors and the move towards convergence of rents within the two social housing tenures. It concludes with a brief consideration of housing benefit. Not only did housing benefit play a pivotal role in the reshaping of housing provision in the late 1980s and the 1990s (by underpinning the growth in housing provided by housing associations and helping to finance the expansion of the private rented sector: DSS, 1998: 34) but it can now also be seen as a major plank in the reforms planned by the current government with respect to choice-based lettings and the best value regime.

Private rented sector rents: legislative background

There have been three generations of rent regulation in the private rented sector. The first, which existed from 1915 until 1965, consisted of compulsory, *national* control. The Increase in Rent and Mortgage Interest (War Restrictions) Act 1915 froze rents at the free market level operative at the outbreak of war and only staggered increases were subsequently permitted. Some decontrol followed in the 1920s and 1930s, but control was reimposed in 1939 for all but highest value properties. Extensive decontrol took place in 1957, but for the most part on a piecemeal basis, as and when properties subject to controlled tenancies were vacated.

The second generation of rent regulation emerged from the Rent Act 1965 which provided for voluntary, *individual* rent regulation, thereby separating regulation of rent from security of tenure. It has been described as 'a watershed in governmental policy towards the private rented sector' which ended 'the violent swings between control and decontrol dictated by party political ideology' and marked 'an implicit acceptance' by the Labour government that the appropriate mechanism for setting private rents is generally the market, with regulation to prevent the exploitation of scarcity by the charging of exorbitant rents (Watchman, 1985: 199). However, as stated in Chapter 5, rent control has been seen as an important reason for the decline of the private rented sector and the poor condition of much of its housing. Ironically, while rent control may operate to reduce supply, it can push up the demand for rented housing by bringing it within the reach of a greater proportion of the population. People whose financial circumstances would otherwise have forced them to live together, are tempted to break away to form new separate households. Its critics also argue that it discourages mobility of labour – an important point in this age of the flexible workforce, the members of which are expected to move to wherever jobs are available. The existence of what has been described as a 'stationary housing subsidy' means that people pass up opportunities for better jobs which are more suited to them, or may even prefer to remain unemployed, if taking up a new job necessitates their moving out of property which is subject to a fair rent to one for which a market rent is payable. For the same reason, rent control is said to encourage an inefficient use of house space because it gives tenants an incentive to stay where they are, rather than to adjust their housing consumption to changes in their circumstances, e.g. the birth of children, children growing up and leaving home, the death of a family member, the need to house and look after an elderly relative (Albon and Stafford, 1988: 12, 18). Arguably, rent control is inherently unfair. Whether it be by blanket control (as was the case until 1965) or individual control (as under the Rent Act 1977), it places the cost of housing subsidy on landlords, regardless of the financial means of the parties and the lack of evidence that, in general terms, tenants are poor and landlords are rich. The current provisions are contained in the Rent Act 1977.

The Housing Act 1988 dispenses with rent control for assured tenancies and provides for only limited regulation for assured shortholds. It is left to the market to determine the level at which rents should be set, the aim being to restore the appeal of rented property as an investment so that existing landlords are dissuaded from leaving the sector and prospective landlords are persuaded to make accommodation available for letting.

The removal of control is generally regarded as one of the reasons why the supply of housing in the private rented sector has increased since 1988. Such a view presupposes that, before 1989, fair rents had been determined in relation to most Rent Act tenancies. However, as is explained in Chapter 13, landlords had become adept at circumventing the Rent Acts by the use of, e.g. so-called 'holiday lets' or 'licences', and an 'informal process of deregulation' had already been taking place. Further, the decline of the private rented sector was not the outcome simply of rent control alone but of a combination of complex circumstances. It is worth remembering that the nearest Great Britain has come to a free market in rented housing was during the first half of the nineteenth century. By the end of the nineteenth century, it had failed to provide satisfactory housing for a large part of the population despite the efforts of the philanthropic bodies to provide decent housing for the 'labouring classes', and the public health legislation aimed at eradicating the worst conditions (Ivatts, 1988: 200).

'Market rent' is a 'problematic concept' which raises 'complex issues of distributive justice and social policy'. Free market theory dictates that 'property rents should provide a satisfactory return in relation to the capital value of the house'. That value is affected by the local availability of 'services, transport facilities and communications networks' (which are mostly paid for out of the public purse), and it reflects planning constraints (including the preservation of the 'green belt') and the resultant land shortages. A market rent means, therefore, that the landlord is profiting from that part of the rent which is attributable to the value of public investment and that tenants are paying rents which include an element relating to the 'artificial restrictions upon land use for housing and commercial development in the most economically active regions in the country' (Ivatts, 1988: 198–9). The geographical distribution of the private rented sector is uneven, with high concentrations in some areas (notably, in London, in and around certain coastal resorts, in certain rural areas, and in Oxford and Cambridge) and little in others. A disproportionately high amount is sub-standard and, in many cases, the rents paid represent poor value for money, compared with property in the public rented sector and owner-occupied housing. The problem is compounded by the fact that many of those who are most dependent on the private sector are those with the fewest resources and the least able to afford market rents. This has significant implications for housing benefit.

Fair rents under the Rent Act 1977

Introduction

Rent regulation under the Rent Act 1977 applies to protected and statutory (i.e. 'regulated') tenancies. It is steadily dying out as (apart from a few exceptions) no new protected tenancies have been created since 15 January 1989 (the date when Part I of the Housing Act 1988 came into force). Of the 117,000 regulated tenancies in existence in 2002/3, 66,000 were subject to a registered rent, compared with 590,000 in 1990 (ODPM, *Housing Statistics 2004*: Table 6.6).

If no rent is registered for a dwelling-house which is let under a regulated tenancy, the parties are free to agree on whatever rent they like, but either the landlord or the tenant, or both jointly, may apply at any time for the registration of a fair rent. Application is made to a rent officer, who must act within the statutory guidelines. Once a fair rent has been determined, the rent officer must enter details in an area register which is available for public inspection (s. 66). Both parties have a right to appeal to a rent assessment committee from the rent officer's decision. The appeal is by way of a re-hearing. Appeal from the decision of a rent officer on a point of law lies to the county court or the High Court (s. 141). The decision of a rent assessment committee can be appealed only on a point of law. The appeal should be made to the High Court.

Section 44(1) of the 1977 Act provides that where a rent for a dwelling-house is registered, 'the rent recoverable for any contractual period of a regulated tenancy of the dwelling-house shall be limited to the rent so registered'. The registration operates to determine the maximum rent payable for premises until:

(a) the demised premises undergo such a change in their structure as to render them no longer the dwelling-house referred to in s. 44 (see, e.g. *Solle v Butcher* [1950] 1 KB 671 in which internal structural alterations and improvements and the addition of a garage were held not to have changed the identity of the dwelling-house); or
(b) there is a cancellation of the registration under s. 73; or
(c) a new registration results from a fresh application under s. 67(3).

Generally, once a fair rent has been registered, it cannot be altered within two years from the effective date of registration (s. 72(1)). Exceptionally, applications seeking different rents may be made during that period where there has been 'such a change in (a) the condition of the dwelling-house (including the making of any improvement therein); (b) the terms of the tenancy; (c) the quantity, quality or condition of any furniture provided for use under the tenancy (deterioration by fair wear and tear excluded); or (d) any other circumstances taken into consideration when the rent was registered or confirmed, as to make the registered rent no longer a fair rent' (s. 67(3)).

Determination of a fair rent

Section 70(1) of the 1977 Act provides that 'in determining ... what rent is or would be a fair rent under a regulated tenancy of a dwelling-house, regard shall be had to all the circumstances (other than personal circumstances) and in particular to –

(a) the age, character, locality and state of repair of the dwelling-house, and
(b) if any furniture is provided for use under the tenancy, the quantity, quality and condition of the furniture'.

Of course not all circumstances will be relevant to the question of how much rent should be payable. As to those which *are* relevant, the courts have said that regard must be had 'to the sorts of factors which tend to push rents up or down on the market' (*Metropolitan Properties v Finegold* [1975] 1 WLR 349, 351). Such circumstances could include, e.g. any restrictions in the tenancy as to use of the premises, or the quantity and quality of any services provided for the tenant by the landlord, whether expressly under the tenancy or under a separate agreement.

As far as the state of repair of the dwelling-house is concerned, there is persuasive authority that a nil or nominal rent should be determined in respect of a property which is unfit for human habitation (*Black v Oliver* [1978] QB 870) but in *Williams v Khan* (1982) 43 P & CR 1, it was held that the rent assessment committee are not bound to assess a nil rent because the property is subject to a closing order. That the landlord cannot afford to keep the property in repair is a 'personal circumstance' which should be disregarded.

There is uncertainty as to whether the possibility of inflation over the two-year period may be taken into account when the rent is initially determined. A rent which was fair when the determination was made will soon become unfair in times of rapid inflation. In *Metropolitan Properties Co (FGC) Ltd v Lannon* [1968] 1 WLR 815, Lord Widgery suggested that some anticipation of inflation is appropriate if sufficient information on inflation trends is available. However, in *Guppys (Bridport) Ltd v Carpenter* (1973) 228 EG 1919, he stated that 'it is not the duty of a rent assessment committee necessarily to assume inflation in the ensuing [two] years or to make provision for it'. In *Wareing v White* (1984) 270 EG 851, it was held that while account could be taken of inflation, it would be quite wrong for the court to lay down principles as to how the question of inflation should be approached.

The Rent Act 1977 makes it quite clear that in determining a fair rent, rent officers and rent assessment committees should ignore personal circumstances (s. 70(1)), scarcity value (s. 70(2)) and any defects caused, or improvements carried out, to the dwelling-house by the tenant (s. 70(3)).

Personal circumstances

The parties' gender, sexual orientation, age, health, ethnicity, religion, and financial standing should all be disregarded as 'personal circumstances', as should security of tenure (*Mason v Skilling* [1974] 1 WLR 1437, 1440).

Scarcity

Arguably the most important disregard falls within s. 70(2). This requires rent officers and rent assessment committees to assume that 'the number of persons seeking to become tenants of similar dwelling-house in the locality ... is not substantially greater than the number of such dwelling-houses in the locality which are available for letting ...'.

If demand for rented accommodation is greater than the available supply, the market rent will be higher than would be the case if supply and demand were evenly balanced. The effect of s. 70(2) is that where there is an imbalance, rent officers or rent assessment committees must determine a rent on the assumption that supply and demand are equal. In contrast to 'the owner of other commodities, the landlord cannot take advantage of shortages in order to increase the rent' (Martin, 1995: 173). Implicit in both subss. (1) and (2) is the notion that the level at which the rent is fixed represents the level of rents if only the current (temporary) housing shortage did not exist. Lord Widgery explained it thus:

> It seems to me that what parliament is saying is this. If the house has inherent amenities and advantages, by all means let them be reflected in the rent under subs. (1); but if the market rent would be influenced simply by the fact that there is a shortage, and in the locality rents are being forced up beyond the market figure, then that element of market rent must not be included when the fair rent is being considered. Parliament, I am sure, is not seeking to deprive the landlord of a proper return on the inherent value and quality of his investment in the house, but parliament is undoubtedly seeking to deprive a landlord of a wholly unmerited increase in rent which has come about simply because there is a scarcity of houses in the district and thus an excess of demand over supply.
> (*Metropolitan Property Holdings v Finegold* [1975] 1 WLR 349, 352.)

In *Metropolitan Property Holdings v Finegold*, the presence of a school in St John's Wood which restricted entry to children of American families in London made the district more attractive to American families and rents went up. The tenant argued that this introduced a scarcity element, which should be disregarded. It was held, however, that the word 'locality' should be interpreted broadly and does not mean the immediate locality. Thus, the scarcity test should be applied over a substantial area, ignoring local scarcity caused by a particular amenity.

Defects or improvements to the dwelling-house

By s. 70(3) of the 1977 Act the rent officer or rent assessment committee must disregard:

(a) any disrepair or other defect attributable to a failure by the tenant under the regulated tenancy or any predecessor in title to comply with any terms thereof; and

(b) any improvement carried out by the tenant under the regulated tenancy or any predecessor in title, otherwise than in pursuance of the terms of the tenancy. A similar provision applies to any improvement to or deterioration in the condition of any furniture which is provided. The word 'improvement' means something more than repair and maintenance and, in this context, includes the replacement of any fixture or fitting (s. 70(4)).

In the case of 'any disrepair or other defect', there must be evidence of negligence or other breach of the terms of the tenancy by the tenant. In *McGhee v London Rent Assessment Panel* (1969) 113 SJ 384, five fires on the demised property, allegedly caused by the activities of a poltergeist, were held not to have been caused by the tenant's negligence or by any failure to comply with the terms of his tenancy. Accordingly the rent officer's reduction in rent from £6 per week to 5 shillings (25p) was restored in place of the rent assessment committee's £4. It makes no difference that the landlord has failed to enforce the tenant's repairing covenant (*Metropolitan Properties Co Ltd v Woldridge* (1969) 20 P & CR 64).

Methods of determining a fair rent

Section 70(1) leaves it up to the rent officer or rent assessment committee to adopt any method of ascertaining a fair rent provided that it is not unlawful or unreasonable (*Mason v Skilling* [1974] 1 WLR 1437, 1439). The registered comparables test, in which regard is had to the recently registered rents of comparable properties in a locality, was described in the House of Lords as 'the most obvious and direct method' of ascertaining a fair rent (*Mason v Skilling* [1974] 1 WLR 1437, 1439; see too *Western Heritable Investment Co Ltd v Husband* [1983] 3 WLR 429, 436). The use of comparables does have limitations in that a true comparable rarely exists unless it is an identical flat in the same block, or a corresponding house on a housing estate of similar properties. Even then, there will always be some differing factors.

Since it is based on existing registered rents, the registered comparables method contains a built-in scarcity deduction. In *London Rent Assessment Committee v St George's Court Ltd* (1984) 48 P & CR 230 the Court of Appeal stated that the rent assessed for a comparable property had to be regarded as 'the best evidence of the rent which would be a fair rent for the property under consideration' unless it could be shown that it had been arrived at upon a fundamental misapprehension. Thus, although already registered rents will be presumed to have been correctly ascertained, either party may show that those comparable rents have been determined on a wrong basis (*Mason v Skilling* [1974] 1 WLR 1437).

The expansion of the sector following the Housing Act 1988 witnessed a steep increase in registered rents, over and above inflation. In 1990 the average weekly rent (excluding housing association tenancies) was £61 for assured tenancies, £66 for assured shorthold tenancies, £27 for regulated tenancies with a registered rent and £33 for regulated tenancies with a non-registered rent (thus suggesting that many non-registered rents for regulated tenancies were not set at 'market levels' but 'in the shadow' of registered rent levels (Davey, 1992: 500). However, in a series of cases (e.g. *BTE Ltd v Merseyside and Cheshire Rent Assessment Committee* [1992] 16 EG 111; *Spath Holme Ltd v Greater Manchester and Lancashire Rent Assessment Committee* (1995) 28 HLR 107; *Curtis and Others v London Rent Assessment Committee* (1995) 28 HLR 841) the courts made it clear that the determination of fair rents would no longer be restricted to a comparison with registered fair rents but that reference could be made to the open market rents at which comparable properties were being let on assured tenancies (including assured shortholds). Between 1989 and 1995, the average annual rate of increase on re-registration in England ranged from 18 per cent to 25 per cent (DoE, 1996: Table 11.6).

Having pledged before the 1997 general election that it would take steps to stem escalating fair rents for Rent Act tenants (many of whom were elderly), the Labour government introduced the Rent Act (Maximum Fair Rent) Order 1999. The Order placed a limit on the amount of rent which rent officers and rent assessment committees could register for regulated tenancies and secure housing association tenancies where a fair rent had previously been registered on the property. The limits were RPI + 7.5 per cent for the first registration after the limit came into force and RPI + 5 per cent for the next and all subsequent registrations. Additional increases were permitted where the landlord had carried out major works to the dwelling.

In a successful challenge by Spath Holme Ltd, a Manchester landlord which owned several flats occupied by Rent Act tenants paying fair rents, the Court of Appeal held that the Order did not come within the scope of the power under which it was made (Landlord and Tenant Act 1985, s. 31) because it was not made for counter-inflationary purposes. However, in *R v Secretary of State for the Environment, Transport and the Regions ex p Spath Holme Ltd* [2001] 2 WLR 15, the House of Lords allowed the appeal, holding that while countering inflation had been part of the mischief at which s. 31 had been aimed, it had not been the sole mischief and the provision could also have been used to alleviate the hardship caused to tenants by increased or excessive rents.

Rents under the Housing Act 1988

Assured tenancies

The policy of the Housing Act 1988 – a measure which 'shattered the 20 year old political consensus on rent regulation' (Davey, 1992: 497) – is to allow freedom of contract to prevail and to limit the degree of statutory intervention. It is left to the parties, therefore, to agree on the level of rent and make provision for rent reviews in appropriate cases. In contrast to the Housing Act 1957, the 1988 Act did not deregulate any existing lettings but provided that, as a general rule, no new registered tenancies could be created on or after 15 January 1989. The only external influences provided for by the 1988 Act operate through the s. 13 review procedure for assured periodic tenancies and via referrals to rent assessment committees by assured shorthold tenants. The aim of these provisions is not to limit rents but to set them at a market level.

Fixed term tenancies

The parties to a fixed-term tenancy may agree on whatever rent they like. Unless there is a rent review clause, a landlord who wishes to increase the original rent will have to wait until the fixed-term tenancy ends and a statutory periodic tenancy arises. The landlord will then be able to serve a notice of increase under s. 13.

Periodic tenancies

The landlord may increase the rent of a periodic or statutory periodic assured tenancy by serving notice under s. 13. However, any provision in the tenancy agreement for rent review will govern rent increases to the exclusion of the statutory procedure (s. 13(1)(b)). Alternatively, the landlord and tenant may agree to vary the rent, regardless of the provisions of ss. 13 and 14 (s. 13(5)). The statutory procedure allows for rent to be increased annually.

The landlord must serve a notice in the prescribed form, proposing a new rent to take effect as from a 'new period of the tenancy specified in the notice' (s. 13(2)). The form advises the tenant of his or her right to refer the rent to a rent assessment committee under s. 13(4). There is no earliest date when the notice can be served, but the increase cannot take effect any earlier than (a) the minimum period after the date of service of the notice, and (b) the end of the first anniversary of the date in which the first period of the tenancy began (s. 13(2)(b)). If the rent has previously been increased by a s. 13 notice or a s. 14 determination by a rent assessment committee, no further notice of increase can be served until one year after the increased rent takes effect (s. 13(2)(c)).

By s. 13(2) and (3), the 'minimum period', from which the new rent is payable, is not to begin earlier than:

(a) in the case of a yearly tenancy, six months;
(b) in the case of a tenancy where the period is less than a month, one month;
(c) in any other case, the period of the tenancy.

Once the period specified in the notice expires, the new rent takes effect as specified in the notice, unless the tenant has referred the notice to a rent assessment committee, by an application in the prescribed form, or the parties have agreed on a different rent, or have agreed that no increase is called for (s. 13(4)). Of course, a periodic tenant who is unwilling or unable to pay a new rent may determine the tenancy by a notice to quit.

Statutory periodic tenancies

A statutory periodic tenancy arises on the termination of an assured fixed-term tenancy (by expiry of the term (s. 5(2)) or the operation of a break clause by the landlord) and also where the tenant has succeeded to a tenancy which was previously regulated by the Rent Act 1977 (s. 39(6)(f)). The rent payable continues at the same level as before (s. 5(3)) but the landlord may propose a rent increase under s. 13. The notice must be served during the final year of the fixed-term assured tenancy, giving a 'minimum period' for the coming into effect of the new rent. The length of the minimum period will depend on the intervals at which rent is payable under the tenancy. Further increases in rent will be governed by the provisions which apply to periodic tenancies.

Determination by a rent assessment committee

There is no procedure which allows a tenant to take the initiative in referring a matter to a rent assessment committee; its jurisdiction arises exclusively on a landlord's attempt to secure an increase. Where there are joint tenants, they must all make the application they authorise one tenant to act as their agent.

The referral must be in a prescribed form and must take place before the beginning of the 'new period' specified in the notice (s. 13(4)). Otherwise the new rent specified in the notice will become payable, however high or unreasonable it may be. The committee must consider the reference under s. 14. Committees are empowered to obtain from both the landlord and the tenant such information as they may reasonably require for the purposes of their functions (s. 4) and the president of every rent assessment panel must keep and make publicly available specified information as to the rents of assured and assured shorthold tenancies (s. 42). Both parties may give written notice that they no longer require a determination (s. 14(8)). Rent does not include a service charge (s. 14(4)) but the committee must consider sums payable for furniture and for services, repairs, maintenance or insurance of the landlord's costs of management, whether or not they are separate from the rent, and whether they are payable under the tenancy or under separate agreements.

By s. 14(1), a rent assessment committee must determine the rent at which they consider the dwelling-house might reasonably be expected to be let in the open market by a willing landlord under an assured tenancy on the assumption that:

(a) the tenancy is periodic with the same periods as the tenancy to which the notice relates,
(b) it begins at the beginning of the period from which the new rent specified in the notice is payable,
(c) the terms are those of the tenancy to which the notice relates (other than that relating to the amount of rent), and
(d) where appropriate, notices under Sch. 2, grounds 1–5 have been given to the tenant.

The rent determined by a rent assessment committee takes effect as from the date specified in the landlord's s. 13 notice, unless the committee considers that this would cause undue hardship to the tenant, in which case they may substitute a later date which cannot be any later than the date of their decision (s. 14(7)).

Statutory disregards

While the rent must be determined as a market rent, s. 14(2) provides that the committee must make the following disregards:

(a) The fact that there is a sitting tenant.
(b) Any increase in the value of the dwelling-house attributable to certain improvements carried out by the person who, at the time they were carried out, was the current tenant. Any improvement carried out pursuant to a contractual obligation will generally be disregarded. Voluntary improvements cannot be disregarded unless they were carried out either during the current tenancy, or under an earlier tenancy provided that (i) they were carried out no more than 21 years before the date of service of the notice; and (ii) at all times since then, the dwelling-house has been let under an assured tenancy and (iii) on the coming to an end of an assured tenancy at any time during that period, the tenant (or one of the joint tenants) did not quit the property (s. 14(3)).
(c) Any reduction in the value of the dwelling-house attributable to a failure by the tenant to comply with the terms of the tenancy. Where a person became an assured tenant by succession under s. 39 of the Housing Act 1988, a failure by the tenant's predecessor to comply with the terms of the tenancy cannot be taken into account as s. 14(2)(c) applies only to the defaults of the *current* tenant (*N&D (London) Ltd v Gadson* [1992] 1 EGLR 112).

Assured shorthold tenancies

The 1987 White Paper which paved the way for the Housing Act 1988 stated that for all new lettings under the proposed Act, landlords should be able to choose to let either on the assured tenancy basis (with rents freely negotiated between landlord and tenant), or on the shorthold basis (with no security beyond the period of the tenancy but with the right for either party to seek registration of an appropriate rent) (DoE, 1987: 3.11). The impression given was that because assured shorthold tenancies carry no security of tenure, assured shorthold tenants would pay less rent. What has happened in fact is that because most lettings have been assured shorthold tenancies, the rent payable under an assured shorthold tenancy has become the market rent and does not reflect the tenant's lack of security.

Periodic assured shorthold tenancies

The tenant who, after 28 February 1997, is granted a periodic assured shorthold tenancy has a right to refer the rent to the rent assessment committee but only during the first six months of the tenancy. The landlord can use the s. 13 procedure to increase the rent.

Fixed-term assured shorthold tenancies

By s. 22 of the 1988 Act an assured shorthold tenant may apply to the rent assessment committee to determine the rent 'which, in the committee's opinion, the landlord might reasonably be expected to obtain'.

Where the tenancy was granted after 28 February 1997, the tenant cannot refer the rent if more than six months have elapsed since the beginning of the tenancy (s. 22(2)(aa)) or, in the case of a replacement tenancy, since the beginning of the original tenancy. The tenant cannot in any case refer the rent if a rent has previously been determined under s. 22 (s. 22(2)(a)).

Determination by a rent assessment committee

A rent assessment committee can only make a determination if by s. 22(3) they consider that:

(a) there is a sufficient number of similar dwelling-houses in the locality let on assured tenancies (whether shorthold or not); and
(b) the rent payable under the assured shorthold tenancy in question is 'significantly higher' than the rent which the landlord might reasonably be expected to be able to obtain under the tenancy, having regard to the level of rents payable under the tenancies of similar dwelling-houses in the locality.

The rent, as determined by the rent assessment committee, takes effect from whatever date the committee directs, but no earlier than the date of the application (s. 22(4)(a)). The landlord cannot serve notice of an increase of rent under s. 13(2) until after the first anniversary of the date on which the determination takes effect (s. 22(4)(c)). The 'closely defined circumstances in which it is available' mean that this 'modest form of consumer protection' which applies to tenants 'who, perhaps through ignorance of local market conditions' have agreed 'an unrealistically high rent', is exercised only infrequently (Law Commission, 2002a: 2.75).

Housing association rents

Part VI of the Rent Act 1977 provides for the registration of 'fair' rents for dwellings let by housing associations, housing trusts and the Housing Corporation before 15 January 1989. However, the vast majority of housing association tenancies are assured tenancies granted on or after 15 January 1989. During the passage of the Housing Act 1988 through Parliament, the government rejected the argument made by representatives of the housing association movement that, because most housing associations were created to provide low-cost housing, there should be a separate regime for housing association rents. However, the new funding regime for housing associations which required them to raise private capital to underpin new development made it desirable – if not essential – to give them freedom 'to determine the rents on their new tenancies in the light of their financial commitments, their plans for future housing and service developments' (Marsh and Walker, 2006: 201). Rents for housing association tenancies created since the 1988 Act came into force are therefore determined in the same way as ordinary private sector tenancies although intervention by the Housing Corporation plays an important role in securing their affordability.

When housing associations first began to grant assured tenancies, the Housing Corporation stated in its 'Tenants' Guarantee' that they should try to set and maintain their rents at levels which were within the reach of those in low-paid employment. It also stated that they should not discriminate in their rent-setting policies between tenants who were eligible for housing benefit and others. The Corporation's *Regulatory Code* (which has superseded the Tenants' Guarantee) makes no reference as such to affordability but requires rents payable for housing association properties to be set at levels which 'are, on average, below those in the private sector for similar properties and which reflect size, property values and local earnings' (HC, 2002: 3.1).

Local authority rents

Local authorities have traditionally enjoyed a wide discretion in fixing the rents for their properties, but their discretion was significantly affected by the financial regime established under the Local Government and Housing Act 1989, and the process of rent-restructuring which is currently taking place with the aim of achieving greater consistency between local authority and housing association rents completely removes their discretion as regards the method by which their rents are set.

In the past, central government has not generally concerned itself with the methods employed by social landlords to set their rents nor with the rents of individual dwellings. Any attempt at interference has often proved either unpopular or unworkable. A notable example is the Housing Finance Act 1972 in which the Conservative government attempted to extend the fair rent system into the public sector. Not only were the fair rent criteria seen as inappropriate in the public sector but also, 'in future, council rents would effectively be set by non-elected, non-accountable committees entirely separate from local authorities themselves' (Malpass, 1992: 125). One of the aims behind this policy was to address the concern over what were perceived to be 'privileged council tenants clinging on to subsidised housing in order to profit from public munificence' (Jacobs et al., 2003: 312). It would also encourage those who could afford to buy to move into owner-occupation and thus create vacancies within the council sector (ibid.). It appeared that fair rents would be substantially higher than existing rent levels and the new regime required authorities to make annual increases in rent, equivalent to 50 pence per week, until the fair rent was achieved. Malpass points out that, although 50 pence per week may sound modest today, in 1972 it represented an increase of around 25 per cent for most tenants. The Act faced considerable resistance from tenants and local authorities, although ultimately only two authorities – Bedwas and Machen and Clay Cross – refused to implement it. The Clay Cross councillors were removed from office, held personally liable for, and surcharged for, the loss of rent income and a commissioner – with whom the authority refused to co-operate – was appointed to run the town's housing service (Malpass, 1992). The Act was repealed when a Labour government was returned to power in 1974.

Section 24 of the Housing Act 1985 empowers local authorities to make 'such reasonable charges as they may determine for the tenancy or occupation of their houses'. By s 24(2), 'the authority shall from time to time review rents and make such changes, either of rents generally or of particular rents, as circumstances may require'. In deciding whether a charge is 'reasonable' the courts have held that local authorities must strike a balance between council tax-payers and tenants (*Belcher v Reading Corporation* [1950] Ch 380) and are entitled to approach it as a matter of social policy (*Luby v Newcastle-under-Lyme Corporation* [1965] 1 QB 214). They are neither obliged to relate their rents to market rents nor to seek to make a profit (*Evans v Collins* [1965] 1 QB 580). Although these principles are still good law they must be viewed in the light of the 'ring-fencing' of the Housing Revenue Account (HRA) by the Local Government and Housing Act 1989 which prohibits authorities from making payments to the HRA from any other revenue account, e.g. the General Fund. The 1989 Act obliges local authorities to prevent a debit balance on the HRA (s. 79) and, as one of the major sources of income to the account is the rental income, the rent levels set will necessarily reflect this duty. Furthermore, the other major source of income – housing subsidy – is now calculated on the account on the basis of the assumed, rather than actual, rent levels and of reasonably efficient management (s. 80).

In 1989 central government sought once more to influence the way local authorities set *relative* rents – that is, the rents on one type of property relative to those of another. Section 24 of the 1985 Act was amended so that local authorities were obliged to 'have regard in particular to the principle that the rents of houses of any class or description should bear broadly the same proportion to private sector rents as the rents of other houses of any other class or description'. 'Private sector rents' are the rents which would be recoverable if the 'houses of any class or description' were 'let on assured tenancies within the meaning of the Housing Act 1988 by a person other than the authority' (s. 24(4)). The aim was that the differential between the rents charged for different types of housing in the public sector should be broadly the same as that in the private sector. Thus, if under an assured tenancy, the rent for a three-bedroom flat is roughly three times the rent charged for a one-bedroom flat, the local authority should try to maintain the same ratio between its own three-bedroom and one-bedroom flats. The motivation for this policy was a desire 'to replicate market-like differentials in the public sector and thereby to present tenants with incentives to consider their housing costs and to optimise their housing consumption' (Marsh, 2002: 289). In practice however very few local authorities made the comparisons they had been directed to make and, even when they did, there appeared to be no obligation to act upon them.

Unlike the Rent Act 1977, the Housing Act 1985 contains no formal machinery for challenging the rent payable. Theoretically, the tenant can seek judicial review of the local authority's exercise of its discretion but, in practice, such a course of action is unlikely to be successful. The discretion given to a local authority is such that the court can interfere only if the tenant can prove that it has been exercised in a manner which no reasonable person could consider justifiable. In only one reported case has the authority's discretion been overturned (see *Backhouse v Lambeth Borough Council, The Times*, 14 October 1972).

The significance of housing benefit

The housing benefit scheme is administered by local authorities under the central direction of the Department of Work and Pensions (DWP). It is a means-tested or income-related payment which provides rent assistance for low-income tenants and licensees (whether in or out of work) in private and social rented housing. For tenants of housing associations and private landlords, the benefit takes the form of a rent allowance paid either to the tenant or, as has more often been the case, direct to the landlord (either at the tenant's request or because the local authority considers it to be in the tenant's best interests). At present, 60 per cent of private and housing association tenants have their housing benefit paid directly to their landlord. For local authority tenants, housing benefit takes the form of a rent rebate.

A decision on a housing benefit claim should be made by the relevant authority within 14 days of receiving all the necessary information or as soon as reasonably practicable thereafter (Housing Benefit Regulations 2006, reg. 89(2)). Yet, in 2000/01 only 63 per cent of claimants received their benefit within the prescribed period (Audit Commission, 2002: 5) and the speed at which claims are processed has worsened over the years, despite the fact that the number of claims has fallen (ibid.). The complexity of the rules and regulations, frequent changes to the system, and difficulties in recruiting and retaining benefit staff all contribute to delays in processing claims. Another contributory factor has been the 'verification framework' (introduced in an attempt to reduce fraud as much as possible, as part of the government's drive to minimise the overall social security bill) which sets a minimum standard of evidence needed for a claim to be assessed and requires the claimant to provide original documentation (e.g. the claimant's birth certificate or passport) to establish his or her identity.

Over 47 per cent of housing benefit claimants in Great Britain live in local authority housing, 33 per cent in housing owned by RSLs and 19 per cent in the private rented sector. These figures account for around two-thirds of local authority and housing association tenants and a fifth of private tenants (DWP, 2004: Table 3.1). In 1978/9, £2.3 billion (at 1998/9 prices) was spent on housing benefit. By 1998/9, this figure had increased to £11.1 billion and it now stands at £12.7 billion (DWP, 2004: Table 2). It can be seen therefore that housing benefit is important not only to the 3.7 million recipients but also, because it comprises a significant share of their rental income, to the private and social landlords who house them (Kemp, 2000: 265).

When the housing benefit scheme first came into existence, local authorities were reimbursed by central government the full cost of paying benefit on reasonable rents. However if (a) the accommodation was deemed to be larger than was reasonably needed for the occupier and anyone who also occupied the accommodation, or (b) the rent was unreasonably high compared with that for suitable accommodation elsewhere within the area, the local authority was required to meet the full cost of the difference. Financial incentives existed, therefore, for local authorities not to pay out full benefit on unreasonably high rents so that claimants had either to find the difference themselves or try to persuade landlords to reduce the rent. Safeguards existed for certain vulnerable claimants (the elderly, disabled and families with children) and the courts were sometimes prepared to exercise some control over landlords (see, e.g. *R v Manchester City Council ex p Baragrove Properties Ltd* (1991) 23 HLR 337).

Concerns that landlords and tenants who were eligible for housing benefit were colluding over the setting of rents led to an amendment of the regulations in January 1996 in relation to new claims made by private sector and
most housing association tenants so that payments of housing benefit are
now limited to a 'maximum rent'. Where a rent is thought to be out of line,
the housing benefit authority (usually a local authority or a private agency to
whom the task has been outsourced) applies to the rent officer for a determination, and the maximum rent is then fixed in the light of that determination. Generally, rent officers will be asked to determine a 'local reference
rent' (arrived at by adding the highest rent which, in the rent officer's opinion,
a landlord might have been able to obtain for the dwelling in question, to the
lowest rent and dividing by two). Councils can meet 50 per cent of the difference between local reference rents and their 'market' equivalents (i.e. the
maximum amount that non-claimant tenants would willingly pay). Arguably,
this process has 'reintroduced a *de facto* element of rent control' back into
private renting (Ball, 2004: 27). The previous safeguards for vulnerable
claimants have been removed, leaving only local authorities' general powers to make provision in cases of exceptional hardship. Rent officers are also
empowered to make pre-tenancy determinations of the maximum eligible
rent at the request of prospective tenants, the idea being that, given such
information, tenants can then seek to renegotiate the asking rent.

Since October 1996, the amount of housing benefit payable to many single
people under the age of 25 living in private sector accommodation has been
severely restricted and covers only the 'average' rent in the area for single-
roomed accommodation with the shared use of toilet and kitchen facilities
and, from 2 July 2001, a shared living room and bathroom. The policy
behind this measure was to deter young people from occupying self-
contained accommodation, freeing it up for families. Plans to extend this
restriction to all single people between the ages of 25 and 59 were scrapped
by the Labour government.

When it came to power in 1997, New Labour made it clear that it
intended substantially to cut back and otherwise reform housing benefit as
part of its wider aim of reducing the cost of and 'modernising' the social security system, and thereby freeing up resources which could then be directed
towards health and education (Kemp, 2000: 266). Although initially it had
radical reform in mind, it subsequently scaled down its plans. In contrast to
the Conservative government in the mid-1980s (which had been able to
make cuts to housing benefit because its attention was still focused on
extending home ownership and the policy of demunicipalisation had yet to be
introduced), New Labour was 'locked in' to the status quo. Its housing policy
depended upon the willingness of private landlords to let accommodation
to tenants on housing benefit and upon private loans for social housing
(which funders made clear was dependent upon 'the continued availability of
housing benefit to underwrite the rental income needed to service the debt')

(ibid.: 272–3). Thus although housing benefit is in the process of reform, the changes are being made on an incremental basis and will come into effect over a longer timeframe than was originally anticipated.

In October 2002 the government announced its intention to replace the present complex mechanisms of housing benefit with a local housing allowance (LHA) (see DWP, 2002).[1] This is currently being trialled in nine 'pathfinder' areas, with a national roll-out planned for 2008. Briefly, claimants receive a flat rate allowance based on the size of their household and the area in which they live. It is calculated in a similar way to 'local reference rents' and – at present – claimants who receive an LHA which is greater than their rent can spend the 'surplus' as they wish. Those claimants with rents which exceed the LHA have to make up the difference. The government is now proposing a number of changes, however, including capping the surplus which claimants can keep and setting the rate at the median rent rather than the mid-point of the rental market. Although it was intended that the reform would eventually be extended to social housing the government now seems undecided as to whether this will actually take place.

In line with the moves towards a more 'consumerist' approach in housing, one of the most significant (and controversial) changes introduced by the LHA regime is the payment of benefit direct to claimants unless they are deemed to be vulnerable, or it is improbable that they will pay their rent or the claimant has built up rent arrears of eight weeks or more. At present, around 60 per cent of private tenants have their housing benefit paid directly to their landlords. In future, however, it is planned that the majority of tenants will receive the benefit themselves and take responsibility for paying it to their landlords. Although it was predicted that this new measure would double the number of tenants who fall into arrears (*The Guardian*, Society, 19 November 2003) the view favoured by government is that direct payments appear to 'remove tenants from the responsibility of having to pay the rent themselves' as a result of which recipients of housing benefit are regarded as 'supplicants more than purchasers' (Kemp and Leather, 2002). Moreover, as indicated above, direct payments must still be made where the claimant has accrued more than eight weeks' arrears and the benefit service can intervene to prevent arrears reaching the eight weeks level. Those who support direct payment argue that it 'reduce[s] the number of tasks involved in processing housing benefit claims which, in turn, results in time and cost savings in the administration of the scheme' (Kemp and Leather, 2002). It can cut the cost of rent collection for landlords and spare tenants the time, trouble and anxiety involved in paying their rent. Nonetheless, direct payment stands in the way of reforms which seek 'to create incentives through more rational pricing mechanisms' and to foster 'a more engaged, critical tenant body'

---

1   For an explanation of the background to, and a critique, of the proposals, see Rahilly (2003).

which will 'hold landlords more closely to account' in delivering 'value for money' (Bramley *et al.*, 2004: 149).

Most recently, under its 'Respect' agenda, the government has proposed to pilot a scheme in 2007 of cutting housing benefit payable to those evicted for anti-social behaviour who refuse to undergo rehabilitation. It is proposed that benefit will be cut by 10 per cent for the first four weeks and 20 per cent for the following four weeks, and will be completely removed for up to five years if claimants still do not co-operate. Normal payments can resume at any time. The government's view is that housing benefit sanctions would have a deterrent effect, act as an additional tool against anti-social behaviour and enable perpetrators to be tracked through different tenures, e.g. where, having been evicted by a social landlord, they move into nearby private rented housing and continue their anti-social behaviour. On the other hand, the proposals may be criticised for unfairly associating anti-social behaviour with social tenants, being at odds with the government's other objectives such as the prevention of homelessness and the promotion of social inclusion, and overlooking the fact that anti-social behaviour is often a consequence of many complex problems involving poverty, unemployment and alcohol and drug dependency.

Rent restructuring

The fact that individual landlords have used different rent-setting methods at different times has produced a plethora of rent levels in social housing. Alder and Handy explain that, for many years, 'competition for steadily reducing grant levels' (and the need to finance the loans from private lenders which make up the difference) has driven up housing association rents at a rate well above those of wages and the cost of living so that they are, on average, around 20 per cent higher than those payable for their local authority counterparts. They state that at the beginning of 2002, housing association rents were about 11 per cent higher than council rents (Alder and Handy, 2003: 1–017). However, this is largely in line with the difference in property values between the two sectors, mainly because housing association stock tends to be newer (DETR, 2000: 10.32). The Housing Corporation responded in 1999 by introducing rent competition for new projects and a cap on rent increases so that the total rental income of each association could increase no more than the RPI plus half a per cent. Alder and Handy describe this as 'a ligature on future rental growth' which, while it has imposed a limit on the overall increase of housing association rents, has also 'reinforced existing differentials of rent between housing associations and between tenure regimes' (Alder and Handy, 2003: 1–017).

However, the government's introduction of the rent restructuring framework – which aims to inject a degree of rationality and consistency into rent setting in social housing by introducing a single formula applied nationally to both local authorities and RSLs – means that by 2012 existing rent differentials between (and sometimes within) local authority and RSL stock should have disappeared. One objective of rent restructuring is to encourage better management by social landlords of their stock but it is also intended to make rents fairer and less confusing for tenants and to reduce 'unjustifiable' differences in rents of similar properties owned by different landlords (DETR, 2000: 10.1). Local authorities and RSLs are required to determine target rents for each of their properties based upon a combination of capital values and average earnings within local areas. Thirty per cent of a property's rent should be based on relative property values and 70 per cent on relative local earnings (ODPM, 2003c: 2.2). A bedroom factor should also be applied so that, other things being equal, lower rents are payable for smaller properties. So as to 'protect tenants from substantial year-on year increases', a restriction has been placed on 'annual rent rises (and reductions) on individual properties, and maximum rents for different sized properties have been specified to protect those living in areas with high earnings and/or high capital values' (Marsh and Walker, 2006: 203). Although rent restructuring does not apply directly to fair rents paid by secure tenants of housing associations, landlords will not be compelled to increase rents to the level assessed by rent officers and rent assessment committees but nor will they be able to raise them above the assessment level. If a fair rent is set below the target rent, the lower amount will prevail. If the fair rent is set above the target rent, RSLs are expected to charge the target rent rather than the fair rent.

Although there is evidence that changes in rent levels have only limited impact upon local authority tenants' choice of dwelling, greater consistency in rent setting can be seen as 'removing artificial distortions from tenants' choice about where to live and from whom to rent their home' (Cowan and Marsh, 2001: 270). As such, rent restructuring can be located within a broader strategy for the social housing sector which includes housing benefit reform and choice-based lettings. As indicated above, the government intends within the next few years to introduce legislation which will replace housing benefit with flat-rate local housing allowances, making it possible for households to make trade-offs between spending on rents and other living expenses. The emergence of a more coherent structure of rents – via restructuring – is intended to ease that transition. Marsh and Walker predict that this is likely to be achieved provided that 'the level of average local target rents is taken as the basis for setting local housing allowances' (Marsh and Walker, 2006: 206). Because rents in an area will generally be similar for comparable types of property irrespective of landlord, restructuring will also act as 'a complement to the introduction of choice-based lettings as a new method of accessing social housing' by enabling (prospective) tenants to make more informed choices. It will also make it easier for stock transfers to take place from local authorities to housing associations (DETR, 2000: 10.36).

Unlike the requirement to set fair rents contained in the Housing Finance Act 1972 and the provisions of s. 162, rent restructuring has been put in place without primary legislation and the legal status of the regime is consequently uncertain (Marsh and Walker, 2006: 206). Nonetheless, Marsh and Walker predict that, despite its lack of legislative force, it arguably has a greater chance of successful implementation than its predecessors. While it does not set out any 'explicit mechanisms with which to ensure compliance', the fact that the subsidy system has been reformed on the assumption that restructuring is taking place has put pressure on local authorities to abide by it. Similarly, in the housing association sector, the calculation of capital subsidy for new developments presupposes that the rents to be set for the new properties accord with the restructuring formula. Alongside these financial incentives, performance review under the Best Value regime includes an assessment of a landlord's strategy for implementing rent restructuring as an indicator of good management (ibid.: 207). Pointing out that central government cannot use its status and legal powers to control RSLs in the same way that it can control local authorities, Mauthe goes so far as to suggest that 'by placing housing finance [of which restructuring is part] at the centre of housing policy', it has provided itself with an alternative mechanism for exercising such control (Mauthe, 2001: 308).

While the rent restructuring framework aims to maintain the total rental income for the RSL sector as a whole, some redistribution is bound to take place. In some cases rents will increase and in others reduce, and rent restructuring will have a differing impact on different associations and their tenants. For some associations, there may be an increase in income, although this is a less likely scenario, particularly for associations operating in areas where there are low capital values and low average incomes. Others will inevitably suffer a reduction in their overall income, resulting in financial restrictions. However, RSLs will have to determine the annual adjustment required to meet their existing contractual commitments and the Housing Corporation has made it clear that 'in deciding whether to take any action to adjust the rent levels or rate of increase of an RSL, our paramount concern will be to protect the public and private investment in its stock and to retain the confidence of its lenders' (HC, 2001: 2.9). It may be therefore that 'convergence will be partial at its best' if RSLs are allowed to operate outside the restructuring regime because their business plans are threatened by the proposed rent cap (Cowan and Marsh, 2001: 270).

Chapter 7

The responsibility for repairs

Introduction

As they grow older, houses deteriorate and are damaged by use, and parts of them wear out. They are 'like old clothes, handed down from earlier generations and remodelled with varying success' (Donnison and Ungerson, 1982: 16–17), a fact which has significant implications for the question of who is to bear the responsibility for their maintenance and repair.

For many years the maintenance of council housing was not regarded as a significant management issue. The focus was on new building, the stock was younger and resources were less constrained. More recently, however, it has become a major concern. The proportion of council housing in a substandard condition has increased since the 'right to buy' provisions introduced in 1980 creamed off the better quality properties into owner-occupation. The financial limitations to which local authorities are now subject mean that they often cannot afford to pay for the maintenance of those which remain. The result is that, 'whether by dint of lack of resources or poor management', much social housing has suffered for years from 'want of routine maintenance', with some landlords unable to comply with even 'the (minimal) repairing obligations imposed by law' (Luba, 2003: 105). A significant number of relatively modern properties suffer problems as a result of poor design, unproven building techniques and bad workmanship, yet expenditure on major overhauls and modernisation of properties with design flaws appears to be a low priority. In the private sector, many rented properties were built around the beginning of the twentieth century and now require extensive and frequent repairs. Around one in 20 homes has severe problems with condensation or mould, and one in 100 suffers seriously from damp. On average more than £6,600 would have to be spent on each of the 6.4 million non-decent homes in England to make them decent (DCLG, 2006: 34). Not surprisingly, given the sums of money which may be involved, liability for the repair and maintenance of rented property provides a rich source of disputes between landlords and tenants. It should not be forgotten, however, that a significant percentage of non-decent homes are in owner-occupation. The benefits of home ownership depend upon income and wealth, and some poor home owners might actually be better off as tenants.

The move towards the achievement of the Decent Homes Standard by 2010 might be thought to have made it less likely that social tenants would need to resort to the law to compel their landlords to carry out repairs. Ironically, however, it seems that it is precisely those tenants whose homes have been refurbished under the decent homes programme who (because of raised expectations) are more likely to demand repairs (*Inside Housing*, 12 October 2006). Furthermore, the Decent Homes Standard has been described as having been set at 'too basic a level [which] by 2010 will be seriously out of step with tenant expectations' (HPLGRC, 2004: 3) and it would seem therefore that tenants will continue to seek legal redress where they are exposed to unsatisfactory housing conditions.

At common law, no covenant is implied by the landlord of an unfurnished house or flat that it is, or will be, reasonably fit for habitation or that the landlord will carry out any repairs during the course of the tenancy. In the absence of express agreement, the landlord is not liable to the tenant for defects in the demised premises which make the premises dangerous or unfit for occupation, nor for personal injury to the tenant caused by such defects even though the landlord knows of their existence (*Lane v Cox* [1897] 1 QB 415). There is no duty to warn the tenant of them. There may be situations in which there is no repairing obligation imposed either expressly or impliedly on anyone in relation to a lease (*Demetriou v Robert Andrews (Estate Agencies) Ltd* (1990) 62 P & CR 536) resulting in deadlock between the parties. The principle of *caveat emptor* applies and it is up to prospective tenants to inspect a property, to satisfy themselves as to its condition and, if possible, to negotiate an appropriate contract. Viewed from a purely property perspective, the landlord's 'service' is ended as soon as the estate is granted to the tenant. Such a view however sits uneasily alongside the notion that residential tenants should be treated as consumers of a housing package.[1] Moreover, as Lord Hoffmann pointed out in *Southwark London Borough Council v Mills* [2001] 1 AC 1, 8 the tenant often lacks 'the bargaining power to exact an express warranty as to the condition of the premises or the freedom of choice to reject housing which does not meet his needs'. There are therefore a number of instances where a repairing obligation or an obligation as to fitness is either implied against a landlord or (as a result of Parliament's aim 'to protect certain tenants from the bleak laissez-faire of the common law') imposed by statute. Local authorities too play an important role in ensuring that residential property is in a habitable condition. The oft-quoted statement that 'fraud apart, there is no law against letting a tumble-down house' (*Robbins v Jones* (1863) 15 CB(NS) 221, 240) is subject to important exceptions. However, the law has developed in a

1   For an interesting discussion of the current state of the law on residential tenancy repairs, see Smith (2003).

haphazard and piecemeal fashion and the Law Commission has recommended extensive reform by the enactment of a new statute, on the ground that there is 'a public interest in seeing that there is an adequate stock of usable rented property, properly maintained and repaired ... and that residential property should be reasonably fit to live in' (Law Commission, 1996: 1.27).

Express obligations

Usually the parties to leases of commercial property or long leases of residential property will make express provision as regards liability for repairs. A long lease normally contains covenants by the tenant to keep the demised premises in repair during the term of the lease and to repair defects within a specified time of being requested by the landlord to do so. These will generally be coupled with a covenant by the tenant to permit the landlord or the landlord's agents to enter and view the state of repair. Private landlords commonly use 'clear' leases where the premises are divided into a number of units which are let to different tenants. The landlord covenants for the repair of the structure, exterior and common parts but the individual tenants bear all the costs of repairing and maintaining by way of service charges so that the rent reaches the landlord clear of all expenses and overheads. The tenant's express covenant for repair will normally extend only to the inside of the premises. Nonetheless, particularly in the social housing sector, the written terms may impose upon the landlord obligations which exceed the statutorily implied minima. For example, in *Welsh v Greenwich London Borough Council* (2001) 33 HLR 40, there was an express obligation to keep the property 'in good condition' and in *Southwark London Borough Council v Long* [2002] HLR 56, an express obligation 'to keep the estate and common parts clean and tidy'. In the more volatile private sector, the premises are more likely to be of poorer quality. Although the express terms again form the starting point there are two important limitations. First, the express terms cannot impose on tenants the obligations which statute places on landlords. Secondly, if the express terms are the landlord's standard terms, they must be 'fair', in accordance with the Unfair Terms Consumer Contract Regulations 1999. For example, an attempt to 'contract-out' of the tenant's usual common law right to set off the cost of repairs against rent might be unenforceable if it is unfair (Luba, 2005a: 62–3).

The meaning of repair

The distinction between repair, renewal and improvement

Repair 'connotes the idea of making good damage so as to leave the subject as far as possible as though it had not been damaged' (*Anstruther-Gough-Calthorpe v McOscar* [1924] 1 KB 716, 734 but it may also involve taking steps so as to prevent damage from occurring, or to prevent recurrence where damage has already occurred (*Stent v Monmouth District Council* (1987) 19 HLR 269). In *McDougall v Easington District Council* (1989) 58 P & CR 193, the Court of Appeal identified three tests which the courts have used in determining whether the works required constitute repair or something more:

(a) whether the alterations went to the whole or substantially the whole of the structure or only to a subsidiary part;
(b) whether the effect of the alterations was to produce a building of a wholly different character than that which had been let;
(c) the cost of the works in relation to the previous value of the building and their effect on the value and lifespan of the building.

These tests may be applied separately or concurrently, but must all be approached in the light of 'the nature and age of the premises, their condition when the tenant went into occupation, and the other express terms of the tenancy' (at p. 201).

The traditional approach has been to distinguish between a repair on the one hand and a renewal or an improvement on the other. In *Lurcott v Wakely and Wheeler* [1911] 1 KB 905, 924 Buckley LJ described repair as 'the restoration by renewal or replacement of subsidiary parts of a whole'. Renewal, he said, is 'the reconstruction of the entirety, meaning by entirety not necessarily the whole but substantially the whole subject-matter under discussion'. Repair always involves the renewal of subsidiary parts but if a house is in such poor condition that substantially the whole of it needs to be renewed, the works cannot properly be described as 'repairs'. Improvement involves rectifying defects by substituting something qualitatively different from, and better than, the original.

The relative costs

A new approach was adopted in *Ravenseft Properties Ltd v Davstone (Holdings) Ltd* [1980] QB 12, in which Forbes J said that whether or not the works amount to repair is always a question of degree, bearing in mind the cost of the disputed work relative to the value or cost of the whole premises. This test was adopted and applied in *Elmcroft Developments Ltd v Tankersley-Sawyer* (1984) 15 HLR 63 in which the replacement of a defective damp-proof course in a flat in a high-class fashionable residential area of London was held to constitute repair. By contrast, in *Wainwright v Leeds City Council* (1984) 270 EG 1289 (in which *Ravenseft* was not cited), it was held that the insertion of a damp-proof course, where none had existed before, in a run-down back-to-back terraced house in a poor part of Leeds would involve giving back something wholly different from that demised, and would not, therefore, be a repair.

The standard of repair

The standard of repair must be sufficient to enable the premises to be used not only with safety but with reasonable (although not excessive) comfort by the appropriate class of persons (*Belcher v M'Intosh* (1839) 2 Mood & R 186, 189). It is such 'as having regard to the age, character and locality of the house, would make it reasonably fit for the occupation of a reasonably minded tenant of the class likely to take it' (*Proudfoot v Hart* (1890) 25 QBD 42, 55). As Lord Esher explained in *Proudfoot v Hart*, a 200-year-old house cannot reasonably be expected to be in the same condition as a house recently built, and the character of the house is relevant in that the class of repair appropriate to a palace would be inappropriate to a cottage. As regards locality, the state of repair necessary for a house in Grosvenor Square would, the judge said, be totally different from that necessary for a house in Spitalfields.

The standard of repair is judged by the condition of the property at the commencement of the lease and is not raised by any improvement in its tenants or its neighbourhood, nor lowered by their deterioration (*Anstruther-Gough-Calthorpe v McOscar* [1924] 1 KB 716).

Landlords' contractual obligations imposed by common law

Furnished accommodation

It is an implied condition of a letting of furnished accommodation that it will be reasonably fit for habitation (rather than in structural repair) when the tenancy begins. The landlord is not obliged to *keep* the premises fit for habitation (*Sarson v Roberts* [1895] 2 QB 122) but will be liable if the premises were unfit at the start of the tenancy but the defect did not become apparent until later on. If the condition is not fulfilled, the tenant may treat the contract as repudiated and quit the premises without any liability for rent or sue the landlord for breach of contract.

Examples of defects which have been held to render premises unfit for habitation in this context include infestation by bugs (*Smith v Marrable* (1843) 11 N&W 5) and recent occupation by a person with an infectious disease (*Collins v Hopkins* [1923] 2 KB 617).

Obligation to repair common or essential parts

Where the tenancy is of a dwelling-house which forms only part of a building and is granted on or after 15 January 1989 for a term of less than seven years, a term will be implied that the landlord will keep in repair the structure and exterior of any part of the building in which the landlord has an estate or interest (Landlord and Tenant Act 1985, s. 11(1A)). Thus the landlord will generally be under a statutory duty to keep in repair the structure and exterior (including the common parts) of a block of flats. Because the common parts are deemed to be within the landlord's control, the tenant is not required to give notice of disrepair before the obligation to repair arises. For those tenants whose tenancies were granted before 15 January 1989, other terms may be implied into the contract unless they are excluded by express terms to the contrary.

Where the landlord retains part of a building, maintenance in proper repair of which is necessary for the protection of the demised premises or the tenant's safe enjoyment of them, there is implied an obligation on the landlord to take reasonable care to maintain the retained parts so as to not to cause damage to the tenant or the premises let. Thus a landlord who retains control of the roof and gutters is obliged to repair them so as to prevent damp getting into the flat (*Cockburn v Smith* [1924] 2 KB 119).

Where the landlord retains control of essential means of access to the demised premises, the insertion of a term may be necessary to give business efficacy to the contract. In *Liverpool City Council v Irwin* [1976] 2 All ER 39, the House of Lords held that the local authority landlord was under a contractual obligation to take reasonable care to maintain lifts, stairways and rubbish chutes serving upper-storey lettings in a 15-storey block of flats. Pointing out that these were not facilities or conveniences provided at discretion but 'essentials of the tenancy without which life in the dwellings, as a tenant, is not possible', Lord Wilberforce said that to leave the landlord 'free of contractual obligation ... and subject only to administrative or political pressure' would be 'totally inconsistent' with the nature of the landlord and tenant relationship. However, their Lordships emphasised that it did not impose an absolute obligation; rather it was a question of what was necessary, so that failure to imply the term would render the contract 'futile, inefficacious and absurd'. Significantly, what was reasonable to expect of a landlord was clearly related to 'what a reasonable set of tenants should do for themselves'. The council was held to have discharged its obligation; it had spent large sums of money to repair the lifts, stairs and rubbish chutes, and the subsequent – almost immediate – disrepair was due to vandalism. The decision might, on the face of it, appear to alter the balance of power between tenant and authorities and reduce 'the sphere of decisions taken in the public interest without acknowledgement of private rights' (McAuslan, 1980: 193). However, in authorising a 'fluctuating standard', it is possible that the House of Lords merely gave 'authoritative legal backing' to existing practices of many local authorities which regarded 'problem families' on 'problem estates' as not behaving reasonably and entitled to lesser standards of maintenance and care (ibid.). The court cannot imply terms it considers reasonable; no contractual obligation could be implied therefore where the lease itself provided for a perfectly workable scheme of repairs (*Duke of Westminster v Guild* [1985] QB 688).

Noise has proved to be a particular problem. In *Southwark London Borough Council v Mills* [2001] 1 AC 1, a lack of soundproofing meant that the tenants were constantly disturbed by the noise of their neighbours' ordinary everyday domestic activities. The tenants could hear 'not only neighbours' televisions and their babies crying but also their coming and going, their cooking and cleaning, their quarrels and their love-making' (p. 7). The House of Lords held that a covenant for quiet enjoyment does not oblige a landlord to rectify acts or omissions pre-dating the grant of a tenancy. The law imposed no obligation, whether express or implied, on a landlord to install soundproofing in an existing dwelling and there could be no extension of the common law, given the extent of Parliament's legislative provisions in this area of the law over the years. Tenants took premises in the condition in which they found them and subject to the uses which the parties contemplated would be made of the parts retained by the landlord. The absence of sound insulation was an inherent structural defect for which the council could not be held responsible. Furthermore, it could not be said to have authorised any nuisance, as the neighbours were merely using their properties in the normal way.

Correlative obligations

In some circumstances, the courts may imply an obligation on the landlord to match a correlative obligation expressly imposed on the tenant (*Duke of Westminster v Guild* [1985] QB 688). Thus in *Barrett v Lounova (1982) Ltd* [1989] 1 All ER 351, the lease provided that the tenant would carry out 'all inside repairs . . . and at the expiration of the tenancy . . . leave the inside of the said premises and fixtures in good repair order and condition . . .'. Neither party was under an express duty to keep the outside of the property in repair. Water penetration had damaged internal plasterwork and timbers. It was obvious, said Kerr LJ, that sooner or later the covenant imposed on the tenant (which was clearly intended to be enforceable throughout the tenancy) could no longer be complied with unless the outside has been kept in repair. In his view it was therefore necessary, as a matter of business efficacy to make the agreement workable, that an obligation to keep the outside in repair must be imposed on someone. And that someone, he said, was clearly the landlord.

Houses in the course of construction

In a lease of a house which is still in the course of construction, there is implied a warranty that it will be built with proper materials in a workmanlike manner and fit for human habitation when completed (*Perry v Sharon Development Co Ltd* [1937] 4 All ER 390). This is because the tenant is in no position to check the physical state of the premises in accordance with the principle of *caveat emptor*.

Landlords' contractual obligations imposed by statute

In general, an express covenant will override or displace an implied one. This is particularly so with implied covenants which derive from case law. However, some of the statutory obligations imposed upon landlords cannot be contracted out of and will apply despite any provision to the contrary.

Premises let at a low rent

Regardless of any express stipulation to the contrary, s. 8 of the Landlord and Tenant Act 1985 implies in certain contracts for the letting of a house (a) a condition that at the commencement of the tenancy the house is fit for human habitation and (b) an undertaking that the landlord will keep it so during the tenancy. As well as the house, the duty embraces 'any yard, garden, outhouse and appurtenances belonging to the house or usually enjoyed with it' (s. 8(6)). However, there are important qualifications to this provision:

(a) It applies only to houses let at very low rent levels (i.e. £80 per annum in London and £52 elsewhere) which have remained unchanged since 1957. The provision was first included in the Housing of the Working Classes Act 1885 to deal with insanitary and overcrowded housing and appears to have encompassed a substantial proportion of leased accommodation. The Law Commission calculated in 1996 that if the upper levels for the implied obligation of fitness were to be restored to a position equivalent to those which applied in 1957, they would be well over £3,000 per annum (Law Commission, 1996: 4.12) but Parliament's failure to increase them may be explained by a number of factors: the extension of local authority housing, the decline in the private rented sector, the rise in owner-occupation, and the introduction of the implied repairing obligation in 1961 of what is now s. 11 of the 1985 Act, all of which appeared to make the implied term redundant and out-dated (ibid.: 4.13). There can be very few lettings, if any, to which s. 8 applies. It was not available to the tenant in *Quick v Taff Ely Borough Council* [1985] 3 All ER 321, even though he was unemployed and lived in a small council house. In *McNerny v Lambeth London Borough Council* (1989) 21 HLR 188, Dillon LJ observed that the limits set by the 1957 Act (which Parliament has 'conspicuously refrained from updating') 'are far below the normal rents for a council house or flat', and in *Issa v Hackney London Borough Council* [1997] 1 WLR 956, 964 Brooke LJ described the statutory covenant (and the consequential value to the tenant's family of s. 4 of the Defective Premises Act 1972) as 'a completely dead letter'.

(b) Section 8 does not apply if the house is let for a term of not less than three years upon the terms that the tenant puts it into a condition reasonably fit for human habitation, and the lease is not determinable by either party within three years.

(c) The landlord's obligation under s. 8 is restricted to cases where the house is capable of being rendered fit for habitation at a reasonable expense (*Buswell v Goodwin* [1971] 1 All ER 418).

Section 10 provides that in determining whether a house is unfit for human habitation regard should be had to repair, stability, freedom from damp, internal arrangement, natural lighting, ventilation, water supply, drainage and sanitary facilities, facilities for the preparation and cooking of food, and the disposal of waste water. The test is whether the state of the house is such that by ordinary use the occupier might be injured in limb or in health (*Morgan v Liverpool Corporation* [1927] 2 KB 131). In *Summers v Salford Corporation* [1943] AC 283, a broken sashcord in the only window of one bedroom was held to be a breach of the undertaking but in *Stanton v Southwick* [1920] 2 KB 642 an invasion of the house by rats did not constitute a breach because liability arises only in relation to the defects *within* the premises let to the tenant.

The landlord's obligation is limited to defects of which he or she has notice and the landlord may, on giving 24 hours' notice in writing to the occupier, enter to view the condition of the premises (s. 8(2)). Breach of the condition makes the lease voidable. Breach of the undertaking gives rise only to a claim to damages or specific performance.

The Law Commission has proposed that a statutory warranty that a dwelling-house is fit for human habitation should be implied into any lease for less than seven years (Law Commission, 1996: 11.16). This would bring English law closer into line with Scottish law, which implies an obligation on the landlord of an urban house (but not a farmhouse) to give the tenant a habitable house and to maintain it in that condition (*Cameron v Young* [1908] AC 176), and that of the US, where each residential lease is deemed to include a warranty that the landlord will deliver the premises in habitable condition and maintain them in that condition during the currency of the lease (see *Javins v First National Realty Corporation* 428 F.2d 1071 (D.C. Cir) (1970)). This common law warranty is largely replicated in the statutes of more than 30 states. As Carr points out, there are a number of arguments in favour of a modernised s. 8. First, it provides a 'clear floor of provision below which no individual should fall' and could therefore 'form part of a valuable universalising discourse of social exclusion which would complement and enforce the new welfare norm of the decent home' (Carr, 2003: 9). Secondly, the imposition of a 'clear and [individually] enforceable standard within the tenancy agreement' would provide 'greater legitimacy' for emphasising the tenant's responsibilities as regards anti-social behaviour, for example (ibid.). Thirdly, legal remedies can compensate individuals for time spent in unacceptable housing conditions in a way in which planned programmes of modernisation cannot.

Sections 11–16, Landlord and Tenant Act 1985

The implied covenant to repair now contained in s. 11 of the Landlord and Tenant Act 1985 was first enacted in 1961 (a) to stop unscrupulous landlords from imposing unreasonable repairing obligations on tenants under short leases, and (b) for public policy reasons, to make someone responsible for getting repairs done (Law Commission, 1996: 5.11). It can be seen as 'a measure which, in part, has the effect of redistributing wealth from the richer landlords to the poorer tenants', with the direct interest of the landlord making him the 'best choice for carrying out structural repairs' (Bright and Gilbert, 1995) and/or one which constructs the landlord 'as potentially harmful to the tenant's position and in need of policing' (Stewart, 1996: 98). Carr is unconvinced by either view, preferring to locate the provision within the decontrolled climate of the private sector brought about by the Rent Act 1957 (Carr, 2003: 3). She argues that it was not about the redistribution of wealth (given that 'an economically rational landlord will raise the rent and recoup his expenditure on repairs') and that a Conservative administration which had decontrolled rents would be unlikely to perceive landlords as harmful to tenants and in need of policing (ibid.: 4). Rather, she says, it was a means of protecting the policy of deregulation at a time when increased immigration had led to an increased demand for rented housing. As such, it be seen as a 'form of consumer protection' (ibid.) and – it might be added – a further example of the historic modification of free market principles in the context of housing standards and quality.

Section 11 is frequently invoked but is unlikely to be utilised by the bulk of private sector tenants who, because they rent on the assured shorthold basis, have virtually no protection from arbitrary eviction by their landlords. It imposes repairing obligations on landlords of dwelling-houses where the lease was granted after 24 October 1961 and is for a term of less than seven years. This includes periodic tenancies. The term 'dwelling-house includes a building or part of a building (s. 16(b)) which means that s. 11 can apply to a flat or bed-sit just as well as it can apply to a whole house.

Section 11(1) implies a covenant by the landlord:

(a) to keep in repair the structure and exterior of the dwelling-house (including drains, gutters and external pipes); and

(b) to keep in repair and proper working order the installations in the dwelling-house for the supply of water, gas and electricity and for sanitation (including basins, sinks, baths and sanitary conveniences but not, except as aforesaid, fixtures, fittings and appliances for making use of the supply of water, gas or electricity); and

(c) to keep in repair and proper working order the installations in the dwelling-house for space heating and heating water.

The landlord's obligation to effect repairs carries with it an obligation to make good any consequential damage to decorations (*Bradley v Chorley Borough Council* (1985) 17 HLR 305).

The landlord is not liable (a) for repairs attributable to the tenant's failure to use the premises in a tenant-like manner; (b) to rebuild, or reinstate the premises as a result of damage by fire, tempest, flood or other inevitable accident; (c) to repair or maintain any tenant's fixtures (s. 11(2)).

Inherent defects

Poor housing conditions are often the outcome of inherent defects brought about by design faults, bad workmanship, etc. Inherent defects fall into two categories: those which cause damage to the demised premises and those which do not. In the former case, repairs may be necessary to put the matter right, as where condensation results in damage to plasterwork, or causes window frames to rot, or where rising damp makes it necessary to repoint a basement wall (*Pembery v Lamdin* [1940] 2 All ER 434), or a slate damp-proof course put in too low leads to rising damp (*Elmcroft Developments Ltd v Tankersley-Sawyer* (1984) 15 HLR 63. In the latter case, the inherent defect may have caused the property to have become uninhabitable but a repairing covenant has no application since no damage has been done. In *Quick v Taff-Ely Borough Council* [1985] 3 All ER 321, specific performance was sought of the local authority landlord's repairing obligation under what is now s. 11 of the 1985 Act. The house had single-glazed metal-framed windows and a central-heating system based on warm air ducts. Severe condensation – caused largely by lack of insulation around the concrete window lintels, and sweating from the windows – made the house virtually unusable during the winter and rotted the tenant's furniture and furnishings. However, the Court of Appeal held, reluctantly, that the landlord was not bound to replace the metal windows nor to insulate the lintels; although they were inherently defective, neither item was damaged or in want of repair, and had caused no damage to the demised premises. The key factor, said Dillon LJ, 'is that disrepair is related to the physical condition of whatever has to be repaired, and not to questions of lack of amenity or inefficiency'. Had the authority failed in its appeal it would have cost £9 million to rectify similar defects in all its properties.

The contribution of the Human Rights Act 1998 in this regard is unclear. *Ratcliffe v Sandwell Metropolitan Borough Council* (2002) 34 HLR 17 concerned two appeals involving separate authorities which had let properties to the claimants. Both properties suffered from severe condensation and consequent mould growth arising from design faults. The principal argument for the tenants was that the houses in which they lived were not fit for human habitation and constituted a risk to health. It was argued that that *Quick* was wrongly decided and that, following the incorporation into domestic law of the European Convention of Human Rights by the Human Rights Act 1998, s. 11 of the 1985 Act should be construed in a way which was compatible with the Convention. The Court of Appeal held that there was no evidence to show that the local authority had breached Art. 8, despite the fact that the property it had let to the appellant was unfit for human habitation or in a state prejudicial to health. The court accepted that s. 6 of the Human Rights Act 1998, obliges a local authority landlord to take steps to ensure that the condition of a dwelling-house which it has let is such that the tenant's Convention right under Art. 8 is not infringed. However, it did not consider that, having regard to 'the fair balance that has to be struck between the competing interests of the individual and of the community as a whole', the condition of the dwelling-house in question was such an infringement had taken place. In the court's opinion, the steps which an authority will be required to take in order to ensure compliance with Art. 8 'must be determined, in each case, by having due regard to the needs and resources of the community and of individuals'. In striking the balance between these competing demands, there is a need (highlighted by Lord Hoffmann in *Southwark London Borough Council v Tanner* [2001] 1 AC 1, 9H–10A), 'to show a proper sensitivity to the limits of permissible judicial creativity' in the field of social housing responsibilities; a field which is 'so very much a matter for the allocation of resources in accordance with democratically determined priorities'. Nonetheless, while the Court of Appeal in *Ratcliffe* was mindful of the resource implications, Chadwick LJ did not rule out the possibility of a local authority landlord being in breach of Art. 8 where a house was unfit for human habitation or in a state prejudicial to health. As Lord Wilberforce pointed out in *Salford City Council v McNally* [1976] AC 379, 389 it is clear that 'a house may well be unfit for human habitation in the statutory sense without being either prejudicial to health or a "nuisance"'. Tenants in such accommodation could be left without a remedy, having neither rights under the 1985 nor a remedy for statutory nuisance.

To 'keep in repair'

A covenant to 'keep in repair' obliges the covenantor (a) to put the premises into repair at the outset (if necessary), and (b) to keep the premises in repair at all times during the currency of the tenancy (*Luxmore v Robson* (1818) 1 B & Ald 584). Liability arises as soon as the premises fall into disrepair and the covenantee can compel repair work to be done during the course of the tenancy.

Structure and exterior

In *Irvine v Moran* [1991] 1 EGLR 262, it was said that 'structure' consists of those elements of the overall dwelling-house which give it its essential appearance, stability and shape' but does not extend to 'the many and various ways in which the dwelling-house will be fitted out, equipped and decorated and generally made to be habitable'. It was held that internal wall plaster was more in the nature of a decorative finish and not part of the essential material elements which go to make up the structure. However, in *Staves v Leeds City Council* (1990) 23 HLR 107, the defendant landlord conceded that plaster was part of the structure and exterior of the house.

The 'exterior' has been held to include the dividing wall between a house and the one adjoining it (*Green v Eales* [1841] 2 QB 225), and steps and a flagstone path leading to, and demised with, the house (*Brown v Liverpool Corporation* [1969] 3 All ER 1345) but not paving slabs in the back yard of a house or a passageway to the rear of the property which was not included in the lease (*Hopwood v Cannock Chase District Council* [1975] 1 All ER 796). 'Structure and exterior' also includes windows (*Irvine v Moran* [1991] 1 EGLR 262).

Installations

The obligation to keep installations in proper working order refers to their mechanical condition and may require the landlord to remedy an inherent defect which prevents them from working properly. They will be considered to be in proper working order if they are able to function under those conditions of supply which are reasonably foreseeable. If, for example, a water company lowers the pressure at which water is supplied to houses then, as this is a foreseeable occurrence, the landlord will be liable under s. 11 if the installation cannot cope adequately with the new reduced pressure. If the ability of the installations to work properly is affected by an unforeseeable external event, much will depend upon the nature of the event and its duration. Thus, if the existing installations cannot work because of a change in the voltage supply or from coal gas to natural gas, they will not be considered to be in proper working order even though they worked perfectly adequately under the previous system of supply. Where however there is a disruption to the supply of an external and transient nature, such as a drop in water pressure caused by drought, then the inability of the system for conveying water properly to the tenanted properly for the duration of the interruption will not mean that the installation is not working properly (*O'Connor v Old Etonian Housing Association Ltd* [2002] Ch 295). A landlord was not in breach for failing to lag the pipes, so that they burst during a spell of very cold weather (*Wycombe Health Authority v Barnett* (1982) 264 EG 619).

The effect of the Housing Act 1988

Where the lease was entered into before 15 January 1989, the repairing obligation applies only to the dwelling-house in question. In *Campden Hill Towers v Gardner* [1977] 1 All ER 739, it was held that where the dwelling-house – typically a flat – formed part of a larger building, the obligation to repair the structure and exterior did not apply to the whole building, but only to that of the particular part included in the lease. Thus, the roof of a block of flats would not form part of the structure and exterior of a ground floor flat, but might do as regards a top floor flat (*Douglas-Scott v Scorgie* [1984] 1 WLR 716). The obligation to keep installations in repair and proper working order was limited to the repair of installations within the physical confines of the dwelling. It would not cover the central heating boiler which supplied hot water to all the flats in the block and was located in the basement.

Section 11(1A) (inserted by s. 116 of the Housing Act 1988) reverses the effect of *Campden Hill Towers v Gardner* so that (a) the obligation to repair the structure and exterior now applies to any part of the building in which the landlord has an estate or interest, and (b) the obligation in relation to installations apply to those which directly or indirectly serve the dwelling-house and which either form part of the building in which the landlord has an estate or interest, or are owned by the landlord or are under his or her control. These extended obligations apply only if the disrepair or failure to maintain affect the tenant's enjoyment of the dwelling-house or any common parts which he or she is entitled to use (s. 11(1)(B)).

If the necessary work requires access to a part of a building or an installation to which the landlord does not have a sufficient right of access, it is a defence if the landlord can prove that 'he used all reasonable endeavours to obtain such rights as would be adequate to enable him to carry out the works or repairs' (s. 11(3A)). The landlord may, however, be able to obtain an access order under the Access to Neighbouring Land Act 1992.

Standard of repair

In determining the standard of repair required by the landlord's repairing covenant, regard must be had to 'the age, character and prospective life of the dwelling-house and the locality in which it is situated' (s. 11(3)). In taking account of the property's prospective life, this differs from the standard of repair in *Proudfoot v Hart* and means that a landlord may not be obliged to carry out repairs which do not make economic sense. In *Newham London Borough v Patel* [1978] 13 HLR 77, the tenant spent five years in a house which had been condemned as both unfit for habitation and a statutory nuisance. The Court of Appeal found no breach of s. 11, as the house had been scheduled for redevelopment and carrying out repairs on it would have been a waste of money. Alternatively, the council had charged the tenant only a very low rent because of the property's poor condition and, even if a breach were established, the tenant could not have the benefit both of a low rent and an award of damages.

If the defect is within the premises let, liability under s. 11 does not arise unless the landlord has actual notice of the want of repair (see *O'Brien v Robinson*

[1973] 1 All ER 583) and is only in breach of covenant if, after a reasonable time from being given notice, fails to remedy the defect. The landlord, or a person authorised by the landlord in writing, may view the state of repair of the premises, at reasonable times of the day and on giving 24 hours' written notice (s. 11(6)). If the defect is outside the demised premises, there is no need to show 'knowledge' or to allow a 'reasonable period' for the work to be carried out (*British Telecommunications plc v Sun Life* [1996] Ch 69).

The landlord cannot contract out of these obligations except with the tenant's consent and the approval of the court (s. 12). Otherwise any repairing covenant by the tenant (including any covenant to put in repair or deliver up in repair, to paint, point or render or to pay money in lieu of repairs by the tenant or on account of repairs by the landlord) is ineffective in so far as it relates to the obligations imposed by s. 11(1) (s. 11(4)).

The landlord who is in breach may be subject to action by the tenant or the local authority.

Consumer protection legislation

Section 13 of the Supply of Goods and Services Act 1982 provides that 'in a contract for the supply of a service where the supplier is acting in the course of a business, there is an implied term that the supplier will carry out the service with reasonable care and skill'. It was argued in *Dunn v Bradford Metropolitan District Council* [2003] HLR 15 that in providing housing accommodation (or permitting former tenants to remain in occupation as 'tolerated trespassers'), a local authority was carrying out a service and that it had breached s. 13 by letting unfit premises. Although it had been held in *Brown v DPP* [1956] QB 369 that the provision of housing by a landlord was not a service, the claimants in *Dunn* pointed to the advance of consumerism (notably in the form of the Unfair Terms in Consumer Contracts Regulations 1994 which they said, justified a change in the law. The Court of Appeal held that any service which had been provided consisted in the fact of the grant itself and the obligations of the parties as to repairs and fitness must be found in the express or implied terms of the tenancy. Section 13 could not have the effect of requiring the landlord to carry out a service which the tenancy would not otherwise require him to do. In any case, the existence of s. 8 of the Landlord and Tenant Act 1985, even though it applied to only 'a very restricted, and diminishing, class of tenancies' demonstrated Parliament's decision not to impose a direct obligation on landlords to ensure that premises are fit for human habitation.

Obligations arising in tort

Nuisance

The habitability of the demised premises may occasionally be affected by a nuisance for which the landlord is liable. However, this will generally be the case only where that nuisance emanates from property retained by the landlord. In *Habinteg Housing Association v James* (1994) 27 HLR 299, infestation by cockroaches was finally eliminated after six years following the service of an abatement notice on the landlord housing association under what is now s. 80 of the Environmental Protection Act 1990. There were no common parts in the block of which the flat in question formed part and no proof that the cockroaches entered the flat from any property controlled by the housing association. The situation was distinguishable from *Sharpe v City of Manchester* (1977) 5 HLR 712 in which the tenant successfully sued his landlords for the nuisance caused by an infestation of cockroaches which had come into the flat through service ducts situated in the common parts of a block of flats.

Negligence

At common law, the landlord owes no duty towards the tenant's family or visitors to ensure that the premises are in a safe condition at the time of the letting (*Tredway v Machin* (1904) 91 LT 310) or during its currency (*Lane v Cox* [1897] 1 QB 415). No liability in negligence arises even where the landlord knows of, or is responsible for, any defect or disrepair in the premises which makes them dangerous or unsafe. As the landlord is liable only for breach of a repairing covenant, those who are not parties to the letting – the tenant's family and visitors – are completely unprotected. While the courts have increasingly imposed liability on the suppliers of goods and services, they have preserved this rule of general immunity in relation to landlords, even though occupiers have been seriously injured or even killed (*Cavalier v Pope* [1906] AC 428). The one exception is where a local authority landlord constructs an unfurnished dwelling-house to its own design and specification (*Rimmer v Liverpool City Council* (1984) 1 All ER 930). However, the common law position has been extensively altered by statute. It was s. 4 of the Occupiers Liability Act 1957 which first imposed on the landlord a tortious duty of care in respect of danger arising from failure to comply with repairing obligations under the lease. This was replaced and significantly extended by the Defective Premises Act 1972.

Occupiers Liability Act 1957

The occupier of premises owes to all lawful visitors a 'common duty of care', i.e. a duty to take 'such care … that visitors will be reasonably safe in using the premises for the purposes for which they were invited or permitted to be there' (s. 2). 'Occupation' in this context focuses on 'control' (*Wheat v Lacon* [1966] 1 All ER 582). Thus, the landlord who retains control over any part of the building, e.g. entrance hall, lifts, forecourt or other common parts, will be the occupier for the purposes of the 1957 Act and will be liable for injury caused by any defects in that part. The landlord who has let the whole of the premises, retaining no control over any part, ceases to be the occupier for the purposes of the 1957 Act but the Defective Premises Act 1972 will then come into play. An owner who grants a licence, rather than a tenancy, and still has the right to do repairs may be regarded as being sufficiently in control for the purposes of the 1957 Act. For example, in *Hawkins v Coulsdon & Purley Urban District Council* [1954] 1 QB 319, the landlord was held liable to a visitor who fell on the defective step to the front door, and in *Greene v Chelsea Borough Council* [1954] 2 QB 127, a defective ceiling fell on the occupier's wife.

The landlord may try to restrict, modify or exclude this statutory duty by agreement, notice or any other means. However, the Unfair Contract (Terms) Act 1977 provides that any such exclusion or modification must be shown to be reasonable (ss. 1, 2(1)) and any purported exclusion or restriction of liability for death or personal injury will be ineffective (ss. 1, 2(2)). The 1977 Act applies to business liability only and a domestic occupier is perfectly free to modify, restrict or exclude liability for negligence.

Section 4, Defective Premises Act 1972

This section imposes a duty of care on the landlord who, under the terms of the tenancy, is under an obligation to the tenant for the maintenance or repair of the premises. The obligation may arise from an express term in the lease or may be implied by statute, e.g. s. 11 of the Landlord and Tenant Act 1985. The duty encompasses 'all persons who might reasonably be expected to be affected by defects in the state of the premises'. It is a duty to take such care as is reasonable in all the circumstances to see that they are reasonably safe from personal injury or from damage to their property caused by a defect within the repairing obligation. Although s. 4 was primarily intended to protect third parties – members of the tenant's household, visitors, neighbours, passers-by and even trespassers – the duty of care it imposes is also owed to tenants (*Smith v Bradford Metropolitan Council* (1982) 44 P & CR 171). It arises if the landlord knows, or ought to have known, of the defect (s. 4(2)) but where the landlord has an express or implied right to enter premises and carry out repairs, the duty of care laid down in s. 4(1) is owed in the same way as if there was an obligation to carry out such work (s. 4(4)).

Significantly, the duty of care under s. 4 arises only where there is some hazard which makes the property unsafe rather than unfit. It does not extend, therefore, to damp in the premises which discolours decorations, leads to the growth of mould, and causes the tenant's children to suffer coughs and colds (see *McNerny v Lambeth London Borough Council* (1989) 21 HLR 188).

The interplay between s. 4 of the 1972 Act and s. 11 of the 1985 Act was demonstrated in *Sykes v Harry* [2001] QB 1014, in which the tenant sought compensation for injuries resulting from carbon monoxide poisoning caused by emissions from a gas fire. Although the landlord appreciated the importance of regular servicing the gas fire and did not expect it to be the tenants' responsibility, he failed to enter into any servicing agreement. The judge at first instance dismissed the claim, concluding that the landlord's lack of knowledge of the actual defect meant that there was no contractual duty to repair under s. 11. Further s. 4, being effectively a 'public policy' provision, gave the tenant no greater protection than that afforded by the lease. The Court of Appeal, allowing the tenant's appeal, ruled that the judge was wrong to equate the claimant's task in establishing a breach of duty under s. 4 with his need under s. 11 to demonstrate actual notice of the defect which had caused the injury. Under s. 4 it merely had to be shown that the landlord had failed to take such care as was reasonable in the circumstances to ensure that the tenant was reasonably safe from injury. By failing to repair or maintain the gas fire over a substantial period before the tenant's injury, and knowing that the tenant was not having it serviced, the landlord was in breach of his duty under s. 4. Because, however, the tenant and his wife were also aware of the desirability of servicing, and knew of defects in the fire (a yellow and inadequate flame, and a one-inch gap between the fire and the closure plate) of which the landlord was ignorant, contributory negligence was assessed at 80 per cent. The case demonstrates that there may be liability under s. 4 if the landlord *ought to have known* of the defect, even though there is no *actual* notice for the purposes of s. 11.

Tenants' obligations

Tenant-like user

There is an implied obligation on every tenant to use the premises in a tenant-like manner. According to Denning LJ in *Warren v Keen* [1953] 2 All ER 1118, 1121:

> The tenant must take proper care of the place. He must, if he is going away for the winter, turn off the water and empty the boiler. He must clean the chimneys, when necessary, and also the windows. He must unstop the sink when it is blocked by his waste. In short, he must do the little jobs about the place which a reasonable tenant would do.

A tenant from year to year must keep the premises wind- and water-tight (*Wedd v Porter* [1916] 2 KB 41). In *Wycombe Health Authority v Barnett* (1982) 264 EG 619, the tenant was held not to have breached her duty to use the premises in a tenant-like manner in leaving unattended a house with unlagged pipes for two nights during which time the pipes froze and burst.

Doctrine of waste

'Waste' is a tort (the abolition of which has been recommended by the Law Commission). Technically, it is any act which alters the premises for better or for worse. It is of two main types: voluntary and permissive. Voluntary waste is the commission of any act which alters or destroys the premises, e.g. a failure to make good damage caused by the tenant's lawful removal of fixtures (*Mancetter Developments Ltd v Garmanson Ltd and Givertz* [1986] 1 All ER 449). Permissive waste is an omission to take action to prevent damage to the premises, e.g. allowing a house to decay; permitting foundations to rot through failing to clear drains (*Herne v Bembow* (1813) 4 Taunt 463). All tenants are liable for voluntary waste. All tenants, apart from weekly tenants, tenants at will and tenants at sufferance, are liable for permissive waste. A defence is available where the tenant can show that his or her use of the premises was reasonable (*Manchester Bonded Warehouse Co v Carr* (1880) 5 CPD 507).

If a tenant commits waste, the landlord may either (a) bring an action for damages or (b) in the case of voluntary waste only, seek an injunction. An injunction will not be granted in respect of permissive waste as it involves supervising the tenant to ensure that omissions are rectified. Damages for waste are based on the damage to the value of the reversion, and not the actual cost of making good the damage to the premises (*Whitham v Kershaw* (1885–1886) LR 16 QBD 613). Thus, if the tenant alters the premises by, e.g. building an extension, an action in damages may well fail since it will be difficult to show that the alteration has diminished the value of the reversion.

Chapter 8

Remedies for disrepair, overcrowding and houses in multiple occupation

Introduction

A number of private remedies are available to the tenant where the landlord is in breach of a repairing obligation. Until recently, a lack of resources on the tenant's part made it likely that he or she was usually in no position to pursue those remedies. However, the introduction of conditional fee agreements has led to a spiralling number of disrepair claims against social landlords, with 'claims farmers' leafleting and cold-calling on tenants in areas of run-down housing, and persuading them – with 'the prospect of early repairs and compensation at "no risk" of costs under a "free service"' – to sign up to credit agreements and conditional fee arrangements (Luba, 2003: 105). Instead of having to resort to litigation, however, most tenants of social housing should be able to secure an effective response by making use of their landlord's complaints procedure and (if they remain dissatisfied after this has been completed) by referring the matter to the Local Government Ombudsman (if their landlord is a local authority) or the Independent Housing Ombudsman (if their landlord is a housing association) (Luba, 2005b: 98). The CPR Pre-Litigation Protocol for Housing Disrepair Claims – the thrust of which is the avoidance of litigation – also encourages the consideration and use of alternative methods of dispute resolution.

Local authorities too have an important role in ensuring the maintenance of minimum housing standards and consideration is given in the second part of this chapter to their powers and duties relating to statutory nuisance and the new Housing Health and Safety Rating System (HHSRS). Overcrowding does not concern disrepair per se but it does, of course, impinge on housing conditions and is, in any case, relevant to issues of security of tenure and homelessness. Houses in multiple occupation (HIMOs) provide accommodation for a large number of people and often pose a significant fire risk. The final part of this chapter outlines the licensing system put in place by the Housing Act 2004 which seeks to ensure that HIMOs are properly managed and health and safety risks thereby reduced.

Tenants' remedies

Damages

Tenants can claim damages whenever their landlords are in breach of their repairing obligations. The aim is not to punish landlords but to put tenants in the position they would have been in had the breach not occurred. General damages are assessed as the loss of the value of the tenancy to the tenant, i.e. the loss of comfort and convenience of living in a property in disrepair. These can be calculated on the basis of a notional deduction in rent for each week of disrepair or by a global award for discomfort and inconvenience or a combination of the two (*Wallace v Manchester City Council* (1998) 30 HLR 1111). If the landlord's breach of covenant deprives the tenant of his or her enjoyment of the property for a significant period, the most appropriate starting point for assessment of damages is the notional loss of rental value caused by the defects, even where there is a long lease and the only rent payable is a ground rent (*Earle v Charalambous* [2006] EWCA Civ 1090). In *Chiodi (Personal Representatives of) v de Marney* [1988] 2 EGLR 64, the tenant had been in poor health, had spent much of her time in the property because of unemployment, and had been unable to escape from the effects of damp and cold since all parts of the flat were affected. The sum of £5,460 for inconvenience and distress was awarded at a rate of £30 per week over three years even though the registered rent was only £8 per week. Special damages may be awarded for the cost of alternative accommodation while the demised property is uninhabitable, reasonable expenditure on redecoration, discomfort, loss of enjoyment and ill-health, the cost of storing furniture while the tenant is in temporary accommodation and the cost of clearing debris and clearing up after repair work has been done (*Calabar Properties v Stitcher* (1983) 268 EG 697; *McGreal v Wake* (1984) 269 EG 1254).

Self-help/set-off against rent

If the landlord fails to respond within a reasonable time to notice of the breach, the tenant may carry out the repairs and withhold rent to recover the money spent (*Lee Parker v Izzet* [1971] 1 WLR 1688). Where set-off applies, it will be a defence to an action for non-payment of rent (*British Anzani (Felixstowe) Ltd v International Marine Management (UK) Ltd* [1980] QB 137).

Specific performance

This is an exception to the rule that a court will not compel performance of an obligation which requires supervision. Specific performance is not available to the landlord to enforce the tenant's repairing obligations (*Hill v Barclay* (1810) 16 Ves 402) and it was assumed by analogy that the same applied to the tenant. It was not until Pennycuick V-C's decision in *Jeune v Queens Cross Properties Ltd* [1974] Ch 97 that it became clear that specific performance was available to a tenant to enforce a landlord's repairing obligations. In this case the breach complained of was failure to reinstate a first-floor stone balcony. In addition, s. 17 of the Landlord and Tenant Act 1985 provides that in any proceedings in which a tenant of a dwelling alleges a breach on the part of the landlord of a repairing covenant relating to any part of the premises in which the dwelling is comprised, the court may, in its discretion, order specific performance of that covenant, whether or not the breach relates to a part of the premises let to the tenant, and notwithstanding any equitable rule restricting the scope of that remedy. It extends to obligations to repair and maintain common parts.

Appointment of a receiver

Section 37 of Supreme Court Act 1981 allows for an application to be made to the court for the appointment of a receiver where it is just and convenient to do so, to carry out some of the functions of the landlord, e.g. *Hart v Emelkirk* (1983) 267 EG 946. This remedy cannot be used, however, in relation to local authority landlords (*Parker v Camden London Borough Council* [1985] 2 All ER 141).

Part II of the Landlord and Tenant Act 1987, which deals with the appointment of a manager, applies to premises consisting of the whole or part of a building containing two or more flats except where the landlord is an exempt landlord (e.g. a local authority or registered social landlord) or a resident landlord in a non purpose-built block of flats. The court may make an order appointing a manager to carry out such functions in connection with the management of the premises or of a receiver, or both, as the court thinks fit (s. 24) thus protecting the interests of the tenants without causing any loss to the landlord. Before an application is made for an order under s. 24, the tenant must serve notice on the landlord (s. 22). The court must be satisfied that either (a) the landlord is in breach of a management obligation (i.e. repair, maintenance, insurance) under the lease, or (b) would be so (but it has not been reasonably practicable for the tenant to give the appropriate notice), and that it is just and convenient to make the order in all the circumstances. These provisions might typically be used where the landlord of a large block of flats occupied under long leases neglects his repairing obligations with regard to common parts, perhaps because returns have become too low. The application would seek the appointment of a manager to collect rents and service charges and carry out such repairs as are or have become necessary.

The right to manage (RTM) introduced by the Commonhold and Leasehold Reform Act 2002 gives tenants of qualifying blocks of flats the right to set up an RTM company which can take over the management of the residential common parts of the premises. There is – in contrast to Part II of the

Landlord and Tenant Act 1987 – no requirement to show any default by the freeholder or manager. Furthermore, no compensation need be paid, and there is no requirement to make an application to a tribunal or the court.[1] Excluded from the RTM provisions of the 2002 Act are any premises where the landlord is a local authority. Local authority tenants already have a separate right to manage which encompasses all tenants (including long leaseholders) and which is more fully dealt with in Chapter 19.

Repudiatory breach

In *Total Oil Great Britain Ltd v Thompson Garages (Biggin Hill) Ltd* [1972] 1 QB 318 Lord Denning said, obiter, that a lease was not capable of determination by repudiation and acceptance. His view was attributable in part to the fact that a lease was not then capable of determination by frustration so that contractual remedies in other cases could not apply. By acknowledging that a lease could be frustrated, the House of Lords in *National Carriers v Panalpina* [1981] 1 WLR 728 effectively paved the way for the application of ordinary contractual principles to leases.

In *Hussein v Mehlman* [1992] 2 EGLR 87, the county court held that a repudiatory breach of a letting is possible. A three-year assured tenancy of a house was subject to the landlord's obligation, implied by s. 11 of the Landlord and Tenant Act 1985, to keep in repair the structure and exterior and the installations for the supply of utilities and space and water heating. After 15 months of the tenancy, one bedroom was uninhabitable owing to the collapse of the ceiling, the sitting room was letting in rainwater and part of its ceiling was bulging dangerously, the outside lavatory was unusable, the hall well was damp, and the doors and windows were ill-fitting. The landlord refused to carry out repairs so the tenant returned the keys to the landlord's agents, vacated the property and sued the landlord for breach of contract. Assistant recorder Sedley QC (as he then was) held that the landlord's breach of the implied repairing covenant amounted to a repudiatory breach of the lease. The landlord had made it clear that he was not going to comply with the covenant and the house as a whole was unfit for habitation. By vacating the premises, the plaintiffs had accepted that the repudiation had terminated the lease and were entitled to damages.

The decision in *Hussein* brings English law into line with other Commonwealth jurisdictions in which it has been held that a lease may be terminated by repudiation and acceptance (see, e.g. the Canadian case of *Highway Properties v Kelly* (1971) 17 DLR 3d 710 and, from Australia, *Progressive Mailing House Pty v Tabah Pty* (1985) 157 CLR 17 and *Wood*

---

1   For further detail on Part II of the Landlord and Tenant Act 1987 and the RTM see Wilkie *et al.* (2006: Ch. 17).

Factory Pty v Kiritos Pty (1985) 2 NSWLR 105). It is important to remember, however, that not every breach of covenant amounts to a repudiatory breach. As Melon J explained in *Progressive Mailing House Pty v Tabah Pty* (at p. 33), it must be one where 'the party evinces an intention no longer to be bound by the contract or ... to fulfil the contract only in a manner substantially inconsistent with his obligations and not in any other way'.

The right to repair scheme for secure and introductory tenants

The Secure Tenants of Local Housing Authorities (Right to Repair) Regulations 1994, as amended, provide that where a secure or introductory tenant applies to the landlord to have a qualifying repair carried out, the landlord must issue a repair notice specifying the nature of the repair, the identity of the contractor and the date by which the work should be carried out. If the work is not carried out on time the tenant will be entitled to compensation. A 'qualifying repair' is one which the landlord is obliged by a repairing covenant to carry out. The scheme applies to small urgent repairs (up to a value of £250) which are likely to affect the occupier's health, safety or security.

Landlords' remedies

Damages

Depending on the wording of the tenant's repairing covenant (whether it is, e.g. to 'keep in repair' or 'to leave in repair'), the landlord may start an action for damages for disrepair during the currency of the tenancy or after its expiry. During the term, the damages may amount to the diminution in the value of the reversion but thereafter it will be the actual cost of the repair. Section 18(1) of the Landlord and Tenant Act 1927 imposes a limit on damages for disrepair on all covenants to put, keep or leave in repair. Whether the action is commenced during the term or at its end, the landlord cannot recover more than the amount of diminution in value of the reversion, and no damages are recoverable for failure to put or leave the premises in repair at the termination of the lease if it is shown that the premises are at, or shortly after, termination to be demolished or altered so as to render the repairs valueless. The onus of proof is on the tenant.

Forfeiture

The lease must contain a proviso for re-entry and forfeiture. By s. 146 of the Law of Property Act 1925, the landlord must serve a notice on the tenant specifying the breach, the remedy and compensation (if required). If the lease is for a term of seven years or more, of which three or more remain, the

Leasehold Property (Repairs) Act 1938 applies. Not less than one month before bringing the action, the landlord must serve a s. 146 notice indicating that the tenant may, within 28 days, serve on the landlord a counter-notice claiming the benefit of the 1938 Act. Should the tenant do this, the landlord cannot proceed further without leave of the court which will not be granted unless the landlord shows that, e.g. an immediate remedy is required to prevent a substantial drop in the value of the reversion, or to give effect to a by-law or court order or any other Act, or to protect another occupier, or would involve relatively smaller cost than if it were postponed, or the special circumstances make it just and equitable to grant leave.

Self-help

The landlord may enter the premises and undertake the repairs provided that the right to do so is reserved in the lease. It is a condition of a statutory tenancy under the Rent Act 1977 (s. 3(2)) and an implied term of every assured tenancy (Housing Act 1988, s. 16) that the tenant shall afford the landlord access and 'all reasonable facilities' to execute such repairs as the landlord is entitled to execute. The cost of the repairs may be recovered from the tenant.

Specific performance

In its Report on *Responsibility for State and Condition of Property*, the Law Commission emphasised the potential importance of specific performance as a remedy to rectify the state and condition of demised property and recommended that it should be made generally available as a discretionary remedy to enforce repairing obligations in all leases to landlords and tenants alike (Law Commission, 1996: 9.32, 11.33; and see cl. 13(1) of the Draft Bill appended to the report). The orthodox view – that a landlord cannot compel a tenant to perform his repairing obligations by mandatory injunction or specific performance stems from a dictum of Lord Eldon LC in *Hill v Barclay* (1810) 16 Ves 402. The original objection to an order for specific performance – that the court could not supervise it – has gradually been eroded and in *Co-operative Insurance Society Ltd v Argyll Stores* [1998] AC 1, the House of Lords distinguished between supervision of an ongoing state of affairs and supervision of work to attain a specific result. Lord Hoffmann explained that in the latter case, 'even if the achievement of the result is a complicated matter which will take some time, the court, if called upon to rule, only has to examine the finished work and say whether it complies with the order'. In *Rainbow Estates Ltd v Tokenhold* [1999] Ch 64, it was held that the remedy should be available to a landlord in appropriate cases. In that case, extensive repairs were needed to a Grade II listed mansion, in respect of which the local authority had served notices under the Housing Act 1985 and the Environmental Protection Act 1990 (see below). Unusually the lease made no provision for forfeiture or for the landlord to enter and carry out the repairs. The court held that the general availability of the right of forfeiture under both commercial and residential leases meant that specific performance would rarely be an appropriate remedy for enforcing a repairing covenant but it could be used – as here, for example – where the landlord faced substantial difficulties in effecting repairs and the property was in danger of deteriorating. The court should be astute, however, to ensure that the remedy was not being sought by the landlord as a means of harassing or otherwise putting pressure on the tenant.

Public law remedies: Environmental Protection Act 1990

General principles

Since the mid-nineteenth century, public health legislation has been the mechanism by which Parliament has sought to deal with the worst effects of slum housing (i.e. disease, overcrowding and dangerous buildings). These early measures were largely consolidated into the Public Health Act 1936, the relevant provisions of which are replaced by Part III of the Environmental Protection Act 1990, as amended. The aim of the public health legislation is to eliminate housing conditions, in both the private and public sectors, which amount to a 'statutory nuisance'. The existence of a statutory nuisance may be proved even though there has been no breach of the landlord's repairing obligations (*Birmingham City District Council v Kelly* (1985) 17 HLR 572) but the legislation may nonetheless be a way of compelling landlords to carry out repairs and improve the condition of their property.

Responsibility for dealing with statutory nuisances rests with the local authority but, where the local authority owns the premises in question or it declines to intervene, an individual occupier may institute proceedings under the Act. So far as local authority landlords are concerned, however, the courts have urged magistrates to act with sense and discretion and to bear in mind that the local housing authorities have many responsibilities and burdens, especially in times of recession and large-scale homelessness. Orders should not be used to give tenants benefits which they did not have when they took up their tenancies (see *Salford City Council v McNally* [1976] AC 379; *Birmingham City District Council v Kelly* (1985) 17 HLR 572). Where a tenant mounts a challenge against a local authority landlord, the law on statutory nuisance is applied in such a way as to emphasise the 'primacy of the public interest' and so preserve 'the authority of the local authority' (McAuslan, 1980: 208). Where, on the other hand, a local authority is proceeding against a private landowner, the courts use the 'ideology of private property' to protect the landowner (ibid.). In the middle sits the tenant, generally living in completely unacceptable housing conditions.

Statutory nuisances

'Statutory nuisances' include 'any premises in such a state as to be prejudicial to health or a nuisance' (Environmental Protection Act 1990, s. 79(1)(a)). 'Prejudicial to health' means 'injurious, or likely to cause injury, to health' (s. 79(7)), i.e. such as would cause a well person to become ill or the health of person who is already ill to deteriorate further (*Malton Urban Sanitary Authority v Malton Farmers Manure Co* (1879) 4 Ex D 302). A mere want of internal decorative repair is not sufficient (*Springett v Harold* [1954] 1 All ER 568).

Premises which are 'prejudicial to health' for the purposes of the Environmental Protection Act 1990 are most likely to be those which are suffering from the effects of serious dampness, whether due to water penetration (see *Salford City Council v McNally* [1976] AC 379) or condensation which gives rise to extensive mould growth and dampness (*Greater London Council v London Borough of Tower Hamlets* (1983) 15 HLR 54). This is particularly useful, given that condensation may not be attributable to any want of repair by the landlord (see *Quick v Taff-Ely Borough Council* [1985] 3 All ER 32. It is necessary to show a risk to health, not simply a risk of injury. In *R v Bristol City Council ex p Everett* [1999] 1 WLR 1170, a house with an unusually steep staircase which posed a danger of accidental physical injury was held not to be prejudicial to health.

A recent, significant decision on the meaning of the term was *Oakley v Birmingham City Council* [2001] 1 AC 617 in which the only lavatory in a council house was too small to accommodate a wash-basin. As a result, after they had used the lavatory, the family (consisting of the tenant, his wife and four young children) had to wash their hands in the kitchen sink or the basin in a bathroom situated on the other side of the kitchen. When the council refused to carry out the remedial works that Mr Oakley had suggested – namely to install a lavatory in the bathroom – he initiated proceedings against them under s. 82 of the 1990 Act. The House of Lords held, by a majority, that the purpose of s. 79 was to deal with foul and filthy conditions which posed a risk of disease and germs or were the source of unpleasant smells. The words 'in such a state' in s. 79 referred to conditions in the premises, such as dampness, excessive dirt or rat infestation, which could be regarded as being prejudicial to health. Thus, for premises to be 'prejudicial to health' within the meaning of s. 79, there had to be present in them some feature, such as the condition of the lavatory or a defective drain, which was, of itself, prejudicial to health in that it was a possible source of infection or disease or illness. On the facts of the instant case, however, there was nothing wrong with the lavatory or with the washing facilities. The fact that there was no wash-basin in the lavatory and that it was only possible to access washing facilities in or through the kitchen was a design and layout problem and was not in itself prejudicial to health. Lord Clyde, supported by Lord Steyn, delivered a powerful dissenting judgment, concluding that the 'state' of the premises could include 'a deficiency due to the absence of a facility or a particular positioning of the facilities'. The majority decision typifies the courts' concern to prioritise the 'public interest' so as to protect local authority landlords, using the financial implications of a finding in the tenant's favour as the reason why it would not be reasonable to require the authority to take certain action.

In *R (on the application of Vella) v Lambeth London Borough Council* [2006] HLR 12, it was held that lack of adequate sound insulation could not cause the premises to be in such a state as to be 'prejudicial to health' for the purposes of s. 79(1). Social and private landlords would have to shoulder immense financial burdens if the court required, by the statutory nuisance route, the immediate upgrading of properties to a standard of sound insulation not required when the properties were constructed or adapted. Accordingly the authority's decision not to serve an abatement notice on the landlord was lawful and legally correct.

The Environmental Protection Act 1990 does not define 'nuisance', although it was said in *National Coal Board v Thorne* [1976] 1 WLR 543 that the act or default complained of must be either a private or public nuisance. On such an interpretation, the problem must emanate from some external source and a statutory nuisance cannot arise if what has taken place affects only the person or persons occupying the premises where the nuisance is said to have taken place. There is some doubt, however, as to whether such a view is correct and it may be sufficient therefore that the premises themselves have a defect which adversely affects those who occupy them (see McManus, 2003: 88–9).

Enforcement

Service of an abatement notice

The environmental health department of the local authority can either act on its own initiative, or in response to a complaint made to it by a person living within its area.

If, after investigations, the authority is satisfied that a statutory nuisance exists, or is likely to occur or recur, it must serve an abatement notice requiring (a) the abatement of the nuisance or prohibiting or its occurrence or recurrence; and (b) the execution of such works, and the taking of such other steps, as may be necessary for any of those purposes (s. 80(1)). The notice must be served on the person responsible for the nuisance, except where the nuisance arises out of a structural defect, or where the person responsible cannot be found, in which case the owner is to be served (s. 80(2)).

The notice may require substantial works of renovation, such as the installation of central heating, rewiring, insulation, or the renewal of defective windows. On the other hand, only minimal works are likely to be specified if the premises in question face imminent demolition. It is only possible to comply with a s. 80 notice by taking some remedial action. Thus, the removal of occupants from premises which are in such a state to be prejudicial to health or a nuisance does not constitute an abatement of the nuisance (*Lambeth London Borough Council v Stubbs* (1980) LGR 650) nor does the fact that a house has been left unoccupied unless it has been effectively rendered incapable of occupation, e.g. by having all the services permanently disconnected and being boarded up prior to demolition (*Coventry City Council v Doyle* [1981] 2 All ER 184). The person upon whom the notice is served may appeal to a magistrates' court within 21 days from the date of service of the notice (s. 80(3)). Failure to comply with the terms of the notice amounts to a criminal offence punishable by a fine. A compensation order can also be made. It is a defence to a prosecution under s. 79 to show that there was a 'reasonable excuse' (s. 80(4)).

Remedy of defects by local authority

Where a local authority considers that an unreasonable delay would result if it proceeded by way of abatement notice under the Environmental Protection Act 1990, it may serve a notice on the appropriate person stating that it intends to remedy the defective state and specifying the defects it intends to remedy (Building Act 1984, s. 76(1)).

Action by tenants and other occupiers

By s. 82 of the 1990 Act a person aggrieved by a statutory nuisance may complain direct to a magistrates' court. The complainant must give at least 21 days' written notice of intention to bring proceedings (s. 82(7)). If the court is satisfied that a statutory nuisance exists, it must make an order in terms similar to an abatement notice and fine the defendant. The court has a wide discretion as to the precise terms of such an order (*Nottingham Corporation v Newton* [1974] 2 All ER 760). Costs must be awarded in favour of the complainant where it is proved that the alleged nuisance existed at the date of the complaint, whether or not it has ceased to exist, or has been abated, by the time of the hearing (s. 82(12)).

Public remedies: Part I, Housing Act 2004

Introduction

For many years local housing authorities have had powers to deal with unfit housing. Until recently, they were under a duty to carry out periodic reviews of housing conditions in their areas in order to decide whether and what action should be taken if a property was unfit for human habitation (Housing Act 1985, s. 605). In deciding whether a particular dwelling was unfit for human habitation, the local authority were required to have regard to the fitness standard (first introduced in 1919 and latterly contained in s. 604 of the 1985 Act). This provided that a property would not be fit for human habitation if, in the opinion of the local authority, it was not reasonably suitable for occupation because it failed to meet one or more of the following requirements: structural stability, freedom from serious disrepair, freedom from damp prejudicial to the health of the occupants (if any), adequate provision of lighting, heating and ventilation, an adequate piped supply of wholesome water, satisfactory facilities for preparing and cooking food (including a sink with a satisfactory supply of hot and cold water), a suitably located water-closet for the exclusive use of the occupants (if any), a suitably located fixed bath or shower and wash hand basin (each with a satisfactory supply of hot and cold water) for the exclusive use of the occupants, and an effective system for the draining of foul, waste and surface water.

The fitness standard was criticised not only for failing to address many known hazards likely to pose a risk in residential property (e.g. poor fire safety and domestic energy efficiency) but also for being fixed and consequently unresponsive to changing needs and aspirations with regard to housing conditions and standards. In its 2000 Green Paper, the government pointed out that local authorities made only limited use of their extensive powers to intervene where dwellings failed the fitness standard, partly because of their labour-intensiveness and partly because of a fear that the strict enforcement would lead to a reduction in much-needed supply. If a local authority considered that a dwelling-house or HIMO was fit for human habitation, but either that (a) substantial repairs were necessary to bring it up to a reasonable standard, having regard to its age, character and locality, or (b) its condition was such as to interfere materially with the tenant's personal comfort, s. 190 of the 1985 Act empowered it to serve a repair notice on the person having control of the house and also on anyone who had an interest in it. The power under s. 190 was first introduced by the Housing Act 1969 at a time when a number of landlords were deliberately allowing properties to fall into such a state of disrepair that they were condemned as unfit for human habitation. Protected tenants could then be evicted, the property repaired and sold at a considerable profit. Meanwhile the local authority would be under an obligation to rehouse the dispossessed tenant (see *Hillbank Properties Ltd v Hackney London Borough Council* [1978] QB 998, 1010–1). However, there were limitations to s. 190. First, it had no application to premises controlled by the local authority (*R v Cardiff City Council ex p Cross* (1981–82) 1 HLR 54) which meant that tenants of council accommodation had to turn either to private remedies, or to the procedure for abatement of a statutory nuisance under the Environmental Protection Act 1990. Secondly, if the local authority failed to take action under s. 190, an aggrieved occupier's only remedy was judicial review (see *R (on the application of Erskine) v Lambeth London Borough Council* [2003] EWHC 2479).

Taking the view that the fitness standard did not relate well 'either to tenants' perceptions of the condition of their homes or to problems which threaten their health and safety' (DETR, 2000: 5.27), the government announced its intention in its 2000 Green Paper to replace the existing pass-or-fail fitness standard with a health and safety rating scale, and to overhaul authorities' powers to intervene. The aim was to aid improvements to the quality of all housing, regardless of tenure, and to move away from the image of the fitness standard as a regulatory tool for the private sector. It predicted that the new rating would help in two ways. First, it would be based directly on the actual hazards threatening the occupants and would therefore give a more accurate measurement of the impact of defects on health and safety. Secondly, it would enable local authorities to tailor the type and degree of their intervention to the severity of the hazards within the dwelling, resulting in 'better-targeted and more effective use of their resources' (ibid.: 5.28).

The Housing Health and Safety Rating System

Part I of the Housing Act 2004 replaces the fitness standard with a new evidence-based risk assessment procedure, the HHSRS which is applicable to all types of residential premises in all tenures. Local housing authorities are required to keep under review the housing conditions in their districts with a view to identifying what, if any, course of action they should take under the 2004 Act, which includes their powers and duties to deal with hazards under HHSRS or provide financial assistance for home repair and improvement (s. 3(1)). The purpose of the review is to ensure that a local authority is aware of the state of the housing stock in its area so that it can make informed judgments as to the action it needs to take. It has a duty to inspect residential premises if, as a result of carrying out its duty under s. 3, it considers that such inspection would be appropriate to determine whether any category 1 or 2 hazards exist on the premises (s. 4).

Unlike the fitness standard, the HHSRS emphasises the effect of a defect rather than its mere presence and, by measuring and ranking the severity of risk, is intended to generate objective information in order to determine and inform enforcement decisions. It introduces a more flexible enforcement framework which means that authorities can now take action against a much broader range of housing conditions, from very severe to relatively minor hazards. The term 'hazard' is defined as 'any risk of harm to the health or safety of an actual or potential occupier of a dwelling or HIMO which arises from a deficiency in the dwelling or HIMO or ... building or land in the vicinity (whether the deficiency arises as a result of the construction of any building, an absence of maintenance or repair, or otherwise' (s. 2(1)). There are 29 'hazard profiles' known to give rise to injury, which fall into four categories: physiological, psychological, protection against infection, and protection against accidents. They include matters such as excessive temperatures, falls, damp and mould, etc, noise, asbestos, entry by intruders, poor provision for food safety and inadequate sanitation or drainage. When carrying out their inspections, environmental health officers use the hazard profiles to assess the condition of the dwelling by addressing first the likelihood of an occurrence and then the range of probable harm consequences. These two factors are combined using a standard method to give each hazard a score. The calculation is based on the risk of harm to the most vulnerable potential occupant of that dwelling whether or not such an applicant is resident in the premises at the time of the inspection. For example, stairs constitute a greater risk to the elderly so, for hazards relating to stairs, they are considered the most vulnerable even though the property may currently be occupied by young and able-bodied students. The assumption is that a dwelling which is safe for the most vulnerable will be safe for everybody. If it were assessed only on the basis of the current occupier(s), then it would have to be re-inspected and re-assessed every time there is a change of occupier. The total score decides the category into which an assessed hazard falls and dictates the action which will follow. If the dwelling is a category 1 hazard, the local authority is under a duty to take, or insist that the landlord takes, action to resolve the problem. For category 2 hazards, local authorities have the power to take action but are not obliged to do so.

Enforcement

The enforcement powers available to local housing authorities are extended and adapted. The Act introduces three new enforcement actions – the improvement notice, the prohibition notice and the hazard awareness notice – which replace the repairs notice, closing order and deferred action notice provided for by the Housing Act 1985. Amendments have been made to the pre-existing powers on demolition orders and clearance areas in order to accommodate the HHSRS.

By s. 5(2), if a local authority considers that a category 1 hazard exists on any residential premises, it must:

(a) serve an improvement notice requiring remedial works (s. 11); or
(b) make a prohibition order (which closes the whole or part of a dwelling or restricts the number of permitted occupants) (s. 20); or
(c) serve a hazard awareness notice (s. 28); or
(d) take emergency remedial action (s. 40); or
(e) make an emergency prohibition order (s. 43); or
(f) make a demolition order (Housing Act 1985, s. 265(1) or (2)); or
(g) declare the area in which the premises concerned are situated to be a clearance area (Housing Act 1985, s. 289(2)).

Options (a) to (e) only apply where the premises in respect of which the notice is to be served are not the subject of a management order made under

Part 4 of the 2004 Act. A local housing authority has a duty to take the best course of action available to it in relation to the hazard. It cannot simultaneously take more than one of the actions set out. This is to ensure that local authorities properly consider the appropriate action and landlords are not asked to comply unnecessarily with more than one requirement.

An improvement notice requires the person on whom it is served to take the remedial action specified within it (Housing Act 2004, ss. 11 and 12). By s. 13(2), the notice must specify:

(a) the nature of the hazard;
(b) the deficiency which gives rise to the hazard;
(c) the premises and the remedial action;
(d) the date for the commencement of the remedial action; and
(e) the period for completion (although no remedial action can commence within 28 days of service of the notice).

Importantly, the notice must contain information about the right of appeal (to a residential property tribunal) and the period within which an appeal may be made (s. 13(4)). Provision is also made for the suspension, operation, revocation and variation of improvement notices (s. 16), and it is an offence for someone to fail to comply with an improvement notice without reasonable excuse (s. 30(1) and (4)). Section 31 of and Sch. 3 to the 2004 Act enable an authority to take the action required by an improvement notice itself, with or without the agreement of the person on whom it was served.

A prohibition order may prohibit the use of all or part of the premises for some or all purposes, or occupation by particular numbers or descriptions of people (s. 22). It can relate to more than one category 1 hazard. It might be appropriate where, for example, the conditions present a serious risk to health or safety but remedial action is considered unreasonable or impractical because of the cost involved or because the remedial work cannot be carried out with the tenant in residence. Part 3 of Sch. 2 provides a right of appeal. It is an offence to use premises, or permit the use of premises, in contravention of the prohibition order so long as that person doing so knows that it has become operative (s. 32(1)). It is a defence that there was a reasonable excuse (ss. 30(4) and 32(3)).

Hazard awareness notices are a wholly new concept. They are advisory in nature and discretionary. A hazard awareness notice under category 1 advises the person on whom it is served of the existence of the hazard which arises as a result of a deficiency in the premises. The notice should also include details of the remedial action which the local authority considers to be practical and appropriate (s. 28(6)). Such a course of action might be appropriate where an owner or landlord has agreed to take remedial action and the authority is confident that the work will be done within a reasonable time. Although no further action is required on the part of the person served with the notice, the authority may monitor any hazard awareness notice which it serves. The service of such a notice does not preclude further formal action should an unacceptable hazard remain. Because of its advisory nature, no provision is made for appeal against a hazard awareness notice.

Emergency remedial action can be taken if there is a category 1 hazard, there is an imminent risk of serious harm to health and safety, and no management order is in effect under Part 4 of the 2004 Act (s. 40(1)), and the authority can take whatever steps it considers necessary to remove the risk. The owner of a property can appeal but any appeal will not prevent the action from being taken or the prohibition put into effect. Where the conditions in s. 43 are fulfilled, an authority may enter the premises at any time to make an emergency prohibition order, prohibiting the use of all or any part of the premises with immediate effect. Once issued, an emergency prohibition order can be reviewed, varied or revoked in the same way as an ordinary prohibition order.

Demolition orders remain available under Part 9 of the Housing Act 1985 as amended but cannot be used in respect of a listed building. In deciding whether to make a demolition order an authority should, e.g. take into account the availability of local accommodation for rehousing the occupants and consider the prospective use of the cleared site.

Section 7 gives the power to local authorities to take similar steps to deal with category 2 hazards. However, emergency measures cannot be used in respect of category 2 hazards and an authority cannot make a demolition order or a slum clearance declaration. The authority must give a statement of reasons for its decision to take a particular course of enforcement action (s. 8).

Part X, Housing Act 1985: overcrowding

A dwelling is overcrowded when the number of people sleeping in the same dwelling contravenes either the room standard or the space standard (Housing Act 1985, s. 324). The room standard is contravened when the available sleeping accommodation is such that two people of opposite sexes over the age of 10 years and who are not living as husband and wife must sleep in the same bedroom (s. 325). The space standard is contravened whenever the number of persons sleeping in the dwelling exceeds the permitted number. The permitted number is arrived at by a formula set out in s. 326(3) and depends on either the number of rooms or the floor area. In this calculation, no account is taken of children under the age of one year; and children between the ages of one and 10 years each count as half a person (s. 326(2)).

The local housing authority has power to require from an occupier information about the number, ages and sexes of the people sleeping in the dwelling (s. 335) and the power of entry to determine the permitted number of people (s. 337).

If a particular dwelling is overcrowded within the meaning of Part X, the local housing authority can serve a notice on the occupier, requiring that the overcrowding be brought to an end within 14 days. If, within three months from the expiry of the 14 days, the person on whom the notice was served or a member of that person's family is still in occupation and the dwelling is still overcrowded, the local housing authority can take its own proceedings in the county court for possession to be given to the landlord, and recover its expenses from the landlord (s. 338). The occupier will be classed as a homeless person and can apply to the local housing authority to be housed under the homelessness legislation.

By s. 331, the offence of 'causing or permitting overcrowding' is committed where:

(a)   the landlord or a person who effected the letting on the landlord's behalf had reasonable cause to believe that the dwelling would become overcrowded; or
(b)   the landlord or a person who effected the letting on the landlord's behalf failed to make inquiries of the proposed occupier as to the number, ages and sex of those who would be sleeping there; or
(c)   the landlord has failed to take reasonable steps to abate overcrowding following the service of an abatement notice.

Overcrowding is permitted where:

(a)   the occupier has obtained a licence under s. 330 from the local housing authority permitting overcrowding for a period not exceeding one year because of exceptional circumstances (e.g. a seasonal increase of population);
(b)   the overcrowding results from temporary use of the dwelling by members of the occupier's family (s. 329);
(c)   a child has reached a relevant age and the occupier has sought alternative accommodation from the local housing authority (s. 328). The overcrowding will become illegal if the offer of alternative accommodation is unreasonably refused, or the occupier fails to require the removal of a member of the household, who is not a member of the occupier's family, the removal being reasonably practicable having regard to all the circumstances (including the availability of suitable alternative accommodation for that person).

Houses in multiple occupation

Introduction

HIMOs are recognised as constituting a particular housing problem and they have been subject to statutory control since 1957. Powers to regulate HIMOs have evolved from the Regulation and Inspection of

Common Lodging Houses Act 1851 which allowed police and sanitary authorities to set standards and control the number of people occupying a dwelling. Common lodging houses – or 'doss houses' as they were sometimes known – provided cheap accommodation usually in the form of straw mattresses rented on a nightly basis in a communal room (Lund, 2006: 163). They are often in a poor state of repair and are especially susceptible to fire and other health and safety risks. Typically HIMOs are occupied by lower-income single people, including some particularly vulnerable and disadvantaged groups, and many lack the facilities needed to cater for the number of occupiers they house.

Part XI of the Housing Act 1985 contained a number of powers and duties in relation to HIMOs. Local housing authorities had the power to serve a 'general works notice' requiring the execution of necessary works where an HIMO failed to provide certain facilities and amenities (e.g. satisfactory facilities for the storage, preparation and cooking of food, an adequate number of baths, showers and WCs, and an adequate means of escape from fire) as a result of which the property was not considered to be reasonably suitable for occupation by the number of persons or households living there. The person who controlled the house and the person managing it were under a duty to take such steps as were reasonably practicable to prevent the occurrence of a state of affairs calling for the service of such a notice. Failure to comply with the duty constituted a criminal offence. Regulations required the manager of an HIMO to 'ensure the repair, maintenance, cleansing and good order' of all means of water supply and drainage in the house, all means of escape from fire and all apparatus, systems and other things provided by way of fire precautions, kitchens, bathrooms and WCs in common use, common staircases, corridors and passage ways, and outbuildings, yards and gardens in common use'. If, in the opinion of the local housing authority, the condition of an HIMO was defective in consequence of a failure to comply with the regulations, it could serve on the manager a notice specifying the works which it felt were required to make good the neglect (Housing Act 1985, s. 372). Failure to comply with the notice constituted a criminal offence. Where the living conditions in the house were so poor as to represent a danger to the safety, health or welfare of the people living in it, the local authority could make a control order (s. 381) allowing it to run the property itself (s. 381) and could ultimately acquire the property by way of a compulsory purchase order. If either type of notice was not complied with, the local housing authority could itself do the work specified in the notice (s. 375) and recover the expenses it incurred from the person having control of the house or the manager (Sch. 10, para. 2). An 'overcrowding notice' could also be served on the occupier or on the person who is responsible for its management and control, where it appears that an HIMO was already accommodating, or was likely to accommodate, an excessive number of people. The notice would specify the maximum number of people who were allowed to sleep in each room, and specify which rooms were considered as unsuitable for sleeping accommodation (s. 359). Contravention of an overcrowding notice was a criminal offence.

Mandatory licensing

Part 2 of the Housing Act 2004 repeals Part XI of the Housing Act 1985 and provides a new scheme for the control of conditions in privately-rented HIMOs. It introduces a mandatory scheme for the licensing of larger HIMOs and 'additional' licensing for others, the aim being the introduction of 'a far more effective regime for stamping out neglect, dishonesty and malpractice but also a much more satisfactory framework for reputable operators, incorporating the principles of better regulation' (DETR, 2000: 5.30). The 'larger' HIMOs which are the subject of mandatory licensing are those of three or more storeys which have five or more occupants. Given however that most HIMOs consist of fewer than three storeys and that there are many three-storey HIMOs with fewer than five occupants, it has been estimated that only 20 per cent of the HIMO stock is likely to be affected (Prevatt and Sergides, 2005: 26).

The definition of an HIMO is set out in ss. 254–259 of the Housing Act 2004. Generally speaking, an HIMO comprises a house occupied by persons who do not form a single household and there is a degree of sharing (such as bathrooms, kitchens, etc). Controversially, local authority and RSL HIMOs are excluded from the definition as are the NHS, police properties, religious communities of several kinds and buildings occupied 'solely or principally by persons who occupy [them] for the purpose of undertaking a full-time course of further or higher education at a specified educational establishment or at an educational establishment of a specified description' (even though 'the living circumstances and the risks associated with them are presumably similar' (Ball, 2004: 44)). Given that it repeals the provisions in the Housing Act 1985 which applied to all HIMOs regardless of their ownership, the 2004 Act may in this regard be considered a regressive measure.

Local authorities may impose additional licensing for HIMOs outside the mandatory scheme in particular parts of their district or for HIMOs of a particular type. An authority must judge that a significant proportion of HIMO (of the type that it is considering licensing) is being managed ineffectively so as to give rise to problems for the occupiers or members of the public. In considering the quality of management, an authority must take into account the degree of adherence to relevant codes of practice (if any). It remains to be seen whether – in view of their limited resources – local authorities will pursue additional licensing. Before the introduction of the 2004 Act, only a third of authorities had introduced a discretionary HIMO registration scheme and there is little to suggest that the take up additional licensing will be more widespread.

Before granting a licence, an authority must be satisfied that the licence holder is a fit and proper person and that the proposed management arrangements for the HIMO are satisfactory. Every licence must include certain conditions. These are listed in Sch. 4 and include the production of a gas safety certificate and the installation and smoke alarms which must be kept in proper working order. Authorities are empowered to include other conditions which they consider appropriate for the regulation of the management, use and occupation of the HIMO and its condition and contents. Section 72 contains a number of offences which may be committed in relation to HIMO licensing and local authorities are given wide powers of enforcement.

Chapter 9

Succession

Introduction

At common law, where there is a joint tenancy and one of the joint tenants dies, the rule of survivorship applies. Otherwise, a tenancy (be it periodic or fixed-term) is an estate in land which passes on the tenant's death to the person who is entitled under the tenant's will or on intestacy. This may be of some value in the case of a fixed-term tenancy which still has some time to run, but the transmission on death of a periodic tenancy is of little practical use as it can generally be terminated by notice. Thus, in recognition of the fact that for many tenants, their homes are 'the core of their existence' (Law Commission, 2002b: 7.42) and to achieve a degree of parity with those who have bought a property interest in their home – be it freehold or leasehold – which they can leave to their successors, the common law rules have been extensively modified by statute. Overly-generous rights to succeed could well harm the operation of the rental market and limit the ability of social landlords to provide accommodation to those most in housing need (ibid.: 7.52). Describing the present legal position as 'undoubtedly confusing and complex' the Law Commission acknowledges that it nonetheless attempts 'to achieve a balance between allowing individuals to retain a sense of security that comes from the right to occupy their homes and allowing landlords flexibility to use their housing stock as efficiently as possible' (ibid.: 7.53).

This chapter charts the history of statutory succession in relation to both private and social rented sectors.

Succession under the Rent Act 1977

Introduction

Succession rights for Rent Act tenants were first conferred by s. 12(1)(g) of the Increase of Rent and Mortgage Interest (Restrictions) Act 1920. As originally drafted, the prospective legislation confined succession to the widow of a male tenant. A few Members of Parliament recognised that this restriction might present a problem in the 'great number of cases of women who earn their living all over the country, journalists and others, who sometimes have old mothers living with them or young sisters ... It would be hard if [the tenant] died and the mother or sister might be turned out' (HC Deb (1920) vol. 130, cols 1929–30 (21 June)).

Section 12(1)(g) therefore defined the word 'tenant' to include 'the widow of a tenant dying intestate who was residing with him at the time of his death' or, where the tenant (a) died intestate leaving no widow or (b) was a woman, 'such member of the tenant's family so residing as aforesaid ...'. It was soon established that a widower was a member of his wife's family (*Salter v Lask* [1925] 1 KB 584). A six months' residence requirement for members of the tenant's family was added in 1933 and a second succession was added by the Rent Act 1965. The Rent Act 1977, which it will be remembered is a consolidating Act, allows for two possible successions – the first to the spouse (or, if none, to a member of the tenant's family), and the second to a member of the tenant's family. The policy underlying these provisions was said to derive from 'the middle-class ideal of owning your own home and garden' which 'so infused English thinking that those who cannot afford to buy their homes are given the next best things: security for one, two or three lives' (Honore, 1982: 59). At the same time it was recognised that 'it is such a serious inroad on the right of the landlord that it runs close to expropriation, at least of the present owner's effective interest' (ibid.).

By conferring long-term security of tenure, the Rent Acts give tenants far greater protection than they would have enjoyed by virtue of their own contractual arrangements. The security conferred by the Act was designed not merely to ensure that the tenant had a roof over his head, but also – perhaps mainly – to provide the tenant with enough security to establish a family home (Zuckerman, 1980: 263). Further, 'it would be inequitable to deny such protection to those whose lives are intimately bound up with that of the statutory tenant, and who would reasonably be expected to share his day-to-day life and home'. In consequence, 'the [Rent] Act gives security to such people at the time when they are most vulnerable (after the tenant's death) by allowing them to "inherit" the protection granted to the tenant' (Berkowits, 1981: 95). The Housing Act 1988 and the Civil Partnership Act 2004 have made significant changes to the rules regarding succession to Rent Act tenancies and these are dealt with below.

A successor may have a claim to a statutory or assured tenancy on the death of a regulated tenant. If there is no successor, a statutory tenancy will come to an end but a protected tenancy will devolve under the will or intestacy of the tenant. Succession under the statutory provisions takes precedence over the rights of any person entitled under the tenant's will (*Moodie v Hosegood* [1952] AC 61), or on the tenant's intestacy. Such rights are suspended until the succession rules have run their course.

Death of the original tenant before 15 January 1989

The Rent Act 1977, in its original form, allowed two successions. Either the tenant's spouse or (if the tenant had no spouse) a 'member of the original tenant's family' could become a statutory tenant by succession. A spouse was entitled to succeed if he or she was 'residing in the dwelling-house immediately before the death of the original tenant'; a member of the tenant's family was entitled only if he or she had been 'residing with' the tenant 'at the time of and for the period of six months immediately before [the tenant's] death'. The Housing Act 1988 extended the length of the residence requirement to two years where the original tenant dies after 15 January 1989. Similarly, the circumstances of the second succession depend on whether the death of the first successor occurs before or after 15 January 1989 (see below).

Spouses and cohabitees

There is no definition of 'spouse' in the Rent Acts but, in effect, it has been interpreted as a person who has gone through a legal ceremony of marriage with the tenant.

Until the Housing Act 1988 amended the succession provisions of the Rent Act, the tenant's unmarried cohabitee was not regarded as a spouse and, in order to become a statutory tenant by succession, had to prove that he or she was a member of the tenant's family. The first occasion on which the Court of Appeal was faced with the issue was in *Gammans v Ekins* [1950] 2 All ER 140, in which the defendant had lived with the deceased tenant for 20 years or so 'in close, but unmarried, association'. He had adopted her name and posed as her husband. The couple had no children. The court held that no ordinary man could on the facts answer 'yes' to the question of whether the surviving partner was a member of the tenant's family. It took a somewhat censorious view of the relationship. Asquith LJ thought it 'anomalous that a person can acquire a "status of irremoveability" by living or having lived in sin ... To say of two people masquerading as these two were as husband and wife ... that they were members of the same family seems to be an abuse of the English language' (at pp. 141–2). The presence of children in such a case appears to have been significant in creating a family unit. Thus, in *Hawes v Evendon* [1953] 2 All ER 737 the claimant who had lived with the tenant for 12 years and had borne him two children was successful.

In *Dyson Holdings v Fox* [1976] QB 503, the Court of Appeal departed from *Gammans v Ekins* and found for the claimant (who had lived with the tenant as his wife for 21 years until his death but had no children with him) on the ground that the popular meaning of 'family' had changed. Bridge LJ spoke of the 'complete revolution in society's attitude to unmarried partnerships of the kind under consideration' which had occurred between

1950 and 1975. 'Such unions', he said 'are far commoner than they used to be' and 'the social stigmas that once attached to them has almost, if not entirely, disappeared' (at p. 512). He felt some hesitation as to whether the court could give effect to the change in social attitude without doing violence to the doctrine of judicial precedent but in the end decided it would be unduly legalistic to allow this consideration to defeat the claim.

In *Helby v Rafferty* [1979] 1 WLR 13, a man who had cohabited with the tenant for five years was held not entitled to succeed to a statutory tenancy, on the ground that the relationship lacked the permanence and stability over a long period necessary to constitute a family relationship. The couple shared expenses, went to shows and the cinema and did the shopping together. When the tenant became ill, the defendant nursed her as a loving husband might have done. However, the parties had no intention of marrying and did not hold themselves out as married. Neither had taken the other's name. In *Watson v Lucas* [1980] 1 WLR 1493, a majority of the Court of Appeal upheld the claim because the relationship was permanent (the couple had lived together for 19 years) even though the woman had not adopted the man's name and the claimant had a wife and children elsewhere. In *Chios Property Investment Co. Ltd v Lopez* (1988) 20 HLR 120 – described as a 'most exceptional case' – the woman had lived with the tenant for two years with the ultimate intention of marrying him as soon as financial circumstances permitted. She was held entitled to succeed despite the comparative brevity of their relationship and the absence of children. The Court of Appeal noted that there could be no hard and fast rule as regards the necessary length of the relationship, although the longer it had lasted, the easier it would be to infer permanence.

The situation with regard to same-sex partners is dealt with below.

Death of original tenant after 15 January 1989

As before, the spouse of the deceased tenant is entitled to be the first successor provided that he or she was residing in the dwelling-house immediately before the tenant's death. However, the Housing Act 1988 extended the term 'spouse' to cover those living together as husband and wife (Rent Act 1977, Sch. 1, para. 2(2)) which means that cohabitants no longer have to try to establish that they are members of the same family. Where the successor is the spouse or a cohabitant, he or she is entitled to a Rent Act statutory tenancy.

In the absence of a spouse or a cohabitant, the first successor is a member of the tenant's family. The residence requirement is increased from six months to two years. A member of the tenant's family succeeds to an assured periodic tenancy under the Housing Act 1988, rather than a statutory tenancy under the Rent Act 1977 and no further succession is possible (Housing Act 1988, s. 17(2)(c)).

Who is 'a member of the original tenant's family'?

None of the Rent Acts has included a definition of the word 'family'. In *Salter v Lask* [1925] 1 KB 584, 587 Salter J predicted that 'it may have to be determined some day what limit is to be put on these words "tenant's family", whether they are equivalent to "household" or whether they are limited as meaning blood relations'. The issue has indeed come before the courts on many occasions, membership of a family being nowhere near as clear-cut as would appear at first glance.

In *Brock v Wollams* [1949] 2 KB 388 Cohen LJ said that in deciding whether the claimant to the tenancy was a member of the tenant's family, the test should depend upon the opinion of the 'ordinary man'. However, in *Carega Properties v Sharratt* [1979] 1 WLR 928, 932 Viscount Dilhorne observed that the ordinary man approach was 'not likely to exact any more than the judge's personal view', and in *Watson v Lucas* [1980] 1 WLR 1493, 1507 Sir David Cairns expressed his doubt as to the value of the test, admitting that on the facts of the case he had no idea what an ordinary man would say.

It has been said that the term 'family' requires 'a broadly de facto familial nexus' which may be 'found and recognised as such by the ordinary man' where the link would be 'strictly familial had there been a marriage, or where the link is through adoption of a minor, de jure or de facto, or where the link is "step-", or where the link is "in-law" or by marriage' (*Ross v Collins* [1964] 1 WLR 425). Not surprisingly, it has been held to include brothers and sisters (*Price v Gould* (1930) 143 LT 333) and a grandchild (*Collier v Stoneman* [1957] 1 WLR 1108).

The courts will take the surrounding circumstances into account and the fact that the claimant is related by blood to the deceased tenant does not necessarily mean that he or she is a member of the tenant's family for the purposes of the Rent Act. *Langdon v Horton* [1951] 1 All ER 60 concerned the tenant's two cousins, the three women having lived together for many years. It was not their consanguinity which was regarded as decisive, but the fact that they were living together for reasons of convenience. It was thought that the ordinary man would not regard as members of the same family two middle aged women who decided to live together, or if one accepted an invitation to live in the house of the other, even if they were cousins and remained together for many years.

In *Jones v Whitehill* [1950] 2 KB 204 the tenant's niece by marriage, having acted out of natural love and affection, was held to have assumed the duties and offices peculiarly attributable to members of a tenant's family, by looking after her uncle and aunt for between 18 months and two years until their deaths. Sir Raymond Evershed MR made it clear, however, that not all nephews and nieces by marriage should be regarded as members of the tenant's family. Caring for the tenant, even for a very long time, and thus performing some of the duties associated with family membership does not, in the absence of consanguinity or a relationship by marriage or de facto adoption, suffice. In *Ross v Collins* [1964] 1 WLR 425 a housekeeper who regarded the tenant as an older relative – partly elder brother, partly father – was held not to be a member of the tenant's family. She had performed all household duties for him, nursed him and arranged his holidays. In return, he had provided her with free accommodation. In *Carega Properties SA v Sharratt* [1979] 1 WLR 3, the defendant lived with the tenant for 18 years until her death at the age of 94. He was some 50 years her junior. The tenant had no children of her own and at one stage had wanted to call the defendant her son. Since his mother was still alive, they reached a compromise: he called the tenant 'Aunt Nora' and she called him 'Bunny'. They were not related in any way. The judge at first instance described their relationship as 'sensitive, loving, intellectual and platonic'. Through their mutual devotion, he concluded, they had achieved 'what must surely be regarded in a popular sense, and in common sense, as a familial nexus'. The Court of Appeal and the House of Lords thought differently. 'The line must be drawn somewhere', warned Browne LJ in the Court of Appeal (echoing the sentiments of Asquith LJ in *Gammans v Ekins*). If the relationship between the deceased tenant and the defendant were held to constitute a family it would be 'difficult, if not impossible, to exclude the cases ... of two old cronies sharing a house'. In rejecting the defendant's claim, the House of Lords made it clear that the only de facto relationships which were recognised for succession purposes were the 'common law' spouse and the 'parent/child' relationship where the child had joined the tenant's household at a young age but had never been legally adopted. Accordingly, in *Sefton Holdings Ltd v Cairns* [1988] 14 EG 58 the claimant was unsuccessful despite having lived with the tenant's family for 45 years and having been treated as a daughter. It was significant that she had moved in with the tenant's family at the age of 23.

Same-sex partners

Fitzpatrick v Sterling Housing Association Ltd [2001] 1 AC 27 was the first case in which the courts were called upon to consider the question whether the homosexual partner of a protected tenant had lived 'with the original tenant as his or her wife or husband' or was 'a member of the tenant's family' for the purposes of the Rent Act 1977, although the issue had already been raised in relation to a secure public sector tenancy in *Harrogate Borough Council v Simpson* (1985) 17 HLR 205 (see below). For 18 years until the tenant's death, the tenant and his partner, Mr Fitzpatrick, lived together in a homosexual relationship, described by Lord Slynn as 'longstanding, close, loving, faithful [and] monogamous' (at p. 32). The Court of Appeal recognised that the interpretation of the statute in a way which would allow all sexual partners, whether of the same or opposite sex, to succeed to Rent Act tenancies would be consistent not only with social justice but also with 'the respect accorded by modern society to those of the same sex who undertake a permanent commitment to a shared life' ([1998] Ch 304, 318). It felt, however, that problems would flow from the extension of succession rights to same-sex partners in a sexually based relationship. Would it then be right to continue to exclude platonic friends? If friends were to be included, how could the stability and permanence of their household be defined? There was also the question of fairness to homeowners whose rights to possession of their property would be more deeply invaded by an enlargement of the class of potential successors to rent controlled tenancies. Reconciling these competing social priorities might in the end require a political judgment and was a task better suited to the legislative function of Parliament than to the interpretative role of the courts.

The House of Lords decided, by a three to two majority, that Mr Fitzpatrick could succeed as a member of the tenant's family, but not as his spouse. He would be entitled, therefore, to an assured periodic tenancy protected by the Housing Act 1988, rather than a statutory tenancy protected by the Rent Act 1977. Lord Slynn, giving the majority verdict, rejected the claimant's contention that a 'spouse' and a person living with the tenant 'as his or her wife or husband' could include a same-sex partner, as these terms could only include a man and a woman. As he explained (at p. 34):

> In the context of this Act ... 'spouse' means ... legally a husband or wife ... [T]he 1988 amendment ... as obviously intended to include persons not legally husband and wife who lived as such without being married. That prima facie means a man and a woman, and the man must show that the woman was living with him as 'his' wife; the woman that he was living with her as 'her' husband. I do not think that Parliament as recently as 1988 intended that these words should be read as meaning 'my same sex partner' ... [I]f that had been the intention it would have been spelled out.

However, the word 'family' was to be applied flexibly. The hallmarks of a family relationship were a degree of mutual interdependence, the sharing of lives, of caring and love, of commitment and support. Provided that, as a matter of fact, these essentials were present, there was no reason why, as a matter of law, a same-sex partner could not be a member of the deceased tenant's family.

Lord Slynn anticipated that the implementation of the Human Rights Act 1998 might require the courts to revisit this issue and, indeed, the opportunity soon presented itself in *Ghaidan v Godin-Mendoza* [2004] 2 AC 557, the facts of which were materially identical to those of *Fitzpatrick*. The House of Lords in *Fitzpatrick* had already established the right of same-sex partners to succeed to assured tenancies by way of family membership. The question in *Mendoza* was whether the claimant was entitled to succeed to the more beneficial statutory tenancy. The advantages of a Rent Act tenancy over a Housing Act assured tenancy manifest themselves in three ways.

First, the Rent Act confers greater security of tenure. Under the Housing Act 1988, the grounds on which possession may be sought may be regarded as more 'landlord-friendly', of most significance in this regard being ground 8, the mandatory rent arrears ground. Secondly, on the death of the survivor, only a statutory tenancy can be transmitted further to a member of the family of both the original tenant and the survivor. Thirdly, only Rent Act tenants are subject to the fair rent scheme under which the rent officer, when determining a fair rent, is obliged to disregard 'scarcity value'. Assured tenants, by contrast, are liable to pay market rents (Mead, 2003: 503).

The House of Lords (Lord Millett dissenting) agreed with the Court of Appeal that the succession provisions in the Rent Act 1977 should be construed, in accordance with s. 3 of the Human Rights Act 1998 so that there would be no breach of Mr Mendoza's Convention rights under Art. 14, thereby allowing him to succeed to a statutory tenancy. Section 3 obliges the court to read and give effect to legislation in a way which is compatible with Convention rights so far as it is possible to do so. Article 14 provides that 'the enjoyment of the rights and freedoms set forth in this Convention shall be secured without discrimination on any grounds such as sex, race, colour, religion, political or other opinion, national or social origin, association with a national minority, property, birth or other status'. Although it does not contain any free-standing or independent guarantee of equal treatment without discrimination, its parasitic nature (insofar as it prohibits discrimination but only in the provision of another Convention right) operates 'as though [it] formed an integral part of each of the provisions laying down rights and freedoms' (*Belgian Linguistics Case (No 2)* (1968) 1 EHRR 252, 283–4, para. 9). As a result, it may often expand the scope of other Convention rights and 'render a greater range of state conduct open to human rights standards than would otherwise be the case' (Livingstone, 1997: 29).

To assist in its task, the House of Lords drew upon the guidance set out in *Michalak v Wandsworth London Borough Council* [2002] 1 WLR 617 which requires the court to address the following four questions when dealing with an Art. 14 claim. First, do the facts fall within the ambit of one or more of the substantive Convention provisions? Secondly, if so, was there different treatment as respects that right between the complainant on the one hand and the other persons put forward for comparison (the 'chosen comparators') on the other? Thirdly, were the chosen comparators in an analogous situation to that of the complainant? Finally, if they were, did the difference in treatment have an objective and reasonable justification: in other words, did it pursue a legitimate aim and did the differential treatment bear a reasonable relationship of proportionality to the aim sought to be achieved? Here it was clear that the facts fell within the ambit of Art. 8, and affirmative answers could obviously be given to the second and third questions. However, the House of Lords (like the Court of Appeal before it) failed to see how the difference in treatment accorded to same-sex couples under Sch. 1 could be objectively justified, and decided that s. 3 could be utilised to re-interpret the wording of the 1977 Act 'as his or her wife or husband' to mean '*as if they were* his or her wife or husband'.

Lord Millett did not dissent on the basis that the existing legal position was non-discriminatory. Indeed, he felt that discrimination against same-sex couples:

> is not only incompatible with the Convention but is unacceptable in a modern democratic society at the beginning of the twenty-first century. That is not to say that it was always, or even until fairly recently, unacceptable; but times change, and with them society's perceptions change also.
>
> (At para. 55.)

Instead he was concerned that the majority's use of s. 3 to take 'judicial activism' too far and (in so doing) subverted the constitutional balance between the legislature and the judiciary.

The changes which were hurriedly made to the Housing Bill 2004 to accommodate these developments were almost immediately rendered redundant as a result of the Civil Partnership Act 2004. The 2004 Act amends the Rent Act succession provisions so as to allow for transmission of the tenancy to the tenant's 'surviving civil partner'. This includes 'a person who was living with the original tenant as if they were civil partners'. In deciding whether such a relationship exists, consideration may be given to *Nutting v Southern Housing Group Ltd* [2005] HLR 25 in which the central issue was whether the claimant had been living in a relationship similar to marriage so as to be treated as the tenant's spouse. Mr Nutting had originally moved in with the tenant in early 2001. Both men were alcoholics and their relationship was volatile and often abusive. In March 2002, the tenant obtained a non-molestation order against Mr Nutting, citing in evidence that the relationship had ended a year previously. Mr Nutting breached the order and was imprisoned. On his release, he returned to live with the tenant. Shortly after, the tenant successfully applied for a transfer, indicating that he intended to live alone. Within a month of moving into the new property, the tenant died. It was accepted that Mr Nutting had been living with the tenant at the date of his death. His claim to succeed to the tenancy was unsuccessful, the court holding that the irreducible minimum required of a homosexual relationship such as to render it equivalent to marriage was that there existed a relationship of mutual lifetime commitment between the partners which is openly and unequivocally displayed to the outside world. Neither at first instance or on appeal did the court seek to suggest that the volatility of the relationship would, of itself, amount to a bar. Indeed, as Lord Millett had pointed out in *Mendoza* (see above), 'it cannot depend on the relationship being a happy, or long-lasting, or stable one'.

Death of the first successor before 15 January 1989

It will be recalled that where the original tenant died before 15 January 1989, the tenant's spouse or a member of the tenant's family (who satisfied the residence requirements) became a statutory tenant by way of succession. If, by the time of the first successor's death, he or she was still a statutory tenant, the tenancy devolved to the first successor's spouse or a member of his or her family (who satisfied the residence requirements). On the death of the second successor (whenever it occurs), the statutory tenancy comes to an end, and the landlord is entitled to recover possession.

A statutory tenant by succession is protected by the Rent Act 1977 'if and so long as he [or she] occupies the dwelling-house as his or her residence' (s. 2(1)(a)).

Death of the first successor after 15 January 1989

Where the first successor was a statutory tenant by way of succession, a further succession is possible but the conditions to be satisfied are stricter than those which applied to deaths before the 1988 Act came into force. The second successor must be a member of the original tenant's family *and* a member of the first successor's family *and* must have resided with the first successor in the dwelling-house for a period of at least two years immediately before the first successor's death. The second successor takes on the tenancies as an assured periodic tenant. These rules are designed to deal with the situation where the claimant is the child of the original tenant and the first successor.

There can be no second succession where the first successor was a member of the tenant's family who succeeded to an assured periodic tenancy. The landlord may recover possession under ground 7 of the Housing Act 1988 where an assured periodic tenancy devolves under the will or intestacy of the tenant.

In the event of there being more than one eligible claimant, the county court can decide who becomes the statutory tenant if the parties themselves fail to agree (Rent Act 1977, s. 2(1)(b); Sch. 1, Part I, paras 2 and 3). In *Dealex Properties Ltd v Brooks* [1966] 1 QB 542 it was held, per curiam, that a statutory tenancy cannot be transmitted to a number of persons jointly, but only to one person who fulfils the necessary qualifications.

Residence with the tenant

As has already been pointed out, a member of the tenant's family who is claiming to succeed to what was originally a tenancy regulated under the Rent Act, must have been 'residing with' the tenant for two years immediately before the tenant's death. In the case of succession to a secure or introductory tenancy, the tenant's spouse or a member of the tenant's family must have been 'residing with the tenant throughout the period of 12 months ending with the tenant's death'. The question arises, therefore, as to what is meant by 'residing with' the tenant.

In *Edmunds v Jones* [1957] 1 WLR 1118 the tenant had sub-let two rooms in the house to her daughter and the two of them shared a kitchen. It was held that the words 'residing with' must be given their ordinary popular meaning. The person claiming to succeed to the tenancy must have lived in, and shared for living purposes, the whole of the premises to which he or she claimed to have succeeded. Since the daughter had no right to go into any part of the house beyond the confines of her own tenancy and the kitchen, she could not be said to have been residing with her mother at the time of her mother's death.

In *Collier v Stoneman* [1957] 1 WLR 1108, the claimant's grandmother was the statutory tenant of a flat consisting of two rooms and a kitchen. One room was occupied by the tenant as her bedroom and other by the claimant and her husband. They all shared the kitchen. The tenant kept very much to her own room and did most of her own shopping and cooking, eating only occasionally with the claimant and her husband in the kitchen. The Court of Appeal held that the claimant (and her husband) were residing with the grandmother up to the date of her death. *Edmunds v Jones* was distinguished. In that case, the daughter was legally entitled to exclusive possession of the two rooms comprised in her sub-tenancy; she could not be said to be residing in them with her mother for she was, in fact, residing in them to the exclusion of her mother. In *Collier*, the fact that the parties led largely independent lives was irrelevant. It might have been otherwise if they had lived 'wholly separate lives without mutual meetings or domestic co-operation' (p. 1118).

In *Foreman v Beagley* [1969] 1 WLR 1387 the tenant spent the last three years of her life in hospital. Her son came to the flat to air the premises and he lived there for the year immediately preceding her death. The Court of Appeal held he had not been 'residing with' her, as he had only moved in as caretaker without any indication of establishing a joint household. The phrase 'residing with' requires some factual community of family living and companionship. There had never been any 'community of living' with his mother. Had he lived in the flat with her before her illness and continued to live there during her absence, the residence requirement would probably have been satisfied. *Foreman v Beagley* was distinguished in *Hedgedale Ltd v Hands* (1991) 23 HLR 158 in which a young man moved into his grandmother's flat in order to help care for her. Soon afterwards, she broke her arm and went to stay with her daughter. After about three months, she returned to the flat where she lived with her grandson for the remaining five months of her life. The young man was held to have resided with her for the requisite period, despite her absence, since he had at all material times the intention to form a family unit with her in the flat.

The issue of residence with the deceased tenant becomes more problematic where the claimant has a home elsewhere. While the Rent Acts recognise that a person may have two homes, it is only rarely that a claimant with his or her own home will be successful. In *Morgan v Murch* [1970] 1 WLR 778, a man left his wife and children in a council house to live with his mother. On her death, six and a half months later, the son was held entitled to remain as a successor since he had made his home with her. He had not attempted any reconciliation with his wife, and there was no immediate prospect of his returning to the matrimonial home. In *Swanbrae v Elliott* (1987) 19 HLR 87 the claimant slept three or four nights a week at the home of her sick mother and spent the other nights in her own house where her adult son continued to live. It was held that she was not residing with her mother. The fact that she had a permanent home of her own was not necessarily fatal to her claim but made it more difficult for her to satisfy the test of residence with her mother. She had moved in for a limited time and for a limited purpose, i.e. to stay with her mother for so long as was necessary. In *Hildebrand v Moon* (1989) 37 EG 123 a woman moved back to nurse her sick mother. She kept her own flat on but contemplated selling it a few months before her mother's death. The Court of Appeal held that, in contrast to the daughter in *Swanbrae v Elliott* she had made her home with her mother and was entitled, therefore, to succeed to her statutory tenancy.

The Rent Act 1977 did not originally specify whether the whole of the qualifying period of residence with the tenant must have taken place in the dwelling-house to which succession was claimed, provided that they had lived together for the required six-month period. However, the amendments made by the 1988 Act provide that the two-year period of residence must have been 'in the dwelling-house' (Housing Act 1988, Sch. 4). Where succession to a secure tenancy (and, presumably an introductory or demoted tenancy) is involved, the period of residence does not need to be in the same property throughout the relevant period (*Waltham Forest London Borough Council v Thomas* [1992] 2 AC 198).

Succession under the Housing Act 1988

Introduction

The Housing Act 1988 permits one succession to an assured tenancy and that to the tenant's spouse only. All new private sector lettings are now effected by assured shorthold tenancies unless steps are taken expressly to create an assured tenancy (see Chapter 12). Although an assured shorthold tenancy is a type of assured tenancy – and therefore subject to the same succession provisions – the fact that it can generally be brought to an end by two months' notice makes the issue of succession academic. All in all, the aim of establishing a measure of security sufficient to encourage and support the formation of a family by the tenant has all but disappeared for the vast majority of Housing Act tenants in the private rented sector. However, most housing association tenants are assured tenants and they, therefore, are the real beneficiaries of the succession provisions of the 1988 Act. Indeed, the Housing Corporation's Regulatory Code requires RSLs to demonstrate their commitment to equal opportunity, specifically including sexual orientation (HC, 2005: 2.7b). The Code replaces the Housing Corporation's old Performance Standards (which expected RSLs to consider offering a tenancy to partners including those of the same sex) and other members of the deceased tenant's household who had been living with the tenant for the year before the tenant's death, and had been looking after the tenant, or had accepted responsibility for the tenant's dependants. It appears that 'the tenancy agreements of many RSLs continue to reflect these expectations' (Blandy, 2004: 52).

Fixed-term assured tenancies

Unlike the Rent Act 1977, the Housing Act 1988 makes no special provision for succession to fixed-term tenancies. When a fixed-term assured tenant dies, the remainder of the term will pass to whoever is entitled under the tenant's will or on intestacy. That person will become the assured tenant provided that the requirements of an assured tenancy are satisfied, e.g. that the dwelling-house is occupied as his or her only or principal home. If not, the tenancy will cease to be assured and the landlord may recover possession at the end of the term.

Periodic assured tenancies (contractual or statutory)

Under the general law, the tenancy will pass under the tenant's will or on intestacy but, in order to prevent the tenancy continuing indefinitely, Ground 7 provides a mandatory ground for succession on the death of a periodic assured tenant. The only exception is to be found in s. 17 which prevails over any devolution under the tenant's will or intestacy. It provides for a statutory transfer of the tenancy to a surviving spouse who, immediately before the tenant's death, was 'occupying the dwelling-house as his or her only or principal home'. The right is limited to sole tenants. In the case of a joint tenancy, the survivor is treated as a successor, so that there can be no further succession on his or her death (s. 17(2)). Section 17(4) extends succession rights to 'a person who was living with the tenant as his or her wife or husband or as if they were civil partners'. If more than one person fulfils the condition relating to the spouse in occupation in s. 17(1) they may agree, or if they do not agree the court may decide, who is to be treated as the spouse. As with Rent Act tenancies, a joint succession is not possible. Only one succession is permitted under s. 17.

Succession to secure tenancies

General principles

While the proper use and allocation of 'public' resources is clearly relevant as regards RSLs and other housing associations, it may be seen as 'even more significant' in the context of local authorities, given that 'the ability to succeed to a secure tenancy has the effect of tying up a public resource for a further period' (Davis and Hughes, 2005: 323).

Limited rights of succession exist on the death of a tenant who is not a 'successor'. By s. 88, the tenant is a successor where:

(a) the tenancy vested in the tenant by virtue of s. 89 (succession to a periodic tenancy), or
(b) the tenant was a joint tenant and has become a sole tenant, or
(c) the tenancy arose by virtue of s. 86 (periodic tenancy arising on the ending of a term certain) and the first tenancy there mentioned was granted to another person or jointly to him and another person, or
(d) he or she became the tenant by virtue of an assignment under s. 92 and was a successor in relation to the tenancy which he or she assigned. If the assignment was made in pursuance of an order made under:

   (i) ss. 23A or 24 of the Matrimonial Causes Act 1973,
   (ii) s. 17(1) of the Matrimonial and Family Proceedings Act 1984, or
   (iii) Sch. 1, para. 1 to the Children Act 1989,

   the tenant is a successor only if the other party to the marriage was a successor.

(e) the tenancy vested in the tenant on the death of the previous tenant, or
(f) the tenancy was previously an introductory tenancy and the tenant was a successor to the introductory tenancy.

In *Walker v Birmingham City Council* [2006] 1 WLR 264, it was held that a former joint tenant who became a sole tenant by the right of survivorship before secure tenancies were created by the Housing Act 1980 was not 'a successor' for the purposes of s. 88 of the 1985 Act and the rule that there could be only one succession to a secure tenancy did not apply.

Who is entitled to succeed?

Under s. 87 of the Housing Act 1985, the successor must fulfil two conditions. First, the dwelling-house must have been the successor's 'only or principal home at the time of the tenant's death', and, secondly, the successor must be either (a) the tenant's spouse or civil partner, or (b) another member of the tenant's family who resided with the tenant throughout the period of 12 months ending with the tenant's death. 'Member of the tenant's family' is defined by s. 113 of the 1985 Act to include those who 'live together as husband and wife or as if they were civil partners' and those who are the parents, grandparents, children, grandchildren, brothers, sisters, uncles, aunts, nephews and nieces of the deceased. Relationships by marriage are treated as relationships by blood, the half-blood as the whole, step-children as children and illegitimate children as legitimate children of their mothers and reputed fathers.

It can be seen therefore that spouses and civil partners take priority and all other 'family' members (including a person with whom the tenant lives together as husband and wife or as a civil partner) have to fulfil a further 12-month residence condition. 'Family' is widely but (apparently) preclusively defined, in that 'a person is a member of the tenant's family' only if he or she can be accommodated within a defined list of 'relations'. In *Michalak v Wandsworth London Borough Council* [2002] 1 WLR 617 a possession claim was made against the brother-in-law of the deceased tenant's first cousin once removed because the relationship was not in the list contained in s. 113. The Court of Appeal held that although Art. 8 was engaged, there was no infringement of Art. 14, and there was an objective justification for Parliament's decision not to extend the right to succeed to distant relatives.

Until recently, the category of those 'living together as husband and wife' did not include same-sex partners. In *Harrogate Borough Council v Simpson* (1985) 17 HLR 205, 210 Ewbank J said that 'the essential characteristic of living together as husband and wife, is that there should be a man and a woman and that they should be living together in the same household'. It did not suffice that the tenant and the claimant (a lesbian couple who had lived together for three years), had regarded and described themselves as husband and wife, nor that they had behaved in some ways as though they were, the tenant being the masculine partner who wore men's clothing and the claimant being 'the female counterpart'. Subsequent proceedings before the European Commission on Human Rights were also unsuccessful (see Loveland, 2003 for a critique of the Commission's decision).

The decision in *Mendoza* was welcomed as a victory for gay rights and it might be assumed that if the facts of *Simpson* recurred in an equivalent case the result would be different today. Davis and Hughes suggest however that this might be wishful thinking, given that those living with the tenant as if they were civil partners must still fulfil a 12-month residence requirement. During the passage of the Housing Act 1996 through Parliament, an attempt to expand the definition of wife or husband to include same-sex partners was overturned on the Third Reading in the House of Commons. It was generally felt however that a more generous approach should be taken that with regard to secure tenancies and the consequence was the publication by the government of guidance to local authorities, requiring them to grant joint tenancies in circumstances where household members have a long-term commitment to the home, e.g. partners (including same-sex partners), friends or unpaid live-in carers. Further, where a tenant dies and another household member (who does not have succession rights) has (a) been living with the tenant for the year prior to the tenant's death; or (b) been providing care for the tenant; or (c) accepted responsibility for the tenant's dependants and needs to live with them in order to do so, the authority should consider granting him or her a tenancy (ODPM, 2002: 3.10). It must be satisifed that '… the allocation has no adverse implications for the good use of the housing stock and has sufficient priority under the allocation scheme' (ibid.) and its decision will inevitably affected by the availability of stock.

Succession by minors

Until the decision of the Court of Appeal in *Kingston upon Thames London Borough Council v Prince* (1999) 31 HLR 794, it was generally accepted that children could not be tenants, because of their inability to hold a legal estate in land (Law of Property Act 1925, s. 1(6)). The issue in *Prince* was whether, on the death of a secure tenant, his 13-year-old granddaughter (who had been living with him for three years, and thereby satisfied the 12–month residence requirement of s. 87 of the Housing Act 1985) was 'a person qualified to succeed the tenant' so that 'the tenancy' vested in her (s. 89(2)). Hale J had no doubt that a minor is quite capable of becoming a tenant (albeit only in equity) of any property, including a council house, and that 'housing legislation may include an equitable tenancy without catering for it expressly'. Referring to *R v Tower Hamlets London Borough Council ex p Von Goetz* [1999] QB 1019 (in which a 10-year assured shorthold tenancy made in writing but not by deed was held to be a valid equitable lease), she pointed out that a would-be landlord is perfectly free to grant an equitable tenancy to a minor. It followed, therefore, that a minor could succeed to the actual tenancy held by a deceased secure tenant. The deceased's estate would hold the legal estate on trust for the minor until he or she reached the age of 18 when a conveyance of the legal estate could be called for.

In *Prince*, the original tenant had been granted a legal tenancy. On the succession by his granddaughter to the equitable tenancy, the legal estate was left in limbo. The Court of Appeal held (without giving reasons) that the granddaughter's mother could succeed to the legal tenancy even though she did not qualify to succeed to the secure tenancy herself as she failed to fulfil the 12-month residence requirement, Hale J simply stating (at p. 802) that 'Marie's mother was declared trustee because she was willing to act and no-one objected'.

In *Newham London Borough Council v Ria* [2004] EWCA Civ 41 the first defendant was aged 15 when her mother died, having made a will leaving her entire estate to her daughter and appointing her sister to be the sole executrix and trustee. The mother had been a secure tenant and she and her daughter had both occupied the premises as their only or principal home.

It was agreed, applying *Kingston BC v Prince*, that the daughter succeeded to an equitable tenancy. There was disagreement, however, as to who (if anyone) held the legal estate. In the Court of Appeal, Sir Martin Nourse took the view that 'the notion of a landlord's being a trustee of a tenancy of the demised premises for the benefit of the tenant is a very curious one, to which effect should not be given without express provision' (para. 14). He also rejected the notion that the vesting of the legal estate would in some way be suspended or in limbo until the daughter attained her majority. Instead it was held that the legal estate vested in the aunt under the express provisions of the deceased tenant's will.

In *Hereford City Council v O'Callaghan* [1996] CLY 3831 the county court declined to follow the first instance decision in *Reading Borough Council v Isley* [1981] CLY 1323 that members of the tenant's family include children whom the tenant has fostered throughout their childhood and has always treated as his or her natural children. It was pointed out that s. 113(1) and (2) defines exhaustively the relationships which can qualify and it was not the intention of Parliament to include a foster child.

Periodic tenancies

Succession to periodic tenancies is governed by s. 89 of the Housing Act 1985. Where more than one person is qualified to succeed, the tenant's spouse is to be preferred to another family member. Where two or more other members of the tenant's family qualify and cannot agree between themselves, the successor is to be selected by the landlord (s. 89(2)(b)).

If there is no person qualified to succeed to the tenant, the tenancy will be disposed of under the terms of the tenant's will or according to the intestacy rules. It ceases to be a secure tenancy unless the vesting or disposal of the tenancy is in pursuance of an order made under:

(i)   s. 24 of the Matrimonial Causes Act 1973 (property adjustment orders in connection with matrimonial proceedings);
(ii) s. 17(1) of the Matrimonial and Family Proceedings Act 1984 (property adjustment orders after overseas divorce); or
(iii) Sch. 1, para. 1 to the Children Act 1989 (orders for financial relief against parents).

Fixed-term tenancies

A fixed-term tenancy will be disposed of under the terms of the tenant's will or according to the intestacy rules. It will cease to be secure unless:

(a) the vesting or disposal of the tenancy is in pursuance of an order made under:

  (i) s. 24 of the Matrimonial Causes Act 1973 (property adjustment orders in connection with matrimonial proceedings);

(ii) s. 17(1) of the Matrimonial and Family Proceedings Act 1984 (property adjustment orders after overseas divorce); or

(iii) Sch. 1, para. 1 to the Children Act 1989 (orders for financial relief against parents); or

(b) the vesting or disposal is to a person qualified to succeed the tenant (s. 90(3)).

Succession to introductory tenancies

Section 131 of the Housing Act 1996 provides that a person is qualified to succeed to a tenancy on the death of an introductory tenant if that person occupies the tenant's house as his or her only or principal home at the time of the tenant's death and was either the tenant's spouse or another member of the tenant's family and has resided with the tenant throughout the 12 months prior to the tenant's death. If the tenant who has died was a successor, no statutory succession can take place. Section 132 sets out the circumstances in which a tenant is himself a successor. The succession will be to an introductory tenancy (s. 133). Where more than one person is qualified to succeed, the tenant's spouse is to be preferred to another family member. Where there is no agreement between two or more other members of the tenant's family, the successor is to be selected by the landlord. An introductory tenancy comes to an end where there is no person qualified to succeed.

Succession to demoted tenancies

In the case of a first succession eligibility to succeed to the tenancy depends on the standard criteria, i.e. the claimant must be the tenant's spouse or civil partner who was occupying the dwelling-house as his or her only or principal home at the time of the tenant's death, or a member of the tenant's family (as defined in s. 113) who resided with the tenant throughout the period of 12 months ending with the tenant's death. The demoted tenancy will become a secure tenancy at the end of the demoted period unless the landlord has successfully sought possession.

Chapter 10

Homelessness: eligibility, homelessness, priority need and intentionality

Introduction

Before a local authority owes its most extensive duty to rehouse an applicant under s. 193 of the Housing Act 1996, it must be satisfied that the applicant has cleared all four obstacles in the 'homeless persons' obstacle race' (see Chapter 2), i.e. is eligible for assistance, homeless, in priority need of accommodation, and did not become homeless intentionally. However, even if the applicant fulfils these requirements, the authority to which application is made may consider whether the applicant has a local connection with the district of another authority to which it may refer the application. Lesser duties may be owed to, e.g. an applicant who is eligible, unintentionally homeless but not in priority need, or one who is eligible, intentionally homeless and in priority need (see Chapter 11). The 1996 Act is supported by a Code of Guidance (CoG) issued by the Department for Communities and Local Government, to which local authorities must 'have regard' (s. 182) but need not follow slavishly (*De Falco v Crawley BC* [1980] QB 460).

Initial inquiries

If the local housing authority has reason to believe that an applicant is homeless or threatened with homelessness, it must make such inquiries as are necessary to establish (a) whether the applicant is eligible for assistance, and (b) if so, whether any duty, and if so what duty, it owes (s. 184).

The authority may also make inquiries as to whether the applicant has a local connection with the district of another local housing authority in England, Wales or Scotland (s. 184(3)). On completion of the inquiries, the authority must notify the applicant of its decision and, if any issue is decided against the applicant's interests, the reasons for the decision. Notification and reasons must also be given to the applicant if the authority has referred, or intends to refer, the case to another authority under s. 198. The applicant must be informed of the right to request a review of the decision and the time within which such a request must be made (s. 202). A local housing authority is under a duty to secure accommodation while the inquiries under s. 184 are being carried out (s. 188).

Eligibility

In the parliamentary debates on the Housing (Homeless Persons) Bill, home-lessness appears to have been viewed as a fundamentally domestic issue. Concern was voiced about British passport holders from troubled countries overseas (Malawi and Uganda were cited as examples) who sought refuge in Great Britain (HC Deb (1977) vol. 926, col. 984) and it was also recog-nised that a duty to accommodate might arise in relation to a couple, one of whom was Italian and the other French, who had become homeless in this country (HC Deb (1977) vol. 926, col. 930). Otherwise, attention seemed to focus on 'rascally Irishmen' who 'popped up again and again throughout the proceedings in Committee' (HC Deb (1976–7) vol. 926, col. 1673). The UK's membership of the EEC seems to have been overlooked, specifically Council Regulation 1612/68, Art. 9(1) of which provides that 'a worker who is a national of a member state and who is employed in the territory of another member state shall enjoy all the rights and benefits accorded to national workers in matters of housing, including ownership of the house he [or she] needs'.

The Housing (Homeless Persons) Act 1977 contained no express restrictions on the kinds or categories of persons who could apply for accommodation. It was soon established, however, that no duty was owed to illegal immigrants to the UK or those who had overstayed the period for which they were granted leave to enter or were in breach of a deportation order. Such persons had com-mitted a criminal offence or were at least in breach of the immigration laws and, as such, were not lawfully here (*R v Hillingdon London Borough Council ex p Streeting* [1980] 1 WLR 1425; *R v Secretary of State for the Environment ex p Tower Hamlets London Borough Council* [1993] QB 632).

The Housing Act 1996 introduced important restrictions and provides that the homelessness provisions contained in Part VII are available only to those who are 'eligible for assistance' (s. 185(1)). There are two main groups of people who are not eligible. The first consists of those who are not British citizens and or do not have full rights to live in Great Britain because of their immigration status (people from abroad). The second consists of people who may have rights to live here but have spent time living somewhere else and therefore fail the 'habitual residence' test. The provisions on eligi-bility are very complex and reference should be made to the CoG (DCLG, 2006a: Ch. 9).

Homelessness

General principles

By s. 175(1) of the Housing Act 1996:

> a person is homeless if he [or she] has no accommodation available for his [or her] occupation, in the UK or elsewhere, which he [or she]—

(a) is entitled to occupy by virtue of an interest in it or by virtue of an order of the court,
(b) has an express or implied licence to occupy, or
(c) occupies as a residence by virtue of any enactment or rule of law giving him [or her] the right to remain in occupation or restricting the right of another person to recover possession.

Section 175(1)(a) includes legal and equitable interests in property and, therefore, covers owners and tenants. Homeless applicants may include those who are no longer entitled to occupy accommodation because their landlord has defaulted on the mortgage of the property (DCLG, 2006a: 8.15). A person will have an express or implied licence to occupy under s. 175(1)(b) if, e.g. he or she is a lodger, or lives in a hostel or hospital or with relatives, or is an employee with a service occupancy. In *Fletcher v Brent London Borough Council* [2006] EWCA Civ 960, the Court of Appeal held that where a local authority secure joint tenancy had been terminated effectively by notice to quit it was necessary – in order to be able to determine whether he was homeless within s. 175 of the 1996 Act – to consider whether the former tenant had a licence to occupy and what the terms of any licence were. Protection given by law (s. 175(1)(c)) will include, e.g. statutory tenants under the Rent Act 1977 who have no proprietary interest in the property but merely 'a status of irremoveability' (see Chapter 12).

Section 175(1) makes no mention of (i) those who have been trespassers from the outset and remain so, and (ii) those who have excluded tenancies and licences (and to whom, therefore, the notice to quit and court order provisions of the Protection from Eviction Act 1977 do not apply) which have been brought to an end. Both will be statutorily homeless even though no possession order has been made against them; they are not 'roofless', but neither do they have accommodation within any of the specified classes (see e.g. *R v Portsmouth City Council ex p Knight* (1983) 10 HLR 115 and *R v Surrey Heath Borough Council ex p Li* (1984) 16 HLR 79).

Section 175(2) provides that a person is also homeless:

if he [or she] has accommodation but—

(a) ... cannot secure entry to it, or
(b) it consists of a moveable structure, vehicle or vessel designed or adapted for human habitation and there is no place where he [or she] is entitled or permitted both to place it and to reside in it.

Subsection (a) could apply to, e.g. those who have been unlawfully evicted or whose accommodation is being occupied by squatters (DCLG, 2006a: 8.16). On a practical level, it has proved to be of little value, however, because local authorities have tended to regard as intentionally homeless applicants who have not used the legal remedies open to them to achieve reinstatement. The effect of subs. 2(b) is that a mobile home, caravan, houseboat, etc. will qualify where there is nowhere both to place it and to live in it. In *R v Chiltern District Council ex p Roberts et al.* (1990) 23 HLR 387 travelling showmen were considered to be neither homeless nor threatened with homelessness whilst moving from fair to fair during the fairground season and residing at each fairground in caravans on a temporary basis. Following the repeal (by the Criminal Justice and Public Order Act 1994), of the Caravan Sites Act 1968, Part II, which imposed upon local authorities a duty to provide sites for them, gypsies and other travellers are increasingly likely to fall within subs. 2(b) although they may prefer to make use of unauthorised sites or to develop their own land without planning permission. The caravan count in January 2006 revealed that around 21 per cent of caravans in England are on unauthorised sites, 31 per cent are on private sites and 42 per cent are on sites owned by local authorities. The number of pitches provided by local authorities has remained static since Part II of the 1968 Act was repealed (DCLG, 2006d: 3 and 4).

Reasonableness

Section 175(3) provides that 'a person shall not be treated as having accommodation unless it is accommodation which it would be reasonable for him to continue to occupy'. The Housing and Planning Act 1986 added the requirement of reasonableness to the definition of homelessness in response to the House of Lords ruling in *R v Hillingdon London Borough Council ex p Pulhofer* [1986] AC 484 in which a couple and their two children occupied a single bedroom in a guest house. The room contained a single and a double bed, and neither cooking nor washing facilities. The House of Lords upheld the local authority's decision that the family was not homeless. The words 'appropriate' or 'reasonable' were not to be imported for the purpose of describing 'accommodation' nor was it relevant that the accommodation might be statutorily unfit or overcrowded. Their Lordships made it clear, however, that not all places in which a person might choose or be constrained to live could properly be regarded as accommodation; it would be 'a misuse of language to describe Diogenes [who lived in a barrel] as having occupied accommodation within the meaning of the Act'.

The CoG acknowledges that there is no simple rule of reasonableness (DCLG, 2006a: 8.18) leaving it to housing authorities to make a judgment on the facts of each case, taking into account the applicant's circumstances. It does however make particular mention of the following factors.

Domestic violence

Section 177(1) provides that it is not reasonable for a person to continue to occupy accommodation if it is probable that this will lead to domestic violence against him, or against:

(a) a person who normally resides with him as a member of his family, or
(b) any other person who might reasonably be expected to reside with him.

For this purpose 'domestic violence' means violence or threats of violence which are likely to be carried out from someone with whom a person is associated. By s. 178, a person is 'associated with another person' if:

(a) they are, or have been, married to each other;
(b) they are, or have been, civil partners of each other;
(c) they are, or have been cohabitants (including same-sex partners);
(d) they live, or have lived, in the same household;
(e) they are relatives (i.e. father, mother, stepfather, stepmother, son, daughter, stepson, stepdaughter, grandmother, grandfather, grandson or granddaughter, brother, sister, uncle, aunt, niece or nephew (whether of the full blood, half blood or by affinity) of a person or a spouse or former spouse, or cohabitee or former cohabite (DCLG, 2006a: 8.20);
(f) they have agreed to marry one another (whether or not that agreement has been terminated);
(g) they have entered into a civil partnership agreement (whether or not that agreement has been terminated);
(h) in relation to a child, each of them is a parent of the child or has, or has had, parental responsibility for the child;
(i) if a child has been adopted or freed for adoption, two persons are associated if one is the natural parent or grandparent of the child and the other is the child of a person who has become the parent by virtue of an adoption order or has applied for an adoption order or someone with whom the child has been placed for adoption.

The violence or threat of violence is not confined to instances within the home (as in *R v Kensington and Chelsea Royal London Borough Council ex p Hammell* [1989] QB 518 where the applicant had suffered alleged violence and harassment by her former husband, who lived nearby). The fact that violence has not yet occurred does not, on its own, suggest that it is not likely to occur. Authorities should not base their assessment of a likely threat of violence solely on whether there has been actual violence in the past. An injunction ordering a person not to molest the applicant or enter the applicant's home will not necessarily prevent such behaviour. Authorities may inform applicants of the option to take out an injunction, but should make it clear that there is no obligation to do so (DCLG, 2006a: 8.23). The CoG also refers to 'people fleeing harassment' which – although severe – falls short of actual violence or threats of violence, e.g. verbal abuse or damage to property. It advises that careful consideration should be given to applicants who may be at risk of witness intimidation (ibid.: 10.34).

General housing conditions

In determining whether it would be, or would have been, reasonable for a person to continue to occupy accommodation, regard may be had to the general housing circumstances in the district of the authority to which application has been made (Housing Act 1996, s. 177(2)). This involves consideration of a range of questions, not confined to the condition of the housing formerly occupied but extending to issues of employment and the availability of welfare benefits. The authority is 'fully entitled to take into account the difficulties of accommodation and the difficulties of employment in their area, and in the context of someone coming from abroad, the difficulties in this country in general' (*R v Hammersmith and Fulham London Borough ex p Duro-Rama* (1983) 9 HLR 71). This calls for a 'balancing exercise' between housing conditions in the authority's area and the accommodation which has been left and involves other questions such as the 'pattern of life' followed by the applicant (*R v London Borough Tower Hamlets ex p Monaf* (1988) 20 HLR 329).

As regards physical conditions, it must be asked whether the condition of the property is so poor compared with other accommodation in the area that it would not be reasonable to expect someone to continue to live there. The cases demonstrate, however, that conditions must often be very poor if an authority's decision on reasonableness is successfully to be challenged. The CoG states that overcrowding should also be considered in relation to general housing circumstances in the area. It points out, however, that statutory overcrowding (within the meaning of Part X of the Housing Act 1985) may not by itself be sufficient to determine whether it is (un)reasonable for the applicant to continue to live there (DCLG, 2006a: 8.28), although where the accommodation seriously infringes the statutory standards relating to unfitness or overcrowding, the general housing circumstances in the area are likely to be less influential in the assessment of reasonableness. The applicant may therefore be 'homeless' while living in unsatisfactory accommodation even though general conditions in the locality are undoubtedly poor. Thus, in *R v Westminster City Council v Ali* (1984) 16 HLR 83, McCullough J found it astonishing that anyone should regard it as reasonable that a family of seven should live in one room measuring 10 feet by 12 feet. As to the general housing circumstances in the area, he commented (at p. 93) that '[n]o evidence has been placed before me that accommodation in the area of the Westminster City Council is so desperately short that it is reasonable to accept overcrowding of this degree'. In *R v Preseli District Council ex p Fisher* (1985) 17 HLR 147 the court held that a one-roomed boat with no bath, shower, WC, electricity, hot water, or kitchen sink, occupied by the applicant, her children and two friends was not accommodation of which it was reasonable to remain in occupation. However, in *R v South Herefordshire District Council ex p Miles* (1985) 17 HLR 82 a couple and their children occupied a rat-infested hut which measured approximately 10 feet by 20 feet. It had no mains services, although services were available in a nearby caravan occupied by relatives. The hut was held to constitute accommodation of which continued occupation could be considered reasonable (albeit on the borderline of what was reasonable) while there were only two children. On the birth of the third child, it crossed the borderline into unreasonableness.

In areas where there is a serious housing shortage, the consideration of general housing circumstances may mean that people end up living in potentially life-threatening conditions. In *R v Kensington and Chelsea Royal London Borough Council ex p Ben-el-Mabrouk* (1995) 27 HLR 564, the applicant, his wife and very young child lived on the top floor of a house in multiple occupation in Kensington. The house was one in which there was a real risk of fire and no adequate means of escape. The local authority decided that the applicant was not homeless as it was accommodation which it was reasonable to continue to occupy, given that the owner had been served with a notice under s. 352 of the Housing Act 1985 requiring him to install an adequate means of fire escape. In the High Court, it was held that it was not reasonable for the applicant to continue living in the flat and that accordingly he was homeless. Effective action was needed either to provide a means of escape or to ensure that the top flat was vacated. Any delay was unacceptable because it left a period during which the applicant and his family were unprotected. On appeal, the authority expressed its concern that, if the judge's decision was upheld, anyone who could demonstrate a lack of adequate fire escape in a house of multiple occupation could in effect demand to be rehoused by the authority at once. The Court of Appeal allowed the council's appeal, acknowledging the difficulties encountered by local authorities in discharging their duties under the homelessness legislation, and the fact that there were 4,500 households in houses in multiple occupation in the council's area alone.

Alternatively, the physical characteristics of the current accommodation may make it unsuitable for the applicant (e.g. the applicant is a wheelchair user and access is limited). In *R v Medina Borough Council ex p Dee* (1992) 24 HLR 562, the accommodation consisted of an elderly prefabricated beach bungalow which was in a poor state of repair, and suffered from persistent dampness. In deciding that it would be reasonable for the applicant and her newborn baby to live there, the authority had failed to take into account (a) the fact that the property was on the borderline of unfitness, and (b) medical advice given to the applicant that it was inappropriate accommodation for a baby. The significance of medical evidence which was available, or could easily have been made so, was also apparent in *R v Wycombe District Council ex p Holmes* (1990) 22 HLR 150, a case which demonstrates that the location of the accommodation may be significant as well as its condition. Here, the accommodation was satisfactory in itself but was situated just off a very steep hill. The applicant suffered from severe back problems which were exacerbated when she became pregnant and meant that during her pregnancy she was effectively housebound. It was held that on all the facts of the case no reasonable authority could have concluded that it was reasonable for the applicant to remain in her previous accommodation.

Affordability

The Homelessness (Suitability of Accommodation) Order 1996 specifies that in determining whether it would be (or would have been) reasonable for a person to continue to occupy accommodation, the housing authority *must* take into account the affordability of the accommodation for the applicant and, in particular, must take account of:

(a) the financial resources available to the applicant;
(b) the costs of the accommodation;
(c) maintenance payments (to a spouse or former spouse, or to or for the benefit of a child); and
(d) the applicant's other reasonable living expenses.

Tenant given notice of intention to recover possession

According to the CoG, a person who has been occupying accommodation as a tenant and who has received a valid notice to quit, or notice that the landlord requires possession of the accommodation, generally has the right to remain in occupation (and is not homeless therefore) until a warrant for possession is executed (DCLG, 2006a: 8.14). The exceptions are tenants with resident landlords and certain other tenants who are excluded from the notice and due process provisions of the Protection from Eviction Act 1977.

If the tenant has received a valid notice to quit but the landlord cannot be persuaded to allow the tenancy to continue or permit the tenant to remain for a reasonable period to enable alternative accommodation to be found, the authority must also consider whether it would be reasonable for the tenant to continue to occupy the accommodation once the notice has expired. Relevant factors may include the general cost to the housing authority and the likelihood that the landlord will actually proceed with possession proceedings.

In *R v London Borough of Croydon ex p Jarvis* (1993) 26 HLR 194 it was held to be reasonable for an applicant who had received notice to terminate her assured shorthold tenancy to remain in occupation until a possession order was made. In *R v London Borough of Newham ex p Ugbo* (1993) 26 HLR 263, the applicant (also an assured shorthold tenant who had been served with notice) ignored the authority's advice to wait for a court order. She sought judicial review of the decision that by vacating the property before a court order was made, she had made herself intentionally homeless. It was held that the authority should have considered whether it was reasonable for her continue to occupy until a possession order was made, given that while she had been resident in the premises – which were overcrowded – she had been subjected to harassment. Now, the CoG makes it clear that where the applicant is an assured shorthold tenant who has received proper notice in accordance with s. 21 of the Housing Act 1988, the housing authority is satisfied that the landlord intends to seek possession and there would be no defence to an application for a possession order, then it is 'unlikely to be reasonable' for the applicant to continue to occupy beyond the date given in the s. 21 notice, unless the housing authority is taking steps to persuade the landlord to withdraw the notice or allow the tenant to continue to occupy the accommodation for a reasonable period to provide an opportunity for alternative accommodation to be found (DCLG, 2006a: 8.32).

Former armed forces personnel required to leave service accommodation

So as to make clear the date on which the entitlement to occupy service accommodation ends and to enable housing authorities to determine whether applicants who are service personnel and who are approaching their date of discharge are homeless or threatened with homelessness, the Ministry of Defence issues a certificate six months before the discharge. The CoG advises that housing authorities should not insist upon a court order for possession in such circumstances to establish that entitlement to possession has ended and should use the six-month period of notice to ensure that service personnel receive 'timely and comprehensive advice' of the housing options available to them when they leave the armed forces (DCLG, 2006a: 8.33).

Type of accommodation

According to the CoG, it should not be regarded as reasonable for someone to continue to occupy on a long-term basis some types of 'crisis' accommodation (e.g. women's refuges, direct access hostels, and night shelters). This is an interesting point given the immediate judicial history to the 1996 Act. Section 175(1) obviously covers a person who is sleeping rough (i.e. one who is 'roofless'), but has also been held to extend to someone occupying temporary accommodation (i.e. one who is 'houseless'). In *R v Ealing London Borough ex p Sidhu* (1983) 2 HLR 45, the applicant was living in a women's refuge and in *R v Waveney District Council ex p Bowers* [1983] QB 238, an alcoholic who had suffered serious brain damage as a result of a road accident was staying at a night shelter, on a night-by-night basis, and could be turned away if the shelter was full. Each of the occupiers was a licensee which, strictly speaking, brought them within what is now s. 175(1)(b) of the 1996 Act. In both cases, however, the applicants were held to be homeless. In *Sidhu*, Hodgson J (reiterating the comments of the judge in the county court) said that it was important that 'refuges be seen as temporary crisis accommodation, and that women living in refuges were still homeless under the terms of the Act' (p. 53). To suggest otherwise would make it necessary for voluntary organisations to issue 28-day notices as soon as women came in, thereby bringing them under the threat of homelessness. That, he said, would be 'totally undesirable and would simply add stress to stress'. If living in crisis accommodation took women out of the homeless category, 'the protection afforded by the Act would be removed from a whole class of persons that it was set up to help and for whom it was extremely important'.

In *R v London Borough of Brent ex p Awua* [1995] 2 WLR 215, the local authority had housed the applicant in private sector leased (PSL) accommodation as a stage in performing its duty to secure her with long-term housing. The House of Lords approved the decision in *Bowers* but held that there was no wording in the Act from which it could be implied that 'accommodation' in what is now s. 175 was to be construed as a 'settled home', nor anything to suggest that a local authority could not reasonably expect a person to continue to occupy temporary accommodation under s. 175. 'Accommodation' meant a place it would be reasonable to occupy with regard to general local authority housing conditions and this was not qualified by any requirement of permanence. Lord Hoffmann, giving the leading speech in *Awua*, referred to *R v Hillingdon London Borough Council ex p Pulhofer* [1986] AC 484. Given their Lordships' rejection in that case of any implication as to physical suitability, it was highly improbable that they would have accepted an implication that the accommodation must in some sense be 'settled'. The concept of being 'threatened with homelessness' deals with precariousness of tenure and does not fit easily, he said, with an implication that a person whose tenure is more secure can be regarded as not merely threatened with homelessness but actually homeless. In *Awua*, the accommodation was temporary but it was, nonetheless, reasonable for Ms Awua to continue to occupy. By refusing the authority's offer of more permanent accommodation, she had made herself intentionally homeless from the PSL accommodation and was owed no further duty.

The temporary accommodation enjoyed by Ms Awua certainly lasted for longer than the stay of those accommodated in refuges and night shelters, but *Awua* does not appear to preclude the acceptance as homeless of some applicants other than the literally roofless. *Bowers* and *Sidhu* are still good law to the effect that short-term occupants in emergency-type accommodation are homeless. It should be borne in mind however that, as Lord Hoffmann explained (at p. 68):

> ... the extent to which the accommodation is physically suitable, so that it would be reasonable for a person to continue to occupy it, must be related to the time for which he has been there and is expected to stay. A local housing authority could take the view that a family like the Pulhofers, put into a single cramped and squalid bedroom, can be expected to make to do for a temporary period. On the other hand, there will come a time at which it is no longer reasonable to expect them to continue in such accommodation. At such a time they come back within the definition of homelessness.

Availability

By s. 176, 'accommodation shall be regarded as available for a person's occupation only if it is available for occupation by him together with:

(a) any other person who normally resides with him as a member of his family, or
(b) any other person who might reasonably be expected to reside with him.'

This requires consideration of two issues: (a) are there persons with whom it is reasonable for the applicant to reside?, and (b) was the accommodation available for the occupation of the applicant and those persons? In addressing the first question, the CoG states that the phrase 'a member of his/her family' in s. 176(a) will clearly cover established households where there is a close blood or marital relationship and cohabiting partners (including same-sex partners) (see *R v Peterborough City Council ex p Carr* (1990) 22 HLR 206). It advises that 'any other person' for the purposes of s. 176(b) will include those who may not have been living as part of the household at the time of the application, but whom it would be reasonable to expect to live with the applicant as part of his or her household. People in this second group could include children who are being fostered by the applicant or by a member of the applicant's family, or housekeepers, companions or carers for elderly or disabled people. It might also include family members who are not living with the applicant at the time of the application (perhaps because there is no accommodation in which they can live together) but who nonetheless might reasonably be expected to form part of it (DCLG, 2006a: 67).

Until the Housing Act 1996 came into force, the local authority could not take into account the existence of any housing abroad which the applicant was entitled to occupy in determining whether or not the applicant was homeless in this country. However, it *was* relevant in deciding whether or not he or she was intentionally homeless (see below). Now, as there is still accommodation available for their occupation elsewhere, only the general duty under s. 179 of providing advice and information may be owed to people who have left their parental or family homes overseas but have found nowhere to live in the UK. Generally, therefore, if they are to remain in the UK, they will have to find their own private sector accommodation or stay with friends or relatives. However, the legal availability, suitability and affordability of the overseas accommodation, family or other personal problems, ill-health, immigration restrictions and physical security are some of the factors which may be relevant as to whether it is reasonable for the applicant to return to occupy overseas accommodation. Clearly financial inability to travel to it will be significant; if the applicant cannot go to a property how can it be regarded as reasonable for him or her to occupy it? However, an authority will not be under a duty to investigate factors which are not self-evident, unless they are brought up by or on behalf of the applicant in the course of the authority's inquiry (*Begum (Nipa) v Tower Hamlets London Borough Council* [2000] 1 WLR 306).

Threatened with homelessness

Section 175(4) provides that 'a person is threatened with homelessness if it is likely that he will become homeless within 28 days'.

Where an applicant is eligible for assistance, threatened with home-lesness unintentionally and in priority need, the local authority must take reasonable steps to secure that accommodation does not cease to be available (s. 195(2)). The CoG states that 'timely advice and assistance' can some-times prevent the loss of existing accommodation. Where there is intention-ality, the local authority must simply provide such advice and assistance as it considers appropriate to prevent the loss of the applicant's existing occupation (s. 195(5)).

Priority need

General principles

When he introduced the Housing (Homeless Persons) Bill, Stephen Ross acknowledged that the 'first call on available resources in areas of housing difficulty should go to those most in need'. The Bill therefore included the notion of priority groups introduced by the 1974 circular. Ross recognised that 'if one is homeless the need for accommodation as just as great as if one is single and healthy as it is if one has children or if one is disabled' but that those who are single and healthy are in a better position to help themselves (HC Deb (1976–7) vol. 926, col. 903).

Authorities are generally either unable and/or unwilling to accept respon-sibility for applicants falling outside the priority need categories. An authority cannot fetter its discretion, however, by adopting a policy that people within specified groups, e.g. the single or childless homeless, should never be con-sidered as being in priority need.

By s. 189(1) of the Housing Act 1996 the following have a priority need for accommodation:

(a) a pregnant woman or a person with who she resides or might reason-ably be expected to reside;
(b) a person with whom dependent children reside, or might reasonably be expected to reside;
(c) a person who is vulnerable as a result of old age, mental illness or hand-icap or physical disability, or other special reason, or such persons with whom such persons reside or might reasonably be expected to reside;

(d) a person aged 16 or 17 who is not a 'relevant child' or a child in need to whom a local authority owes a duty under s. 20 of the Children Act 1989;

(e) a person aged under 21 who was (but is no longer) looked after, accommodated or fostered between the ages of 16 and 18 (except a person who is a 'relevant student');

(f) a person aged 21 or more who is vulnerable as a result of having been looked after, accommodated or fostered (except a person who is a 'relevant student');

(g) a person who is vulnerable as a result of having been a member of HM regular naval, military or air forces;

(h) a person who is vulnerable as a result of:

   (i)   having served a custodial sentence;
   (ii) having been committed for contempt of court or any other kindred offence; or
   (iii) having been remanded in custody.

(i) a person who is vulnerable as a result of ceasing to occupy accommodation because of violence from another person or threats of violence which are likely to be carried out;

(j) a person who is homeless or threatened with homelessness as a result of an emergency such as flood, fire or other disaster.

Pregnancy

The priority given to dependent children and pregnant women is, it has been said, an indication of 'the centrality of the family to housing' (Watson, 1986: 12) which is 'particularly important to the new right's ideology of the family' (Clapham *et al.*, 1990: 121). Pregnancy, however, proved the most controversial of the priority need groups when the Housing (Homeless Persons) Bill was being debated in the House of Commons. It was claimed that teenage girls would deliberately become pregnant to improve their chances of obtaining council housing and that, having been allocated housing, some women would then proceed to have an abortion. Some Conservative MPs predicted that giving housing rights to pregnant women would lead to a large increase in lone parent families.

Pregnancy qualifies as a priority irrespective of its length. The relevant time is when the authority makes its decision. 'A person with whom she resides or might reasonably be expected to reside' would obviously include the father of the unborn child even if he has never previously lived with the mother, unless she is aged under 16, in which case he might not 'reasonably be expected to reside with her' (Hoath, 1989: 82), given that sexual intercourse with a girl aged under 16 is a criminal offence (Sexual Offences Act 2003, ss. 9–24).

Dependent children

This is the most common category of priority need. The Act does not define 'dependent' but, according to the CoG, it means all children aged under 16 and those between 16 and 18 who are in, or are about to begin, full-time education or training or are otherwise unable to support themselves and who live at home (DCLG, 2006a: 10.7). A person aged 16 or 17 may not be financially dependent on his or her parents, but may be not be sufficiently mature to live independently. The children need not be the applicant's own children but may be, e.g. adopted children or foster children. In *Ekinci v Hackney London Borough Council* [2001] EWCA Civ 776, the Court of Appeal held that that the applicant's 17-year-old wife (who was in full-time education) was not a dependant child, on the basis that s. 189(1)(b) concerned a parent/child relationship and did not cover a dependent spouse. The applicant's wife was capable of being a dependent child in relation to her parents but not her husband.

The priority is accorded to the parents or those caring for dependent children; dependent children are not classified as in priority need in their own right, nor will they qualify as vulnerable merely because of their youth or because of any disability. To hold otherwise would allow for the circumvention of the intentional homelessness provisions so that they would have to practical application to households with dependent children. Dependent children rely on their parents or those looking after them to decide where they are to live. Further, the offer of accommodation can only sensibly be made to those in charge of them. Thus, while a child is entitled to apply under the Act, 'the duty to make an offer of accommodation is owed only to those who are capable of understanding and responding to such an offer and if they accept it to undertake the responsibilities that will be involved' (*R v Oldham Metropoliton Borough Council ex p Garlick; R v Bexley London Borough Council ex p Bentum; R v Tower Hamlets London Borough Council ex p Begum (Ferdous)* [1993] AC 509).[1] Whether a person has sufficient mental capacity to be an 'applicant' is a matter for the authority's discretion, challengeable by judicial review on grounds of *Wednesbury* unreasonableness.

Where the child's parents are living apart, court orders are a starting point from which to determine residence and dependency. However, in many cases the parents reach agreement between themselves as to how the child is to be cared for and a court order will not be made or required. Thus, where children are in fact residing with a parent, the grant of a residence order is irrelevant (*R v Ealing London Borough Council ex p Sidhu* (1981–2) 2 HLR 45). Section 189(1)(b) does not require that the child be 'wholly and exclusively' dependant on the applicant, nor does it refer to 'whole and exclusive' or 'full-time' residence, but only in exceptional cases will a child have two

---

1   For a critical analysis, see Loveland (1996).

residences enabling both parents to fall within the definition of priority need (*R v Port Talbot Borough Council ex p McCarthy* (1991) 23 HLR 207).

Vulnerability

Vulnerability is one of the most contentious areas of the law on homelessness with many county court appeals concerning 'single people with mental health problems, often former asylum-seekers suffering from post-traumatic stress disorder and depression' (Dymond, 2005: 26). Therefore, those who are vulnerable 'have, for the most part, no direct relationship with the labour market' and 'can be defined as deserving of assistance, in that the provision of state help would not be expected to inhibit the qualities of initiative and self-reliance which the undeserving homeless (those who could, theoretically compete in the labour market and provide for themselves) are deemed to lack' (Clapham *et al.*, 1990: 121).

In *R v Camden London Borough Council ex parte Pereira* (1998) 31 HLR 317, it was established that the test for the authority to apply was whether, when homeless, the applicant will be 'less able to fend for himself than an ordinary homeless person so that injury or detriment to him would have resulted when a less vulnerable man would be able to cope without harmful effect'. However, it was made clear in *Osmani v Camden London Borough Council* [2005] HLR 22 that the *Pereira* test was merely a judicial guide to the interpretation and application of s. 189(1)(c) and should not be used as if it were a statutory formulation. The Court of Appeal emphasised that a decision as to vulnerability is primarily a matter for the authority and that the courts should rarely intervene. A local housing authority has to apply s. 189(1)(c) in its broad and immediate statutory context. This involves a matter of 'priority' as between homeless persons, and a scheme of social welfare conferring benefits at public expense on grounds of public policy on those who are identified as entitled to such priority. Applicants will be vulnerable only if they have a less than normal ability to fend for themselves such that they would suffer more harm than would an 'ordinary' homeless persons. The assessment of an applicant's ability to cope is a composite one taking all the circumstances into account. Vulnerability must be assessed on the assumption that applicants have or would become street homeless, not on their ability to fend for themselves while they were still housed.

Old age

Old age is not, by itself, sufficient for the applicant to be regarded as vulnerable. However, the CoG suggests that authorities should look at whether age has made it hard for the applicant to fend for himself or herself, and that all applications from people over 60 should be considered carefully, especially where the applicant is leaving tied accommodation (DCLG, 2006a: 10.15). A lesser age may be one factor in a number which make up vulnerability as a result of special reason (*R v Waveney District Council ex p Bowers* [1983] QB 238).

Mental illness or learning disability or physical disability

The CoG advises that in considering whether such applicants are vulnerable authorities will need to take account of all relevant factors including:

(a) the nature and extent of the illness and/or disability which may render the applicant vulnerable;

(b) the relationship between the illness and/or disability and the individual's housing difficulties; and

(c) the relationship between the illness and/or disability and other factors such as drug/alcohol misuse, offending behaviour, challenging behaviours, age and personality disorder.

The CoG notes that people discharged from psychiatric hospitals and local authority hostels for people with mental health problems are likely to be vulnerable (DCLG, 2006a: 10.18). A distinction may be drawn between psychotic illness and learning disability. The latter will not necessarily amount to vulnerability (*R v Bath City Council ex p Sangermano* (1984) 17 HLR 94). Whether epilepsy renders a person vulnerable is a question of fact and degree and the position of any particular sufferer may need to be reassessed from time to time (*R v Sheffield City Council ex p Leek* (1994) 26 HLR 669). Vulnerability will be established if grand mal attacks take place with intense regularity (*R v Wandsworth London Borough Council ex p Banbury* (1987) 19 HLR 76; *R v Reigate and Banstead Borough Council ex p Di Dominico* (1988) 20 HLR 153; *R v Lambeth London Borough Council ex p Carroll* (1988) 20 HLR 142).

Other special reason

The phrase 'other special reason' should not be construed using the eiusdem generis rule. The word 'vulnerable' relates to a need for housing and is not limited to physical or mental conditions suggested by the other categories. The word 'special' points to the fact that the circumstances of the applicant are particularly serious and different from those of other homeless persons. In *R v Kensington and Chelsea Royal London Borough Council ex p Kihara* (1996) 29 HLR 147 (decided after in-country asylum seekers had been stripped of their entitlement to welfare benefits but before the eligibility provisions of the Housing Act 1996 came into force), it was held that the applicants were in priority need for some 'other special reason'. Their financial impecuniosity did not amount to a special reason on its own but should be considered in the light of other circumstances, i.e. the lack of access to income or capital, the absence of friends and family in the UK and an inability to speak English, which stood them apart from most homeless persons.

The CoG states that chronically sick people, including those with AIDS and HIV-related illnesses, may be vulnerable not only because their illness has progressed to the point of physical or mental disability but because the manifestations or effects of their illness, or common attitudes to it, make it very difficult for them the find stable or suitable accommodation (DCLG, 2006a: 10.32).[2]

The likelihood of relapse into drug addiction may amount to a special reason making an applicant vulnerable for the purposes of s. 189(1)(c). In *Crossley v Westminster City Council* [2006] EWCA Civ 140, the appellant was a recovering drug addict who had been in care from the ages of three to 17 and had been addicted to drugs from the age of 13. His drug addiction had affected his mental health, causing him to self-harm and to suffer from depression as well as hepatitis C. Having lived on the streets after leaving care he applied to the authority for accommodation as a homeless person. The Court of Appeal held that the authority should reconsider its decision that he was not in priority need as it had overlooked the evidence about the appellant's history of relapse into substance abuse and the conclusions of his support workers that he would be unlikely to remain free from drugs if he remained homeless.

The CoG acknowledges that there are many young homeless people who fall outside the categories for whom specific provision is made. It states that 'most young people can expect a degree of support from families, friends or an institution (e.g. a college or university) with the practicalities and costs of finding, establishing and managing a home for the first time'. There are others, however, 'who are forced to leave the parental home or who cannot remain there because they are being subject to violence or sexual abuse' and who will therefore 'lack this back-up network and be less able ... to establish and maintain a home for themselves' (see *Kelly v Monklands District Council* 1986 SLT 165 in which a homeless girl aged 16 with no assets or income had left home because of violence). Furthermore, a young person on the streets may be at risk of abuse or prostitution.

An earlier version of the CoG recognised that childless adults may be vulnerable if they have suffered or been threatened with harassment or violence on account of their gender, race, colour, ethnic or national origin, or religion. The 2006 version directs authorities to consider whether applicants who have fled their home because of non-violent forms of harassment are vulnerable as a result. It advises that careful consideration should be given to applicants who may be at risk of witness intimidation.

The CoG states that former asylum seekers who have been granted refugee status or exceptional leave to remain, humanitarian protection, or discretionary leave will be eligible for homelessness assistance and may be

---

2   See Cowan (1995).

at risk of homelessness as a result of having to leave accommodation which has been provided for them, by e.g. the National Asylum Support Service, while a decision was being reached on their asylum claim. It states that they may well have experienced persecution or trauma in their country of origin or severe hardship in their efforts to reach the UK and may be vulnerable as a result (DCLG, 2006a: 10.35).

People aged 21 or over who have been looked after, accommodated or fostered

Unless he or she is a 'relevant student', a person aged 21 or over who is vulnerable as a result of having been 'looked after, accommodated or fostered' has a priority need. By s. 24 of the Children Act 1989, the terms 'looked after, accommodated or fostered' include any person who has been:

(a) looked after by a local authority (i.e. has been subject to a care order or accommodated under a voluntary agreement);
(b) accommodated by or on behalf of a voluntary organisation;
(c) accommodated in a private children's home;
(d) accommodated for a consecutive period of at least three months:
  (i) by a health authority, special health authority, primary care trust or local education authority; or
  (ii) in any care home or independent hospital or in any accommodation provided by an NHS trust; or
(e) privately fostered.

A 'relevant student' means a care leaver aged under 24 who is in full-time further or higher education and whose term-time accommodation is not available during a vacation. Where a social services authority is satisfied that a person is a relevant student and needs accommodation during a vacation, it must provide accommodation or the means to enable it to be secured (Children Act 1989, s. 24B(5)).

In determining whether there is vulnerability, the CoG suggests that the housing authority may wish to consider:

(a) the length of time for which the applicant was looked after, accommodated or fostered;
(b) the reasons why the applicant was looked after, accommodated or fostered;
(c) the length of time since the applicant was looked after, accommodated or fostered, and whether the applicant had been able to obtain and/or maintain accommodation during any of that period;

(d) whether the applicant has any existing support networks, particularly including family friends or mentor.

Former members of the armed forces

The CoG suggests that in considering whether former members are vulnerable as a result of their time spent in the forces, a housing authority may wish to take into account:

(a) the length of time the applicant spent in the armed forces (although it should not assume that vulnerability could not occur as a result of a short period of service);
(b) the type of service in which the applicant was engaged (those on active service might find it more difficult to cope with civilian life);
(c) whether the applicant spent any time in a military hospital (which could be indicative of a serious health problem or of post-traumatic stress);
(d) whether HM Forces' medical and welfare advisers have judged the applicant to be particularly vulnerable and have issued a summary of the circumstances which caused the vulnerability;
(e) the length of time since the applicant left the armed forces, and whether her or she had been able to obtain and/or maintain accommodation during that time;
(f) whether the applicant has any existing support networks, particularly by way of family and friends.

Having been in custody or detention

This category applies to applicants who are vulnerable as a result of having:

(a) served a custodial sentence within the meaning if s. 76 of the Powers of Criminal Courts (Sentences) Act 2000;
(b) been committed for contempt of court or any other kindred offence; or
(c) been remanded in or committed to custody by an order of the court, or to housing authority accommodation under the Children and Young Persons Act 1969 and placed and kept in secure accommodation, or to hospital under the Mental Health Act 1993.

The CoG suggests that, in reaching its decision as to vulnerability, the housing authority may wish to take into account:

(a) the length of time the applicant served in custody or detention (although it should not be assumed that vulnerability could result from a short period therein);

(b) whether the applicant is subject to supervision from a criminal justice agency, e.g. the Probation Service or the Youth Offending Team or the Drug Intervention Programme;

(c) the length of time since the applicant was released from custody or detention, and the extent to which whether the applicant had been able to obtain and/or maintain accommodation during that time;

(d) whether the applicant has any existing support networks, e.g. family or friends, and how much of a positive influence they are likely to be in the applicant's life.

Violence

The CoG suggests that in considering vulnerability in this regard, a housing authority may wish to take into account:

(a) the nature of the violence or threats of violence (there may have been a single but significant incident or a number of incidents over an extended period of time which have a cumulative effect);

(b) the impact and likely effect of the violence or threats of violence on the applicant's current and future well-being;

(c) whether the applicant has any existing support networks, particularly by way of family and friends.

Young people

In the past, the emphasis placed by successive governments on the responsibility of the state towards families has given rise to questions about the legitimacy of young people wishing to form independent households, and to obtain secure housing in the social sector if they cannot afford to buy or rent in the private market. As Anderson explains, young single people seem to have been viewed as 'individuals who are not yet families' who do not require the same security and independence in their housing as family households' (Anderson, 1999: 38). Such an attitude, she says, results in the assumption that young people who do not live with their parents are adequately housed in temporary, shared accommodation. She also points out that if young people on low incomes are to achieve independent living as part of their transition to adulthood, access to secure, affordable accommodation must be a realistic prospect. She explains that 'transitional' accommodation such as foyers and other supported housing can play a valuable role in times of crisis and in preparing young people for independent housing, but eventually many young people will look to social rented housing as a long-term option, increasingly so as access to the private rented sector is curtailed through housing benefit restrictions (ibid.: 47).

Until recently, the law focused on homeless young people in the context of 'other special reason' and the CoG recognised that they may be at risk in a variety of ways, e.g. violence or sexual abuse from a person with whom they are associated, or from drug or alcohol abuse or prostitution. The CoG suggested that certain groups of young people will be less able to fend for themselves: those leaving or who have been in local authority care, young offenders (including those discharged from young offender institutions), those who have been physically or sexually abused, those with learning disabilities, those who have been the subject of statements of special educational need, those who lack family contact and support. It highlighted the responsibilities of social services departments under ss. 20 and 27 of the Children Act 1989 in providing accommodation for certain children. However, the priority need categories were extended by the Homelessness (Priority Need for Accommodation) (England) Order 2002 and now include (subject to certain exceptions) a person aged 16 or 17. Those who are over this age but are vulnerable and have been looked after, accommodated or fostered are considered above.

All 16 and 17-year-old homeless applicants, irrespective of vulnerability, have a priority need for accommodation except those who are 'relevant children' or children in need who are owed a duty under s. 20 of the 1989 Act, in which case the responsibility for providing suitable accommodation will rest with the children's service authorities. A person is a relevant child in two situations. The first is where he or she is aged 16 or 17 and has been looked after by a local authority for at least 13 weeks since the age of 14 and at some time while 16 or 17 but is not currently being looked after. The second is where he or she would have been looked after by the local authority but for the fact that on his or her sixteenth birthday, he or she was detained through the criminal justice system, or in hospital, or was at home on a family placement which has broken down (Children Act 1989, s 23A; Children (Leaving Care) Regulations 2001, reg. 4). Section 20(1) of the Children Act 1989 requires social services authorities to provide accommodation for 'children in need' within their areas who appear to require accommodation because no one has parental responsibility for them, or they are lost or have been abandoned, or whoever has been caring from them (whether or not permanently and for whatever reason) is prevented from providing suitable accommodation and care. Subsection (3) obliges them to house children over the age of 16 whose welfare will otherwise be 'seriously prejudiced'.

In *Robinson v Hammersmith and Fulham London Borough Council* [2006] EWCA Civ 1122, the 17-year-old applicant presented herself to the local housing authority as homeless, having been asked by her mother to leave the family home. The authority sought to reconcile them, but having initially agreed to mediation, the mother then changed her mind. The authority's letter, informing the applicant that she was not in priority need, arrived on her eighteenth birthday. The decision was upheld on review.

The Court of Appeal held that the original decision was unlawful; the applicant was aged under 18 when the decision was taken, and therefore in priority need. The authority could not base its decision on the fact that she was aged so nearly 18 that the difference should be ignored. It is unlawful for an authority to postpone making a decision even for a short period on the basis that, by postponing the decision, the child will have reached the age of 18 before it is taken. The mediation process is wholly independent of the inquiry process, and the authority has no power to defer making inquiries on the ground that there is a pending mediation. Finally, it was wrong for an authority to persuade a family into mediation while a child was 17 and then use the time that the mediation would take to deprive the child of a right that he or she would have had without mediation.

Emergency

The 'emergency' cases fall into the 'unforeseen homelessness' situation, reminiscent of the National Assistance Act 1948. If not actually flood or fire, the emergency must be of a similar nature and does not include unlawful eviction. Emergencies which can give rise to priority need are not confined to those amounting to 'force majeure' but embrace all emergencies consisting of physical damage, even fires or floods deliberately or accidentally caused by human beings (*R v Bristol City Council ex p Bradic* (1995) 27 HLR 584). In *Higgs v Brighton and Hove City Council* [2003] EWCA Civ 895, the applicant had been living in a caravan placed unlawfully on local authority land. Returning one day from a walk, he found the caravan had vanished without trace. He argued that the disappearance of his caravan constituted an 'emergency' for the purposes of s. 189(1)(d) and that he therefore had a priority need for accommodation. The Court of Appeal held that although the sudden and completely unexpected loss of the applicant's home in circumstances wholly outside his control represented an emergency similar to those expressly referred to in s. 189(1)(d), his homelessness had resulted not from the disappearance of his caravan but from the circumstances which had led him to live in a caravan which he had had no right to park anywhere. As such, he had been homeless before the caravan's disappearance and, for the purposes of s. 189(1)(d), had not become so 'as a result of' its disappearance.

Intentionality

General principles

The Housing (Homeless Persons) Bill 1977, as originally drafted, contained no provision for intentionality but the local authority lobby forced through amendments, fearing that people would jump the waiting list queue for council housing by making themselves deliberately homeless. The Bill was attacked as 'a charter for scroungers and scrimshankers' (HC Deb (1976–7) vol. 926, col. 929), a 'charter for queue jumpers' (ibid.) and 'a charter for the rent-dodger, for the scrounger and for the encouragement of the homeleaver'

(HC Deb (1976–7) vol. 926, col. 972). Most homelessness cases have involved the issue of intentionality. An application cannot be made by minors where there is intentionality on the part of their parents (*R v Oldham Metropoliton Borough Council ex p Garlick*; *R v Bexley London Borough Council ex p Bentum*; *R v Tower Hamlets London Borough Council ex p Begum (Ferdous)* [1993] AC 509.

The two ways in which a person can become homeless or threatened with homelessness intentionally are by (a) deliberate acts or failures to act (s. 191(1)); or (b) collusion (s. 191(3)). Section 196 deals with the issue of intentionality when a person is 'threatened with homelessness'.

Deliberate acts or failures to act

A person becomes homeless intentionally 'if he deliberately does or fails to do anything in consequence of which he ceases to occupy accommodation which is available for his occupation and which it would have been reasonable for him to continue to occupy' (s. 191(1)). The elements of the subsection are:

(a) the applicant must deliberately have done something or failed to do something;
(b) the loss of accommodation must be in consequence of the act or omission;
(c) there must be a cessation of occupation as distinct from a failure to take up accommodation;
(d) the accommodation must have been available for the occupation of the homeless person; and
(e) it must have been reasonable for the homeless person to continue to occupy the accommodation.

The onus is on the local authority to satisfy itself of intentionality. It is not for applicants to prove that they are unintentionally homeless (*R v Woodspring District Council ex p Walters* (1984) 16 HLR 73). The enquiries which the authority makes need not be detailed 'CID-type' enquiries (*Lally v Royal Borough of Kensington and Chelsea*, *The Times*, 27 March 1980) and the court should intervene 'only if no reasonable authority could have been satisfied on the basis of the enquiries made' (*R v Royal Borough of Kensington and Chelsea ex p Bayani* (1990) 22 HLR 406).

Whose act or omission resultsf in intentional homelessness?

The 'person' referred to in s. 191(1) is the applicant. This means that a person who is found to be intentionally homeless does not lose all chance of being rehoused under the Act because the application can then be made by someone who resides or might reasonably be expected to reside with the applicant and who is unintentionally homeless. The issue first arose in *R v North Devon*

District Council ex p Lewis [1981] 1 WLR 328 in which a man had become intentionally homeless by leaving his job and thereby losing his tied accommodation. The woman with whom he was living then applied in her own name. The court held that her case was not governed by the decision on his application and that she was entitled to separate consideration. However, her acquiescence in his decision to leave his job meant that she, by association, had committed an act of intentionality. *Lewis* (and the concept of 'infectious intentionality' to which it gave rise) has been applied in a number of cases, among them *R v West Dorset District Council ex p Phillips* (1984) 17 HLR 336 in which the applicant's husband had spent the rent money on drink, resulting in the family's eviction. It was held that the applicant was entitled to be found unintentionally homeless. She had not acquiesced in her husband's behaviour, but had lost her temper and attacked him when she learned of the debt. Further, where the debt is so great by the time the applicant finds out about it that it is too late to do anything, mere knowledge of the debt cannot be said to amount to acquiescence (*R v East Northamptonshire District Council ex p Spruce* (1988) 20 HLR 508) unless the applicant is aware of the commitments and has a sound grasp of the financial situation (*R v London Borough of Barnet ex p O'Connor* (1990) 22 HLR 486). In *R v Cardiff City Council ex p John* (1982) 9 HLR 55, nuisance and annoyance by a man with whom the tenant had lived for some time resulted in the tenant's eviction, even though it occurred only when she was out of the flat, he was both younger and considerably larger than her, and she was unable to control his behaviour. She was held to have acquiesced in his conduct by failing to evict him. The CoG now recommends however that in considering whether the applicant has acquiesced in certain behaviour, the housing authority should take into account whether he or she could reasonably be expected to have done so because of fear of actual or probable violence (DCLG, 2006a: 11.9). 'Infectious intentionality' is not confined to cohabitants but may extend to conduct by lodgers or children whom the tenant has failed to control (*Smith v Bristol City Council* [1981] LAG Bull 287; *Devonport v Salford City Council* (1983) 8 HLR 54; *R v Rochester upon Medway City Council ex p Williams* [1994] EGCS 35).

What is a 'deliberate' act or omission?

The CoG (DCLG, 2006a: 11.17) states that, in general, an act or omission should not be considered as deliberate where:

(a) it consists of non-payment of rent which was the result of housing benefit delays, or financial difficulties beyond the applicant's control;
(b) the authority has reason to believe that the applicant is incapable of managing his/her own affairs, e.g. on account of age, mental illness or disability;

(c) it was the result of limited mental capacity, or a temporary aberration or aberrations caused by mental illness, frailty, or an assessed substance abuse problem;

(d) it was made when the applicant was under duress;

(e) homelessness was the result of imprudence or lack of foresight on the applicant's part but the act or omission was in good faith.

Acts or omissions which may be regarded as deliberate could include situations in which someone:

(a) chooses to sell his/her home in circumstances where there is no risk of losing it; or

(b) has lost his or her home because of wilful and persistent refusal to pay rent or mortgage instalments, when he had the money to do so and could be said to have neglected his/her affairs having disregarded advice from qualified persons;

(c) voluntarily surrenders adequate accommodation in this country or abroad which it would have been reasonable for the applicant to continue to occupy (see *R v London Borough of Ealing ex p Sukhija* (1994) 26 HLR 726);

(d) is evicted because of anti-social behaviour such as nuisance to neighbours, harassment, etc.; or

(e) is evicted because of violence or threats of violence by them towards another person;

(f) leaves a job with tied accommodation and the circumstances indicate that it would have been reasonable to continue in the employment and reasonable to continue to occupy the accommodation;

(g) chooses to sell his/her home in circumstances where he/she is under no risk of losing it; or

(h) has lost his/her home because of wilful and persistent refusal to pay rent or mortgage instalments, when he/she had the money to do so;

Some of these 'grounds' of intentionality are considered further below.

Rent and mortgage arrears

The CoG advises that an applicant's actions would not amount to intentional homelessness where he or she has lost his or her home, or was obliged to sell it, because of rent or mortgage arrears arising from significant financial difficulties (e.g. because he/she became unemployed or ill or suffered greatly reduced earnings or family breakdown) and genuinely could not keep up rent payments or loan repayments even after claiming benefits, and no further financial help is available. When approaching the question of arrears, the authority must enquire into why the arrears have arisen and whether or not there has been 'wilful default' (*R v Wyre Borough Council ex p Joyce* (1983) 11 HLR 73). If the applicant has taken on financial commitments knowing full well that there is little prospect of keeping up the necessary payments, it will go beyond the stage of honest incompetence and amount to intentionality (*R v Wandsworth London Borough Council ex p Onwudiwe* (1993) 26 HLR 302). However, it cannot be reasonable to continue to occupy accommodation if the applicants can no longer pay the rent or make the mortgage payments without depriving themselves of the ordinary necessities of life, such as food, clothing, heat and transport (*R v London Borough Hillingdon ex p Tinn* (1988) 20 HLR 305). A conscious decision to devote what resources the applicant has to his or her children, rather than the payment of rent, is not to be treated automatically as a 'deliberate' act, and inability to pay is a relevant matter in deciding whether a failure to pay is 'deliberate' (*R v Wandsworth London Borough Council ex p Hawthorne* [1994] 1 WLR 1442). What amounts to a necessity is a matter for the authority. In *R v Brent London Borough Council ex p Baruwa* (1997) 29 HLR 915, the Court of Appeal upheld the local authority's decision that expenditure on university fees and childcare costs were not necessities.

Failure to pursue other remedies

Two common examples of omission which are alleged to amount to intentional homelessness are:

(a) failure of an illegally evicted private tenant to take action against the landlord to gain entry; and
(b) failure by a spouse or cohabitee to use remedies offered by family law in order to secure peaceful occupation of the home. In *R v Wandsworth London Borough Council ex p Nimako-Boateng* (1984) 11 HLR 95, it was suggested that there might be circumstances where it would be reasonable for a woman to seek to remain in occupation by obtaining a court order to restrain her partner. However, failure to take such proceedings should not be regarded as 'deliberate' if they are unlikely to protect the applicant sufficiently to enable her to return to the former matrimonial home (*Charles v Charles* [1984] LAG Bull 81).

Loss of tied accommodation

Departure from a person's job may result in the loss of tied accommodation. There will be intentional homelessness only if there is a sufficient link, or proximity, between the act which caused the loss of the job, and the loss of the accommodation (*R v Thanet District Council ex p Reeve, The Times,* 25 November 1981). Thus, a direct act, e.g. theft from an employer, which could reasonably be foreseen to lead to loss of job and accommodation, may amount to intentional homelessness. Someone who loses his job for incompetence, which will usually be a course of conduct spread over a period of time, cannot be said to be carrying out a deliberate act. The necessary intention or state of mind is absent unless proof exists that a course of incompetent conduct had been adopted in order to provoke dismissal. The fact that someone appears to have resigned from his or her job voluntarily does not necessarily indicate intentional homelessness; it may be a case of constructive dismissal.

Was an act or omission in good faith?

An act or omission in good faith on the part of the person unaware of any relevant fact is not to be treated as deliberate (s. 191(2)). Examples of acts or omissions which could be made in good faith might include situations where an owner occupier, faced with foreclosure or possession proceedings to which there is no defence, sells before the lender recovers possession or surrenders the property to the lender, or where a tenant, faced with possession proceedings to which there is no defence and the granting of a possession order would be mandatory, surrenders the property to the landlord. However, in *R v Leeds City Council ex p Adamiec* (1991) 24 HLR 138, a sale of their home by the applicants before the building society sought repossession was upheld as intentional, even though in the long run the applicant could probably not have afforded to continue living in the house, having been unable to work following an industrial accident.

In *R v Exeter City Council ex p Tranckle* (1994) 26 HLR 244, the applicant and her husband found a pub to run. The landlord had recently died, the pub was in poor condition and no accounts were available but the brewery assured the couple that it could be turned into a profitable venture. The applicant's husband became the tenant and they obtained a business loan secured on their house. The business failed and the couple fell into arrears with their loans. They separated and the brewery obtained a possession order in respect of the pub. At the same time the house was also being repossessed. The local authority decided that the applicant was intentionally homeless because of her decision to secure a loan on her house without properly assessing the business's profitability. The Court of Appeal held that the applicant had not become homeless intentionally. Although she had entered into imprudent financial arrangements, she had done so in good faith, unaware of a relevant fact, i.e. that the pub's prospects of success were very slender indeed.

If it is established that the applicant was ignorant of a relevant fact, the authority must not ask whether that ignorance was unreasonable but whether it was in good faith. There is a distinction here between honest blundering and dishonesty; a fraudulent act can never be in good faith. In *R v London Borough of Barnet ex p Rughooputh* (1993) 25 HLR 607, the applicant, who owned a flat, was persuaded to buy a grocery store. She obtained a mortgage for £46,000, having convinced the building society that she was working although she was actually unemployed. When the business failed, the building society repossessed her flat and she applied to local authority for housing. The court upheld the authority's decision that she was intentionally homeless, having obtained the mortgage by giving false information. In *F v Birmingham City Council* [2006] EWCA Civ 1427, a finding of intentional homelessness was upheld where the applicant had given up her council tenancy (ignoring advice from her social worker that in doing so she risked being intentionally homeless) and taken privately rented accommodation without considering whether she would be able to afford to pay the rent. May LJ explained that:

> the statutory dividing line comes not at the point where the applicant's ignorance of a relevant fact was due to his own unreasonable conduct but at the point where, for example, by shutting his eyes to the obvious he can be said not to have acted in good faith. Wilful ignorance ... must fail the 'good faith test' ... If the prospect of future housing rests on little more than a wing and a prayer, it cannot be said that an original decision-maker or a review panel falls into legal error by failing to invoke s. 191(2) in favour of the applicant.
>
> (At para. 17.)

Causation and the chain of intentionality

In *R v Hammersmith & Fulham London Borough Council ex p P* (1989) 22 HLR 2, Schiemann J described causation as 'a notorious minefield in jurisprudence and philosophy'. As Lord Fraser explained in *Din v Wandsworth London Borough Council* [1981] 3 All ER 881 (at p. 890), the fundamental principle is that there must be a 'continuing causal connection between the deliberate act [or omission] in consequence of which homelessness resulted ...'. The present homelessness must be a consequence of a past act or omission. Earlier versions of the CoG pointed out that, in assessing whether someone has become intentionally homeless, 'it is open to the authority to look beyond the most immediate cause of that homelessness' and a particularly controversial matter has been just how far back an authority can look for the original cause of the homelessness. If there is a *novus actus* which breaks the chain of causation, the original act or omission which gave rise to intentional homelessness from previous accommodation cannot be regarded as the effective cause of the applicant's present homelessness or being threatened with homelessness. The *novus actus* is most likely to consist of a period, between the act of intentionality and the application, spent in other accommodation.

In *De Falco v Crawley Borough Council* [1980] QB 460, the De Falcos had left Naples to come to England to work. They stayed with two sets of relatives while they looked for (and found) jobs. When the second relative eventually asked them to leave, they approached Crawley BC for assistance. The housing authority decided they were intentionally homeless because they had come to England without having ensured that they had permanent accommodation to come to.

In *Dyson v Kerrier District Council* [1980] 1 WLR 1205, Ms Dyson shared a council flat with her sister in Huntingdon. Soon after the birth of Ms Dyson's baby, her sister moved to Cornwall. It was not long before Ms Dyson followed her, surrendering the tenancy of her council flat in order to take on what she knew to be an insecure 'winter let' of private sector accommodation next door to her sister. Before her landlord recovered possession, she applied to Kerrier District Council for assistance. After her eviction, the council decided that she was homeless intentionally as she had voluntarily terminated the tenancy of her council flat in Huntingdon. The Court of Appeal dismissed her argument that the housing authority was only entitled to have regard to acts or omissions immediately preceding her homelessness and was not entitled, therefore, to have regard to what had happened in Huntingdon.

In *Din v Wandsworth London Borough Council* [1983] AC 657, the applicants left secure accommodation in Wandsworth despite advice from the local housing aid centre that they should stay where they were as they had a possible defence to a claim by their landlord for possession. They moved in with a relative in Uxbridge but, after a short time, he asked them to leave and Mr Din approached Wandsworth London Borough Council for assistance. The House of Lords upheld the authority's decision that he was intentionally homeless because he had voluntarily terminated his tenancy. It made no difference that by the time of the application the family would have been homeless in any event. Their Lordships explained that, first, '... there must be a continuing causal connection between the deliberate act in consequence of which homelessness resulted and the homelessness existing at the date of the inquiry' and secondly that the continuation might be broken by 'settled', but not by 'temporary, accommodation occupied by the applicant in the intervening period' (at pp. 672, 688).

Lambert v Ealing London Borough Council [1982] 2 All ER 394 concerned M Lambert ('a real Frenchman', in the words of Lord Denning MR, with 'three charming daughters'). Having sold his business in Grenoble because of financial problems, he and his daughters came to England in a motor caravan. He arranged their education and put his name on the council waiting list. He then entered into a series of 'holiday' letting agreements. During this period he obtained a job as a van driver for a patisserie. When his rental agreements expired he tried, unsuccessfully, to obtain alternative accommodation. He then applied to Ealing Borough Council which decided that he had become intentionally homeless. Following *De Falco* and *Dyson*, the Court of Appeal upheld the authority's decision, on the ground that:

> When M Lambert sold up and left France, he became homeless. He was intentionally homeless because he had given up his home in France.

That intentional homelessness was the effective cause of his becoming homeless in England. The intervening 18 months do not alter the fact that he was intentionally homeless.

This line of authority appeared to suggest that the chain of causation could be broken only by a period spent in 'settled' accommodation. However, in *R v London Borough of Brent ex p Awua* [1995] 2 WLR 215, Lord Hoffmann doubted whether 'the occupation of a settled residence' was the 'sole and exclusive method by which the causal link can be broken' and in *R v Harrow London Borough Council ex p Fahia* (1997) 29 HLR 974, it was held by the Court of Appeal (albeit left open on subsequent appeal to the House of Lords) that, as Lord Hoffmann had predicted, the chain of causation could be broken other than by the obtaining of intervening settled accommodation.

Availability

The accommodation which has been lost must have been 'available for the applicant's occupation' (s. 191(1)). Availability has already been considered above in relation to homelessness. In *Re Islam* [1983] 1 AC 688 (a case on intentionality), the applicant had spent 16 years living and working in Uxbridge. He returned to Bangladesh to marry and went back to visit his wife on five subsequent occasions, resulting in the birth of four children. While they waited for clearance to join him in the UK, his wife and children lived with his parents in Bangladesh. He lived in a rented room which he shared with another man. He had never lived with his family. In the Court of Appeal, Lord Denning MR held that Mr Islam had been in notional occupation, through his wife and children, of the family home in Bangladesh. When they left the family home to join him in the UK, he, albeit notionally, had also left and rendered himself (and them) intentionally homeless. Sir Denys Buckley took the view that either (a) the accommodation in Uxbridge and Bangladesh could together constitute the available accommodation, or (b) by bringing his family over to the UK, Mr Islam had become intentionally homeless from his rented room. The House of Lords disagreed and allowed Mr Islam's appeal. Mr Islam had never occupied accommodation which was 'available' within the meaning of what is now s. 191(1). The shared room in this country was clearly not 'available', and there was no evidence that the accommodation in Bangladesh was ever available to the applicant himself, nor that he was ever in occupation of it. Further, rooms in two separate continents could not be combined to make up 'available accommodation'.

Was it reasonable to continue to occupy the accommodation?

Reasonableness has already been considered above in relation to 'homelessness'.

Collusion

Where a person enters into an arrangement which requires him or her leave accommodation which it would have been reasonable to continue to occupy, and the purpose of the arrangement is to enable that person to become entitled to assistance under Part VII, he or she will be treated as becoming homeless intentionally unless another 'good reason' for the homelessness exists (s. 191(3)). Collusion is not confined to arrangements between friends and relatives but can also occur between landlords and tenants. The CoG advises authorities that they should not rely merely on hearsay or unfounded suspicions in satisfying themselves that it exists. Examples of other 'good reasons' for the applicant's homelessness would include 'overcrowding or an obvious relationship breakdown between the applicant and his or her host or landlord' (DCLG, 2006a: 11.28).

Chapter 11

Homelessness: duties of local authorities, local connection and the right to a review

Duty to formulate a homelessness strategy

For the first time, the Homelessness Act 2002 has attempted to engender a proactive approach among local authorities towards homelessness, with s. 1 obliging them to carry out a homelessness review of their district and to formulate and publish a homelessness strategy based on the results of that review. The purposes of the review are:

(a) to prevent homelessness in the authority's district;
(b) to secure that accommodation is or will be available for people in the district who are or may become homeless;
(c) to provide support for people in the district—

   (i) who are or may become homeless; or
   (ii) who have been homeless and need support to prevent them becoming homeless again.

Duty to provide advisory services

The 1996 Act makes information and advice a key component of the strategy for dealing with homelessness, both for people in general who need advice and for homeless applicants specifically.

For the first time, therefore, the 1996 Act imposed a duty on local authorities to secure that advice and information about homelessness and its prevention is provided free of charge to any person in their district. They may provide the advice and information themselves or arrange for it to be provided by, or in conjunction with, another organisation (s. 179). It is up to each authority to determine what precisely an advisory service covers, but homelessness might be prevented by information and advice on, e.g. obtaining accommodation in the private rented sector, allocation of accommodation through the social housing waiting list or choice-based lettings scheme, debt management, rights of occupation, harassment and illegal eviction, possession proceedings, grants available for housing repair and/or adaptation (DCLG, 2006a: 2.12).

Only the general duty contained in s. 179 is owed to a person who is eligible for assistance but who is neither homeless nor threatened with homelessness. In the case of a person who is not eligible for assistance, however, the CoG advises that homelessness strategies should aim to prevent homelessness amongst all households in the district and points out that authorities may also choose to offer other assistance, such as a rent deposit, to help ineligible applicants obtain accommodation (DCLG, 2006a: 14.3).

Interim duty to accommodate

Where an authority considers that an applicant may be eligible for assistance, is homeless and in priority need, it comes under a duty under s. 188 to secure accommodation while it carries out enquiries under s. 184 to establish the applicant's status and what further duty under Part VII (if any) may be owed. This duty arises even if the authority considers that the applicant may not have a local connection with its district but may have one with that of another authority.

A local housing authority which owes any duty under the homelessness legislation to provide accommodation to a homeless person is required to secure accommodation in its own area so far as is reasonably practicable (s. 208(1)) but may discharge its housing functions by securing that the applicant obtains suitable accommodation from 'some other person' (s. 206(1)(b)). That 'other person' does not have to be within the authority's area and an authority will often have to turn to another 'host' authority because it has insufficient housing available on a temporary basis within its own area. The fact that the completion of s. 184 inquiries can take months, rather than days or weeks, means that interim accommodation in the area of the host authority is often no longer available for homeless applicants who will be placed in the area of yet another authority, and so on. The 'shuttling' of households between different local authorities is, once again, a common feature of homelessness. Now, however, it is caused partly by an increase in the number of applications but, equally significantly, no commensurate increase in social housing provision.

The duty to provide interim accommodation ends once the authority has notified the applicant of its decision on his or her application. Any further duty towards a homeless applicant is determined by the outcome of the local authority's enquiries. If the authority decides that no further duty is owed, the applicant should be given a reasonable period of notice to enable him or her to make alternative accommodation arrangements (DCLG, 2006a: 7.10) but it may also continue to secure that the accommodation is available pending the outcome of a review (s. 188(3)). When considering an application for interim accommodation pending an appeal against a review decision, a local authority must consider the grounds for appeal (*Lewis v Havering London Borough Council* [2006] EWCA Civ 1793).

It is generally the case that no court order is required to terminate the right to occupy the interim accommodation. In *Mohamed v Manek and Royal Borough of Kensington and Chelsea* (1995) 27 HLR 439, it was held that where a council had arranged for temporary bed-and-breakfast accommodation in a hotel owned by a third party, it was not in breach of s. 3 of the Protection from Eviction Act 1977 in seeking to terminate the occupier's right to remain in that accommodation. *Manek* was applied in *Desnousse v Newham London Borough Council* [2006] 3 WLR 349, in which a majority of the Court of Appeal held that once a local authority had decided that no duty was owed, it should not have to take proceedings to evict any applicant who failed or refused to vacate the temporary accommodation provided. Lloyd LJ, dissenting, took the view that *Manek* should no longer be followed in so far as its reasoning extends to self-contained accommodation which constitutes the occupier's home. The court also rejected the submission that to interpret s. 3 of the 1977 Act in a way which denied its application to recovery of possession from someone in Mrs Desnousse's position was incompatible with Art. 8. There was no doubt that – had the accommodation become the applicant's home – an eviction would constitute an interference with his or her right to respect for it but the question then became one of proportionality, i.e. whether the possibility of eviction without the procedural safeguards contained in the 1977 Act could be justified. The court held that it could – given that local authorities (under whose control evictions were likely to take place) could be trusted to act lawfully and responsibly, that they were likely to give 28 days' notice and there were safeguards built into the 1996 Act (e.g. for review of any decision made by the authority and the general duty to provide advice and assistance). To hold otherwise would significantly impair the authority's ability to discharge its duties in the general interest as it the period of occupation would be prolonged by months rather than weeks in most cases and the process might be further delayed by 'unmeritorious defences' being raised to the claim for possession.

The CoG advises that the use of bed and breakfast accommodation should be avoided wherever possible and, where it has been provided as emergency accommodation, applicants should be moved to more suitable accommodation as soon as possible (DCLG, 2006a: 7.6). In recent years government policy has aimed significantly to reduce the use of bed and breakfast accommodation in the housing of homeless families with children. Where accommodation is made available for occupation under ss. 188 and 193 for applicants with 'family commitments' who are pregnant or with whom a pregnant woman or dependent children reside or might reasonably be expected to reside, bed and breakfast accommodation is not to be regarded as suitable unless it is the only type of accommodation which is available for occupation and the applicant occupies it for a period, or a total of periods, which does not exceed six weeks (the Homelessness (Suitability of Accommodation) (England) Order 2003). The right to request a review contained in s. 202 can be used in respect of any decision of a local authority as to the suitability of accommodation which has been offered.

Duties owed to applicants who are threatened with homelessness

Where the authority is satisfied that the applicant is *eligible for assistance, threatened with homelessness unintentionally, and in priority need*, it has a duty to take reasonable steps to secure that existing accommodation does not cease to be available for his or her occupation (s. 195(2)). Such steps may include, e.g. negotiating with the applicant's landlord or, in cases where the applicant has been asked to leave by family or friends, exploring the possibility of mediation and the provision of support to the household to help ease any pressures which may have led to the applicant being asked to leave. As soon as an authority has become subject to a duty under s. 195(2) it must give the applicant a copy of the statement included in its allocation scheme about its policy on offering choice to people allocated accommodation under Part VI of the 1996 Act (s. 195(3A)).

Where an applicant is *eligible for assistance and threatened with homelessness unintentionally but has no priority need*, the local authority has a *duty* to provide advice and such assistance as it considers appropriate to prevent loss of the applicant's existing accommodation (s. 195(5)). It also has a *power* to take reasonable steps to secure that accommodation does not cease to be available for the applicant's occupation (s. 195(9)).

In the case of an applicant who is *eligible for assistance and in priority need but threatened with homelessness intentionally*, the local authority must provide advice and such assistance as it considers appropriate to prevent loss of the applicant's existing accommodation (s. 195(5)).

Duties owed to applicants who are homeless

Where an applicant is *eligible for assistance, intentionally homeless and not in priority need*, the local authority must provide the applicant with advice and such assistance as it considers appropriate in any attempt by the applicant to find accommodation for himself or herself (s. 190(3)). This might include, e.g. assistance with a rent deposit or guarantee to help the applicant obtain accommodation in the private sector, or advice on applying for an allocation of long-term social housing accommodation, possibly through another social landlord. The local authority owes no duty of care that any premises to which it directs the applicant are reasonably safe, especially as regards fire (*Ephraim v London Borough of Newham and Mirza* (1993) 25 HLR 207).

Two duties are owed to an applicant who is *eligible for assistance and in priority need but intentionally homeless*. First, the authority must provide applicants, or ensure that they are provided with, advice and assistance in any attempts which they may make to secure that accommodation becomes available for their occupation (s. 190(1)(b)). Secondly, the authority must secure that accommodation is available for their occupation for such period as it considers will give them a reasonable opportunity of securing accommodation (s. 190(2)(a)). The accommodation must be suitable and each case must be considered on its merits when determining the period for which accommodation will be secured. The CoG notes that a few weeks may provide applicants with a reasonable opportunity to find their own accommodation but it recognises that some applicants may need longer and others less (particularly where the authority provides 'proactive and effective advice and assistance'). Account will need to be taken of the housing circumstances in the local area, including how readily other accommodation is available in the district, and the applicant's particular circumstances (including his or her financial resources) (DCLG, 2006a: 14.28).

Where an applicant is *eligible for assistance and unintentionally homeless but not in priority need*, the local authority is under a duty to provide advice and assistance as above (s. 192(2)). It also has a *power* to secure that accommodation is available for the applicant's occupation (s. 192(3)).

The most extensive duty is owed to an applicant who is *eligible for assistance, unintentionally homeless and in priority need* and it is worth spending some time in consideration of its legislative antecedents and how it came to be in its present form. It should be noted that acceptance of a duty under s. 193(2) does not prevent an immediate allocation of accommodation through the normal allocations route via Part VI of the 1996 Act if the applicant has the necessary priority under the authority's allocation scheme. As soon as an authority has become subject to a duty under s. 193(2) it must give the applicant a copy of the statement included in its allocation scheme about its policy on offering choice to people allocated housing accommodation under Part VI (s. 193(3A)).

The main duty

As stated in Chapter 2, s. 21(1)(b) of the National Assistance Act 1948 required local authority welfare departments to provide 'temporary accommodation' to those whose urgent need for such accommodation could not reasonably have been foreseen. By 1977, however, there was strong support for the view that, instead of a short stay in temporary accommodation to tide them over their difficulties, what most homeless people really needed was 'a permanent solution to their problem which they had been unable to arrange for themselves' (HC Deb (1976–7) vol. 926, cols 898–9).

The Housing (Homeless Persons) Act 1977 provided that where a local housing authority was satisfied that an applicant for accommodation had a priority need and was not satisfied that he became homeless intentionally, it had a duty to 'secure that accommodation becomes available for his occupation'. That duty, subsequently incorporated into s. 65(2) of the Housing Act 1985, was commonly referred to as the 'full' duty. Lesser duties (of securing that accommodation was made available for the applicant's occupation for such period as would provide a reasonable opportunity of securing accommodation for him- or herself, and/or of furnishing the applicant with advice and assistance to enable this to be accomplished) were owed to those who had a priority need but were intentionally homeless, or those who were unintentionally homeless but had no priority need.

The then CoG stated that the accommodation secured in order to discharge the full duty must be 'long term settled accommodation, commonly referred to as permanent' but the duty was diluted as the depletion of council stock and the increase in the number of people applying to local authorities for housing made its execution more difficult to achieve. The accepted construction following *Dyson v Kerrier District Council* [1980] 1 WLR 1205 was that the full duty required the provision of indefinite accommodation while in *R v Slough Borough Council ex p Ealing London Borough Council* [1981] QB 801, 811 Lord Denning MR said that the local authority was 'to secure that accommodation is available for [the applicant] indefinitely and not merely for a short time'. Lord Lowry's statement in *Din v Wandsworth London Borough Council* [1983] 1 AC 657, 677 that 'there is no temporal adverbial qualification of the word "occupation"' was relied upon in, for example, *R v London Borough of Camden ex p Wait* (1986) 18 HLR 434, in which it was held that the accommodation to be provided must be 'indefinite in length'. In more recent cases the courts inclined to use the phrase 'settled' accommodation (e.g. *R v Rushcliffe Borough Council ex p Summerson* (1992) 25 HLR 577) and in *R v Wandsworth London Borough Council ex p Crooks, The Independent*, 30 March 1995, it was held that the obligation to provide 'settled' accommodation had been fulfilled by placing a homeless person in private rented accommodation under an assured shorthold tenancy. In *R v London Borough of Brent ex p Awua* [1995] 2 WLR 215, the House of Lords held that there was, in fact, no duty to provide 'settled' accommodation at all. What there did appear to be was an indefinite duty to secure accommodation but in discharging that duty, no account need be taken of the security of tenure of the accommodation provided so long as it lasted for at least 28 days (otherwise the applicant would be regarded as 'threatened with homelessness').

Taking the view that homelessness is a consequence of an emergency or crisis, the 1995 White Paper stated the government's intention that, in future, local authorities would have a duty merely to secure suitable accommodation for not less than 12 months for 'families and vulnerable people who have nowhere to go' and who were found to be unintentionally homeless. This 12-month period was intended to tide people over 'the immediate crisis of homelessness, and to give them time to find longer term accommodation'. It was felt that in many parts of the country, 12 months would be long enough for a household with real housing need to be offered a long-term tenancy by means of the housing register with a local authority, housing association or other social landlord.

Much of the responsibility for the current housing malaise was placed with the courts, their interpretation of the legislation having enabled anyone who was accepted by the local housing authority as statutorily homeless to be given priority in the allocation of 'a life-long tenancy' (DoE, 1995: 36). This disingenuous statement was misleading on two counts. First, as indicated above, there has never been any legal entitlement to a 'life-long' tenancy. Indeed, despite the exhortation of the then CoG, the courts had gone to great lengths to avoid using the words 'permanent' or 'life-long' to denote the type of accommodation to be secured in discharging the full duty. In fact they had recognised that, in the light of new forms of housing provision such as private sector leasing (PSL) which had emerged since the CoG was drafted, the notion of 'permanence' was outdated (see, e.g. *R v Brent London Borough Council ex p Macwan* (1994) 26 HLR 528), and that to interpret 'accommodation' in s. 65(2) as 'permanent' would result in the imposition on local authorities of duties which, given their depleted housing stocks, they would not be able to fulfil – hence the liberal interpretation of the word 'settled' in *Crooks*.

Secondly, even if the courts had interpreted s. 65(2) as imposing a duty to provide permanent accommodation, there is no evidence to be found from the parliamentary debates during the passage of the Housing (Homeless Persons) Bill that Parliament ever intended anything different. Such was the concern among MPs who opposed the Bill as to what they perceived as the likely outcomes of the legislation – that those who were not genuinely homeless, or who did not belong to the area in which they were applying for accommodation, would be given council house tenancies in preference to local applicants whose names had been on the waiting list for some time – that attention was centred on the issues of intentionality and local connection. The type of accommodation to be secured by the local authority in what was to become s. 65(2) was virtually ignored but the very presence of the lesser duty owed to the intentionally homeless in priority need (of securing that accommodation is made available for the applicant's occupation 'for such period as the local authority considers will give him a reasonable opportunity of securing accommodation for himself') makes it quite clear that Parliament intended something different (and, presumably, longer term) to be provided via s. 65(2) for the unintentionally homeless in priority need.

While the Housing Act 1996 was being debated in the House of Commons, the minimum period was extended from 12 months to two years. Soon after coming to power in 1997, however, the Labour government began to dismantle the changes made to the homelessness legislation by the previous Conservative administration. Now, therefore, subject to the power to refer to another authority with which the applicant has a local connection, s. 193

effectively restores an open-ended duty to provide suitable accommodation. It comes to an end if at any time the applicant:

(a) refuses an offer of suitable accommodation, having been informed by the local housing authority of the possible consequence of refusal. The authority must notify him or her that it regards itself as having discharged its duty under this section (s. 193(5)); or

(b) ceases to be eligible for assistance under Part VII, as defined in ss 185 and 186 (s. 193(6)(a)); or becomes homeless intentionally from the accommodation made available for his or her occupation (s. 193(6)(b)); or

(c) accepts an offer of accommodation under the general allocation provisions of Part VI (including an offer of an assured tenancy of an RSL property via the housing authority's allocation scheme) (s. 193(6)(c)); or

(d) accepts an offer of an assured tenancy (other than an assured shorthold tenancy) from a private landlord (or RSL) (s. 193(6)(cc)); or

(e) voluntarily ceases to occupy as his or her only or principal home the accommodation made available under s. 193 (s. 196(3)(d)); or

(f) having been informed of the possible consequence of refusal, refuses a final offer of accommodation under Part VI (s. 196(7)). The duty does not end unless the applicant is informed of the possible consequences of refusal and of his or her right to ask for a review of the suitability of the accommodation (s. 193(7)), the offer is in writing and states that it is a final offer (s. 193(7A)), and the authority is satisfied that the accommodation is suitable and that it would be reasonable for the applicant to accept it (s. 193(7F)). An applicant may reasonably be expected to accept an offer of accommodation under Part VI even though he or she is under contractual or other obligations in respect of existing accommodation, provided that those obligations can be brought to an end before the applicant is required to take up the offer. In considering whether or not it is objectively reasonable for an applicant to refuse an offer of accommodation which the housing authority has found to be suitable, the decision-maker must first have regard to and take account of all the applicant's personal characteristics and particular needs, e.g. to be protected from domestic violence and to be located near support networks (*Slater v Lewisham London Borough Council* (2006) HLR 37); or

(g) accepts a qualifying offer of an assured shorthold tenancy which is made by a private landlord in relation to any accommodation which is, or may become, available for the applicant's occupation (s. 196(7B)). An offer of an assured shorthold tenancy is a qualifying offer if:

(i) it is made, with the approval of the authority, in pursuance of arrangements made by the authority with the landlord with a view to bringing the authority's duty under this section to an end;

(ii) the tenancy being offered is a fixed term tenancy (within the meaning of Part I of the Housing Act 1988); and

(iii) it is accompanied by a statement in writing which states the term of the tenancy being offered and explains in ordinary language that there is no obligation to accept the offer, but if the offer is accepted the local housing authority will cease to be subject to the duty under this section in relation to the applicant (s. 196(7D)).

A person who ceases to be owed the duty under this section may make a fresh application to the authority for accommodation or assistance in obtaining accommodation (s. 193(9)).

Local connection

Introduction

One of the principal objectives of the Housing (Homeless Persons) Act 1977 was to end the 'shuttling' of homeless people between different local authorities, each alleging that the applicant had a stronger connection with the other. The notion of 'local connection' – seemingly a legacy of the Poor Law – did not feature in the original draft of the Bill. It was introduced during its passage through Parliament at the insistence of the Association of District Councils, the members of which were concerned that 'scroungers, scivers, scrimshankers, rent dodgers, queue jumpers and beach bums' would be attracted to the areas of certain 'magnet authorities', making those authorities responsible for housing such people (HC Deb (1977) vol. 926, cols 905, 921, 972 and 973). They predicted that authorities in seaside areas would have to accommodate those who 'come off the beach' and apply for housing (HC Deb (1977) vol. 926, col. 973). To avert such an outcome, the local connection provisions of the homelessness legislation enable a local housing authority to refer to another authority an application which it has received under the homelessness legislation (s. 198(1)). A referral can be made only where the most extensive housing duty under s. 193 is owed (i.e. the authority to which application is made is satisfied that the applicant is eligible for assistance, unintentionally homeless and in priority need). However, arrangements can still be made with another authority under s. 213 of the 1996 Act for assistance in securing accommodation in discharge of any other duty under Part VII.

Before a referral under s. 198 can be made, it must be determined that (a) neither the applicant, nor any person who might reasonably be expected to reside with the applicant has a local connection with the district applied to; and (b) the applicant, etc. does have such a connection with the area of another authority. It should be noted that that the referral procedure does not arise if the applicant has a local connection with the area of the authority to which application has been made, but a greater or closer local connection elsewhere (*Eastleigh Borough Council v Betts* [1983] 2 AC 613). In such a case, however, the first authority will be obliged to secure accommodation but it may seek assistance from the second under s. 213 in doing so. If a person accepted as eligible for assistance, unintentionally homeless and in priority need has no local connection with the area of any housing authority in Great Britain, then the duty to secure accommodation rests with the authority to which application for assistance has been made (*R v Hillingdon London Borough Council ex p Streeting* [1980] 3 All ER 413). Not surprisingly, this puts considerable pressure on those authorities in whose districts are situated international airports and ferry terminals.

No referral may take place where there is a risk of the applicant (or any person who might reasonably be expected to reside with the applicant) being exposed to domestic violence in the other authority's district (s. 198(2)). 'Violence' for the purpose of s. 198 means actual physical violence and not acts or gestures which lead someone to fear physical violence (*Kensington and Chelsea Royal London Borough Council v Danesh* [2006] EWCA Civ 1404, para. 14).

The applicant and the members of the applicant's household may between them have local connections with a number of different areas, and there may therefore be several authorities to which responsibility could properly be referred. In such a case the first authority has a discretion to choose to which of those authorities to notify of the case, and the chosen authority will not be able to disclaim responsibility merely because there is a stronger local connection with the area of a third authority (Carnwath, 1978: 32). Further, an authority to which a referral is made under the local connection provisions is bound by the decision of the referring authority on the question of intentional homelessness even if it has determined, as the result of a previous application made to it directly, that the applicant is intentionally homeless. An authority to which a reference is made under s. 198 may be acting unlawfully if it refuses to accept responsibility for it (see *R (on the application of Bantamagbari) v City of Westminster* [2003] All ER (D) 163).

Each local authority to which an application is made must make its own inquiries about the applicant's homelessness and form its own view as to whether the homelessness was intentional or unintentional. The concept of intentional homelessness is subjective and an authority's decision on the matter can only be challenged on the ground that no reasonable authority acting reasonably in the discharge of its functions could have reached that decision. This principle was established in *R v Slough Borough Council ex p Ealing London Borough Council* [1981] QB 801 in which former council tenants who had been evicted by Slough BC applied to be re-housed. On a finding by Slough that they were intentionally homeless, the applicants then approached Ealing London Borough Council. Ealing decided they were unintentionally homeless but, because of their lack of local connection with Ealing, referred them back to Slough. The Court of Appeal held that Slough, being the appropriate area of local connection, was bound by Ealing's decision that the applicants were unintentionally homeless. Lord Denning MR likened the situation to the disputes under the Poor Law (as to which parish was to be responsible for the relief of those who were poor and unable to work) which created an infinity of expensive law-suits between contending neighbourhoods, concerning those settlements and removal, predicting that 'another dose of the same medicine' was likely to occur in the future (pp. 807–8).

A person who is refused permanent accommodation by one authority can proceed to apply to others until one of them accepts (a practice described as 'forum shopping' by Henry J in *R v London Borough of Tower Hamlets ex p London Borough of Camden* (1988) 21 HLR 197). Alternatively, applications may be made to several authorities simultaneously (see Cowan, 1993: 222). Thus, In *R v Newham London Borough Council ex p Tower Hamlets London Borough Council* [1992] 2 All ER 767, 771 Lord Donaldson said that although the applicant had 'confined himself to Newham', he 'might well have chosen any, or possibly all, of the many housing authorities in this country'. Furthermore, every authority applied to is entitled, if the circumstances warrant it, to decide that the applicant has a local connection with a different authority. The applicant has the right to request an internal review of, *inter alia*, any decision of a local housing authority to notify another authority under the local connection provisions (s. 202). The legislation is framed on the basis that application will apply to the applicant's preferred authority and there is, however, no statutory right of a review of a local housing authority's decision *not* to refer an application under s. 198 of the Act to another authority (*Hackney London Borough Council v Sareen* [2003] EWCA Civ 351).

Where there is a dispute between two or more authorities as to which of them is to bear the responsibility for securing accommodation, it may be resolved by reference to the Local Authority Association Joint Local Connection Agreement (the 'Referral Guidelines'). If the housing authorities fail to reach agreement, the matter must be referred to arbitration (s. 198(5)). Until the dispute is resolved, it is the authority to which application was initially made that must accommodate the applicant.

Meaning of 'local connection'

By s. 199(1) of the Housing Act 1996 a person has a local connection with the district of a local housing authority:

(a) because he or she is, or in the past was, normally resident in that district, and that residence is or was of his or her own choice;
(b) because he or she is employed there;
(c) because of family associations; or
(d) because of special circumstances.

The correct date for deciding whether a person has a local connection is that of the initial decision or (if a review takes place) the date of the review

(*Mohamed v Hammersmith and Fulham London Borough Council* [2002] 1 AC 547). In assessing the merits of an application, the reviewing officer can have regard to information relevant to the period before the initial decision but only obtained after it and also to matters occurring after the initial decision. In addition, account can be taken of a local connection which develops during the period between the initial decision and the review.

Residence

Most applicants under the homelessness legislation become homeless in the area in which they have previously lived for a considerable period and in their cases the local connection provisions as to residence will not come into play. Residence must be 'of choice'. It is not of choice if the applicant, or any person who might reasonably be expected to reside with the applicant, is serving in the regular armed forces, or is imprisoned or is detained under the Mental Health Act 1959 (s. 199(3)). The Referral Guidelines suggest a working definition of 'normal residence' as being established by six months in the area during the previous 12 months, or not less than three years during the previous five-year period.

In *Mohamed v Hammersmith and Fulham London Borough Council* [2002] 1 AC 547, the House of Lords held that the period spent in interim accommodation provided under s. 188 of the 1996 Act could be used to count towards establishing a local connection, thereby obliging the authority to which application for accommodation had been made to house the applicant on a long-term basis (even though the applicant had no previous local connection with the authority). Lord Slynn explained that normal residence is a place where at the relevant time the person in fact resides. So long as he voluntarily accepts the place where he eats and sleeps, the reason why he is there rather than somewhere else does not prevent it from being his normal residence and the fact that it is provided subject to statutory duty does not prevent it from being such. The local authority had argued that interim accommodation was not intended to give an applicant the chance to build up a local connection and to count it as normal residence would defeat the purpose of the 1996 Act and benefit those whose cases demanded lengthy enquiries to the disadvantage of those whose cases could be dealt with quickly. Lord Slynn acknowledged the Act's re-distributive purpose but felt that it should be read with the other statutory purpose of providing for people to stay in an area with which they have established a local connection and that there was no overriding reason or principle why interim accommodation should not count as normal residence for this purpose.

The Immigration and Asylum Act 1999 excludes those who are subject to immigration control from access to the mainstream welfare system and provides in its place a system of support administered by the National Asylum Support Service (NASS). To qualify for NASS support, an asylum seeker must show that he is destitute (that is, has no other means of support), or is likely to become so within 14 days (the Asylum Support Regulations 2000, para. 7(a)). When exercising his power under s. 95 of the Immigration and Asylum Act 1999 to provide accommodation, the Secretary of State is specifically directed to disregard 'any preference that the supported person or his dependants (if any) may have as to the locality in which the accommodation is to be provided' (Immigration and Asylum Act 1999, s. 97(2)). The White Paper which paved the way for the 1999 Act had declared that accommodation would be on a 'no-choice basis', stating that 'asylum seekers would be expected to take what was available, and would not be able to pick and choose where they were accommodated' (Secretary of State for the Home Department, 1998: 8.22). In *Al-Ameri v Kensington and Chelsea Royal London Borough Council* [2004] 2 WLR 354, the House of Lords held that accommodation occupied in Glasgow by virtue of the NASS dispersal scheme was not residence of choice and could not therefore give rise to a local connection under s. 199(1)(a). This meant that the London housing authorities to which the applicants subsequently applied under the homelessness legislation were not entitled to refer their applications back to Glasgow. The government was quick to respond to the decision by amending the local connection provisions of the 1996 Act. Now, s. 199(6) provides that people have a local connection with the district of a housing authority if they were at any time provided with accommodation there under s. 95 of the Immigration and Asylum Act 1995 unless (a) they have subsequently been provided with s. 95 accommodation in a different area; or (b) they have been provided with s 95 accommodation in an accommodation centre in the district.

Employment

A person who is serving in the regular armed forces is not regarded as being employed in an area. There is no indication that 'employment' for the purposes of s. 199 excludes self-employment or that employment need be full-time.

Family associations

The Referral Guidelines limit family associations to parents, adult children, or brothers and sisters who have been in the area for a period of at least five years at the date of application and the applicant indicates a wish to be near them. They state that only in exceptional circumstances will the residence of other relatives be taken to establish a local connection. In *Ozbek v Ipswich Borough Council* [2006] EWCA Civ 534 the applicant – a former asylum seeker who had been granted indefinite leave to remain – had a local connection with Portsmouth, having been provided with NASS accommodation there under s. 95 of the Immigration and Asylum Act 1999 (see above). However, he and his wife wished to live in Ipswich where, although he had extensive family connections, only his two brothers fell within the class of relationship which would ordinarily constitute a family connection and they had been resident there for only 18 months. Although sympathetic to the applicant's plight, the Court of Appeal upheld the local authority's decision that he had no local connection with Ipswich. Chadwick LJ made it clear (at para. 48) that 'the fact that the welfare need of the applicant and his family might be better served by the help and support which would or might be provided by his extended family than by voluntary or statutory agencies had little or no relevance'. The relevant question was whether, in the particular circumstances of the individual case, the bond between the applicant and one or more members of the extended family – whose period of residence in Ipswich exceeded five years – was of such a nature that it would be appropriate to regard them as 'near relatives'. He held that the authority had been entitled to conclude that the question should receive a negative answer. Sedley LJ expressed doubt as to whether 'the presence within the locality of a parent or sibling with whom the applicant has had little contact for years will ordinarily be sufficient to constitute a family association within s. 199(1)(c)' (para. 63) and suggested that the character of the family asso-ciation must be at least as relevant – probably more relevant – than the degree of consanguinity. The CoG (amended in the light of this decision) suggests that family associations may extend to step-parents, grandparents, grandchildren, aunts or uncles provided that there are sufficiently close links in the form of frequent contact, commitment or dependency. It states that family associations may also extend to unmarried couples, provided that the relationship is sufficiently enduring, and to same-sex couples (DCLG, 2006a 18.10).

Special circumstances

This phrase is not defined in the Act and the only assistance given by the CoG is that it may include the need to be near special medical or support services which are available only in a particular district (DCLG, 2006a: 18.1). The Referral Guidelines mention families returning from abroad, those leaving the armed forces or those who wish to return to an area where they were brought up or lived for a considerable length of time in the past. In *R v Vale of White Horse District Council ex p South and Hay* (1984) 17 HLR 160, an unsuccessful attempt was made to establish a local connection by the applicants' involvement with an evangelical church which was the most importance influence on their lives. In *R v Hammersmith & Fulham London Borough Council ex p Advic* (1996) 28 HLR 897, the residence of a first cousin once removed in a neighbouring borough was held not to be sufficient to amount to a special circumstance.

No local connection

As is explained above, if a person accepted as eligible for assistance, unintentionally homeless and in priority need has no local connection with the area of any housing authority in the UK, then the duty to secure accommodation rests with the authority to which application has been made for assistance. However, s. 206(1)(b) provides that a local housing authority may discharge its housing functions by securing that the applicant obtains suitable accommodation from 'some other person'. That 'other person' does not have to be within the authority's area and means that the authority to which the application is made may even be able to arrange accommodation with an agency in the country from which the applicant comes. In *R v Bristol City Council ex p Browne* [1979] 3 All ER 344, the duty to secure accommodation lay with Bristol but the 'other person' from which the council sought to secure accommodation was the authority in the Republic of Ireland from whose district Mrs Browne had fled to escape her violent husband. It was not, therefore, a referral under what is now s. 198 as it was outside the legislation's jurisdiction. The Divisional Court ruled that Bristol had acted neither unlawfully nor unreasonably, despite the fact that the decision to return Mrs Browne to the Republic of Ireland was based merely on an assurance made over the telephone by a welfare officer in Tralee that Mrs Browne could be safely accommodated there.

Sources of accommodation

Introduction

By s. 206 of the 1996 Act, a local authority may discharge its housing functions under Part VII of the 1996 Act by:

(a) securing that suitable accommodation provided by it is available for the applicant;
(b) securing that the applicant obtains accommodation from 'some other person'; and
(c) giving the applicant such advice and assistance as will enable him or her to secure accommodation from some other person.

In each case, the accommodation must be 'suitable' and authorities may make reasonable charges for it (s. 206(2)). The Act requires authorities to secure accommodation in their own areas, so far as reasonably practicable (s. 208(1)). If they provide accommodation in another area, they must notify the local authority in that other area within 14 days of the provision of the accommodation, of the applicant's name, address, number and description of other people who normally reside with the applicant or might be expected to do so, the date on which the accommodation was made available and the duty which the authority was discharging (s. 208(2)–(4)).

Accommodation provided by the housing authority

The CoG states that, generally, it is inappropriate for social housing to be used as temporary accommodation other than for short periods and that where the main duty is owed, the authority should consider offering the household a settled home under the terms of its allocation scheme as soon as possible (DCLG, 2006a: 16.6). Otherwise, the housing authority may place the applicant in, e.g. a house or flat from its own stock, or a hostel which it owns, or in accommodation which it leases from another landlord (e.g. under a private sector leasing agreement). The CoG states that in considering whether to provide accommodation from their own stock, authorities will have to balance the (limited, short-term) requirements of homeless people against the need to provide accommodation for others who have priority for an allocation under Part VI of the 1996 Act. A tenancy granted by a housing authority in pursuance of any function under Part VII is not a secure tenancy unless the housing authority notifies the tenant that it is such (Housing Act 1985, Sch. 1, para. 4).

Accommodation secured from another person

Where an authority secures accommodation from another landlord, it must ensure that the accommodation is 'available' and 'suitable'. The CoG identifies the main options as follows.

Registered social landlords

In an area in which a whole stock transfer has taken place, the housing authority will still retain duties under the homelessness legislation but will have no stock of its own in which to accommodate homeless applicants. It will need to approach RSLs and other providers in the area therefore for assistance in its discharging statutory duties. If asked, RSLs are obliged under s. 213 to assist local authorities in carrying out their duties under the homelessness legislation by cooperating as far as is reasonable in the circumstances. Where accommodation is provided to assist a housing authority in discharging an interim duty a tenancy granted cannot be an assured tenancy unless the landlord notifies the applicant that it is, or unless 12 months have elapsed since the applicant was notified of the decision which brought the interim duty to an end. Where an RSL assists a housing authority to discharge any other homelessness duty, the tenancy granted will be an assured shorthold tenancy. Such a tenancy cannot be converted to an assured tenancy unless it is allocated through the housing register under Part VI (s. 209(3)).

Private renting

Local authorities are permitted to provide financial assistance to private landlords in order to secure accommodation in the private sector for people who are homeless or at risk of homelessness. According to the CoG, this could involve the authority paying the costs of leases, making small one-off grants ('finders' fees') to landlords to encourage them to let their properties to homeless households, paying rent deposits or indemnities to ensure that accommodation is secured for such households, and making one-off grant payments to prevent an eviction. They may also make discretionary housing payments to a private landlord to meet a shortfall between the rent and the amount of housing benefit to which a person who is at risk of homelessness is entitled (DCLG, 2006a: 16.20).

Other social landlords

Section 213 obliges other social landlords, e.g. new town corporations and housing action trusts, to co-operate, as far as is reasonable in the circumstances, with a local authority in carrying out its homeless functions under the 1996 Act if asked to do so.

Lodgings

The CoG regards lodgings provided by private householders as suitable for some young and/or vulnerable single people and advises that housing authorities may wish to establish a network of such providers in their district, and to liaise with social services which may operate supported lodgings schemes for people with support needs (DCLG, 2006a: 16.24).

Hostels

The CoG points out that some people may benefit from the supportive environment provided by managed hostels which can offer short-term support to those at crisis point to enable them to move on to independent living. It warns however that housing authorities should not assume that a hostel will automatically be the most appropriate form of accommodation for vulnerable people, particularly young vulnerable people, people with mental health problems and those who have experienced violence and/or abuse, and states that vulnerable young people or families with children should not be accommodated alongside adults with chaotic behavioural problems (DCLG, 2006a: 16.25).

Women's refuges

Securing accommodation in a refuge may not count as a discharge of an authority's duty. Refuges should be used for the minimum time necessary before securing suitable accommodation elsewhere. Authorities should not delay securing other accommodation for an applicant placed in a women's refuge in the hope that she might return to her partner. It is also important to ensure that places in refuges continue to be available for others in need. If the refuge terminates a licence because the household no longer needs to be in the refuge, the authority has a duty to secure alternative accommodation immediately.

Bed and breakfast

The CoG notes that bed and breakfast accommodation caters for very short-term stays only. It will usually provide only limited privacy and lack important amenities, such as cooking and laundry facilities.

Other housing authorities

Another housing authority which is under less housing pressure may be able to assist in the provision of temporary or settled accommodation, especially where victims of violence and/or serious harassment do not wish to return to the area where the perpetrator of the violence/harassment lives. Other authorities may also be able to provide accommodation where the applicant has special housing needs.

Mobile homes

Although mobile homes may sometimes provide emergency accommodation, e.g. to discharge the interim duty, they may not be satisfactory for households with children, or for elderly or disabled people. The CoG urges authorities to satisfy themselves that the accommodation is suitable for the applicant and his or her household, paying particular regard to their needs, requirements and circumstances and the conditions and facilities on the site. It states that caravans designed primarily for short-term holiday use should not be regarded as suitable as temporary accommodation for homeless people (DCLG, 2006a: 16.30).

Occupiers of caravans, houseboats, etc. including gypsies

If a duty to secure accommodation arises where a person has become homeless because there is nowhere he or she is entitled or permitted to put and live in a caravan, houseboat, or other moveable structure (s. 175(2)), an authority is not required to make equivalent accommodation available (or provide a site or berth for the applicant's own accommodation), although of course it may do so if resources permit. It may nonetheless have to provide an alternative, temporary solution until a suitable site – or some other suitable option – becomes available. The CoG directs authorities to consider the needs and lifestyles of applicants of gypsies and travellers when considering their application and how best to discharge a duty to secure suitable accommodation in line with their obligations to act in accordance with the Human Rights Act 1998, in particular the Art. 8 right to respect for private and family and the home (DCLG, 2006a: 16.38).

Advice and assistance

Housing authorities may secure accommodation by giving advice and assistance to an applicant which will secure that accommodation becomes available for him or her from another person but, if they do so, they must make sure that the advice and assistance results in suitable accommodation actually being secured. Examples of securing accommodation in this way may be through the provision of advice on all options for financing house purchase (if this appears to be a viable possibility for the applicant) or shared equity schemes.

Availability

The Housing Act 1996 requires that the accommodation must be 'available'. It must be capable, therefore, of accommodating the whole household, that is, the applicant and any other person who normally resides with the applicant as a member of his or her family, and any other person who might reasonably be expected to reside with the applicant, e.g. a carer.

Suitability

The accommodation provided by, or found for, the applicant for the purposes of Part VII of the Housing Act 1996 must be suitable (s. 210). In assessing suitability, the local housing authority must have regard to Parts IX and X of the Housing Act 1985 (slum clearance, overcrowding) and Parts I to IV of the Housing Act 2004 (housing conditions, houses in multiple occupation). The accommodation must be suitable not only for the applicant but also for anyone who normally resides with the applicant, or might reasonably be expected to do so. It was said by Leggatt LJ in *R v Brent London Borough Council ex p Macwan* (1994) 26 HLR 528, 534 that 'suitability imports questions of fact and degree, and is dependent upon all the circumstances of the case, including the size, composition and health of the applicant's household, and the applicant's preferences as to area and type of accommodation, as well as the availability of housing and the pressures upon the local housing authority from competing applicants. In *London Borough of Newham v Khatun* [2005] QB 37, the Court of Appeal held that the authority's policy of requiring applicants to accept or refuse the accommodation without giving them an opportunity to view the property first was not unlawful. It was said that the applicant's subjective view of suitability was not a factor which a reasonable council was obliged in principle to regards as relevant and he or she was given protection by the right to a review of the accommodation's suitability.

Affordability

The Homelessness (Suitability of Accommodation) Order 1996 specifies, *inter alia*, that in determining whether accommodation is suitable for a person an authority must take into account the affordability of the accommodation for the applicant and, in particular, must take account of:

(a) the applicant's financial resources, including (i) salary, fees and other remuneration, (ii) social security benefits, (iii) payments due under a court order for the making of periodical payments to a spouse or to, or for the benefit of, a child, (iv) payments of child support maintenance under the Child Support Act 1991, (v) pensions, (vi) contributions to accommodation costs made by other members of the household, (vii) financial assistance towards the cost in respect of the accommodation, including loans, provided by a local authority, voluntary organisation or other body, (viii) benefits derived from a policy of insurance, (ix) savings and other capital sums;

(b) the costs of the accommodation, including (i) rent or (ii) payments in respect of a licence or permission to occupy the property, (iii) mortgage costs, (iv) service charges, (v) mooring charges payable for a houseboat, (vi) pitch fees for a caravan or mobile home, (vii) council tax, (viii) payments by way of deposit or security, and (ix) payments required by an accommodation agency;

(c) payments which the applicant is required to make under a court order for the making of periodical payments to a spouse or former spouse, or to or for the benefit of a child, and payments of child support maintenance under the Child Support Act 1991; and

(d) the applicant's other reasonable living expenses.

Location

The location of the accommodation is a relevant consideration as to its suitability. Where, for example, the applicant is in paid employment, account will need to be taken of the need to reach his or her normal workplace. In *R v Newham London Borough Council ex p Sacupima* [2001] 1 WLR 563, the applicant and her five children had lived for five years in Newham. The Court of Appeal held that the local authority's decision to house them in bed and breakfast accommodation in Great Yarmouth had failed to take account of the family's relevant characteristics, particularly the educational requirements of the three older children (who were attending schools and colleges in London) and the medical requirements of the youngest child. Similarly, in *R v Enfield London Borough Council ex p Yumsak* [2002] EWHC 280, the local housing authority was held to have failed to provide the applicant with suitable interim accommodation when it placed her in bed and breakfast accommodation in Birmingham, given that she was a single mother who spoke little English and had no friends or family there. In most cases, however, housing authorities will have a free rein in placing applicants in out-of-district accommodation while they carry out their s. 184 inquiries. The CoG now advises that housing authorities should try to minimise disruption to the education of young people, particularly at critical points in time such as the run-up to their GCSE examinations. Authorities should also avoid placing applicants in isolated accommodation away from transport, shops and other facilities and, wherever possible, secure accommodation which is as close as possible to where they were previously living so that they can retain established links with schools, doctors, social workers and other key service and support (DCLG, 2006a: 17.41).

Challenging the decision of a local authority

Introduction

No private law mechanism exists for challenging a homelessness decision by means of an action for breach of statutory duty (*O'Rourke v Camden London Borough Council* [1998] AC 188). In *R v Newham London Borough Council ex p Morris* [2002] EWHC 1262), the High Court refused to award damages under s. 8 of the Human Rights Act 1998 for the authority's failure to provide suitable accommodation under s. 193(2) of the 1996 Act. It was held that there had been no violation of Art. 8 even though the claimant and her family had been forced to live in grossly overcrowded conditions.

Internal review

The Housing Act 1996 introduced a right for an aggrieved applicant to have the decision reviewed by the authority. Since 1991, the CoG had recommended that authorities put in place arrangements to allow applicants to review decisions made in relation to homelessness cases, and it appears that nearly 60 per cent of local authorities developed written internal appeal procedures (Cowan and Halliday, 2003: 23). However, there remained concern (probably unfounded) that the High Court was being subjected to an unnecessarily high number of judicial review cases in homelessness. The internal review process was intended therefore to provide 'a local, simple and immediate' mechanism through which homeless applicants could express their grievances – 'one which would detect and remedy deficiencies in initial decision-making and so reduce the extent to which ... external review by [the] courts was required' (ibid.: 37). However, despite the fact that 'it does not cost anything, legal representation is not required, no forms have to be filled in, [and] the applicant does not have to attend a hearing' (ibid.: 5) the take up of rights to review is quite low and the drop-out rate between internal review and the county court is very high (ibid.: 37).

A review may be carried out by the housing authority itself or by someone acting as an agent of the housing authority where the authority has contracted out its homelessness functions. Where the review is to be carried out by an officer of the housing authority, the officer must not have been involved in the original decision, and must be senior to the officer(s) who took that decision. An application for review may be made:

(a) on the applicant's eligibility for assistance under ss. 185–186;
(b) on what duty (if any) is owed under ss. 190–193 and 195–197 (duties to persons found to be homeless or threatened with homelessness);
(c) on any decision to notify another authority that the conditions for a referral of the applicant under s. 198(1) are met (i.e. to refer the applicant to another housing authority in accordance with the local connection provisions);
(d) on whether the local connection conditions are met under s. 198(5) for the referral of the applicant's case;
(e) as to the duties owed to an applicant whose case is considered for referral or referred under the local connection provisions in s. 200(3) or (4);
(f) on the suitability of accommodation offered under (b) or (e) above. (Although there is no right of review of a decision on the suitability of accommodation secured under ss. 188 or 200(1), such decisions could nevertheless be subject to judicial review.)

The application for a review must be made before the end of the period of 21 days beginning with the day on which the applicant was notified of the local authority's decision. The housing authority may specify, in writing, a longer period during which a review may be requested. The applicant is only entitled to one internal review, after which alternative means of redress must be sought (s. 202(4)).

Right of appeal

If the applicant is (a) dissatisfied with the decision on the review, or (b) not notified of the decision on the review within the time prescribed in the regulations, s. 204 of the 1996 Act provides a right of appeal to the county court on a point of law. The jurisdiction of the country court in this regard 'is in substance the same as that of the High Court in judicial review' (*Begum (Runa) v Tower Hamlets London Borough Council* [2003] 2 AC 430).

In *Begum (Runa) v Tower Hamlets London Borough Council*, the applicant (to whom the authority owed the main duty under s. 193) rejected as unsuitable the flat which she was offered on the ground that the area in which it was situated suffered from drugs and racism. An internal review under s. 202 was carried out by a more senior housing officer who found that the applicant's refusal of the offer was unreasonable. The applicant appealed to the county court under s. 204. The county court quashed the decision, holding that the local authority's failure to refer the matter to an independent tribunal was incompatible with the applicant's rights under Art. 6 of the Human Rights Act 1998 to have her 'civil rights and obligations' conducted by an 'independent and impartial tribunal established by law'. In allowing the authority's appeal, the Court of Appeal held that a determination on a review under s. 202 was a determination of an applicant's civil rights and obligations and that the reviewing officer could not be an independent and impartial tribunal for the purposes of Art. 6. However, even though it did not involve a fact-finding exercise, the appeal to the county court gave the applicant access to an independent judicial body with full jurisdictional control over the procedure. The applicant appealed to the House of Lords. The House of Lords agreed that the reviewing officer could not be regarded as an independent and impartial tribunal because her position as an employee of the authority meant that she could not be independent when deciding whether the authority had discharged its duty to the applicant. However, they further held that the county court possessed 'full jurisdiction' so as to guarantee compliance with Art. 6(1), notwithstanding that s. 204 did not enable it to examine the merits of the case but only questions of law. Delivering the main speech, Lord Hoffmann said (at para. 59) that, in deciding whether a particular statutory scheme is compatible, the question was whether, 'consistently with the rule of law and constitutional propriety', the relevant decision-making powers might be entrusted to administrators. If they could, it did not matter that there were 'many or few occasions on which they need to make findings of fact'. Furthermore, their Lordships held that the normal grounds for judicial review ensured that the housing officer's decision had been lawful and fair and did not advocate a 'more intensive' form of judicial review as being appropriate for the s. 204 appeal.

Provision of accommodation pending review or appeal

The authority may continue to secure that accommodation is available for the applicant's occupation until the determination of an appeal (s. 204(4)). In *R v London Borough of Camden ex p Mohammed* (1998) 30 HLR 315, the High Court reviewed Camden's policy of providing accommodation pending a review in exceptional circumstances only. At the time of the hearing, the council had carried out 51 reviews of decisions, but only four had been successful. The judge agreed that the authority's restrictive policy was justified in view of the low success rate. He stated that the relevant matters which local authorities must take into account include the merits of the case, new material or information provided by the applicant which could have a real effect upon the decision under review, and the impact on the applicant of an adverse decision.

Local Government Ombudsman

An applicant who is aggrieved about the decision on review may complain to a Local Government Ombudsman if he or she considers that unfair treatment has resulted from maladministration, e.g. the authority has delayed taking action without good reason, has not followed its own rules or complied with the law, has not fulfilled undertakings given to the applicant, has given the applicant the wrong information, or treated the applicant unfairly (DCLG, 2006a: 19.26).

Part III

The private rented sector

Chapter 12

Protection for private tenants: the Rent Act 1977 and the Housing Act 1988

Introduction

Both the Rent Act 1977 and the Housing Act 1988 provide protection where there is 'a tenancy of a dwelling-house . . . let as a separate dwelling' (Rent Act 1977, s. 1; Housing Act 1988, s. 1). This wording also appears in s. 79(1) of the Housing Act 1985 (which confers security of tenure, together with many other rights, upon tenants of local authority landlords) and the Housing Act 1996 (which governs introductory tenancies). In addition, the 1977 and 1988 Acts will apply only if the tenancy (a) complies with the rateable value and rental limits and (b) is not excluded either by the Acts themselves or one of the miscellaneous exceptions set out elsewhere. Protection under the 1988 Act is also conditional upon the tenant (or, in the case of a joint tenancy, each of the joint tenants) (a) being an individual and (b) occupying the dwelling-house as his or her only or principal home.

As indicated in Chapter 5, the Rent Act 1977 deals with regulated tenancies, while the Housing Act 1988 deals with assured tenancies. Regulated tenancies are of two types: protected and statutory tenancies. The former tenancy lasts so long as the contractual tenancy lasts while the latter comes into existence when the contractual tenancy comes to an end, e.g. by effluxion of time in the case of a fixed-term tenancy or on expiry of the landlord's notice to quit in the case of a periodic tenancy.

Concepts common to residential tenancies

There must be a 'tenancy'

Taking the view that the lease/licence distinction is 'out of place in a modern system of housing law', the Law Commission has recommended that its scheme should apply to all contractual agreements and not just those classifiable as tenancies (Law Commission, 2002a: 6.19) although it points out that the distinction will still be significant in the determination (in accordance with property law principles) of certain third-party rights. Until such time as the Commission's proposals reach the statute book, the term 'tenancy' includes periodic and fixed term tenancies of any length, equitable tenancies, express tenancies at will in respect of which rent is being paid (*Chamberlain v Farr* [1942] 2 All ER 567), tenancies at sufferance, tenancies by estoppel (*Stratford v Syrett* [1958] 1 QB 107), and sub-tenancies (Rent Act 1985, s. 152(1); Housing Act 1988, s. 45(1)). A genuine licence falls outside the protection of both Acts but certain types of contractual licence created before 15 January 1989 may be protected as restricted contracts under the 1977 Act (s. 19).

The extensive protection given to tenants by the Rent Acts made many landlords anxious to avoid creating leases which might not be terminable for the foreseeable future. Since protection hinged on the existence of a tenancy, landlords often granted what appeared to be licences instead of tenancies. For many years the courts generally adhered to the principle that the relationship between the parties was determined by the law, rather than the label attached to it. To depart from this approach would, said Lord Denning, 'make a hole in the Rent Acts through which could be driven – I will not say in these days a coach and four – but an articulated vehicle' (*Facchini v Bryson* [1952] 1 TLR 1386, 1389–90).

In the 1970s and early 1980s, however, 'the courts may have allowed the boundary between legitimate avoidance and illicit evasion of the Rent Act to shift in response to a perceived need to stimulate the supply of rented accommodation in large urban centres' (Gray and Gray, 2005: 7.183, n. 1). Perhaps they saw themselves as adopting a pragmatic and fundamentally humane approach, the problem of homelessness, and the housing shortage generally, having been the subject of considerable publicity for some time. More probably, they wanted to put a stop to what they considered to be an unreasonable interference by the Rent Acts with the property rights of landlords and thus took a somewhat blinkered view of the housing situation, ignoring the fact that people would agree to and sign anything in order to get a roof over their heads. In a string of cases (e.g. *Somma v Hazelhurst and Savelli* [1978] 1 WLR 1014; *Buchman v May* [1978] 2 All ER 993; *Aldrington Garages v Fielder* (1979) 37 P & CR 461), the Court of Appeal held (despite the transparent intention to avoid Rent Act protection) that the intentions of the parties – as manifested in the tenancy agreement – were paramount in determining whether an agreement was a lease or a licence. In only a few cases (e.g. *Walsh v Griffiths-Jones and Durant* [1978] 2 All ER 1002; *Demuren v Seal Estates Ltd* (1978) 249 EG 440; *O'Malley v Seymour* (1978) 250 EG 1083; *R v Rent Officer for London Borough of Camden ex p Plant* (1981) 257 EG 713) were the labels attached to evasive devices overturned. The turning point was *Street v Mountford* [1985] 1 AC 809 in which the House of Lords made it clear that what the parties call their agreement is by no means conclusive and that the intention of the parties will be deduced from the realities of the arrangement in practice, rather than that which is expressed in the agreement. As Lord Templeman said: 'The manufacture of a five-pronged implement for manual digging results in a fork, even if the manufacturer ... insists that he intended to make and has made a spade' (p. 819).

The hallmarks of a tenancy

The 'hallmarks' of a tenancy have been identified as exclusive possession for a period of time which is certain or capable of being rendered certain (*Street v Mountford* [1985] 1 AC 809). While rent is usually payable, it is not an essential ingredient of a tenancy (Law of Property Act 1925, s. 205(xxvii); *Ashburn Anstalt v Arnold (W J) & Co* [1988] 2 All ER 147) although it is an essential ingredient of Rent Act and Housing Act 1988 protection. As regards certainty, a finite point must either be expressed or implied from the outset or be capable of being rendered certain (*Prudential Assurance v London Residuary Body* [1992] 3 All ER 504). Thus in *Lace v Chantler* [1944] KB 368, an agreement that a house should be let 'furnished for the duration' (meaning the duration of the war) was void for uncertainty because, at the time when the lease took effect, no one knew how long the war would last.

In *Street v Mountford*, the House of Lords stated that, in order to determine an occupier's status, the courts need only enquire 'whether as a result of an agreement relating to residential accommodation, the occupier is a lodger or a tenant'. A person will be a lodger only where 'the landlord provides attendance or services (such as cleaning the room or changing the linen) which require the landlord or his servants to exercise unrestricted access to and use of the premises'. The decision in *Abbeyfield (Harpenden) Society Ltd v Woods* [1968] 1 WLR 374 (in which the occupier of a room in an old people's home was held to be a licensee even though he had exclusive possession of his room) was approved. A broader approach is appropriate, however, and a combination of factors should be taken into account, when the fact of exclusive occupation is in issue. Where this is the case, the court must ask itself:

(a) Is there a grant of exclusive possession to the occupier? Exclusive possession is the right to exclude everyone from the premises, including the landlord. In the words of Lord Donaldson MR it is 'the touchstone by which the "spade" of tenancy falls to be distinguished from the "fork" of lodging (*Aslan v Murphy* [1989] 3 All ER 130, 133). The fact that the landlord has reserved a right to enter any part of the accommodation to inspect or repair it does not destroy the occupier's exclusive possession.

(b) If there is exclusive possession, is it referable to some relationship other than a tenancy? There may be occasions when an occupier has exclusive possession but nonetheless is merely a licensee. The occupier may be a service occupier, i.e. an employee who occupies the employer's premises in order better to perform the duties as an employee (*Norris v Checksfield* (1991) 23 HLR 425), or there may have been something in the circumstances, e.g. a family arrangement, or act of friendship or generosity, which negatives any intention to enter into legal relations. Examples can be found in *Cobb v Lane* (1952) 1 TLR 1037 (where the owner of a house allowed her brother to live in it rent-free), and *Booker v Palmer* [1942] 2 All ER 674 (where evacuees were allowed to stay in a cottage rent-free for the duration of the war) but a transaction between family members does not always indicate a lack of intention to enter into legal relations (*Ward v Warnke* (1990) 22 HLR 496). In *Gray v Taylor* [1998] 1 WLR 1093 the Court of Appeal decided that the occupier of an almshouse owned by a charitable trust was a licensee. The existence of a tenancy – and the consequent enjoyment of security of tenure – might be inconsistent with the objects of the trust and could make it impossible for the trustees to ensure that occupation of the almshouse was restricted to persons who satisfied the qualifications required. The court concluded that it was only the relationship of trustee and beneficiary which empowered the trustees to grant an almsperson a right of occupation. Their power did not allow them, however, to grant a right which would or might infringe the charity's objects by permitting the grantee to remain in occupation after she had ceased to qualify as a beneficiary. On this analysis it was clear that the almsperson's occupation and her right to exclusive possession were referable to a legal relationship other than a tenancy, thus bringing the case outside the general category identified in *Street v Mountford*.

In *Errington v Errington and Woods* [1952] 1 KB 290, Denning LJ also stated that there could be no tenancy (even if the occupier had exclusive possession) where the grantor had no power to grant a tenancy. It was not made clear however whether this was confined to want of capacity, or if it extended to want of title. The question was settled in *Bruton v London & Quadrant Housing Trust* [2000] 1 AC 406, the outcome of which is that if the grantor has legal capacity but lacks title, the existence of the landlord and tenant relationship will depend on the terms of any agreement between the parties. In *Bruton*, Lambeth council had compulsorily purchased a number of properties as part of a redevelopment scheme which was intended to regenerate the centre of Brixton. In the meantime, Lambeth granted the London & Quadrant Housing Trust (the Trust) a licence to use the properties as temporary accommodation for homeless persons. Mr Bruton signed an agreement with the Trust for occupation of a self-contained flat in one of the properties on a weekly licence. The agreement noted that the Trust held the premises on licence from the local authority pending development and that, until such development took place, they were being used to provide temporary housing accommodation. It required the occupier to vacate the premises upon receiving reasonable notice from the Trust (which would not normally be less than four weeks) and provided that the Trust could enter the premises to inspect the state of repair, etc. at all reasonable hours of the day. The redevelopment scheme was shelved and the properties continued to be used as short-term accommodation for the homeless (although, by the time the case reached the House of Lords, Mr Bruton had been living in his flat for 10 years). Mr Bruton brought proceedings in the county court claiming that he was a tenant of the premises and seeking specific performance by the Trust of an implied repairing covenant under s. 11 of the Landlord and Tenant Act 1985 (see Chapter 8). The question to be answered was whether Mr Bruton occupied the premises as a tenant or licensee.

One of the reasons given by the Court of Appeal for rejecting Mr Bruton's argument was that Mr Bruton did not have exclusive possession, because the Trust could not grant him such a right. Millett LJ took the view that:

> in this context ... exclusive possession means possession to the exclusion of the whole world, not merely of the grantor and those claiming through him. If the grantor has no power to exclude the true owner from possession, he has no power to grant a legal right to exclusive possession and his grant cannot take effect as a tenancy.

The House of Lords, however, allowed Mr Bruton's appeal. Basing its decision on *Street v Mountford*, it found that the three indicia of a tenancy were present in the arrangement between Mr Bruton and the Trust. Exclusive possession existed because 'there was nothing to suggest that [Mr Bruton] was to share possession with the [T]rust, the council or anyone else'. Further, the Trust's lack of title was held to be irrelevant since it was the character of the agreement rather than the nature of the landlord or its estate which determined whether a lease had been created.

The conclusion reached by the House of Lords has provoked extensive debate (see, e.g. Bright, 2000a; Pawlowski, 2002; Hinojosa, 2005) and its full implications are still being worked through. A number of observations can be made. First, the House of Lords appears to have created a new type of contractual, non-proprietary tenancy, the existence of which depends neither on the grantor having an estate or interest in the land, nor upon estoppel. According to Lord Hoffmann, 'the term "lease" or "tenancy" describes a legal relationship between two parties who are designated landlord and tenant' and 'is not concerned with . . . whether the agreement creates an estate or other proprietary interest which may be binding upon third parties'. The creation of such an estate or interest 'will depend upon whether the landlord had an interest out of which he could grant it . . . But it is the fact that the agreement is a lease which creates the proprietary interest'. However, such an analysis fails to address the question of whether there can truly be said to be a grant of exclusive possession where the grantor has no exclusive possession to give. The grantor's lack of title is surely a 'special circumstance' to be considered in determining whether or not a tenancy has been granted or, as second best, a tenancy by estoppel has come into being.

Secondly, the decision has far-reaching practical implications. Lords Slynn and Jauncey shared the concern expressed by Slade LJ in *Family Housing Association v* Jones [1990] 1 All ER 385 that the result would be substantially to reduce the choice of methods available to . . . [housing associations] for dealing with their always limited supplies of housing stock' which would not 'necessarily inure to the benefit of the class of homeless persons in this country viewed as a whole' (p. 396). The fact that in *Bruton* the Trust existed to provide accommodation for the homeless and 'to that end to maintain a stock of housing over which it [had] maximum control, which a licence rather than a tenancy might be more likely to give' did not constitute 'special circumstances' negativing the grant of a tenancy (p. 410). In this regard, a contrast may be made with *Westminster City Council v Clarke* [1992] 2 AC 288 (in which emergency housing was provided by the council) and *Gray v Taylor* [1998] 1 WLR 1093 (in which charitable purposes surrounded the grant of occupation).[1] As a result, there is every chance that social landlords will have to pay even greater attention to the degree of control they exert over their premises if they wish to deny occupants exclusive possession.

Thirdly, the extent to which a 'contractual' licence may be enforced (if at all) against the freeholder of the property – or indeed against third parties generally – was left open. Given the decision in *Dutton v Manchester Airport plc* [1999] 2 All ER (that a licensee with a contractual right to occupy could sue to recover possession against a trespasser), Harwood suggests that 'there can be little doubt that [a *Bruton* tenancy] would be enforceable against a stranger' (Harwood, 2000: 512). However, Lord Hoffmann declined to express a view on whether Mr Bruton was a secure tenant under the Housing Act 1985 or on the rights of the council to recover possession of the flat, although in his dissenting judgment in the Court of Appeal, Sir Brian Neill concluded that Mr Bruton's tenancy would not affect the rights of the council ([1998] QB 834, 842). The point has since been addressed by the House of Lords in *Lambeth London Borough Council v Kay* [2006] 2 WLR 570. Lambeth's response to the House of Lords decision in *Bruton* was to terminate the lease with which, in 1995, it had replaced the original licence to the Trust and to begin possession proceedings against the individual occupiers on the basis that they were trespassers. The occupiers argued that on the termination of the lease they had become tenants of the local authority and, alternatively, that Art. 8 of the Human Rights Act 1998 afforded them a defence to the claim. The House of Lords held that since the tenancies were granted by the Trust when it was itself merely a licensee, they did not at any stage amount to derivative estates. While the Trust could not surrender its licence so as to give away or prejudice the rights of the *Bruton* tenants against

---

1 This point is made by Dixon who concludes that a 'non-proprietary lease' is 'a contradiction in terms' and 'otherwise better called a licence!' (Dixon, 2000: 27).

itself, those rights were never enforceable against Lambeth. Once the Trust's licence had been terminated, the occupiers were – vis-à-vis Lambeth – trespassers. Further, when in 1995 Lambeth granted the Trust a term of years, the *Bruton* tenancies were 'fed' by the estate which the Trust acquired but because they were derived from the 1995 lease, they could not (in the absence of statutory intervention) survive its termination. The House of Lords also rejected unanimously the occupiers' submission that compliance with Art. 8 required the court to consider proportionality with each and every possession claim. Where the occupier's right to possess has come to an end or he never had such a right in the first place, it will only be in highly exceptional circumstances that interference will not be justifiable in accordance with Art. 8(2). The implications of finding to the contrary would have been far-reaching; the ability of public landowners to manage housing stock would have been impeded while the administrative burden on the county courts of dealing with possession claims would have increased immeasurably.

In *Islington v Green and O'Shea* [2005] HLR 35 (the facts of which were analogous to those of *Bruton*), the Court of Appeal rejected the occupiers' argument that, in entering into the tenancy, the landlord housing association was acting as the council's agent and was able to bind its principal to the contract made within the scope of its actual or ostensible authority under the licence. On the contrary, the terms of the licence made it clear that, upon termination, the association was to give up vacant possession and that the council would not accept responsibility to re-house occupiers of the property unless it had a legal obligation to do so. Blackburne J also concluded that even if the association had a sufficient estate in the property (or the requisite authority to grant a sub-tenancy binding on the council), the sub-tenancy would automatically have come to an end with the ending of the head tenancy. This begs the question, however, as to the nature of the tenancy created between the association and the occupiers, i.e. the statutory code (if any) to which it was subject. The normal common law rule is indeed that if a head lease comes to an end, any sub-lease granted out of it will also determine. For assured tenancies, however, the rule is varied by s. 18 of the Housing Act 1988 which provides that where a dwelling-house is lawfully sub-let on an assured tenancy and the head lease comes to an end for whatever reason, the sub-lease will continue. The assured sub-tenant will, therefore, become the direct tenant of the head landlord with full security of tenure.

Non-exclusive possession agreements

One way in which landlords have purported to disguise the grant of a tenancy has been by way of 'non-exclusive possession agreements' under which rights of shared occupation only are granted to two or more people, reserving to the landlord the right to select another occupier if one should vacate the premises, or to introduce another occupier at any time, or to use the whole or part of the accommodation him or herself. The House of Lords decision in *Street v Mountford* concerned a single occupier and the owner had conceded that there was exclusive possession. The judgment, therefore, was not directly concerned to analyse purported non-exclusive occupation licences. Nonetheless, Lord Templeman exhorted the courts to be astute in detecting and frustrating 'sham devices and artificial transactions whose only objective is to disguise the grant of a tenancy and to avoid the Rent Acts'.

The leading authority on non-exclusive occupation agreements is the decision of the House of Lords in *Antoniades v Villiers* [1988] 3 WLR 1205 in which an unmarried couple occupied an attic flat, comprising a bedroom, a bed-sitting room, a kitchen and a bathroom. The furniture in the bed-sitting room consisted of a bed settee, a table-bed, a sideboard and a chair. When the owner showed the flat to the couple, he agreed to put a double bed in the bedroom. Each of the proposed occupants concurrently signed identical agreements described as licences which reserved a right to the owner to occupy the flat himself or permit others to do so. The House of Lords held that the two agreements were interdependent. The couple had acquired, and enjoyed, exclusive occupation of the whole of the flat in consideration for periodical payments. They had a tenancy. The clause giving the landlord power to share occupation with them was only designed to disguise the grant of a tenancy. It was a sham or pretence. The flat was situated in an attic with a sloping roof and was too small for sharing between strangers and was not suitable for multiple occupation.

In *A. G. Securities v Vaughan* [1988] 3 WLR 1205 (consolidated with *Antoniades v Villiers* for the purposes of the House of Lords hearing), the flat in question consisted of four bedrooms, a kitchen and a bathroom. The company customarily granted short-term licence agreements to individual occupiers. At different times between 1982 and 1985, it entered into four separate agreements with four different people. The agreements, each for six months, were in the same form – except for the amount payable – and gave each occupant the right to use the flat in common with up to three others. They did not reserve a right for the company to share the flat, but they did provide that further licences could be granted, up to four in total. When one occupant left, the company could nominate a replacement and had the final say on who should fill each vacancy even though, in practice, it was willing to accept someone put forward by the remaining occupiers. The company never specified that any occupant should have a particular bedroom, and from time to time people changed rooms. In the House of Lords, Lord Templeman said that if the four occupants had been jointly entitled to exclusive possession then, on the death of one of them, the right of survivorship would have come into play and the remaining three would have been entitled to joint and exclusive occupation. In fact, however, they could not exclude a fourth person nominated by the company. The four agreements were independent of one another. The four unities necessary to create a joint tenancy – possession, interest, time and title – were not all present, nor was there any suggestion of sham or pretence in respect of the individual agreements.

The effect of *A. G. Securities v Vaughan* is that where individuals join the sharing arrangement at different times – so that there is a genuine turnover in the occupation of the premises and the separate agreements can in reality be seen as a series of individual rights of occupation – there will be no joint tenancy unless at some subsequent time it is expressly granted. If each of the occupiers has exclusive possession of a particular room, it might be possible to argue that he or she is a tenant of that room. The fact that there is shared use of, e.g. a sitting room or bathroom does not of itself prevent a protected or an assured tenancy from arising. This argument was not made in *A. G. Securities v Vaughan*, but Lord Oliver in any event felt that individual tenancies would arise only 'if the facts support the marking out with the landlord's concurrence of a particular room as the exclusive domain of a particular individual'.

A joint tenancy involves jointly liablity for the rent. This last point formed the central issue in *Mikeover Ltd v Brady* [1989] 3 All ER 618 where cohabitees were each required to sign separate but identical agreements which required them to make separate payments to the owners as consideration for the right to occupy. When one of them later moved out of the flat, the remaining occupant offered to pay her share of the monthly payment. The owners rejected this offer. The Court of Appeal held that the effect of the two agreements was to confer on the couple together a right of joint exclusive occupation. There was no unity of interest, however, because the provisions for the payment of rent created separate obligations, rather than a joint obligation to pay the whole rent.

In *Aslan v Murphy (No 1)* [1989] 3 All ER 130 the credibility of a non-exclusive occupation agreement was stretched to the limit. However, the Court of Appeal did not consider whether the provisions as to non-exclusive occupation were pretences, its decision focusing instead on the owner's retention of keys. Mr Murphy occupied a basement room measuring $4^r\ 3^{rr} \times 12^r\ 6^{rr}$ under an agreement which stated that the 'licensor' was not willing to grant the 'licensee' exclusive possession of any part of the room. The use of the room given to Mr Murphy was, according to the document, in common with the licensor and/or such other licensees or invitees as the licensor might permit from time to time to use it (presumably, given the size of the room, only if they arranged themselves into a human pyramid!). The agreement limited Mr Murphy's use of the room to the hours between midnight and 10.30 am, and between noon and midnight. It also provided for various services, including house-keeping, the cleaning of rooms and windows, the collection of rubbish, the provision of household supplies, and the provision and laundering of bed linen. It was stipulated that the 'licensor' would retain the keys to the room and had an absolute right of entry at all times. Lord Donaldson, delivering the judgment of the Court of Appeal, stated that provisions as to keys 'do not have any magic in themselves'. What matters is why a provision for keys appears in the bargain. If it appears that the owner is retaining keys in case of emergency, or to read the meters or to carry out repairs 'none of these underlying reasons would of themselves indicate ... that the occupier was in law a lodger'. If, on the other hand, the true bargain is that the owner will provide genuine services (such as frequent cleaning, daily bed-making and the regular provision of clean bed-linen) for which the retention of keys is necessary, it would be possible to infer that the occupier is a lodger rather than a tenant. Since in *Aslan* virtually no services were provided during the currency of the agreement, there were no underlying reasons for access from which it was possible to infer that Mr Murphy was a lodger.

Simply because there a number of cases in which non-exclusive possession agreements have been overturned, does not mean that such agreements are always held to be ineffective. A non-resident landlord can validly reserve the right to share, even if he or she does not actually exercise that right, nor have a clear intention of doing so, so long as the possibility of moving into the premises is genuinely within his or her contemplation at the time of the tenancy. The question which must be addressed is whether or not there is a real prospect of the landlord's doing so at some future time (*Gray v Brown* (1993) 25 HLR 144). It is important to remember, however, that the need for landlords to use such evasive measures has all but disappeared since the advent of assured shorthold tenancies under the Housing Act 1988.

There must be a 'dwelling-house'

There is no statutory definition of 'dwelling-house', but the term covers anywhere immobile which is constructed or adapted for use as or for the purposes of a dwelling (*Ashridge Investments Ltd v Minister of Housing and Local Government* [1965] 1 WLR 1320). Thus an immobilised caravan can constitute a dwelling-house (*Makins v Elson* [1977] 1 WLR 687), but not a moored houseboat because it is not annexed to the land to the extent that it has become part of the land (*Chelsea Yacht & Boat Co Ltd v Pope* [2000] 1 WLR 1941). The time at which it has to be judged whether premises are entitled to protection is when the proceedings are brought (*Prout v Hunter* [1924] 2 KB 736).

Traditionally, a dwelling-house was viewed as a place where the tenant could carry on all the 'ordinary activities of daily existence': sleeping, cooking and eating. If one or more of the ordinary activities of daily existence could not take place on the premises, they could not amount to a dwelling-house and a tenancy of them was not, therefore, protected under the Rent Acts or assured under the Housing Act 1988 (e.g. *Wright v Howell* (1948) 92 SJ 26). The question for the House of Lords in *Uratemp Ventures Limited v Collins* [2002] 1 AC 301 was whether a room could be a 'dwelling-house' if it had no cooking facilities. Mr Collins moved into a residential hotel in 1985. His room contained a single bed, some furniture, a shower and a basin, but no cooking facilities. The only meal provided was breakfast, and even that ceased to be available after 1988 when the hotel's restaurant closed. Mr Collins brought into his room various items of electrical equipment which he used to prepare simple meals: a pizza warmer, a toasted sandwich maker, a warming plate, a kettle, and what he described as an 'underlight'. He also ate takeaway meals there. In 1993 the hotel published rules which, on safety grounds, prohibited cooking in rooms otherwise than by the use of microwaves and kettles. Residents were required to accept the rules by signing them but Mr Collins never did so. No services were provided. In acknowledging that 'the legislative purpose of the Rent and Housing Acts is to protect people in the occupation of their homes, not to encourage them to cook their own meals', the House of Lords decided that the 'ordinary activities of daily life' did not include cooking; a room will constitute a dwelling if the occupier can merely sleep and eat there. Lord Millett summarised the position as follows: if the subject-matter of the tenancy agreement is a house or part of a house of which the tenant has exclusive possession with no element of sharing, the only question is whether it is the tenant's home. If so, it is his dwelling. The presence or absence of cooking facilities is irrelevant. In reaching their decision, their Lordships were mindful of the social changes which had taken place (including the growth in the number of single person households and the proliferation of 'self-service cafeteria, sandwich shops, takeaway shops, home delivery services and other fast food outlets') which made it necessary to interpret the legislation 'in the world of today'. While Lord Bingham of Cornhill voiced his reluctance to regard as a dwelling-house a room which was 'so small and cramped as to be unable to accommodate a bed', Lord Irvine even went so far as to suggest that '… one could live in a room, which is regarded and treated as home, although taking one's sleep, without the luxury of a bed, in an armchair, or in blankets on the floor' (para. 4).

Under the Rent Act 1977, the dwelling-house 'may be a house or part of a house'. Of course, it is common for more than one dwelling-house to exist within the walls of a single building. In *Luganda v Service Hotels Ltd* [1969] 2 Ch 209 (a case on restricted contracts) a single furnished room equipped with a gas ring was held to be 'part of a house'. The 'house' in question had formerly consisted of four houses but was now a hotel with 88 rooms.

The dwelling-house must be 'let as a separate dwelling'

Rent

Fundamental to the Rent Act 1977 (and to a lesser extent, the Housing Act 1988) is the provision of machinery for the regulation and control of the rent. This could not operate if the rent payable was not quantifiable in money terms.

Rent could not, therefore, include the value of services rendered by the tenant for the benefit of the landlord such as the cleaning of rooms, and the payment of gas and electricity bills (*Barnes v Barratt* [1970] 2 QB 657). However, in *Montagu v Browning* [1954] 1 WLR 1039 Lord Denning stated that:

> ... in cases where rent is not payable in money but in kind, as in goods or services, then, so long as the parties have by agreement quantified the value in terms of money, the sum so quantified is the rent of the house within the meaning of the [Rent Acts]; and if it exceeds two-thirds of the rateable value, the house is within the Acts.

Thus, where the tenant who was employed by his landlord, occupied rent-free accommodation provided by his employer, and received a smaller wage as a result, it was proper to quantify the rent by reference to the reduction in wages. In *Bostock v Bryant* (1990) 22 HLR 449, where the accommodation was provided on the basis that the occupier paid the gas and electricity bills, Stuart Smith LJ said that:

> it would be a most unsatisfactory arrangement if a tenancy could be a protected tenancy one moment and an unprotected tenancy the next, depending on the fluctuating fuel bills of summer and depending on when notice terminating the tenancy was served.
>
> (At p. 455.)

The purpose of the letting

For the purposes of a Rent Act *protected* tenancy, it is irrelevant that the tenant never lives there (*Horford Investments v Lambert* [1976] 1 Ch 39). However, a *statutory* tenant under the Rent Act must continue to occupy the property as a 'residence' in order to enjoy protection (s. 2), while a person can be an assured tenant under the Housing Act 1988 only if the premises in question are occupied as his or her 'only or principal home' (s. 1).

Premises are let as a dwelling if the lease provides that they will be occupied for residential purposes. Where the use of a building changes during the course of the lease, the general rule is that the original terms of the tenancy, and not subsequent actual user, determine the purpose of the letting. Conversely, if the lease describes the premises as let for business purposes (*Ponder v Hillman* [1969] 3 All ER 694), or contains user covenants expressly prohibiting residential user, or clearly contemplates a particular, non-residential purpose (*Court v Robinson* [1951] 2 KB 60), or there is a verbal agreement that they will not be used as a dwelling (*Williams v Perry* [1924] 1 KB 936), neither the Rent Acts nor the Housing Act can apply to the tenancy at any time unless the landlord consents to, or accepts, a change from business to residential user. Similarly, where a business tenant unilaterally changes the use of the premises from business to residential, the tenancy will be neither protected nor assured (*Pulleng v Curran* (1982) 44 P & CR 58) unless the landlord by an express or implied consent (such as a prolonged acceptance of the rent with knowledge of the change) or waiver, agrees to the change and varies the terms of the lease.

Where the purpose of the letting is not discernible from the tenancy agreement, the courts will look at the surrounding circumstances and whether the property is constructed as a dwelling-house or as business premises, e.g. a lock-up shop. If the construction of the property does not indicate one way or another the intended use of the property, then the actual user of the premises must be considered (see, e.g. *Wolfe v Hogan* [1949] 2 KB 194; *Russell v Booker* (1982) 263 EG 513; *Gidden v Mills* [1925] 2 KB 713).

If the tenancy agreement permits both business and residential user, the letting will be subject to Part II of the Landlord and Tenant Act 1954, unless the business user is merely incidental to the residential user (*Cheryl Investments Ltd v Saldhana, Royal Life Saving Society v Page* [1978] 1 WLR 1329). Section 24(3) of the Rent Act 1977 states that a tenancy cannot be a regulated tenancy if it is one to which Part II of the 1954 Act applies, i.e. if the property comprised in the tenancy is or includes premises which are occupied by the tenant for the purpose of a business carried on by him, or for those and other purposes (Landlord and Tenant Act 1954, s. 23(1)). A letting of a dwelling-house to a tenant for the purpose of the tenant making a profit from subletting is not a letting for business purposes as no business is carried on there (*Horford Investments v Lambert* [1976] 1 Ch 39).

The dwelling-house must be let as 'a' separate dwelling

Both Acts can apply only to lettings of one unit. However, two or more physically separate units, demised together, may together constitute a single dwelling as in *Langford Property Co. v Goldrich* [1949] 1 KB 511 in which two self-contained but not adjoining properties (which had previously been separately let) were let together for the first time under one tenancy and occupied by the tenant as a home for himself and his family. The properties were held to constitute one dwelling-house for the purpose of the Rent Acts. This decision was followed in *Whitty v Scott-Russell* [1950] 2 KB 32 where a house, cottage and land attached thereto were demised in one lease, the tenant covenanting to use the whole premises as 'a private dwelling-house only'.

In *Horford Investments v Lambert* [1976] 1 Ch 39, two houses (which had already been converted into a number of units of accommodation) were leased separately by the landlords to the same tenant who covenanted not to use them other than as residential premises in multiple occupation. The court held that the term 'dwelling' should be given a singular construction and that neither tenancy fell within the definition of a protected tenancy as both houses had been let as a number of separate dwellings. This principle was followed in *St Catherine's College v Dorling* [1979] 3 All ER 250 in which the college rented a large house for sub-letting to persons 'pursuing or intending to pursue a course of study'. The house contained rooms suitable for use as study/bedsitting rooms by five students who would share the kitchen and bathroom. It was held that the Rent Act did not apply, the property having been let not let as 'a' dwelling but as several dwellings.

In cases such as *Horford Investments v Lambert* and *St Catherine's College v Dorling* where the head tenancy fails to fulfil all the criteria for statutory protection, the sub-tenancies may (unless they are excluded) be protected as against the tenant.

The dwelling-house must be let as a 'separate' dwelling

Most tenants will have exclusive possession of all the accommodation they use, being totally separate from other occupiers. Further, as indicated above, joint tenants are not regarded as sharers but are deemed to occupy their accommodation as a single entity (*Antoniades v Villiers* [1988] 3 WLR 1205). It is often the case, however, that the demised premises are not self-contained and the tenant is given the right to share certain rooms (such as a kitchen or bathroom), either with the landlord or with other tenants.

Accommodation shared with the landlord

Before 1974, a tenant who shared 'living' accommodation with his landlord was not fully protected under the Rent Acts but had the benefit of what is now a restricted contract. A tenant who shared accommodation other than living accommodation with the landlord was fully protected.

The Rent Act 1974 introduced the resident landlord rules, which do not require any element of sharing of living or other accommodation, but merely that the landlord should be resident in the same building. These rules, which are more fully explained in Chapter 13, operate to give the tenant a restricted contract instead of a protected tenancy where the arrangement was entered into before the 15 January 1989. Under the Housing Act 1988, no new restricted contracts can be created and a tenancy granted by a resident landlord cannot be an assured tenancy. It will, however, be subject to ss. 3 and 5 of the Protection from Eviction Act 1977 unless the landlord or any member of his family share accommodation with the tenant, in which case the tenancy will be excluded and the provisions of ss. 3 and 5 will not apply. (See Chapter 15.)

Accommodation shared with other tenants

Where a non-resident landlord grants a tenant exclusive occupation of, say, a bedroom but the tenant shares the remainder (kitchen, bathroom, sitting room) with someone else, the separate accommodation cannot be regarded as a dwelling-house since the 'ordinary activities of daily existence' will be carried on in the house as a whole rather than in the room by itself (see above). No distinction is drawn between 'living' and other accommodation.

However, the tenant will have a protected or assured tenancy of the separate accommodation despite the sharing element if the basic requirements set out in s. 1 of the Rent Act 1977 or the Housing Act 1988 as appropriate are met. Protection is secured in two ways: first, whilst the tenant is in possession of the separate accommodation, any term or condition purportedly modifying his right to use the shared living accommodation is ineffective (Rent Act 1985, s. 22(3); Housing Act 1988, s. 3(3)). That is to say that the landlord cannot exclude the tenant from the shared areas without lawfully evicting him from the whole. Secondly, a possession order cannot be made in respect of the shared accommodation unless an order is also made in respect of the separate accommodation (Rent Act 1985, s. 22(5); Housing Act 1988, s. 10).

The statutory tenancy under the Rent Act 1977

Introduction

The statutory tenancy is a concept unique to the Rent Act. At common law, the expiry or termination of a contractual tenancy ends the tenant's rights of occupation. The Rent Act, however, confers a statutory tenancy where (a) the tenant holds over from a contractual tenancy which has terminated by expiry of a fixed term, notice to quit, or forfeiture; (b) the tenancy was a protected tenancy at the date of its termination; (c) the tenant was occupying the premises as a residence at the date of termination (regardless of whether or not he or she was living in the premises throughout the contractual period of the tenancy); and (d) the tenant continues to occupy the dwelling-house as his or her residence (s. 2).

A landlord's acceptance of rent from a statutory tenant who holds over after the tenancy has ended, does not create a new or renewed contractual tenancy because the landlord has no choice but to accept it (*Davies v Bristow* [1920] 3 KB 428; *Morrison v Jacobs* [1945] KB 577). The tenant cannot contract out of the statutory entitlement but may ask for, or receive, payment from the landlord as a condition of giving up possession. A request to, or payment from, anyone other than the landlord constitutes an offence (Sch. 1, para. 12).

The nature and value of the statutory tenancy

Statutory tenants are not true tenants since they have no estate or interest in the premises, no existing contract of tenancy and no right at common law to retain possession. Instead, they possess what Lush J described in *Keeves v*

Dean [1924] 1 KB 685, 686 as a statutorily protected 'status of irremoveability', i.e. a right as against all the world to remain in possession until they are turned out by an order of the court. They can also bring an action in trespass against anyone who enters the premises without their permission. In the same case, Bankes LJ explained that the statutory tenant's right is 'a purely personal one, and as such ... must cease the moment [the tenant] parts with the possession or dies' (at p. 690).

Generally speaking, a statutory tenancy is not assignable and cannot be transmitted by will (*John Lovibond and Sons v Vincent* [1929] 1 KB 687). However, up to two statutory transmissions may take place in favour of the spouse and/or members of the family of the deceased tenant (see Chapter 9). Furthermore, the landlord may agree to a transfer of a statutory tenancy to a third party (Sch. 1, para. 13) and Sch. 7 to the Family Law Act 1996 enables the court, during divorce proceedings, judicial separation, etc. to make an order directing that a formerly non-tenant spouse, civil partner or cohabitant is deemed to be the statutory tenant. A statutory tenant may sublet part of the premises and remain a statutory tenant of the retained part (*Berkeley v Papadoyannis* [1954] 2 QB 149) but if the whole is sublet, the statutory tenancy will cease, as the residence requirement of s. 2 will no longer be satisfied (*Haskins v Lewis* [1931] 2 KB 1; *Brown v Bestwick* [1950] 2 All ER 338).

A statutory tenancy is a valuable asset despite the fact that it 'cannot be bought and sold on the open market' and, because of the residence requirements, 'cannot be seen as an income-producing asset' (Hand, 1980: 355–6). In *Murray v Lloyd* [1989] 1 WLR 1060, the claimant recovered damages of £115,000 from the solicitors who gave negligent advice which led to her losing the opportunity of becoming a statutory tenant. Most regulated tenants are people of much more modest means so that 'in the circles in which these parties move possession of [a flat subject to a statutory tenancy] is one of the most significant rights of property that any of them ever see in their lives' (*Mafo v Adams* [1970] 1 QB 548, 557).

Continued residence

Until 1968 the Rent Acts did not themselves require that the statutory tenant should continue to occupy the dwelling-house in question as a residence but the courts soon recognised the intention of the legislation and insisted on such a condition being met. As Scrutton LJ pointed out in *Skinner v Geary* [1931] 2 KB 546, 564, the Rent Acts were intended 'to provide as many houses as possible at a moderate rent' and it followed that somebody who did not live in a house and never intended to do so was 'withdrawing from circulation [a] house which was intended for occupation by other people'; to treat such a person as entitled to protection would be 'completely to misunderstand and misapply the policy of the Acts'. The only person who can become a statutory tenant is the person who was the protected tenant on termination of the tenancy and it is his or her residence which must continue in order to keep the statutory tenancy alive. If a statutory tenant ceases to reside in the property, the protection of the Rent Act is lost completely and a landlord bringing possession proceedings need only prove ownership of the property, the termination of the contractual tenancy and the fact that the tenant no longer resides there. A limited liability company can be a protected tenant within the 1977 Act, but it cannot 'reside' in a dwelling-house personally and is incapable, therefore, of becoming a statutory tenant (*Hiller v United Dairies (London) Ltd* [1934] 1 KB 57). Even if the tenancy was granted to a company on the basis that someone else was to reside in the property, no statutory tenancy exists in favour of that other person (*S.L. Dando Ltd v Hitchcock* [1954] 2 QB 317; *Firstcross Ltd v East West (Export/Import) Ltd* (1980) 41 P & CR 145).

Where the statutory tenant leaves the matrimonial home, security of tenure is not lost so long as the tenant's spouse or civil partner continues to occupy the property as a residence (Family Law Act 1996, s. 30(4)(a)). The tenant remains liable under the tenancy but the landlord is obliged to accept payments from the occupier as if they were from the tenant (s. 30(3)). Unlike married couples, non-tenant cohabitants have no automatic right to pay rent and the landlord can therefore refuse payment but they can apply for occupation orders and acquire the right to remain in occupation (s. 36). Orders are for up to six months, and may be extended for a further period not exceeding six months (s. 36(10)).

As Widgery LJ explained in *Mafo v Adams* [1970] 1 QB 548, 557 'to retain possession or occupation for the purpose of retaining protection the tenant cannot be compelled to spend twenty-four hours in all weathers under his own roof for three hundred and sixty-five days in the year'. Thus, the tenant of a house in London who spends his weekends in the country or his summer holiday in Scotland does not necessarily cease to be in occupation. Nevertheless, absence may be continuous and sufficiently long to raise an inference that possession or occupation has come to an end. The question is one of fact and degree. A tenant may be absent from the dwelling for several years but still regarded as occupying the premises as a residence within the meaning of s. 2(1)(a) provided that, in accordance with the principles laid down in *Brown v Brash and Ambrose* [1948] 2 KB 247, he or she can show both (a) a continuing physical presence and (b) an intention to return. These will be dealt with in turn.

A physical presence (*corpus possessionis*) requires some outward and visible evidence of the tenant's intention to return, e.g. furniture; a caretaker to look after the premises, or relatives. In *Brown v Brash and Ambrose* the tenant was sentenced to two years' imprisonment, leaving his partner and children in occupation. Soon afterwards the partner moved out, taking the children and all but three items of furniture. Thereafter, the tenant's relatives came in for a few hours each week to clean. Ten months after his partner had left, the tenant was released from prison. The Court of Appeal held that the tenant had stopped residing at the premises when his partner and children left. Although he possessed the *animus possidendi*, he lacked any *corpus possessionis*, because there was no intention that the three items of furniture should constitute symbols of possession. The fact that his absence was involuntary did not assist him. Once lost, his Rent Act protection could not be revived.

At the time of the hearing in *Gofor Investments v Roberts* (1975) P & CR 366 – a case described as 'the salvation of many an absent tenant' (Bridge, 1988: 302) – the tenants had been living in Morocco and Malta for five years and were intending to return within three to five years. They had left their furniture and two sons in the premises. In *Brickfield Properties Ltd v Hughes* (1988) 20 HLR 108, a statutory tenant of a flat in London (in which he kept books and furniture) lived most of the time with his wife in a cottage in Lancashire. Between 1978 and 1987 he did not visit the flat at all. His wife visited it three times. During this period the flat was occupied by his three adult children and a son-in-law. The tenant's wife was in poor health and the tenant intended to return to London if her health became worse or she died. As Bridge observes, 'it demands an inordinately metaphysical construction of the role of the furniture to describe it, after nearly ten years, as the deliberate symbol of the father's continuing occupation, and a supremely unrealistic view of the children's residence as being primarily for the benefit of safeguarding the flat for his eventual return' (Bridge, 1988). However, the court had to contend with the 'insurmountable obstacle' of *Gofor Investments* and, because there was a real possibility of the tenant's return to the flat within a reasonable time, the landlord's application for possession was dismissed.

An intention to return (*animus revertendi*) must involve more than a vague wish or 'pipe-dream' (*Baron v Phillips* (1978) 38 P & CR 91). It must be 'a real hope, coupled with the practical possibility of its fulfilment within a reasonable time' (*Tickner v Hearn* [1960] 1 WLR 1406). What is a reasonable time depends on the circumstances. If the tenant is forced to leave by 'some sudden calamity', such as hospitalisation, a sentence of imprisonment or a flood, it will be regarded as a temporary expedient (*Bushford v Falco* [1954] 1 All ER 957). In *Tickner v Hearn* the tenant, a schizophrenic, was hospitalised for five and a half years. That she was 'mentally unsound' did not mean, on the facts, that she was incapable of forming an intention to return to the premises.

Residence in two homes

The notion of the 'two-home man' reflects the fact that, not so very many years ago, the private rented sector provided long-term housing for many middle-class households. A tenant may occupy two properties at the same time, maintaining Rent Act protection in either or both. Comparatively short periods of occupation in one home may suffice, as in *Landford Property Co. v Athanassoglou* [1948] 2 All ER 722, in which the claimant had a cottage in the country but was also the tenant of a flat in London where he slept (but rarely took a meal) on an average of twice a week, and *Bevington v Crawford* (1974) 232 EG 191 where the tenants lived mainly in Cannes and spent approximately two to three months each year in their rented accommodation in Harrow. However, 'occupation merely as a convenience for ... occasional visits' is not sufficient (*Beck v Scholz* [1953] 1 All ER 814). In *Hampstead Way Investments Ltd v Lewis-Weare* [1985] 1 WLR 164, the statutory tenant's new wife and stepchildren joined him in his flat. Some years later they bought and moved into a house situated half a mile away. The flat was then occupied by the tenant's stepson, but the tenant carried on sleeping there five times a week so that he did not disturb his wife when he returned home early in the morning from his job at a night club. He kept his work clothes at the flat, his mail was delivered there and he paid the rent and all other outgoings except the gas bill, which his stepson paid. He did not eat there, however, nor entertain his friends there. The House of Lords held that the house and flat could not together constitute a single unit of living accommodation since they were half a mile apart. The tenant's limited use of the flat, and the fact that an essential activity of daily life, i.e. eating, was not carried out there, meant that his occupation was insufficient to make it his second home. There was not therefore the required residence and thus no security of tenure.

Occupation as the tenant's 'only or principal home'

The requirement of occupation by the tenant as his only or principal home is shared by assured tenancies under s. 1 of the Housing Act 1988 and s. 81 of the Housing Act 1985. However, the decided cases indicate that there are similarities with the 'occupation as a residence test' which is applied in relation to statutory tenancies under s. 2 of the Rent Act 1977. In *Crawley Borough Council v Sawyer* (1988) 20 HLR 98 a weekly tenant left his council flat sometime in 1995 to live with his girlfriend in a property he was helping her to buy. The gas and electricity supplies to the flat were cut off but the tenant carried on paying the rent and rates, visited the flat about once a month, and once spent a week there. The council served a notice to quit. By the time of its expiry, the relationship between the tenant and his girlfriend had ended. He returned to the flat soon afterwards. The council brought possession proceedings. The Court of Appeal upheld the decision of the county court judge that the flat had always remained the tenant's principal home, even while he was living with his girlfriend. The tenant asserted throughout that he had every intention of returning to the flat and did not intend to give it up. To suggest, however, that the flat remained the tenant's only or principal home while he was living with his girlfriend would suggest that there is little meaningful difference between occupation as a residence and occupation as the tenant's principal home (Bridge, 1988).

However, this requirement contrasts with the conditions of protection under the Rent Act 1977 in two respects. First, there is no need for the tenant to occupy the premises for the purposes of a Rent Act protected tenancy (i.e. during the contractual term). Secondly, occupation for the purposes of a Rent Act statutory tenancy is as 'a' residence, rather than as the only or principal home. However, the *Brown v Brash* test (intention to return coupled with some physical sign of that intention on the premises) still applies and where the tenant's absence is caused by residence somewhere other than in a different 'home', the requirement may still be satisfied. In *Notting Hill Housing Trust v Etoria* [1989] CLY 1912 (in which *Brickfield Properties v Hughes* was applied), the tenant was serving a life sentence for murder but there was a real possibility that he would be released on licence in 1995. It was held that he had retained his secure status. His intention to return was obvious from the presence of his furniture and the continued occupation of his brother. *Etoria* can be contrasted with *Ujima Housing Association v Ansah* (1998) 30 HLR 831 in which the tenant lived in the flat before subletting it on an assured shorthold tenancy. The Court of Appeal held that he was not in physical occupation nor entitled to occupation on the expiry of the notice to quit, and he had left no personal possessions in the property. Viewed objectively, therefore, he did not have the necessary intent to maintain occupation of the flat as his principal home.

As with statutory tenancies under the Rent Act 1977, occupation by the tenant's spouse or civil partner as his or her only or principal home is treated as occupation by the tenant (Family Law Act 1996, s. 30(4)(b)).

The tenant must be an individual

Under the Housing Act 1988, a letting to a company cannot be an assured tenancy, nor can a letting to a company and an individual as joint tenants.

Assured shorthold tenancies

Introduction

An assured shorthold tenancy is a species of assured tenancy and must comply, therefore, with all the requirements for an assured tenancy set out in s. 1 of the Housing Act 1988. The main difference between the two types of tenancy lies in the security of tenure which tenants obtain. A landlord who seeks possession of premises let under an assured tenancy must serve a notice of seeking possession and obtain a court order on one of a number of mandatory or discretionary grounds for possession. In the case of an assured shorthold tenancy, however, provided that the landlord has served the requisite notice under s. 21

of the 1988 Act (see Chapter 14), possession is automatic and may be obtained through the accelerated paper procedure in the county court (see Civil Procedure Rules, Part 55, Part II).

As originally enacted, an assured shorthold tenancy was an assured tenancy which was granted for an initial fixed period of not less than six months and contained no power for the landlord to determine the tenancy within that period, other than by way of forfeiture. There was no upper limit as to its duration. By s. 20 of the 1988 Act, notice in the prescribed form (or one which was 'substantially to the like effect') that there was an assured shorthold tenancy had to be given to the tenant before entering into the agreement. Failure to serve a s. 20 notice resulted in the creation of an assured tenancy.

The 1995 White Paper described the 'procedures' (*sic*) which have to be gone through to create a valid assured shorthold tenancy (service by the landlord of the s. 20 notice on the tenant) as 'a trap for inexperienced landlords' which 'may deter owners of empty properties from putting them to use' (DoE, 1995: 22). It might have been thought that service of a single notice on the prospective tenant (albeit one which had to comply with the Assured Tenancies and Agricultural Occupancies (Forms) Regulations 1988) would not be imposing a particular burden upon landlords, let alone deterring them from letting their empty properties. That assured shorthold tenancies constituted 8 per cent of tenancies in the private rented sector in 1990, 40 per cent in 1994/5, and some 70 per cent in 1996 (DoE, 1996b) suggests that most private sector landlords grasped the basic principles of assured shorthold tenancy creation without too much difficulty, but there have been a number of reported cases which demonstrate that some landlords did indeed manage to fall foul of s. 20. In *Panayi and Pyrkos v Roberts* (1993) 25 HLR 421 the landlords granted a tenancy of a flat for a term of 12 months from 7 November. Prior to the grant they served the tenant with a s. 20 notice in a non-prescribed form, which gave 6 May as the termination date. The Court of Appeal held that a notice with an incorrect date is not 'substantially to the like effect' as a notice with a correct date. The notice was therefore invalid and the consequence was that the tenant had been granted an assured, rather than an assured shorthold, tenancy (see, also, *Bedding v McCarthy* (1993) 27 HLR 103; *Lower Street Properties v Jones* (1996) 28 HLR 877).

Creation of an assured shorthold tenancy

The Housing Act 1996 removed the requirement to serve prior notice with the result that assured shorthold tenancies have become the default form of tenancy. Section 19A of the Housing Act 1988 (inserted by s. 96 of the 1996 Act) provides that an assured tenancy which is entered into on or after 28 February 1997 is an assured shorthold tenancy. No longer is there any requirement that the tenancy is for a fixed term. Further, an assured shorthold tenancy will arise when a fixed-term assured tenancy comes to an end in accordance with s. 5 of the 1988 Act after that date.

Exceptions

All new assured tenancies are assured shorthold tenancies unless they are made pursuant to a contract entered into before 20 April 1997 or fall within the list of exceptions contained Sch. 2A to the 1988 Act.

(a) *Tenancies excluded by notice*   The landlord can still grant a fully assured tenancy but must serve prior notice on the tenant, stating that the assured tenancy is not an assured shorthold (Sch. 2A, para. 1). The landlord can also choose to grant the greater security after the tenancy has been entered into (Sch. 2A, para. 2). Assured tenancies are most likely to be used by registered social landlords, who are also subject to the security regime of the 1988 Act. However, when housing the homeless they will have to use assured shorthold tenancies (Housing Act 1996, s. 209).

(b) *Tenancies containing a provision to the effect that the tenancy is not an assured shorthold tenancy (Sch. 2A, para. 3).*

(c) *Tenancies under s. 39 (Sch. 2A, para. 4)*   This concerns the succession provisions under the Rent Act 1977. The first succession to a member of the deceased tenant's family and all second successions will continue to take effect as fully assured rather than assured shorthold tenancies (see Chapter 9).

(d) *Former secure tenancies (Sch. 2A, para. 5)*   Where housing is transferred from local authorities to housing associations (e.g. by way of stock transfer) or to the private sector (e.g. on the termination of a Housing Action Trust), tenants will move from being secure to assured but not assured shorthold tenants (see Chapter 16).

(e) *Tenancies under Sch. 10 to the Local Government and Housing Act 1989 (Sch. 2A, para. 6)*   Where a long tenancy at a low rent expires, security of tenure is governed either by Part I of the Landlord and Tenant Act 1954, in which case the tenancy becomes a statutory tenancy under the Rent Act 1977, or by Sch. 10 to the 1989 Act, in which case it becomes assured. In the latter case, such tenancies will not become assured shorthold tenancies.

(f) *Tenancies replacing non-shortholds (Sch. 2A, paras 7, 8)* Where an assured tenant is offered a replacement tenancy by the landlord, the tenant may serve a prescribed form notice on the landlord that it is to be an assured shorthold tenancy.

(g) *Assured agricultural occupancies (Sch. 2A, para. 9).*

Written statement of terms

Because all assured shorthold tenancies were formerly for a fixed term, and notice had to be served before the tenancy was entered into, nearly all assured shorthold tenancy agreements were in writing. Now that no notice need be served and no fixed term is required, an assured shorthold tenancy can be created orally. The government resisted attempts by the Opposition to require landlords to provide a written tenancy agreement for all shortholds but did concede that tenants should have the right to a written statement of certain terms of the tenancy when demanded by the tenant. Section 20A of the Housing Act 1988 (inserted by s. 97 of the 1996 Act) imposes a duty on landlords to provide statements of the terms of assured shorthold tenancies, i.e. (a) the date the tenancy began or came into being; (b) the rent payable and the dates on which it is payable; (c) any term providing for an express rent review; and (d) if the tenancy is fixed term, its length.

It is a criminal offence for a landlord to fail without reasonable excuse to comply with the tenant's request for 28 days as from receipt of the notice (s. 20A(4)).

Tenancy deposit schemes

Sections 212–215 of the Housing Act 2004 contain provisions to protect deposits received in connection with assured shorthold tenancies and are aimed at removing the risk of their misappropriation by landlords and their letting agents. These measures are prompted by the poor take-up of a voluntary tenancy deposit scheme administered by the Independent Housing Ombudsman. Deposits are usually taken by landlords, the idea being that in the event of any loss or damage or rent remaining unpaid at the end of a tenancy, the whole or part of the deposit may be withheld. There is evidence however that some landlords or their agents unjustifiably withhold deposits (DCLG, 2006c: 7), thus (further) 'damaging the image of the private rented sector' (ibid.: 6). Two types of schemes are available and landlords can choose which type to join: a single custodial scheme (where deposits are paid into and held in a separate account by the scheme administrator), or an insurance-based scheme (where the landlord or agent retains the deposit and any failure on their part to repay it to the tenant is covered by the scheme's insurance arrangements). Schemes must provide means of alternative dispute resolution as an alternative to court action to determine disputes about the return of a deposit at the end of a tenancy. Tenancy deposit schemes must make provision for the return of deposits within 10 days of the scheme administrator being notified of agreement between landlord and tenant or of a court/alternative dispute resolution decision.

Within 14 days of receiving a deposit, the landlord must comply with the initial requirements of a scheme and provide the tenant (or the person who paid the deposit on the tenant's behalf) with information as regards the scheme which applies. A landlord who fails to comply with any of these requirements will lose the right to serve a s. 21 notice for recovery of possession until such time as they are complied with. The tenant can apply for a court order requiring the deposit to be safeguarded or the prescribed information to be provided. Where the court is satisfied that the landlord has failed to comply with these requirements, or is not satisfied that the deposit is being held in accordance with an authorised scheme, the court must either order the landlord to repay the deposit within 14 days of the making of the order or to pay into a designated account held under an authorised scheme. It must also order the landlord to pay the tenant, within 14 days of the making of the order, an amount equivalent to three times the deposit.

Chapter 13

Avoiding full protection under the Rent Act 1977 and the Housing Act 1988

Introduction

It is well established that the parties cannot contract out of the Rent Acts for to do so would mean ousting the jurisdiction of the court under s. 8. Thus, in *Barton v Fincham* [1921] 2 KB 291 it was held that an order for possession could not be made against the tenant, even though he had freely agreed in writing to give up possession on a certain day and had received payment in return. Atkin LJ emphasised that the statutory fetter had been placed not upon the landlord's action but upon the court's, on the ground that 'parties cannot by agreement give the Courts jurisdiction which the Legislature has enacted they are not to have' (at p. 299).

In *R v Bloomsbury and Marylebone County Court ex p Blackburne* (1984) 14 HLR 56 it was held that the court could not make a consent order for possession of a dwelling-house subject to a statutory tenancy unless the judge had obtained from the tenant or his legal representative the concession that the tenant was not entitled to the protection of the Rent Acts (see, also, *R v Newcastle upon Tyne County Court ex p Thompson* (1988) 20 HLR 430). In *Appleton v Aspin* (1988) 20 HLR 182, an agreement by the protected tenant to give up possession to an intending purchaser was held to be rendered inoperative by s. 98(1). In *Woolwich v Dickman* [1996] 3 All ER 204, consent forms signed by protected tenants agreeing that a subsequent mortgage should take priority over their tenancy were held to be ineffective for the same reason.

Further, s. 34(1)(b) of the Housing Act 1988 provides that 'a tenancy which is entered into on or after the commencement of this Act cannot be a [Rent Act] protected tenancy unless ... it is granted to a person (alone or jointly with others) who, immediately before the tenancy was granted, was a protected or statutory tenant and is so granted by the person who at that time was the landlord ...'. In *Secretarial and Nominee Co Ltd v Thomas* [2005] EWCA Civ 1008, the landlords had granted in 1988 a one-year Rent Act protected tenancy of a flat to three tenants, one of whom was M. By the time the tenancy expired, the 1988 Act had come into effect and a one-year assured shorthold tenancy of the flat was granted to M and two new joint tenants. In 1990 another tenancy was granted to M, together with S and others. In 1991, M left and S took a new tenancy together with the respondent (R) and two others. Between 1991 and 1999 – when the final tenancy was granted – R was a joint tenant under a series of annual tenancy agreements with a succession of other tenants. Finally, the landlords served a s. 21 notice to terminate the tenancy. R remained in possession claiming that he enjoyed Rent Act protection and was thus entitled to remain. He argued that s. 34(1)(b) had conferred Rent Act protection upon M and his joint tenants under both the 1989 and 1990 tenancies. Since then there had been a succession of joint tenancies by which protection passed from M to S and then to R. The claim was upheld by the district judge but the Court of Appeal allowed the appeal, holding that the tenancy granted in 1999 was not protected by s. 34(1)(b). The statutory language showed that the protection related to a particular person. Thus, the grant of joint tenancies to M (who was a protected tenant) and others would have resulted in protected tenancies. Once M had left, however, the grant of further joint tenancies to persons who may have been joint tenancies under earlier tenancies with M did not suffice.

Any surrender, notice to quit or other document executed, signed or given by the tenant, before or at the time the tenancy is entered into, to bring the tenancy to an end in the future, will be of no effect (Housing Act 1988, s. 5(5)). Any attempt to contract out after the date of the tenancy will probably be unenforceable by the landlord, the same rules applying to attempts by the parties to oust the jurisdiction of the court under s. 7(1) as those which apply in relation to s. 98 of the Rent Act 1977. If, however, the tenancy cases to be assured (for example where the tenant ceases to occupy the property as his or her only or principal home), the landlord may terminate it under the general law by notice to quit.

It might be thought that the deregulation of the private rented sector by the 1988 and 1996 Acts and the availability of the assured shorthold tenancy would have removed the need for landlords to seek to avoid the statutory scheme. However, in *Bankway Properties Ltd v Penfold-Dunsford* [2001] 1 WLR 1369, the tenancy was granted under the Business Expansion Scheme and the landlords qualified for tax concessions only if a fully assured tenancy was granted. The tenancy agreement provided for an initial rent of £4,680 per annum but also contained a rent review clause under which the rent was increased from to £25,000. The landlords were aware that the tenants were in receipt of housing benefit when they entered into the tenancy and had no prospect therefore of meeting the increased rent liability. In the Court of Appeal, Arden LJ held that the clause was not a genuine provision for the payment of rent but a contracting out of the statutory scheme. Taking a slightly different approach, Pill LJ said that the tenancy had to be construed as one intended to give effect to the statutory purpose of long-term protection for the tenant and that the clause, being inconsistent with that purpose, should be ignored.

Even if a tenancy fulfils all the requirements of a protected or assured tenancy, it may nevertheless be excluded from protection by the express exceptions contained in ss. 4–16 of the 1977 Act or Sch. 1 to the 1988 Act, or one of the miscellaneous exceptions set out elsewhere. This does not necessarily mean, however, that the tenant is completely unprotected. For example, lettings made before 15 January 1989 by a resident landlord or where the rent includes payments for board and attendance may be restricted contracts under the Rent Act 1977, while tenants of properties outside the rateable value limits may have rights to stay in occupation at the end of the contractual term of the lease, or to extend the lease, or even to buy the freehold.[1]

Exclusions from the status of protected tenancy

Such is the extent of the protection afforded by the Rent Acts to regulated tenants that landlords and their advisers have displayed considerable ingenuity in using some of the exceptions in order to circumvent their provisions. It was said that 'every time Parliament acts to protects tenants from excessive rents or eviction ... the more cunning and unscrupulous landlords embark on the search for loopholes in the law' (HC Deb (1974–5) vol. 896, col. 297).

From 1920 until 1974, full Rent Act protection was reserved for unfurnished tenancies. If rent for a dwelling included payment for the use of furniture, then the tenancy would be a furnished letting within the jurisdiction of the rent tribunal, which merely had the powers to set a reasonable rent and to postpone a notice to quit. Many landlords sought to exploit this exception by supplying linoleum (*Wilkes v Goodwin* [1923] 2 KB 86) or a few sticks of second-hand furniture. In *Woodward v Docherty* [1974] 2 All ER 844, 846 Scarman LJ observed that the housing shortage could force a tenant 'to accept furniture he does not want in order to obtain accommodation he desperately needs, even though by accepting it he loses security of tenure which he would dearly love to have'. He also remarked on the ready availability of 'furniture of a sort, capable in a way of furnishing flats and rooms ... available at junk shops and other emporia at no very great price'.

The Rent Act 1974 brought furnished tenancies into the full protection of the Rent Acts, thereby blocking off a convenient escape route for landlords. It also introduced exceptions in respect of (a) student lettings by educational institutions, (b) holiday lettings and (c) resident landlords. The new exceptions

---

1   See Part I of the Landlord and Tenant Act 1954; the Leasehold Reform Act 1967; the Local Government and Housing Act 1989, s. 186 and Sch. 10; the Leasehold Reform, Housing and Urban Development Act 1993, ss. 11–61.

created new loopholes. A particularly popular ploy was the so-called 'holiday let' (the locations of the properties concerned being places such as Brixton, Lambeth and East Ham), for which landlords required references from employers, parents and banks (Weir, 1975).

Some landlords utilised the exclusion which applied where the dwelling-house was let at a rent which included payments for board and attendance (s. 7). Usually such tenancies constituted restricted contracts but if the payments for board formed a substantial proportion of the rent, the tenancy was outside the Act altogether. In *Wilkes v Goodwin* [1923] 2 KB 86 Younger LJ took the view that 'board' suggested 'a provision by the landlord of such food as ... would ordinarily be consumed at daily meals and would be obtained and prepared by the tenant himself'. However, the majority in that case considered that, subject to the *de minimis* rule, any amount of board would do and this approach was followed in *Otter v Norman* [1989] AC 129, in which the House of Lords held that a breakfast of two bread rolls with butter, jam and marmalade, unlimited tea or coffee with milk and sugar, additional milk for cornflakes (which the tenant provided himself), and a glass of milk which the tenant drank in his own room amounted to 'board'. Even though the meal was a modest one, its regularity of serving prevented any finding of bad faith. Given the uncertainty over the status of residential licences raised by *Street v Mountford* [1985] 1 AC 809 it was suggested that the decision in *Otter v Norman* would lead to board and attendance achieving new significance as a means of avoiding the 1977 Act (Rodgers, 1988: 642). However, as Lord Bridge commented, serving even such a modest daily meal as the continental breakfast was hardly likely to appeal to the unscrupulous landlord as a soft option. It would involve not only the cost of the food and drink provided but also shopping for provisions, preparation and service of meals on the premises and cleaning and washing up afterwards. Nonetheless a minority of landlords appeared to feel that raw provisions would be enough and contracted, therefore, to provide their tenants 'with a weekly box of groceries containing such items as milk, cornflakes, bread and eggs' (Waite, 1981: 460).

In an attempt to avoid the Rent Acts, landlords sometimes required prospective tenants to buy 'off-the-shelf' limited companies (which licensed or authorised an individual to occupy a house or flat), to which the lease was then granted. The advantage of the arrangement from the landlord's point of view was that the company's inability to occupy the premises as a residence meant that it could not claim a statutory tenancy and had no security of tenure, therefore, after the contractual tenancy had expired. In *Hilton v Plustitle* [1988] 1 WLR 149, the fact that the company had no assets of its own and was incapable of performing the covenants other than through the occupier (who paid the rent and other outgoings) was regarded as irrelevant. The court was not entitled to hold that the whole arrangement was a 'sham' merely because the letting was to a company so as to avoid the 1977 Act.

While the company tenant is entitled to the benefit of the fair rent provisions (*Carter v SU Carburetter Co Ltd* [1942] 2 All ER 228), an application to the rent officer to fix a fair rent may, of course, result in a notice to quit.

It is difficult to ascertain the extent to which agreements were manipulated so as to give the appearance of coming within one of the statutory exclusions, but a survey in 1976 found that the landlords of 48 per cent of the sampled lettings had altered their lettings policies as a result of the Rent Act 1974. Of these, 15 per cent would only be relet on licence agreements or 'rent-free', 14 per cent would only be let on holiday agreements and a further 16 per cent no longer provided furniture (Paley, 1978).

Exclusions from the status of assured tenancy

The exclusions contained in the Housing Act 1988 bear a close resemblance to those of the Rent Act 1977, but they are not identical. In particular, a letting which includes payments in respect of board or attendance can be an assured tenancy so long as all the other conditions are satisfied. Nor does the list of exclusions contained in Sch. 1 to the 1988 Act mention 'shared ownership leases', which were expressly excluded from Rent Act protection (s. 5A). The shared ownership lease was a method by which sitting tenants could buy council houses on an instalment basis under the right to buy (RTB) legislation (see Chapter 19). The object of excluding such leases from the Rent Act was to ensure that the tenant could not rely on the Act instead of the terms of the lease if, for example, the tenant were to default. Such tenancies could not in any event be protected tenancies by reasons of ss. 14 and 15 of the 1977 Act (see below) as they were restricted to tenants of local authorities and other bodies whose tenants were secure tenants under the Housing Act 1985.

The general rule is that tenancies entered into before 15 January 1989, the date on which Part I of the Housing Act 1988 came into force, or pursuant to a contract made before that date, cannot be assured (Housing Act 1988, Sch. 1, para. 1). Further, if a local authority enters into an arrangement with a private landlord or housing association to discharge its duties to homeless households under Part VII of the Housing Act 1996, the tenancy cannot be an assured tenancy for 12 months unless the landlord notifies the tenant that the tenancy is to be regarded as an assured or an assured shorthold tenancy (Housing Act 1996, s. 209(2)).

Provided that it does not amount to a sham, an exclusion can legitimately be employed as a avoidance device. In *Samrose Properties v Gibbard* [1958] 1 WLR 235, 239 Lord Evershed accepted that 'a landlord is entitled to arrange his affairs (so) that the legal result will bring him outside the statutory provisions ... If they fail, that does not, therefore, reflect on the ethics of their business methods ... '. However, there is little point in landlords and their advisers trying to avoid the Housing Act 1988. Assured shorthold tenancies (which have become the default form of tenancy since the Housing Act 1996 came into effect) give tenants virtually no security of tenure. The exceptions to the 1988 Act are, therefore, much more likely to cover genuine situations, rather than those which have been manipulated to fit them, as was often the case under the Rent Acts.

Exclusions applicable to both the Rent Act 1977 and the Housing Act 1988

Tenancy of a dwelling-house outside rateable value limits (Rent Act 1977, s. 4; Housing Act 1988, Sch. 1, para. 2)

Although some Rent Acts brought virtually all tenancies under control (see Chapter 5), statutory protection has not generally applied to the most expensive housing. Tenants who can afford to rent more expensive housing are usually in a better position to negotiate their own terms. The Rent Acts function, therefore, as 'Parliament's recognition of tenants' weaknesses as negotiators and their inability to buy a fair bargain' (Nicol, 1998: 37).

To enjoy statutory protection, a tenancy granted prior to 1 April 1990 must fall within certain rateable value limits. Domestic rating was abolished on the 1 April 1990 and replaced by the community charge, itself since replaced by council tax. A tenancy granted after that date will be protected or assured if the rent payable for the time being does not exceed £25,000 per annum. Since, with very few exceptions, no new protected tenancies can be created after 15 January 1989, the rental value limits will rarely be applicable to tenancies created under the Rent Act 1977.

Tenancy at no/low rent (Rent Act 1977, s. 5(1); Housing Act 1988, Sch. 1, para. 3)

Again a distinction must be made between tenancies granted before 1 April 1990 and those granted afterwards. As regards the former, a tenancy will not be protected or assured if either no rent is payable or the rent payable is less than two-thirds the rateable value on the appropriate day. In respect of post-1990 protected tenancies, the minimum annual rent payable is at least £1,000 in Greater London or £250 elsewhere.

Two types of situation are covered by this exclusion. The first is where the tenant is being allowed to occupy the property rent-free or for a nominal payment. No doubt this has something to do with the fact that the Rent Acts have always dealt first and foremost with rent control, and only secondarily with security of tenure. (As to what constitutes rent for the purpose of the 1977 and 1988 Acts, see Chapter 12.) A rent-free tenancy granted after the commencement of the Housing Act 1988 is an 'excluded tenancy' for the purposes of the Protection from Eviction Act 1977 (see Chapter 15).

The second type of situation in which the exclusion operates is where the tenant has bought a long lease of the property for a lump sum or premium and pays only a small, annual ground rent. The payment of premiums or the making of loans as a condition of the grant, renewal, continuance or assignment of a Rent Act protected tenancy is unlawful, and anyone who requires or receives such a premium or a loan commits a criminal offence (Rent Act 1977, ss. 119, 120). An established exception to this general rule applies to long tenancies (defined in s. 2(4) of the Landlord and Tenant Act 1954, as terms certain exceeding 21 years). Most long tenancies will be excluded from Rent Act protection by virtue of being at a low rent but where the rent is sufficiently high, so that the tenancy is protected, premiums and loans will be lawful as long as the conditions listed in s. 127 of the 1977 Act are satisfied.

The Housing Act 1988 contains no prohibition on the demand of a premium prior to entry into an assured tenancy and it is left to the market to dictate whether premiums can be charged as part of the consideration for the tenancy being granted. However, an attempt to avoid regulation by charging the tenant a large sum on entering into the tenancy while reserving only a low rent might be viewed as a pretence and ineffective to exclude protection. In *Samrose Properties Ltd v Gibbard* [1958] 1 WLR 235, the tenant paid a large premium for the grant of a fixed term of one year's duration, and then a quarterly rent which was less than two-thirds of the rateable value of the dwelling-house. In the written agreement the landlord stated that it did not wish to grant a lease to which the Rent Acts would apply. The Court of Appeal held that the premium should be added to the annual total of the quarterly rent to calculate the annual rent. On this basis, the tenant was entitled to the protection of the Rent Acts.

Tenancy of dwelling-house let with other land (Rent Act 1977, s. 26; Housing Act 1988, Sch. 1, para. 6)

Under both Acts special provision is made where the dwelling-house is let together with land other than the site of the dwelling-house. If the main purpose of the letting is to provide a home for the tenant or, where there is a joint tenancy, at least one of the joint tenants, then the other land will be treated as part of the dwelling-house. It will not be protected or assured, however, if it consists of agricultural land exceeding two acres in extent. Most of the case law has dealt with mixed lettings of business and residential property. In *Feyereisel v Parry* [1952] 2 QB 29, the Rent Act was held not to apply to the letting of a campsite which included a bungalow, because the bungalow was an adjunct to the campsite.

Lettings to students (Rent Act 1977, s. 8; Housing Act 1988, Sch. 1, para. 8)

If students had protected or assured tenancies they would be able to stay in halls of residence even after their courses had come to an end, leaving little or no accommodation available for new students. The Acts provide therefore that a tenancy granted to a person who is pursuing (or who intends to pursue) a course of study at a specified educational institution is not protected or assured if it is granted either by the institution itself or by another specified institution or body of persons. Specified educational institutions include all universities and publicly funded establishments of further education and certain other associated bodies (Assured and Protected Tenancies (Lettings to Students) Regulations 1988). It has been pointed out that the phrase 'person who is pursuing or intends to purse a course of study' is not necessarily an apt description for all students so that an objective test should be applied, rather than one 'which might be an incentive for constructive laziness' (Farrand, 1974).

Private landlords may also utilise the exclusion by letting premises to a university or college which in turn sub-lets to its students. Under the Rent Act 1977 the head tenancy might be protected (enabling use to be made of the fair rent provisions), but no statutory tenancy could arise on the termination of the contractual tenancy because the institution would be incapable of residing on the premises. As far as the Housing Act 1988 is concerned, a letting to an educational institution for sub-letting to students cannot be an assured tenancy because the tenant is not an individual. It may also be that the letting is subject to the rules on business tenancies contained in Part II of the Landlord and Tenant Act 1954. In *Groveside Properties Ltd v Westminster Medical School* (1984) 47 P & CR 507, the landlord let a furnished flat to the school to be occupied by its students. The school paid the outgoings, kept the keys and its secretary frequently visited the premises. It was held that the school had the necessary degree of occupation and was running a business for the purpose of the 1954 Act. It is possible too that there was no letting as a 'separate' dwelling (*St Catherine's College v Dowling* [1979] 3 All ER 250).

Mandatory grounds for possession apply under both Acts to the letting of the premises during vacations (see Chapter 14).

Holiday lettings (Rent Act 1977, s. 9; Housing Act 1988, Sch. I, para. 9)

Lettings for the purpose of conferring on the tenant the right to occupy the dwelling-house for a holiday were first excluded in 1974. The object of this exclusion is to enable landlords to let out premises for a holiday and to recover possession of them when it is over. Such lettings fell outside full Rent Act protection and the provisions regarding restricted contracts. As a result, landlords who could show that their tenants were 'holiday-makers' were given the opportunity 'to operate in the uncontrolled free market' (Lyons, 1984: 286). Not surprisingly, this led to 'a remarkable boom in holiday lets in places not noted for the quality of their waters or the mildness of their sea breeze' (Widdison, 1982: 29).

The leading case on the effectiveness of 'artificial' holiday lets is *Buchmann v May* [1978] 2 All ER 993. Mrs May, a New Zealand national, had a residence permit to live in Great Britain until December 1974. In October 1974 she agreed with Mr Buchmann to take a further three-month letting of premises in Norbury which she and her husband and child had occupied for about two years under a series of short lets. The tenancy agreement stated that the letting was 'solely for the purpose of the tenant's holiday in the London area'. At the end of the tenancy she refused to vacate, claiming that she had a protected tenancy. In reasoning typical of pre-*Street v Mountford* cases, the Court of Appeal felt that it could not look beyond the actual agreement; the statement it contained as to the purpose of the letting prevailed. While the court should be on its guard to detect a sham, the onus was on the tenant to establish that a provision had been inserted so as to deprive him or her of Rent Act protection; it was not for the landlord to establish that the purpose expressed in the agreement was the true purpose. Whether or not the letting in *Buchmann* was in fact a sham is unclear: Mrs May was in the country on a series of temporary resident permits, she had been abroad for several months before signing the disputed agreement and had told the landlord that she wished to stay in England for only two months more.

As there is no statutory definition of 'holiday', the Court of Appeal in *Buchmann v May* resorted to the definition given in the *Shorter Oxford English Dictionary* of 'a period of cessation from work or a period of recreation'. It has been held in the county court that a working holiday can come within the definition of a holiday (*McHale v Daneham* (1979) 249 EG 969). However, in *R v Rent Officer for London Borough of Camden ex p Plant* (1981) 257 EG 713, it was held that the landlord could not have intended a genuine six-month holiday letting, because he knew that the prospective occupiers were student nurses. In *Francke v Hakmi* [1984] CLY 1906 it was said that 'a holiday is a temporary suspension of one's normal activity not necessarily implying a period of recreation ... [involving] such a period of time as would indicate that one intends to resume one's normal activity at its conclusion and ... is not so long as to imply that another activity had taken its place' (see Lyons, 1984).

A holiday letting granted after 15 January 1989 is an excluded tenancy so that the court order and four-week notice to quit rules contained in ss. 3 and 5 of the Protection from Eviction Act 1977 do not apply. It is lawful, therefore, for the landlord to recover possession, once the tenancy has expired, without an order of the court.

As is explained in Chapter 14, off-season lets of holiday accommodation may be protected or assured but are subject to mandatory grounds for possession provided the landlord complies with a notice requirement and the letting is for a term not exceeding eight months.

Tenancies of agricultural holdings (Rent Act 1977, s. 10; Housing Act 1988, Sch. 1, para. 7)

A tenancy is not protected or assured if the dwelling-house is comprised in an agricultural holding (within the meaning of the Agricultural Holdings

Act 1986) or in a farm business tenancy (within the meaning of the Agricultural Tenancies Act 1995) and is occupied by the person responsible for the control of the farming or management of the holding, whether as a tenant or the tenant's employee or agent.

Licensed premises (Rent Act 1977, s. 11; Housing Act 1988, Sch. 1, para. 5)

A tenancy of a dwelling-house which consists of or comprises premises licensed for the sale of intoxicating liquors for consumption on the premises (e.g. a public house) cannot be a regulated or assured tenancy. However, since the introduction of the Landlord and Tenant (Licensed Premises Act) 1990, a tenancy of licensed premises will probably be a business tenancy under Part II of the Landlord and Tenant Act 1954.

Lettings by resident landlords (Rent Act 1977, s. 12; Housing Act 1988, Sch. 1, para. 10)

The resident landlord exemption was introduced by the Rent Act 1974 to encourage owners to let any spare rooms in their homes safe in the knowledge that they could recover possession at the end of the contractual tenancy as they might 'very understandably wish to do so should the tenant prove incompatible' and to enable them to sell with vacant possession 'what is probably their major asset' (*Barnett v O'Sullivan* [1995] 4 EG 141, 143. It was also intended to avoid the 'social embarrassment arising out of close proximity ... which the landlord had accepted in the belief that he could bring it to an end at any time allowed by the contract of the tenancy' (*Bardrick v Haycock* (1976) 31 P & CR 420, 424). Further impetus has been given to the letting of spare rooms by homeowners by the 'rent a room scheme' which permits rent to be received from the lettings of furnished accommodation in the landlord's only or main residence free from income tax up to a limit of £4,250. In 1995, about one household in every 100 had lodgers (DoE, 1995: 204) but it appears that number of lettings by resident landlords has since declined.

Tenancies granted on or after 14 August 1974 (but before 15 January 1989) are not fully protected under the Rent Act 1977 if:

(a) the dwelling-house forms part only of a building and, *except in a case where the dwelling-house also forms part of a flat*, the building is not a purpose-built block of flats; and

(b) at the grant of the tenancy the landlord occupied as his/her residence another dwelling forming part of the building; and

(c) at all times since the grant of the tenancy the landlord (or successor) has occupied as his/her residence another dwelling forming part of the building.

The words in italics were added by s. 65 of the Housing Act 1980 so that the resident landlord exception also applies (as to tenancies granted on or after 28 November 1980) where the landlord lives in an individual flat in a purpose-built block and has let off part of that flat to a tenant. If, however, a landlord owns all or several flats in a purpose-built block, occupying one and letting the others, the resident landlord exception does not apply.

Purpose-built blocks are excluded because, in accordance with *Bardrick v Haycock*, they are likely to be places where the occupiers lead separate lives. A purpose-built block of flats is one which as originally constructed contained, and now contains, two or more flats (Rent Act 1977, Sch. 2, para. 4). Thus, in *Barnes v Gorsuch* (1982) 43 P & CR 294, a house which had been converted into flats did not satisfy the definition. However, it might be possible to argue that the identity of the building has changed, e.g. where it was completely gutted and rebuilt inside.

There is no statutory definition of the term 'building'. In *Bardrick v Haycock* the landlord lived in an extension which had its own entrance and no means of internal communication with the main house, which had been converted into flats. The Court of Appeal upheld the county court decision that the extension and house did not comprise one building and the resident landlord exemption did not, therefore, apply. In *Griffiths v English* (1981) 2 HLR 126, an extension had been built on either side of the main house, which was divided into flats. The landlord lived in one extension and the tenant lived in the other. The Court of Appeal held that, despite the absence of any internal communication, there was the necessary element of close proximity which the exclusion was designed to avoid. That the appearance was that of one building and had once been in single occupation, and the absence of separate gardens for the main house and the extensions were all material facts which the trial judge was entitled to take into account. In *Wolf v Waddington* (1989) 22 HLR 72, the Court of Appeal declined to interfere with the judge's finding that an extension on the first floor of a property which was partly above a garage and partly above the ground floor of the house was part of the same building even though the extension was self-contained and had its own entrance and an alleyway ran at ground level between the two parts of the house (see, also, *Lewis-Graham and Lewis-Graham v Canachar* (1992) 24 HLR 132).

As regards occupation by the landlord as a residence, reference should be made to the case law on residence for the purpose of a statutory tenancy under the Rent Acts. As a result, liberal interpretations of the residence requirement which operate in the tenant's favour, namely the 'two homes' cases, can be used in this context by the landlord.

The requirement of continuous residential occupation by the landlord is relaxed where the building is sold or transferred to trustees, or vested in the landlord's personal representatives after his or her death (Rent Act 1977, Sch. 2, para. 1(a) and (b); Housing Act 1988, Sch. 2, para. 2A).

The conditions of the resident landlord exemption under the Housing Act 1988 are very similar to the resident landlord provisions of the Rent Act 1977. However, they differ in three significant respects:

(a) The landlord can only satisfy the residence requirements (at the grant and subsequently) if he occupies a dwelling in the same building as 'his only or principal home' (Housing Act 1988, Sch. 1, para. 10(1)(b) and (c)). Thus, in contrast to the position under the Rent Act 1977, a landlord cannot establish resident landlord status in respect of more than one home.

(b) The tenant of a resident landlord under the 1977 Act enjoyed the protection of a restricted contract. Restricted contracts cannot be created after the commencement of the 1988 Act, and a tenancy granted by a resident landlord after that date cannot be assured. The court order and notice to quit requirements of ss. 3 and 5 of the Protection from Eviction Act 1977 will nevertheless apply.

(c) A tenancy granted after the commencement of the 1988 Act will be an excluded tenancy if the tenant shares accommodation with the landlord or a member of his family. Sections 3 and 5 of the Protection from Eviction Act 1977 will not apply. This means that once the tenancy has expired, the landlord may lawfully recover possession without having to take court proceedings.

Crown lettings (Rent Act 1977, s. 13; Housing Act 1988, Sch. 1, para. 11)

Where the property is owned by the Crown or by a government department, a residential letting cannot be protected or assured. However, this does not apply to lettings by the Crown Estate Commissioners.

Lettings by (quasi-) public bodies (Rent Act 1977, ss. 14–16; Housing Act 1988, Sch. 1, para. 12)

Lettings by local authorities, housing associations and housing cooperatives cannot be protected tenancies under the Rent Act 1977. Before the Housing Act 1988 came into force most such lettings were secure tenancies governed by the Housing Act 1985. It should be noted, however, that as from 15 January 1989, new lettings by housing associations are generally assured tenancies governed by the Housing Act 1988.

Business tenancies (Rent Act 1977, s. 24(3); Housing Act 1988, Sch. 1, para. 4)

Section 24(3) of the Rent Act 1977 provides that a tenancy cannot be regulated if it is a tenancy to which Part II of the Landlord and Tenant Act 1954 applies. However, the fair rent provisions contained in the Rent Act meant that it would be to the tenant's advantage to establish that he was a protected tenant, even though the premises were used for the purposes of a business. The exclusion has lost its significance under the 1988 Act as landlords are able to charge a market rent under both regimes. The procedure for obtaining possession of premises let on a business tenancy is highly technical and fraught with pitfalls: it may be that a tenant may on advice see himself in a stronger bargaining position as a business tenant than as an assured tenant.

Miscellaneous exceptions

Tenancies of overcrowded dwellings

Section 101 of the Rent Act 1977 provides that at any time when a dwelling-house is overcrowded within the meaning of the Housing Act 1985 (see Chapter 8), in such circumstances as to render the occupier guilty of an offence, nothing in the Act shall prevent the immediate landlord from obtaining possession. The tenant is deprived of his security while overcrowding lasts, but rent control still applies until such time as a possession order is made. Overcrowding is not dealt with in the Housing Act 1988 in relation to assured tenancies.

Parsonage houses

Church of England parsonage houses are excluded from the Rent Act 1977 and presumably from the Housing Act 1988 by virtue of the Pluralities Act 1838 (*Bishop of Gloucester v Cunnington* [1943] 1 All ER 101). There is no such exception in respect of other denominations, although both the 1977 and 1988 Acts provide mandatory grounds for possession where the dwelling is held for the purpose of being available for occupation by a minister of religion, and is required for such occupation.

Tenancies granted by borrower without consent of mortgage lender

A lease which is granted by a borrower whose statutory power of leasing is excluded or curtailed, binds the landlord and tenant. However, the tenant will not be protected as against a prior legal mortgage lender by either 1977 or the 1988 Acts (*Dudley and District Benefit Building Society v Emerson* [1949] 2 All ER 252).

Chapter 14

Repossession under the Rent Act 1977 and the Housing Act 1988

Introduction

This chapter focuses on security of tenure for private sector tenants. While it is possible for private landlords to grant assured tenancies under the Housing Act 1988, most will opt instead for assured shortholds and the vast majority of assured tenants are those whose landlords are housing associations. For this reason, security of tenure for assured tenants is dealt with in Chapter 18 alongside the Housing Act 1985 which applies to secure tenants of local authorities.

Both the Rent Act 1977 and the Housing Act 1988 give the tenant security of tenure by preventing the exercise of the landlord's common law rights to end the tenancy and providing that the landlord can only regain possession of the premises with a court order. As this chapter seeks to make clear, Rent Act tenants enjoy extensive security because the court can only make an order if the landlord satisfies one or more of the grounds set out in the 1977 Act. By contrast, the assured shorthold tenancy confers virtually no security.

By s. 98(1) of the 1977 Act, a court cannot make an order for possession of a dwelling-house which is let on a protected tenancy or subject to a statutory tenancy unless it considers it reasonable to make such an order and either (a) it is satisfied that suitable alternative accommodation is available for the tenant or will be when the order in question takes effect; or (b) the circumstances are as specified in any of the cases in Part I of Sch. 15 to the Act. By s. 98(2), the court *must* make an order for possession if the circumstances of the case are as specified in any of the cases in Part II of Sch. 15.

In the case of an assured shorthold tenant, an order will be granted if the landlord either establishes one or more of the grounds for possession in Sch. 2 to the 1988 Act or, as is more likely, serves notice under s. 21.

Termination by the tenant

If a Rent Act protected tenancy is brought to an end by a notice to quit served by the tenant upon the landlord or by surrender and the tenant vacates the property with the intention of no longer living there, there is no need for the landlord to bring possession proceedings. If, however, the tenant continues to occupy the dwelling-house as a residence, a statutory tenancy comes into being. If, in the latter scenario, the landlord has contracted to sell or to lease the property in reliance on the tenant's notice to quit, case 5 provides the opportunity to apply to the court for an order for possession conditions provided that certain conditions are satisfied.

A tenancy may be surrendered by express agreement or by operation of law (implied surrender). If the term is for more than three years, an express surrender must be by deed (Law of Property Act 1925, s. 52(1)); otherwise it must be in writing (Law of Property Act 1925, s. 53(1)). It must operate immediately and cannot be expressed to take effect on a future date. Surrender by operation of law arises where there is unequivocal conduct of the parties which is inconsistent with the continuation of an existing tenancy and it is inequitable for one of them to maintain that, just because the due formalities have not been observed ('whether because of laziness, ignorance, double-dealing or a number of other causes': *Proudreed v Microgen Holdings plc* (1996) P & CR 388, 389), a tenancy still exists. The doctrine of surrender by operation of law is founded on the principle of estoppel, the parties having acted towards each other in a way which is inconsistent with the continuation of the tenancy and which precludes either of them from subsequently asserting its continued existence (*Tarjomani v Panther Securities Ltd* (1983) 46 P & CR 32). Examples of surrender by operation of law occur where the tenant agrees to give up the tenancy, in consequence of which the landlord resumes possession of the premises (*Phene v Popplewell* (1862) 12 CB(NS) 334), the tenant returns the keys to the landlord who, a few days later, demolishes the building (*Furnival v Grove* (1860) 8 CB(NS) 496, *cf Boynton-Wood v Trueman* (1961) 177 EG 191 in which the landlord took the keys to carry out repairs), a new lease is created between landlord and tenant or between the landlord and a third party with the tenant's agreement (*Lyon v Read* (1844) 13 M&W 285; *Wallis v Hands* [1893] 2 Ch 75). In *Preston Borough Council v Fairclough* (1983) 8 HLR 70, Griffiths LJ suggested that a court might regard the tenancy as surrendered by operation of law 'if it could be shown that a tenant had left owing a very substantial sum of money and had been absent for a substantial time'. In *Bellcourt v Adesina* [2005] EWCA Civ 208 however, Peter Gibson LJ expressed 'serious reservations' over this 'tentative suggestion' to the extent that it was based on a failure by the landlord to assert his rights for a substantial time. Such inference will be easier to make where the landlord peaceably re-enters, changes the locks of the premises and relets them to a different tenant; in other words has altered its position in reliance upon the supposed surrender (*R v London Borough of Croydon ex p Toth* (1988) 20 HLR 576).

Statutory tenants may surrender their tenancy or, subject to s. 5 of the Protection from Eviction Act 1977, bring it to an end by giving the notice to quit specified in the original lease. If no notice is specified, not less than three months' notice must be given (Rent Act 1977, s. 3(3). Disclaimer by the tenant's trustee in bankruptcy brings the statutory tenancy to an end and the whole of the bankrupt's former interest is then reinvested in the landlord (*Reeves v Davies* [1921] 2 KB 486). Otherwise, a statutory tenancy can be terminated only by court order which will be granted only if the landlord can provide suitable alternative accommodation for the tenant or establish one of the grounds for possession contained in Sch. 15 to the 1977 Act (see below).

Unlike an assured tenant, an assured shorthold tenant has no statutory right to terminate a fixed-term tenancy early by notice, nor is this permitted by the vast majority of fixed-term tenancy agreements. The Conservative government resisted an Opposition amendment to include such a right on the basis that it would deprive the landlord of the expectation of a rent during an initial fixed term (HC Standing Committee G, col. 256 (7 March 1996)).

Rent Act tenancies: termination by the landlord

Introduction

First of all, any contractual tenancy must be brought to an end at common law, by notice to quit (in the case of a periodic tenancy) or effluxion of time or forfeiture (in the case of a fixed-term tenancy). In proceedings to forfeit a Rent Act protected tenancy, the judge has to decide whether the lease should be forfeited and, if appropriate, whether relief should be given. If the lease is forfeited, a statutory tenancy is created. The judge should then consider whether a Rent Act ground for possession has been proved.

Once the contractual tenancy has been terminated, a statutory tenancy arises (s. 2). Where the landlord is seeking to recover possession from a person who is already a statutory tenant, a notice to quit is not necessary but a failure to warn the tenant by, e.g. a letter before action, may affect the issue of reasonableness if possession is sought on a discretionary ground.

The landlord need not serve a notice to quit before seeking possession from a person who is already a statutory tenant nor a notice under s. 146(1) of the Law of Property Act 1925 where the tenant is in breach of covenant. As was explained in *Brewer v Jacobs* [1923] 1 KB 528, the statutory tenant 'must find his protection, if any, within the [Rent Acts] and other Acts do not apply at all'. A landlord cannot lawfully evict a statutory tenant against whom he has a possession order, except by execution of a warrant of possession (*Haniff v Robinson* [1992] 3 WLR 875).

An order for possession will be made only if the landlord can:

(a) satisfy the court that *suitable alternative accommodation* is available for the tenant and the court considers it *reasonable* to make an order for possession; or
(b) establish one or more of the *discretionary* cases listed in Part I of Sch. 15 and the court considers it *reasonable* to make an order for possession; or
(c) establish one or more of the *mandatory* cases listed in Part II of Sch. 15.

Reasonableness

Reasonableness is not an issue if a landlord is seeking an order of possession by establishing a mandatory ground for possession but it must always be considered if the landlord is pleading one of the discretionary grounds for possession or, alternatively, seeking to establish, in the case of a Rent Act regulated tenant, that suitable alternative accommodation is available. Even where a ground or case itself in terms involves a requirement of reasonableness, the general issue of reasonableness must itself be separately considered. Failure by the court to consider reasonableness means that the order can be set aside and in *Peachy Property Corporation Ltd v Robinson* [1967] 2 QB 543, where the tenant did not enter an appearance or serve any defence, a judgment entered in default was held by the Court of Appeal to be ineffective.

The onus is upon the landlord to convince the court that it is reasonable to order possession. In *Cumming v Danson* [1942] 2 All ER 653, Lord Greene MR explained that:

> the judge is to take into account all relevant circumstances as they exist at the date of the hearing . . . in . . . a broad commonsense way as a man of the world . . . giving such weight as he thinks right to the various factors. Some factors may have little or no weight, others may be decisive, but it is quite wrong for him to exclude from his consideration matters which he ought to take into account.
>
> (At p. 655.)

There appears to be virtually no limit to the factors which the court can take into account. They include such matters as the health of the parties (*Briddon v George* [1946] 1 All ER 609), their ages (*Battlespring v Gates* (1983) 268 EG 355), the financial consequences if an order for possession is made (*Williamson v Pallant* [1924] 2 KB 173), the public interest (*Cresswell v Hodgson* [1951] 1 All ER 710), loss of amenities (*Siddiqui v Rashid* [1980] 1 WLR 1018) and the conduct of the parties (*Yelland v Taylor* [1957] 1 WLR 459). The judge must look at the effect on each party of the court making or withholding the order (*Cresswell v Hodgson* [1951] 1 All ER 710).

Adjournment, postponement and suspension

Where possession is sought on discretionary grounds, the court may adjourn proceedings for possession for such period as it thinks fit, or, on the making of a possession order or, at any time before its execution, stay or suspend execution of the order or postpone the date of possession for such period as it thinks fit (s. 100(1)(2)). On any such adjournment, stay, suspension or postponement, the court must impose conditions as to the payment of any rent arrears or mesne profits, or such other conditions as it thinks fit, unless it considers that this would cause exceptional hardship to the tenant or would otherwise be unreasonable (s.100(3)). The court commonly exercises its discretion to suspend the operation of a possession order, especially where possession is sought on the basis of rent arrears. If the tenant fails to comply, the landlord may re-apply for a possession order.

The court has no power to adjourn, etc. where the landlord has been able to prove a *mandatory* ground nor to recovery of possession against assured shorthold tenants under s. 21 of the Housing Act 1988. In these situations the reasonableness (or otherwise) of making the order is irrelevant and possession is potentially instantaneous unless the court can be prevailed upon to exercise its inherent powers to postpone.

After the court has granted the landlord an order for possession, it must grant a warrant for possession before the tenant can be evicted. Once the warrant has been executed, it can be set aside (and the tenant re-instated) only where (a) the order on which it is issued is itself set aside, (b) the warrant has been obtained by fraud, or (c) there has been an abuse of process or oppression in its execution (*Jephson Homes v Moisejevs* [2001] 1 All ER 901).

Suitable alternative accommodation

Strictly speaking, this is a ground for possession but it is dealt with separately here because it does not appear in the list of grounds contained in Sch. 15 to the 1977 Act.

Subject to the requirement of reasonableness, the court may make an order for possession if the landlord can show that suitable alternative accommodation is available for the tenant or will be so when the possession order takes effect. Although s. 98(1) makes it clear that the issues of reasonableness and alternative accommodation should be established independently of each other, the courts have inclined to the view that it is easier to show reasonableness where alternative accommodation is offered. As Scott LJ stated in *Cumming v Danson* [1942] 2 All ER 653:

> There is a fundamental difference . . . between an application for possession where no alternative accommodation is offered and an application where it is offered. In my view, the measure of reasonableness to be established by the landlord is much smaller in regard to the burden of proof in the case where alternative accommodation is offered.

A certificate from the local housing authority stating that it will provide suitable alternative accommodation for the tenant by a specified date is conclusive evidence that such accommodation will be available (Sch. 15, Part IV, para. 3) but 'suitability' remains a question within the discretion of the judge (*Jones and Massey v Cook and Cook* (1990) 22 HLR 319) and the question of whether it is reasonable to make the order must still be addressed (*Dame Margaret Hungerford Charity Trustees v Beazeley* [1993] 2 EGLR 143).

Because demand for local authority housing outstrips supply, such certificates are rarely issued. Thus, the landlord must either provide the accommodation himself or arrange for it to be made available from another private landlord. Either way, it will be up to the landlord to establish its suitability (*Nevile v Hardy* [1921] 1 Ch 404).

Suitability

To be suitable, the accommodation offered must consist of premises which are:

(a) to be let on a protected tenancy or an assured tenancy (as appropriate) or, in the court's opinion, provide equivalent security of tenure; and

(b) reasonably suitable to the needs of the tenant and his family as regards proximity to place of work, and either:

> (ii) similar as regards rental and extent to the accommodation afforded by dwelling-houses provided in the neighbourhood by any housing authority for persons with like needs to the tenant and his family, or
>
> (iii) reasonably suitable to the means of the tenant and to his and his family's needs as regards extent and character; and

(c) provided with similar or reasonably suitable furniture, where furniture was provided under the tenancy (Sch. 15, Part IV, paras 4–5).

The word 'family' bears the same meaning as it does in the context of succession to a Rent Act statutory tenancy (see Chapter 9).

'Alternative' accommodation

Although the Acts refer to 'alternative' accommodation, part of the existing premises can suffice, as in *Mykolyshyn v Noah* [1970] 1 WLR 1271 in which the landlord offered the same flat minus the sitting-room which the tenant had used merely for storing furniture. In *Yoland Ltd v Reddington* (1982) 5 HLR 41 the court held that the part currently occupied by the tenants, less the part which they had (lawfully) sublet, was suitable but it was not reasonable to make the order. The lavatory and bathroom were shared with the subtenants who were friends of the family. If the order was made, the tenants might find themselves left in part of a house, the rest of which remained empty and uncared for or, if the landlords relet the part currently occupied by the subtenants, having to share the bathroom and lavatory with strangers.

Security of tenure

Whether the security of tenure offered is 'reasonably equivalent' will depend upon the facts of the case. Where the tenant is currently a protected or statutory tenant, the court may direct that the alternative accommodation should be held on a protected tenancy if 'in the circumstances, the grant of an assured tenancy would not afford the required security' (Housing Act 1988, s. 34(1)(c)(iii)). This is one of the few situations in which a protected tenancy can be created after 15 January 1989.

Place of work

'Place of work' refers to the place where the work is largely carried out (*Dakyns v Price* [1948] 1 KB 22). It need not be a single place of work such as an office or factory, but may be an area in which the tenant travels to carry out his or her work. The distance, the means of transport available, the amount of time and degree of inconvenience in making the journey between home and the place of work may all be considered (*Yewbright Properties v Stone* (1980) 40 P & CR 402).

Extent and character

Suitability as regards extent and character is decided by reference to objective criteria and the court will consider the particular tenant's housing needs, rather than any incidental advantages enjoyed with the present accommodation, or the tenant's own peculiar wishes and desires. In *Hill v Rochard* [1983] 1 WLR 478, the tenants had spent 16 years in a 'handsome period country house' with 1.5 acres of land, including a paddock and outbuildings, which enabled them to keep a pony and a number of cats and dogs. The alternative accommodation offered was a modern, detached, four-bedroomed house on a housing estate on the outskirts of a nearby village. It was the 'character' of this accommodation which was challenged, rather than its 'extent'. The Court of Appeal held that the alternative accommodation was 'suitable'. In considering the tenants' housing needs, the court may look at the environment to which the tenants have become accustomed in their present accommodation, and to see how far the new environment differs. Here, however, the court was being asked to say that the character was unsuitable, not from the point of view of the tenants' needs, but in relation to 'their own particular taste for amenities, which go . . . beyond their needs even for a person who is entitled to sustain a high standard of living'.

Account should be taken, however, of the tenant's professional needs as in, for example, *De Markozoff v Craig* (1949) 93 Sol Jo 693 (accommodation offered unsuitable for tenant to entertain business acquaintances and had no garden for the tenant's child), *McDonnell v Daly* [1969] 3 All ER 851 (proposed accommodation would not enable the tenant to carry out his profession as an artist because it lacked a studio), and *Warren v Austen* [1947] 2 All ER 185 (the alternative accommodation lacked the amenities to enable the tenant to continue to take in paying guests in order to supplement his low income).

Environmental factors, such as noise and smells, are also relevant to whether or not the accommodation is suitable as regards character. In *Redspring v Francis* [1973] 1 All ER 640, it was held that an order of possession would not be reasonable where an elderly lady, who had occupied a flat in a quiet residential street for 30 years, was offered a flat in a very noisy street next door to a fried fish shop, and near to a hospital, cinema and public house, a yard at the back being scheduled for use as a transport depot. However, environmental factors can only be taken into account if they relate to the character of the property itself, as opposed to personal factors. *Redspring v Francis* was distinguished in *Siddiqui v Rashid* [1980] 1 WLR 1018 in which the alternative accommodation (situated in Luton) was held to be suitable despite the objections of the tenant (who lived in London but worked in Luton) that it would take him away from his friends, mosque and cultural interests. In *Dawncar Investments Ltd v Plews* (1993) 25 HLR 639 the tenant, who had a young child, occupied a flat in a quiet road in a pleasant part of Hampstead. She was offered a flat in Kilburn which was internally superior to her present accommodation but it was in a busy road used by heavy lorries and near to a timber yard, railway and two public houses. The trial judge expressed his concern over 'a woman like Miss Plews' having to live in the alternative accommodation 'because of the noise, traffic, heavy lorries, proximity of railway lines, general roughness of the area and of the inhabitants', and the Court of Appeal accepted his decision that for environmental reasons it was not suitable.

Availability

So far as availability is concerned, it was held in *London City Properties v Goodman* (19 May 1978, unreported) that the tenant's own (empty) property can be 'available' accommodation. In *Amrit Holdings Co Ltd v Shahbakhti* [2005] HLR 30, the landlords sought to recover possession on the ground that, in accordance with s. 98(1), suitable alternative accommodation was available for the tenant in the form of one of his five investment properties which was currently occupied under an assured shorthold tenancy, the contractual term of which had expired. The Court of Appeal held that the alternative accommodation would be available only if it was reasonable to expect the owner to take steps to recover it. It also held that, in considering the reasonableness of making the order, the judge had been entitled to take into account the financial implications of requiring a tenant to reorder his affairs in order to accommodate his landlord. Although the landlords had a legitimate financial interest in getting a higher rent from the premises than they were getting from the tenant, he would lose his investment in his own flat and would have the expense and trouble of bringing proceedings against his tenants.

Grounds for possession

The Rent Act 1977 contains 20 grounds ('cases') for possession. If the landlord proves one of the discretionary grounds, the court will grant possession only if it considers that it is reasonable to make the order. If the landlord proves the requirements of one of the mandatory grounds, the court must grant possession (s. 98(2)) and the question of whether it is reasonable to grant an order for possession is irrelevant (*Kennealy v Dunne* [1977] QB 837).

All the mandatory cases under the Rent Act 1977 require the landlord to serve written notice upon the tenant not later than 'the relevant date' stating that possession may be recovered under the case in question. In most cases the 'relevant date' will be the start of the tenancy (Sch. 15, Part III, para. 2) but the court may dispense with the requirement of notice if it is of the opinion that it is just and equitable to do so. Obviously it is in the landlord's interest to make out a case for one of the mandatory grounds.

Non-payment of rent or breach of any other obligation

Case 1 of the Rent Act 1977 allows the landlord to recover possession where 'any rent lawfully due from the tenant has not been paid'. Rent is not due until a notice under s. 48 of the Landlord and Tenant Act 1987 has been served which contains the landlord's address for the service of notices. Before commencing possession proceedings, the landlord should send the tenant a 'letter before action' demanding payment and threatening legal action if the arrears are not paid by a certain date. The court is unlikely to consider it reasonable to make a possession order if the landlord has failed to warn the tenant and so provide an opportunity to pay what is owed. However, no order can be made if the rent is then paid because the rent is no longer 'lawfully due'; the commencement of proceedings is the date at which the breach must exist (*Bird v Hildage* [1948] 1 KB 91). If payment is made after the start of proceedings, the court can order possession but is unlikely to do so unless there is a long history of non- and late payment of rent (*Dellenty v Pellow* [1951] 2 All ER 716). If arrears are still unpaid at the time of the hearing, the court will take into account all the surrounding circumstances and will probably not order possession in the case of an isolated breach or if only a small sum is owing. It may not be reasonable to order possession against a tenant who is withholding rent because the landlord has breached a repairing covenant (*Televantos v McCulloch* (1991) 23 HLR 412) or if the landlord has failed to comply with the obligation under s. 48 of the Landlord and Tenant Act 1987 (*Hussain v Singh* [1993] 2 EGLR 70; *Dallhold Estates (United Kingdom) Pty Ltd v Lindsey Trading Properties Inc* [1994] 1 EGLR 93).

Breach of a tenancy obligation

Case 1 of the Rent Act 1977 applies where 'any obligation of the ... tenancy ... has been broken or not performed'. This includes a breach of any of the obligations of the tenancy, except those of a personal nature, e.g. to remain in the landlord's employment. It applies to breach of implied as well as express obligations, and whether or not the breach still exists at the date of the hearing. If the breach as been remedied, however, this will be significant to the issue of reasonableness. In *Commercial General Administration v Thomsett* (1979) 250 EG 547, a term of the tenancy required the tenant 'not to do or permit to be done anything which may be or become a nuisance or annoyance or be injurious or detrimental to the reputation of the premises'. An over-persistent admirer of the tenant, who was an actress, had annoyed adjoining occupiers by telephoning, ringing the entry phone and shouting. The tenant held rowdy parties and gave newspaper interviews which, it was said, 'lowered the tone'. The court refused to order possession. 'Permit' means to give leave for an act which could not otherwise legally be done, or to abstain from taking reasonable steps to prevent the act where it is within a person's power to prevent it. The tenant had installed an Ansaphone, disconnected the entry phone, called the police to eject party-goers and conducted interviews off the premises.

Nuisance, immoral or illegal user

A court may order possession under case 2 of the Rent Act 1977 'where the tenant or any person residing or lodging with him or any sub-tenant has been guilty of conduct which is a nuisance or annoyance to adjoining occupiers, or has been convicted of using the dwelling-house or allowing it to be used for immoral or illegal purposes'.

'Nuisance' was defined by Knight-Bruce V-C in *Walter v Selfe* (1851) WDeG & Sm 315 (at p. 322) as being 'an inconvenience materially interfering with the ordinary comfort physically of human existence, not merely according to elegant or dainty modes and habits of living, but according to plain and sober and simple notions among the English people'. 'Annoyance' is a wider term than nuisance and has been described as something which 'reasonably troubles the mind and pleasure . . . of the ordinary English inhabitants of a house even though it may not appear to amount to physical detriment to comfort' (*Todd-Heatley v Benham* (1888) 40 Ch D 80). It may consist of a physical interference, e.g. making excessive noise, producing a lot of dust, allowing water to overflow onto someone else's premises (*Ferguson v Butler* [1918] SLT 228; *Chapman v Hughes* (1923) 129 LT 223) or it may be the result of conduct (such as allowing the premises to be used for prostitution as in *Yates v Morris* [1951] 1 KB 77) or verbal abuse and obscene language (*Cobstone Investments Ltd v Maxim* [1984] 2 All ER 635). Nuisance and annoyance includes anything which disturbs adjoining occupiers, i.e. those who live sufficiently close to be affected by the tenant's conduct on the demised premises, and does not have to take place on the demised premises or even in a property which physically touches them. Thus, in *Whitbread v Ward* (1952) 159 EG 494 the tenant's 'undue familiarity' with the landlord's 16-year-old daughter in an alley some 200 yards away from the premises was held to be an annoyance.

As regards conviction for immoral or illegal purposes, the landlord must show that the premises themselves were connected with the crime; it is 'not enough that the tenant has been convicted of a crime with which the premises have nothing to do beyond merely being the scene of its commission' (*Schneiders & Sons v Abrahams* [1925] 1 KB 301, 311). If the tenant has been convicted of the possession of drugs but the drugs were merely found in the tenant's pocket or handbag, this would not amount to using the premises. It would be different if the premises were used as storage or as a hiding-place (*Abrahams v Wilson* [1971] 2 QB 88).

In *Heglibiston Establishment v Heyman* (1977) 76 P & CR 351, it was held that a term in the tenancy agreement not to use the premises for immoral purposes was intended to prevent the flat in question from being used as a brothel or for prostitution. The tenant was not in breach, therefore, by permitting his son to live with him, together with a woman to whom he was not married.

Deterioration of the dwelling-house or furniture as the result of the tenant's neglect

Possession may be recovered under case 3 of the Rent Act 1977 where the condition of the dwelling-house has, in the opinion of the court, deteriorated owing to acts of waste by, or the neglect of default of, the tenant or any sub-tenant or any person residing or lodging with the tenant, where the court is satisfied that the tenant has not, before the making of the order in question, taken such steps as ought reasonably to have been taken for the removal of the lodger or subtenant as the case may be. Case 3 can apply even if there is no breach of any term of the tenancy or of any common law duty (*Lowe v Lendrum* (1950) 159 EG 423). The tenant cannot be held responsible for any neglect prior to the tenancy (*Holloway v Povey* (1984) 271 EG 195). Case 4 is worded similarly to case 3 but applies to 'any furniture provided for use under the tenancy'.

Dwelling previously occupied, or required for future occupation, by the landlord or the landlord's family

Case 9 (a discretionary ground) permits recovery of possession where the dwelling-house is reasonably required for occupation as a residence for the landlord (which includes the landlord's spouse and any minor children

(*Ritcher v Wilson* [1963] 2 QB 426; *Smith v Penny* [1947] KB 230) or by one of the landlord's adult children, father or mother, or a parent-in-law. This case cannot be utilised by a person who became the landlord by purchase when the tenant was already in occupation. The landlord must need the premises 'with a view to living there for some reasonable period, definite or indefinite, and not so that the property can be sold' (*Rowe v Truelove* (1976) 241 EG 533).

The landlord will have to show that one of the specified categories of relative has a genuine need for the dwelling-house in order to satisfy a court that it is 'reasonably required' for their occupation. Factors to be taken into account include the size and health of the landlord's family, their present housing needs (*Kennealy v Dunne* [1977] QB 837), their current residence (or lack thereof), a probable change of circumstances (*Kidder v Birch* (1983) 265 EG 773), and the proximity of the property to the landlord's place of work (*Jackson v Harbour* [1924] EGD 99). The requirement for accommodation need not be immediate but in *Kissias v Lehany* [1979] CLY 1625 possession was refused where the landlord stated that he required a basement for his daughter to live in on her marriage which might take place in two years' time.

The court must not make an order for possession under case 9 if it is satisfied that, having regard to all the circumstances of the case, including the question whether other accommodation is available for the landlord or the tenant, greater hardship would be caused by granting the order than by refusing to grant it (Sch. 15, Part III, para. 1). The burden of proof is on the tenant. The court should consider all who may be affected – 'relatives, dependants, lodgers, guests, and the stranger within the gates – but should weigh such hardship with due regard to the status of the persons affected, and their "proximity" to the tenant or landlord, and the extent to which, consequently, hardship to them would be hardship to him' (*Harte v Frampton* [1948] 1 KB 73, 79).

The question is: who will suffer the greater hardship? The court must take into account all the relevant circumstances of the case, e.g. the financial means of both parties (*Kelley v Goodwin* [1947] 1 All ER 810), their mental and physical health (*Thomes v Fryer* [1970] 1 WLR 845), and the availability of other accommodation (*Coombs v Parry* (1987) 19 HLR 384; *Chandler v Strevett* [1947] 1 All ER 164; *Manaton v Edwards* [1985] 2 EGLR 159; *Baker v MacIver* (1990) 22 HLR 328).

Mandatory case 11 comes into play where the landlord occupied the dwelling-house as a residence at some time before the letting and it was then let to the tenant on a regulated tenancy. It can apply where joint owner-occupiers are reclaiming possession of premises as a residence for only one of them (*Tilling v Whiteman* [1980] AC 1). Not later than the relevant date the landlord must have served notice on the tenant that possession might be required on this ground. The notice requirement may be dispensed with by the court if it considers it just and equitable to do so. The court must grant possession if one of the conditions (a), or (c)–(f) outlined in Part IV of Sch. 15 are satisfied, namely:

(a) the dwelling-house is required as a residence for the owner or any family member who resided with the owner when he or she last occupied the dwelling-house as a residence;

(b) the owner has retired from regular employment and requires the dwelling-house as a residence;

(c) the owner has died and the dwelling-house is required as a residence for a family member who was residing with the owner at the time of death;

(d) the owner has died and the dwelling-house is required by a successor in title as the successor's residence or for the purpose of its sale;

(e) a mortgage was granted before the beginning of the tenancy and the lender requires vacant possession for the purpose of exercising the power of sale conferred by the mortgage or by s. 101 of the Law of Property Act 1925. Notice must have been given that possession might be required on this ground or the court must be satisfied that it is just and equitable to dispense with such notice. Most mortgages expressly prohibit letting by the borrower without the lender's prior consent. If such consent is not obtained, the tenancy will not normally be binding on the lender, even where the tenant is protected as against the borrower by the 1977 Act (*Dudley and District Building Society v Emerson* [1949] Ch 707; *Quennell v Maltby* [1979] 1 WLR 318);

(f) the dwelling-house is not reasonably suited to the needs of the owner, having regard to the owner's place of work, and he or she wants to dispose of it with vacant possession and use the sale proceeds to acquire a more suitable residence.

There has been sufficient occupation as a residence where, before the letting, the landlord lived mainly in South Africa but occupied the property when visiting the UK on business and for holidays (*Naish v Curzon* (1986) 51 P & CR 229) and used the property on weekdays for a period of eight or nine weeks before the letting, during which he had no home elsewhere (*Mistry v Isidore* [1990] 2 EGLR 97).

Mandatory case 12 applies where the dwelling-house was let by an owner who intended to occupy it on his retirement from regular employment and possession is now required. Unlike case 11, there is no requirement that the owner previously occupied the premises as his or her residence. The tenant must have been given notice not later than the relevant date that possession might be required under this case and one of the conditions in paras (b) to (e) of Part V of Sch. 15 must be satisfied (see above).

Out-of-season holiday lettings

Case 13 of the 1977 Act applies where the dwelling-house is let under a tenancy for less than eight months and the dwelling-house was, at some time within the period of 12 months immediately preceding the tenancy, occupied under a right to occupy it for a holiday. Not later than the beginning of the tenancy, the landlord must have served written notice on the tenant that possession might be claimed under this ground. Since 15 January 1989, no lettings have been granted which would enable this case to be utilised.

Student lettings

Possession may be claimed on case 14 of the Rent Act 1977 where the dwelling-house is let under a tenancy for a term of years certain not exceeding 12 months and at some time within the period of 12 months ending on the relevant date the dwelling-house was let by a specified educational institution as student accommodation. The tenant must have been informed in writing not later than the relevant date that possession might be required on this ground. It enabled colleges and universities to let its residential accommodation during vacations but, as with case 13 above, it will not have been possible since 15 January 1989 to grant any lettings which would enable this case to be utilised.

Ministers of religion

Lettings of Church of England parsonages are excluded from the 1977 Act. There is no such exclusion for other religions but case 15 provides a mandatory ground for possession where the dwelling-house is available for occupation as a residence by a minister of religion for the performance of his or her duties. The tenant must have been given written notice that possession might be required on this ground and the court must be satisfied that the dwelling-house is required for occupation by a minister of religion as such a residence.

Dwelling required for the landlord's employee

Under case 8 of the Rent Act 1977, the landlord must satisfy the court that (a) he or she employed the present tenant to whom the dwelling-house was let in consequence of that employment; and (b) the tenant has ceased to be in that employment, and (c) the dwelling-house is reasonably required for someone engaged in full-time employment by the landlord or by one of the landlord's tenants, and that the contract of employment was made conditional on the provision of housing.

Notice to quit by the tenant

Possession may be recovered under case 5 'where, in consequence of a notice to quit given by the tenant, the landlord has contracted to sell or let the dwelling-house or has taken any other steps as the result of which he would, in the opinion of the court, be seriously prejudiced if he could not obtain possession'. The purpose of this case is to protect a landlord who might otherwise be liable to a third party for breach of a contract of sale or an agreement for a lease. Thus, it could not be relied upon by a landlord who intended to sell but had not contracted to do so (*Barton v Fincham* [1921] 2 KB 291). Notice to quit here means the service of a valid notice; it does not apply where the tenant disappears and returns the keys (*Standingford v Bruce* [1926] 1 KB 466) or where the tenant informally agrees to leave (*De Vries v Sparks* (1927) 137 LT 441).

Assigning or sub-letting without the landlord's consent

The purpose of case 6 is 'to give some protection to a landlord against the risk of finding some person wholly unknown to him irrevocably installed in his property' (*Hyde v Pimley* [1952] 2 QB 506, 512). It can be relied upon against both the tenant and a sub-tenant (*Leith Properties Ltd v Springer* [1982] 3 All ER 731) and applies even where the tenancy agreement contains no prohibition against assignment or sub-letting. From a practical point of view, case 6 applies only to contractual tenants; a statutory tenant cannot assign a tenancy and a statutory tenant who sub-lets the whole of the premises will cease to occupy the premises as his or her residence.

Sub-letting of part at an excessive rent

The landlord can claim possession under case 10 where the tenant is charging a sub-tenant more than the maximum recoverable rent for the premises sub-let by virtue of the fair rent provisions (see Chapter 6).

Agricultural property

Cases 16, 17 and 18 contain complex provisions which apply to property occupied by agricultural employees and tenants who occupy premises of former agricultural employees. They are outside the scope of this book.

Protected shorthold tenancies

As stated in Chapter 5, the protected shorthold tenancy was a creation of the Housing Act 1980. Such tenancies had to be for a fixed term of between one and five years and at the end of the term, case 19 provided landlords with a mandatory ground for possession in addition to all the other cases. Since no new protected shorthold tenancies have been created since 15 January 1989, all protected shorthold tenancies existing at that date will by now have run their course. If, however, on or after that date, a landlord grants a tenancy to a tenant who, before the grant, held a protected shorthold tenancy, the new tenancy will be an assured shorthold tenancy (Housing Act 1988, s. 34(3)).

Landlord is a 'member of the regular armed forces of the Crown'

The landlord must have been a member of the armed forces when he or she (a) acquired and (b) let the dwelling-house. Written notice (which the court may dispense with if it considers it just and equitable to do so) must have been served on the tenant prior to the grant of the tenancy that possession might be required under case 20. The court must be satisfied that the property is now required as a residence for the owner.

Assured shorthold tenancies: termination by the landlord

Assured shorthold tenancies created before 28 February 1997 (the date on which s. 19A of the Housing Act 1988 came into force) must be for a minimum term of six months and there must be no power for the landlord to bring the tenancy to an end any earlier than six months, other than by forfeiture or a power of re-entry. The court cannot make an order for possession of such an assured shorthold tenancy unless the fixed term has come to an end (s. 21(1)(a), (4)). This confers upon the tenant a minimum period of security of tenure (unless there is provision for forfeiture or re-entry, and one of the grounds for possession for an assured tenancy can be relied upon). As there is no requirement of a fixed term of six months for ASTs created since 28 February 1997, s. 21 was amended to prevent possession being ordered until at least six months has elapsed from the grant of the tenancy (s. 21(5)–(7)). The six months runs from the grant of the original tenancy, and not the start of any replacement tenancy whether this arises by virtue of an agreement with the landlord or as a statutory periodic tenancy under s. 5 of the Housing Act 1988.

An assured shorthold tenancy may be terminated in the same ways (i.e. using the same grounds for possession) as any assured tenancy but s. 21 contains what is, in effect, an additional mandatory ground for possession enabling the landlord (or at least one of them, in the case of a joint tenancy) to recover possession by giving the tenant not less than two months' written notice stating that he requires possession of the dwelling-house (s. 21(1)(b), (4)(a)). The court cannot use its discretion to consider the issue of reasonableness, nor to suspend the making of the order.

An accelerated possession procedure, which came into force on 1 November 1993, abolishes court hearings in many cases relating to assured shorthold tenancies (both fixed term and periodic) and to certain mandatory grounds for possession (i.e. cases 1, 3, 4, 5) but only if there is no other claim for relief (such as rent arrears) besides possession and costs. A court order is still required.

Chapter 15

The Protection from Eviction Act 1977, harassment and unlawful eviction

Introduction

Most policy attention and intervention with regard to anti-social behaviour has tended to focus on the occupants of social housing and measures have only recently been introduced – via the selective licensing provisions of the Housing Act 2004 – to address the anti-social activities of private sector tenants in low demand areas. Yet anti-social behaviour – although not labelled as such – has long been a problem in the private rented sector, often stemming from unacceptable behaviour by or on behalf of landlords. The main purpose of this chapter is to explore the ways in which the law seeks to protect residential occupiers against harassment and unlawful eviction by criminalising both activities, and by enabling a person who has been harassed or unlawfully evicted to claim damages or re-instatement through the civil courts.

The number of prosecutions for unlawful eviction and harassment is, and always has been, low given that they are 'persistent problem[s] seemingly endemic within this residualised sector in which understanding of the consequences of letting is often poor and respect for the law limited' (Stewart, 1996: 101). Many judges and magistrates '[fail] to take harassment and unlawful eviction seriously and to punish it to the degree it [warrants]' (Marsh et al., 2000: 11) but it does not follow that the law in this area is wholly ineffective. Consideration is given here to the efficacy of the law in this area within the context of the rights and interests of the actors who operate within the private rented sector, including the statutory security of tenure system to which they are subject.[1] The opportunity is taken in the first part of the chapter to set out the notice, due process and forfeiture provisions of the Protection from Eviction Act 1977 and to explore the legal position of those who remain in the property after expiry of a joint tenant's notice to quit.

---

1 For a further discussion of the reasons why few complaints are made to local authorities by private sector tenants, and why only a small number of these actually result in prosecution, see Cowan (2001).

Notice to quit

A notice to quit is required for the determination of periodic tenancies. At common law it need not be in writing but must be clear and unambiguous (*Gardner v Ingram* (1890) 61 LT 729). The length of the notice required depends upon the express terms of the tenancy. If there are none, six months' notice must be given to end a yearly tenancy, one quarter's notice to end a quarterly tenancy, one month's notice to end a monthly tenancy, and one week's notice to end a weekly tenancy. The appropriate notice must be expressed to expire at the end of the period or on the anniversary date.

Statutory provisions may require longer periods of notice. As regards residential tenancies, s. 5(1) of the Protection from Eviction Act 1977 requires that a minimum of four weeks' notice to quit be given in writing. By s. 5(1A) the same rule applies to periodic licences, but not to a licence which is expressed to be terminable with the licensee's employment (e.g. *Norris v Checksfield* [1991] 4 All ER 327). Section 5 does not apply to excluded tenancies or licences, nor to tenants at will. A landlord's notice must provide certain information, in accordance with the Notices to Quit (Prescribed Information) Regulations 1988. Put simply it should inform the occupier that if he does not leave the dwelling, there can be no lawful eviction without a possession order from the court, that the landlord or licensor cannot apply for such an order before the notice to quit or notice to determine has run out, and that if the occupier is uncertain of his or her right to remain in possession, information and advice is available from a solicitor, a citizen's advice bureau, a housing aid centre or a rent officer. Legal aid may be available to help with all or part of the cost of legal advice and assistance.

There may be particular problems where a notice to quit is given by one joint tenant, a situation which is most likely to arise in the case of relationship breakdown. The tenant leaving the property will often turn for accommodation to the local authority, which may also be the landlord of the existing accommodation. As a precondition of housing the applicant, the authority will generally require the termination of the existing tenancy, a step which when the notice expires will have the effect of turning the tenant who is left into a trespasser against whom possession can be sought. In *Hammersmith and Fulham London Borough Council v Monk* [1992] 1 AC 47, Mr Monk and Mrs Powell were joint tenants of a council flat. Following a domestic dispute, Mrs Powell moved out and the local authority agreed to rehouse her if she would terminate the tenancy by giving the requisite four weeks' notice to quit. This she did without Mr Monk's consent or even his knowledge. The authority immediately notified Mr Monk that the tenancy had been determined and, in due course, brought possession proceedings against him. The House of Lords upheld the effectiveness of the notice. It said that, unless the tenancy agreement provides otherwise, a joint tenant can validly determine the tenancy by notice without the agreement of the other joint tenant or tenants.

Lord Browne-Wilkinson spoke of 'two instinctive reactions' to the case which lead to 'diametrically opposed conclusions'. The first was that the flat in question was the joint home of Mr Monk and Mrs Powell: it could not be right, therefore, that one of them unilaterally could join with the landlords to put an end to the other's rights in the home. The second view – which the House of Lords favoured – was that Mr Monk and Mrs Powell undertook joint liabilities as tenants for the purpose of providing themselves with a joint home and that, once they no longer wanted to live together, the one who left the home should not be made to continue indefinitely to be liable for the discharge of the obligations to the landlord under the tenancy agreement.

Such a notice will only have this effect, however, if it is a valid notice to quit, i.e. it complies with s. 5 of the 1977 Act. In *Hounslow London Borough Council v Pilling* (1993) 25 HLR 305, the local authority undertook to rehouse any tenant who had experienced domestic violence, provided that the tenant surrendered his or her tenancy. The tenancy agreement required four weeks' written notice 'or such lesser period as the council may accept'. With the landlord's consent, Ms Doubtfire, a joint tenant acting unilaterally, gave three days' notice to quit. The Court of Appeal rejected the notice as inappropriate and therefore ineffective. In relying on the landlord's discretionary acceptance of a shorter period, the tenant had not exercised a power of determination by notice to quit but had instead sought to operate what amounted to a break clause in the tenancy agreement. A break clause cannot be unilaterally invoked by one joint tenant. In any event, the court held that it was not possible to override the Protection from Eviction Act 1977 requirement of at least four weeks' notice.

Unsuccessful challenges in land law and family law have been mounted against the rule in *Hammersmith v Monk*. In *Notting Hill Housing Trust v Brackley* (2001) 35 EG 106, the Court of Appeal held that a notice to quit was no more than the exercise by one joint tenant of his or her right to withhold consent to the continuation of the tenancy into a further period. It did not constitute the exercise of a 'function' for the purposes of the Trusts of Land and Appointment of Trustees Act 1996 and the first joint tenant was not, therefore, in breach of s. 11 of the Act by having failed to consult the second before serving the notice to quit. In *Crawley London Borough Council v Ure* [1996] QB 13, an argument based on s. 26(3) of the Law of Property Act 1925 (effectively replaced by s. 11 of the 1996 Act) was similarly unsuccessful. In *Newlon Housing Trust v Alsulaimen* [1998] 3 WLR 451 the defendant tried to persuade the court to invalidate the notice to quit given by his former joint tenant by means of s. 37(2)(b) of the Matrimonial Causes Act 1973 which empowers a court to set aside any 'disposition' of the matrimonial property where a party to divorce proceedings disposes of property in order to defeat the other party's financial and property claims. The House of Lords held that, although a subsisting periodic tenancy is capable of being the subject of a property adjustment order, a unilateral termination by one joint tenant through a notice to quit terminating the tenancy was not a disposition of the property.

More recently, the House of Lords in *Harrow London Borough Council v Qazi* [2004] 1 AC 983 considered the possible impact of Art. 8 of the ECHR. Following the breakdown of her marriage, Mrs Qazi left the council house (of which she and her husband were joint secure tenants) and – like Mr Monk's partner – served notice to quit upon the council. Mr Qazi remained in occupation with his new wife and children but the council declined to grant him a sole tenancy. Mr Qazi defended the proceedings subsequently brought by the council to recover possession from him on the basis that his eviction would amount to a breach of Art. 8. The House of Lords unanimously accepted that the property was Mr Qazi's 'home' as he had sufficient and continuous links to satisfy the test put forward in *Buckley v United Kingdom* (1997) 23 EHRR 101 even though he had no legal or equitable entitlement to be there. They took different approaches, however, as to whether Art. 8 could be used to defend the council's claim for possession. Lords Bingham and Steyn, dissenting, took the view that any action by a public authority seeking possession of residential property occupied by a defendant as his home would ordinarily engage Art. 8(1). Thus, the question of justification – if raised – would fall to be considered even though considerations of domestic property law were likely to be crucial and the occasions on which a court would be justified in refusing to make a possession order would be highly exceptional. The majority held, however, that the exercise of an absolute proprietary right to possession in accordance with domestic law either did not infringe Art. 8 or, alternatively, it automatically ensured that any interference with the occupier's right to 'respect for his home' was justifiable under Art. 8(2). The reason of the majority was the subject of some criticism (see Loveland, 2004; Davis and Hughes, 2004) and *Qazi* was recently re-considered by the House of Lords in *Kay v Lambeth London Borough Council* [2006] 2 WLR 570 in the light of *Connors v United Kingdom* (2005) 40 EHRR 9. In the latter case, the European Court of Human Rights (ECtHR) held that the making of the possession order which led to eviction from a local authority gypsy site violated Art. 8 because it was not accompanied by the procedural safeguards which were required to establish that the interference with the applicant's Convention rights was properly justified. (The authority had simply terminated by notice his licence to occupy.) In *Kay*, Lord Hope, giving the leading speech of the majority, pointed out that *Connors* is the only case in which the ECtHR has held that the making of a possession order in favour of a public authority, in accordance with domestic property law, failed to establish that the measure employed was proportionate to the aim being pursued. In his opinion, it left untouched *Qazi*, where the judgment of the legislature on issues of property law met this requirement. Lord Hope explained that the effect of *Qazi* is that where an order for possession is made by the court in keeping with domestic property law, the essence of Art. 8(1) will not be violated. Most importantly for housing authorities, the county courts need only consider in 'highly exceptional' cases whether the interference is permitted by Art. 8(2). Instead, they should proceed on the assumption that the domestic law is compatible. The only matters which the court needs to consider are whether the requirements of the law and the procedural safeguards which it lays down for the protection of the occupier have been fulfilled. The absence of any statutory protection in such cases is the result of a deliberate decision by Parliament.

The Law Commission takes the view that – as is the case in Scotland – joint occupiers should be able to withdraw from a joint occupation agreement by serving notice but without artificially destroying the whole occupation agreement (Law Commission, 2002b: 3.68). It accepts that social landlords should be able to seek repossession where the occupier who is left is not appropriate to the home in question, e.g. does not have the 'degree of housing need' normally required for occupation of the property, and is a person to whom the landlord would not offer an occupation agreement if the occupier intended to live there alone (ibid.: 3.72).

Forfeiture

Section 2 of the Protection from Eviction Act 1977 provides that 'where any premises are let as a dwelling on a lease which is subject to a right of re-entry or forfeiture, it shall not be lawful to enforce that right otherwise than by proceedings in court while any person is lawfully residing in the premises or part of them'. In *Pirabakaran v Patel* [2006] EWCA Civ 685, it was held that the phrase 'let as a dwelling' in s. 2 of the 1977 Act meant 'let wholly or partly as a dwelling' and so applied to premises which were let for mixed residential and business purposes. The Court of Appeal added that to interpret s. 2 so as to allow a landlord to exercise an alleged right of re-entry upon such premises other than by court proceedings would also be incompatible with the tenant's rights under Art. 8.

This provision is of particular significance for tenants who have no security of tenure. Forfeiture of a protected tenancy under the Rent Act 1977 does not of itself entitle the landlord to possession, and a court order based on a ground for possession must be obtained. Assured tenancies cannot be terminated by forfeiture alone but the presence of a forfeiture clause in a fixed-term assured or assured shorthold tenancy in conjunction with the statutory procedure may enable the tenancy to be brought to an end before the expiry of the term on grounds 2, 8 and 10 to 15.

Eviction without due process of law

Section 3(1) of the Protection from Eviction Act 1977 provides that 'where any premises have been let as a dwelling under a tenancy which is neither a statutorily protected tenancy nor an excluded tenancy and –

(a) the tenancy ... has come to an end, but
(b) the occupier continues to reside in the premises or part of them,

it shall not be lawful for the owner to enforce against the occupier, otherwise than by proceedings in the court, his right to recover possession of the premises.'

By s. 3(2B) of the 1977 Act, inserted by the Housing Act 1988, the section is extended to any premises occupied as a dwelling under a licence, other than an excluded licence.

Section 3, as amended, provides a minimum protection for certain residential occupiers who otherwise have no security of tenure. Breach of s. 3 is a tort. The 'statutorily protected' tenancies are listed in s. 8(1) of the 1977 Act and include, within the residential sector, Rent Act protected tenancies, assured and assured tenancies under the Housing Act 1988, and long tenancies within Part I of the Landlord and Tenant Act 1954, all of which have their own schemes of protection. Secure tenancies (under Part IV of the Housing Act 1985) and statutory tenancies under the Rent Act 1977 are not 'statutorily protected' tenancies, however, and are subject, therefore, to s. 3. In *Haniff v Robinson* [1992] 3 WLR 875 it was held that the landlord had carried out an unlawful eviction by forcibly entering the premises and removing a statutory tenant, even though he had obtained a possession order and a warrant of execution of the order. The Court of Appeal held that the effect of s. 3 was to protect the occupier until there had been proper execution of the order by the court bailiff. The tenant was awarded damages, calculated in accordance with s. 28 of the 1988 Act (see below).

Excluded tenancies and licences

The Housing Act 1988 provides for a new class of 'excluded tenancies and licences' to which s. 3 does not apply. They are set out in s. 3A of the Protection from Eviction Act 1977 and are as follows.

Accommodation shared with the owner or a member of the owner's family

Section 3A(2) provides that 'a tenancy or licence is excluded if (a) under its terms the occupier shares any accommodation with the landlord or the licensor; and (b) immediately before the tenancy or licence was granted and also at the time it comes to an end, the landlord or licensor occupied as his only or principal home premises of which the whole or part of the shared accommodation formed part.'

Section 3A(3) is worded similarly but refers to 'a member of the family of the landlord or licensor' in place of 'the landlord or the licensor' and contains the additional requirement that 'immediately before the tenancy or licence was granted and also at the time it comes to an end, the landlord or licensor occupied as his only or principal home premises in the same building as the shared accommodation and that building is not a purpose-built block of flats.'

The exception in s. 3A(2) differs from the 'resident landlord' exclusions under the Rent Act 1977 and Housing Act 1988 in that it requires the actual sharing of accommodation. It is not confined to the sharing of living accommodation, but extends to a right to share the use of any accommodation, except storage areas, staircases, passages, corridors or other means of access (s. 3A(5)(a)). Thus, where a tenancy granted before 15 January 1989 falls within the resident landlord provisions of the Rent Act 1977, the tenant will have a restricted contract, which requires a court order for possession under s. 3 of the Protection from Eviction Act 1977. In the case of a tenancy granted by a resident landlord after the commencement of the 1988 Act, the tenant can have neither a restricted contract nor an assured tenancy. If the conditions of s. 3A are satisfied, no court order is required. If they are not, a possession order must still be obtained under s. 3.

If the tenant shares accommodation with a member of the landlord's family, but the landlord himself does not reside at the premises, the tenant may have an assured tenancy, as the resident landlord rules would not be satisfied. In such a case, neither ss. 3 nor 3A would apply, recovery of possession being governed by the assured tenancy rules, which require a possession order (and a ground for possession). If, however, the tenant shares accommodation with a member of the landlord's or licensor's family and the landlord occupies as his only or principal home premises in the same building (which is not a purpose-built block of flats), no possession order under s. 3 is required.

Trespassers

A tenancy or licence is excluded by s. 3A(6) if it was granted as a temporary expedient to a person who entered the premises in question, or any other premises, as a trespasser (whether or not, before the beginning of that tenancy or licence, another tenancy or licence to occupy the premises had been granted to him). This provision will be significant mainly to local authorities who may allow trespassers to remain in occupation of its property as a temporary measure.

Holiday occupation

A tenancy or licence is excluded by s. 3A(7)(a) if it confers on the tenant or licensee the right to occupy the premises for a holiday only. Holiday lettings are excluded from protection under the Rent Act 1977 and the Housing Act 1988. Prior to the enactment of s. 3A of the Protection from Eviction Act 1977, tenants with holiday lettings had the protection of the court order requirement. Such tenants (and licensees) are now denied the opportunity of arguing that the exception has been used as an evasion device unless they are willing themselves to initiate the proceedings.

Rent-free occupation

A tenancy or licence is excluded if it is granted otherwise than for money or money's worth (s. 3A(7)(b)). See *West Wiltshire County Council v Snelgrove* (1998) 30 HLR 57.

Hostel accommodation

A licence (but not a tenancy) is excluded if it confers rights of occupation in a hostel within the meaning of the Housing Act 1985, i.e. a building in which 'residential accommodation otherwise than in separate and self-contained sets of premises' (s. 622) is provided by various specified public bodies such as local authorities, the Housing Corporation, and housing trusts which are either charities or registered housing associations (s. 3A(8)). In *Rogerson v Wigan Metropolitan Borough Council* [2005] 2 All ER 1000, the occupier was allocated one bedroom in a two-bedroomed flat (in what had originally been a block of flats rather than a purpose-built hostel) and would have to share the rest of the unit with anyone who happened to be in the other bedroom. The licence expressly provided that occupiers could be moved from one unit of accommodation to another at the will of the authority, and they could be required to share their unit with a stranger. Elias J took the view that a person could not appropriately be described as being in separate accommodation if he or she was compelled to share some of the facilities with someone not of their own choice. The separate bedroom did not amount to separate residential accommodation and, although nobody had in fact been required to share the accommodation whilst the occupier was there, he felt that 'the potential to require sharing was no different to actual sharing' (para. 26).

Unlawful eviction and harassment: legislative history

As stated in Chapter 5, regulation of private renting since 1915 has consisted of a series of measures moving from control to decontrol and back again, reflecting responses by various governments to perceived housing shortage or sufficiency. Until the late 1980s, the private rented sector was in decline and the Rent Act 1957 – one of the most controversial measures passed by the Macmillan government – was 'a last ditch attempt to revive private investment in rented housing' (Kemp, 1992: 110–11). The 1957 Act immediately decontrolled rents of more expensive dwellings, while the rents of the rest became decontrolled when the sitting tenant left – a process known as 'creeping decontrol'.

This gave landlords an incentive to dispose of sitting tenants and to replace them with tenants paying higher rents.

The 1957 Act is associated with 'Rachmanism', a term which has become virtually synonymous with harassment and unlawful eviction. Perec Rachman started to build up his property empire in 1954 by buying up long leases which had only a short time left to run. The houses he bought, which were often in a poor state of repair, were divided up into flats of three or four rooms and let to controlled tenants at low rents. Rachman paid these tenants large sums of money to leave (a practice sometimes referred to as 'winkling') and then converted the flats into furnished single room dwellings. Even though furnished tenants possessed lesser rights than controlled tenants as regards security of tenure and rent control, the housing shortage in Inner London made it easy for Rachman to let his properties at high rents, often to immigrants who found it difficult to obtain accommodation elsewhere. In due course, he realised that there was no point in paying controlled tenants to leave, if they could be persuaded to go by some other means. Rachman and his hirelings certainly used harassment, but it 'belonged to a brief episode in his career and constituted no more than a small and unrepresentative aspect of his normal commercial operations' (Nelken, 1983: 4). Thus, while the Rent Act 1957 gave Rachman's activities some further impetus, it should be remembered that he had been carrying out his dubious business practices some time before the Act was passed, most of his profits deriving from his policy of charging high rents but carrying out few repairs. An interesting question is why certain of his activities were made illegal while others – such as winkling – were not, even though they ultimately achieved the same end. More importantly, Rachman's story should perhaps be remembered 'more for highlighting the fact that regulation can channel behaviour in unfortunate and unintended ways, rather than as an illustration of any innate temperament of landlords' (Ball, 2004: 30).

Rachman was only one of many similar landlords, but he came to public attention because of his connection with the 'Profumo affair' which involved Christine Keeler, a call girl who had formerly been Rachman's mistress, John Profumo, one of her clients and the then Secretary of State for War, and Eugene Ivanov, an assistant Russian Naval Attaché at the Russian Embassy in London. The matter led to questions in the House of Commons and the so-called Rachman debate in July 1963 on the 'Rent Act 1957 and Property Profiteering'.

Harold Wilson, then leader of the Opposition, pointed out that Rachman's was 'a lurid version of a story which goes on in more sombre, sepia tones in other slum empires and in other cities as well as London'. The photophobic world of slimy creatures revealed when a stone is turned over had nothing, he said, to compare with 'the revolting creatures of London's underworld, living there, shunning the light, growing fat by battening on human misery'. He explained how, so as to avoid 'the palsied hand of official control', loopholes in the Companies Act were used – with the assistance of lawyers and accountants – to create 'a proliferation of interlocking companies' so that any official action which might be taken – sanitary notices, certificates of disrepair, or compulsory acquisition – could be frustrated by a total inability to identify the property's owner (HC Deb (1962–3) vol. 681, cols 1058–9).

A Labour government – which had pledged to give urgent assistance to tenants – was returned to power in October 1964. Soon afterwards, the Protection from Eviction Act 1964 was passed, the first piece of legislation to make it an offence to evict a tenant without first obtaining a court order. This temporary measure was replaced by Part III of the Rent Act 1965 which created the criminal offences of unlawful eviction and harassment. The relevant provisions were consolidated in the Protection from Eviction Act 1977, which remains the principal statutory provision in this area, although Part I of the Housing Act 1988 made a number of important changes.

The fair rent provisions of the Rent Act 1977 meant that landlords stood to make significant financial gain if they could persuade protected or statutory tenants to move out and then relet them under the Housing Act 1988 at market rents. Accordingly the 1988 Act – representing the second stage in the development of the law on unlawful eviction and harassment – created a new offence of harassment, amended the existing one, and strengthened the civil law to enable residential occupiers who have been evicted illegally or forced out by harassment to claim greater compensation. At the same time, however, it excludes certain categories of occupant from the protection afforded by ss. 3 and 5, thus sanctioning the use of peaceful self-help. Determining the occupier's status is crucial, therefore, as it dictates whether or not there is entitlement to any protection and, if so, the course of action which is most appropriate. It also has a bearing on the amount of damages which the occupier is likely to recover.

Criminal liability

Unlawful eviction

By s. 1(2) of the Protection from Eviction Act 1977 'if any person unlawfully deprives the residential occupier of any premises of his occupation of the premises or any part thereof, or attempts to do so, he shall be guilty of an offence unless he proves that he believed, and had reasonable cause to believe, that the residential occupier had ceased to reside in the premises'.

A residential occupier means 'a person occupying premises as a residence, whether under a contract or by virtue of any enactment or rule of law giving him the right to remain in occupation or restricting the right of any person to recover possession of the premises' (s. 1(1)). Thus, it includes not only tenants covered by the Rent Act 1977 and Housing Act 1988, but also those whose dwelling-houses have a rateable value outside the limits of those Acts, licensees, and tenants of local authorities. Trespassers receive no protection because they have no right to be in occupation, but they may nonetheless seek recourse to the Criminal Law Act 1977.

In *R v Yuthiwattana* (1984) 128 SJ 661, it was held that the offence under s. 1(2) must have the 'character of eviction' which need not be permanent, but may be for months or weeks during which the evicted occupier has to find other accommodation. Locking the tenant out for a day and a night would not suffice but could well be harassment within the scope of s. 1(3)(a) or (b). In *Costelloe v London Borough of Camden* [1986] Crim LR 249, it was held that exclusion of the occupier for an hour could be within s. 1(2) if the landlord intended it to be permanent but for some reason (e.g. after intervention by the police) the occupier was readmitted. In *Uckuzular v Sandford-Hill* [1994] CLY 1770, an unlawful eviction was held to have taken place where the tenant returned home at 12.30 a.m. to discover her landlord and an unknown companion inside it. The locks had been changed. The police declined to intervene. The claimant spent the night with friends, returning to the house at 4.30 a.m. in an unsuccessful attempt to retrieve some of her valuables. She eventually gained entry, via the intervention of her solicitors, at 5 p.m. Reinstatement may be ordered by mandatory interlocutory injunction (*Parsons v Nasar* (1991) 23 HLR 1).

Section 1(2) applies to 'any premises' (which may consist of one room only: *Thurrock Urban District Council v Shina* (1972) 23 P & CR 205) or 'any part thereof', so that the offence will have been committed if the landlord bars the occupier's access merely to, e.g. the bathroom or kitchen. Since the premises need not have been let as a dwelling, it appears that 'a boat, cave, pigsty, cart shed, green house or cow house' could all constitute 'premises' so long as they are occupied as a residence (Farrand, 1978: 431). It should also be noted that the offence can be committed by people other than landlords, e.g. managing agents, and perhaps even solicitors who serve invalid notices to quit. The offence of unlawful eviction was not amended by the Housing Act 1988.

Harassment

What is harassment?

Harassment can take a wide variety of forms, and perceptions of what behaviour by a landlord constitutes harassment and what is reasonable may be interpreted quite differently by the other actors involved: tenants, local authority officers, the police and magistrates. While they have 'a considerable amount of discretion in interpreting landlords' behaviour, the severity of the case and how it should be dealt with' (Marsh *et al.*, 2000: 3.3), their understanding may not accord with what is covered by legislation. According to local authority officers, as well as physical violence and assault, harassment includes disconnecting services, calling at the property constantly or at unreasonable hours, stopping the occupier from having guests or visitors (including partners), denying access to parts of the property (e.g. bathrooms or kitchens in HIMOs), unjustified withholding of deposits at the end of a tenancy, not providing a rent book, serving invalid notices seeking possession, interfering with telephones or mail, removing fixtures such as doors or staircases, removing furniture, failing to carry out necessary repairs or starting but not finishing them, and sending abusive or threatening letters (ibid.: 3.4). Actual physical violence appears to be rare, but threats of violence and verbal abuse are frequent (Jew, 1994: 15). What in isolation may be comparatively minor actions can accumulate and cause the occupier considerable anxiety and distress.

The culprits, causes and casualties of harassment

Harassment (and unlawful eviction) are persistent problems within the private rented sector. When the 1965 Act was passed, profiteering commercial landlords were thought to be the main culprits. However, the Milner Holland Committee on Housing in Greater London which reported in 1965 concluded that the type of landlord guilty of such conduct 'bears little resemblance to the big business stereotype' and that 'relatively few abuses can be attributed to companies' (Holland, 1965: 256–60). As such, the law on harassment and unlawful eviction rarely affects the ways in which commercial landlords operate because harassment is not, and never has been, a common business practice (Nelken, 1983: 8). Where tenants fail to meet their obligations, the difficulty and/or expense of removing them may be a nuisance for commercial landlords yet, on the whole, they can either afford to tolerate them or to remove them – either via the legal process or by offering a financial incentive. However, for small-scale landlords (as, of course, the majority are) far more is at stake and often, for them, 'property ownership must include physical control if it is to mean anything, especially once they are in dispute with their tenants' (ibid.: 19). This has implications too for what both tenants and landlords may perceive as acceptable behaviour on the landlord's part. They are often under the impression that landlords have complete control over their properties and can evict a tenant at any time, using force if necessary. It is commonly thought that little can be done if the landlord 'threatens, intimidates, abuses or even steals for the tenant' (Jew, 1994: 21). The legislation, therefore, is most relevant to small-scale landlords who are often ignorant of their own obligations and of tenants' rights.

In spite of the tarnished reputation which private landlords have historically endured (and not infrequently deserved), the 'official' view tends to be that despite their:

> ordinary human instincts of kindliness and courtesy, [they] may often be afraid to allow to a tenant the benefit of those natural instincts in

case it may afterwards turn out that the tenant has thereby acquired a position from which he cannot subsequently be dislodged.

(*Marcroft Wagons v Smith* [1951] 2 KB 496, 501.)

The Green Paper recognises that 'the larger-scale operations of some unscrupulous landlords, often linked to housing benefit fraud, drug-dealing and prostitution, are destabilising local communities, creating a range of social and economic problems, and seriously hampering efforts at regeneration' (DETR, 2000a: 5.32). However, it regards most private landlords as 'basically well-intentioned and anxious to do a good and responsible job' (ibid.: 5.8) and, mindful of the 'great mass of legislation' with which they have to come to terms and their lack of any previous knowledge of property management, sees their lapses from the law as stemming from inadvertence rather than intentionality. Unless they employ the service of managing agents (whose 'standards of competence and probity' vary greatly: ibid.: 5.3), small-scale landlords are less likely to vet tenants before they accept them and are more likely to conduct their arrangements on an informal basis. Even where private landlords seek legal advice, the understanding of housing law possessed by many solicitors in private practice ranges from 'inadequate to non-existent' (Burrows, 1990: 17).

An upturn in the property market may encourage landlords who want to sell the property to use harassment or unlawful eviction to obtain vacant possession. Landlords who have had action taken against them by local authorities to force compliance with repairing obligations, amenity standards, fire safety or planning notices, or whose rents have been lowered by rent officers may also try to remove occupiers, without going through the appropriate legal channels (Jew, 1994: 9). On the other hand, landlords may 'fall victim to irresponsible or unscrupulous tenants' (who, for example, may refuse to move after their tenancy has ended, even if they have no statutory security of tenure, or fail to pay the rent or to treat the property in the way in which the landlord expects it to be treated). They may be in need therefore of 'encouragement, support and education rather than further heavy regulation' if they are to 'raise their standards and prosper' (DETR, 2000a: 5.10).

Rent arrears, the housing benefit system, and delays in possession proceedings are the most important specific triggers for unlawful action by landlords (Marsh *et al.*, 2000: 3.96). Particularly significant in this regard is the change which has taken place in the social composition of the private rented sector. Most notably in areas where there is lower demand for rental accommodation from working households, it is increasingly the preserve of vulnerable households with complex social or behavioural problems who are in receipt of housing benefit. It is that part of the sector which local authority officers most closely associate with issues of harassment and unlawful eviction (ibid.: 2.5, 3.71). A significant number of those living in the private rented sector rely on housing benefit to pay all or part of their rent (see Chapter 6).

It follows that 'the dynamics of the sector are intimately affected by changing the structure and generosity of the benefit system' (Marsh *et al.*, 2000: 2.4). In the early 1990s, households who would be in priority need under the homeless persons' legislation accounted for around half of all harassment and unlawful eviction complaints made to local authorities. People from racial minorities were disproportionately affected as were single parents and households with low incomes in receipt of housing benefit (Jew, 1994: 9). Since then, the housing benefit system has been subject to a number of changes which have imposed further strains on landlord and tenant relations (see Chapter 6).

A survey carried out on behalf of Shelter in 1989 found, not surprisingly, that tenancies created before the implementation of the Housing Act 1988 figured more prominently in the statistics than those tenancies created after 15 January 1989 (Burrows, 1990). It might be expected that the advent of the assured shorthold tenancy and the limited security it confers might have led to a decline in incidences of unlawful eviction and harassment. However, as early as 1993, research carried out for the Campaign for Bedsit Rights revealed that assured and assured shorthold tenants were the most likely to be harassed. While one of the aims of the Housing Act 1988 was to strengthen the law on harassment, it is possible that assured shorthold tenancies serve merely to exacerbate the reluctance of tenants to pursue their legal rights. As Jew points out:

> if it is only a short time anyway before the tenancy ends, many tenants will silently endure their landlord's criminal actions in the hope that the tenancy will be renewed. As a result and, not least, because harassment often results in the tenant being in a constant state of fear, the majority of incidents and offences remain hidden, unreported to statutory authorities.
>
> (Jew, 1994: 21–2.)

Many unlawful eviction cases arise from informal, verbal tenancy agreements (Carter and Dymond, 1998: 49). Before the changes put in place by the Housing Act 1996, a landlord wishing to grant an assured shorthold tenancy had to serve notice on the prospective tenant. As a result, nearly all assured shorthold tenancy agreements were in writing. Since the relevant part of the 1996 Act came into effect, no prior notice need be served and an assured shorthold tenancy can be created verbally, although tenants can demand a written statement of certain terms of the tenancy (see Chapter 3). This, of course, puts the onus on tenants, many of whom are unlikely to be aware of their entitlement to a written statement. As Cowan neatly puts it, 'paper has a particular currency for tenants' (Cowan, 2001: 254) and it may well appear to many tenants that an arrangement so easily entered into can be terminated with equal ease and lack of formality. Whereas under the Rent Act regime, landlords used a variety of methods to try (often successfully) to avoid conferring security of tenure upon the occupiers of their properties, the 1988 Act has replaced insecurity via extra-legal means with legally sanctioned insecurity (in the form of the assured shorthold tenancy). As history shows, it has been those with the least security who have been most affected by unlawful eviction and harassment. As Kemp maintains, 'Rachmanism will not return because it never really went away' (Kemp, 1990: 152).

Harassment: the offences

By s. 1(3) of the Protection from Eviction Act 1977:

'if any person with intent to cause the residential occupier of any premises —

(a) to give up occupation of the premises or any part thereof; or
(b) to refrain from exercising any right or pursuing any remedy in respect of the premises or part thereof;

does acts likely to interfere with the peace or comfort of the residential occupier or members of his household, or persistently withdraws or withholds services reasonably required for the occupation of the premises as a residence, he shall be guilty of an offence.

Two changes were made by the Housing Act 1988 which, theoretically, should have made prosecution more readily achievable. First, as regards the existing offence, the word 'likely' was substituted for the word 'calculated'. The offence is now easier to establish, but still requires an intent to cause the occupier to give up his occupation or to refrain from exercising his rights. As regards the former, one issue is whether or not the tenant has to give up occupation permanently or whether an offence will have been committed if he gives it up only temporarily. In *Schon v Camden London Borough Council* (1987) P & CR 361, the installation of a bathroom immediately above the tenant's room involved strengthening the floor underneath. Access could be gained from above by pulling up the floor boards or from below via the tenant's room. The landlord and tenant failed to agree on alternative accommodation for the two weeks during which the work was to be carried out, so that the tenant remained in situ. The building works brought the ceiling down and the tenant's room was rendered uninhabitable. It was held that no offence under s. 1(3)(a) had been committed. The landlord had no intention that the tenant should give up her room permanently, nor had the ceiling been brought down with the intent of causing her to go. There was said to be strong argument that 'occupation' had the same meaning as for the purposes of a statutory tenancy under the Rent Act 1977, so that the tenant was still in occupation during her absence if her possessions remained on the demised premises and she intended to return. The landlord's acts could have connoted an intent to cause the tenant 'to refrain from exercising any right' (i.e. her right to occupy in person for the two-week period), thus falling within s. 1(3)(b), but this was not pleaded.

It has been established that the 'rights' referred to in s. 1(3)(b) are not confined to those arising out of the contractual relationship between the claimant and defendant. In *R v Burke* [1991] 1 AC 135, the landlord prevented the tenant from using a bathroom and lavatory situated outside his room in the basement by storing furniture in the bathroom and corridor. He padlocked the door to another lavatory and deliberately disconnected the front door bell which connected with the basement floor. The judge found that the tenant had no contractual right to use a particular lavatory or bathroom, nor that the landlord should maintain a system of front door bells. Thus, the landlord's actions were not in breach of the tenancy agreement but the House of Lords nonetheless upheld his conviction.

For the offence to be committed, either (a) acts likely to interfere with the residential occupier's peace and comfort must have been committed, or (b) services persistently withdrawn or withheld. Although the plural 'acts' is used, a single act suffices (*R v Evangelo Polycarpou* (1978) 9 HLR 129). In *R v Bokhari* [1974] 59 Crim LR 559, the acts (ostensibly 'repairs') consisted of knocking holes in walls and ceilings, disconnecting mains services, blocking sinks and drains, removing fittings and leaving rubble. In *R v Spratt, Wood and Smylie* [1978] Crim LR 102, rent was owing and the house was in an insanitary and dirty state. Accompanied by two friends (one of whom was armed with a monkey wrench and a cleaver), the landlord went to the house where the tenant's brother was made to strip off (to prevent him from escaping) and to reveal what he believed to be the tenant's whereabouts. In due course, he was also made to clean and tidy the house. The three men, all without previous convictions, were each given six months' imprisonment for harassment.

In *R v Zafar Ahmad* (1986) 18 HLR 416, the landlord asked the tenant to vacate her flat for three months while improvements were being carried out. The tenant had agreed in principle to the landlord's plans, but no agreement had been reached over whether the rent would continue to be payable while the work was taking place. She came home one day to find that all her bathroom fittings had been removed. Over the next year the landlord did no further work and the bathroom remained out of use. It was held that the landlord's failure to complete the building works, although a breach of the tenancy agreement, did not fall within s. 1(3). There was evidence that once the landlord had removed the bathroom fittings he formed the intention of evicting the tenant. Afterwards, however, he did not 'do acts' but merely failed to rectify damage already caused.

It was emphasised by Ormrod J in *McCall v Abelesz* [1976] 2 WLR 151, 159–60 that, where 'services' are concerned, something more than a 'hopeful inactivity' has to be shown and in *R v Abrol* [1972] Crim LR 318, the

Court of Appeal said there must be 'an element of deliberate continuity in withholding [them]'.

Often the prosecution has been unable to prove that the defendant landlord specifically intended to cause the occupier to leave, rather than just make life unpleasant in the hope that he or she might decide to go. To counter these problems s. 1(3A) Introduced by the Housing Act 1988) provides that:

> the landlord of a residential occupier or an agent of the landlord shall be guilty of an offence if—
>
> (a) he does acts likely to interfere with the peace or comfort of the residential occupier or members of his household; or
> (b) he persistently withdraws or withholds services reasonably required for the occupation of the premises in question as a residence;
>
> and (in either case) he knows, or has reasonably cause to believe, that the conduct is likely to cause the residential occupier to give up the occupation of the whole or part of the premises or to refrain from exercising any right or pursuing any remedy in respect of the whole or part of the premises.

Thus s. 1(3A) creates an offence which can be committed only by certain individuals, i.e. the landlord of the residential occupier concerned ('landlord' being defined as including any superior landlord: s. 1(3C)) or an agent of the landlord. The *actus reus* is identical to s. 1(3); the only difference is the *mens rea*. Whether or not the landlord intended the occupier to leave is not relevant; what matters is whether a reasonable person (having at his or her disposal the facts known to the landlord) would believe the occupier to be likely to give up possession as the result of the landlord's behaviour.

Section 1(3B) provides that a person shall not be guilty of an offence under subs. 3A if it can be proved that there were reasonable grounds for doing the acts or withdrawing or withholding the services in question. In *R v Phekoo* [1981] 1 WLR 1117, the owner had threatened two men found on the property that he would 'bring his mates round' and 'carve up' one of them. He believed, honestly but mistakenly, that the two men had no right to be there. The Court of Appeal held that the prosecution must prove specific intent to harass someone whom the defendant knew or believed to be a residential occupier and not merely a squatter.

It should be noted that the offence is not limited to the occupier and members of the ocupier's family but extends to members of his or her 'household'.

A person found guilty of an offence under s. 1(1) or s. 1(3), as amended, is subject to a maximum penalty of six months' imprisonment or a £2,000 fine or both. If convicted on indictment, imprisonment may be for up to two years and/or an unlimited fine may be imposed (s. 1(4)).

Enforcement

The law on harassment and unlawful eviction has been criticised for being ineffective. The number of prosecutions and the consequent convictions has always been low, rarely reaching more than 100 each year.

The police can prosecute s. 1 offences but tend to take the view that the responsibility for bringing prosecutions lies with local authorities. They do not normally intervene unless physical violence is involved and, if they do intervene, prefer to charge landlords/licensors with 'ordinary' criminal offences such as assault, obstructing a police officer, conduct likely to provoke a breach of the peace or criminal damage. The response of the police seems to depend on station and/or officer concerned. It has been maintained, however, that a lack of awareness of anti-harassment and illegal eviction laws often leads to police officers declining to intervene in landlord and tenant disputes and sometimes actually assisting landlords in evicting tenants illegally (Jew, 1994: 11).

Section 6 also gives local authorities the power to bring prosecutions. Following the criminalisation of harassment and unlawful eviction, the Francis Committee recommended the establishment within local authorities of tenancy relations officers (TROs) to implement the unlawful eviction and harassment provisions of the Rent Act 1965 and to police the private rented sector, investigating complaints and either settling disputes or collecting the necessary evidence to support a prosecution (Francis, 1971: 111). However, local authorities were never placed under a statutory duty to employ TROs nor to investigate complaints of harassment or unlawful eviction. Consequently, tenancy relations services have developed sporadically, and some authorities have failed to provide any service at all (Strudwick, 1991: 9). It is worth noting, however, that failure by a local authority to introduce policies, procedures and services to deal with harassment and unlawful eviction may result in a finding of maladministration by the Local Government Ombudsman (Commission for Local Administration) (see e.g. complaint nos 90/A/1356 and 94/A/3711).

Very often the task of dealing with harassment and unlawful eviction complaints is given to other officers within local authorities, including environmental health officers, homeless persons' officers and members of the legal department. Some authorities have contracted out the tenancy relations role to other independent agencies such as local large scale voluntary transfer (LSVT) housing associations or housing advice centres (Marsh et al., 2000: 4.11). Wherever the precise location of the tenancy relations role, however, local authorities rather than the police may be regarded as the regulatory agencies charged with the responsibility of enforcing the law on unlawful eviction and harassment.

Local authorities generally prosecute wherever there is any real chance of success. Unlawful eviction is relatively easy to prove but harassment is more problematic, especially in the absence of corroborative evidence which will be particularly difficult to obtain where there is a long delay between the commission of the alleged offence and the court hearing (Burrows, 1990: 59). In a minority of authorities the decision to prosecute is made by a council committee which causes further delays in processing complaints (Jew, 1994: 11). Authorities sometimes have difficulty in discovering the landlord's true identity or address. Prosecutions may also fail because the charges as framed did not convey to the court the real nature of the alleged offence. The significance of a single act, which might appear justifiable when viewed in isolation may only become appreciated when set in the context of all the defendant's activities. Older victims of abuse and harassment may feel that 'by dealing with the situation themselves, or not dealing with it, they retain a sense of control over their lives' (Carlton *et al.*, 2004: 139).

The low level of fines for successful prosecutions may discourage authorities from instituting criminal proceedings, although heavier fines may well be imposed where there is evidence of financial motivation (Nelken, 1983: 9). In *R v Brennan and Brennan* [1979] Crim LR 603, in which the landlord, accompanied by a 'very large man and an Alsatian dog', evicted a group of students from their rented premises, it was said that 'loss of liberty should be the usual penalty where landlords use threats or force, in the absence of unusual mitigation'. In *R v Khan (Jahinger)* [2001] EWCA Crim 912, the Court of Appeal held that concurrent sentences of 15 months' imprisonment for unlawful eviction and harassment, were not excessive, given the wanton damage inflicted on the tenant's property, as well as threats made to her boyfriend (that, e.g. the tenant's face would be 're-arranged' if she were to return to the property). Where the police or local authority is unwilling to initiate proceedings, the individual occupier may bring a private prosecution.

The low number of prosecutions for unlawful eviction and harassment is sometimes seen as proof that the law in this area is ineffectual. Such a view, however, fails to take into account that, especially in the regulatory sphere, 'enforcement' may involve a more holistic approach, relying upon negotiation, education, advice and – as a last resort – prosecution as ways of securing compliance. Thus TROs may incline to mediation rather than prosecution because of the increasingly important role played by private landlords in providing housing for homeless applicants and the consequent development of a mutually reliant (and potentially beneficial) relationship between private landlords and local authorities (particularly where tenants are in receipt of housing benefit). Indeed, the *Homelessness Code of Guidance* encourages authorities to maximise their use of accommodation leased from a private landlord as temporary accommodation and highlights the powers which authorities have to incur expenditure on rent deposits and guarantees to private landlords to help people secure accommodation in the private sector (DCLG, 2006a: 16.15–16.16). The change of emphasis from prosecution to preventative work – through conciliation and mediation – may be evidenced by the practice in some local authorities of locating tenancy relations functions in the homelessness section. However, homelessness is not always the driving force behind a local authority's private rented sector strategy. It may also be concerned to improve the condition of accommodation in this sector, to bring empty properties back into use, and to instigate area regeneration (DETR, 1998b) all of which will be facilitated by the development and maintenance of a workable relationship between the two sectors.

Although some acts of harassment may accord with traditional notions of criminal activity (e.g. physical violence), others, given the ambivalent feelings generated by the surrender of control over the property which has been let, may not have the taint of criminality at all, e.g. serving invalid notices to quit. Moreover, the changing nature of the tenant population in the private rented sector – in which 'increased poverty, hard drugs and deinstitutionalisation' (Marsh *et al.*, 2000: 3.71) all play a part – means that infringements of 'normal' tenant behaviour are more likely to occur. Acts of harassment may be 'legitimated', therefore, by transgressions on the part of the tenant, e.g. non-payment of rent, or nuisance and annoyance.

Prosecution is central to a sanctioning strategy and 'as such it may well be used as an indicator of work undertaken and a sign of success' (Hutter, 1988: 7). The number of prosecutions and convictions should not, however, be seen as the only indicator of how well the law is working. A rigorous prosecution strategy, together with the imposition of tough criminal penalties might be a deterrent to some landlords who would otherwise be inclined to take the law into their own hands. However many landlords are unaware that their conduct is criminal and it is hardly surprising, therefore, that mediation and education have become more important components of tenancy relations work with a strong focus upon the value of compliance.

Using violence to secure entry to premises

Section 6 of the Criminal Law Act 1977 makes it an offence for a person without lawful authority (such as a bailiff executing a warrant of possession) to use or threaten violence for the purpose of securing entry to premises upon which, to his knowledge, someone is present who is opposed to the entry. It is not necessary that there should be any entry; the crime can be committed even if the intruders are unsuccessful. The violence may be directed against the person or the property. 'Violence' covers:

> any application of force to the person, but it carries a somewhat restricted meaning in relation to property ... [F]orcing a Yale-type lock with a piece of plastic or a window catch with a thin piece of metal, would almost certainly amount to force, but not to violence ... On the other hand, splintering a door or a window or its frame would be.
>
> (Law Commission, 1976: 2.61.)

Even an excluded tenant or licensee (see above) or a trespasser cannot be evicted whilst actually within the premises. Eviction can only occur through a bailiff or sheriff and with a court order. The landlord or licensor can, however, wait until the occupier leaves the premises, e.g. to go to work, and then remove his or her belongings and change the locks. There will be no criminal offence.

Civil liability

The complexity, cost and length of time involved may deter tenants from bringing a civil action. Reductions in the availability of legal aid over recent years mean that many tenants cannot afford civil action and the easiest solution is simply to find somewhere else to live.

It was held in *McCall v Abelesz* [1976] 1 All ER 727 that what is now s. 1(3) of the Protection from Eviction Act 1977 did not create a cause of action for breach of statutory duty on the basis of which a residential occupier could take action, e.g. for damages or reinstatement. Instead action had to be taken under other causes, the primary objective of most civil proceedings in this area being to obtain an injunction from the court ordering the landlord to reinstate the residential occupier in the premises.

Contract

Where there is a lease, the tenant can sue the landlord for breach of contract, usually the landlord's implied covenant for quiet enjoyment. Although a covenant for quiet enjoyment will not be implied into a mere licence to occupy property, the court may imply some term preventing the landlord from unduly interfering with the licensee's occupation and use of the property. An example can be found in *Smith v Nottingham County Council, The Times*, 13 November 1981, in which students living as licensees in a hall of residence were unable to study for their exams because of noise and other disturbance caused by urgent building works to another nearby hall.

As regards quiet enjoyment, the traditional view is that the tenant must have suffered physical interference with his enjoyment of the property. However, in *Kenny v Preen* [1963] 1 QB 499 a breach of covenant was said to occur when anything was done which was an invasion of the tenant's right to remain in possession undisturbed even if it caused no direct physical interference. Here the landlord had served a purported notice to quit on the tenant (an elderly widow), sent her letters threatening to evict her and to put her property into the street, and knocked at her door, shouting threats. The landlord's 'deliberate and persistent attempt' to drive the tenant out by 'persecution and intimidation' was held to constitute a breach of covenant even if there was no direct physical interference with the tenant's possession and enjoyment. In so far as such interference was a necessary element in the breach of covenant, it was present in the form of knocking on the door and shouting threats. Other examples of a breach of the covenant include cutting off the tenant's gas and electricity (*Perera v Vandiyar* [1953] 1 WLR 672) and the removal of doors and windows (*Lavender v Betts* [1942] 2 All ER 723). These would now amount to the criminal offence of harassment.

Neither exemplary nor aggravated damages (see below) can be awarded for breach of contract because it cannot be described as a contract to provide peace of mind or freedom from distress (*Branchett v Beaney, Coster and Swale Borough Council* [1992] 3 All ER 910). Therefore the tenant who can establish a tort may be in a better position.

Tort

A tenant or licensee can sue the landlord in tort, the landlord having committed trespass (to the person, land or personal property) and possibly assault and/or nuisance. In *Caruso v Owen* (1983) LAG Bulletin 106, the landlord – in the mistaken belief that the tenant had given up possession – burned the tenant's PhD notes on a bonfire. In assessing damages of £3,000 for the loss of the research material (for the tort of wrongful interference with goods) the judge accepted the tenant's evidence that it would take at least another year to redo the work which had been destroyed and that he had been in receipt of a maintenance grant of £3,000 for the year.

Types of damages

The claimant may obtain:

(a) *General damages*: these are unliquidated damages which can be claimed for, e.g. any personal injury sustained by the claimant, loss of enjoyment, and loss of the right to occupy (*Millington v Duffy* (1985) 17 HLR 232). In *Shafr v Yagambrun* [1994] CLY 1450 the landlord told the tenant a month before her 'A' level examinations, that she must leave the house the next day as it was about to be repossessed by the building society. General damages of £3,000 were based in part on the adverse effect the disruption must have had on the tenant's studies.

(b) *Special damages*: the aim of special damages is to compensate the evicted occupier for specific losses such as reasonable accommodation costs incurred after the eviction, the cost of items taken from the property (*Ramdath v Daley* (1993) 25 HLR 273) and return of any premium paid (*Ayari v Jetha* (1991) 24 HLR 639).

(c) *Aggravated damages*: these are intended to compensate the claimant for 'injury to his proper feelings of dignity and pride' (*Ramdath v Daley* (1993) 25 HLR 273, 279), and feelings of outrage, indignation and distress, which the claimant incurred as a result of the eviction (see, e.g.

Nwokorie v Mason (1993) 26 HLR 60; *McMillan v Singh* (1984) 17 HLR 120; *Asgar v Ahmed* (1984) 17 HLR 25).

(d) *Exemplary damages*: these are payable where the defendant has calculated that the wrongful conduct will make a profit which may well exceed the compensation payable to the claimant (*Ramdath v Daley* (1993) 25 HLR 273; cf. *Sampson v Wilson* (1994) 26 HLR 486). In *Cassell & Co v Broome* [1972] AC 1027, 1029 Lord Hailsham gave as an example 'the late Mr Rachman, who is alleged to have used hired bullies to intimidate statutory tenants by violence or threats of violence into giving vacant possession of their residences and so placing a valuable asset in the hands of the landlord'. This, he said, amounted to 'a cynical calculation of profit and cold-blooded disregard of a [claimant's] rights'. The objective of exemplary damages is punitive rather than compensatory and they can properly be awarded 'whenever it is necessary to teach a wrongdoer that tort does not pay' (*Rookes v Barnard* [1964] AC 1129, 1221). Awards of exemplary damages have been upheld in several eviction cases but they have not been particularly high (see, e.g. *Drane v Evangelou* [1978] 1 WLR 455; *Guppy (Bridport) Ltd v Brookling* (1984) 269 EG 846; *Asghar v Ahmed* (1984) 17 HLR 25). Since the claim for damages is at common law, it is irrelevant that the claimant may have failed to behave with the utmost propriety. Thus, in *McMillan v Singh* (1984) 17 HLR 120, the fact that the claimant had fallen into arrears from time to time had no bearing on his claim for exemplary damages.

Sections 27 and 28, Housing Act 1988

Section 27 of the Housing Act 1988 effectively overturned the decision in *McCall v Abelesz* and created a new statutory tort. It gives the residential occupier evicted after 9 June 1988 a right to sue his landlord, or any person acting on his behalf, for committing an act which amounts to a criminal offence under s. 1 of the Protection from Eviction Act 1977 and which has caused him to give up occupation of the premises as a residence. Awards of damages under these provisions have, in some circumstances, been considerable. The remedy provided by s. 27 does not replace the traditional causes of action in tort and contract which can still be used where, e.g. the occupier did not give up occupation or has been reinstated (see *McCormack v Namjou* [1990] CLY 1725) or had little or no security of tenure so that the damages recoverable by him under s. 28 would be low.

Defences under s. 27

Three defences are made available to the landlord by s. 27:

(a) Before proceedings are finally disposed of, the claimant has been reinstated in the premises and has again become a residential occupier with the full rights of which he or she was deprived (Housing Act 1988, s. 27(6)(a)). However, 'reinstatement does not consist in merely handing the tenant a key to a lock which does not work and inviting her to resume occupation of a room which has been totally wrecked' (*Tagro v Carfane* [1991] 2 All ER 235, 242–3). The occupier is not obliged to accept an offer of reinstatement by the landlord but if one is made before proceedings are commenced then an unreasonable refusal thereof by the occupier may result in a reduction of damages awarded (see below). If the occupier is reinstated a claim for damages under the general law may still be made.

(b) The court has acceded to the claimant's request for reinstatement, so that the claimant is once more the residential occupier (s. 27(6)(b)).

(c) The landlord believed, and had reasonable cause to believe, that the occupier had ceased to reside in the premises, or that there were reasonable grounds for withdrawing or withholding services (s. 27(8)).

Section 27(7) imposes on the claimant a statutory duty to mitigate his or her loss but damages will be reduced in two instances only:

(a) if the landlord made an offer of reinstatement prior to the commencement of proceedings which the claimant did not take up;

(b) where the conduct of the occupier or any person living with him in the premises in question was such that it is 'reasonable' to mitigate the damages payable.

The measure of damages

By s. 28 the measure of damages is the difference in value, as at the date when the residential occupier left the premises, between the property with the occupier in it and the property with vacant possession. In other words, it is the profit which the landlord stood to make by acting unlawfully, whether or not in fact such profit was made. That which is to be valued is the whole building in which the premises are situated so that the potential gain to, e.g. the last protected tenant of a bedsit in a house with the potential for conversion into flats or resale for owner-occupation, will be considerable as in *Guppy's (Bridport) Ltd v Brookling* (1983) 14 HLR 1. However, against that must be set the assumptions that the landlord's interest is being sold in the open market to a willing buyer, that neither the occupier nor a member of the occupier's family want to buy, and that there is no extant 'substantial development' or demolition permission. Thus 'there shall be no increase in the damages because the effect of the tenant being dispossessed is that it enables some very valuable development to take place' (see *Tagro v Carfane* [1991] 2 All ER 235, 242–3 in which the landlord, himself a business tenant, argued unsuccessfully that the value of his interest was nil because his lease prohibited assignment and sub-letting).

It is the right of occupation which is to be valued so that eviction of someone with a lesser right, e.g. a restricted contract or an assured shorthold tenancy, will produce a lower amount of damages than an assured or protected tenant with full security of tenure. In *Melville v Bruton* [1996] EGCS 57, the landlord unlawfully evicted the claimant a few weeks after the start of her assured shorthold tenancy. The county court judge awarded damages of £15,000 under ss. 27 and 28, representing the difference in the value of the property immediately before and after the eviction, even though two other people (tenants or licensees) were still living at the property. The Court of Appeal allowed the landlord's appeal on the basis that nothing in ss. 27 and 28 justified disregarding the existence of the other residential occupiers. The tenant's eviction made no difference to the value of the property as it was still encumbered. The purpose of the 1988 Act was not so comprehensive as to provide damages for evicted tenants in all circumstances and it should be interpreted to reflect the fact that the eviction had not materially increased the value of the landlord's interest. The award of £15,000 was set aside and £500 substituted for inconvenience, discomfort and distress.

As stated above, an agent of the landlord can be found guilty of the criminal offences in s. 1(2), (3) and (3A) of the Protection from Eviction Act 1977 and it follows, therefore, that civil liability under s. 27 can be imposed jointly on a principal and an agent acting within the scope of his or her employment (see *Sampson v Wilson* [1995] 3 WLR 455).

Part IV

Social housing

Chapter 16

The eclipse of council housing

Introduction

The eclipse[1] of council housing by both Conservative and Labour governments in recent years has taken broadly three forms: first, the sale of council houses to their tenants; secondly, the disposal of council stock to housing
associations, trusts and private companies; and thirdly, the assumption of local
authorities' housing management functions by other agencies. Attempts have
also been made to inject private funding into the provision of social housing by means of the Private Finance Initiative. The sale of council houses is
considered in Chapter 19. This chapter deals with the different methods by
which councils have been forced or encouraged to dispose of the whole or
parts of their stock to other landlords, and/or to relinquish their housing
management functions. While demunicipalisation continues apace, with the
expectation that council housing, traditionally owned and managed, is set
to become the exception rather than the rule, it is predicted that by 2010
the sector will still contain around 1.5 million houses (Audit Commission,
2005: 8–9). However, even where local authorities *retain* housing stock,
they are being encouraged to improve the quality of housing services by separating the management and ownership roles. With the change in emphasis
during the past 25 years 'from building as many dwellings as possible to
managing a rapidly deteriorating stock with ever smaller resources', the role
of housing management has been subject to close scrutiny and governments
have used legislation to impose a 'contract ethos' on social landlords with the
role of housing management being seen as mainly that of property management, e.g. allocations, voids and rent-collecting (Papps, 1998: 652). While
on the face of it, social landlords are free to provide housing services by
whatever means they choose, they may be unable in practice to be able to
demonstrate that '"traditional" in-house delivery' (Vincent-Jones, 2001:
251) provides the best, most cost-efficient service and may be forced therefore
to outsource management service to the private sector, 'with increased quality

---

1   For a summary of the different views as to whether or not local authority housing has
    been, and is being' 'privatised', see Daly *et al.* (2005: 331–2).

and efficiency supposedly being ensured by the competitive conditions of the market' (ibid.).

Context

Following the Second World War, it was 'more or less taken for granted that general purpose, multi-functional local authorities' were playing, and should play, a leading role in the implementation of public policy and the delivery of a wide range of key services in the newly developed welfare state (Malpass, 2005: 185). Importantly, the involvement of local authorities provided a formal mechanism of accountability: their staff were answerable to the councillors and the councillors themselves were answerable to the public at regular elections. However, 'the crisis of the welfare state' in the mid-1970s prompted criticisms that municipal services were 'inefficient and remote from the public'. For their critics 'the remedy was to redress the balance through a more market oriented approach in which competition would empower consumers' (ibid.: 186). The past two decades have therefore witnessed a radical restructuring in the organisation and delivery of public services, which are increasingly carried out by 'multiple providers . . . drawn from both the private and public sectors, [and] from a third group . . . made up of religious and charitable associations as well as various public and private partnerships' (Morison and Livingstone, 1995: 68). Instead of 'taking on the tasks that became its traditional role during the height of the welfare state', the state is now seeking to reduce its involvement and responsibility 'by restricting its role to providing for the regulation of privatised activities and to setting the policies, mission statements and framework documents with which it hopes to exercise some measure of control' (ibid.).

Social housing provides a clear example of this shift in policy. Formerly, local authorities dominated the provision of social housing, enjoying considerable (though never unfettered) autonomy with regard to investment, rent-setting, allocations and the organisation of housing management. There was minimal central government involvement in local decision-making. However, since the early 1970s, when central government first attempted to remove the freedom of local councillors to set rents, 'the trend has been consistently towards less public housing, less municipal control over social housing as a whole and greater central government prescription, direction and regulation' (ibid.: 189). Since 1997 New Labour has taken it forward, with the introduction of Best Value (BV) and the establishment of the Housing Inspectorate further extending centralised monitoring and surveillance of both local government and the 'independent' RSL sector, i.e. the spread of the so-called 'audit state'. The fact that 'funding and flexibility to act' is progressively more dependent upon 'satisfactory performance within this regime' means that 'the ability of local actors to follow local priorities' is necessarily limited

(Cowan and Marsh, 2001: 269). It has been argued that these measures are increasingly turning local government into a 'policy-free zone', the role of local authorities 'like many of their non-elected local counterparts' being confined to the delivery of 'centrally determined policies in a strategic way' (Maile and Hoggett, 2001: 512).

From one viewpoint, the emergence and development of local authority housing in Great Britain in the twentieth century can be regarded as a success story. By the late 1970s, local authorities were responsible for managing around a third of the housing stock. Local government had made a major contribution to the general improvement of housing conditions. They had cleared nearly two million sub-standard houses since the 1930s and provided grants, since 1949, to renovate more than three million others (Loughlin, 1996: 100). A contrasting view is that the historical failings of council housing have largely been responsible for its demise. It was argued that 'council housing should have become the Marks and Spencer of housing' but it appeared instead that management was often monolithic and bureaucratically insensitive, tenants lacked choice, and there was little mobility in or between authorities, transfers normally being confined to households of special need (Kilroy, 1979: 453).

The Conservative government (which was committed to 'rolling back the frontiers of the state') set out its agenda for public sector housing in its 1987 White Paper. Taking the view that local authorities had been inefficient and bureaucratic managers of their housing, that tenants had been deprived of choice, that public investment in housing had been at the expense of other public sector spending programmes and that party political considerations had often operated at local level to the detriment of housing (DoE, 1987a: 1.11) the government sought to change their role. No longer were they to be the main providers of social housing; instead '[they] should increasingly see themselves as enablers who ensure that everyone in their area is adequately housed; but not necessarily by them' (ibid.: 1.16). Theirs was to be strategic role which included 'identifying housing needs and demands' and 'encouraging innovative methods of provision by other bodies to meet such needs' (ibid.: 5.1). Housing associations were henceforth to be the main providers of social housing, their housing projects being financed mainly (and increasingly) by private funding from financial institutions. Two initiative – Tenants' Choice (providing for the acquisition of local authority housing by other landlords) and Housing Action Trusts (HATs) (to take over areas of run-down local authority housing) – were identified as the means by which housing stock was to be transferred out of local authority control. Although both initiatives were failures – essentially because of a lack of tenant enthusiasm – fear of what they might entail spurred a number of local authorities into taking pre-emptive action by transferring their stock to housing associations.

Tenants' choice

Tenants' Choice (also known as Pick a Landlord) was presented in the White Paper as a scheme which would offer a remedy to tenants who received a poor service from their council. Even those who chose not to transfer would, it was said, benefit from a better general standard of services resulting from the exposure of councils to 'healthy competition'. If tenants wished to transfer, they could decide when to set the process in motion (DoE, 1987a: 5.9). They would need to identify a new landlord willing to take them on and arrangements would be made to put tenants and prospective new landlords in touch. Landlords – established housing associations, commercial landlords, tenants' co-operatives – would require formal approval by the Housing Corporation or Housing for Wales to ensure that they were 'financially stable and capable of managing their homes to a high standard while giving value for money' (DoE, 1987b: 16).

The White Paper placed the emphasis on tenants taking the initiative, but the scheme which emerged in Part IV of the Housing Act 1988 appeared, by contrast, to confer something resembling a 'predatory private landlord's choice' (Hoath, 1989: 372) which gave tenants very little choice indeed. Any approved person or body could acquire the freehold in any relevant buildings occupied by qualifying tenants of a public sector landlord. Various categories of property were excluded from the scheme. A detailed and lengthy procedure culminated in affected tenants being balloted on their wishes. If (a) fewer than 50 per cent of eligible tenants responded; or (b) a majority voted against the proposal, the application could not proceed. If, however, at least 50 per cent responded, an 'inertia' vote in favour of the proposed acquisition was deemed to have been registered by any tenant who failed to respond, or who indicated no strong feelings either way. All existing tenants would then be transferred to the new landlord and would become assured tenants but with a preserved right to buy. Given the unusual system of inertia voting involved in the scheme, the effective exercise of such choice as there was – the right to reject given applicants – would, it was said, require 'an extraordinarily high degree of organised resistance to the proposals concerned', requiring 'meticulous planning, forceful campaigning and careful organisation' (Bridge 1989: 107–8).

In its passage through Parliament, Part IV was 'the most politically controversial and potentially divisive part of the whole statute' (Bridge, 1989: 106). Critics believed it could lead to the complete dismantling of council estates. However, despite the fears it provoked, only 921 homes (belonging to Westminster City Council) were transferred under the Tenants' Choice scheme (*The Guardian*, Society, 10 April 2002) and it was finally laid to rest by the Housing Act 1996.

Housing action trusts

The Conservatives were returned to government in 1987 having pledged in their election manifesto to revive the inner cities. Earlier attempts to target certain underprivileged areas had been made in the introduction of urban development corporations and enterprise zone authorities. Urban development corporations were devised to tackle largely derelict industrial areas in need of regeneration, while enterprise zones aimed to encourage private sector commercial and industrial expansion. Recognising that some council estates were so run down that Tenants' Choice could not be implemented, the government stated in the 1987 White Paper its proposal to establish bodies similar to urban development corporations in designated areas. The new bodies, to be known as housing action trusts HATS, would take over responsibility for local authority housing, renovate it and pass it on new owners, including housing associations, tenants' co-operatives, and approved private landlords. As well as improving housing conditions, they would act as 'enablers and facilitators' for the provision of other community needs such as shops, workshops and advice centres, and for encouraging local enterprise (DoE, 1987a: 6.3). Areas suitable for HAT treatment were identified as those containing large numbers of poor quality public sector dwellings in deprived environments with high vandalism rates and other social problems such as unemployment, a high proportion of residents in receipt of state benefits, poor estate design, and general decay.

The initiative to establish a HAT over a particular area comes from the Secretary of State who is empowered to 'designate an area of land for which, in his opinion, it is expedient that a ... housing action trust ... should be established' (Housing Act 1988, s. 60). The four statutory objectives of a HAT are (a) to secure the repair and improvement of housing accommodation for the time being held by the trust; (b) to secure its proper and effective management and use; (c) to encourage a greater diversity of tenure and in the identity of landlords; and (d) generally to improve the living conditions of those living in the area, and the area's social conditions and general environment (s. 63(1)). In order to achieve these objectives, they may provide and maintain housing accommodation, facilitate the provision of shops, advice centres and other community facilities, acquire, hold, manage, reclaim and dispose of land, carry out building and other operations, seek to ensure the provision of main services, and carry on any business or undertaking. To enable a HAT to achieve its objectives, the Secretary of State may order the transfer from a local housing authority to a HAT of all or any of the authority's local authority housing situated in the designated area, and any other land held or provided in connection with it (s. 74). It was initially proposed that tenants in the proposed designated area would merely be consulted before any transfer took place but, in fact, the 1988 Act gave them a right to be balloted (s. 61). The Secretary of State could not proceed if a majority of the tenants were opposed to the proposal.

A HAT is not intended to act as a provider of housing and housing repair for the indefinite future but must use its best endeavours to secure that its objects were achieved as soon as practicable. Once it has done so, it is dissolved by the Secretary of State (s. 88). Since local authorities were regarded as being at least partly to blame for the decline of the inner cities, the first step in the rejuvenation process was to remove completely from their control the areas which were of most concern. It was predicted that homes removed from municipal control would not be returned to it once purposes of the HAT had been accomplished (Bridge, 1989: 90–1) because this would be at odds with the 'diversity of landlord and ownership' sought by the 1987 White Paper. In fact, the law was altered to allow the local authority to repurchase the stock on the dissolution of the HAT. Where a HAT proposes to dispose of one or more dwellings let on secure or introductory tenancies to 'another person' who is not a local housing or other authority, the tenants must be notified of the proposed disposal and the name of the person to whom disposal is to be made, the consequences of the disposal for secure or introductory tenants, and their right to make representations to the Secretary of State or the HAT. Any general representations must be taken into account. More importantly, if the tenant of a house, or the majority of tenants in a block of flats make representations that they wish to become tenants of the local housing authority, the Secretary of State must by order transfer the house or block of flats from the HAT to the local housing authority.

In theory, HATs were an important means whereby central government could interfere in local government issues. In practice, however, proposals to set them up for certain areas met with considerable resistance from tenants and only six HATS were ever established (in Waltham Forest, Hull, Liverpool, Tower Hamlets, Castle Vale (Birmingham) and Stonebridge (Brent London Borough Council). The Liverpool HAT was the largest with 5,332 properties in 67 tower blocks. It was given 12 years and £260m of government money to complete its designated projects. All except Stonebridge have now been wound up, their properties generally being transferred to tailor-made housing associations.

Stock transfer

Throughout the history of council housing, local authorities have been empowered, subject to ministerial consent, to dispose of housing land and stock to the private sector. The powers to carry out transfers – called large-scale voluntary transfers (LSVTs) where an authority's entire housing stock is disposed of – are contained in ss. 32–34 and 43 of the Housing Act 1985. Consultation provisions were added by the Housing and Planning Act 1986, and restrictions on LSVTs imposed by the Leasehold Reform, Housing and Urban Development Act 1993. Stock transfer did not feature, therefore, in the mechanisms identified in the 1987 White Paper to extend housing choice to council tenants but were promoted by local authorities themselves. Indeed, the purpose of several early transfers was to circumvent the proposals contained in the White Paper (especially Tenants' Choice which, it had been feared, could lead to the complete dismantling of local authority housing), and the effects of the new financial regime introduced by the Local Government and Housing Act 1989.

When a voluntary transfer takes place, the new landlord takes over all the stock involved. The tenants whose homes have been transferred cease to be secure tenants and if, as is usually the case, the transfer is to a housing association, they become assured tenants (Housing Act 1988, s. 38). They do, however, retain the 'preserved right to buy' (Housing Act 1985, s. 171A-H). Although a whole stock transfer 'terminates council housing as an institution', it is important to remember that a local authority which disposes of its stock still retains important responsibilities in relation to housing matters. These include housing allocation, obligations under the homelessness legislation, the promotion of effective management and maintenance of housing in the private sector, and broader strategic duties such as the duty to undertake a periodic review of housing conditions and to consider aggregate housing need.

The first LSVT took place in 1988 when Chiltern District Council (a Conservative controlled authority) transferred its stock to the newly created Chiltern Hundreds Housing Association. Typically, until 1997, LSVTs occurred in rural, Conservative-run local authorities in the south of England which were also politically motivated 'to advance the then government's privatisation agenda, whilst escaping from an unattractive financial regime' (Walker, 2001: 688). However, New Labour has also embraced stock transfer, setting out in the 2000 Green Paper its plans to 'expand and modernise' the transfer programme (DETR, 2000a: 7.16). More recently, stock transfer has moved into urban areas where it is expected that large housing stocks will be divided between several new landlords. Thus, in 2002 tenants of Glasgow City Council voted in favour of the proposed transfer of the city's 83,000 council homes to 62 local housing organisations under the parent body, Glasgow Housing Association (see *The Independent*, 6 April 2002). By February 2003, 143 local authorities had transferred all or part of their housing stock to RSLs (NAO, 2003: 1). The transfers, involving over 738,000 dwellings, raised over £11.6 billion of private finance of which £5.4 billion was used to purchase the stock and the remainder being available to the new landlords to meet the costs of their long-term improvement programmes (NAO, 2003: 2). By October 2004, the number of authorities which had transferred their stock had risen to 194 (ODPM, 2004b: 7) but the pace of transfer had slowed down. It has been far less popular in Wales, the first whole-stock transfer taking place only in 2004.

Restrictions on stock transfer

The popularity of stock transfer has had a significant impact on public sector costs. As a result of changes made to local authority housing revenue accounts by the 1989 Act, some authorities now obtain negative housing subsidy because the housing revenue account subsidy does not fully compensate for the payments they make by way of housing benefit. Once the stock moves out of local authority ownership on a voluntary transfer, the cost of the housing benefit must be met by the Department of Work and Pensions, thereby placing a much greater burden on the Exchequer (Stewart, 1996: 173), especially if the tenants transferred are required to pay higher rents than those payable whilst they were local authority tenants. These Exchequer implications spurred the government into imposing restrictions on LSVTs. The Secretary of State is now empowered to prepare a disposals programme limiting the number of voluntary transfers which will be allowed each year, and based on an estimate of the Exchequer costs of the disposal, including any increase attributable to housing benefit (Leasehold Reform, Housing and Urban Development Act 1993, s. 135). Further, a one-off levy of 20 per cent, in favour of the Secretary of State, may be charged on any capital receipt arising from LSVT, as a way of recouping some of the extra housing benefit cost (Leasehold Reform, Housing and Urban Development Act 1993, s. 136).

The terms on which a transfer is made to an RSL are intended to be cost neutral (i.e. to generate neither a surplus nor a loss) for the RSL. The price which it pays for the housing it acquires through transfer must have regard to its 'tenanted market value', a method of valuation which assumes that the stock is transferred as a going social housing concern. Put simply, it equates to the income the RSL is likely to receive over 30 years by way of rents, less the estimated expenditure necessary on repair and improvement works, maintenance and supervision and management. It also takes into account the fact that transferring tenants retain their right to buy. Invariably, therefore, the price paid by the new landlord is significantly lower than the amount which the houses would fetch if sold individually under the right to buy. Where the properties are in relatively good repair, the authority will obtain a substantial capital receipt. However, at least 75 per cent of the net capital receipts generated by housing transfers must be set aside to pay off any outstanding loans and only 25 per cent may be used for capital expenditure.

Generally, local authorities may dispose of the property on such conditions as they think fit but, by s. 33(2) of the Housing Act 1985, the Secretary of State's consent is required if the proposed transfer is to include:

(a) a condition limiting the resale price;
(b) in the case of a sale, a condition reserving a right of pre-emption (i.e. a requirement that the purchaser cannot sell the property or grant a lease on it without giving the vendor authority one month to refuse, or fail to accept, an offer of sale or lease back); or
(c) on the grant of a lease, a condition which prohibits assignment or the grant of a sub-lease.

Reasons for use of stock transfer

There have been a number of reasons for the growth of stock transfer. It has found favour with successive governments primarily because it provides a mechanism for escaping the borrowing restrictions placed on local authorities by the public expenditure regime. Whereas 'loans taken out by local authorities to invest in public sector housing must be included in the Public Sector Borrowing Requirement (PSBR) calculations, and are effectively prevented by the Local Government and Housing Act 1989' those taken out by housing associations are not included in the PSBR and are not subject to statutory control (Law Commission, 2002: 2.111). Housing associations can therefore use the asset base of the transferred stock as security to borrow from banks and other lending institutions in order to fund the construction of new properties, and to carry out repairs and improvements to existing stock. Furthermore, stock transfers can not only bring in capital receipts and enable local authorities to fulfil their housing duties, without having to own and manage housing stock directly, but they are also 'one of the few effective ways open to local authorities of investing in their housing stock' (ibid.).

In the early days, transfers were geographically concentrated in rural, suburban and resort areas mostly in the south of England, where housing stock was in reasonable repair, there was a positive transfer value and outstanding loan debt relatively low. The PSBR rules precluded local authorities from borrowing money to finance the rehabilitation of council estates and inner city regeneration funds were not available in suburban and rural areas (Ginsberg, 2005: 119). Transfer not only released the transferring authorities from the burden of future expenditure on repairs and improvements but also meant that they could use the capital receipts to pay off their existing debts and to cushion their other financial commitments. It was a less feasible option for (mainly urban) authorities with poor quality stock, the sale of which would result in a negative transfer value, leaving them still to service the debt after their stock had been sold (Mullen, 2001: 48–9). Since 1999, however, the Treasury has agreed to make a one-off payment to clear such 'overhanging' debt and any early redemption penalties. Even though such payments merely 'facilitate transfer . . . [and] represent no additional investment in the stock and no increase in provision' (Cowan and Marsh, 2001: 268), this debt write-off, together with 'a perception that there is no alternative method for obtaining the investment necessary to improve stock', has resulted in 'the recent conversion of large Labour-controlled authorities to stock transfer' (Mullen, 2001: 48–9) even though it involves 'a huge subsidy from the taxpayer' (Ginsberg, 2005: 123). Although there is less incentive to maximise the transfer value in such cases, the government predicts that a significant proportion of future transfers will involve overhanging debt because such authorities were unable to transfer all of their stock earlier in the transfer programmes (NAO, 2003: 3.25). Often (and increasingly) therefore authorities have used stock transfer to avoid the responsibility of having to manage increasingly dilapidated housing stock. The government has estimated the cost of the repairs and maintenance backlog in the sector at £19 billion and acknowledged that it will take 10 years to bring properties up to the desired standard.

It is for a local authority to decide on whether to embark on a transfer of its homes, having taken account of its tenants' views and other options available to it, and to apply to the Secretary of State for a place on the annual transfer programme. The Secretary of State assesses the application and, if accepted, the local authority is then responsible for developing the details of its transfer scheme, consulting and balloting tenants, and negotiating a transfer price at which an RSL will take over the authority's stock. The legislation does not prescribe in any detail the criteria according to which the Secretary of State's decision to grant or withhold consent should be made although it does state that the Secretary of State may have regard to the extent to which (a) the intending purchaser is controlled or influenced by members or officers of the authority, and (b) the proposed disposal would result in the intending purchaser becoming the predominant or a substantial owner in any area of housing accommodation let on tenancies or subject to licences (Housing Act 1985, s. 34(4A)). The policy on approval has always been contained in non-statutory guidance which, in earlier versions, suggested that consent would not be given unless the intended transferee was suitable (which among other things, meant being independent of the local authority) and the transfers did not exceed prescribed size limits. In around two-thirds of transfers, local authorities have disposed of their stock to new organisations created out of the authorities' own housing departments. While in recent years there have been more transfers to existing RSLs or to newly-created subsidiaries of existing RSLs, it seems that specifically created associations will continue to be the preferred option, partly because of the desire among authorities to retain an element of control over their former housing, partly because of concerns that social landlord organisations should not become too large, and partly as a result of concerns over the structures and practices of traditional housing associations. Local authorities have long been suspicious of the 'apparent lack of accountability' of housing associations and their tendency 'to recruit new board members informally from within their own social circles' (Malpass, 2005: 195). In the past, housing associations have demonstrated scant commitment to tenant involvement or representation on boards, and 'although there are shareholders (each entitled to just one share) with the formal power to elect board members, it is the board itself which decided how many shares to issue and to whom' (Malpass, 2005: 195–6). By contrast, stock transfer organisations have adopted a more 'open and democratic' approach, with places on the board reserved for tenants and local councillors. Until 1996 councillors could not constitute more than 20 per cent of the board of the purchasing body. However, since the Housing Act 1996, councillors and tenants may each make up as much as 49 per cent; typically this results in equal numbers of tenants, local authority representatives and 'independent' members.

One of the stated purposes of giving housing associations an enhanced role in the provision of social housing – by replacing large monopolistic landlords with 'smaller organisations operating in competition' (Mullins and Pawson, 2005: 207) – was to allow (prospective) tenants better quality housing and a wider range of landlords from which to choose. However, their being selected for such a role probably had less to do with their manifest suitability (certainly from the viewpoint of organisational structure) and more to do with the then government's antipathy towards local authorities. Ironically, however, the number of housing associations has fallen by about a third since 1989 'through a combination of mergers between medium and larger associations trying to strengthen their financial base and the deregistration of smaller organisations, unable or unwilling to compete in the new era dominated by private finance' (Lowe, 2004: 57). It appears that most stock transfer associations have considered setting up or joining some form of group structure and a third have also considered merger (Pawson and Fancy, 2003). They may do so on business grounds (economies of scale, ability to borrow at lower rates) for active RSLs to merge or form alliances in group structures but also because of the approach taken by the Housing Corporation towards funding. As soon as the new Funding regime for housing associations was put in place in 1975, the Corporation tended to channel development funds to a relatively small group of associations and the more recent suggestion that it was developing a 'super league' was borne out by the announcement that in 2004–6, some 80 per cent of development programmes in England would be carried out by just 70 RSLs. This represents an extension of existing practice, for although in recent years some 300–400 housing associations have received development grants, in 2003 approximately 56 per cent went to just 42 associations (Malpass, 2005: 200). The fact that such mergers and alliances have taken place across 'ever-wider geographical boundaries' means that any sense of 'local' identity (together with any semblance of local accountability) is lost, and it becomes harder to enforce promises made at the time of transfer (HCCHG, 2005: 5.1.3).

Commensurate with the aim of breaking up local authorities' monopoly of social housing and to avoid replacing 'one large, mostly anonymous landlord with another' (Bright and Gilbert, 1995: 539; DETR, 2000a: 7.23), transfers were, until recently, subject to a size limit. The original limit of 5,000 dwellings was extended to 12,000 but – because there were strong organisational reasons for not dividing up the stock or there were to be significant levels of demolition in areas of low demand – there were a number of occasions on which the ODPM gave its approval to transfers that exceeded the guideline maximum size (NAO, 2003: 2.4). The formal upper limit has now been removed, although the government states that it still bases 'great importance on delivery and locally based management' (ODPM, 2004d: 3.20). It suggests that an authority proposing to transfer a large stock holding should consider splitting its stock and transferring it to two or more distinct RSLs with clearly separate identities, possibly as part of a group structure, or putting in place 'significant and meaningful devolved local management' (ibid.).

Because whole stock transfers have been the primary transfer vehicle, transfer RSLs have displaced local authority landlords as the principal suppliers but without necessarily expanding choice for tenants. There is a tension therefore between the argument that transfer would lead to smaller and more locally responsive organisations, and the way in which these independent organisations respond to the business pressures on them' (Malpass, 2005: 196).

Consultation

Only exceptionally will a local authority seek to transfer property with vacant possession. Where the purchaser plans to redevelop, the court can order possession of the properties concerned under ground 10A of the Housing Act 1985 (see Chapter 18) to enable the transfer to proceed. It must be satisfied that suitable alternative accommodation is available for the displaced tenants and that the local authority will dispose of the properties in accordance with the development scheme within a reasonable time of obtaining possession.

Before a local authority applies to the Secretary of State for the approval of a redevelopment scheme involving tenanted properties, it must consult the secure tenants of any dwelling-houses affected by the proposal and consider their views (Housing Act 1985, Sch. 2, Part V). In considering whether or not to approve such a scheme, the Secretary of State must also have regard to the tenants' representations, as well as:

(a) the effect of the scheme on the extent and character of housing accommodation in the neighbourhood,
(b) the period of time over which it is proposed that the disposal and redevelopment will take place, and
(c) the extent to which the scheme includes provision for housing provided under the scheme to be sold or let to existing tenants or persons nominated by the landlord.

The Housing Act 1985 contains provisions requiring consultation to take place where a local authority is seeking to dispose of dwelling-houses subject to secure or introductory tenancies and the proposed disposal is to a landlord which does not fulfil the 'landlord condition' of s. 80 of the Act (s. 106A; Sch. 3A). These provisions replace the normal consultation requirements contained in s. 105. There is no requirement to consult, however, where the local authority has acquired the property by means of a compulsory purchase order which provides for onward disposal to an RSL, and the disposal is made within a year of the acquisition (s. 106A(3)). The authority must serve written notice, informing the tenants of the proposed purchaser's identity, the likely consequences of the disposal (e.g. changes in security of tenure and in rent), the fact that (in the case of secure tenants) their right to buy is preserved, and the effect of the consultation provisions. They must also be notified of their right to make representations to the authority within a reasonable, specified time (Sch. 3A, para. 3(1), (2)). The authority must then consider any representations and serve a further notice on the tenants of any significant changes to the plan, their right to make representations to the Secretary of State, and the duty of the Secretary of State to withhold consent if a majority of the tenants oppose the scheme. The Secretary of State may require the authority to carry out further consultation with its tenants. Consent must not be given if it appears that a majority of the tenants concerned do not wish the disposal to proceed (Sch. 3A, para. 5). The requirement that the consultation process should involve a formal test of tenant opinion has been met in all cases by a ballot of tenants. Most authorities have employed a straight majority voting system but a few have used the system of 'intertia voting' devised for Tenants' Choice ballots (Mullins *et al.*, 1993: 179–80; Stewart, 1996: 171).

By 2003, tenants had chosen to transfer rather than remain with their local authority in all but 46 of the proposed transfers (NAO, 2003: para. 1.4) but the fact that the majority of ballots have favoured transfer does not necessarily mean that tenants have been particularly keen to leave the local authority sector (Mullen, 2001: 51–2).[2] Indeed, it has been important for authorities proposing a sale to work with prospective purchasers in making transfers sufficiently attractive to encourage tenants to vote for them. Given that local authorities are subject to tight capital allocations, which often mean that they are in no position to improve and modernise the stock themselves, transfer proposals have invariably involved 'a new investment programme over five to seven years' together with a rent guarantee and 'some empowerment of tenants via representation on management boards and consultation machinery' (Ginsberg, 2005: 121). Tenants living in housing which needed repair and/or modernisation were faced with a simple choice: to accept 'a definite offer of major investment in their homes in the short term on condition that they chose a new landlord, or . . . to stay with the local authority', knowing that they might spend many more years in sub-standard accommodation (Mullen, 2001: 52).

Sometimes the proposed purchaser will go so far as to 'guarantee' a minimum package of further rights for the sitting tenants, thus suggesting that '. . . on transfer the tenants will be "cushioned" or "protected" from the loss of secure status and their Tenant's Charter of associated statutory rights' (Luba, 2000: 117). Whether such guarantees are legally enforceable is another matter. In any event they are usually offered to (and therefore only enforceable by), the transferring authority rather than to the tenants whose homes are being transferred. Were they to be included in the formal contract of sale, they might later be directly relied upon by the tenants (by means of the

2   See Daly *et al.* (2005: 333) for the various factors which are likely to influence the outcome of a tenants' ballot.

Contracts (Rights of Third Parties) Act 1999). Alternatively, if the transferring authority wished to ensure that its tenants were fully protected in the hands of the new owner(s), it could in the lead-up to the transfer use the statutory mechanism provided by s. 103 of the Housing Act 1985 to vary its tenancy agreements, 'setting out as a matter of contract' the 'rights' the new owner had indicated would be honoured (ibid.).

Because transfer has involved tenants moving from the local authority rent regime to that of the RSL sector, another incentive which has been presented to existing secure tenants has been the offer of rent guarantees which have usually limited rent increases in the first five years. As new tenants had no such guarantee, the cumulative impact on the average rent could be significant, and once a home had been renovated or substantially improved, new charges could be applied. However, in the context of rent convergence (which seeks to achieve greater fairness and coherence in the structure of social rents, so that comparable homes within an area have comparable rents), rent guarantees are no longer seen as meaningful. Instead, RSLs are now including new rent rules to limit increases to inflation plus 0.5 per cent a year in their offer at the time of transfer. Finally, the preserved right to buy is an important benefit for those tenants who might be able to finance a purchase in future; even if their properties are currently in need of repair and/or renovation, their value will increase on completion of the development programme.

Mullen points out that the various amendments made to the LSVT rules – including the consultation provisions – have produced 'a greater quantity of legislation' which, he says, might have been expected to result in greater recourse to the courts. The fact that this has not occurred is primarily because 'the interests of central government and those of local authorities who have promoted stock transfer have coincided' and the process of balloting has weeded out those proposals to which there has been the most extensive tenant opposition. The cost of financing challenges and the highly discretionary nature of the legal framework has meant that applications for judicial review of local authority actions or of ministerial consent by or on behalf of 'disappointed tenants and tenants' groups who wanted to remain with the council, or . . . other interested parties such as public sector workers' have not materialised (Mullen, 2001: 54–5). An exception is *R v Secretary of State for the Environment ex p Walters* (1998) 30 HLR 328 in which a council tenant applied for judicial review of a proposed sale, redevelopment and leaseback of the housing estate on which he lived on the ground that the consultation process had been flawed. The judge accepted that it had been flawed because it had originally been undertaken on the basis that only those properties occupied by tenants who voted in favour of the scheme would be affected and it had not addressed the question of the leaseback to the council. However, having taken into consideration the approval of the vast majority of tenants who wished the scheme to go ahead, the benefit which would be brought about by the scheme, and the minimal effect on the applicant's legal rights, he refused to grant relief. The Court of Appeal dismissed the appeal, holding that the judge was fully entitled to exercise his discretion so as to refuse the application despite finding that the consultation process had been flawed.

As Mullen points out, tenants have led 'neither the general drive towards transfer to non-local authority landlords nor the specific proposals brought forward for particular transfers'. Further, while the legal framework appears to let the local authority take the initiative in proposing transfers but leave the final decision with the tenants, the choice given to tenants has been presented within very narrow constraints: 'the choice between a change of landlord with major new investment in their homes, and keeping the same landlord without the same scale of investment' (Mullen, 2001: 53).

While it is true that 'the policy of stock transfer has been pursued in spite of the wishes of many citizens to remain as council tenants' (Mullen, 2001: 53), tenants have nonetheless successfully opposed proposed transfers in over 40 cases. In April 2002, for example, tenants of Birmingham City Council rejected what would have been England's largest stock transfer, involving 84,000 homes (*Housing Today*, 11 April 2002). In order to make it possible for authorities to achieve the Decent Homes Standard, the New Labour government has been compelled to offer alternatives to stock transfer. Arguably, therefore, its policy of demunicipalisation can be seen as being based on pragmatic rather than ideological foundations although, conversely, the Decent Homes Standard can be seen as 'a Trojan horse' which the government is using in its 'dogmatic quest to minimise the proportion of housing stock managed by local authorities' (HPLGRC, 2004: 3). If the ownership or management of council housing can be transferred to other agencies, new investment funded by private finance can be introduced to carry out renovation and new construction without counting as public spending (Kemp, 2000: 272–3).

The delegation of housing management functions

Compulsory competitive tendering

Throughout the 1980s, attempts to dismantle the near monopoly enjoyed by local authorities in the ownership and management of social housing focused on ownership. Attention was also given, however, to the separation of ownership and management through compulsory competitive tendering (CCT) for housing management services, a concept 'based on the assumption that it is appropriate or possible to manage public sector stock on a commercial basis' which 'marginalise[d] the social collective elements of public housing' (Stewart, 1996: 177).

Local authorities have always had the power to contract with the private sector for the provision of services. Until the introduction of CCT in 1980, core services were usually provided by directly employed council staff, and the private sector was invited to tender only for specialist work or to assist at times of high demand. It was generally agreed by central and local government, and across the party political divide, that this was the most effective method of public service delivery. Only gradually did the government come to realise the potential of competitive tendering, as part of its broader, political strategy of privatisation. The public justification for competitive tendering hinged on the maintenance of standards and the reduction of costs, but it appealed to the government on other grounds, including the encouragement of businesses in the service sector and the reduction of public expenditure. The reluctance of most local authorities voluntarily to subject themselves to competitive tendering led to the enactment of the Local Government Act 1988, which significantly extended CCT and was specifically designed to make it very difficult for authorities to circumvent the Act's provisions (Radford, 1988: 747–9). The 1988 Act specified household and commercial refuse collection, cleaning of buildings, street cleaning, school, welfare and other catering, ground maintenance and the repair and maintenance of vehicles as the 'defined activities' which had to be put out to tender. The housing management functions which became subject to CCT (from 1 April 1994), and therefore had to be put out to tender included rent and service charge collection, letting of properties, dealing with vacant properties, repairs and maintenance, and caretaking and cleaning (Local Government (Competition) (Defined Activities) (Housing Management) Order 1994). Local authority landlords were required to specify and cost the services involved and could continue to provide these services only if their own in-house management teams won the contract following a CCT exercise with other would-be providers. Functions which authorities could continue to exercise themselves without putting them out to tender included setting the council's housing strategy and its housing investment programme, rent setting, allocation policies, tenancy conditions, maintenance, waiting lists, assessing housing need and allocating tenancies.

It was predicted that the introduction of CCT to the management of local authority housing would have a profound impact in relation to local authority housing management functions, potentially transforming the landlord and tenant relationship (Stewart, 1996: 176) and resulting both in 'a fragmentation of ownership and enhanced complexity' (Driscoll, 1994: 796). However, it was widely resented by local government and its 'formalistic regulatory schema . . . encouraged many local authorities in the 1990s to divert their energies from the improvement of services into undermining the process of CCT' (Vincent-Jones, 2001: 245). In consequence, its effects were not (on the fact of it) as far-reaching as had been feared and the first round of housing management CCT, which ended in the spring of 1996, resulted in councils losing only 16 contracts (generally to housing associations). Ninety-five per cent of those tendered remained in-house. At the same time, however, it has had an enduring legacy by inculcating New Public

Management values in local authority housing departments, with the result that target-setting and performance indicators 'have developed a powerful status in the assessment of housing departments' operations' (Cowan and Halliday, 2003: 22).

Best value

The change of government in May 1997 appeared to signal the final demise of CCT, New Labour having expressed the view while in Opposition that councils should be allowed to put services out to tender if they wish, but should not be forced to do so. Once in government, they argued not only that CCT had failed but also that 'a culture in which authorities decide what services are to be provided on the basis of what suits them is no longer an option' (DETR, 1988: 1.6). Improvements in services were more likely to be achieved where 'those who use and pay for them are given a greater say in how they are run', e.g. in setting the appropriate standards and in deciding how they should be met and by whom (ibid.: 1.7). As a result, since spring 2000, local authorities have been subject to BV, a regime which has subsequently been extended to include RSLs.

The BV scheme involves a framework of 'performance indicators' set by central government against which performance (and thus progress towards achieving a 'continuous improvement') can be monitored, and 'performance standards' which authorities are required to meet (Local Government Act 1999, s. 4). It is administered by the Audit Commission which carries out regular inspections of services to ensure that BV is being achieved. A separate housing inspectorate within the Commission deals with housing services. Since one of the aims of BV is to inform the public about local authority performance, the Commission publishes inspection reports (in the form of Comprehensive Performance Assessments bringing together the results of assessments by OFSTED, the Commission for Social Care Inspectorate and the Audit Commission) which give each local authority a star rating based on performance, ranging from no stars for poor performance to three stars for excellent performance. These ratings effectively create a league table of local government performance, with those with an excellent rating receiving more control over their budgets and more freedom to sell services, and those who fare poorly being forced to accept an intensive package of government help. One of the aims of BV is 'to stimulate competition' between local authority and other social landlords as providers and managers of rented housing and to 'increase sensitivity to consumer choice through mechanisms allowing easier comparability and read-across between different providers'. Rather than prescribing the exact mix of forms of social housing, the objective is to create the conditions which will allow such a balance 'to be locally determined by market forces in particular areas' (Vincent-Jones, 2001: 253).

The principal duty imposed on authorities by s. 3 of the 1999 Act (which, it has been suggested, is 'deliberately vaguely worded to minimise the possibility of legal challenge': Vincent-Jones, 2001: 242) is to 'make arrangements to secure continuous improvement' in the way in which all their functions are exercised, 'having regard to a combination of economy, efficiency and effectiveness' – values to which local government had been compelled to pay regard under CCT. However, while under CCT housing management was narrowly defined in terms of the council's landlord responsibilities, the broader BV duty under s. 3 involves an obligation to consult and be accountable to all local service users, whether council tenants, leaseholders, owner-occupiers or private tenants. While this 'emphasis on involving a range of stakeholders in the common pursuit of quality . . . resonates with Labour's broader political agenda of social inclusion' (Maile and Hoggett, 2001: 510), it is also the case that BV 'extends market-like disciplines to the many local authority functions which were not covered by CCT' (Geddes and Martin, 2000: 380). Guidance has been issued centrally on the consultative duty, including the persons to be consulted, and the form, timing and content of consultations (ODPM, 2003c). Local authorities are expected to put in place Tenants' Participation Contracts, negotiated and agreed with tenants, which set out, e.g. how tenants will be involved; the support, facilities, training and advice to help tenants to take part effectively; how disagreements and disputes will be dealt with; and the ways in which participation arrangements will be monitored and reviewed.

By s. 5, the 'arrangements' referred to in s. 3 include undertaking a programme of reviews of all their functions over a maximum five-year period. In carrying out their reviews, local authorities are required to apply the so-called four Cs: challenge, consult, compare, and compete. They must ask themselves whether they really need certain services and identify customer needs for each activity. They have to show that they have consulted local people and key local stakeholders as part of their BV reviews, and have monitored customer satisfaction. They have to compare their services against other local authorities, and private and not-for-profit service providers, and demonstrate how their performance fares against national performance indicators. Finally, and most significantly, they must show that in-house services are the most cost effective by subjecting them to external competition. If in-house services are more expensive, they may have to switch control of that activity to a private firm or the voluntary sector. It is this final area where BV has, arguably, the most congruence with the CCT regime.

The reviews provide the basis for setting establishing authority-wide objectives and performance measures and a programme of fundamental performance reviews to be published in an annual BV performance plan (BVPP) (s. 6). Local accountability on the provision of services is achieved by requiring BVPPs to provide local people with a summary of the extent to which their authority was successful in meeting the previous year's targets and objectives, a comparison of its performance with other relevant authorities, a statement of targets to be set for the following and future years and a statement of the outcome of any review carried out, e.g. by way of a revision of targets and the programme for achieving them. The Secretary of State is also able to prescribe the content of BVPPs. BVPPs are subject to local audit under s. 7 as to their accuracy and with a view to recommending remedial action. The initial audit is carried out by each authority's own auditor, but may give rise to later action undertaken by the housing inspectorate or the Secretary of State. Section 9 of the 1999 Act obliges each authority to respond to an auditor's report on its BVPP where it has identified serious deficiencies in the BVPP and the auditor has recommended that the Secretary of State should intervene. The response must be made as soon as practicable and must state what action the authority proposes to take and the proposed timetable for action. It must be forwarded to the Secretary of State and be incorporated in the next edition of the BVPP.

Sections 10 and 11 of the 1999 Act empower the Audit Commission to inspect authorities with respect to their compliance with BV policy, e.g. to ensure that they have reviewed their performance as required and have set sufficiently challenging performance targets to achieve BV in the future. Inspections are carried out on a programmed basis but provision is also made for non-programmed ad hoc or 'spot check' inspections where an authority's performance is considered to be falling well below required levels and the authority has no immediate plans to review the function in question. The Secretary of State has power under s. 10(2)–(4) to issue guidance to the Audit Commission in this regard, and may direct it to carry out an inspection of an individual authority. In carrying out inspections the Commission has extensive powers to obtain papers and other relevant information. The Housing Inspectorate carries out inspections in three key areas of local authority housing functions, i.e. strategy and enabling, community services (such as homelessness and housing advice), and landlord services (such as repairs and maintenance, and tenant participation). Early criticisms that the BV scheme was unnecessarily heavy-handed and imposed too many inspections on even the best performing authorities, have led to streamlining. Now, the number of inspections an authority undergoes will more closely reflect its performance, with the best local authorities receiving a 'light touch' approach and inspection focusing on poorer-performing authorities (DTLGR, 2001). Authorities are no longer required to review all their services as a matter of course but must focus instead on the services which are highlighted as being in need of review.

Following an inspection, the Commission issues a report to the authority concerned. If it concludes that the authority is failing in its functions, but not sufficiently seriously for referral to the Secretary of State, the authority will be required to record its failure and the action taken to remedy the situation within the next performance plan. Where there are found to be serious failures, the Commission will also send its report to the Secretary of State. This will be one potential 'trigger' for the Secretary of State to utilise enforcement powers under s. 15 to require an authority to prepare or amend a performance plan, or to follow specified procedures with regard to such a plan, or to carry out a review of the performance of specified functions, or to take such other action as the Secretary of State considers necessary to meet BV criteria. The Secretary of State may hold a local enquiry into the performance of specified functions of an authority and, having given the relevant authority an opportunity to make representations, direct that he or she or some other nominated person shall exercise a specified function for a specified period, or for so long as he considers appropriate. Serious mismanagement of an authority's housing stock could thus lead to the authority losing its housing functions to another provider nominated by the Secretary of State. This is a very considerable extension of central powers with regard to local government.

It can be seen therefore that BV is a comprehensive system for setting targets and monitoring progress and although the 'rhetorical emphasis' is placed on 'local responsibility' for standard- and target-setting, and the means by which they are to be achieved, the fact that there is a 'centrally imposed framework' of performance indicators enables 'central government to exert pressure on local performance' (Malpass, 2005: 204). As Cowan and Marsh point out, the 'softer' forms of government under BV, which ostensibly allow greater freedom to local authorities, have been combined with stricter financial controls for the past 20 years or more so that 'with performance measured, compared and individual organisations held up to scrutiny, the pressure to perform is considerable' (Cowan and Marsh, 2005: 39). They also suggest that 'in the context of a diminished, residualised sector whose stock in many parts of the midlands and north' faces low demand or is hard to let, it becomes more difficult to manage and deliver the continuously improving performance expected by government (ibid.: 40). Indeed, close control over expenditure by central government requires local government increasingly to focus on finding innovative ways to use its resources. Others suggest however that instead of encouraging 'new local policy initiatives' and 'challenging traditions of uniformity in service provision', BV represents (at least in part):

> an attempt to deal with some of the fragmenting and complex organisational issues which arise in the context of a proliferation of regulations and interorganisational relationships between the public, private and voluntary sectors (all of which is the direct consequence of policy choices made by successive governments).
>
> (Maile and Hoggett, 2001: 512.)

What is more, while BV is held out as a means of disseminating information and developing public participation, it may be regarded as 'participation-lite', in that it is not about 'power over policy and resource questions' but rather 'social inclusion (or rather, being given the feeling of inclusion) and effective feedback'. Geddes and Martin, on the other hand, maintain that there are three important respects in which BV appears to differ from what went before. First, it involves an attempt to 'repair relations' between central and local government, and to secure support for BV principles from a broad range of interest groups including local government itself, trade unions and the voluntary sector. Secondly, in contrast to previous Conservative administrations whose aim was 'to place public sector activities under the direction of business-led organisations', New Labour sees those local authorities which demonstrate a capacity to improve as having a 'key community leadership and service delivery role'. Finally, it has allowed different interpretations of its principles and approaches to emerge (Geddes and Martin, 2000: 380) although 'the arrangements for auditing BV appear to be based on an assumption that most authorities will adopt a fairly uniform approach' (ibid.: 381). Indeed, the creation of new audit and inspection regime together with the creation of nationally applicable performance indicators suggests a 'strong centralising instinct' (ibid.).

Arm's length management organisations

Two alternatives to stock transfer – arm's length management organisations (ALMOs) and private finance initiative (PFI) – have emerged partly 'in response to tenant ballots which turned down transfer, leaving few options except to make the most of the 'old system' housing investment programme' (Lowe, 2004: 53–4) but also – and primarily – as means of achieving the decent homes standard. It has been made clear that unless local authorities use one of these three options, they cannot expect increased investment in their housing stock outside the housing investment programme. By the time the decent homes standard was introduced in 2000, 101 out of 354 stock-owning authorities had already transferred all of their stock. A further 57 did so before the government announced in 2003 that the remaining authorities would be required to undertake an 'options appraisal' (involving tenants) to deciding which of the three options to pursue.

ALMOs were introduced in the 2000 Green Paper in which it was stated that authorities which were 'delivering high-quality housing services, . . . making effective use of resources and [which had] put [their] housing management at arm's length . . . would be able to retain and use more of their rental income to finance borrowing for investment in stock improvements' (DETR, 2000a: 7.39–7.41). Additional capital funding is also available. This option is not available to all local authorities but only to those which have received a 'good' or 'excellent rating' from the Audit Commission's Housing Inspectorate for its current services under the BV regime and have been accepted onto the government's annual ALMO programme. The 2000 Comprehensive Spending Review budgeted £460 million for 2002/3 and 2003/4 to finance improvements to around 90,000 dwellings. In February 2003 the government announced a total of nearly £2 billion to be spent between April 2003 and March 2006. Not all authorities receive the same level of extra subsidy, the amount available depending on, e.g. demand for resources, the mix of dwelling types in the stock under arm's length management, and regional cost differences. An individual authority may use the extra revenue to finance additional borrowing for investment in the housing stock.

An ALMO is specifically set up by a local authority (usually as a company limited by guarantee which does not trade for profit) to manage, maintain and improve all or part of its housing stock, thereby separating its housing management role from its strategic housing function. Ownership of the housing stock remains with the local authority and, in contrast to stock transfer therefore, there is at least the possibility of housing management being returned to direct local authority control. Again unlike stock transfer, the authorities operating ALMOs retain their housing revenue accounts over which they (and not their ALMOs) exercise ultimate control. Tenants remain secure tenants of their landlord authority and their rights – such as the right to buy, the right to repair and the right to manage – are unaffected. However, in common with most recently-established transfer housing associations, ALMOs have a significant degree of independence from their parent local authorities and are governed not by municipal housing committees but by quasi-autonomous boards composed of equal numbers of tenants, local authority nominees and independent members.

The relationship between a local authority and an ALMO is regulated in a management agreement which should cover: the functions to be delegated to and carried out by the ALMO; the standards to which they are to be carried out; arrangements for reporting on and monitoring performance; requirements for the involvement of tenants in decision-making; the financial relationship and obligations of each party; arrangements for consultation and liaison between the authority and the ALMO; the ALMO's role in helping to deliver the authority's housing strategy, including means to ensure that the authority, as ALMO shareholder, can achieve its objectives without unduly inhibiting the ALMO's freedom to manage the stock; the length of the agreement (e.g. an initial period of five years renewable, or 10 years, renewable, with provision for a break after five years); actions to be taken where there is non-compliance or failure; and arrangements for termination (ODPM, 2004b: 2.6).

This combination of public money and freedom to borrow from the private market has become an attractive alternative for several authorities which had previously resisted the transfer model (or for whom stock transfer was not financially viable). A total of 66 local authorities have set up ALMOs which now have responsibility for managing one million homes. However, while ALMOs have proved popular, concerns have been expressed about their high set-up costs, their democratic accountability and governance, and the extent of tenant involvement in making the decision as to whether an ALMO should be created in the first place.

Section 27 of the Housing Act 1985 entitles a local housing authority to transfer specified management functions to 'another person' and in order to delegate such functions to an ALMO, local authorities must apply to the Secretary of State for consent (unless the ALMO is also a TMO). As the establishment of an ALMO comprises a matter of housing management, the tenants likely to be affected by it are entitled to be consulted (Housing Act 1985, s. 105), i.e. to be informed of the authority's proposals and given the opportunity to make their views known on the reasons for setting up the ALMO, the functions to be transferred and the continuing role of the local authority, the composition and status of the ALMO and its board, including the selection and role of the tenant board members, tenants' and leaseholders' rights, and performance standards for ALMOs. Before giving consent, the Secretary of State must be satisfied that such consultation has taken place and that the tenants show a balance of support for the proposal.

There is no legal requirement that tenants be balloted and although most local authorities have held tenant ballots, others have simply held 'consultation exercises' in order to canvas tenants' views. Even where ballots are held, there is disquiet that the information given to tenants beforehand is presented in such a way as to deprive them of the opportunity to make a real choice. In *R (on the application of Beale) v Camden London Borough* [2004] HLR 48, the claimants sought judicial review of the local authority's consultation process prior to a ballot of tenants and leaseholders on its plan to transfer the management of its council houses to an ALMO. They contended that the consultation process was unfair and unlawful because, in only presenting the arguments in favour of the proposal, the local authority had failed to provide voters with the information that was reasonably required to enable them to choose. Refusing the application, the court held that that the local authority had no legal duty to set out in its publicity materials the case against its proposals. On the contrary, it was obliged merely to inform tenants and leaseholders of its own proposals. Section 105(1) did not oblige the court to determine whether the material put out by the local authority was fair. A court could only interfere if it was satisfied that no reasonable local authority could deem the arrangements adopted to be appropriate, and on the facts, a reasonable authority could have concluded that this consultation process would enable the tenants and leaseholders to be reasonably informed about its proposals.

Finally, and importantly, there are worries that ALMOs are a staging-post to privatisation. Although it may be that 'the emergence of [ALMOs] has the potential to slow the flow of stock from the public to the RSL sector if it establishes itself as a viable alternative' (Cowan and Marsh, 2001: 267) the fear that they represent the first step in separating a council from its stock has been fuelled by the Housing Act 2004 which empowers the Housing Corporation to make grants for social housing to bodies other than RSLs. ALMOs will thus be able to bid for SHG alongside RSLs and private companies, enabling them to carry out new build development.

The private finance initiative

The third but far less common option put forward by the government for achieving the Decent Homes Standard is the PFI. Since its introduction by the Conservative government in the early 1990s, PFI has been adopted and developed by New Labour as a means of levering private finance into various parts of the public sector and promoting efficiency. The most significant users of PFI funding in the UK are transport (principally because of the London Underground contract but also involving road-building), health (including the construction of new hospitals) and defence.

As in other sectors, social housing PFI schemes are structured as long-term contracts (typically with a 30-year lifespan) which involve the renovation and ongoing repair of a number of estate-specific properties and the building of replacement homes. The parties to the contract will be a public service purchaser (a local authority) and a private sector operator (typically a consortium which includes a construction firm to manage the renovation, maintenance or building work, a housing association to provide housing and estate management services and a bank or building society to provide the finance for the scheme). There are, broadly speaking, two types of housing PFI. The first is the non-HRA PFI which a local authority funds entirely from its own resources and is accounted for in the General Fund. The second is the HRA PFI, where credits from central government meet – in full or in part – a local authority's capital obligations under the contract, and the transaction is included in the local authority's HRA. The authority's rental income provides revenue support. In order to qualify for credits from central government, the project in question must satisfy the two essential characteristics of value for money and risk transfer. Risk transfer will include the passing on of future legal risks (e.g. because of changes in housing law which have a cost or other implication), operational risks (e.g. responsibility for rent collection and the letting of properties) and development risk (e.g. the price fluctuations associated with refurbishment, maintenance and rebuild). (See Handy, 2004, for an explanation of the funding mechanism and its statutory framework.) The local authority retains – throughout the duration of the contract – the 'demand risk'. In other words, so long as the consortium achieves and maintains the agreed refurbishment standards, the properties are regarded as being available for letting (whether or not they are actually occupied and generating rental income) and the consortium must be paid. This may be particularly significant in poorer areas where there is low demand for housing (Anon, 2003).

The consortium is paid by way of a unitary charge (normally on a monthly basis). Deductions may be made for unavailability (if all or part of a dwelling is unavailable for use as defined in the contract) and failures in service performance (in relation to activities such as rent collection, repairs and maintenance and tenancy and estate management based upon service levels defined in the contract). Continued failure in either availability or service performance will normally bring about the operation of a 'ratchet mechanism' which increases the amount of the deduction (Hodges and Grubnic, 2005: 65). PFI is a means whereby local authorities can achieve a consistent level of availability and service quality over the contract period. However they are committed to the annual service charges and these may rise to excessive levels because of poor pre-contract negotiation, falling demand so that properties remain unoccupied, or as a result of unanticipated costs which have not been expressly provided for in the contract. If continuing low demand leads to a high number of vacant properties, the local authority may be forced to transfer resources from other parts of its housing budget to meet its PFI obligations and it may be therefore that PFI housing contracts are likely to be restricted to areas which do not suffer from low inherent demand. Furthermore, the impact of the PFI schemes on the future rent levels cannot be predicted with certainty given that any shortfall of revenue cost to the local authority will have to be made good in some way. As all or part of the rent of many social housing tenants is paid through housing benefit, any rent increases will have implications as regards social security costs, and the transfer of repair work and estate management previously undertaken by local authority staff may make it more difficult for the authority to support the remainder of its housing services (ibid.: 66).

Arguably, PFI has certain advantages over stock transfer, primarily in so far as the cost of refurbishment can be spread over the full contract period rather than requiring the funding of a stock transfer deficit (Hodges and Grubnic, 2005: 63). In addition, because the local authority retains ownership of the properties and there is no change in the identity of the landlord, a PFI arrangement does not require tenants' approval. However, a number of problems associated with the procurement of PFI schemes in general have emerged, including the lack of experience of managers involved in their development, high procurement costs, difficulties with the identification and measurement of risk, and increasing costs over the lifetime of the contract resulting in an affordability gap (ibid.: 62). Furthermore, the negotiation of PFI contracts in the context of social housing presents particular challenges which may result in its being a minority solution, leaving stock transfer and management through ALMOs as preferred policy options. Thus, while users of services (and indeed taxpayers) are arguably always significant stakeholders in PFI schemes, hospital patients and motorists will not be directly involved in negotiations for PFI hospitals or road schemes. By contrast, the involvement of tenants in PFI HRA social housing schemes is inevitable, either as tenant representatives or as occupiers of houses which are to be demolished or surveyed and renovated (ibid.: 74). Indeed, one of the major issues arising out of the ongoing Pathfinder pilots is that the stock condition survey (of properties continually occupied by tenants) must be sufficiently comprehensive to allow contractors accurately to determine both their costs and the level of risk they may be expected to assume. A further area of concern, which is unique to HRA PFI schemes, is the management of the right to buy (RTB) during the period of contract. As the RTB tends to be exercised in respect of better quality housing stock, guidance published by the Department for Communities provides that the HRA PFI standard contract should make provision for adjustments to be made to the unitary charge following of the exercise of an RTB and indicates that, in some, circumstances compensation should be paid to the consortium during both the construction and service periods of the contract. A final issue is uncertainty as to nature of the consortium, i.e. whether its decisions are judicially reviewable or open to challenge under the Human Rights Act 1998.[3]

The fourth option

The government has refused to provide specific funding for the achievement of the Decent Homes Standard for stock retained under the management of local authorities. However, there exists significant support for the so-called fourth option, i.e. the retention of housing stock by local authorities with direct additional public investment for the repair and maintenance of existing housing and the construction of new housing. Indeed, 99 authorities responded to the 2005 options appraisal by choosing stock retention. While a proposal to provide councils with an 'investment allowance' as part of the calculation of their HRA subsidy was rejected, the Local Government Act 2003 puts in place a new 'prudential borrowing regime' which allows local authorities to borrow without the consent of central government (provided that they remain within their own affordable borrowing limits) either from the Public Works Loan Board or directly from the market if they can obtain a better rate. While most applications have been for transport projects, some have also involved housing, with the so-called 'prudential borrowing' powers providing an alternative to ALMOs as regards stock improvement.

3   Handy (2003: 31) suggests that an HRA PFI may well be a functional public authority, given that the work it undertakes is so 'enmeshed' in the functions and activities of the local authority in question.

Chapter 17

The allocation of social housing

Introduction

Allocations and lettings combine to represent one of the core activities of social landlords. In 2003/4, local authorities and housing associations in England together let 383,000 'general needs' properties (DCLG, 2007b: Table 601). How social housing is allocated – or let – and to whom is, therefore, of fundamental importance (Brown and Yates, 2005: 345).

In the private market (both rented and owner-occupied), individuals must take an active part in finding accommodation. Properties are advertised and prospective occupiers (who can consider and accept or reject what is available) are required to take the initiative in contacting the owner or the owner's agent. By contrast, the allocation of housing by social landlords has traditionally been bureaucratic, with the landlord selecting a suitable applicant to whom a tenancy can be offered from the housing register. Prompted perhaps by the growing emphasis on 'management efficiency' as measured by best value performance indicators and an increased pressure to cut voids, there has been a tendency among some authorities to adopt a take-it-or-leave-it approach as regards offers made to non-homeless and transfer applicants, sometimes accompanied by a threat that, if an offer is rejected, the application may be 'deferred, de-prioritised or even cancelled' (Pawson and Kintrea, 2002: 649–50, 657–8). Curiously, despite two decades of public sector reform, social housing allocations remained outside the choice debate until the end of the 1990s, with consideration of choice in access policies usually 'firmly embedded in a culture of rationing' (Mullins and Niner, 1998: 179). Recently, however, the emphasis has shifted to giving applicants a greater degree of choice, while at the same time reducing bureaucracy, encouraging better use of the housing stock and developing sustained and more balanced communities. Before examining these developments and their statutory underpinnings in more detail, this chapter starts with an outline of the legal basis on which local authorities provide housing generally.

The legal framework for the provision of council housing

There is an obvious link between the amount of housing which an individual authority has available and the policies it uses to allocate that housing and to allow transfers. It is useful, therefore, to consider the legal position governing the provision of council housing.

Local authorities have a duty to 'consider housing conditions in their district and the needs of the district with respect to the provision of further housing accommodation' (Housing Act 1985, s. 8). As to 'conditions', s. 3 of the Housing Act 2004 obliges local housing authorities to keep under review the housing stock in their areas to determine what, if any, action they should take to deal with hazards under the Housing Health and Safety Rating System or to provide financial assistance for home repair and improvement (Housing Act 2004, s. 3(1)). The 'needs' of the district are not confined to the needs of the people already living there, but extend to residents in nearby areas who might want to live, or who might be more conveniently housed, there in the future (*Watson v Minister of Local Government and Planning* [1951] 2 KB 779) as, for example, where the development of new industry in the area is planned. The special needs of the chronically sick and disabled must also be taken into account (Chronically Sick and Disabled Persons Act 1970, s. 3).

In 1980 the duty of local authorities (which had existed since 1919) to prepare and submit plans for the provision of new housing with which to meet the 'needs' referred to in what is now s. 8 was removed. It is now left to the discretion of the individual authority to decide how much and what sort of housing (if any) it will actually provide. Increasingly, however, the financial restraints imposed upon them by central government make it impossible for authorities to provide the housing which they perceive to be necessary, and a number of authorities have disposed of their entire stock (see Chapter 16).

By s. 9(1) of the 1985 Act a local housing authority may provide housing accommodation by way of erection, conversion and acquisition. By subs. (2) it may alter, enlarge, repair or improve a house it has built, converted or acquired under subs. (1). A local authority is not required to hold any housing land or stock (s. 9(5)) but it should be noted that those authorities which have disposed of all their stock remain housing authorities for a variety of purposes, most importantly with regard to homelessness, in respect of which they have to make appropriate arrangements.

A local housing authority may provide 'furniture, fittings and conveniences' (s. 10), 'meals and refreshments', 'laundry and laundry services' (s. 11) and welfare services (s. 11A) in connection with the housing accommodation it provides. By s. 12, either solely or jointly with another person (such as a private company), it may provide and maintain shops, recreation grounds and other buildings which, in the opinion of the Secretary of State, will serve a beneficial purpose in connection with the requirements of the persons for whom the housing accommodation is provided. In *Conron v London City Council* [1922] 2 Ch 283, it was held that a beer-house could be provided to meet the requirements of people living on an estate.

The tension between allocations and homelessness

Section 21(1) of the Housing Act 1985, by which the general management, regulation and control of a local housing authority's houses is vested in and exercised by the authority, appears to give authorities complete freedom in determining how and to whom they should let their housing. As Laurie explains, 'successive governments have realised that local circumstances demand a local response' (Laurie, 2004: 49) and while central government may 'legislate and guide', it has long been accepted that 'allocations policies should be determined and applied locally' (Stirling and Smith, 2003: 146). Thus, since 1924, local authorities have been obliged merely to secure that, in the selection of their tenants, a 'reasonable preference' is given to, e.g. people who are occupying insanitary and overcrowded houses, those who have large families or are living in unsatisfactory housing conditions. While the original 'reasonable preference' categories tended to focus on the physical attributes of the current accommodation, homeless households were brought into the 'reasonable preference' obligation by the Housing (Homeless Persons) Act 1977, greater attention to social need having been urged in the Cullingworth Report (CHAC, 1969).

Until the Housing Act 1996 came into force, the duty of local authorities to provide long-term accommodation to people who were unintentionally homeless and in priority need resulted in two routes into 'permanent' social housing: one via the waiting list and the other via the homelessness legislation. Most local housing authorities maintained housing registers (more commonly known as 'waiting lists') on which general applicants for council housing could register, and from which the authorities made their allocations in accordance with their individual selection schemes. People accepted as statutorily homeless could not register. By the early 1990s, many people, who previously would have been rehoused from the general waiting list, were surfacing as homelessness cases and virtually all of the properties owned by some local authorities were being taken up by homelessness allocations. Research revealed that nationally, homelessness was a factor contributing to the allocation of council houses in 59 per cent of all cases and 78 per cent in London (DoE, 1994). The government interpreted these figures as indicating a failure by the homelessness legislation to fulfil its original function as a safety net. It was seen rather as a queue-jumping device into social housing which created 'a perverse incentive for people to have themselves accepted by a local authority as homeless' (ibid.: 4). However, it is possible that such fears were unfounded given that, according to Shelter, 59 per cent of homeless acceptances were made in respect of applicants who were already on the waiting list (Shelter, 1994).

In its 1995 White Paper, the government expressed its commitment to maintaining a safety net (in the form of the homelessness legislation) 'for families and vulnerable people' but asserted that this should be separate from a fair system of allocating long-term accommodation in a house or flat owned by a local authority or housing association. Achieving that separation would be by reforming the homelessness legislation and the introduction of new arrangements for the allocation of social housing. It stated that allocation schemes should reflect 'the underlying values of our society', balancing 'specific housing needs' against 'the need to support married couples who take a responsible approach to family life, so that tomorrow's generation grows up in a stable home environment' (Department of the Environment, 1995: 36). To this end, Part VI of the Act (which marked a significant departure from the earlier, non-interventionist attitude) introduced a comprehensive statutory framework for the allocation of social housing by local authorities, reserving to the Secretary of State numerous and broadly-stated regulation-making powers which gave potential for significant central control (Laurie, 2004: 49). As such, the 1996 Act can be understood, at least in part, as symptomatic of 'a restructured and less consensual central-local government relationship' (Laurie, 2004: 50–1).

Central to the government's aim of creating a single route into social housing, was the duty imposed by the 1996 Act on local housing authorities to set up and maintain a housing register and to make allocations therefrom to 'qualified persons' through an allocations scheme. Households accepted as statutorily homeless who were provided with temporary accommodation by the local authority were able to register and, indeed, the local authority could apply for registration on their behalf. An important response during the 1990s to 'the fragmentation of housing supply' between local authorities and housing associations was the establishment of common housing registers, which pooled arrangements for access to the housing of local social landlords. An unfortunate consequence of this development, however, was the standardisation of access criteria between landlords which maintained bureaucratic rationing systems and made it harder for consumers 'to make direct approaches to providers of their choice' (Mullins and Pawson, 2005: 208).

Only those eligible for housing accommodation could be allocated accommodation, eligibility being largely concerned with immigration status. Otherwise, as in the past, authorities could decide for themselves who qualified for (or was disqualified from) inclusion on their registers (Housing Act 1996, s. 161). The CoG encouraged them not to be too rigid in determining their qualification criteria; in short, they should not 'fetter their discretion' so as to expose their decisions to the possibility of a challenge by way of judicial review.

While exclusions from the housing register for 'offences' such as rent arrears or a history of anti-social behaviour appear to have become more common, the use of other eligibility criteria (involving residence in the district of the authority for a specified period, minimum age requirements, maximum income limits) has varied regionally, being more frequently found in London and the South of England than in the North (Mullins and Pawson, 2005: 219).

Section 167, which set out the 'reasonable preference' groups, placed greater emphasis on the socio-economic and welfare characteristics of prospective tenants than its predecessors had done but, until amended by regulations in 1997, made no reference to homeless applicants at all. Under Part VII of the Act, the most extensive duty owed to homeless households was reduced to providing temporary accommodation lasting a minimum of two years. Soon after coming to power, the Labour government used secondary legislation to restore certain homeless households as reasonable preference groups but, in future, allocations of long-term housing were to come from the register.

Allocations under Part VI, Housing Act 1996

General principles

Section 159 of the Housing Act 1996 sets the scene for the allocation of social housing, obliging local housing authorities to comply with the provisions of the Act in 'allocating housing accommodation'. An authority 'allocates' accommodation when (a) it selects someone to be a secure or introductory tenant of one of its dwellings, or (b) it nominates someone to be a secure or introductory tenant of another landlord (e.g. a housing action trust), or (c) it nominates someone to be an assured (including an assured shorthold) tenant of housing accommodation held by an RSL (s. 159(2)). The redefinition of 'allocation' by the 2002 Act to include a transfer which follows from an application made by a secure or introductory tenant (s. 159(5)) has brought many more people into the allocations process. The provisions of Part VI do not apply in cases of succession to introductory or secure tenancies on death, the mutual exchange of secure tenancies, or where introductory or secure tenancies are disposed of in consequence of orders made on relationship breakdown (s. 160).

The Homelessness Act 2002 amends Part VI of the Housing Act 1996, leaving in place the framework set up by the earlier statute. Certain of its provisions have their roots in the first legislation to control local authorities' activities in this area of housing practice. At the same time, however, the 2002 Act can also be seen as 'a radical attempt to shift the culture of public sector housing allocations, and particularly to alter the way in which authorities select their tenants' (Laurie, 2004: 48). It maintains the distinction drawn in the 1996 Act between those who are eligible and ineligible persons for housing but also gives local authorities the power to treat an applicant as ineligible because of 'unacceptable behaviour'. Thus, by s. 160A(7) of the 1996 Act, a local housing authority may decide that an applicant is to be treated as ineligible if it is satisfied that:

(a) the applicant, or a member of the applicant's household (clearly a wider term than 'members of the family') has been guilty of unacceptable behaviour serious enough to make him or her unsuitable to be a tenant of the authority; and

(b) in the circumstances at the time the application is considered, the applicant is unsuitable to be a tenant of the authority by reason of that behaviour.

An authority is not allowed to allocate a tenancy to a person who is ineligible, nor a joint tenancy to such a person with someone who is eligible (s. 160A(1)(c)). However, an allocation may still be made to an eligible person, even if a member of that person's household is ineligible. Where an authority decides that an applicant is ineligible, it must notify the applicant in writing of the decision and the grounds therefore (s. 160A(9) and (10)).

Unacceptable behaviour is defined as behaviour which, if the tenant were a secure tenant, would entitle the housing authority to a possession order under grounds 1 to 7 of the Housing Act 1985 (s. 160A(8)). Although these are 'fault' grounds (which include conduct likely to cause nuisance or annoyance), they are also discretionary grounds and the authority must therefore address the issue of reasonableness. A further consideration is whether the behaviour was such that a court would have awarded an outright possession order or would have used its powers to postpone possession. Arguably, in this regard, account should also be taken of the Human Rights Act 1998, Art. 8(1) of which provides everyone with 'the right to respect for ... his home'. It has been accepted in a number of cases that 'a legal threat to a secure home' will, in the ordinary way, engage Art. 8 (see, e.g. *Lambeth London Borough Council v Howard* [2001] EWCA Civ 46, para. 32). However, interference with the primary right will be justifiable by virtue of Art. 8(2) where it is 'in accordance with the law and ... necessary in a democratic society ... for the protection of the rights and freedoms of others'. Nonetheless, the interference must be proportionate to the aim pursued (*Handyside v United Kingdom* (1976) 1 EHRR 737) on the basis that 'however compelling the social goal, there are limits to how far the individual's interest can be legitimately sacrificed to achieve it' (*International Transport Roth GmbH v Secretary of State for the Home Department* [2002] 3 WLR 344, para. 29). It is possible therefore that an applicant who feels that past conduct is insufficiently serious to justify a decision of ineligibility or to deny preference may be able to mount a challenge on the ground that his or her Convention rights have been breached.

Allocation schemes

Housing authorities are required by s. 167 of the 1996 Act to have in place an allocation scheme for determining priorities between applicants, and for defining the procedures to be followed in allocating housing accommodation. An authority must not allocate housing accommodation except in accordance with its allocation scheme (s. 167(8)).

'Procedure' includes all aspects of the allocation process, including the people, or descriptions of people, by whom decisions are to be taken. The CoG states that the scheme must reflect 'all the housing authority's policies and procedures, including information on whether the decisions are taken by elected members or officers acting under delegated powers' (ODPM, 2002a: 5.1). The Cullingworth Committee recommended that the selection of individual tenants for council houses should in general be undertaken only by housing officers (CHAC, 1969) but in 1994, it was reported that in 19 out of 37 Welsh local authorities, councillors were involved in decisions about the allocation of properties, directly or in consultation with officers (Stirling, 1994: 12). While councillors can, of course, make a valuable contribution to the allocation process, their involvement carries the risk of discrimination and exploitation of the process for personal or political gain. In *R v Port Talbot Borough Council ex p Jones* [1988] 2 All ER 207, a councillor, who lived outside the ward she represented, applied for a council house. In the normal course of events, she would have been allocated a one- or two-bedroomed flat, but the chair of the housing tenancy committee pressurised the borough officer into offering her a tenancy of a three-bedroomed house in the ward. The court allowed the application by another councillor for judicial review because the decision to allocate the house to her had been made in breach of the council's published allocation rules (and not, therefore, in a lawful and authorised manner) and it was based on irrelevant considerations (that she would be in a better position to fight an election from the house). This type of situation is now subject to the Allocation of Housing (Procedure) Regulations 1997 which state that the decision-making body shall not include a councillor in whose electoral division or ward is situated (a) the housing accommodation in relation to which an allocation decision falls to be made, or (b) the sole or main residence of the person in relation to whom the decision falls to be made.

Although the idea of housing need may be said to have occupied 'a hegemonic position' within the housing profession, the word 'need' is nowhere to be found in the relevant legislation (Cowan and Marsh, 2004: 28). Cowan *et al.* label it as a 'neat but empty concept, which has enabled successive governments to pay lip service to a welfarist principle whilst ... providing [them] with [sufficient] latitude to ignore need whenever they deem [it] necessary' (Cowan *et al.*, 1999: 404). Different indicators of need have been expressed in terms of 'reasonable preference'. Section 167(2) provides that, in framing their allocation schemes, authorities must ensure that reasonable preference is given to:

(a) people who are homeless (within the meaning of Part VII of the 1996 Act);
(b) people owed a homelessness duty under ss. 190(2), 193(2) or 195(2) of the 1996 Act or are occupying accommodation secured by any housing authority under s. 192(3);
(c) people occupying insanitary or overcrowded housing or otherwise living in unsatisfactory housing conditions;
(d) people who need to move on medical or welfare grounds (including grounds relating to a disability);
(e) people who need to move to a particular locality in the district of the housing authority, where failure to meet that need would cause hardship (to themselves or to others).

A 'reasonable preference' involves giving applicants 'a reasonable head start' (*R v Wolverhampton Metropolitan Borough Council ex p Watters* (1997) 29 HLR 931) but it may be weighed against other factors which may diminish or even nullify the preference. It implies the power 'to choose between different applicants on "reasonable grounds" [and] it is not unreasonable to prefer good tenants to bad tenants' (*R v Newham London Borough Council ex p Miah* (1995) 28 HLR 279). It allows for a wide degree of discretion, and does not restrict authorities to taking into account only the factors listed in s. 167(2). An allocation scheme must be able to take into account multiple categories of need so as to reach a composite assessment of the applicant's needs. The categories of need made be cumulative and are not to be treated separately (*R v Islington London Borough Council ex p Reilly and Mannix* (1998) 31 HLR 651). It follows that an applicant who needs to move on medical grounds and is living in overcrowded accommodation should be given a higher priority than one who falls into only one of the reasonable preference categories.

Local authorities were previously obliged but, since the 2002 Act, are empowered to give 'additional preference' to particular descriptions of people who fall within the reasonable preference categories and who have urgent housing needs. This involves giving 'additional weight' or 'an extra head start' to those applicants to whom the additional preference is applied (*R (on the application of L) v London Borough of Lambeth* [2001] EWHC Admin 900, para. 62). Examples of such people could include (a) those owed a homelessness duty as a result of violence or threats of violence likely to be carried out and who as a result require urgent housing and (b) those who have to move because of urgent medical reasons (ODPM, 2002a: 5.18).

However, no preference need be given to applicants where either they or members of their household have been guilty of unacceptable behaviour (s. 167(2B) and (2C)). This is decided in the same way as for (in)eligibility and requires the authority to conclude not only that the applicant (or a member of the applicant's household) has been guilty of serious unacceptable behaviour but also that he does not deserve (by reason of his behaviour) to be treated as someone to whom preference should be given.

In order to determine priorities between applicants who fall within the reasonable and additional preference categories, allocation schemes may take into account any behaviour of a person (or of a member of the household) which affects suitability to be a tenant, as well as the financial resources available to the applicant to meet his or her housing costs, and any local connection which exists between a person and the authority's district (Housing Act 1996, s. 167(2A)). It has been said that 'at no time since the advent of social housing has more effort been put into dividing the anti-social from those who conform to the norm' and that the notion of the state as 'the citizens' provider of last resort no longer holds' (Cowan and Marsh, 2005: 40–1). It is true that the unacceptable behaviour provisions introduced by the 2002 Act may indeed have contributed to the exclusion and 'segregation' of 'the anti-social'. However, it should be remembered that local authorities have for some time used 'unacceptable behaviour' as a reason for restricting access to their housing and even in the early days of municipal housing, it was intended primarily to house the respectable working class. In *R v Wolverhampton Metropolitan Borough Council ex p Watters* (1997) 29 HLR 931, Mrs Watters, her husband and five children were evicted from their council house for non-payment of rent arrears. They moved into privately rented housing which, the council agreed, was statutorily overcrowded. This, together with the size of the family, and the fact that they were living in unsatisfactory housing conditions, brought them within three of the reasonable preference categories. Mrs Watters applied to be placed on the council housing list but her application was turned down because of the council's policy of not registering people with at least two weeks' rent arrears outstanding from previous council tenancies. There was a right of appeal where tenants had made substantial efforts to reduce the arrears, or they had a substantial social or medical need or if other exceptional circumstances existed. The Court of Appeal upheld the dismissal of Mrs Watters' application for judicial review on the ground that the requirement of a 'reasonable' preference (as opposed to an 'absolute' one) envisaged that other factors might weigh against, and so diminish and even nullify, the preference. In fixing the criteria for allocation, the council was entitled to balance the seriousness of the history of behaviour as a tenant, as against the severity of the circumstances identified in s. 167 which applied in the particular case. The weight given to each factor was a matter for the council to determine and the court would only rarely intervene. The council also had a duty to have regard to the financial consequences of its actions, and to balance its housing revenue account (*R v Newham London Borough council ex p Miah* (1995) 28 HLR 279). The existence of the right of appeal meant that it had not fettered its discretion.

The exclusion of 'anti-social' applicants may be regarded therefore as exemplifying Cowan *et al.*'s earlier thesis that risk, rather than need, has become a primary determinant in the selection for, and allocation of, social housing with selection processes designed to assess the risks posed by particular individuals both to the management of social housing and the safety of the community (Cowan *et al.*, 1999: 404).

Types of allocation scheme

As the supply of social housing in many parts of the country is often insufficient to satisfy demand, the need for housing has to be prioritised. The point on the spectrum at which the definition of need is drawn depends partly on the available resources but it also involves making value judgments. Reporting in 1969, the Cullingworth Committee expressed surprise that some housing authorities 'took up a moralistic attitude towards applicants: the underlying philosophy seemed to be that council tenancies were to be given only to those who "deserved" them and that the "most deserving" should get the best houses. Thus unmarried mothers, cohabitees, "dirty" families, and "transients" tended to be grouped together as "undesirable". Moral rectitude, social conformity, clean living and a "clean" rent book on occasion seemed to be essential qualifications for eligibility – at least for new houses' (CHAC, 1969: 96). Today, a less judgmental view is taken of some of those who would formerly have been regarded as 'undesirable' but the use of 'objective' allocation schemes has not prevented the segregation of, and discrimination against, certain types of household. There is, for example, a long and well documented history of racial discrimination in the allocation of council housing (see Hughes *et al.*, 1978–9; Henderson *et al.*, 1984) and there has also been a tendency to concentrate so-called 'problem families' in particular sections of the housing stock. Such a policy may exacerbate the difficulties of the families involved and the deterioration of the areas in which they are housed, while their arrival is resisted by 'existing residents, often struggling themselves with the consequences of local economic decline' (Cole and Furbey, 1994: 141). Among the recommendations which emerged from these discoveries 'was a stress on the need to minimise the scope for housing staff, elected councillors and housing association committees to exercise unaccountable discretion in the allocation process' (Pawson and Kintrea, 2002: 648). The consequence was 'an increasingly professionalised, detailed, rule-bound approach with strict limits on discretion by officials, and with councillors and committee members restricted to policy-making and monitoring rather than having any day-to-day operational involvement. Allocations systems seemingly have become ever more complex, designed to reflect the range of nuances of housing need, a trend made possible by ... computerisation [which] is now universal, except among the smallest housing associations' (ibid.).

Traditionally, there has been a wide variation between the allocation schemes employed by different authorities but they can generally be classified as falling within three models: 'date order', 'points' and 'group'. In the past, when there was generally less pressure on public housing, date order schemes (which operated on a 'first come, first served' basis) were popular. However, as the groups of people to whom a reasonable preference was to be given increased, the type of scheme most commonly used came to be some type of 'points' scheme. Here, applicants are awarded 'points' according to their housing needs and circumstances. Once applicants are registered, the higher the number of points they amass, the sooner they are rehoused. Points may be given for, e.g. overcrowding, having to share facilities (kitchen, lavatory, bathroom, hot running water) with another, unrelated household; badly situated facilities (a cooker on the landing, an outside lavatory or a bath or shower in the kitchen); living in temporary or insecure accommodation (with friends or relatives who have asked the applicant to leave, as a lodger sharing facilities with the landlord who has asked the applicant to leave; and medical problems. Additional points may be awarded to reflect time spent on the waiting list while living in particularly difficult housing conditions (e.g. in overcrowded or insanitary accommodation). The factors normally selected for 'pointing' have meant that families with children and the elderly have a much higher priority than single people of below retirement age, childless couples, or other adult households. It has been found, however, that prioritising applicants on the basis of need may contribute to problem estates with the rehousing of 'vulnerable households in relatively low demand neighbourhoods (see Brown and Yates, 2005: 345–6).

'Group' frameworks involve broad categories of applicants regarded as having similar degrees of priority, or a common access route (e.g. homelessness). Such an approach, particularly where within-group priority is ranked according to waiting time, have recently been advocated on the grounds of providing a relatively 'transparent' approach from an applicant's perspective. Many authorities have also used 'quota schemes', setting aside a quota of anticipated allocations for groups with particular characteristics. The 'apparent disappearance' of 'merit' systems (in which each application was treated on its own merits and officers or councillors made decisions based on their local knowledge) 'reflects the reduced involvement of elected council members in day-to-day local authority practice' although it seems that their 'direct involvement in lettings decisions ... have not been entirely eradicated' (Mullins and Pawson, 2005: 216).

Allocations and choice

The 1996 Act (as amended by the Homelessness Act 2002) provides that, so long as the duty concerning reasonable preference categories is fulfilled, a local authority's scheme may provide for the allocation of particular housing accommodation, first, to a person who makes a specific application for that accommodation; and, secondly, to persons of a particular description (whether or not they are within the reasonable preference categories) (Housing Act 1996, s. 167(2E)). The 2002 Act thus signals the government's apparent change of emphasis away from strictly needs-based allocations decisions and towards a system for bidding for properties in accordance with choice-based letting (CBL) and for local letting schemes. As Hunter points out, however, the changes read more obviously as 'a parliamentary belief that power to engage in choice-based lettings already exists' rather than as 'a source of power' (Hunter, 2003: 1). The Homelessness Act 2002 abolishes the duty to maintain a housing register (s.14(1)), and requires authorities to consider *all* applicants for re-housing (s. 166(3)). Before looking more closely at these new developments, however, it is useful to consider some of the problems encountered by the use of the traditional allocation schemes in the current housing climate.

In allocating their housing, local authorities have long had to contend with 'fewer houses to rent [in the private rented sector], an increasing dependence upon [social] housing, more single person and elderly households, [and] a decreasing supply of large family-type houses' (CHAC, 1969: 447). Recent years have witnessed a decline in rates of council house-building, the introduction of the right to buy for public sector tenants and the transfer of council housing stock to other bodies via, e.g. large-scale voluntary stock transfers. The most desirable homes have become absorbed into owner-occupation through the right to buy, and the fact that few new council houses have been built since 1980 means that a limited range of inferior and unpopular properties have been left for those who rent. As a result, many authorities have little or no housing stock to allocate and have to rely on nomination rights to housing associations or agreements with private sector landlords. Mullins and Pawson describe how, while the 'voice' of existing tenants was being increased through management reforms (e.g. 'increased opportunities for participation, performance indicators, reports to tenants and customer charters') and 'the right to buy was facilitating "exit" from social renting ... there was little real change for people seeking access to social housing'. Instead, they 'continued to experience bureaucratic rationing and only limited ability to express or exercise real choice'. Although most social landlords have allowed housing applicants to express housing preferences in general terms (e.g. with respect to the area or type of property they wish to live in), applicants have 'typically faced a limited number of offers of accommodation, made sequentially, thereby preventing comparison or choice' (Mullins and Pawson, 2005: 207). In 2000, for example, 75 per cent of London boroughs (compared with 1 per cent of authorities in the North of England) imposed a one-offer-only limit on non-homeless applicants (ibid.: 217). This 'take it or leave it' approach and the lack of any opportunity for comparison did not sit easily alongside New Labour's modernisation agenda (ibid.: 224).

Such 'coercive' practices (possibly a consequence of the growing focus on 'management efficiency') may be said to signify that 'to apply for social housing is to act as a supplicant for welfare, and therefore serve to deter potential applicants who see themselves primarily as consumers' (Pawson and Kintrea, 2002: 657). Further, the prioritisation of applicants on needs-based criteria – including the use of points-based approaches – combined with 'the expansion of alternative housing options' (such as the right to buy) has meant that new entrants to the sector come from a 'much narrower range of social groups than in earlier periods', with the rehousing of vulnerable households in relatively low demand neighbourhoods contributing to the creation and continuation of problem estates. A consequence of this narrower social base has been the tendency of some critics to regard social housing 'as part of a process of exclusion from rather than enjoyment of citizenship rights' (Mullins and Niner, 1998: 176). A series of initiatives which was were put in place in the 1990s in response to these concerns included the marketing of difficult-to-let properties on a first come first served basis, the establishment of common housing registers covering all the social housing landlords in an area, community lettings policies to help build sustainable neighbourhoods by allocating properties on criteria other than needs, and the promotion of cross-boundary moves through national mobility schemes. A more significant development has been the upsurge of interest in CBL which, by offering customers greater choice compared with traditional bureaucratic rationing approaches, represents 'a radical step change' (Brown and Yates, 2005: 334–6).

While demand for social housing outstrips supply in certain parts of the country (notably London and the South of England), there are other areas in which low demand and even abandonment place different demands upon the allocations process. In the former situation, bureaucratic allocation based on need may be an appropriate mechanism of rationing access and discriminating between households. However, in those areas in which there is a surplus of social housing, the operation of bureaucratic rationing has become increasingly untenable. Thus, while 'the top-down influence of legislation and regulation [has] become increasingly important over the past ten years in setting the framework within which policies are developed and implemented ... there has been a growing recognition that bottom-up factors – in particular, supply and demand in local housing markets – constrain landlords' ability to implement government policies' (Mullins and Pawson, 2005: 209).

Choice-based lettings

The lack of choice associated with conventional allocation models, together with problems of low demand in particular parts of the country and a desire to achieve sustainable communities, has prompted an interest in 'alternative' systems of housing allocations, all of which depart from the traditional model with its focus on allocating housing according to measured need. Two distinct, but related, approaches have emerged: CBL (which aims to introduce a consumerist ethic into allocations) and the use of 'community' or 'sensitive' lettings (which aim to expand neighbourhood social and/or demographic mix). Neither of them are new ideas (see Smith *et al.*, 2001: Chapter 3) but both (the latter under the heading of 'Local lettings policies') were flagged up in the 2000 Green Paper, with the government emphasising the importance of giving applicants a greater role in selecting their housing (DETR, 2000a: 9.5). Indeed, significant claims were made for the principle of choice, including an increased likelihood of longer-term commitment to the locality, with the consequence of more sustainable communities, increased personal well-being, and a reduction in anti-social behaviour, crime, stress and educational under-achievement (ibid.: 9.7). Criticisms were levelled at the way in which some local authorities had adopted 'complex points systems' for prioritising needs which were difficult to explain to applicants (ibid.: 9.8).

CBL, as adopted by growing numbers of British social landlords in recent years, was largely inspired by the so-called 'Delft model', initially developed in the Netherlands in the late 1980s, and subsequently adopted by most Dutch social landlords (see Kullberg, 2002). In Britain, Harborough District Council and its housing association partners developed the first district-wide scheme covering all the social rented housing in an area. It went 'live' in 2000. By 2005 more than a quarter of local authorities in England were operating CBL systems, with two-thirds of the remainder planning to do so (Pawson *et al.*, 2006: 7). In recognition of the fact that 'housing markets do not follow local authority boundaries', the government is keen that CBL should operate regionally or sub-regionally and has set aside funding to enable housing authorities to develop such schemes.

There is no clear definition of CBL and no formal statutory attempt has been made to clarify what it entails, most of the literature focusing – because of CBL's relative youth – on 'detailed processes and procedures' (Brown and Yates, 2005: 343). As a result, the detail of how a CBL scheme operates is largely left to individual authorities so that 'each scheme has set its own priorities based on the views of local stakeholders, and the nature of the local housing market' (ibid.: 344). The general idea however is that vacant properties are openly advertised (usually in a weekly newspaper but also, perhaps, on the internet or in other media). Instead of waiting for an offer to be made by a housing officer, applicants are expected to be active in bidding for properties in which they are interested and for which they are eligible.

The CoG urges authorities to adopt 'a simplified system of applicant prioritisation in place of a complex points-based approach' (ODPM, 2002a: 5.11). It suggests, first, the banding of applicants into a number of groups, each band consisting of applicants with broadly similar housing needs, priority depending on the length of time they have spent in that particular group, and secondly, giving priority over other applicants to those in the most urgent need (often by time limited 'priority cards') (ibid.). This type of scheme is intended to enhance applicants' choice by enabling them to balance their own 'felt' need – as measured by the time they felt able to wait – against the availability of the properties they might be able to secure. In practice, however, it has proved difficult to operate banding systems which reconcile choice and need in areas where there is a serious mismatch between supply and demand (see *R v Lambeth London Borough Council ex p A* [2002] EWCA Civ 1084; Cowan and Marsh, 2004) and CBL schemes will typically prioritise on a combined basis of needs (often measured by 'points') and waiting-time. Nonetheless, most organisations which have introduced CBL have experienced improved tenancy sustainment rates (as measured by the proportion of tenancies enduring for at least 12 months) and an increase in lettings to ethnic minority households outside existing areas of concentration. In addition, landlords appear to have developed their policies and practices so that formerly homeless households are less likely to be rehoused in low-demand areas than was previously the case and have developed strategies of giving targeted assistance to groups who are potentially disadvantaged by CBL's requirement of active participation. High set-up and operating costs are generally perceived as being off-set by non-quantifiable benefits such as improved customer satisfaction and freeing up front-line staff to concentrate more on core estate management functions such as organising repairs and managing rent arrears (Pawson *et al.*, 2006: 8.17).

Local lettings

The other type of system proposed by the government in the Green Paper is that of Local Lettings, a concept which builds upon existing practice in the form of 'community' and 'sensitive' lettings, both of which tend to be associated with difficult-to-let estates or areas. Where low demand for social housing is pronounced, the relationship between landlords and housing applicants changes fundamentally. The 'bureaucratic rationing philosophy' becomes irrelevant and 'the lettings process necessarily begins to involve a greater emphasis on marketing and negotiation' (Mullins and Pawson, 2005: 223). A common response is the alteration of allocations policies. The aim of community lettings is to engineer the social or demographic composition of particular areas by discouraging or preventing lettings to certain groups of people while encouraging lettings to others (Pawson and Kintrea, 2002: 662). Cowan and Marsh accuse such systems of involving 'the abandonment, or at the very least the suspension ... of the universalist notion of need' in order to achieve 'sustainable communities' (Cowan and Marsh, 2001: 272, 274). Allen and Sprigings take a similar line, arguing that New Labour's championing of community lettings demonstrates that the 'suspension of welfare principles' is now being 'promoted nationally as a matter of housing policy, rather than on an ad hoc basis by individual landlords' (Allen and Sprigings, 2001: 394). It should be remembered however that housing authorities can allocate accommodation to 'persons of a particular description' (whether or not they fall within the reasonable preference categories) only on condition that first they fulfil their duty concerning reasonable preference. The promotion of 'more cohesive and settled communities' has not therefore replaced 'the key objective of meeting housing need' but, for many social landlords, can rather be seen as a 'legitimate additional consideration' (Stirling and Smith, 2003: 147). The aim is to facilitate 'socio-economic balance in particular areas or on specified estates, achieving appropriate child densities or allowing households to move nearer to other relatives to provide or receive care, or to move closer to employment' (Griffiths *et al.*, 1996: 1). It means that, e.g. 'essential workers such as teachers, nurses and police officers' can be allocated accommodation within a reasonable travelling distance from their work in areas where high housing costs might otherwise price them out of the communities they serve. It could also be used to lower 'the child to adult ratio ... on an estate where there is high child density' or, conversely, to integrate 'young single people ... into an estate'.

Closely related to community lettings are 'sensitive' lettings. These occur where, for social reasons, there is an explicit departure from routine practice in the selection of tenants. Instead, housing officers use their discretion to match applicants to particular properties or areas. The concerns underpinning such an approach might include the need to house people in appropriate locations (e.g. older people or families with young children near to public transport links); the need to avoid, where possible, clashes of lifestyle (e.g. rehousing a former tenant with a record of playing loud music in a property known to have poor sound insulation); and the need to avoid over-concentration of a particular household type (e.g. families with young children) or housing need type (vulnerable people) in one area or estate. Again, a housing authority which seeks to implement such a system must first prioritise reasonable preference applicants. However, the way in which such a system operates not only runs the risk of 'heightening the social exclusion of some individuals' but it also runs counter to the prevailing ethos of minimising officer discretion so as to reduce possible discrimination (Pawson and Kintrea, 2002: 663).

Information

The requirement to provide certain information made its first appearance in the Housing Act 1980, as part of the Tenants' Charter, which imposed on authorities a duty to publish a summary of their allocations policies. The duty was expanded under the 1996 Act, which provided that anyone on the housing register was entitled to see his or her entry and to be given 'such general information' as would enable an assessment of how long it was likely to be before appropriate accommodation was allocated. The 2002 Act goes further than its predecessors, in making the provision of information central to the structure of the allocation scheme itself. It can be seen as a key aspect of the 'empowerment' aspect of the allocations process, helping applicants to make informed decisions and to exercise choice about their available housing options. In the words of the Green Paper, 'People should understand what housing is available and what their chances are of getting it'.

First, all authorities must make available, free of charge, advice and information about the right to make an application for housing (Housing Act 1996, s. 166(1)(a)). This duty extends to assisting applicants who are likely to experience difficulties in making their application (s. 166(1)(b)) although it is acknowledged that the level of assistance which will be required is related to whether the authority adopts an applicant-driven system (ODPM, 2002a: 6.9).

Secondly, authorities must publish summaries of their allocation schemes and supply a copy free of charge to any member of the public who asks for one (Housing Act 1996, s. 168(1)). When they make an alteration to their scheme reflecting a major change of policy, they are obliged within a reasonable period of time take such steps as they consider reasonable to bring the effect of the alteration to the attention of those likely to be affected by it (s. 168(3)).

Thirdly, allocation schemes must include the rights of applicants to request such general information as will enable them to assess how their application is likely to be treated under the scheme. This must include that he is likely to be a member of a group to which preference is given (s. 167(4A)). The information must be sufficient to assess whether accommodation appropriate to his needs is likely to be made available and, if so, how long it is likely to be before it actually becomes available. It must give applicants an opportunity to request information regarding the facts of their case (e.g. their previous behaviour) which is likely to be, or has been, taken into account in considering whether to allocation housing accommodation to them (s. 167(4A)(b)).

By s. 166(2) all applicants must be informed of the right:

(a) to request information about their application and about any decisions made in relation to them; and
(b) to seek an internal review.

Challenging the authority's decision

Cowan and Halliday point out that the past 50 years have witnessed a trend towards informal mechanisms – in the shape of tribunals, ombudsmen and the use of conciliation and arbitration in the civil court system – for seeking redress in the event of a grievance. The right to a review in relation to all allocations decisions (which bears a passing resemblance to the review machinery which can be utilised as regards homelessness decisions by local authorities) was introduced by the 2002 Act. However, there are 'strong grounds for doubting whether ... the existence of internal review' should be regarded as part of this trend. Instead of being 'a planned feature of a coherent system of administrative justice', it can perhaps be more realistically regarded as 'a preliminary disputing stage, internal to an organisation, which mimics external review' (Cowan and Halliday, 2003: 22).

The right to a review does not extend to all allocations decisions. Applicants have the right to a review where the authority has decided that they are ineligible because of unacceptable behaviour or has decided that applicants are ineligible for housing either because of their unacceptable behaviour or because they are subject to immigration control (Housing Act 1996, s. 160(3) and (5)). They can also seek a review of the facts of their case on which the authority is basing its (non-) allocation decision. However, because the powers of authorities in this context are those of general management and create no rights for individuals (*R v London Borough of Newham ex p Dawson* (1994) 26 HLR 747), there is no duty to give reasons for a decision on reasonable preference.

If a review is sought, the applicant has the right to be informed of the review decision and the grounds there for (s. 167(4A)(d)). In contrast to the homelessness provisions, there is no statutory right of appeal to a county court and it is arguable therefore that a human rights challenge might be mounted, given that Art. 6 ECHR provides that 'in the determination of his civil rights ... everyone is entitled to a fair and public hearing within a reasonable time by an independent and impartial tribunal established by law'.

The courts are reluctant to intervene in allocation decisions by way of judicial review but will do so if an authority is operating a blanket policy which fetters discretion and is *Wednesbury* unreasonable. *In R v Canterbury City Council ex p Gillespie* (1987) 19 HLR 7, the applicant and her partner were joint secure tenants of a council house. When their relationship broke down, she moved to accommodation which was both 'overcrowded' and gave rise to 'unsatisfactory housing conditions' within what is now s. 167(2). However, the local authority for the area to which she had moved (the 'first' authority) refused her application to join the waiting list unless she relinquished the secure tenancy. Her landlord authority would not allow her to do so, however, because there were rent arrears outstanding. The first authority later admitted her to the waiting list but refused to consider her for allocation of accommodation, again because of its stated policy of debarring those who held secure tenancies elsewhere. Its decision was quashed because it constituted 'a rule which was required to be followed slavishly rather than merely a stated general approach which is always subject to an exceptional case and which permits each application to be individually considered'.

The existence of a procedure for dealing with special cases on an exceptional basis enables authorities to reach what often appear to be very harsh decisions. In *R v Bristol City Council ex p Johns* (1993) 25 HLR 249, the applicant and her husband were the outright owners of a two-bedroomed, two-storey terraced house. The applicant, who was suffering from osteoarthritis, applied unsuccessfully to Bristol City Council for housing. Three years later, she was diagnosed as suffering from multiple sclerosis which progressed to the extent that she was effectively confined to a wheel-chair. Bristol changed its allocation policy to the effect that owner-occupiers could not be considered for rehousing under their points scheme unless they were in 'severe difficulties'. An occupational therapist from Avon County Council reported that the applicant was 'housebound and socially isolated' which, together with the unsuitability of the property in which she was liv-ing, had resulted in her becoming very depressed. She reapplied unsuccess-fully for rehousing and was told that, as an owner-occupier, she could not be considered for rehousing under the points scheme. Her application for judi-cial review was based on the argument that the authority had fettered its dis-cretion by having this blanket policy. The court dismissed the application because the authority retained some discretion despite the exclusion from the points system of owner-occupiers other than those in severe difficulties.

Registered social landlords

The allocations and lettings practices of housing associations have assumed a new significance given the increasing proportion of the housing stock which they own and manage. Most RSLs maintain their own housing reg-isters (although common housing registers have been established in some areas) to which local authorities have nomination rights, often for 50 per cent or more of true vacancies. Yet, while housing associations are required to work with local authorities to enable the latter to fulfil their obligations to the homeless and those in priority need (Housing Act 1996, s. 213), they are not governed directly by the 1996 or 2002 Acts. Instead, the Corporation's Regulatory Code states that RSLs should seek to offer a choice of home, while giving reasonable preference to those in priority housing need, and using lettings policies which are fair and reflect the diversity of their client groups (HC, 2005: 3.5.1, 5.5.5). Growing numbers of housing associations are becoming involved with CBLs and by the end of 2005, 77 associations in England were letting most of their vacant properties through CBL (Pawson *et al.*, 2006: 7). Often, however, housing association involvement is limited to vacancies earmarked for local authority nominees under exist-ing nomination arrangements, the remainder being filled by the traditional model of housing officers (rather than applicants themselves) matching peo-ple to properties (ibid.). Indeed, although no published empirical evidence is available to support it, there is anecdotal evidence that 'housing associations, despite their new role in providing housing for the poorest as a result of the transfer of local authority housing, continue to select tenants in ways that leave the most disadvantaged with worse choices' (6, 2003: 255). This may be in part because the financial risks to which they are exposed means that the allocations process provides them with an opportunity 'to weed out bad payers', e.g. anyone with a history of rent arrears (Cowan *et al.*, 1999: 411). In cases where local authorities have transferred their entire stock to an RSL, 'complaints have been made that some such RSLs have refused to accept nominations of homeless applicants either on grounds of their conduct or because the RSL considers them to be unsuitable for mainstream accommodation', leaving such applicants in a legal no-man's-land between the local housing authority and the RSL (Latham, 2005: 18). As Latham argues, 'If there is to be equality of access to social housing, local housing authorities should develop common allocation schemes with the RSLs which have housing within their districts' (ibid.).

Conclusion

From the consumer-choice perspective, 'the empowerment of home-seekers inherent in the CBL approach arguably represents a decisive break with the paternalist tradition'. Indeed, at first sight it appears to represent a major reconfiguration of the way in which social housing is allocated (Cowan and Marsh, 2005: 44). However, it is important to scrutinise more closely the 'new' statutory framework. The aim of introducing choice into the process of allocations is to place applicants, as far as is possible, on the same footing as purchasers or renters of private housing. Potential occupiers can 'choose housing in the same way as those looking for housing in the private sector, reducing their sense of dependency and social exclusion' (DETR, 2000a: 9.2). CBL can be seen therefore as 'an attempt to create a "social market" ... enabling housing applicants to weigh up different housing options available to them, and [encouraging] a greater sense of ownership of lettings decisions by tenants as consumers' (Mullins and Pawson, 2005: 209). Yet it is clear that 'while CBL systems involve a much expanded consumer role, they are *managed* rather than *free* markets. Applicant priority remains dependent on administratively defined criteria [rather than] ability to pay' (ibid.: 218). The degree of choice offered to applicants is limited by the retention of the statutory duty to give reasonable preference to certain categories of applicant. Housing need therefore remains 'the priority for lettings and transfers policies' (DETR, 2000a: 9.16). Housing officers still act as bureaucratic gatekeepers in determining eligibility and the priority of applicants on the basis of assessed need, and in this regard they may well want to restrict access in cases where there are risks of anti-social behaviour or rent arrears.

Considering the allocations provisions in the 2002 Act from the viewpoint of the central-local government relationship, Laurie suggests that there does indeed appear to be 'a shift towards a more consensual approach with greater emphasis being placed (again) on local government's right to exercise considerable autonomy' (Laurie, 2004: 64). Notable by their absence, she says, are 'the numerous and broad regulation-making powers that were such a prominent feature of the 1996 Act'. Further, given that 'the relevant provisions are predominantly expressed as powers, rather than [as] duties, with a concomitant impact on local authorities' discretion', there is 'considerable latitude within the legislation to develop and implement ... local responses' (ibid.). Finally, she says, the government's policies can in certain respects be seen to build on housing practice dating back to the 1990s, suggesting that they may have emanated at least in part from local government.

A local housing authority is free to decide the structure of its allocations scheme (i.e. whether it is points-based, date-order, etc.), what indicators to use, and what weighting to give to the reasonable preference categories (s.167(6)). However, by s. 167(1A) an authority's allocations scheme must include a statement of the authority's policy on offering eligible applicants a choice of accommodation or the opportunity to express preferences about the accommodation offered to them. While this provision does not explicitly require authorities to offer choice, it is intended to 'to have a motivating or hortatory effect' (Laurie, 2004: 60). More significantly perhaps, the targets have been set for the number of authorities to have choice-based lettings schemes in operation by certain dates. By 2005, 25 per cent of local authorities should have a CBL scheme and this should reach 100 per cent by 2010 (ODPM, 2002b: 1.1). Thus, while the 2002 Act ostensibly leaves local authorities a free hand to achieve the 'right' balance between choice and need and, as such, to respect local autonomy, the targets 'appear to run counter to [its] generally permissive nature' and it may be that 'in practice authorities will have little choice but to incorporate the Government's preferred consumerist principles in their housing allocations policies' (Laurie, 2004: 60, 66).

The amount of discretion which remains vested in local authorities, together with the absence of any precise definition of CBLs or of any 'directive regulation' as to the form CBL schemes should take, suggest that 'practice may be as diverse in the new world as in the old' (Mullins and Pawson, 2005: 226).

Chapter 18

Introductory, secure and assured tenancies

Introduction

This chapter sets out to explore the different types of tenancies to which occupiers of social housing may be subject and the security of tenure which they enjoy as a result of legislative intervention. Their further rights are discussed in Chapter 19 and recovery of possession for reasons connected with anti-social behaviour is dealt with in Chapter 20. The final part of this chapter looks at the curious concept of the tolerated trespasser.

The Increase of Rent and Mortgage Interest (Restrictions) Act 1920 conferred security of tenure on local authority tenants whose housing was constructed before 1919, but most local authority housing was removed from regulation in 1939. It was thought 'safe and proper' to give local authority landlords a complete discretion with regard to the eviction of their tenants, and to rely on them to exercise such discretion fairly and wisely (*Harrison v Hammersmith & Fulham London Borough Council* [1981] 1 WLR 650). It was not until the Housing Act 1980 that local authority tenants were given 'the same kind of protection from being evicted from their homes without good and sufficient cause' as had been enjoyed by private sector Rent Act tenants for many decades (ibid.). Until then, their rights were dictated by the common law and the terms of their tenancy agreements. In truth, however, tenancy agreements simply reflected the imbalance of power between council tenants and their landlords; they contained few undertakings by landlords, offered limited rights to tenants and usually amounted to little more than a list of tenants' obligations (Cole and Furbey, 1994: 39). The absence of statutory security of tenure meant that possession actions were effectively incapable of being defended and only featured in law reports where landlords had allegedly abused their discretion (Hughes, 2000: 168). Even then, the courts were disinclined to accept any notion that tenants had property rights which merited protection, preferring instead to regard evictions 'as examples of the exercise of power by public authorities in the public interest which should if possible be supported against challenge' (McAuslan, 1980: 190). Thus, in *Shelley v London County Council* [1948] 2 All ER 898, the tenant was served with notice of eviction even though no evidence was offered of any breach of the tenancy agreement. The House of Lords, however, declined to intervene on the basis that housing authorities could 'pick and choose their tenants at will' and could similarly 'oust' them after 'due notice'. Judicial reluctance to interfere with councils' decisions with regard to public housing persisted through the 1960s and into the 1970s, Lawton LJ stating in *Cannock Chase District Council v Kelly* [1978] 1 WLR 1 that 'the duty to assess need and to allocate resources may necessitate notices to quit being given to persons who have paid their rent and complied with the terms of their tenancies'. The Court of Appeal held that the local authority was not required to particularise its deliberations in the exercise of its statutory powers and an inference of error could only be made if the decision was so unreasonable that no reasonable authority could have come to it. Authorities should 'stay within the limits of fair dealing' but this did not generally require them to give reasons for their decision to evict a tenant or 'to do anything in the nature of holding a formal inquiry ... into the question of who was right and who was wrong' (*Sevenoaks District Council v Emmott* (1980) 39 P & CR 404, 412). The non-interventionist approach adopted by both Parliament and the courts towards the administration of public housing was characteristic of central-local government relations between 1945 and 1975, with councils being expected to '*govern* their local areas, rather than simply administer centrally defined services on an agency basis' (Loveland, 1992: 344).

By the late 1970s, there was a growing feeling that long-established tenants were being exploited by local authorities (Jacobs *et al.*, 2003: 314–15). Statutory intervention was seen as necessary not only to compel authorities to meet their obligations but also to improve the public image of tenants and the regard in which their landlords held them (Stewart, 1996: 154). Local authority autonomy was necessarily curtailed by the introduction in 1980 of a number of legally enforceable rights, including security of tenure and the right to buy, collectively referred to as the Tenants' Charter. They were consolidated into Part IV of the Housing Act 1985 and further amended by the Housing and Planning Act 1986 and the Housing Acts of 1988 and 1996.

It has been suggested that even today the emphasis placed by tenancy agreements on tenants' duties and responsibilities and the 'absence of substantive discussion' (*sic*) of tenants' rights or landlords' duties reflects 'the imbalance of power relations' between the parties. This 'imposition of a moral framework in the tenancy agreement' (which is not replicated in other tenures) is said to be at odds with the desire to 'empower' tenants which characterised the Tenants' Charter and lay behind initiatives such as Tenants' Choice introduced by the Housing Act 1988 (Haworth and Manzi, 1999: 159–60). Certainly, social landlords are increasingly using tenancy agreements to make tenants aware of their responsibilities and the possible consequences of anti-social behaviour. Regardless of the tone they adopt in their tenancy agreements, the behaviour of local authority landlords is subject to statutory constraints.

Nonetheless, even though their decisions may be subject to judicial review, the courts may still be reluctant to question them.

Until the Housing Act 1988 came into force, the Housing Corporation, charitable housing trusts and housing associations could all grant secure tenancies. This means that tenancies granted by such bodies before 15 January 1989 will be secure tenancies under the Housing Act 1985, while those granted after 15 January 1989 will be assured tenancies under the 1988 Act. If the landlord's interest is transferred to a landlord who is not listed as satisfying the landlord condition of s. 80, the tenancy is no longer secure. Thus, when a local authority transfers its stock to a registered social landlord (RSL), the tenants whose homes have been transferred cease to be secure tenants and become assured tenants (Housing Act 1988, s. 38) although they retain the 'preserved right to buy' (Housing Act 1985, s. 171A–H). In practice, as part of the transfer process, existing rights are normally preserved by their inclusion in the new tenancy agreement.

Introductory tenancies

Local authorities and housing action trusts (see Chapter 16) may elect to operate an introductory tenancy regime under which all new periodic tenants and licensees are granted introductory tenancies rather than secure tenancies (Housing Act 1996, s. 124). By April 2003, some 119 local authorities – half of those still owning housing stock – had chosen to do so.

Part V of the 1996 Act – in which the introductory tenancy appears – is entitled 'Conduct of Tenants'. The 1995 White Paper described the scheme as one for 'tenancies on a probationary basis' to allow landlords at any time during the probationary period to be able to terminate the tenancies of 'the minority of tenants who do not behave responsibly' (DoE, 1995: 44). It remains unclear whether they can be brought to an end for other reasons, e.g. a change in the landlord's allocation policy, or under-occupation.

In contrast to households in other tenures who are not required to earn their security, the introductory tenancy involves the withholding of a secure tenancy until such time as the tenant has shown himself to be 'deserving' of a settled home (Haworth and Manzi, 1999: 161). On the one hand, this distinctive treatment may be said to reinforce images of a 'marginalised underclass' in social housing which facilitates the use of 'punitive solutions' (ibid.). Another view is that introductory tenancies can help to build sustainable communities, the existence of which depends on tenants feeling confident that compliance with their tenancy agreements will enable them to 'keep their long-term family homes' (Law Commission, 2002a: 1.21, 1.22).

An introductory tenancy lasts for a trial period of one year beginning with the date the tenancy is entered into or, if later, the date when the tenant is first entitled to possession (s. 125(2)). The introductory period may be extended for a further six months beyond the trial period (s. 125(2A)). The landlord must first serve a notice of extension on the tenant at least eight weeks before the original expiry date and either the tenant must have not requested a review or, if a review has been requested, its outcome must be to confirm the decision to extend. The notice must state that the decision has been made to extend the period, set out the reasons for this decision and the time within which the request for a review must be made. The request for a review must be made within 14 days (s. 125B(1)) and the landlord must complete it and notify the tenant before the original expiry date.

At the end of the trial period, the tenancy automatically becomes a secure tenancy unless the landlord has already begun possession proceedings and obtains possession either during or after the first year of the tenancy. By s. 125(5), a tenancy ceases to be an introductory tenancy if, before the end of the trial period:

(a) the circumstances are such that the tenancy would not otherwise be a secure tenancy (e.g. the tenant ceases to occupy the dwelling-house as his or her only or principal home); or
(b) a person or body other than a local housing authority or Housing Action Trust becomes the landlord; or
(c) there is no one qualified to succeed on the tenant's death.

A court order is necessary if the landlord wishes to bring an introductory tenancy to an end during the trial period (s. 127(1)). No ground(s) for possession need be proved but the court cannot entertain proceedings for possession unless the landlord has served a notice which:

(a) sets out the landlord's reasons for seeking possession (s. 128(3));
(b) specifies a date for the beginning of proceedings, which must be no earlier than that of a common law notice to quit (s. 128(4)); and
(c) informs the tenant or licensee of the right given by s. 129 to seek a review and thereby challenge the reasons given by a landlord for its decision.

In *Manchester City Council v Cochrane* [1999] 1 WLR 809, the Court of Appeal held that an introductory tenancy only conferred a right to possession until such time as the court made an order for possession and, once the notice requirements of s. 128 had been met, the court was obliged, by virtue of s. 127(2), to make such an order. The county court could not entertain a defence based on a denial of the allegations contained in the s. 128 notice but it could grant an adjournment to allow the tenant to apply for judicial review of the council's conduct of the review. From a human rights perspective, the Court of Appeal held in *R (on the application of McLellan) v Bracknell Forest Borough Council* [2002] QB 1129 that the existence of the statutorily determined internal review process before an application to the county court for a possession order, coupled with judicial review while proceedings in the county court were adjourned, entailed compliance with Arts 6 and 8 of the Human Rights Act 1998.[1]

Not surprisingly, introductory tenancies have a number of features in common with secure tenancies, including a right of succession on the death of the original tenant subject to conditions similar to those which apply to secure tenancies (ss. 131–134), and rights under the secure tenants' repair scheme (s. 135). By s. 134, an introductory tenancy cannot be expressly assigned except:

(a) by court order in cases of relationship breakdown; or
(b) to a person who would be qualified to succeed if the tenant died immediately before the assignment.

Introductory tenancies have never been available to RSLs but in 1998 the Housing Corporation gave them permission to create 'starter' tenancies where this was 'compatible with the purpose of the housing and the sustainability of the community'. Starter tenancies operate as assured shorthold tenancies. They can be used to provide the same probationary period as introductory tenancies and can be ended without proof of a ground for possession using s. 21 of the Housing Act 1988 (see Chapter 14).

Secure tenancies

Definition

A secure tenancy is 'a tenancy under which a dwelling-house is let as a separate dwelling ... at any time when the conditions described in ss. 80 and 81 as the landlord condition and the tenant condition are satisfied' (Housing Act 1985, s. 79). A landlord will satisfy the landlord condition if it belongs to the list of bodies set out in s. 80(1), i.e. it is a local authority, a new town corporation, a housing action trust, an urban development corporation, the Development Board for Rural Wales, or a housing co-operative. By s. 81, the tenant condition is satisfied where (a) the tenant is an individual and occupies the dwelling-house as his or her only or principal home; or (b) where the tenancy is a joint tenancy, each of the joint tenants is an individual and at least one of them occupies the dwelling-house as his or her only or principal home.

The requirement of occupation as the tenant's only or principal home has already been considered in Chapter 12 in relation to the Housing Act 1988. So far as the 1985 Act is concerned, a secure tenancy is conferred *at any time* 'the tenancy condition' is satisfied. Section 81 has therefore an 'ambulatory effect', allowing for the tenant to move in and out of protection. Thus in *Hussey v Camden London Borough Council* (1995) 27 HLR 5, the tenant

---

1   For a discussion of the decision in *R (on the application of McLellan) v Bracknell Forest Borough Council* [2002] QB 1129, see Laurie (2002).

had moved out of the flat in question but had resumed occupation by the date the notice to quit expired and was held therefore to have regained security.

Like the Rent Act 1977 and the Housing Act 1988, there must be 'a tenancy' of 'a dwelling-house' which is 'let as a separate dwelling' (see Chapter 12). However, in contrast to the 1977 and 1988 Acts, the 1985 Act confers secure status upon certain licensees (see below) and contains no equivalent provision to s. 22 of the 1977 Act or s. 3 of the 1988 Act where the dwelling-house is not 'let as a separate dwelling'. Thus, an occupier who shares essential living accommodation cannot be a secure tenant. In *Central YMCA Housing Association Ltd v Saunders* (1991) 23 HLR 212, the Court of Appeal held that a room (with a small bathroom attached) in a hostel was not a separate dwelling. The occupants, who had access to a communal kitchen, were expressly forbidden to cook in their rooms (although Mr Saunders did confess to boiling eggs in his electric kettle!).

Licences

Section 79(3) of the Housing Act 1985 states that 'the provisions of this Part apply in relation to a licence to occupy a dwelling-house (whether or not granted for a consideration) as they apply in relation to a tenancy'. However, not all residential licences fall within the statutory regime but even where they do, advantage cannot be taken of the right to buy provisions. There will be no security where:

(a) the licence is granted as a temporary expedient to a person who entered the dwelling-house as a trespasser (s. 79(4)). This concerns former squatters who may have been granted short-life licences of the properties in which they squatted, or of other properties destined for improvement, conversion or redevelopment; or

(b) there is no exclusive possession of the premises. The inclusion of licences was originally enacted in the Housing Act 1980, at a time when some private landlords were dressing up tenancies as licences to avoid the Rent Acts. In *Westminster City Council v Clarke* [1992] 2 AC 288, Mr Clarke was given temporary accommodation in a hostel for single homeless men. A resident warden was present during the daytime to supervise the hostel and, if necessary, to assist the occupants (some of whom had personality disorders or physical disabilities). Mr Clarke's 'licence to occupy' gave him no right to exclusive occupation of any particular room and it contained a 'mobility clause' which allowed the council to change the allotted accommodation and to require him to share accommodation with any other person. His self-contained bed-sitting room had its own lockable door to which both Mr Clarke and the warden had a key. Occupants had to be in their rooms by 11 p.m., by which time any visitors had to have left. Because of Mr Clarke's unacceptable behaviour, the council gave him notice, maintaining that he had a mere licence which could be revoked at any time. Mr Clarke contended that he was a tenant. The House of Lords confirmed that s. 79(3) applied only to those licences which granted a right of exclusive possession of a dwelling-house. (To hold otherwise would make it difficult for bodies which were responsible for housing the homeless, to enter into any arrangement which allowed a person to enjoy exclusive occupation of premises, however temporarily, without conferring security of tenure.) In deciding that Mr Clarke was not a tenant, their Lordships took into account the authority's need to retain total control over all rooms in the hostel in order to discharge its homelessness duties, the considerable limitations on the occupier's enjoyment of any room allotted to him, the need to obtain approval before guests could be entertained, and to comply with instructions from resident staff. Lord Templeman pointed out that these provisions were not inserted in the licence to avoid the creation of a secure tenancy, but to enable the council to discharge its responsibilities to the vulnerable people accommodated at the hostel.

Exclusions from secure status under the Housing Act 1985

Schedule 1 to the Housing Act 1985 lists the tenancies which cannot be secure. Not surprisingly these number introductory tenancies (Sch. 1, para. 1A) including those which cease to be introductory because there is no one qualified to succeed or because the residence requirement is no longer fulfilled. Other tenancies which are excluded because they may attract security under other codes include long leases (Sch. 1, para. 1) (i.e. those granted for a term certain exceeding 21 years whether or not determinable before the end of the term by a tenant's notice or by forfeiture), on-licensed premises such as public houses (Sch. 1, para. 9), business tenancies within Part II of the Landlord and Tenant Act 1954 (Sch. 1, para. 11) and agricultural holdings (Sch. 1, para. 8).

Also excluded are premises occupied in connection with employment (Sch. 1, para. 2) where the landlord employs the tenant and the contract of employment requires occupation of the dwelling-house for the better performance of the tenant's duties. Even if the contract of employment did not originally require such occupation, it may subsequently be varied so as to bring the tenant within the exclusion. Such a situation arose in *Elvidge v Coventry City Council* [1993] 4 All ER 903 where, on the tenant's promotion from water bailiff to assistant ranger of a countryside park, his conditions of employment were altered so as to require him to live in the cottage he was already occupying. In *South Glamorgan County Council v Griffiths* (1992) 24 HLR 334, a retired school caretaker was held not to be, and never to have been, a secure tenant, as he was *impliedly* required to live in a house adjacent to the school for the better performance of his duties. His 'insecure' status remained, notwithstanding his recent retirement. However, in *Hughes v*

Greenwich London Borough Council [1993] 4 All ER 577, the House of Lords was not prepared to imply a term into a headmaster's contract of employment to the effect that he was required to occupy a house in the school grounds for the better performance of his duties. He was therefore a secure tenant with the right to buy. In *Greenfield v Berkshire County Council* (1996) 28 HLR 691, a former school caretaker who had been made redundant was allowed to remain in tied accommodation until a house provided with his new job became available. It was held that his continued occupation was not referable to his former employment but to a decision by the council to let him stay there. He had therefore obtained a secure tenancy even though his tenancy was not secure at its commencement. A dwelling-house which has been let on a tenancy within this exclusion may be kept out of security for a period or periods not exceeding three years even if it is re-let to a non-employee provided that written notice is served on the tenant not later than the grant (Sch. 1, para. 2(4)).

A further category of excluded tenancies involves temporary arrangements, including land required for development which in the meantime is being used by the landlord as temporary housing accommodation (Sch. 1, para. 3). The landlord need not be the body which acquired the land for development and in *Hyde Housing Association v Harrison* (1990) 23 HLR 57, the exclusion was held to apply where a housing association had granted a temporary weekly licence to occupy a flat on land which the Department of Transport had acquired for a road-widening scheme. An authority may change the nature of the development envisaged without losing the protection of the exception (*Attley v Cherwell District Council* (1989) 21 HLR 613) but where permission for development has been refused and no development is subsequently pending, it will not apply (*Lillieshall Road Housing Co-operative Ltd v Brennan & Brennan* (1992) 24 HLR 195). Similarly, a tenancy granted in pursuance of any duty discharged under Part VII of the Housing Act 1996 to secure accommodation for homeless persons is not secure unless the local housing authority has notified the tenant to the contrary (Sch. 1, para. 4). People accommodated as homeless will remain insecure, therefore, unless and until the authority decides otherwise. Notification that the tenancy will be secure amounts to an allocation under Part VI of the Housing Act 1996. This exemption also applies to temporary lettings by a housing association discharging the authority's duty by arrangement (*Family Housing Association v Miah* (1982) 5 HLR 94). Short-term arrangements, i.e. where the dwelling-house has been leased to the landlord with vacant possession for use as temporary housing accommodation are also excluded (Sch. 1, para. 6). The terms on which the property has been leased must provide for the head landlord (which is not a body capable of granting secure tenancies) to obtain vacant possession from the landlord on the expiry of a specified period or when required, e.g. pursuant to a break clause in the lease, and the landlord's only interest in the dwelling-house must be under the lease in question or as a mortgagee. Despite the use of the word 'leased', this exception includes the situation in which the owner of a house makes it available to the local authority under a licence agreement (*Tower Hamlets London Borough Council v Miah* (1992) 24 HLR 199). This exception for temporary accommodation made available to the tenant or to a predecessor in title (who is not a secure tenant) while works are carried to his or her principal home (Sch. 1, para. 7) will come into play where, for example, the tenant's home is subject to compulsory improvement works. The final type of arrangement which comes within this category relates to temporary accommodation for persons taking up employment (Sch. 1, para. 5). Four conditions must be satisfied. First, the tenancy must be granted to a person who, immediately before the grant, did not live in the local housing authority's district; secondly, prior to the grant of the tenancy, the tenant obtained employment, or an offer thereof, in the district or in its surrounding area; thirdly, the tenancy was granted to meet the tenant's need for temporary accommodation in the district or its surrounding area in order to work, and to enable the tenant to find permanent accommodation there; and, fourthly, the landlord notified the tenant in writing of the circumstances in which this exception applies. Student lettings (Sch. 1, para. 10), almshouses (Sch. 1, para. 12) and tenancies at will (*Banjo v Brent London Borough Council* [2005] EWCA Civ 292) are also excluded.

Secure and assured tenancies: termination by the tenant

The Housing Acts of 1985 and 1988 restrict only the landlord's rights to end a tenancy. The tenant can still, at any time, terminate a periodic tenancy by notice to quit (provided that the tenant complies with the Protection from Eviction Act 1977) and can end a fixed-term tenancy by surrender or other action, such as the exercise of a break clause.

Abandonment of the premises is a problem commonly encountered by social landlords, with tenants simply vacating the premises without notifying their landlords (either in the manner provided for by the tenancy agreement or at all), that they intend to do so. Essentially, from a legal viewpoint, abandonment can be regarded as an offer by the tenant to terminate the lease or tenancy prematurely. English law affords the landlord two possible responses. First, it may treat the term as still subsisting and sue for the instalments of rent as they fall due. Alternatively, it may accept the tenant's offer so that the lease is surrendered. Surrender is discussed in Chapter 14.

Secure and assured tenancies: termination by the landlord

Fixed-term tenancies

Possession during the currency of a fixed-term tenancy, secure or assured, can only be sought if the terms of the tenancy provide for it to be brought to an end prematurely by a right of re-entry by way of forfeiture, determination by notice or otherwise. (A landlord will nearly always reserve a right of re-entry for the tenant's breach of covenant.) An assured tenancy can be terminated during the currency of its fixed term only on grounds 2, 8 or 10–15 (Housing Act 1988, s. 7(6)). Both statutes require the landlord to apply to the court for an order terminating the tenancy (Housing Act 1985, s. 82(3); Housing Act 1988, s. 5(1)). This will necessitate compliance with the notice procedure unless the court considers it 'just and equitable' to dispense with it.

The other principal mechanism for bringing a fixed-term tenancy to an end before its expiry date is a break clause. Break clauses entitle the landlord (or the tenant) to terminate the tenancy by notice at specific intervals during the term. Operation of the break clause by the tenant will be effective to terminate the tenancy. Operation by the landlord, however, results in the fixed-term tenancy ending on the date specified in the landlord's notice and the creation of a statutory periodic tenancy (see below).

Statutory periodic tenancies

When a fixed-term secure or assured tenancy comes to an end other than by order of the court or by a surrender or other action on the part of the tenant, a statutory periodic tenancy automatically arises (Housing Act 1985, s. 86(1); Housing Act 1988, s. 5(2)) unless the landlord grants the tenant a further fixed-term or periodic tenancy of the same dwelling-house to begin on the termination of the original tenancy. The terms of the statutory periodic tenancy are the same as those of the tenancy which immediately preceded it, in so far as they are compatible with a periodic tenancy and make no provision for re-entry or forfeiture (Housing Act 1985, s. 86(2); Housing Act 1988, s. 5(3)). The landlord may vary the terms of a statutory periodic assured tenancy within the first complete year of its coming into being (Housing Act 1988, s. 6). A qualified covenant against sub-letting or assignment is implied into every periodic assured tenancy, whether statutory or not (s. 15). The statutory periodic tenancy will continue until the landlord obtains an order for possession, or the tenant is granted a new tenancy of the same or substantially the same dwelling-house (s. 5(4)). In the case of a fixed-term assured tenancy granted after 28 February 1997, the statutory periodic tenancy which arises on its termination under s. 5 will be an assured shorthold, provided that it does not fall within any of the exceptions contained in Sch. 2A to the 1988 Act (s. 19A).

Periodic tenancies

A periodic secure or assured tenancy (whether contractual or statutory) can only be brought to an end by the landlord obtaining an order of the court (Housing Act 1985, s. 84(1); Housing Act 1988, s. 5(1)).

Procedure

The court cannot entertain proceedings for possession against a secure or assured tenant unless the landlord has served a notice seeking possession. In the case of an assured tenancy, the notice may validly be served by one of two or more joint landlords (Housing Act 1988, s. 8(1)(a)).

The court may dispense with the need to serve the notice if it considers it just and equitable to do so (Housing Act 1985, s. 83(1)(b); Housing Act 1988, s. 8(1)(b)). In *Fernandes v Pavardin* (1982) 5 HLR 33, it was held on the facts that oral notice was enough to justify waiver of the requirement for written notice, there being no suggestion of misunderstanding by the tenants and no injustice or inequality resulting from failure to serve written notice. Stephenson LJ, in the minority, considered that the approach need not be restricted to considerations of injustice or inequality. In *Bradshaw v Baldwin-Wiseman* (1985) 17 HLR 260, the court expressed the view that the minority approach in *Fernandes* was to be preferred, and the court should look at all the circumstances of the case affecting both landlord and tenant, and those in which the failure to give written notice arose. In *Boyle v Verrall* (1997) 4 EG 145, the landlord had intended to create an assured shorthold tenancy but the district judge was not satisfied that the requisite s. 20 notice had been served. The result was the creation of an assured tenancy which was terminable only on one of the grounds specified in Sch. 2 to the 1988 Act. Recovery of possession on ground 1 depended on its being 'just and equitable' to dispense with the service of written notice on the tenant, at the time the tenancy was created, that the landlord might require the property back for her own or her husband's use. The Court of Appeal held that all the circumstances of the case should be considered. The giving of oral notice might be an important factor favouring dispensation but was not necessarily a pre-requisite of dispensation. Nor, if oral notice was absent, was dispensation restricted to 'exceptional cases'. Had the judge applied the correct test, he could only have concluded that it was just and equitable to dispense with the requirement of notice. This power to dispense does not apply where possession is sought from an assured tenant on the basis of ground 8 (two months' rent arrears).

The notice must be in the prescribed form or a form substantially to the same effect (Secure Tenancies (Notices) Regulations 1987; Assured Tenancies and Agricultural Occupancies (Forms) Regulations 1997). It must:

(a)   state on which ground or grounds the landlord intends to rely. The court cannot make an order for possession based on a ground which is not specified in the landlord's notice but the grounds which are specified may be altered or added to with the leave of the court (Housing Act 1985, s. 84(3); Housing Act 1988, s. 8(2)). The power to alter or add grounds imports a power to alter or add to particulars (*Camden London Borough Council v Oppong* (1996) 28 HLR 701);

(b) give particulars of the ground(s);
(c) state the date after which proceedings may be begun (Housing Act 1985, s. 83(2); Housing Act 1988, s. 8(3)(b)). In the case of a secure tenancy, the specified date cannot be earlier than the date on which a periodic tenancy could be brought to an end by notice to quit. In most cases concerning an assured tenancy, the specified date should be not earlier than two weeks from the date of the service of the notice. If the landlord seeks to rely on ground 1 (owner-occupier), ground 2 (mortgagee's power of sale), ground 5 (occupation required for minister of religion), ground 6 (intention to demolish or reconstruct), ground 7 (death of tenant), ground 9 (suitable alternative accommodation) and ground 16 (employee), the date specified in the notice should be not less than two months from the date of service of the notice and, in the case of a periodic tenancy, the earliest date on which the tenancy could be brought to an end by notice to quit given by the landlord on the same date as service of the notice (Housing Act 1988, s. 8(4A)). Where the landlord is relying on ground 2 or 14 of the 1985 and 1988 Acts respectively, the notice must state that possession proceedings may be begun immediately after service of the notice seeking possession and specify the date sought by the landlord as the date on which the tenant is to give up possession (Housing Act 1985, s. 83(3); Housing Act 1988, s. 8(4)).

A notice served on an assured tenant must also inform the tenant that the landlord intends to bring possession proceedings and that those proceedings will not begin later than 12 months from the date of service of the notice (Housing Act 1988, s. 8(3)(c)). The notice served on a secure tenant lapses 12 months after the specified date (Housing Act 1985, s. 83(4). The court cannot allow the landlord to bring a claim for possession until after the specified date has passed and the notice remains in force (s. 83A(1)) and possession cannot be ordered to take effect any earlier than the date specified in the landlord's notice (s. 84(4)).

Minor errors in the prescribed form of the notice will not be fatal provided that the notice is substantially to the same effect as that statutorily required. It will not be invalidated by a mistake in the particulars if the landlord has in good faith stated the ground and given the particulars at the time the notice was served (see *Dudley Metropolitan Borough Council v Bailey* (1990) 22 HLR 424). Given however that the purpose of the notice is to give the tenant an opportunity to rectify any breaches under the tenancy, sufficient particulars must be provided of the ground on which the landlord intends to seek possession. In *Torridge District Council v Jones* (1987) 19 HLR 526, a statement that 'the reasons for taking this action are non-payment of rent' did not suffice. The court held that the notice of seeking possession is a 'warning shot across the bows', the purpose of which is to enable the tenant to know what has to be done to put matters right before proceedings are commenced. In *Mountain v Hastings* (1993) 25 HLR 427, the landlord was seeking possession of an assured tenancy on a number of grounds, including ground 8. The notice summarised the text of each ground instead of giving the full text as was required by the prescribed form of notice. It would be valid if it set out fully the substance of the ground so that it gave the tenant such information as would enable her to do what she could to protect herself against the loss of her home. The notice in question was defective, however, because it did not convey the substance of ground 8. It simply stated that 'at least three months' rent is unpaid', omitting to mention that the rent must be unpaid for three months (since reduced by the Housing Act 1996 to two months) at the date of service of the notice *and* at the date of the hearing.

A landlord seeking to recover possession from an assured tenant will be able to obtain an order for possession only if the landlord can establish one or more of the mandatory grounds 1 to 8, in which case the court must grant a possession order (Housing Act 1988, s. 7(3)) or one or more of the discretionary grounds 9 to 16 and the court considers it reasonable to grant a possession order (s. 7(4)).

A court is only entitled to grant the landlord possession against a secure tenant on one or more of the statutory grounds 1–16 set out in Sch. 2 to the 1985 Act. Unlike the Rent Act 1977 and the Housing Act 1988, the 1985 Act contains no mandatory grounds. Instead, the grounds for possession are divided into three categories. The court will make an order for possession on grounds 1 to 8 (i.e. those in Part I) only if it considers it reasonable to do so. It will do so in respect of grounds 9 to 11 (Part II) only if it is satisfied that suitable alternative accommodation will be available for the tenant when the order takes effect. So far as grounds 12 to 26 (Part III) are concerned it will make an order if considers it reasonable to do so and it is satisfied that suitable alternative accommodation will be available for the tenant when the order takes effect. The court cannot make an order for possession under Parts II and III unless a member of the tenant's family who lives in the premises has been joined as a party to the proceedings (*Wandsworth London Borough Council v Fadayomi* [1987] 3 All ER 474).

Reasonableness

Reasonableness has already been considered in relation to the Rent Act 1977 and reference should be made to Chapter 14. Special considerations apply where possession is sought under the 'nuisance and annoyance' grounds (see Chapter 20).

Suitable alternative accommodation

For the purposes of the Housing Act 1985, suitable alternative accommodation is not a ground in itself but is an additional requirement for possession under the grounds contained in Parts II and III of the Act.

Accommodation will be suitable if it consists of premises which are to be let as a separate dwelling under:

(a) a secure tenancy; or
(b) a protected tenancy, not being a tenancy under which the landlord might recover possession under one of the mandatory cases in the Rent Act 1977; or
(c) an assured tenancy which is neither an assured shorthold tenancy nor a tenancy under which the landlord might recover possession under any of the grounds 1 to 5; and, in the opinion of the court, the accommodation is reasonably suitable to the needs of the tenant and the tenant's family (Sch. 2, Part IV, para. 1).

In *Enfield London Borough Council v French* (1985) 17 HLR 211, it was held that although a garden can qualify as one of the 'needs' of a tenant, accommodation may nonetheless be regarded as reasonably suitable even if one particular need cannot be met. A one-bedroomed flat constituted suitable accommodation for a bachelor, even though it had no garden and he was a dedicated gardener who had created 'a beautiful garden' out of a 'wilderness' at his existing home, with fish in a pond and birds in an aviary.

In determining whether the alternative accommodation is 'suitable' the court shall have regard to:

(a) the nature of the accommodation which it is the practice of the landlord to allocate to persons with similar needs;
(b) the distance of the accommodation available from the place of work or education of the tenant or any members of the tenant's family;
(c) its distance from the home of any member of the tenant's family if proximity to it is essential to that member's or the tenant's well-being;
(d) the needs (as regards extent of accommodation) and means of the tenant and the tenant's family;
(e) the terms on which the accommodation is available and the terms of the secure tenancy;
(f) if furniture is provided by the landlord for use under the secure tenancy, whether furniture is to be provided for use in the other accommodation, and if so the nature of the furniture to be provided.

It will be observed that, unlike the private sector provision, the Housing Act 1985 makes no reference to the character of the proposed accommodation, so that no account may be taken of environmental factors.

The requirements of suitable alternative accommodation for discretionary ground 9 of the Housing Act 1988 are similar to those contained in the Rent Act 1977. Where the tenant is an assured tenant, the alternative accommodation must be let on an assured tenancy (but not an assured shorthold tenancy or subject to one of the mandatory grounds dependent upon service of a notice, i.e. grounds 1 to 5) or, alternatively, on terms which give the tenant reasonably equivalent security (Sch. 2, Part III, para. 2(a)). Further, where the landlord obtains an order for possession under ground 9, the tenant is entitled to reasonable removal expenses from the landlord, and can sue the landlord if he or she fails to pay them (s. 11).

Adjournment, postponement and suspension

Where proceedings are brought on any of the grounds contained in Parts I or III of the 1985 Act or the discretionary grounds of the 1988 Act, the court may make an outright order or it may adjourn the proceedings, or stay or suspend the execution of any order or postpone the date of possession for such period or periods as it thinks fit (Housing Act 1985, s. 85; Housing Act 1988, s. 9).

In *Canterbury City Council v Lowe* (2001) 33 HLR 53, the court stated that in cases of anti-social behaviour 'the issue of whether to suspend must be very much a question of the future' and that 'there is no point suspending an order if the inevitable outcome is a breach' (para. 25).

In *Norwich City Council v Famuyiwa* [2004] EWCA Civ 1770, although the judge accepted that the tenant's conduct had caused a nuisance and annoyance to, and constituted harassment of, her neighbours, he concluded that it would not be reasonable to make an order for possession: a postponed order would not control her behaviour and an outright order would put her at risk of losing the right to buy or actually losing her home altogether. Allowing the local authority's appeal, the Court of Appeal held that it was not right in principle to refuse an order for possession. If a postponed order were made, the tenant's right to buy would also be postponed but if she behaved she would in due course be able to get the possession order removed and proceed with her right to buy.

On any adjournment, postponement, stay or suspension, the court must impose conditions with respect to the payment of rent arrears and rent or payments in respect of occupation after the termination of the tenancy (mesne profits) unless it considers that to do so would cause exceptional hardship to the tenant or would otherwise be unreasonable (Housing Act 1985, s. 85(3), Housing Act 1988, s. 9(3)). Where a tenant complies with conditions which have been imposed, the court may, if it thinks fit, discharge or rescind the possession order (Housing Act 1985, s. 85(4); Housing Act 1988, s. 9(4)). The tenancy will not be automatically revived by fulfilment of the conditions (*Marshall v Bradford Metropolitan District Council* [2002] HLR 15) nor from an extension of the currency of a postponed possession order (which occurs as a result of the exercise of case management powers rather than from a consideration of the substantive rights of the parties) (*Richmond v Kensington and Chelsea London Borough Council* [2006] 1 WLR 1693).

Where the tenant breaks the terms of a postponed possession order, the order becomes effective and the tenancy is terminated from that moment.

The local authority may then apply for a warrant for possession and need not warn the tenant of its intention to do so (*Thompson v Elmbridge Borough Council* (1987) 19 HLR 526). The court bailiff issues the warrant and fixes an eviction date. However, right up until time until the order is executed, the court may stay or suspend the execution of the order or postpone the date given for possession (Housing Act 1985, s. 85(2)). Tenants often make (repeated) applications further to stay or suspend warrants. The granting of the warrant is a matter entirely for the judge's discretion.

No powers to adjourn, etc. are available where the landlord makes out a *mandatory* ground under the Housing Act 1988 (s. 9(6)). In such a situation the reasonableness (or otherwise) of making the order is irrelevant and possession is potentially instantaneous unless the court can be prevailed upon to exercise its inherent powers to postpone. Particular difficulties may arise in relation to mandatory ground 8. In *North British Housing Association Ltd v Matthews* [2005] 1 WLR 3133, the Court of Appeal acknowledged that there are a number of situations in which, even where the landlord is seeking to rely on ground 8, it would be perfectly proper for the court to adjourn the date of the hearing (i.e. before being satisfied that the landlord is entitled to possession). It might be that no judge is available on the date for which the case has been listed, or there has been an overlisting, or the tenant is too ill to attend court. The tenant might intend to claim damages which could be set off against the arrears of rent and bring them below the eight-week limit. The tenant might show an arguable defence based on accord and satisfaction or estoppel, the landlord having allegedly accepted an offer by the tenant to pay off the current rent and arrears at a certain rate in return for not pursuing the claim for possession. Finally if before or at the hearing date, the landlord accepts a cheque from the tenant for a sufficient sum to bring the arrears below the ground 8 threshold, then the court could properly adjourn the claim for possession to see whether the cheque would be honoured (*Coltrane v Day* [2003] 1 WLR 1379). The court confirmed however that only in exceptional circumstances should a hearing be adjourned to enable a tenant to reduce the outstanding rent arrears below the ground 8 threshold. An example might be where a computer failure prevented the housing benefit authority from paying the arrears of benefit until after the date of the hearing. Pointing out the 'sad feature of contemporary life that housing benefit problems are widespread', Dyson LJ concluded that maladministration on the part of the housing benefit authority was not an exceptional circumstance.[2]

In *Circle 33 Housing Trust v Ellis* [2006] HLR 7, the assured tenant's housing benefit was paid directly to the landlord. When the benefit payments ceased, the landlord sought possession because of rent arrears. The tenant did not attend court and an outright order was made. After the tenant's

---

2   For discussion of the human rights considerations, see Morgan (2005).

eviction, the housing benefit department confirmed that he had, in fact, been entitled to benefits at all material times. His rent account was credited with the benefit payments, leaving arrears of just over £200. The Court of Appeal refused to reinstate the tenant, holding that a finding of oppression in the execution of an order cannot be made unless the court's process has been misused. The housing benefit department had informed the landlord that the tenant was not eligible for benefit. Only when the tenant himself pursued the matter after his eviction did the truth emerge. Chadwick LJ explained that a time must come when the landlord can re-let the property confident that the scheme for protecting the former tenant has run its course. In the case of the 1988 Act, that time was when eviction took place.

Grounds for possession: general

Many of the cases for possession contained in the Rent Act 1977 and the Housing Acts of 1985 and 1988 are identical – or at least very similar. However, the 1988 Act contains a number of 'new' or revised ones, notably ground 1 (a revised owner-occupier ground); ground 6 (a new ground, enabling the landlord to obtain possession for redevelopment); ground 8 (a new ground based on proof of 'serious' rent arrears); ground 11 (a new ground which permits recovery of possession for persistent rent arrears). Given that the 1988 Act is targeted primarily at the private rented and housing association sectors, some of its grounds are not found in the 1985 Act, e.g. mandatory ground 2 which allows for repossession by a mortgage-lender. Variations of the following grounds appear in both the 1985 and 1988 Acts.

Rent arrears

Although social landlords appear to have been changing their management practices and taking a firmer stance as regards rent arrears (Pawson *et al.*, 2005: 32), 'overall, the performance of rent/arrears collection services has been seen as weak by housing inspection reports' (Evans, 2003: 11). Despite the fact that, between 1997 and 2002, the proportion of local authority tenants in arrears with their rent remained more or less constant at around 40 per cent, current arrears increased by 20 per cent (ibid.). The Right to Buy and stock transfer have effectively removed from council stock many of the 'good' payers and increased the proportion of indebted and benefit-dependent tenants. In 2000/1 only 31 per cent of council benefits were in paid work (full or part time) (ibid.: 7). There is a generally greater acceptance of debt, and it is likely that the entry into the sector of younger households is likely to exacerbate the problem. Key areas for improvement have been identified as 'better working relationships between housing services and housing benefit departments, more advice and support for tenants, more consistent application of procedures, the extension of payment options, strengthening performance management and a better understanding of the problem' (ibid.: 11).

The present procedure for recovering possession on grounds of rent arrears has been subject to some criticism. A six-week wait for a court hearing is typical (Evans, 2003: 37). Fixed date hearings are usually a mere formality because the majority of defendants do not attend and those who do are rarely represented (Nixon *et al.*, 1996). They are wasteful, therefore, of both court time and legal costs. Further, the objective of the procedure tends not to be possession of the property but the payment of arrears. In theory, the landlord may recover what is owed by a claim for debt against the tenant or the 'archaic' remedy of distress (*Abingdon Rural District Council v O'Gorman* [1968] 2 QB 811) but neither of these is really satisfactory: it is not worth bringing an action in debt against a tenant who seemingly cannot afford to pay the rent, and the amount yielded by distraint is often inadequate to cover arrears. The threat of possession is, therefore, the only effective weapon landlords have against recalcitrant tenants. However, arrears are usually caused by illness, unemployment, relationship breakdown and the late payment of housing benefit, and these will all be taken into consideration when possession is sought of a discretionary ground and the court is addressing the issue of reasonableness and/or deciding whether to make an outright or a postponed order. Judges will often give the tenant a last chance by making a possession order postponed so long as the current rent is paid and a further sum is paid off the arrears (unless, for example, the tenant makes no proposals for paying off serious rent arrears (*Haringey London Borough Council v Stewart* [1991] 2 EGLR 252)). Thus, in *Woodspring v Taylor* (1982) 4 HLR 95, the Court of Appeal dismissed an appeal against a refusal by the county court to grant an outright order against the tenants even though the arrears amounted to more than £550 by the date of the hearing. The tenants had been satisfactory tenants for almost 20 years and had fallen into arrears only because of illness and unemployment. A large money judgment payable by small weekly instalments will result in the possession order being postponed for lengthy periods – possibly years. In 2002, the Law Commission reported concerns that '[postponed] possession orders for rent have too readily been given out, made in hearings listed in bulk, with very low attendance rates and poor participation by occupiers' (Law Commission, 2002a: 12.34). The tenant's (non)-attendance at the hearing appears to be an important factor in determining the type of order which is made and the terms of any postponed order (see Hunter *et al.*, 2005).

Discretionary ground 1 of the Housing Act 1985 applies where rent 'lawfully due' from the tenant has not been paid or an obligation of the tenancy has been broken or not performed. It bears a close resemblance to case 1 under the Rent Act 1977 and the same considerations apply (see Chapter 14). The 1988 Act takes a much tougher stance, and contains no less than three separate grounds for possession: one mandatory and two discretionary.

Discretionary ground 10 corresponds in material aspects to case 1 of the 1977 Act, requiring that 'some rent lawfully due' from the tenant (a) is unpaid on the date on which the proceedings for possession are begun; and (b) was in arrears at the date when the s. 8 notice was served. Ground 11 (which is based on s. 30 (1)(b) of the Landlord and Tenant Act 1954) applies even if no rent is outstanding on the date on which proceedings for possession are begun but the tenant has persistently delayed paying rent. Thus in *Hopcutt v Carver* (1969) 209 EG 1069, the court refused to grant a new business tenancy, the tenant of some 20 years standing having been persistently late in paying his rent over the last two years, at one time delaying for five months.

Mandatory ground 8 – the most contentious ground contained in the 1988 Act – applies where both at the date when the s. 8 notice is served *and* at the date of the hearing, at least two months' rent (eight weeks' where rent is payable weekly or fortnightly) is unpaid. Its operation can be particularly harsh where tenants have fallen into arrears because of non- or late payment of housing benefit to which they are entitled. However, when the former period of three months (13 weeks) was reduced to two by the Housing Act 1996, Parliament failed to 'mitigate the consequences of that reduction by making any special provision to deal with the particular and well-known problems occasioned by non-payment of housing benefit' (*North British Housing Association Ltd v Matthews* [2005] 1 WLR 3133, para. 34). Some authorities take over 100 days on average to process new claims (Audit Commission, 2002: 5). However, the Minister for Housing recently confirmed that there were no plans to amend ground 8, given that a range of housing benefit reforms had been introduced which 'are improving the performance of local authorities in administering housing benefit' so that 'the average time taken to process housing benefit claims in 2003–04 was 49 days compared to 55 days in 2002–03' (HC Deb (2004) vol. 423, col. 876W).

In its Regulatory Circular 07/04, the Housing Corporation has set out its expectations of housing associations when working to prevent or respond to breaches of tenancy. The Circular states that:

> possession proceedings for rent arrears should not be started against a tenant who can demonstrate that they have (1) a reasonable expectation of eligibility for housing benefit; (2) provided the local authority with all the evidence required to process a housing benefit claim; (3) paid required personal contributions towards the charges. Associations should make every effort to establish effective ongoing liaison with housing benefit departments and to make direct contact with them before taking enforcement action. A certificate should be obtained, if possible, to confirm that there are not outstanding benefit enquiries, according to Department of Work and Pension good practice guidance.
> (HC, 2004: 3.1.1.)

If, by the date of the hearing, the tenant has paid the arrears or at least enough to reduce the amount outstanding to below the level necessary for possession to be granted under ground 8, the landlord will no longer be able to rely on the mandatory ground. It is in the landlord's interest, therefore, to include grounds 10 and 11 as alternatives in the s. 8 notice.

Breach of tenancy obligation

Discretionary grounds 1 of the 1985 Act and 12 of the 1988 Act both allow the landlord to recover possession where an obligation of the tenancy has been broken or not performed. They are usually used in cases involving anti-social behaviour and are therefore considered in Chapter 20.

Nuisance or annoyance, etc.

Discretionary grounds 2 of the 1985 Act and 14 of the 1988 Act are explored in detail in Chapter 20.

Domestic violence

Discretionary grounds 2A of the 1985 Act and 14A of the 1988 Act (the latter applying to assured tenancies of social landlords rather than private sector tenancies) were introduced by the Housing Act 1996. They can be used where the dwelling-house was occupied (whether alone or with others) by a married couple, a couple living as civil partners, a couple living together as husband and wife or a couple living together as if they were civil partners. One or both of the partners must be the tenant. It covers situations where one of them has left because of the other's violence either to the departing partner or to a child residing with that person immediately before departure. The court must be satisfied that the person who has left is unlikely to return.

Deterioration of the dwelling-house or furniture as the result of the tenant's neglect

Ground 3 of the 1985 Act may be used where the condition of the dwelling-house or any of the common parts (e.g. staircases, corridors, lifts, etc.) has deteriorated owing to acts of waste by, or the neglect or default of, the tenant or a person residing in the dwelling-house and, where the tenant's lodger or sub-tenant is responsible, the tenant has failed to take such steps as ought reasonably to have been taken for that person's removal. It is virtually identical to ground 13 of the 1988 Act. The wording of grounds 4 and 15 of the 1985 and 1988 Acts is very similar but it applies instead to furniture provided by the landlord.

Grant of tenancy induced by tenant's false statement.

Discretionary grounds 5 of the 1985 Act and 17 of the 1988 Act come into play where the tenant is the person, or one of the persons, to whom the tenancy was granted and the landlord was induced to grant the tenancy by a false statement made knowingly or recklessly by the tenant or by another person at the tenant's instigation, e.g. where a secure tenant of a housing association obtained housing from the local authority by stating on her application form that she was currently living with family and friends (*Rushcliffe Borough Council v Watson* (1991) 24 HLR 124). In *Islington v Uckac* [2006] 1 WLR 1303, the local authority had granted a secure tenancy to the second defendant who subsequently assigned it to the first defendant (his wife). The authority sought possession under ground 5 or, alternatively, rescission because of fraudulent misrepresentation. The Court of Appeal upheld the judge's decision that ground 5 was only available where a defendant from whom the possession was sought was the person to whom the tenancy was granted. It was unavailable where the tenancy had been assigned to another person, even where that person had been party to the fraud. Further, as Parliament had specifically included fraudulent misrepresentation as a ground for possession, it could not have intended that a landlord could claim possession for fraudulent misrepresentation by a different route based on a different set of rules, e.g. rescission. The court added, *obiter*, that the 1985 Act contained a lacuna and created the unpalatable result that an assignee of a secure tenancy, who had participated in the fraudulent misrepresentation which induced the landlord to grant the tenancy to the original tenant, was able to resist an order for possession and thereby take advantage of his (or her) own fraud.

In deciding the question of reasonableness, the court can take into account, *inter alia*, the nature and degree of the untrue statements, and the tenant's attitude when the deception is discovered (*Shrewsbury and Atcham Borough Council v Evans* (1997) 30 HLR 123).

Demolition or reconstruction

Ground 10 of the 1985 Act applies where the landlord intends, within a reasonable time of obtaining possession of the dwelling-house (a) to demolish or reconstruct the building or part of the building comprising the dwelling-house, or (b) to carry out work on that building or on land let together with, and thus treated as part of, the dwelling-house. It is a requirement of both this and mandatory ground 6 of the 1988 Act that the landlord cannot reasonably carry out the proposed works without obtaining possession of the dwelling-house. These very similar grounds are modelled on s. 30(1)(f) of the Landlord and Tenant Act 1954 which applies to business tenancies.[3]

3   For an explanation and analysis of s. 30(1)(f) of the 1954 Act, see Wilkie *et al.* (2006: Ch. 19).

Grounds for possession: Housing Act 1985

The following grounds for possession are peculiar to the Housing Act 1985.

(a) Ground 6 (which is designed to prevent the exploitation of s. 92 which permits secure tenants to exchange tenancies) may be used where a premium was paid in connection with the assignment of the tenancy to (a) the tenant, or (b) a predecessor in title who is a member of the tenant's family and is residing in the dwelling-house. A 'premium' in this context means any fine or other sum and any other pecuniary consideration in addition to rent.

(b) Ground 7 enables a landlord to regain possession where an employee of the landlord who lives within a building used for non-housing purposes (e.g. a school or hospital) is guilty of misconduct which makes continued occupation inappropriate.

(c) Ground 8 applies where the dwelling-house was made available for occupation by the tenant (or a predecessor in title) while works were carried out on the dwelling-house which was previously occupied as the tenant's only or principal home and:

(i) the tenant (or predecessor) was a secure tenant of the other dwelling-house at the time when occupation as a home ended,

(ii) the tenant (or predecessor) accepted the tenancy of the dwelling-house of which possession is sought on the understanding that occupation would be given up when the works were completed, and the other dwelling-house was again available for occupation under a secure tenancy, and

(iii) the works have been completed and the other dwelling-house is so available.

(d) Ground 9 applies where the dwelling-house is overcrowded, within the meaning of Part X of the 1985 Act (see Chapter 8), in such circumstances as to render the occupier guilty of an offence.

(e) Ground 10A (which was added by the Housing and Planning Act 1986), may be used where the whole or part of the dwelling-house is in an area which is subject to a redevelopment scheme approved by the Secretary of State or the Housing Corporation in accordance with Sch. 2, Part V and the landlord intends, within a reasonable time of obtaining possession, to dispose of the dwelling-house in accordance with the scheme and for that purpose reasonably requires possession of the dwelling-house.

(f) Ground 11 applies where the landlord is a charity and the tenant's continued occupation of the dwelling-house would conflict with the objects of the charity.

(g) Ground 12 of the 1985 Act applies where the dwelling-house forms part of a building which is mainly used for non-residential purposes or is situated in a cemetery and the landlord requires it for an employee.

(h) Ground 13 applies where the dwelling-house has features which are substantially different from those of ordinary dwelling-houses and which are designed to make it suitable for occupation by a physically disabled person who requires accommodation of a kind provided by the dwelling-house and (a) there is no longer such a person residing in the dwelling-house, and (b) the landlord requires it for occupation (whether alone or with members of his or her family) by such a person. The features must be of a type not normally present in ordinary dwellings, e.g. ramps instead of steps, cooking surfaces at a special height, but not an additional downstairs lavatory (*Freeman v Wansbeck District Council* [1984] 2 All ER 746).

(i) Ground 14 may be used where the landlord is a housing association or housing trust which lets dwelling-houses only for occupation (whether alone or with others) by people whose circumstances (other than merely their financial circumstances) make it especially difficult for them to satisfy their need for housing, and:

  (i) either there is no longer such a person residing in the dwelling-house or the tenant has received from a local housing authority an offer of accommodation in premises which are to be let as a separate dwelling under a secure tenancy, and,

  (ii) the landlord requires the dwelling-house for occupation (whether alone or with members of his or her family) by such a person.

(j) Ground 15 applies where the dwelling-house is one of a group of dwelling-houses which it is the practice of the landlord to let for occupation by persons with special needs and (i) a social service or special facility is provided in close proximity to the group of dwelling-houses in order to assist persons with those special needs, (ii) there is no longer a person with those special needs residing in the dwelling-house, and (iii) the landlord requires the dwelling-house for occupation (whether alone or with members of the landlord's family) by a person who has those special needs.

(k) A landlord may recover possession under ground 16 if it can be established that the accommodation afforded by the dwelling-house is more extensive than is reasonably required by the tenant who, as a member of the previous tenant's family, succeeded to a *periodic* tenancy by virtue of s. 89. Notice of seeking possession must have been served under s. 83, or proceedings for possession begun, between six and 12 months after the date of the previous tenant's death. In determining whether it is reasonable to make an order on this ground, the court must take into account:

  (i) the tenant's age,

  (ii) the period during which the tenant has occupied the dwelling-house as his or her only or principal home, and

  (iii) any financial or other support given by the tenant to the previous tenant.

Grounds for possession: Housing Act 1988

The following grounds appear in the 1988 Act but not in the 1985 Act, reflecting the fact that assured tenancies can be used by private landlords as well as housing associations:

(a) Ground 1 can be used if 'not later than the beginning of the tenancy the landlord gave notice in writing to the tenant that possession might be recovered on this ground or the court is of the opinion that it is just and equitable to dispense with the requirement of notice and (in either case):

   (i) at some time before the beginning of the tenancy, the landlord who is seeking possession or, in the case of joint landlords seeking possession, at least one of them occupied the dwelling-house as his only or principal home; or

   (ii) the landlord who is seeking possession or, in the case of joint landlords seeking possession, at least one of them requires the dwelling-house as his or his spouse's only or principal home and neither the landlord (or in the case of joint landlords, any one of them) nor any other person who, as landlord, derived title under the landlord who gave the notice mentioned above acquired the reversion for money or money's worth.'

Although this ground bears a passing resemblance to the discretionary case 9 and the mandatory case 11 under the Rent Act 1977, it differs from both in significant respects. To succeed in recovering possession under this ground, the landlord may rely on either:

   (i) past occupation of the dwelling-house as his or her only or principal home (which need not have immediately preceded the grant of the tenancy). No intention to occupy in the future need be proved: the landlord may simply want to sell with vacant possession; or

   (ii) a need for the dwelling-house presently as his or his spouse's only or principal home. No past use of it as such need be shown, unless he is a landlord by purchase (for money or money's worth).

(b) Provided that there has been no statutory succession by the former tenant's spouse, civil partner or cohabitant (see Chapter 9), the tenancy can devolve under the former tenant's will or intestacy. Mandatory ground 7 may be used to recover possession where a person has thus inherited a *periodic* tenancy. Where there has been a statutory succession under s. 17, ground 7 will become available on the death of the successor. Proceedings for the recovery of possession must be begun not later than 12 months after the death of the former tenant or, if the court so directs, after the date on which, in the court's opinion, the landlord (or any one of them, in the case of joint landlords) became aware of the former tenant's death. If the landlord accepts rent from the new tenant, a new periodic tenancy is not created unless the landlord agrees in writing to a change in the terms of the tenancy (e.g. as to the rent payable, the period of the tenancy, the premises which are let).

Finally, ground 16 of the 1988 Act is very similar to case 8 of the Rent Act 1977 except in so far as the dwelling house need not be required as a residence for a new employee.

Tolerated trespassers

As indicated above, a secure tenancy determines either on the date specified in an absolute order or when the terms of a postponed order are breached (*Thompson v Elmbridge Borough Council* (1987) 19 HLR 526). The landlord may then apply for a warrant for possession. However, few warrants are actually executed. If the tenant vacates voluntarily, the eviction is made purely technical. More frequently, although the tenancy has ended, landlords allows former tenants to remain in occupation so long as they continue to pay for occupation (in the form of mesne profits) and make regular payments towards the arrears. Indeed, because possession proceedings are often used as a 'rent payment mechanism rather than as a means to recover possession of property' (Bright, 2006b: 52), many thousands of households find themselves in this situation – and often for many years. Unless an intention on the part of both parties to create a new tenancy can be found, eviction is effectively at the landlord's discretion so that the occupier is dependent 'more on the exercise of administrative discretion than on definable legal rights' (Driscoll, 1988: 376).

Former tenants and their families who find themselves in such circumstances are known as 'tolerated trespassers', a term coined by Lord Browne-Wilkinson in *Burrows v Brent London Borough Council* [1996] 1 WLR 1448. Here, Ms Burrows, a secure tenant, made an arrangement to pay off rent arrears days before the court awarded possession to her local authority landlord. She failed to keep up payments and two years later the authority issued a possession warrant which was executed. Ms Burrows then applied for a declaration that she was still a secure tenant because the agreement to pay arrears had had given her a new right of occupation, either by way of a new tenancy or as a licensee. The House of Lords rejected her argument, holding that prior to the execution date the parties could indeed have created a new tenancy or licence or could have reached an alternative arrangement, depending on their intention. In this case, however, the only intention was to defer execution of the possession order as long as Ms Burrows complied with the agreed conditions. Had her argument succeeded, it would have meant not only that a new tenancy would have been created but also that the landlord would have to have made a fresh application for a further possession order. As Lord Browne-Wilkinson explained, this would either discourage local authorities from making 'reasonable and humane concessions by agreement' or would oblige them to make an application to the court in every case to vary the existing order to ensure that the old tenancy was not brought to an end. It was impossible, he said, to believe that Parliament would have intended 'to produce such an unreasonable regime, penalising sensible agreements out of court, and requiring repeated applications to an already over-stretched court system' (at p. 1454). *Burrows v Brent* concerned an absolute possession order but the Court of Appeal subsequently held that the concept is equally applicable where the terms of a postponed order have been breached (*Lambeth London Borough Council v Rogers* (2000) 32 HLR 361) or where the order provides that the tenant should give up possession on or before a specified date but the court directs that the order will not be enforced provided that the tenant complies with the requirements set out therein (*Harlow District Council v Hall* [2006] 1 WLR 2116).

Tolerated trespassers live in a curious social and legal limbo. They have no security of tenure, are not entitled to any of the other common law or statutory rights of a tenant, and are unable to enforce any covenants in the former tenancy against their landlords. There can be no succession if the former tenant dies while a tolerated trespasser and the potential successor will have no defence to possession proceedings (*Newham London Borough Council v Hawkins* [2005] HLR 42). Similarly, without an application to reinstate the tenancy, it will not be possible to exercise the right to buy, to assign the tenancy or to effect a mutual exchange. The landlord cannot enforce any covenant with regard to the tolerated trespasser's behaviour or any other covenant of the former tenancy agreement. Once the occupier has become a trespasser, the statutory framework for increasing the rent payable by a secure tenant does not apply. Problems may arise where a local authority transfers its stock to an RSL because it is only the rights of *tenants* which survive the transfer (see *Bristol City Council v Hassan* [2006] 1 WLR 2582, para. 34). Tolerated trespassers can however claim damages for breaches which occurred during the tenancy and, because these causes of action emanate from the law of tort rather than from the tenancy agreement, they can still claim damages from the landlord for nuisance, negligence (*Pemberton v Southwark London Borough Council* [2000] 1 WLR 1672) and trespass to property. In the absence of an application under s. 85(4) to have the possession order discharged, their secure status will be revived only if the intention of both parties was to create a new tenancy. This will require more than the acceptance of rent by the landlord or, indeed, the service of notice of rent increases upon the tenant (*Lambeth London Borough Council v O'Kane* [2006] HLR 2) but was held to have occurred in *Swindon Borough Council v Aston* [2003] HLR 42 in which the local authority had not only received the rent but had also provided the occupier with a new tenancy agreement.

A solution (albeit perhaps only a partial one) to the problems associated with tolerated trespassers appears to have emerged from the decision in *Bristol*

City Council v Hassan [2006] 1 WLR 2582. Here, the Court of Appeal held that judges are not obliged to set out an absolute date for possession on the face of their orders and can lawfully make orders which provide that the date for possession is postponed to a date fixed by the court on an application by the landlord. The defendant's secure tenancy will continue until that date. The approach adopted by the Law Commission in clause 154 of its Rented Homes Bill is that an occupation contract will end on the date on which the contract-holder gives up possession (Law Commission, 2006).

Chapter 19

Rights and duties of social tenants

Introduction

Quite apart from security of tenure, secure tenants have a number of other rights which are incorporated in the so-called 'Tenants' Charter'. Rights relating to rent and repairs and rent and rights of succession and are dealt with in Chapters 6 to 9 but the others are considered here. Of most significance is the right to buy (RTB).

Assignment

Because the allocation of social housing is generally based on need, it is important that public sector landlords are able to control the occupation of their housing. Therefore, s. 91 of the Housing Act 1985 prohibits assignment except in the following circumstances:

(a) under the 'right to exchange' provisions contained in s. 92;
(b) by court order in cases of relationship breakdown;
(c) to a person who would be qualified to succeed if the tenant died immediately before the assignment.

Exchange

Section 92 implies a term into every secure tenancy that the tenant may assign the tenancy:

(a) to another secure tenant, or
(b) to an assured tenant whose landlord is either the Housing Corporation, Housing for Wales, a registered social landlord, or a charitable housing trust.

The landlord must give written consent to the assignment. Consent can be withheld only on one or more of the following grounds which are set out in Sch. 3 to the Housing Act 1985:

(a) the assignee is already obliged by a court order to give up possession;

(b) a notice of seeking possession under s. 83 has been served, or proceedings for possession have begun, on any of grounds 1 to 6 in Sch. 2;

(c) an injunction against anti-social behaviour (see Chapter 20) or a postponed ground 2 or ground 14 possession order is in force or an application for either of these or an application for a demotion order is pending before the court;

(d) the accommodation afforded by the dwelling-house is substantially more extensive than is reasonably required by the proposed assignee;

(e) the extent of the accommodation is not reasonably suitable to the needs of the proposed assignee and the assignee's family;

(f) the accommodation has been let to the tenant in consequence of employment, related to non-housing purposes;

(g) the landlord is a charity and the proposed assignee's occupation of the dwelling-house would conflict with the charity's objects;

(h) the dwelling-house is adapted for a disabled person;

(i) occupation of the dwelling-house by the proposed assignee would conflict with the purposes of a specialist housing association or trust;

(j) the dwelling-house is one of a group of houses which the landlord lets for the occupation of people with special needs;

(k) the proposed assignee refuses to become a member of the tenants' housing association which is managing the property.

Within 42 days of the tenant's application for consent, the landlord must serve on the tenant a notice specifying and giving particulars of the ground on which consent is withheld (s. 92(4)). If it is withheld for any reason other than one of the grounds set out in Sch. 3, the tenant may treat it as having been given (s. 92(3)). Consent can be made conditional upon the tenant paying any outstanding rent or remedying any breach of obligation (s. 92(5) and (6)).

Relationship breakdown

Assignment of a secure tenancy is possible by virtue of court orders made under:

(a) ss. 23A or 24 of the Matrimonial Causes Act 1973;

(b) s. 17(1) of the Matrimonial and Family Proceedings Act 1984; or

(c) para. 1 of Sch. 1 to the Children Act 1989.

On granting a decree of divorce, nullity or judicial separation, the court can make a property adjustment order under ss. 23A or 24 of the Matrimonial Causes Act 1973 transferring the tenancy from one spouse to another. An assignment of the tenancy by the tenant is necessary to give effect to the court's order. In deciding whether or not to make an order under the 1973 Act, the court should take into account the policy of the local housing authority with regard to housing need and its effect on the parties concerned and the circumstances of security of tenure. In *Jones v Jones* [1997] 2 WLR 373 the wife had access to a loan which would probably enable her to find accommodation in the private rented sector. The husband's need to retain the tenancy was greater as he was disabled and the property was particularly suited to his needs. It was also felt that he should have priority, given that he had been the tenant for 20 years and his wife had only lived in the flat for the 15 months of the couple's marriage. The Family Law Act 1996 extends the power to transfer between cohabitants and former cohabitants civil partners whose relationship has broken down. When considering whether to transfer a tenancy, the court must have regard to all the circumstances, e.g. the parties' respective housing needs and resources, their financial resources and their suitability as tenants (Housing Act 1985, Sch. 7, para. 5). Further, the transferee may be ordered to pay compensation to the transferor for the loss of the transferor's rights under the tenancy (Sch. 7, para. 10).

Assignment to a successor

This provision may be used where the tenant wishes, e.g. to pre-empt any dispute which may arise upon the tenant's death between the potential successors, or to assign to a potential successor and then leave the premises. In *Peabody Donation Fund (Governors) v Higgins* [1983] 1 WLR 1091, the tenancy agreement contained an absolute prohibition against assignment. The tenant, intending to retire to Ireland, executed an assignment by deed in favour of his daughter (who would have qualified to succeed upon the tenant's death). The assignment was effective but, because it contravened the terms of the tenancy, there was nothing to prevent the landlord from starting proceedings afresh to recover possession on ground 1 (breach of the term of the tenancy).

To be effective, the assignment must be by deed (Law of Property Act 1925, s. 52(1)) even if writing was not necessary for the tenancy itself because it is for less than three years. Thus, in *Crago v Julian* (1991) 24 HLR 306, a wife's appeal against a possession order was unsuccessful where her husband had given a written undertaking to transfer the weekly tenancy to her within 14 days of the granting of their decree absolute, but had failed to incorporate the assignment in a deed. In *City of Westminster v Peart* (1991) 24 HLR 389, Sir Christopher Slade doubted, *obiter*, that Parliament had intended to impose the formality and expense of executing a deed upon those who wished to take advantage of s. 91(3)(c) but the approach taken in *Crago* was confirmed by the Court of Appeal in *London Borough of Camden v Alexandrou* (1997) 74 P & CR D33.

Taking in lodgers and sub-letting

It is a term of every secure tenancy that the tenant:

(a) may allow any persons to reside as lodgers in the dwelling-house, but

(b) will not, without the landlord's written consent, sub-let or part with possession of part of the dwelling-house (s. 93(1)).

If a secure tenant parts with possession of the dwelling-house or sub-lets the whole of it (or sub-lets part of it and then the remainder), the secure status of the tenancy is lost and cannot subsequently be resurrected (s. 93(2)).

Consent to sub-letting must not be unreasonably withheld. If it is with-held unreasonably it will be treated as given. A tenant must always seek con-sent before sub-letting but it may be validly given even after the sub-lease has been granted (s. 94(4)). If consent is refused, the landlord must give the ten-ant a written statement of the reasons for refusal (s. 94(6)). The burden of proof is on the landlord to show that the withholding of consent was not unreasonable (s. 94(2)). In determining the matter of reasonableness, the court should take into account whether granting consent would lead to over-crowding of the dwelling-house within the meaning of Part X of the 1985 Act (see Chapter 8), or whether the landlord proposes to carry out works on the premises which would affect the accommodation likely to be used by the sub-tenant (s. 94(3)(a) and (b)).

Improvements

The improvement programmes of local authority landlords have been severely affected by cuts in capital spending. The right given to secure ten-ants to carry out improvements to their properties might have been expected therefore to have assumed an increased significance but the residualised nature of local authority housing means that most secure tenants cannot afford to do so (Stewart, 1996: 153).

It is a term of every secure tenancy that the tenant will not make improve-ment without the written consent of the landlord (s. 97(1)). 'Improvement' means any alteration in, or addition to, a dwelling-house, and includes any addition or alteration to the landlord's fixtures and fittings or connected with the provision of services to the dwelling-house, the erection of a wireless or TV aerial, and the carrying out of external decoration (s. 97(2)).

Consent to improvements must not be unreasonably withheld. If it is withheld unreasonably it will be treated as given (s. 97(3)). The burden of proof will be on the landlord to show that consent was not withheld unreasonably (s. 98(1)). In determining whether consent has been withheld unreasonably, the court should consider the extent to which the improvement would be likely:

(a) to make the dwelling-house, or any other premises, less safe for the occupiers;
(b) to cause the landlord to incur expenditure which it would be unlikely to incur if the improvement were not made; or

(c) to reduce the price which the dwelling-house would fetch if sold on the open market or the rent which the landlord would be able to charge on letting the dwelling-house (s. 98(2)).

Consent to an improvement may be made subject to conditions (s. 99(1)) but if the condition is not reasonable, consent will be taken to have been unreasonably withheld (s. 99(2)). A secure tenant who fails to satisfy a reasonable condition will be treated as having breached an obligation of the tenancy (s. 99(4)).

If the improvements have added to the value of the property or the rent that the landlord can charge, the tenant may be entitled to compensation. Depending on whether the improvements were begun before or after 1 February 1994, compensation will be governed by s. 100 of the Housing Act 1985 or ss. 99A and 99B of the 1985 Act.

Variation

Terms which have been implied by statute cannot be varied (s. 103(3)(a)). Otherwise, by s. 102, the terms of a secure tenancy may be varied only:

(a) by agreement between the landlord and tenant;
(b) by the landlord or tenant in accordance with a provision in the lease or tenancy agreement, or in an agreement varying it, provided that the variation relates to rent or to payments in respect of rates, council tax or services;
(c) in accordance with s. 103.

In *Kilby v Basildon District Council* [2006] EWHC 1892, a clause in the existing tenancy agreement provided that the landlord authority could only change the terms of the agreement if a majority of the tenants' representatives agreed. A new tenancy agreement – which the local authority had approved and decided to implement – contained no such provision. In judicial review proceedings brought by one of the authority's secure tenants, McCombe J held that the clause contravened s. 102 in that it attempted to provide for variation 'otherwise' than in a manner permitted by the section and thus (even though 'it might be in the best interest of good tenant relations so to organise its affairs') it unlawfully fettered the statutory powers of variation.

Section 103 applies only to secure periodic tenancies. It provides that the landlord who wishes to vary the terms of a secure tenancy must serve on the tenant a preliminary notice which (a) informs the tenant of the landlord's intention to serve a notice of variation; (b) gives details of the proposed variation and its effect; and (c) invites the tenant to comment on the proposed variation within a specified time. The landlord must consider any comments made by the tenant.

Information

Tenancy agreements need not be in writing but s. 104 of the 1985 Act requires landlords to publish information about their secure tenancies, explaining in simple terms the effect of:

(a) the express terms of their secure tenancies,
(b) the provisions of Part IV; and
(c) the provisions of ss. 11 to 16 of the Landlord and Tenant Act 1985 in respect of the landlord's repairing obligations (see Chapter 7).

They should also ensure that, so far as is reasonably practicable, the information so published is kept up to date (s. 104(1)) and should make available a statement of the tenancy terms in so far as they are neither expressed in the written tenancy agreement (if any) nor implied by law (s. 104(2)(b)). Where the landlord is a local housing authority, it should supply its secure tenants with a copy of the information at least once a year (s. 104(3)).

Section 106 requires landlords to publish information about housing allocation. As is explained in Chapter 17, this duty is bolstered by the Housing Act 1996 (as amended by the Homelessness Act 2002) which contains further duties as regards the provision of advice and information about making an application for housing, the publication of summaries of allocation schemes, and notifying tenants of, *inter alia*, their right to request information about the progress of their application.

Sections 121AA and B govern the provision of information regarding the right to buy.

Consultation

Section 105 of the 1985 Act requires landlords who fulfil the landlord condition to maintain such arrangements as they consider appropriate to enable secure tenants who are likely to be substantially affected by a matter of housing management:

(a) to be informed of proposed changes and developments, and
(b) to make their views known to their landlord within a specified time.

A matter is one of 'housing management' if, in the landlord's opinion,

(a) it relates to the management, maintenance, improvement, or demolition of municipal dwellings, or to the provision of services or amenities to such dwellings, and
(b) it represents a new programme of maintenance, improvement or demolition, or some change in the landlord's practice, and

(c) it is likely substantially to affect either its secure tenants as a whole or a group of them. A group is defined as a group of secure tenants who form a distinct social group, or who occupy dwelling-houses which constitute a distinct class, whether by reference to the kind of dwelling, or the housing estate or larger area in which they are situated. Thus, in *Short v London Borough of Tower Hamlets* (1986) 18 HLR 171, the Court of Appeal held that a decision taken 'in principle' to dispose of an estate to a private developer was not a matter of 'housing management' requiring consultation nor, in *R v London Borough of Hammersmith and Fulham ex p Beddowes* [1987] 1 All ER 369, was the identity of the prospective developer.

The authority has a duty to consider any representations made by secure tenants before making any decisions on a matter of housing management.

Section 106A gives a right to secure and introductory tenants whose local authority landlord is intending to dispose of its dwellings to a private sector landlord, to be consulted prior to the disposal. A further duty is imposed by s. 27BA, which requires local housing authorities to consult with tenants with respect to the management of their housing management functions.

Management

Section 27 of the 1985 Act empowers a local housing authority, with the Secretary of State's approval, to transfer specified management functions over specified houses to 'another person'. Such delegation is by way of a management agreement which sets out the terms on which the authority's functions are exercisable by the manager, the geographical areas for which it has responsibility and such provisions as are prescribed by regulations made by the Secretary of State. 'Another person' can include the tenants (in the form of a Tenant Management Organisation (TMO)) or other professional managers such as housing associations. The management functions which can be delegated under these powers are widely defined and include maintenance, repair, allocation of tenancies and rent collection.

Until 1987, there was only one type of TMO: the tenant management co-operative (TMC). The estate management board model (EMB) was developed in the 1980s, coinciding with the introduction of Estate Action which aimed to revitalise run-down estates. TMC boards are usually composed entirely of tenants and directly employ their own staff. EMB boards contain a majority of tenants but may also include councillors and officers and their staff is usually seconded from the local authority. Like TMCs, they are either registered as industrial and provident societies or as companies limited by guarantee. There is no legal distinction between the two forms of TMO and, in practice, the difference between them is blurred.

Local authorities have been able to delegate budgets and responsibility for housing management and maintenance to TMOs since the Housing

(Rents and Subsidies) Act 1975. For some years, however, they were slow to use their powers and, by 1993, only 62 estates had passed to TMOs (about 2 per cent of all local authority housing). In a series of consultation papers produced in the early 1990s, the government proposed that certain tenant organisations would have the right to insist on delegation. Their proposals were given legislative force by the Leasehold Reform, Housing and Urban Development Act 1993. Now, all tenants groups covering 25 or more properties have a right to insist that a local authority delegates its housing management functions and maintenance responsibilities to them in defined circumstances (Housing Act 1985, s. 27AB). After serving a Right to Manage notice, the tenants group receives training, and opinion is tested to ensure sufficient support exists to proceed to the development stage. This stage, usually lasting for between 18 and 24 months, is when the management agreement is negotiated and the Management and Maintenance Allowances agreed. There follows a ballot which, if it is successful, leads to the establishment of the TMO. Responsibility for some or all of the day-to-day management and maintenance then passes to the TMO board. The TMO and local authority sign the legally-binding management agreement. Once the TMO is established, tenants vote every five years on whether it should continue.

There are now more than 200 TMOs (over 60 per cent of which are to found in London) covering an estimated 84,000 homes. They range in size from 12 to more than 9,000 properties, with an average of just over 400 properties (ODPM, 2002c: 7). Although they cover less than 3 per cent of the total council stock in England, they have always attracted a disproportionate amount of interest as examples of tenant participation and control. Nationally, there has been all-party support for TMOs, which has not always existed at the local level. Some local authorities have actively promoted TMOs, while others have taken a passive approach.

The right to buy

Introduction

The sale of council houses to tenants has been possible throughout the history of council housing. It really took off, however, with the Housing Act 1980 which gave the RTB to secure tenants who fulfilled the qualifying period. Since its inception in 1980, the RTB has generated over two million sales in Great Britain (Wilcox, 2005: Table 20d).

In previous periods of high discretionary sales, the amount of new building was considerably higher than disposals but since the introduction of the RTB, hardly any local authority housing has been built. This so-called 'sale of the century' has resulted in the largest ever transfer of public assets into the private sector, the receipts from council house sales having contributed almost as much in terms of capital receipts as the rest of the Conservative government's privatisation programme put together. When the RTB was introduced, it was assumed that sales would be spread evenly across the country. In fact, the pattern of sales has been uneven, both geographically and socially. It is typically in those areas where home ownership was already high that it has grown the most (Forrest and Murie, 1992: 144–6).

Council house sales before 1980

When local authorities were first empowered to build houses, they were not intended to remain the owners of those houses forever. The Artisans and Labourers' Dwellings Improvement Act 1875 and the Housing of the Working Classes Act 1890 both provided that housing built by local authorities should be sold within 10 years of its completion but very little council housing was produced under this legislation, and the obligation to sell was in any case removed by the Housing and Town Planning Act 1909. Local authorities were still permitted to sell council houses with ministerial consent but, even though the inter-war years witnessed council house building on an unprecedentedly large scale, the volume of sales was small. Where sales did take place, they had to be for the best price obtainable.

A refusal of consent to the sale of council houses during the Second World War was maintained after 1945 by the Labour government, which considered that in the current circumstances as many houses as possible should be kept available for letting to those people who most needed them (HC Deb (1947–8), vol. 445, col. 1167; vol. 468, col. 186). There was also the view that 'where public money and public facilities have been found to provide houses for letting to those in the greatest need, those houses should [not] now be sold to others merely because they have the money to buy them' (HC Deb (1947–8) vol. 445, col. 1167). By contrast, the Conservative party leadership promised to increase home-owning as part of their plan to create 'a property-owning democracy', a phrase coined in 1946 by Anthony Eden, then deputy leader of the Opposition.

Following their election victory in 1952, the Conservatives removed the requirement that local authorities obtain ministerial consent to sales. Instead the 'general consent', contained in MHLG Circular 64/52, allowed them to sell their housing and simply to notify the Minister on completion. No longer were local authorities obliged to obtain the best price for the houses they sold. For pre-1945 houses, the price was to be at least 20 times the net annual rent. For post-war houses, the price was to be not less than the all-in cost of providing the house. Authorities were also required to impose conditions on sale, limiting the resale price for a period of five years and reserving a right of pre-emption so that they could buy back the property at its original price if the purchaser resold it within five years. Between 1953 and 1959 local councils sold an annual average of only 2,003 houses, which included houses built for sale as well as those bought by sitting tenants (Merrett, 1979: 119).

The next general consent, given by a Conservative government in 1960, stated that the terms of the 1952 Circular were minima and cautioned authorities not to sell at 'sacrificial' prices. It also asked authorities to consider carefully the effect that sales would have on their ability to accommodate poorer families at rents within their means.

In the lead up to the 1964 general election it was Labour which made the running on housing and home ownership. The new Labour government let the 1960 general consent continue in force and actively supported council house sales in the new towns in order to achieve a social and economic balance. The encouragement of home ownership was desirable but was 'primarily a matter for the private sector to deal with' (HC Deb (1967) vol. 740, col. 1336). In the private rented sector, the Leasehold Reform Act 1967 gave long leaseholders the right to purchase freeholds or extend leases by 50 years. At the same time, however, the government increased building targets and specified that 50 per cent of new building should be by local authorities for letting. The number of council house sales was too low to pose a threat to the government's housing programme (Forrest and Murie, 1991a: 47).

The rate of sales stayed at around 2,000 to 3,000 per year until the late 1960s, when the Conservatives won control of many major local authorities (notably Greater London and Birmingham) and began to mount enthusiastic sales campaigns. Circular 24/67 was a response to this substantial growth in sales in certain areas. It replaced the 1952 minima and, for the first time, required sale prices to be based on market valuations. Because of the problems involved in making valuations and the restrictions on resale, authorities were allowed to reduce values by up to 20 per cent below the vacant possession market value provided that no loss on the sale was incurred. It attempted to dissuade local authorities from selling accommodation in areas where there was a pressing social need for rented housing.

In 1968 over 8,000 sales were recorded, despite the Labour government's Circular 42/68 which imposed a limit on the proportion of municipal stock to be sold annually in the major conurbations. On the return of a Conservative government in 1970, these restrictions were removed and a general consent was given to local authorities that houses could be sold at full market value, or at a discount of up to 20 per cent on condition that the house was offered back to the council if it was re-sold within five years (MHLG Circular 54/70). Sales figures rose by what was then quite a dramatic rate, peaking at 45,000 in 1972 when the government issued a circular stating that applications to buy should only be refused in exceptional local circumstances. A further circular issued in 1973 enabled councils to increase the discount to 30 per cent, but only with ministerial consent.

The Conservative party's 1974 election manifesto contained a commitment that it would place a duty on every council to sell tenants their homes at a price one-third below market value (Conservative Party, 1974: 16–17). In the event, however, a Labour government – which had pledged to provide every family with 'a decent home' – was returned. Circular 70/74 maintained that in general, local authorities should not sell council houses in areas where there were substantial needs to be met for rented dwellings, as in large cities. While the sale of council houses into owner-occupation might be appropriate in some areas to achieve a better housing balance, it should not occur where there was an unmet demand for rented accommodation. The general consent was reissued, however, although the government's apparent lack of concern may be explained by the dominance of Labour in the large urban authorities (Forrest and Murie, 1991a: 54). Certainly, annual sales did not exceed 5,000 between 1974 and 1976.

The rise in the number of council house sales during the late 1970s was attributable to the Conservatives regaining control of many urban local authorities. In March 1979, therefore, the Labour Secretary of State for the Environment announced restrictions to prevent 'indiscriminate and irresponsible' sales of stock at discounts by some Conservative-controlled authorities. There was a tension in the Labour party, however, between those with a traditional allegiance to council housing and those who supported owner-occupation.

In 1979, the Conservatives won the general election, having made clear in their manifesto their commitment to the sale of council houses. In the Debate on the Queen's Speech in 1979, the new Prime Minister, Margaret Thatcher, spoke enthusiastically about the 'thousands of people in council houses and new towns [who] came out to support us for the first time because they wanted a chance to buy their own homes' and of making 'a giant stride towards making a reality of Anthony Eden's dream of a property-owning democracy' (HC Deb (1979–80), vol. 967, cols 79–80). The government lost no time in putting its pre-election promises into effect. During the second

Table 19.1 Local Authority dwellings sold 1970–79 (England and Wales)

1970	6,231
1971	16,851
1972	45,058
1973	33,720
1974	4,153
1975	2,089
1976	4,582
1977	12,020
1978	29,100
1979	40,550

Source: DoE, 1981: Table 82.

reading of the Housing Bill (which was to go on to confer the RTB), Michael Heseltine, then Secretary of State for the Environment, spoke of the 'deeply ingrained desire for home ownership' which 'ensures the spread of wealth through society, encourages a personal desire to improve and modernise one's home, enables parents to accrue wealth for their children and stimulates the attitudes of independence and self-reliance that are the bedrock of a free society'. The proposed legislation, he said, laid the foundations 'for perhaps as profound a social revolution as any of our history' (HC Deb (1979–80) vol. 976, cols 1444–5). Nonetheless, at its heart, the RTB was simply a mechanism for increasing owner-occupation, and little or no thought appears to have been given to 'the loss of re-lets, the financial implications of the policy' or its contribution to 'the development of welfare housing' (Murie and Ferrari, 2003: 8).

The Housing Act 1980 provided for a system of centrally directed, compulsory sales with a more generous level of discount. Tenants of three years' standing were entitled to an immediate 33 per cent discount and for every additional year of tenancy a further 1 per cent discount was added, up to a maximum of 50 per cent of the property valuation. The discount was justified on two grounds: first, it was common practice to give discounts to sitting tenants in the private sector who bought their homes and, secondly, it was claimed that tenants should be compensated for past rent payments. The Housing and Building Control Act 1984 reduced the residence qualification and increased the maximum discount, leading to the observation that the discount rate had become simply 'a balancing act between providing sufficient incentive to maintain sales and generating a certain level of capital receipts' (Forrest and Murie, 1992: 141). The current provisions regarding the discount to which the tenant may be entitled are dealt with below. The frequent changes meant that what had started off as a relatively simple scheme soon became much more complex (see Murie and Ferrari, 2003: 11–13).

While it was undoubtedly the case that a number of local authority landlords were guilty of 'poor management, bureaucratic incompetence and petty restriction', such problems were probably not widespread, and could have been rectified by measures such as the extension of tenant participation, greater self-management by tenants, and improved transfer and allocations policies, rather than by the disposal of council stock (Lansley, 1979: 173). The eager take-up by tenants of the RTB has probably owed less to their dissatisfaction with their local authority landlords than to the opportunity they have been given to buy – at knock-down prices – generally well-built and maintained housing which would almost certainly appreciate and which they could pass on to their children (see Murie and Ferrari, 2003: 21). Whether or not 'the encouragement of working-class owner occupation is, at least, partly motivated by the desire to subvert revolutionary and militant activity' (Jacobs, 1981) is a moot point. A survey of people who had bought their council houses between 1968 and 1973 provided no evidence either way that moving into owner-occupation had influenced their political loyalties (Forrest and Murie, 1991b).

Council house sales since 1980

Not surprisingly, sales of local authority housing accelerated rapidly after the RTB provisions came into force. The scheme was highly publicised and 'made more attractive by the expectation that rents would rise' (Murie and Ferrari, 2003: 9). The Conservative government's support for the extension of the 'property owning democracy' continued throughout the 1980s. Its commitment to home ownership was reaffirmed in its election manifesto of 1987 and, in the 1987 White Paper, one of its four main objectives for future housing policy was stated to be the 'spread [of] home ownership as widely as possible, through encouraging suitable market conditions, continuing tax relief on mortgage interest, and pressing on with the right to buy' (DoE, 1987a: para. 1.4).

Rising real incomes for households in employment, lower levels of unemployment and rising rents ensured the continuation of high levels of council house sales in 1988 and 1989 despite an escalation in house prices and rising interest rates followed by a general recession in the property market. Moreover, high discounts helped cushion RTB purchasers from rising prices and mortgage interest rates, and the uncertainty over the future of council housing raised by various provisions in the Housing Act 1988 and the Local Government Act 1989 may also have encouraged tenants to move into home ownership (Forrest and Murie, 1992: 142). Sales have averaged 91,000 per annum but there was a temporary upsurge in 2002–3, with over 230,000 sales taking place after the prospective capping of discounts was announced.

The RTB has expanded the socio-economic base of home ownership, extending to many tenants an opportunity they would not otherwise have had to enter owner occupation. However, as indicated in Chapter 3, home ownership has become a more hazardous enterprise than in previous decades. Unemployment, the spread of atypical employment, high interest rates, cuts in mortgage interest tax relief and in income support for unemployed borrowers have seriously affected the ability of many people to enter or maintain owner-occupation, particularly in areas where sales have traditionally been high. There are also those who have found themselves saddled with virtually worthless properties, design defects having come to light since the purchases took place, or facing drastic increases in service charges (see *The Guardian*, Society, 9 August 1995; Murie and Ferrari, 2003: 34). The fact that the more desirable, better-maintained dwellings have been sold off has compounded the process of 'residualisation', whereby the disadvantaged have become increasingly concentrated in council housing – ironically at the same time as this sector has been starved of investment funds and subsidies, housebuilding has dropped to a very low level, whilst rents (and by necessity means-tested benefits) have increased (Malpass and Murie, 1999: 123–30).

Nonetheless, while it may have contributed less than half of the growth in owner-occupation since 1980 (and may therefore be less significant in this regard than is commonly supposed), the RTB been a political success; it has supported tenant purchasers whose household incomes can sustain mortgages, demonstrated government commitment to reducing 'dependency' on the state, bolstered public support for 'private enterprise', and exposed 'the political weakness of tenants, trade unions and other lobbyists such as academics and Shelter' who had pointed out some of the adverse effects of the scheme (Goodlad and Atkinson, 2004: 453).

Although New Labour has declared itself to be 'committed' to maintaining the RTB scheme (ODPM, 2003a: 34), government support in recent years has been relatively subdued and a number of reforms have made purchase less financially attractive to prospective buyers, most notably by capping the discount in those parts of the country where housing demand is particularly high (see below). Clearly, this has had, and will continue to have, a dampening effect on RTB sales. Powers under s. 157 have also been used to designate particular areas as 'rural'. This means that RTB sales in such areas can be subject to a covenant which either permits resale only to a person who has lived or worked in a 'rural area' for at least three years immediately prior to the sale or – with the Secretary of State's consent – gives the landlord a right of first refusal if the purchaser wishes to sell the property within 10 years.

Significant amendments to the RTB scheme have also been made by the Housing Act 2004 which inserts a number of new provisions into the Housing Act 1985. One of the most important changes made by the 2004 Act would appear to be the introduction into the 1985 Act of a new covenant which gives the former landlord (or some other body prescribed by the Secretary of State – most probably another local social landlord) a right of first refusal when properties are resold within 10 years of the date of the initial sale (s. 156A). This measure – which has been introduced as a result of the government's concern about 'the scheme's impact on the availability of affordable housing' (ODPM, 2004: para. 5) – applies to the tenant purchaser or any successor in title. However, given that the landlord will have sold the property at a discount, but the offer will be to sell it at current market value, there are doubts as to whether many local authorities will be able to afford to buy back their stock – even if, as Loveland points out, they are 'ideologically willing' to do so, especially as an authority may soon find itself having to resell the property at a discount to another tenant who has RTB status. While some RSLs which are prescribed as nominees under the system may have the resources to buy back former council properties, it is unlikely that this provision will affect many properties.

The dominance of owner-occupation and local authority housing by the end of the 1970s meant that there was very little choice for households which had difficulty in accessing loans to finance house purchase but also fell outside the priority categories for local authority housing. A large part of the appeal of the RTB therefore was element of choice it introduced into people's housing options, by enabling council tenants to choose their tenure. Over the past 25 years, however, owner-occupation has become generally more accessible and changes in both the social and private rented sectors (including in the latter instance, its expansion and the portability of housing benefit) have introduced greater choice. The case for the RTB has consequently become less strong (Murie and Ferrari, 2003: 16). The recent legislative changes to the scheme should be considered in a context in which many of the circumstances which led to its introduction no longer exist.

The subject-matter of the right to buy

Secure tenants have the right to either pay the freehold or be granted a long lease of the dwelling-house in which they are living. If the dwelling-house is a house and the landlord owns the freehold, the tenant will acquire the right to purchase the freehold. If the dwelling-house is a house and the landlord does not own the freehold, or if the dwelling-house is a flat, the tenant will acquire the right to be granted a long lease (s. 118(1)). This will usually be for a minimum term of 125 years at a rent not exceeding £10 per annum.

The 'qualifying tenant' and the 'qualifying period'

The RTB can only be enjoyed by a secure *tenant* and not, therefore, a *licensee* who has acquired statutory protection under s. 79(3) of the 1985 Act. The tenant must have held a public sector tenancy (i.e. one where the 'landlord condition' and the 'tenant condition' of ss. 80 and 81 are satisfied) for the 'qualifying period,' as defined by Sch. 4. The Housing Act 2004 has extended the qualifying period from two to five years, but only for secure tenancies entered into since 18 January 2005.

The qualifying period does not have to be a continuous period (Housing Act 1985, Sch. 4, para. 1) and it need not immediately precede the tenant's exercise of the RTB (Sch. 4, para. 2(a)). The tenant need not have had the same landlord for the whole of the period, nor the tenancy of one particular dwelling-house. Where the secure tenancy is a joint tenancy, the qualifying period has only to be satisfied with respect to one of the joint tenants (s. 119(2)). Secure tenants of local authorities who are transferred to the private sector following a voluntary transfer, for example, retain a 'preserved RTB', even though they are no longer secure tenants (s. 171).

If the secure tenancy is a joint tenancy, the RTB belongs jointly to all of the tenants, or to such one or more of them as they may agree, provided that the person or at least one of the persons to whom the RTB is to belong occupies the dwelling-house as his or her only or principal home (s. 118(2)).

A sole secure tenant may require that the RTB is shared with not more than three members of the tenant's family who occupy the dwelling-house as their only or principal home (s. 123) but only if that member is:

(a) the tenant's spouse or civil partner or has been residing with the tenant throughout the period of 12 months ending with the giving of notice; or
(b) a family member who does not satisfy the residence requirement but the landlord consents.

The joint purchasers will then be treated as joint tenants of the property.

The RTB cannot be exercised if the tenant purchaser (a) is obliged to give up possession of the dwelling-house in pursuance of an order of the court or will be so obliged at a date specified in the order; or (b) has a bankruptcy petition pending against him, or is an undischarged bankrupt, or has made a composition or arrangement with creditors which has not been finalised; or (c) is the subject of a suspension order (s. 121A).

Suspension orders were introduced by the Housing Act 2004 as part of the government's anti-social behaviour strategy. In order to make a suspension order, the court must be satisfied that (a) the tenant, or a person residing in or visiting the dwelling-house, has engaged or threatened to engage in conduct to which ss. 153A or 153B of the Housing Act 1996 apply (anti-social behaviour or use of premises for unlawful purposes), and (b) it is reasonable to make the order. When making a decision as to reasonableness, the court must consider, in particular (a) whether it is desirable for the dwelling-house to be managed by the landlord during the suspension period; and (b) where the conduct in question consists of conduct by a person which is capable of causing nuisance or annoyance, the effect that the conduct (or the threat of it) has had on other persons, or would have if repeated (s. 121A(4)).

Properties excluded from the right to buy

Section 120 of the Housing Act 1985 provides that the RTB will not arise in the following cases, which are set out in Sch. 5:

(a) the landlord is a charitable housing association or housing trust (Sch. 5, para. 1);
(b) the landlord is a co-operative housing association or a housing association which has at no time received public funds (Sch. 5, paras 2 and 3);
(c) the landlord does not own the freehold or does not have an interest sufficient to grant a lease (21 years for a house and 50 years for a flat);
(d) the dwelling-house is let in connection with employment;

(e)   the dwelling-house has features which are substantially different from those of ordinary dwelling-houses and are designed to make it suitable for occupation by physically disabled persons and (i) it is one of a group of dwelling-houses which it is the practice of the landlord to let for occupation by physically disabled persons, and (ii) a social service or special facilities are provided in close proximity wholly or partly for the purpose of assisting those persons (Sch. 5, para. 7). In *Freeman v Wansbeck District Council* [1984] 2 All ER 746, it was held that the introduction of an indoor downstairs lavatory was not a feature 'substantially different', even though introduced by the use of powers contained in the Chronically Sick and Disabled Persons Act 1970 for the benefit of the tenants' daughter who suffered from spina bifida. 'Designed' was held to refer to the architectural process; it does not mean 'intended'. A similar exclusion exists in respect of dwelling-houses occupied by people who are suffering, or have suffered, from a mental disorder (Sch. 5, para. 9). There is no requirement for physical adaptation of the property. Only grouped accommodation will qualify;

(f)   the dwelling-house is one of a *group* of dwelling-houses (i) which are particularly suitable, having regard to their location, size, design, heating systems and other features for occupation by elderly persons, and (ii) which it is the practice of the landlord to let for occupation by persons aged 60 or more, or for occupation by such persons and physically disabled persons (Sch. 5, para. 10(1)). The services of a resident warden must be provided or a non-resident warden, a system for calling and the use of a common room in close proximity to the group of dwelling-houses (Sch. 5, para. 10(2));

(g)   the property is an *individual* dwelling-house (Sch. 5, para. 11) subject to the same conditions as in para. 10 (above);

(h)   the dwelling-houses is held on a Crown Tenancy;

(i)   a final demolition notice is in force in respect of the dwelling-house and the proposed demolition date falls within the period of 24 months beginning with the date of service of the notice (Sch. 5, para. 13). This exclusion, (introduced by the Housing Act 2004) is designed to stop tenants from buying the property during the consultation stage of a regeneration scheme and, when the local authority subsequently acquires the property under a compulsory purchase order, from receiving full market value compensation (despite having bought the property at a discount) together with disturbance payments and a potential entitlement to rehousing (ODPM, 2003b: para. 1.4).

The purchase price

The price payable for the dwelling-house is its market value at the time when the tenant serves notice under s. 122 claiming to exercise the RTB, less the discount to which the purchaser is entitled (s. 126). If a dispute arises as to the value of the dwelling-house, it must be referred to the district valuer for determination under s. 128.

The value of the dwelling-house is the price it would realise if sold on the open market by a willing vendor. Section 127 sets out the assumptions that should be made in reaching a valuation. If the freehold is to be conveyed the assumptions are that:

(a) the vendor was selling an estate in fee simple with vacant possession;
(b) neither the tenant nor a member of the tenant's family residing with the tenant wanted to buy; and
(c) the dwelling-house was to be conveyed with the same rights and subject to the same burdens as it would be in pursuance of Part V of the Act (s. 127(2)).

If a lease is to be granted the assumptions are that:

(a) the vendor was granting a lease with vacant possession for a term of 125 years (or if the landlord's interest is less than 125 years, for a term of five days less than the length of the landlord's term);
(b) neither the tenant nor a member of the tenant's family residing with the tenant wanted to take the lease;
(c) the ground rent would not exceed £10 per annum; and
(d) the grant was to be made with the same rights and subject to the same burdens as it would be in pursuance of Part V of the Act (s. 127(3)).

Any improvements made by the tenant will be disregarded, as will a failure by the tenant to keep the dwelling-house in good internal repair (s. 127(1)(b)). Service charges or improvement contributions will be assumed not to be less than the amounts specified in the landlord's notice under s. 125 (s. 127(1)(c)).

The discount

The amount of the tenant's discount depends on the length of the 'qualifying period', i.e. the amount of time that the tenant has been a public sector tenant (see above).[1] Originally, the same discount rates applied to both flats and houses, but the disproportionately poor take-up of flats led to the introduction of a preferential discount. At their most generous levels, the discount

---

1   For a discussion of the legal and policy ramifications where the purchase is funded partly by the discount and some or all of the remainder by somebody other than the tenant, see Hopkins and Laurie (2006).

for a house was 33 per cent plus 1 per cent for each complete year by which the qualifying period exceeded two years, up to a maximum of 60 per cent; for a flat, it was 44 per cent plus 2 per cent for each complete year by which the qualifying period exceeded two years up to a maximum of 70 per cent. The maximum discount was £50,000. However, New Labour has twice used the powers under s. 131 to cap the discount in those parts of the country where housing demand is particularly high. First, in 1998, total discounts were capped on a range between £24,000 and £38,000 depending upon the region in which the property was located (Housing (Right to Buy) (Limits on Discount) Order). In 2003, the discount was further capped in London and much of the South East of England at just £16,000 (Housing (Right to Buy) (Limits on Discount) (Amendment) Order 2003).

Where joint tenants are seeking to exercise the RTB, the discount is calculated by reference to the joint tenant who satisfies the longest qualifying period (s. 129(3)). A full discount is not available where the tenant has exercised the RTB on a previous occasion (s. 130). Where, before completion of the sale, another person become the secure tenant other than by way of exchange under s. 92, 'the new tenant shall be in the same position as if the notice had been given by him and he had been the secure tenant at the time it was given' (s. 136). In *McIntyre v Merthyr Tydfil District Council* (1989) 21 HLR 320, the Court of Appeal held that the new tenant is in the same position as if he or she had been the secure tenant, with all the secure tenant's qualities and characteristics. The secure tenant's daughter (who succeeded to the tenancy on her mother's death) was thus entitled to the same discount as her mother, rather than a lesser one based on her own period of residence.

Repayment of the discount

The RTB is not intended to give tenants the opportunity of making a quick profit by buying at a discount and then selling the property on at a full market price. Section 155 of the 1985 Act therefore provides for RTB discounts to be repaid – by way of a covenant in the conveyance or (in the case of flats) the long lease – if the property is sold. Thus, where the dwelling-house has been purchased at a discount, the purchaser must covenant to repay some or all of the discount to the landlord if there is a 'relevant disposal' within five years of the conveyance or grant. A 'relevant disposal' is:

(a) a further conveyance of the freehold or an assignment of the lease; or
(b) a grant of a lease or sub-lease for more than 21 years otherwise than at a rack rent, whether the disposal is of the whole or part of the dwelling-house (s. 159(1)).

The liability to make a repayment does not arise in the case of exempt disposals, e.g. on the vesting of the property under a will or on intestacy, or a disposal under ss. 23, 24 or 24A of the Matrimonial Causes Act 1973,

s. 17(1) of the Matrimonial Homes and Family Proceedings Act 1984 or para. 1 of Sch. 1 to the Children Act 1989. Where, however, the property is *sold* pursuant to an order of the court in matrimonial proceedings, the sale is not an exempt disposal (*R v Rushmoor Borough Council ex p Barrett* (1988) 20 HLR 366).

Previously, the covenant required payment of the discount if the re-sale took place within three years of the exercise of the RTB, with the amount reduced by one-third for each complete year which had elapsed since the conveyance or grant of the lease. There was concern however that the three-year period 'encourage[d] tenants in high demand areas to buy with the intention of selling as soon as possible, to take advantage of rising prices' (Standing Committee E, 16th sitting, 12 February 2004, col. 574 (Keith Hill, Minister for Housing and Planning)). The Housing Act 2004 therefore extended the period to five years but gave landlords greater flexibility by providing that the covenant shall be to pay the landlord such sum (if any) as the landlord may demand as is considered 'appropriate' to the specified maximum (Housing Act 1985, ss. 155(2), 155A). Guidance published in January 2005 advises that the discretion to waive repayment should be exercised only in circumstances where, for example, the owner wishes to move because there is a demonstrable threat of violence or of significant harm, or a move is essential because of the sudden onset of a severe medical condition or serious deterioration of an existing condition , or to enable a return to employment (e.g. because there is a firm offer of a job in another area), or because of a traumatic personal event such as a sudden bereavement. It also suggests that any waiver of discount should only be made where the purchaser cannot afford to repay the full sum due (ODPM, 2005: 5, 9).

The changes made to the repayment provisions by the 2004 Act mean that the sum repayable may now be expressed in 'relative and mobile rather than absolute and static terms' with discount repayment being linked for the first time to house price inflation (Loveland, 2004: 409). By s. 155A(2), the discount is expressed as a percentage of the dwelling-house under s. 127 and the maximum amount of repayment will be an equivalent percentage of the resale price. Section 155A(3) provides that 'for each complete year which has elapsed after the conveyance or grant and before the disposal the maximum amount which may be demanded by the landlord is reduced by one fifth'. In calculating the maximum amount to be demanded, the landlord may disregard any amount of the resale price which is attributable to improvements made since the exercise of the RTB by the person selling the property (s. 155C(1)). If the amount to be disregarded cannot be agreed, the district valuer may make a determination if it is reasonable and the seller pays the costs (s. 155C(2)).

The 2004 Act also aims to discourage 'deferred resale agreements' where private companies offer incentives (usually in the form of a lump sum) to council tenants to take up their RTB. The former tenants then lease the property to the company with a commitment to sell it to them at below market price after the three-year discount repayment period has passed (see ODPM: 2003b, 4.24–4.55). Such schemes appear to have been confined to inner London and the number of properties acquired in this way are probably in the low thousands (ibid.: 8.32). Although the tenants themselves could have exercised their RTB without entering into such arrangements, they may have been unwilling to do so because they were intending to emigrate or to move away from London or because 'their property is not mortgageable by standard sources' or because 'they are unhappy with its characteristics' (ibid.: 8.35). As a result, many of the properties bought under these schemes are flats in high rise blocks or on problem estates but which, having become part of the private rented sector, are then let (predominantly to younger non-family households) at high rents. Contrary to the spirit of the RTB legislation, deferred resale agreements mean that there is 'no increase in owner occupation ... despite the public subsidy' (ibid.: 1.6). Section 163A of the 1985 Act therefore makes an agreement between the secure tenant and his successor in title and any other person a 'relevant disposal' (so that repayment of the discount can be demanded under the covenant imposed by s. 155) if it is an agreement:

(a) which is made (expressly or impliedly) in contemplation of or in connection with, the tenant exercising or having exercised the RTB;
(b) which is made before the end of the discount repayment period; and
(c) under which a relevant disposal (other than an exempted disposal) is or may be required to be made to any person after the end of that period.

The right to buy procedure

A tenant wishing to exercise the RTB must serve a notice on the landlord (s. 122). This notice, which can be withdrawn at any time before completion, must be in the form prescribed in the Housing (Right to Buy) (Prescribed Forms) Regulations 1986, as amended. The landlord has four weeks in which to serve a written notice in reply either (a) admitting the RTB, or (b) denying it and stating the reasons why, in the landlord's opinion, the tenant does not have the RTB (s. 124). If the landlord denies the tenant's right to exercise the RTB, the tenant can apply to the county court for a declaration (s. 181).

If the landlord admits the tenant's RTB, or approval is given by the county court, the landlord must serve notice upon the tenant in accordance with s. 125. This notice should be served within eight weeks if the tenant has the right to acquire the freehold, or within 12 weeks if the tenant has the right to be granted a lease (s. 125(1)). Where the RTB was first claimed on or after 11 October 1993, the notice must, *inter alia*, describe the dwelling-house, state the price payable and show how that price was arrived at, contain estimates of service charges or improvement contributions (where appropriate), state the provisions which, in the opinion of the landlord, should be contained in the conveyance or grant, and contain a description of any structural defect known to the landlord (s. 125(2)).

Within 12 weeks of receiving the s. 125 notice, the tenant must serve a further notice on the landlord stating whether the tenant intends to pursue his or her claim to exercise the RTB, or to withdraw the claim (s. 125D). Alternatively, the tenant may serve notice under s. 144 claiming to exercise the right to acquire on rent to mortgage terms.

As soon as all the matters relating to the purchase of the freehold or the grant of the lease have been agreed or determined, the landlord is under a duty to complete (s. 138(1)). However, the landlord may become entitled to possession at any time up to completion on any of the grounds contained in Sch. 2 to the 1985 Act. This is because the exercise of the RTB is not a once and for all step but a continuing process which is 'exercised' each and every time the tenant takes any step towards its implementation (*Enfield London Borough Council v McKeon* [1986] 1 WLR 1007).

The tenant can withdraw from the process at any time up to the completion or grant by serving written notice on the landlord (s. 122(3)). If all relevant matters have been agreed or determined, the landlord can serve a notice at any time on the tenant requiring completion within a specified period of not less than 56 days (s. 140). If the tenant fails to comply with this preliminary notice, the landlord may serve a further and final notice (s. 141). If the tenant fails to comply with the second notice within the specified time (which must be at least 56 days) the RTB is deemed to have been withdrawn.

Enforcing the right to buy

There are a number of ways in which the landlord's duty to complete the purchase or grant the lease can be enforced. The following are the most important:

(a) As soon as all matters relating to the grant have been agreed or determined in accordance with s. 138(1), the tenant is entitled have the freehold conveyed or the lease granted and can seek an injunction (ss. 138(3), 150(3)) or a decree of specific performance. However, the landlord's duty to complete the transaction will be suspended while an application is pending for a demotion order under s. 82A, a possession order under ground 2 of Sch. 2 or a suspension order under s. 121A (Housing Act 1985, s. 138(2B)).

(b) The tenant can utilise the self-help remedy contained in ss. 153A and 153B. This involves service of an initial notice of delay followed by an 'operative notice of delay' if the landlord fails to serve a counter-notice within the time allowed. Thereafter, all future payments of rent can be credited against the eventual purchase price.

(c) The Secretary of State has extensive default powers to intervene when it is apparent that 'tenants generally, a tenant or tenants of a particular landlord have or may have difficulty in exercising effectively or expeditiously the RTB' (s. 164). The Secretary of State may directly vest the freehold or long leasehold interest, recover the costs with interest from the local authority (ss. 165–166) and provide assistance to the tenant, including legal assistance and arranging legal representation (s. 170). The decision to intervene under the default powers can only be challenged on judicial review.

In *Norwich City Council v Secretary of State for the Environment* [1982] 2 QB 808, Norwich City Council received some 900 applications claiming the RTB during the first year that the Housing Act 1980 was in force. The council, with a long history of Labour control, was opposed to the sale of council houses and had not used its powers voluntarily to dispose of its purpose-built council housing. However, its members did not oppose the expansion of home ownership and, in the past, the council had sold some acquired council dwellings. In most cases, the council admitted the RTB within the prescribed four-week period but there began to be complaints of delay, particularly with regard to valuation of the properties and obligatory counselling interviews arranged by the council for all prospective purchasers. From May 1981 the Department of the Environment took the matter up with Norwich City Council which led, after correspondence, negotiation and meetings, to a demand by the Secretary of State that all outstanding valuations be completed by February 1982. The council would not promise to complete them before June 1982. The Secretary of State exercised formal powers and Norwich applied unsuccessfully to the Divisional Court for an order of certiorari to quash the decision to intervene. The Court of Appeal dismissed Norwich's appeal. Lord Denning MR held that intervention should occur only if the authority's default was unreasonable or inexcusable. The remainder of the Court of Appeal, however, held that the Secretary of State could intervene whenever it appeared that tenants have or may have difficulty in exercising RTB effectively or expeditiously, regardless of whether or not the authority's behaviour was reasonable, provided that the Secretary of State's own decision was one to which a reasonable man might come in accordance with normal administrative law principles.[2]

Section 164 – described by the Court of Appeal as 'coercive', 'Draconian' and 'clearly framed by Parliament to maximise the minister's power and to minimise any power of review by the court' – can be seen as 'perhaps one of the strongest indications of the way in which the Thatcher Governments used Parliament's legislative power to depart from conventional post-war conventional understandings of the proper nature of the relationship between central and local government' (Loveland, 2004: 404, n. 7).

---

2   See Malpass and Murie (1999: 214–17), for an account of the so-called 'Battle for Norwich'.

Housing association tenants

When a local authority transfers its stock to an RSL, the tenants whose homes have been transferred cease to be secure tenants and become assured tenants. They do, however, retain the 'preserved RTB' (Housing Act 1985, ss. 171A–H).

In its 1995 White Paper, the government expressed its full commitment to 'the continued growth of sustainable home ownership, which gives people more opportunities and choice' (DoE, 1995: 12). The Housing Act 1980 had already introduced the RTB for tenants of non-charitable housing associations and one way of continuing the growth of home ownership was made possible by ss. 16 and 17 of the Housing Act 1996 which gives the 'right to acquire' to some tenants of registered social landlords on a similar basis to the RTB. In contrast to the old scheme, under which the sale proceeds went to the Housing Corporation, the newer scheme provides for sale proceeds to be paid to the RSL itself and must be used to replace the stock which has been sold. There are a number of conditions:

(a) The tenant must be an assured tenant (other than an assured shorthold tenant or of a long tenancy), or a secure tenant, of the dwelling-house in question.
(b) The dwelling must have been provided with public money. (A dwelling is provided with public money for this purpose only if it is (i) funded either wholly or in part out of Social Housing Grant under the 1996 Act; (ii) funded out of sales assets from disposals; or (iii) acquired after the commencement of the Act from a public authority.)
(c) The dwelling must have remained in the social rented sector.
(d) The tenant satisfies any further qualifying conditions applicable under Part V of the Housing Act 1985. Thus for new tenancies created on or after 18 January 2005, the tenant must have spent at least five years as a public sector tenant. For those whose tenancies started before 18 January 2005, the qualifying period continues to be two years.

Section 17 gives extensive powers to the Secretary of State to specify the amount or rate of discount to be given on the exercise of the right to acquire, and to designate rural areas where the right is not to apply. The discount currently ranges from £9,000 to £16,000 depending on the local authority area in which the property is situated but are capped at 50 per cent of the value of the property. Since assured tenants of pre-1996 Act stock have neither the RTB nor the right to acquire, the latter has been dismissed as 'a decaffeinated RTB' which 'like too many housing measures since 1980 ... seems designed not so much to solve housing problems but to avoid causing offence by not working' (Coleman, 1996). Around 100,000 housing association tenants have bought their homes, either through the preserved RTB or the right to acquire.

Chapter 20

Anti-social behaviour

Introduction

Anti-social behaviour covers a wide range of activities many of which, taken individually, would probably not amount to breaches of the tenancy agreement or even be regarded as anything more than a relatively minor inconvenience. Cumulatively, however, when experienced on a regular and frequent basis, they may become intolerable. Most reported anti-social behaviour complaints involve domestic noise but others relate to 'violence and verbal abuse, complaints about children, teenagers and pets and problems with misuse of alcohol and drugs . . . as well as . . . graffiti and vandalism' (Pawson *et al.*, 2005: 30). Landlords regard it as covering situations 'from poor garden maintenance right through to assaults on staff or neighbours' (ibid.). Clearly, therefore, anti-social behaviour can include both criminal and non-criminal behaviour. It should also be borne in mind that it 'is not in itself a behaviour but a social construct that can and does vary over space and time' (Card, 2001: 208). As such, behaviour, which might be perfectly acceptable to one person or group of people in a particular setting at a particular time, may be unacceptable to another person or group of people in a different setting and/or at a different time (ibid.).

The Crime and Disorder Act 1998 effectively defines anti-social behaviour as behaviour which causes or is likely to cause 'harassment, alarm or distress to one or more persons not in the same household' (s. 1(1)) while the Housing Act 1996 refers to conduct 'capable of causing nuisance and annoyance to any person' and/or 'use of the premises for unlawful purposes' (s. 153A). The elasticity of the term and the fact that there is no commonly agreed definition – let alone a consistent legal definition – has two consequences. First, taken with the absence of any reliable recording by landlords and other agencies, it makes it difficult to assess the size and severity of the problem. For most people in England and Wales, anti-social behaviour is not a major concern. It is, however, a serious issue for a sizeable minority in some areas, notably those in inner city and deprived areas (Millie *et al.*, 2005: 11, 13). Nonetheless, although 'there is little hard evidence as to the extent of anti-social behaviour and whether this has changed over time' (HCHAC, 2005: 12), there does seem to be a consensus among social landlords that there is a genuine upward trend which is often associated with drug and alcohol misuse and disruptive behaviour by mental health sufferers (Pawson *et al.*, 2005: 30). Whether, however, there has been an actual rise in misconduct is unclear. That victims are increasingly inclined to report incidents may stem in part from the publicity given by the media to anti-social behaviour which has, in turn, raised its political profile but it may also be that social landlords are more willing to respond to it (ibid.: 30). Possibly too communities are less able or willing to reach an informal solution to problems and disputes between their members, thus making anti-social behaviour 'a community as well as an individual problem' (ibid.).

Secondly, the absence of a standard definition makes it more difficult to develop an effective policy response or to judge the effectiveness of legal or other remedies.[1] It is clear, however, that since the 1990s, anti-social behaviour has become a common feature in politics and the media, and a range of strategies has emerged. Flint suggests that the problem has been, and will continue to be, addressed on at least four levels: prioritisation within rhetoric and discourse; changes in the housing management practices and policies of landlords; multi-agency partnerships; and an increasing range of legislative powers (Flint, 2004b: 4). It is the last of these on which this chapter will focus. However, before exploring them in more detail, it is worth considering why – although problems can arise in any tenure – social housing is where they appear to be most commonly encountered and why it has been the focus of government interventions. While 'greater responsibility and self-regulation in the owner-occupied sector' (Flint, 2004a: 903) are said to be notable by their absence – perhaps because it is the sector in which 'active citizenship is represented as normalised conduct' (ibid.: 901), concern has widened more recently to embrace the private rented sector, the response being – as is pointed out in Chapter 5 – the introduction of selective licensing.

Anti-social behaviour and social housing

Areas of bad urban housing have existed in Britain ever since the industrialisation of the nineteenth century encouraged mass migration to the towns and cities (Papps, 1998: 640). Until the development of council housing, the urban poor lived in privately rented accommodation situated near centres of industry and commerce (ibid.). Well into the post-war period, crime and social disorganisation tended to be associated with these declining neighbourhoods which were dominated by deteriorating housing and high levels

---

1   But see HCHAC (2005: 44) for reasons against more specificity in the definition(s) of anti-social behaviour.

of turnover (Murie, 1997: 24). The expectation that such problems would be solved by slum clearance proved to be ill-founded. Nevertheless, even though parts of the council stock in most cities had a poor reputation and were avoided by all except those who had no choice (ibid.: 28), most areas of council housing consisted of stable neighbourhoods occupied by respectable employed working class families, their 'informal and formal processes of social control' often being linked to 'family and kinship networks, and workplace relationships' (ibid.: 24). In estates where there was a dominant local employer, neighbours often worked together – frequently belonging to the same trade union – 'and the disciplines and relationships associated with work spilled over into the organisation of neighbourhoods' (ibid). The association of crime (and, it may be added, anti-social behaviour) with council housing is not therefore 'inherent in council housing provision' but can be explained in terms of the sector's changing role (ibid.: 25).

Even though it has declined in size over the last 25 years and now accommodates some of the most economically deprived households, social housing is expected to deal with and manage the consequences of 'risks that are being decontainerised as a result of welfare restructuring' (Allen and Sprigings, 2001: 392–3). Thus, as well as having to house sexual offenders, individuals requiring care in the community, refugees and asylum seekers (often in the most difficult to let local authority stock), it is also expected 'to tackle the perpetrators of anti-social behaviour' (Flint, 2004b: 4). A reason exists therefore for government intervention. This, however, tends to be based on the premise that problems occur in social housing because of 'deficiencies in the conduct and cultural and social capital of residents', rather than a recognition that 'the actions of government and the utilisation of resources by more affluent and powerful populations' are themselves partly responsible for 'the spatial concentration of social problems' (Flint and Rowlands, 2003: 216). Governmental intervention is made possible because social housing provides a legal, organisational and often geographical framework which is absent from other tenures.

Card maintains the changing nature of 'the political discourse surrounding anti-social behaviour' has contributed to the identification of social housing and its tenants as 'marginalised or excluded', such labels allowing for 'more punitive and rehabilitative measures to be applied to those who fail to conform or fail to act responsibly towards the community in which they live' (Card, 2001: 201). Hawarth and Manzi take a similar view, suggesting that the concepts of 'social exclusion' and 'residualisation', although not themselves explicitly judgmental, 'nevertheless allow an implicit agenda to be shaped, within which traits of stigma and culpability can be introduced' (Hawarth and Manzi, 1999: 158). The designation of social housing as a 'safety-net' limited to those in greatest housing need has, they argue, contributed to the shift in housing management practice towards more interventionist policies designed to deal with a 'marginalised underclass' (ibid.: 159).

Because the allocation of local authority housing is subject to the discretion of local authority officers and members, their role as 'gatekeepers' and 'the designation of tenants and housing applicants as "deserving" and "undeserving"' has become more explicit in housing discourse. The categorisation of local authority residents as 'passive recipients of welfare' may mean that they are more inclined to accept 'authoritarian intervention' in their private lives and the fact that these interventionist policies have been introduced against the background of reduced funding means that 'moral values' can assume a greater prominence (ibid.: 153). At the same time, however, the role of social landlords as agents of social control sits uneasily alongside the 'consumer-oriented' approach to the delivery of housing services in which social tenants are portrayed as active citizens who should be involved in decision-making processes and be able to exercise choice.

The notions of 'social protection, social rights and collective provision' associated with a post-war welfare state in which universal access to health, education and social insurance was seen as a passport towards social citizenship (Marshall, 1950) have given way in recent years to market-oriented policies and a focus on individual responsibilities. Flint highlights the increased emphasis on civic responsibilities of individuals (e.g. to behave with respect for other people), the identification of local neighbourhoods as the most appropriate location of government intervention (hence the focus on neighbourhood renewal and neighbourhood management) and the greater weight placed on 'social and communal relations . . . in the success and sustainability of policy interventions' (Flint, 2004b: 7). While the affluent who are seen as successful citizens and consumers, increasingly live 'an individualistic and privatised existence', poorer groups, including social housing tenants are urged 'to adopt collective neighbourhood-based responses to their social exclusion' (Flint and Rowlands, 2003: 223). At the same time, however, the limitations of these 'community processes' may explain why an increasing emphasis on tenant participation has coincided with more intensive housing management and the greater use by local authorities of 'formal, punitive forms of social control' (ibid.: 222) such as introductory tenancies and repossession. The metamorphosis from what Card describes as 'social' to 'community' government in which 'governments no longer govern from a "social" point of view but through individuals as members of the many and various communities to which they belong' results in a differentiation between the 'affiliated' and the 'marginalised' (Card, 2001: 203). Thus, instead of accepting the existence of an 'environment of diversity and value pluralism', 'politicians and professionals have attempted to narrow the boundaries of "acceptable behaviour" and to become increasingly prescriptive in their approaches' (Hawarth and Manzi, 1999: 157).

Deacon takes a slightly different approach, arguing that 'New Labour's response to anti-social behaviour should also be seen in the context of a broad and far-reaching shift towards greater conditionality in welfare', i.e. that welfare assistance should be made available only to those who fulfil certain conditions regarding their own behaviour and that of their children. He maintains that the primary purpose of such welfare conditionality is to change behaviour rather than to determine entitlement or to establish need. He suggests that this 'marks the abandonment of the largely structural explanations of deprivation and exclusion which dominated left and centre left thinking for much of the post war period', and also recognises the role played by 'the choices, lifestyle and culture of the poor themselves' (Deacon, 2004: 912). The 'non-judgmentalism' on which the provision of welfare rights was formerly based has thus been replaced by the adoption of a more moralistic approach which emphasises the obligations and responsibilities of welfare recipients. However, as Deacon asserts, measures which seek to enforce the obligations which people owe to each other are 'not incompatible with policies to widen opportunities for self-fulfilment and to reduce social exclusion'; it is a mistake to view them therefore as 'necessarily disciplinary in intent or in effect' (ibid.: 911). A recent example of this conditionality is the proposal that local authorities should be empowered to reduce housing benefit for 'unruly tenants' as an alternative or as part of the process of pursuing an Anti-Social Behaviour Order (ASBO), with the restoration of full benefit once the tenant's behaviour had improved (DETR, 2000a: 5.47; DWP, 2003).

Legal responses

Legal responses to anti-social behaviour may be seen as having taken two forms. The first is premised on the belief that, as discussed above, anti-social behaviour is a problem of social housing, and more particularly those who occupy it. The second does not link the problem to a particular tenure or even housing in general but acknowledges that it affects the wider community (Hunter, 2001: 223). Nonetheless, the government has continued to introduce housing-specific measures to deal with anti-social behaviour. Some of these may be regarded as sitting uneasily alongside the pressure being placed on local authorities to adopt a 'holistic' approach by developing strategies which address the underlying causes of anti-social behaviour and which therefore involve 'prevention and resettlement as well as enforcement action' (Hunter and Nixon, 2001: 90). However, they may also be said to recognise the fact that social landlords are 'senior stakeholders' in the community which can 'demand and . . . draw in other service provision when necessary' (DTLR, 2002: 7).

Throughout the history of social housing, landlords have sought to control access to their housing and the conduct of their tenants (Burney, 1999) but they have become increasingly dominant concerns in recent years. By controlling access and excluding 'undesirable' applicants from their housing, landlords can avoid potential anti-social behaviour. We have seen, in Chapter 17, how local authorities may, as a result of changes made to the allocations process by the Homelessness Act 2002, treat an applicant as inel-igible for housing or deny him or her 'reasonable preference' because of 'unacceptable behaviour'. At the same time, the move towards CBL and local lettings is aimed towards the creation of sustainable communities in which a sense of community cohesion can be fostered and social control exerted over standards of behaviour.

Once tenants have been able successfully to access social housing, one of the most effective tools which the landlord has for influencing and control-ling their conduct is the tenancy agreement. Tenancy agreements may be said to have assumed a renewed significance 'in today's individualistic con-sumer age' in which 'contractual governance . . . represents a pre-eminent form of social regulation' (Crawford, 2003: 480). Crawford maintains that there exists a 'complex mesh' of 'parochial contracts' in which people are involved in their 'everyday encounters and interactions' (ibid.). These 'contract-like instruments' – which are not necessarily legal constructs in the strict sense and are often therefore legally unenforceable – are nonetheless 'binding social arrangements' and share a number of common characteristics: the distribution of responsibilities and obligations (which thus facilitate the 'responsibilisation' within civil society); the implication of reciprocity and mutuality; the treatment of the parties as 'self-maximising rational choice actors'; and the assumption of a 'sense of choice' (albeit sometimes through 'the voluntary acceptance of imposed obligations') (ibid.: 489–90). Of course, tenancy agreements *are* legal constructs and *are* legally enforceable. However, by expanding them 'to include more explicit and wide-ranging sections on prohibited behaviours and setting out the desired and expected conduct of tenants' (Flint, 2004b: 8), they can be 'a [pro-active] mode of social control', encouraging self-regulation and self-policing and active rather than merely passive responsibility. This increased emphasis on the use of the tenancy agreement as a means of encouraging responsible behaviour has been bol-stered by the introduction of a range of quasi-legal techniques which aim to achieve a similar objective. An example is the Acceptable Behaviour Contract. This is a written agreement between a perpetrator of anti-social behaviour and a local authority, RSL or the police. It contains a list of anti-social acts which the perpetrator agrees not to continue and sets out the consequences if the agreement is breached. Contracts usually last for six months but can be extended if the parties agree and, although they are not legally binding, they can be used as evidence to support an application for an ASBO or in possession proceedings.

Over the last 10 years or so, concern that anti-social behaviour is a wide-spread and possibly growing problem has led to the introduction of a range of legislative measures to deal with those who perpetrate it (e.g. introduc-tory or starter tenancies (see Chapter 18)) and a wider emphasis on the responsibility of individuals, families and communities for their own well-being. This is reflected in the government's 'Respect' agenda – which locates anti-social behaviour as a community concern with everyone being urged to 'play their part in setting and enforcing standards of behaviour' (Home Office, 2003: 1.14).

Recovery of possession

The procedural aspects of recovery of possession are dealt with in Chapter 18. Here the focus is on the two sets of grounds contained in the Housing Acts of 1985 and 1988 which social landlords can use in cases of anti-social behaviour.

Breach of tenancy obligation

Possession proceedings under this part of ground 1 of the 1985 Act and ground 12 of the 1988 Act are invariably concerned with anti-social behaviour. 'Nuisance clauses' are increasingly used by social landlords to attempt to modify tenants' behaviour. They can cover general harassment, racial, sexual and homophobic harassment, domestic violence, criminal behaviour, the abuse of housing staff, drug-dealing, noise nuisance including loud music, the keeping and behaviour of dogs and other animals, rubbish and litter dumping, untidy gardens, the repair of cars and other vehicles in the street and their unsocial parking. It is often easier to prove 'breach of a clearly worded agreement specifying certain behaviour as unacceptable . . . than establishing the likelihood that such behaviour will cause a nuisance or annoyance' (Sylvester, 2005: 2).

   In considering whether or not it is reasonable to make the order, the court must take into account all the circumstances, including the seriousness of the breach, whether it is capable of remedy, whether it is likely to happen again, and the availability of other remedies such as an injunction. In *Wandsworth London Borough Council v Hargraves* [1994] EGCS 115, one of the conditions of the tenancy was that the tenant should 'not permit to be done anything which may increase the risk of fire'. A visitor brought a can of petrol into the tenant's flat, made petrol bombs and threw them out of the window, damaging a car parked outside. A fire started in the flat from some spilt petrol. The Court of Appeal upheld the decision at first instance that, even though the terms of the tenancy had been broken, it was not reasonable to make an order for possession. The tenant had not taken an active part in the events leading to the fire and there had been no misconduct on his part since the event. In *Sheffield City Council v Jepson* (1993) 25 HLR 299 however, the Court of Appeal overturned a county court judge's decision that it could not be reasonable to make an order for possession against a tenant who had kept a dog in breach of covenant, because the breach was deliberate and persistent. In *Bristol City Council v Mousah* (1998) 30 HLR 32, the Court of Appeal held that only rarely would it be unreasonable to make a possession order where there had been serious breaches of the tenancy conditions. The tenancy agreement provided that the tenant must not 'supply from or in the neighbourhood of the premises any controlled drug'. Within nine months of the start of the tenancy, the premises had been subject to repeated police raids in respect of drug use, surveillance had established a steady stream of visitors calling at the house, many people had been arrested, and drugs, including crack cocaine, had been found hidden on the premises together with the accessories of dealing such as foil, pipes and cling film. The judge at first instance found that if an order was made the tenant would become homeless. Were he to apply to the council as a homeless person, he would probably be regarded as intentionally homeless and cast upon the private market. The judge held that the public interest in ensuring the properties were not used to supply drugs was outweighed by the interest in keeping Mousah off the streets when he might become dangerous because of his schizophrenia. The Court of Appeal held that the judge had been wrong to speculate as to the council's response to any application for housing which Mousah might make after the order was made, and there was no evidence that he would become a danger to the public if rendered homeless. The possession order would be made.

Nuisance or annoyance, etc.

Grounds 2 of the 1985 Act and 14 of the 1988 Act apply where 'the tenant or a person residing in *or visiting* the dwelling-house:

(a) has been guilty of conduct causing or likely to cause a nuisance or annoyance to a person residing, visiting or otherwise engaging in a lawful activity in the locality; or
(b) has been convicted of

    (i)   using the dwelling-house or allowing it to be used for immoral or illegal purposes; or
    (ii) an indictable offence committed in, or in the locality of, the dwelling-house.'

The meaning of 'nuisance' and 'annoyance' has already been considered in Chapter 14. The changes made to both grounds by the Housing Act 1996 (which are shown in italics) would seem to make tenants more vulnerable to eviction on grounds of anti-social behaviour than was previously the case. It must be borne in mind however that grounds 2 and 14 are discretionary and the court will order possession only if it is *reasonable* to do so. Generally, some culpability on the part of the tenant will be required even if the principal perpetrator is a member of the tenant's household or even a visitor. Indeed, recent research has shown that the courts will not entertain possession actions to remove 'anti-social' tenants unless it is evident that the

landlord has tried to resolve the problem by nor
ation (Pawson *et al.*, 2005: 80). Nevertheless, m(
cations based on anti-social behaviour result in
(Hunter *et al.*, 2000). Where the court is cons
able to make an order for possession on th
grounds, the court must consider, in particula

(a) the effect that the nuisance or annoyance
    the person against whom the order is sc
(b) any continuing effect the nuisance or annoyance is
    such persons;
(c) the effect that the nuisance or annoyance would be likely to have on such
    persons if the conduct is repeated (Housing Act 1985, s. 85A; Housing
    Act 1988, s. 9A).

Generally speaking, landlords will consider possession proceedings only in respect of 'serious' offences, e.g. violence or threats of violence, racial harassment and illegal possession of drugs or drug-dealing. Occasionally, however, where other measures have been unsuccessful and the perpetrator's behaviour remains unchanged, some landlords will – as a 'last resort' – serve notices seeking possession in cases of less serious but persistent nuisance, e.g. noise nuisance or dog fouling, hoping that 'the "shock value of a notice" can help to alter a tenant's conduct where all other means . . . have failed' (Pawson *et al.*, 2005: 79). Deciding whether or not a case should be pursued via possession action will also depend on, e.g. how confident the landlord is that the complainant (and/or aggrieved and frightened neighbours) will be able and/or willing to provide credible evidence in court, and whether the alleged perpetrator was subject to any form of vulnerability such as mental ill-health which could affect his behaviour.

In *Camden London Borough Council v Hawkins* (1996) 29 HLR 507, the Court of Appeal dismissed an appeal by the council against a refusal to order possession, one of the reasons being that it would not have been reasonable to order possession against a tenant of 24 years' standing by reason of the activities of her teenage son. In *Ealing Family Housing Association v Taylor* (1996) 29 HLR 507, the judge declined to order possession despite the fact that evidence had been given by two neighbours, an arresting police officer and a visitor to the premises who had been assaulted, and statements made by two officers of the claimant association. The judge found the evidence to be grossly exaggerated, holding that if there had been a nuisance, it was 'slight in all the circumstances'. However, in *Kensington and Chelsea Royal London Borough Council v Simmonds* (1996) 29 HLR 507, the Court of Appeal rejected a submission that some degree of fault on the part of the tenant must be shown before an order for possession can be made. If that submission were right, repossession could not be sought from the parents of an ill-disciplined and uncontrollable old to control but too young to be put out of the house, who had the nuisance and annoyance. An order for possession was upheld, ore, against the tenant (a single parent) whose 13-year-old son had jected neighbours to racial harassment (see too *Bryant v Portsmouth City Council* (2000) 32 HLR 906).

The seriousness of the nuisance and annoyance will be relevant and it may be appropriate to order immediate possession if the tenant makes no assurance as to future behaviour. For example, in *Woking Borough Council v Bistram* (1995) 27 HLR 1 the tenant had allegedly used 'vile and abusive language' in respect of race and sexual orientation and there was no evidence that she intended to mend her ways. In *Lambeth London Borough Council v Howard* (2001) 33 HLR 58, the tenant appealed against a decision not to make a postponed order following a history of harassment against his female neighbour and her daughter. He contended that, for 11 months after his arrest and charge, he had shown that he could behave properly towards his victim. The Court of Appeal dismissed the appeal, holding that the judge had correctly weighed up the fact that during the period pending trial only one minor incident had occurred, against the fear and tension which would be caused to his victim by the tenant's return to his flat under a postponed order. The response was proportionate and did not breach the tenant's rights under Art. 8 of the Human Rights Act 1998. In *London and Quadrant Housing Trust v Root* [2005] HLR 28, the tenant did not challenge the decision to make an order but argued that the judge (who had made a 28-day final order) should instead have postponed it. The main perpetrator of the anti-social behaviour was the tenant's partner who had been made the subject of an ASBO excluding him from the immediate area. Even after his departure, however, the outside of the premises remained in an unacceptable state and the tenant refused access to officers from the Trust to inspect the inside. The Court of Appeal held that the judge had taken into account the factors contained in s. 9A and, in considering whether to postpone the order, had correctly stated that the needs of the tenant and her three children had to be balanced against the very considerable hardships (including threats and intimidation) to which the neighbours had been exposed. There had been a total breakdown in the relationship between the tenant and her landlord (and her neighbours) so that, in the words of Sedley LJ in *Lambeth London Borough Council v Howard*, 'the shadow of the past [was] too heavy upon the present' to allow for those relationships to be repaired (para. 39).

In *Manchester City Council v Romano and Samari* [2005] 1 WLR 2775, the Court of Appeal was called upon to consider the interface between housing legislation and the Disability Discrimination Act 1995. Section 22(3) of the 1995 Act makes it unlawful to discriminate 'by evicting the disabled person [or] subjecting him to any other detriment'. By s. 24(3), a person discriminates against a disabled person if 'for a reason which relates to the disabled person's disability, he treats him less favourably than he treats or would treat others to whom that reason does not or would not apply' and he cannot show that the treatment in question is justified. The only relevant justification in the context of anti-social behaviour is that the occupier poses a danger to others. In *Romano* the local authority landlord had obtained orders for possession against two secure tenants under ground 2. The tenants – one of whom was suffering from a depressive illness and the other from a borderline personality disorder – contended that they were discriminated against under s. 22(3). The Court of Appeal held that, in order to interpret s. 24(3) in a way which was compatible with the ECHR, a court had to ask (a) whether the landlord felt that it was necessary to seek possession in order that the health of a person or persons would not be endangered and (b) if so, whether that opinion was objectively justified. Brooke LJ, delivering the judgment of the court, pointed out that there were evident difficulties in ss. 22 and 24 which – unless Parliament took remedial action – could result in the courts being confronted with 'a deluge of cases in which disabled tenants are resisting possession proceedings'. He suggested that, for example, a tenant could challenge a claim of possession for non-payment of rent because mental disability prevented the efficient management of the tenant's financial affairs. Even where a private landlord relied on a mandatory ground, a disabled tenant could assert that detriment had been caused by his or her selection for eviction. The provisions might also 'preclude social landlords from enforcing injunctions or ASBOs against the mentally disordered' and prevent providers of supported housing from 'evicting or refusing to allocate it in the best interests of the individual or the housing project' (Cobb, 2006: 266).

Subject to the issue of reasonableness, a possession order can be made against a tenant if the tenant or another resident or visitor, is convicted of committing an arrestable offence in the premises or its locality. The extension of the 'conviction' limb was a response to opposition amendments to strengthen local authorities' powers to deal with drug-dealers who operate in the common parts of the estate rather than in a person's home. It extends far beyond drug-dealing, however, as arrestable offences include murder, theft, handling stolen goods, criminal damage, taking a motor car without consent and various sexual offences (Police and Criminal Evidence Act 1984, s. 24).

Demoted tenancies

Demoted tenancies – which temporarily reduce the security of tenure of, and remove several other rights from, an existing tenant – were introduced by the Anti-social Behaviour Act 2003. The idea of such a tenancy was first put forward in the Law Commission's 2002 Consultation Paper. Given that the aim of the Commission was to simplify the existing systems of tenure, there is a certain irony in the fact that its proposals have resulted in the emergence of yet another form of tenancy as part of the statutory armoury against anti-social behaviour.

Since 30 June 2004, local housing authorities, housing actions trusts (HATs) and registered social landlords (RSLs) have been able to apply to the county court for a demotion order in circumstances related to anti-social behaviour (Housing Act 1985, s 82A; Housing Act 1988, s. 6A). If the order is made, a secure tenancy of a local authority or HAT will become a demoted tenancy (Housing Act 1996, s. 143A(5)) while an assured or secure tenancy of an RSL will become a demoted assured shorthold tenancy (Housing Act 1988, s. 20B). The demoted tenancy will last for one year (starting with the day when the demotion order takes effect) during which – as with an introductory tenancy – the tenant may be evicted without the landlord having to prove any grounds for possession. If no notice seeking possession is served by the end of the demotion period or the tenancy has not been terminated, the tenancy reverts to its former status (except for secure housing association tenancies which become assured tenancies). The demotion period may be extended for up to six months by serving a notice of proceedings for possession before the end of the demotion period (Housing Act 1985, s. 143B(3)(4); Housing Act 1988, s. 20B(3)(4)). In those circumstances the demoted or demoted assured shorthold tenancy continues until the notice is withdrawn, the proceedings are determined in favour of the tenant, or no possession proceedings have been brought within six months from the date the notice is given. In effect, demoted tenancies 'remove the time constraints from the probationary period' associated with the introductory tenancy' (Sylvester, 2005: 4) although, unlike introductory or starter tenancies, demoted tenancies can only be made by order of the court.

The court will only make a demotion order if, first, the tenant or a person residing in or visiting the property has engaged or threatened to engage in conduct capable of causing nuisance and annoyance to any person and which directly or indirectly relates to or affects the landlord's housing management functions; or involves using or threatening to use, for an unlawful purpose, housing accommodation owned or managed by the landlord (Housing Act 1996, ss. 153A or B). Secondly, it must be reasonable to make the order.

Local authority landlords or HATs seeking demotion must first serve the secure tenant with a notice in the prescribed form under s. 83 of the 1985 Act. It must specify the date after which proceedings may be begun and state that no proceedings will be begun after the end of 12 months from the date when proceedings first began. RSLs must service notice (for which there is no prescribed form) under s. 6A of the 1988 Act and the period will run from the date of service of the notice. Proceedings to end a tenancy cannot be started earlier than the date on which the tenancy could be brought to an end by notice to quit. Unlike proceedings to seek possession on the grounds of nuisance or annoyance which can begin as soon as the notice has been served (Housing Act 1985, s. 83(4)–(5); Housing Act 1988, s. 8(4)), the minimum length of notice to seek demotion is four weeks for a secure tenant (Housing Act 1985, s. 83(4A), (5)) and two weeks for an assured tenant (Housing Act 1988, s. 6A(7)). The court may dispense with the service of the demotion notice if it considers it just and equitable to do so (Housing Act 1985, s. 83(1)(b); Housing Act 1988, s. 6A(5)(b)).

Landlords are likely to seek a demotion order in two sets of circumstances: either as a stand-alone order or as an alternative to seeking a possession order. A stand-alone demotion order may be sought where there has been anti-social behaviour but the landlord does not wish to evict outright. This may be because there has been 'a gradual increase in the frequency or seriousness of the behaviour' or it has followed from changes in the tenant's circumstances, e.g. someone new moving in with him or her (ODPM, 2004c: 29). Alternatively or additionally, the landlord may want to give a 'strong warning' to the tenant but also to continue to work with him or her to change the behaviour, e.g. 'where the problems are caused by a mental illness and the person is now seeking treatment, or the problems are caused by a child and the parent is now attending parenting classes' (ibid.: 30). If the tenant is unable or unwilling to accept the last chance offered by the demotion order, it provides the landlord with a reliable route to possession given that, once it is granted, demoted status can be extended without further application to the court. The landlord may also chose to seek a demotion order because the facts of the case do not meet the stricter requirements of grounds 2 and 14 of the 1985 and 1988 Acts respectively. In contrast to grounds 2 and 14, the landlord is not required to establish actual conduct; threats of nuisance conduct will suffice. Further, the conduct need only be *capable* of causing nuisance or annoyance and, because there is no requirement for it to be directed at someone residing, visiting or otherwise engaging in lawful activity in the area, it can be directed at anyone, regardless of whether they have any connection with the area, the landlord or the other tenants. The focus now goes beyond behaviour emanating from tenants disrupting the community and encompasses all behaviour by tenants, their families and visitors, subject to the limitation that it must relate to or affect either directly or indirectly the landlord's housing management functions.

Landlords can apply for a demotion order at the same time as a possession order. The court can therefore consider the evidence produced by the landlord in order to seek possession or demotion and to decide upon which option would present the best solution. The court cannot however make a demotion order unless the landlord has specifically requested one. In common with postponed possession orders, demotion orders look to the future and the courts are unlikely to grant them where breach seems to be inevitable. Furthermore, the court may decline to make a demotion order where the tenant's children are likely to be seriously affected (Sylvester, 2005: 6).

Unlike a postponed possession order, a demoted tenancy changes the legal status of the tenant, affecting not only security of tenure but also removing a number of other rights, e.g. the right to buy (RTB) and the right to exchange. Demotion is intended to make clear the 'link between acceptable behaviour and the rights held by the tenant' (ODPM, 2004c: 64). It remains unclear however whether those who were formerly secure tenants of RSLs or those with a preserved RTB, will recover their RTB on promotion and it is possible that Human Rights Act 1998 challenges will be mounted in this regard (Holbrook and Underwood, 2004: 1225). Otherwise, many of the terms of the demoted tenancy remain the same as those of the pre-demotion tenancy, including of course any terms which are implied by law. The parties to the tenancy, the amount of the rent and the dates on which rent is payable will also remain the same, as will the period of the tenancy (although a fixed term tenancy will become a weekly tenancy). Any rent arrears or credits will be transferred to the demoted tenancy (Housing Act 1985, s. 82A; Housing Act 1988, s. 6A(3)(c)(d)). The landlord may also apply any other terms of the pre-demotion tenancy by serving a statement of those terms on the demoted tenant (Housing Act 1985, s. 82(7); Housing Act 1988, s. 6A(10)). Because however there is no obligation to do so, the demoted tenant's only protection may be terms implied by statute or common law (Holbrook and Underwood, 2004: 1225).

Should a local housing authority or HAT decide to end a demoted tenancy, it may apply to the county court for a possession order, having first served on the tenant a notice of possession proceedings. The notice must:

(a) state that the court will be asked to make an order for the possession of the property;
(b) set out the reasons for the landlord's decision to apply for the order;
(c) specify the date after which proceedings for the possession of the property may be begun; and
(d) inform the tenant of the right to request a review of the landlord's decision and of the time within which the request must be made (Housing Act 1996, s. 143E).

The request for an internal review must be made within 14 days of receipt of the notice. The landlord must then give the tenant not less than five days' clear notice of the date of review and inform the tenant of the time and place at which it will be heard. At the hearing the court can only consider whether the appropriate procedure was followed, and not the facts on which the decision was based, or on the merits of its decision. The tenant's remedy for challenging the decision to end the tenancy is judicial review.

A demoted assured tenant of an RSL can be evicted on normal assured tenancy possession grounds. There is no restriction on the landlord obtaining a possession order during the first six months. The RSL can therefore serve the tenant with two months' notice and, provided that the tenancy agreement is in writing, use the accelerate possession procedure. Demoted tenants of RSLs, whose landlord decides to move to possession are not entitled to a review of their landlord's decision but must rely on the standard complaints procedure if they wish to challenge it. If this does not deal with their complaint, they can refer the matter to the Independent Housing Ombudsman. The decision of an RSL may not be susceptible to judicially review (see Chapter 4).

It can be seen therefore that the implications of the demotion order for the tenant are more serious than those of the postponed possession order because they deprive the tenant of a final right to have the court review the case before making an absolute order. Further, the postponed order allows the court to prescribe the type of behaviour which will allow the landlord to enforce possession and therefore allows some flexibility of approach in an area where 'individual tenant's circumstances are often precariously dependent on external factors and are rarely predictable'. By contrast, the demoted tenancy can be ended in much wider circumstances, even if the tenant's behaviour improves or for reasons unconnected with behaviour, e.g. rent arrears.

Injunctions and anti-social behaviour

In cases involving very serious anti-social behaviour, eviction may 'resolve major management problems on estates and ensure more efficient use of resources' but it rarely solves the underlying causes (Hunter and Nixon, 2001: 98) and, indeed, can simply result in the relocation of the problem to another area and/or tenure. Since the mid-1990s therefore many local authorities have used injunctions against their tenants as an alternative to eviction in an attempt to combat nuisance and annoyance on their estates. Originally, they were sought under a variety of provisions: tenancy agreements, ss. 111 and 222 of the Local Government Act 1972, actions in trespass and nuisance, and under the race relations legislation. However, while injunctions could be made in respect of tenants on the basis of a breach of the tenancy agreement, it was very difficult for landlords to take action against non-tenants (Hunter, 2001: 225). The Housing Act 1996 dispensed with the need to use powers which had not originally been intended to deal with the anti-social behaviour of tenants, by introducing a new free-standing injunction which could be sought by a local authority where the person in question (not necessarily a tenant) had committed or threatened to commit violence against someone 'residing in, visiting or otherwise engaging in a lawful activity in or in the locality of local authority housing'. Again in cases of violence or threatened violence, the courts were given the power to add a power of arrest to injunctions based on breach of local authorities' and RSLs' tenancy agreements, with the result that overall responsibility for the problem would be passed on to the police.

Injunctions have a number of advantages: they can be obtained quickly (often within only a few hours) and at the start of possession proceedings for anti-social behaviour (to protect victims and/or other witnesses). The hearing takes place in private rather than in open court and is less intimidating therefore for witnesses. Interim injunctions can be obtained without the need for witnesses to appear in person provided they are prepared to sign an affidavit. An injunction can avoid the need to threaten eviction, but if eviction later becomes necessary, it will help a landlord's case if the terms of an injunction have been breached. However, witnesses may be unwilling to become involved and an injunction may jeopardise a possession action if the judge believes that the injunction itself is adequate. It may prove difficult to enforce an injunction unless the police are prepared to co-operate or the judge is willing to punish breaches of its terms. An injunction lasts only the length of the tenancy and its deterrent effect can be very limited unless breach of the injunction carries a threat of arrest (Pawson, 2005: 83).

The original provisions contained in the Housing Act 1996 were shown to be inadequate in a number of respects and have been replaced by new provisions introduced by the Anti-Social Behaviour Act 2003. Thus, while the original provisions allowed only local authorities to apply for injunctions, the new provisions apply not only to local authority landlords but also to housing actions trusts and, more importantly, RSLs. Now, three different types of injunction are available: the anti-social behaviour injunction, the injunction against unlawful use of the premises, and the injunction against breach of the tenancy agreement. The combined effect is that social landlords can obtain injunctions against a wide range of perpetrators – whether or not violence is involved – in order to protect a wide range of victims. An injunction may be made for a specified period or until varied or discharged and have the effect of excluding a person from his normal place of residence (s. 153E). It may be varied or discharged by the court on an application by the person in respect of whom it is made or the relevant landlord (s. 153E(3)).

The anti-social behaviour injunction may be made where there is conduct which is capable of causing nuisance or annoyance to any person, and which directly or indirectly relates to or affects the relevant landlord's housing management functions (s. 153A). This includes functions conferred by or under any enactment and the powers and duties of the landlord as the holder of an estate or interest in housing accommodation (s. 153E(11)). Formerly, the injunction and power of arrest could be granted against anyone for the benefit of any victim in the 'locality' of local authority premises which were subject to a secure or introductory tenancy or accommodation provided in accordance with Part VII of the 1996 Act (see *Manchester City Council v Lawler* (1998) 31 HLR 119). Now, however, it is immaterial where the conduct occurs (s. 153A(5)). Two conditions must be satisfied. First, the person against whom the injunction is sought must be engaging, have engaged or be threatening to engage in conduct to which the section applies. Secondly, the conduct must be capable of causing nuisance or annoyance to a person who is a member of at least one of four specified groups, i.e:

(a) a person with a right to reside in or occupy housing accommodation owned or managed by the relevant landlord, or in other housing accommodation in the neighbourhood (e.g. owner-occupiers or tenants of other landlords); or

(b) a person engaged in lawful activity in or in the neighbourhood of housing accommodation owned or managed by the relevant landlord; or

(c) a person employed (whether or not by the relevant landlord) in connection with the exercise of the relevant landlord's housing management functions.

An injunction may also be granted under s. 153B where the conduct consists of or involves using or threatening to use housing accommodation owned or managed by a relevant landlord for an unlawful purpose (such as drug-dealing or as a brothel).

Section 153D applies if a social landlord (including a charitable housing trust) applies for an injunction against a tenant in respect of the breach or anticipated breach of a tenancy agreement on the grounds that the tenant is engaging or threatening to engage in conduct that is capable of causing nuisance or annoyance to any person, or is allowing, inciting or encouraging any other person to engage or threaten to do so.

In addition, where it is satisfied that either the conduct includes the use or threatened use of violence, or there is a significant risk of harm, the court may include in the injunction a provision excluding the person in respect of whom it is granted from any specified premises or any specified area (s. 153D(3)) and it may also attach a power of arrest (ss. 153C and 153D(2–4)).

Significantly, the court (either the High Court or a county court) may – if it thinks it just and convenient – grant or vary an injunction without giving the person against whom the injunction is made such notice as is otherwise required by rules of court (s. 153E(4)). It must, however, give that person an opportunity to make representations in relation to the injunction as soon as it is practicable for to do so (s. 153E(5)). In *Moat Housing Group–South Ltd v Harris* [2005] 2 WLR 691, an assured tenant of a housing association lived with her four children (aged between six and 14) in a property which was frequently visited by the children's father (from whom she was estranged). The family was served with 'without notice' anti-social behaviour injunctions which ordered immediate ouster and exclusion. The tenant had never received any warning from her landlord about her or her children's behaviour or that of their father. Giving detailed guidance on anti-social behaviour injunctions, the Court of Appeal said that it was hard to envisage a more intrusive 'without notice' order than one which requires a mother and her four young children to vacate their home immediately and it was 'clearly necessary to restate certain principles' governing the grant of such injunctions.

The court advised that judges in the county courts should bear in mind, first, that to grant an injunction without notice departs from the normal rules as to due process and requires the existence of exceptional circumstances; secondly, that one such exceptional circumstance is a risk of significant harm if the order is not made immediately; and thirdly, that the order must not be wider than is necessary to avoid the apprehended harm. It might be acceptable to restrain a person from anti-social behaviour for a short time until a hearing could be arranged at which both sides could be heard but to make a 'without notice' order directing defendants to leave their home immediately and banning them from re-entering a large part of the area where they live was quite different. It concluded that the extent of the injunction in the instant case was much too wide, and that it should have been restricted to what was necessary to protect prospective witnesses from acts of violence or threats of violence and to restrain acts of nuisance. The impact which the order would have upon the tenant and her family was also significant. For children, to become part of an 'intentionally homeless' family, with the bleak prospect of being allotted sub-standard accommodation with their parents or being taken into care, is such a serious prospect that every RSL should be alert to intervene creatively at an early stage, in order to do everything possible to avoid eviction. Inherent in the right to respect for a home is the principle that procedural fairness will be observed before the home is taken away (see, e.g. *Connors v United Kingdom* (2004) 40 EHRR 189, para. 83), so that an RSL should be slow to short-circuit its normal procedures in nuisance cases by proceeding straight to seeking possession without prior notice.

General legal responses to anti-social behaviour

The Crime and Disorder Act 1998 introduced a variety of provisions to deal with anti-social behaviour. First, it places a general obligation on each local authority 'to exercise its various functions with due regard to the likely effect of those functions on, and the need to do all that it reasonably can to prevent, crime and disorder in its area' (s. 17). It also requires the formation of 'responsible authorities' to work with other local agencies and organisations to develop and implement strategies to tackle crime and disorder and the misuse of drugs in their area (ss. 5–7). Currently, this is carried out under the auspices of Crime and Disorder Reduction Partnerships (CDRPs), which bring together local authorities (including social services and youth offending teams), fire authorities, police authorities and primary care trusts (health authorities in Wales). CDRPs must work in co-operation with local probation boards and other bodies specified by the Secretary of State, and must invite the participation of a variety of local private, voluntary, other public and community groups, as prescribed by the Secretary of State. Section 6 of the 1998 Act obliges CDRPs to formulate and implement a strategy for the reduction of crime and disorder in their area once every three years.

Before doing so, they must carry out a review of the levels and patterns of crime and disorder (including anti-social behaviour) in the area, and publish a report analysing the results of that review. While CDRPs are probably the most important bodies concerned tackling anti-social behaviour at local level, others include Children's Strategic Partnerships, youth offending teams and local criminal justice boards

One of the most notable measures introduced by the 1998 Act is the ASBO. Originally only local authorities or the police could apply for ASBOs on a civil basis in the magistrates' court. The Police Reform Act 2002 made a number of significant amendments, with the result that ASBOs can now be sought by RSLs as well. Application may be made to the magistrates' court, the county court as part of other (e.g. possession) proceedings, or on conviction in other criminal proceedings. Even though ASBOs may be seen as blurring the boundaries between civil and criminal law, the standard of proof to be applied in applications for ASBOs is that required for criminal liability, i.e. beyond all reasonable doubt (R *(on the application of McCann) v Manchester Crown Court* [2003] 1 AC 787). The order may prohibit the defendant from doing anything which the court considers necessary '... for the purpose of protecting [a] person in the . . . area from further anti-social acts by the defendant'. An order lasts for at least two years. Breach of an ASBO without a reasonable excuse is a criminal offence and, on conviction, can be punished with imprisonment for up to five years. However, imprisonment is unlikely and it has been suggested that breach of an ASBO may be used instead by local authorities together with 'techniques of surveillance and investigation' primarily as a way of demonstrating the justification of seeking eviction (Brown, 2004: 209). Certainly, the Court of Appeal has made it clear that if the misconduct by the tenant or even by a member of the tenant's household is 'serious and persistent enough to justify an ASBO then that will be strong but not conclusive evidence that the tenant will have forfeited his right to retain possession' (*Manchester City Council v Higgins* [2006] 1 All ER 841, para. 36).

Before granting an ASBO the court must be satisfied that the person has acted in an anti-social manner, i.e. in a way which causes or is likely to cause 'harassment, alarm or distress to one or more persons not in the same household' (s. 1(1)), and that the order is necessary to protect relevant persons from further anti-social acts or conduct. ASBOs may be obtained therefore against anti-social owner-occupiers – a group in respect of whom most other statutory interventions are unavailable despite the fact that owner-occupation would appear increasingly to be a source of anti-social behaviour. Initially, the limited use of ASBOs by local authorities led to the observation that there were limits to the involvement in crime control of agencies other than the police (Burney, 2002). However, by 2003, some 65 per cent of local authorities and 35 per cent of housing associations had applied for ASBOs against their own tenants (or members of their households) (Pawson *et al.*, 2005: 81)

and in the past three years or so the number of orders has grown significantly, giving some credence to the assertion of that the use of measures
such as ASBOs is indicative of the increasing role played by social housing in
crime control (Cowan *et al.*, 1999). ASBOs can be made in respect of anyone
over the age of 10 and can be used as a means of 'targeting action on disruptive young people rather than (necessarily) seeking a possession order
against the whole household' (Pawson *et al.*, 2005: 81).

Local housing authorities, housing action trusts and RSLs are required to
prepare, publish and keep under review their anti-social behaviour policies,
and their procedures for dealing with occurrences of anti-social behaviour
(Housing Act 1996, s. 218A). Further legal responses to anti-social behaviour are available to local authorities using legislation which is not specifically connected to their role as landlord. For example, they may serve
abatement notices under s. 80 of the Environmental Protection Act 1990 (see
Chapter 8) to try to tackle noise nuisance (probably the most common form
of reported anti-social behaviour). The 1990 Act has been amended by the
Clean Neighbourhoods and Environment Act 2005 which gives a plethora
of new powers to local authorities to deal with litter, noise, graffiti, abandoned vehicles and other anti-social behaviour and to make 'gating orders'
to close highways (s. 2). Whether authorities decide to use their powers is
another matter. The question then becomes one of whether those affected
by anti-social behaviour have any legal redress against a local authority
which fails to tackle it.

The liability of landlords

During the past decade there have been signs of a significant change in the
response of social landlords to anti-social behaviour, with the instigation of
legal action at an earlier stage and a greater commitment to seeing it through
by, e.g. 'developing a greater expertise in court proceedings, deploying professional witnesses and introducing a range of strategies, including protection schemes and the use of anti-social behaviour diaries, to encourage
tenants to provide levels of evidence required in legal proceedings' (Flint,
2004b: 9). Such developments may be attributable in part to 'evolving management practices, perhaps stimulated by changes in regulatory pressures or
obligations' (Pawson *et al.*, 2005: 31). A survey carried out between 1989 and
1992 encountered landlords who were willing to intervene only if blame
could clearly be attributed to one of the parties or who responded to disputes by seeking voluntary rehousing for one or other of the parties (usually the complainant) – a step which clearly ran the risk of transferring the
problem to a new set of neighbours (Hughes *et al.*, 1994: 204). It appears
that there are still a handful of landlords who spend a minimal amount of
time dealing with neighbour disputes (perhaps because they are unsure how
best to deal with them) and rarely take legal action (Hunter and Nixon,
2001: 95). Alternatively, landlords may make half-hearted responses by

asking offenders to modify their behaviour and making 'vague threats' as to the legal consequences if such modification does not occur.

Where a landlord refrains from taking action to address specific instances of anti-social behaviour or there is dissatisfaction with the measures which *are* taken to address it, questions arises as to the private law remedies available to (potential) victims. The first point to note is that the landlord owes no duty of care to enforce a clause in a tenancy agreement, for the benefit of another tenant. Nor will the courts imply a term into the tenancy agreement that the landlord will enforce the nuisance clause against other tenants who are subject to the same obligation, should they commit any breach (*O'Leary v Islington London Borough Council* (1983) 9 HLR 91). Of course, the victim can sue the perpetrator directly (perhaps in nuisance or under the Protection from Harassment Act 1997) but there are obvious attractions in trying to impose liability on the landlord, whether in contract or in tort.

Loveland explains that a money judgment for damages will be a worthless remedy against most social tenants whereas a successful claim against a social landlord will not only provide the claimant with compensation for any loss but might also prompt the landlord to take steps to end the nuisance in question. The ending of the nuisance will be the claimant's primary concern and that such an outcome is more likely to result from a court granting a possession order to a landlord than an injunction against the perpetrator followed by committal for contempt if the terms of the injunction are breached. Only rarely will the courts imprison defendants in such circumstances (but see *Tower Hamlets London Borough Council v Long* (1998) 32 HLR 219), especially where there are children living with the tenant, the imprisonment would be temporary and there is the possibility of nuisance continuing in the future (Loveland, 2005: 273–4).

Where the landowner is the complainant's landlord, there are a number of possible causes of action and two or more of them may be pleaded on the same set of facts. The first relates to the covenant for quiet enjoyment which is implied (if not expressly included) into every tenancy. It is broken 'if the landlord, or someone claiming under him, does anything that substantially interferes with the tenant's title to or possession of the demised premises or with his ordinary and lawful enjoyment of the demised premises. The interference need not be direct or physical' (*Southwark London Borough Council v Mills* [2001] 1 AC 1). The landlord will be liable however only if the interference results from a use of the land by the tenant which is authorised by the terms of the agreement (*Sanderson v Berwick on Tweed Corporation* (1884) 13 QBD 547). Thus, where the tenancy expressly forbids anti-social behaviour or, in the absence of such a term, the landlord attempts to curb it, there cannot be said to have been any authorisation and no breach will have occurred.[2]

2   For an informative discussion of quiet enjoyment in this context, see Davey (2001).

Several cases have been brought in the past few years against landlords and other landowners for the nuisance behaviour of their tenants or licensees, but the courts have been unwilling to impose liability. The starting point here is *Sedleigh-Denfield v O'Callaghan* [1940] AC 880 in which the House of Lords held that occupiers of land are liable for nuisances created by others if they continue or adopt them. 'Continuance' occurs if with knowledge or presumed knowledge of the existence of the nuisance, the occupier fails to take any reasonable means to bring it to an end though with ample time to do so. However, the law makes a distinction between a nuisance caused by a trespasser or a licensee (in which case the landowner is deemed to be in occupation of the land concerned) and nuisance caused by a tenant (in which case the landowner is regarded as having parted with occupation by granting the tenancy). It appears that unless there is neither actual or constructive knowledge of the problematic behaviour emanating from the land, the former can adopt or continue a nuisance by omission (i.e. by leaving the wrongdoers on the land or by failing to exercise its power to turn them out once their habitual misbehaviour became apparent) (*Lippiatt v South Gloucestershire Council* [2000] 1 QB 51). However, the latter can only adopt or continue the nuisance by active participation. The rationale for the distinction is that where the land is occupied by a trespasser or licensee, the landowner nonetheless retains 'possession and control' of it, whereas such possession and control is relinquished by the grant of exclusive possession to a tenant. Why the two scenarios should be treated differently is unclear. If their ability to control and abate the nuisance is the reason why landowners can be held responsible for the nuisance behaviour of those on their land, then landlords too should potentially be liable for the acts of their tenants, given that social landlords in particular have extensive powers to control their tenants' behaviour. For example, the tenancy agreement may expressly allow the landlord to enter and abate the nuisance (Morgan, 2001: 386) and, although the right of possession might not be 'immediate', all of the relevant statutory codes allow for repossession on 'nuisance and annoyance' grounds. By contrast, a licensor's ability to control a licensee is by no means absolute, and the courts may be willing to be prepared to grant both negative injunctions and specific performance (*Verrall v Great Yarmouth Borough Council* [1981] QB 202) to enforce compliance with the terms of a contractual licence (Morgan, 2001: 387).

In *Smith v Scott* [1973] Ch 314, the Smiths, an elderly couple, were the owner-occupiers of a house in an area scheduled for demolition. Lewisham had acquired a number of houses in the same road, using them for the time being as short-term accommodation for homeless families. The authority moved the Scotts (a 'large and unruly family') into the house next door to the Smiths. Finding it impossible to continue to live next to the Scotts, whose behaviour was 'altogether intolerable both in respect of physical damage and of noise', the Smiths went to live elsewhere with relatives. Despite the

Smiths' protests, the authority took no effective steps either to control the Scotts or to evict them. The Smiths sued both the Scotts and the authority, contending that the authority was liable in nuisance, *Rylands v Fletcher* (1868) LR 3 (HL) 330 and negligence.

Regarding *Rylands v Fletcher*, the Smiths argued that the authority had brought onto the land a 'thing' likely to do mischief if it escaped. Pennycuick V-C explained however that 'the person liable under the rule in *Rylands v Fletcher* is the owner or controller of the dangerous "thing"', i.e. normally the occupier rather than the owner of the land. It was explained that a landlord parts with possession in favour of the tenant and could not therefore be regarded as controlling the tenant on property which the landlord still occupied. So far as negligence was concerned, while recognising the extensive development of the law as to duty of care situations having evolved since *Donoghue v Stephenson* [1932] AC 562 and culminating in *Home Office v Dorset Yacht Co Ltd* [1970] AC 1004, Pennycuick V-C declined to hold that any owner of a property owes a duty of care to the neighbours when selecting a tenant. Given that 'the relationship of landowner, tenant and neighbour is . . . of the most widespread possible occurrence' it was felt that 'the introduction of the duty of care in this connection would have far-reaching implications in relation to business as well as to residential premises'.

Turning to the claim in nuisance, the authority knew when it placed the Scotts in the house that they were likely to cause a nuisance but Pennycuick V-C found that the authority had not been actuated by any improper motive in so doing. He reiterated the principle that the person to be sued in nuisance is the occupier of the property from which the nuisance emanates. Referring to *Harris v James* (1876) 35 LT 240, he explained that a landlord is not generally liable for nuisance committed by a tenant unless the landlord has expressly authorised it or it is certain to result from the purposes for which the property is let. Here, the terms of the tenancy expressly prohibited the committing of a nuisance and although the authority knew that the Scotts were likely to cause a nuisance, it could not be said to have authorised it.

Bright suggests that a landlord will not be responsible for the tenant's nuisance merely because there has been some express or implied authorisation. There must also, she says, be a 'sufficient nexus between the tenant's behaviour and [the tenant's] land' (although it is debatable as to whether it is only use of the tenanted land itself which can create an actionable nuisance), this second requirement being the only way satisfactorily to explain the decision in *Hussein v Lancaster City Council* [1999] 4 All ER 125. Here, the claimants were the freehold owners of a shop and residential premises on a housing estate populated largely by local authority tenants, some of whom had, along with other residents of the estate, subjected the claimants for several years to racial harassment, property damage and physical violence. Some, though not all, of the acts of harassment involved groups of people gathering on common parts of the estate, in particular the road outside the claimants' shop. The claimants argued that the council was liable in both negligence and nuisance for failing to take possession proceedings or other appropriate action against those of its tenants, or those living with them, who were responsible. Applying *Smith v Scott*, the Court of Appeal emphasised that landlords do not incur responsibility merely because they could foresee that the tenant might act in a way which causes nuisance to neighbouring occupiers, but only where some kind of authorisation has been given to the tenant to act in that way. In the present case, the claimants' complaint did not relate to the use by the other tenants of the property they had leased, but rather to their general behaviour. Further, given that the council's standard form tenancy agreement required tenants to covenant 'not to discriminate against or harass any resident or visitors', it could not be said that the council had 'authorised' the nuisance behaviour. Moreover, while the acts complained of unquestionably interfered persistently and intolerably with the claimants' enjoyment of their land, they did not involve the tenants' use and occupation of the tenanted property (i.e. they were not acting in their capacity as tenants) and therefore fell outside the scope of the tort.

Loveland advances various ways in which the orthodox principle could be 'stretched' and 'challenged' (Loveland, 2005). He suggests, for example, that there might be liability where the landlord has let the property with the nuisance already on it. Thus, if it allows an introductory tenancy to continue despite the tenant causing a nuisance to neighbours, it will be 'continuing' the nuisance and liable for acts occurring after the secure tenancy starts at the end of the introductory period. Another of his suggestions is that a claimant suffering from noise nuisance might have a remedy against a landlord if the noise emanated from another tenant's activities in the common parts of the premises, e.g. stairwells, lifts, hallways or communal gardens, the landlord having granted tenants only a licence to pass over the area concerned and remaining in actual occupation of them itself.

The possibility of assistance being provided by the Human Rights Act 1998 was touched upon in *Mowan v Wandsworth London Borough Council* (2001) 33 HLR 56. Mrs Mowan had obtained a long lease of her home by exercising her RTB. Wandsworth let the flat above on a secure tenancy to a person who suffered from a severe mental disorder. For more than 10 years, the neighbour had regularly committed nuisances. For example, she blocked her lavatory so as to cause Mrs Mowan's property to flood with sewage, she jumped up and down, and she banged, chanted and moaned late at night pursuant to her activities as a clairvoyant. There was no question that the neighbour's behaviour constituted an actionable nuisance (although there was some doubt as to whether, given her mental condition, a court would grant an injunction) but again the question was whether the local authority could be held to be liable in nuisance for having caused, continued or adopted it. The Court of Appeal held, citing *Smith v Scott* and *Hussain v Lancaster City Council*, that the council was not liable.

While Sir Christopher Staughton acknowledged that the neighbour's conduct was 'certainly a breach of Mrs Mowan's rights and I would hope of her human rights too' he would 'say nothing' as to whether it would be a breach of Art. 8 and, in any case – on the basis that the principles were 'too well-established' – rejected the argument that the court should interpret the common law as providing Mrs Mowlam with an effective remedy against the council. Even if it was unlikely that an injunction would be granted against the neighbour, Mrs Mowlam could pursue an action for judicial review.

Bibliography

Albon, R. and Stafford, D. (1988) 'Rent control: its costly repercussions', 22(1), *Social Policy and Administration*: 10–21.

Alder, J. (1997) 'Obsolescence and renewal: Judicial review in the private sector' in P. Leyland and T. Woods (eds) *Adminstrative Law Facing the Future: Old Constraints and New Horizons*, London: Blackstone Press.

Alder, J. and Handy, C. (2001) '*Donoghue v Poplar Harca*: Housing associations and the Human Rights Act 1998', 4(5), *Journal of Housing Law*: 69–72.

—— (2003) *Housing Associations: Law and Practice*, London: Sweet & Maxwell.

Allen, C. and Sprigings, N. (2001) 'Housing policy, housing management and tenant power in the "risk society": Some critical observations on the welfare politics of "radical doubt"', 21(3), *Critical Social Policy*: 384–412.

Anderson, I. (1999) 'Young single people and access to housing' in J. Rugg (ed.) *Young People, Housing and Social Policy*, London: Routledge.

—— (2004) 'Housing, homelessness and the welfare state in the UK', 4(3), *European Journal of Housing Policy*: 369–89.

Anderson, S. (ed.) (2004) *Mortgage Market Manifesto*, London: CML.

Anon (2003) 'Public procurement PFI in social housing: the way ahead?', 10(11), *Housing Law Monitor*: 2–3.

Archbishop of Canterbury's Commission on Urban Priority Areas (1985) *Faith in the City: A Call for Action by Church and Nation*, London: Church House Publishing.

Audit Commission (2002) *Housing Benefit: The National Perspective*, London: Audit Commission.

—— (2005) *Financing Council Housing*, London: Audit Commission.

Aughton, H. and Malpass, P. (1994) *Housing Finance: A Basic Guide*, London: Shelter.

Bailey, R. and Ruddock, J. (1972) *The Grief Report*, London: Shelter.

Balchin, P. and Rhoden, M. (2002) *Housing Policy: An Introduction*, London: Routledge.

Ball, M. (2004) *The Future of Private Renting in the UK*, London: Social Market Foundation

Ball, M. and Harloe, M. (1998) 'Uncertainty in European housing markets' in M. Kleinman, W. Matznetter and M. Stephens (eds) *European Integration and Housing Policy*, London: Routledge.

Barker, K. (2004) *Delivering Stability: Securing our Future Housing Needs*, London: HMSO.

—— (2006) *Barker Review of Land Use Planning: Final Report – Recommendations*, London: HMSO.

Bates, J. (2005) 'Housing and community care legislation', *Legal Action* 23–4, December.

Belcher, A. and Jackson, V. (1998) 'Housing association governance in Scotland and England', 2, *Juridical Review*: 104–18.

Bengtsson, B. (2001) 'Housing as a social right: implications for welfare state theory', 24(4), *Scandinavian Political Studies*: 255–75.

Benjamin, T. (2002) 'Housing rights of 16- and 17-year olds', 183, *Childright*: 18–20.

Berkovits, B. (1981) 'The family and the Rent Acts: Reflections on law and policy', *Journal of Social Welfare Law*: 83–100.

Berry, F. (1974) *Housing, the Great British Failure*, London: Charles Knight.

Best, R., Kemp, P., Coleman, D., Merrett, S. and Crook, T. (1992) *The Future of Private Renting: Consensus and Action*, York: Joseph Rowntree Foundation.

Blandy, S. (2004) 'Succession to tenancies for same-sex couples: more confusion ahead?', 7(4), *Journal of Housing Law*: 51–5.

Blandy, S. and Robinson, D. (2001) 'Reforming leasehold: Discursive events and outcomes, 1984–2000', 28(3), *Journal of Law and Society*: 384–408.

Bowley, M. (1945) *Housing and the State, 1919–1944*, London: George Allen & Unwin.

Braisby, D., Echlin, R., Hill, S. and Smith, H. (1988) *Changing Futures: Housing and Support Services for People discharged from Psychiatric Hospitals*, London: King's Fund Publishing Office.

Bridge, S. (1988) 'The security of tenure of absent tenants', 52, *The Conveyancer*: 300–5.

—— (1989) *Blackstone's Guide to the Housing Act 1988*, London: Blackstone Press Ltd.

—— (1993) 'Barking up the wrong trees: the charmed existence of protected shortholders', *The Conveyancer*: 238–41.

Bright, S. (2000) 'Leases, exclusive possession and estates', 116, *Law Quarterly Review*: 7–11.

—— (2003) 'Landowners' responsibility in nuisance for anti-social behaviour', *The Conveyancer*: 171–6.

—— (2006a) 'Article 8 again in the House of Lords: *Kay v Lambeth LBC*; *Leeds CC v Price*', *The Conveyancer*: 294–308.

—— (2006b) 'Tolerated trespass or a new tenancy', 122, *Law Quarterly Review*: 48–52.

Bright, S. and Gilbert, G. (1995) *Landlord and Tenant: The Nature of Tenancies*, Oxford: Clarendon Press.

Brown, T. and Yates, N. (2005) 'Allocations and lettings – taking customer choice forward in England?', 5(3), *European Journal of Housing Policy*: 343–57.

Burke, G. (1981) *Housing and Social Justice*, London and New York: Longman.

Burnett, J. (1978) *A Social History of Housing, 1815–1970*, Newton Abbott: David & Charles.

Burney, E. (1999) *Crime and Banishment: Nuisance and Exclusion in Social Housing*, Winchester: Waterside Press.

—— (2002) 'Talking tough, acting coy: what happened to the anti-social behaviour order?', 41(5), *Howard Journal of Criminal Justice*: 469–84.

Burrows, L. and Hunter, N. (1990) *Forced Out!*, London: Shelter.

Burrows, R. (2003) *Poverty and Home Ownership in Britain*, Bristol: The Policy Press.

Buyse, A. (2006) 'Strings attached: the concept of "home" in the case law of the European Court of Human Rights', 3, *European Human Rights Law Review*: 294–307.

Card, P. (2001) 'Managing anti-social behaviour – inclusion or exclusion?' in D. Cowan and A. Marsh (eds) *Two Steps Forward: Housing Policy into the New Millenium*, Bristol: The Policy Press.

Carlton, N., Fear, T. and Means, R. (2004) 'Responding to the harassment and abuse of older people in the private rented sector: legal and social perspectives', 26(2) *Journal of Social Welfare and Family Law*: 131–45.

Carnwath, R. (1978) *A Guide to the Housing (Homeless Persons) Act 1977*, London: Knight.

Carr, H. 'Fulfilling limited expectations: an exploration of the law of disrepair', paper presented at Housing Studies Association Conference on Community, Neighbourhood, Responsibility, Bristol, September 2003.

Carter, D. and Dymond, A. (1998) *Quiet Enjoyment*, London: Legal Action Group.

Central Housing Advisory Committee (CHAC) (1969) *Council Housing: Purposes, Procedures and Priorities*, Report of the Housing Management Sub-Committee, London: HMSO.

Clapham, D., Kemp, P. and Smith, S. (1990) *Housing and Social Policy*, Basingstoke: Macmillan.

Clarke, A. (1983) 'Further implications of section 36 of the Administration of Justice Act 1970', *The Conveyancer*: 293–305.

Clarke, A. and Kohler, P. (2005) *Property Law: Commentary and Materials*, Cambridge: Cambridge University Press.

Cobb, N. (2006) 'Patronising the mentally disordered? Social landlords and the control of "anti-social behaviour" under the Disability Discrimination Act 1995', 26(2), *Legal Studies*: 238–66.

Cole, I. and Furbey, R. (1994) *The Eclipse of Council Housing*, London: Routledge.

Coleman, D. (1996) 'Two cheers for the Act', *Roof*: 10, November/December.

Conservative Party (1974) *Putting Britain First: A National Policy from the Conservatives*, London: Conservative Central Office.

Cowan, D. (1993) 'Local connection and disconnection', 56(2), *Modern Law Review*: 218–24.

—— (1995) 'HIV and homelessness: lobbying, law, policy and practice', 17(1), *Journal of Social Welfare and Family Law*: 43–66.

—— (2001) 'Harassment and unlawful eviction in the private rented sector – A study of law in(-)action', 65, *The Conveyancer*: 249–64.

Cowan, D. and Fionda, J. (1994) 'Back to Basics: the Government's Homelessness Consultation Paper', 57(4), *Modern Law Review*: 610–19.

Cowan, D. and Halliday, S. (2003) *The Appeal of Internal Review: Law, Administrative Justice and the (non)-emergence of Disputes*, Oxford: Hart Publishing.

Cowan, D. and McDermot, M. (2006) *Regulating Social Housing: Governing Decline*, Oxford: Routledge-Cavendish.

Cowan, D. and Marsh, A. (2001) 'New Labour, same old Tory housing policy?', 64(2), *Modern Law Review*: 260–80.

—— (2004) 'From need to choice; *R (A) v Lambeth LBC; R (Lindsay) v Lambeth LBC*', 67(3), *Modern Law Review* 478–90.

—— (2005) 'From need to choice, from welfarism to advanced liberalism? Problematics of social housing allocation', 25(2), *Legal Studies*: 22–48.

Cowan, D., Gilroy, R. and Pantazis, C. (1999) 'Risking housing need', 26(4), *Journal of Law and Society*: 403–26.

Coyle, S. and Morrow, K. (2004) *Philosophical Foundations of Environmental Law: Property, Rights and Nature*, Oxford: Hart Publishing.

Craig, P. (2002) 'Contracting out, the Human Rights Act and the scope of judicial review', 18, *Law Quarterly Review*: 551–68.

Crawford, A. (2003) '"Contractual governance" of deviant behaviour', 30(4), *Journal of Law and Society*: 479–505.

Crook, A. and Kemp, P. (2002) 'Housing Investment Trusts: A new structure of rental housing provision?', 17(5), *Housing Studies*: 741–53.

Crook, T., Hughes, J. and Kemp, P. (1995) *The Supply of Privately Rented Homes: Today and Tomorrow*, York: Joseph Rowntree Foundation.

Dabbs, D. (2004) 'Mortgage shortfalls: drawing the line', 154, *New Law Journal*: 1370–1.

Damer, S. (1980) 'State, class and housing: Glasgow 1885–1919' in J. Melling (ed.) *Housing, Social Policy and the State*, London: Croom Helm.

Daunton, M. (1987) *A Property Owning Democracy? Housing in Britain*, London: Faber.

Davey, M. (1992) 'Rent control: a farewell to fair rents', 14, *Journal of Social Welfare and Family Law*: 497–510.

—— (2001) 'Neighbours in law', *The Conveyancer*: 31–60.

Davis, M. and Hughes, D. (2004) 'An end of the affair – social housing, relationship breakdown and the Human Rights Act 1998', *The Conveyancer*: 19–40.

—— (2005) 'What's sex got to do with it? The ever contentious issue of succession to tenancies', *The Conveyancer*: 318–44.

Deacon, A. (2004) 'Justifying conditionality: the case of anti-social tenants', 19(6), *Housing Studies*: 911–26.

Department for Communities and Local Government (DCLG) (2006a) *Homelessness Code of Guidance for Local Authorities*, London: DCLG.

—— (2006b) *English House Condition Survey 2004*, London: DCLG.

—— (2006c) *Tenancy Deposit Protection: Secondary Legislation*, London: DCLG.

—— (2006d) *The Social Landlords Order 2006 relating to the Provision of Gypsy and Traveller Sites*, London: DCLG.

—— (2007a) '*Housing Statistics*', online. Available HTTP: www.communities.gov.uk/index.asp?id=1155991 (accessed 16 January 2007).

—— (2007b) '*Survey of English Housing Live Tables*', online. Available HTTP: www.communities.gov.uk/index.asp?id=1154799 (accessed 16 January 2007).

Department for Transport, Local Government and the Regions (DTLGR) (2001) *Strong Local Leadership: Quality Public Services*, London: DTLGR.

Department for Work and Pensions (DWP) (2002) *Building Choice and Responsibility: A Radical Agenda for Housing Benefit*, London: DWP.

—— (2003) *Housing Benefit Sanctions and Anti-Social Behaviour: A Consultation Paper*, London: DWP.

—— (2004) 'Housing Benefit and Council Tax Benefit Annual Summary Statistics: May 2004', online. Available HTTP www.dwp.gov.uk/asd/asd1/hbctb/hbctbannualmay04.asp#tables.

Department of the Environment (DoE) (1986) *Housing and Construction Statistics 1975–1985*, London: HMSO.

—— (1987a) *Housing: The Government's Proposals*, Cm 214, London: HMSO.

—— (1987b) *Tenants' Choice: The Government's Proposals for Legislation*, London: HMSO.

—— (1990) *The Government's Expenditure Plans 1990–91 to 1992–93*, Cm 1009, London: HMSO.

—— (1993) *English House Condition Survey 1991*, London: HMSO.

—— (1994) *Access to Local Authority and Housing Association Tenancies: a Consultation Paper*, London: DoE.

—— (1995) *Our Future Homes: Opportunity, Choice Responsibility*, Cm 2901, London: HMSO.

—— (1996a) *Household Growth: Where Shall We Live?*, London: HMSO.

—— (1996b) *Housing and Construction Statistics 1985–1995*, London: HMSO.

Department of the Environment, Transport and the Regions (DETR) (1998a) *Residential Leasehold Reform in England and Wales: A Consultation Paper*, London: DETR.

—— (1998b) *How Local Authorities used the Private Rented Sector Prior to the Housing Act 1996* (Housing Research Summary No 86) London: DETR.

—— (1998c) *Modernising Local Government: Improving Local Services Through Best Value*, London: DETR.

—— (2000a) *Quality and Choice: A Decent Home for All: The Housing Green Paper*, London: DETR.

—— (2000b) *Our Towns and Cities: the Future – Delivering an Urban Renaissance*, London: DETR.

—— (2002) *Tackling Anti-social Tenants: A Consultation Paper*, London: DETR.

Department of Social Security (DSS) (1998) *New Ambitions for Our Country*, London: The Stationery Office.

Dickens, P. (1977) 'Social Change, Housing and the state – some aspects of class fragmentation and incorporation: 1915–1946' in M. Harloe (ed.) *Urban Change and Conflict*, London: Centre for Environmental Studies.

Director-General of Fair Trading (1991) *Unjust Credit Transactions*, London: OFT.

—— (1997) *Non-Status Lending: Guidelines for Lenders and Brokers*, London: OFT.

Dixon, M. (2000) 'The non-proprietary lease: the rise of the feudal phoenix?', 59, *Cambridge Law Journal*: 25–8.

Doling, J. (1984) 'Have the Rent Acts become irrelevant?', 270, *Estates Gazette*: 1148–50.

Doling, J. and Davies, M. (1984) *Public Control of Privately Rented Housing*, Aldershot: Gower.

Donnelly, C. (2005) 'Leonard Cheshire again and beyond: private contractors, contract and s 6(3)(b) of the Human Rights Act', *Public Law*: 785–805.

Donnison, D. and Ungerson, C. (1982) *Housing Policy*, Harmondsworth: Penguin.

Driscoll, J. (1988) 'Rent arrears, suspended possession orders and the rights of secure tenants', 51(3), *Modern Law Review*: 371–7.

—— (1994) 'The Leasehold Reform, Housing and Urban Development Act 1993: The public sector housing provisions', 57, *Modern Law Review*: 788–98.

Dymond, A. (2005) 'Legal update: Housing Law', 102(16), *Law Society's Gazette*: 26.

Engels, F. (1958) *The Condition of the Working Class in England*, Oxford: Oxford University Press.

Englander, D. (1983) *Landlord and Tenant in Urban Britain 1838–1918*, Oxford: Clarendon Press.

Evans, A. (2003) *Local Authority Housing Rent Income: Rent Collection and Arrears Management by Local Authorities in England and Wales*, London: Audit Commission.

Farrand, J. (1978) *The Rent Act 1977. The Protection from Eviction Act 1977*, London: Sweet and Maxwell.

Financial Services Authority (FSA) (2003) 'Mortgages: Conduct of Business Sourcebook', online. Available HTTP: www.fsahandbook.info/FSA/handbook/LI/2003/200371.pdf (accessed 15 January 2007).

Fitzpatrick, S. and Kennedy, C. (2001) 'The links between begging and rough sleeping', 16(5), Housing Studies: 549–68.

Flint, J. (2004a) 'The responsible tenant: housing governance and the politics of behaviour', 19(6) *Housing Studies*: 893–909.

—— (2004b) 'On the new front line: Social housing and the management of "problematic populations"', paper presented at Housing Studies Association Conference on Transforming Social Housing, Sheffield, April 2004.

Flint, J. and Rowlands, R. (2003) 'Commodification, normalisation and intervention: cultural, social and symbolic capital in housing consumption and governance', 18(3), *Journal of Housing and the Built Environment*: 213–32.

Ford, J. (1997) 'Who is most at risk?' in CIH, *Sustainable Home Ownership: The Debate*, CIH and JRF.

Ford, J., Quilgars, D., Burrows, R. and Rhodes, D. (2004) *Homeowners, risk and safety nets: Mortgage Payment Protection Insurance and Beyond*, London: ODPM.

Forrest, R. and Leather, P. (1998) 'The ageing of the property owning democracy' 18, *Ageing and Society*: 35.

Forrest, R. and Murie, A. (1991a) *Selling the Welfare State: The Privatisation of Public Housing*, London: Routledge.

—— (1991b) 'Transformation through tenure: the early purchasers of council houses, 1968–1973', 20(1), *Journal of Social Policy*: 1–25.

—— (1992) 'The right to buy', in C. Grant (ed.), *Built to Last*, London: Shelter.

—— (1995) 'Housing and family wealth in Britain' in R. Forrest and A. Murie (eds) *Housing and Family Wealth: Comparative International Perspectives*, London: Routledge.

Fox, L. (2002) 'The meaning of home: a chimerical concept or a legal challenge?', 29(4), *Journal of Law and Society*: 580–610.

Francis, H. (1971) *Report of the Committee on the Rent Acts*, Cmnd 4609, London: HMSO.

Friedman, M. (1962) *Capitalism and Freedom*, Chicago: University of Chicago Press.

Gauldie, E. (1974) *Cruel Habitations: A History of Working Class Housing, 1780–1918*, London: Allen and Unwin.

Geddes, M. and Martin, S. (2000) 'The policy and politics of Best Value: currents, crosscurrents and undercurrents in the new regime', 28(3) *Policy and Politics*: 379–95.

Gilroy, R. (1994) 'Women and owner-occupation in Britain' in R. Gilroy and R. Woods (eds), *Housing Women*, London: Routledge.

Ginsburg, N. (1989) 'The Housing Act 1988 and its policy context: a critical commentary', 9(1), *Critical Social Policy*: 56–81.

—— (2005) 'The privatization of council housing', 25(1), *Critical Social Policy*: 115–35.

Glastonbury, B. (1971) *Homeless near a Thousand Homes: A Study of Families without Homes in South Wales and the West of England*, London: Allen and Unwin.

Goodchild, B. (2001) 'Applying theories of social communication to housing law: towards a workable framework', 16(1), *Housing Studies*: 75–95.

Goodlad, R. and Atkinson, R. (2004) 'Sacred cows, rational debates and the politics of the right to buy after devolution', 19(3), *Housing Studies*: 447–63.

Gray, K. and Gray S.F. (2005) *Elements of Land Law*, 4th edn, Oxford: Oxford University Press.

Green, H., Thomas, M., Iles, N. and Down, D. (1996) *Housing in England 1994/95*, London: HMSO.

Greve, J. (1991) *Homelessness in Britain*, York: Joseph Rowntree Foundation.

Greve, J., Page, D. and Greve, S. (1971) *Homelessness in London*, Edinburgh, London: Scottish Academic Press.

Hand, C. (1980) 'The statutory tenancy: an unrecognised proprietary interest', 44, *The Conveyancer*: 351–60.

Handy, C. (2004) 'The Private Finance Initiative and housing: an introduction to law and practice', 7(2), *Journal of Housing Law*: 28–32.

Harriott, S. and Matthews, L. (1998) *Social Housing: An Introduction*, Harlow: Longman.

Harwood, M. (2000) 'Leases: are they still not really real?', 20(4), *Legal Studies*: 503–16.

Haworth, A. and Manzi, T. (1999) 'Managing the underclass: interpreting the moral discourse of housing management', 36(1), *Urban Studies*: 153–65.

Henderson, J. and Karn, V. (1984) 'Race, class and the allocation of public housing in Britain', 21, *Urban Studies* 115–28.

Hinojosa, J-P. (2005) 'On property, leases, licences, horses and carts: revisiting *Bruton v London & Quadrant Housing Trust*', *The Conveyancer*: 114–22.

HM Treasury and Inland Revenue (2004) *Promoting More Flexible Investment in Property: A Consultation*, London: HMSO.

—— (2005) *UK Real Estate Investment Trusts; A Discussion Paper*, London: HMSO.

Hoath, D. (1989) *Public Housing Law*, London: Sweet and Maxwell.

Hodges, R. and Grubnic, S. (2005) 'Public policy transfer: the case of PFI in housing', 1(1/2), *International Journal of Public Policy*: 58–77.

Holbrook, J. and Underwood, D. (2004) 'Getting demotion right – part 2', 154, *New Law Journal*: 1224–5.

Holland, Sir Milner (1965) *Report of the Committee on Housing in Greater London*, Cmnd 2605, London: HMSO.

Holmans, A. (1987) *Housing Policy in Britain: A History*, London: Croom Helm.

Home Office (2003) *Respect and Responsibility: Taking a Stand against Anti-social Behaviour*, London: Home Office.

Honore, T. (1982) *The Quest for Security: Employees, Tenants, Wives*, London: Stevens.

Hopkins, N. and Laurie, E. (2006) 'Housing or property? The dynamics of housing policy and property principles in the right to buy', 26(1), *Legal Studies*: 65–87.

House of Commons Council Housing Group (HCCHG) (2005) 'Support for the "Fourth Option" of Council Housing', online. Available www.support4council-housing.org.uk/report/resources/HoCCHGreport.pdf.

House of Commons Home Affairs Committee (HCHAC) (2005) *Anti-social Behaviour: Fifth Report of Session 2004–05* (HC 80-1), London: The Stationery Office.

Housing Corporation (HC) (2001) *Rent Influencing Regime: Implementing the Rent Restructuring Framework*, London: HC.

—— (2004) *New Partnerships in Affordable Housing: A Pilot Investment Programme open to Housing Associations and Unregistered Bodies*, London: HC.

—— (2005) *The Regulatory Code and Guidance*, London: HC.

Housing, Planning, Local Government and the Regions Committee (HPLGRC) (2004) *Decent Homes: Fifth Report, Vol. 1*, HC 46-1, London: The Stationery Office.

Hughes, D. (2000) 'The use of the possessory and other powers of local authority landlords as a means of social control, its legitimacy and some other problems', 29(2), *Anglo-American Law Review*: 167–203.

Hughes, D. and Jones, S. (1978–9) 'Bias in the allocation and transfer of local authority housing: a study of the Commission for Local Administration in England', *Journal of Social Welfare Law*: 273–95.

Hughes, D. and Lowe, S. (1995) *Social Housing Law and Policy*, London: Butterworths.

Hughes, D., Karn, V. and Lickiss, R. (1994) 'Neighbour disputes, social landlords and the law', 16, *Journal of Social Welfare and Family Law*: 201–28.

Hunter, C. (2001) 'Anti-social behaviour and housing – can law be the answer?' in D. Cowan and A. Marsh (eds), *Two Steps Forward: Housing Policy into the New Millenium*, Bristol: The Policy Press.

—— (2003) 'Choice-based lettings and the law', 6: *Journal of Housing Law*, 1–3.

Hunter, C. and Nixon, J. (2001) 'Social landlords' responses to neighbour nuisance and anti-social behaviour: from the negligible to the holistic', 27(4), *Local Government Studies*: 89–104.

Hunter, C., Blandy, S., Cowan, D., Nixon, J., Hitchings, E., Pantazis, C. and Parr, S. (2005) *The Exercise of Judicial Discretion in Rent Arrears Cases*, London: DCA.

Hunter, C., Nixon, J. and Shayer, S. (2000) *Neighbour Nuisance Social Landlords and the Law*, Coventry: CIOH.

Hutter, B. (1988) *The Reasonable Arm of the Law*, Oxford: Clarendon Press.

Ivatts, J. (1988) 'Rented housing and market rents: a social policy critique', 22(3), *Social Policy and Administration*: 197–209.

Jacobs, S. (1981) 'The sale of council houses: does it matter?', 4(3), *Critical Social Policy*: 35–48.

Jew, P. (1994) *Law and Order in Private Rented Housing*, London: Campaign for Bedsit Rights.

Karnavou, E. (1981) 'Defending the council housing system or opposing the sales?', 1(2), *Critical Social Policy*: 50–3.

Kemp, P. (1990) 'Deregulation, markets and the 1988 Housing Act', 24(2), *Social Policy and Administration*: 145–55.

—— (1992) 'The Ghost of Rachman' in C. Grant (ed.) *Built to Last*, London: Roof.

—— (1993) 'Rebuilding the Private Rented Sector?' in P. Malpass and R. Means (eds) *Implementing Housing Policy*, Buckingham: Open University Press.

—— (2000) Housing benefit and welfare retrenchment in Britain', 29(2), *Journal of Social Policy*: 263–79.

Kemp, P. and Leather, P. (2002) *Housing Benefit Reform: Price Incentives*, York: Joseph Rowntree Foundation.

Kilroy, B. (1979) 'Labour housing dilemma', *New Statesman*: 451–3, 28 September.

Kullberg, J. (2002) 'Consumers' responses to choice-based letting mechanisms', 17(4), *Housing Studies*: 549–79.

Langstaff, M. (1992) 'Housing associations: a move to centre stage' in J. Birchall (ed.) *Housing Policy in the 1990s*, London: Routledge.

Lansley, S. (1979) *Housing and Public Policy*, London: Croom Helm.

Latham, R. (2005) 'Allocating accommodation: reconciling choice and need: Part 2', *Legal Action*: 15–19, May.

Laurie, E. (2002) 'The compatibility of introductory tenancies with the Human Rights Act 1998', *The Conveyancer*: 414–20.

—— (2004) 'The Homelessness Act 2002 and housing allocations: all change or business as usual?', 67(1), *Modern Law Review*: 48–68.

Law Commission (1976) *Report on Conspiracy and Criminal Law Reform*, Law Com 76, London: HMSO.

—— (1996) *Landlord and Tenant: Responsibility for State and Condition of Property*, Law Com 238, London: HMSO.

—— (2002a) *Renting Homes 1: Status and Security*, Law Com Consultation Paper 162, London: The Stationery Office.

—— (2002b) *Renting Homes 2: Co-occupation Transfer and Succession*, Law Com Consultation Paper 168, London: The Stationery Office.

—— (2006) *Renting Homes: The Final Report*, London: The Stationery Office.

Leather, P. (2001) 'Housing standards in the private sector' in D. Cowan and A. Marsh (eds) *Two Steps Forward: Housing Policy into the New Millennium*, Bristol: The Policy Press.

Livingstone, S. (1997) 'Article 14 and the prevention of discrimination in the ECHR', 1, *European Human Rights Law Review*: 25–34.

Longmate, N. (1974) *The Workhouse*, London: Temple Smith.

Loughlin, M. (1996) *Legality and Locality*, Oxford: Clarendon Press.

Loveland, I. (1992) 'Square pegs, round holes: the "right" to council housing in the post-war era', 19(3), *Journal of Law and Society*: 339–64.

—— (1996) 'The status of children as applicants under the homelessness legislation – judicial subversion or legislative intent?', 8(2), *Child and Family Law Quarterly*: 89–104.

——— (2003) 'Making it up as they go along? The Court of Appeal on same sex spouses and succession rights to tenancies', *Public Law*: 223–35

——— (2004) 'The impact of the Human Rights Act on security of tenure in public housing', *Public Law*: 594–611.

——— (2005) 'Fixing landlords with liability for the anti-social behaviour of their tenants', *Journal of Planning Law*: 273–82 and 405–18.

Lowe, S. (2004) *Housing Policy Analysis: British Housing in Cultural and Comparative Context*, Basingstoke: Palgrave MacMillan.

Luba, J. (2000) 'Large scale voluntary transfer: not all honey and roses', 4(6), *Landlord and Tenant Review*: 116–18.

——— (2005a) 'Landlords' repairing obligations in the residential sector: Part 1 – liability issues', 9(3), *Landlord and Tenant Review*: 62–7.

——— (2005b) 'Landlords' repairing obligations in the residential sector: Part 2 – remedies', 9(3), *Landlord and Tenant Review*: 96–9.

Lund, B. (2006) *Understanding Housing Policy*, Bristol: The Policy Press.

Lyons, T. (1984) 'The meaning of "holiday" under the Rent Acts', *The Conveyancer*: 286–95.

McAuslan, P. (1980) *The Ideologies of Planning Law*, Oxford: Pergamon Press.

McManus, F. (2003) 'Statutory nuisance: success or failure out of a myth?', 24(1), *Statute Law Review*: 77–90.

Maile, S. and Hoggett, P. (2001) 'Best Value and the politics of pragmatism', 29(4), *Policy and Politics*: 509–19.

Malpass, P. (1992) 'The road from Clay Cross' in C. Grant (ed.) *Built to Last: Reflections on British Housing Policy*, London: Shelter.

——— (2000) *Housing Associations and Housing Policy: A Historical Perspective*, Basingstoke: Macmillan Press Ltd.

——— (2001) 'The uneven development of social rented housing', 16(2), *Housing Studies*: 225–42.

——— (2004) 'Fifty years of British housing policy: leaving or leading the welfare state?', 4(2), *European Journal of Housing Policy*: 209–27.

——— (2005) *Housing and the Welfare State: The Development of Housing Policy in Britain*, Basingstoke: Palgrave Macmillan.

Malpass, P. and Murie, A. (1999) *Housing Policy and Practice*, Basingstoke: Macmillan.

Marsh, A. (1998) 'Processes of change in housing and public policy' in A. Marsh and D. Mullins (eds) *Housing and Public Policy*, Buckingham: Open University Press.

——— (2002) 'Restructuring social housing rents' in D. Cowan and A. Marsh, *Two Steps Forward: Housing Policy into the New Millenium*, Bristol: The Policy Press.

Marsh, A. and Walker, B. (2006) 'Getting a policy to "stick": centralising control of social rent setting in England', 34(2), *Policy and Politics*: 195–217.

Marsh, A., Niner, P., Cowan, D., Forrest, R. and Kennett, P. (2000) *Harassment and Unlawful Eviction of Private Rented Sector Tenants and Park Home Residents*, London: DETR.

Marshall, T.H. (1950) *Citizenship and Social Class and other Essays*, Cambridge: Cambridge University Press.

Martin, J. (1995) *Residential Security*, London: Sweet and Maxwell.

Mauthe, B. (2002) 'The politicisation of social rents' in D. Cowan and A. Marsh (eds) *Two Steps Forward: Housing Policy into the New Millenium*, Bristol: The Policy Press.

Mead, D. (2003) 'Swallowing at the camel, straining at the gnat: the implications of *Mendoza v Ghaidan*', 5, *European Human Rights Law Review*: 501–14.

Merrett, S. (1979) *State Housing in Britain*, London: Routledge and Kegan Paul.

—— (1992) 'Housing legislation and the future of the private rental sectors' in R. Best (ed.) *The Future of Private Renting*, York: Joseph Rowntree Foundation.

Millie, A., Jacobson, J., McDonald, E. and Hough, M. (2005) *Anti-social Behaviour Strategies*, Bristol: The Policy Press.

Ministry of Housing and Local Government (MHLG) (1965) *The Housing Programme 1965 to 1870*, Cmnd 2838, London: HMSO.

Morgan, J. (2001) 'Nuisance and the unruly tenant', 60, *Cambridge Law Journal*: 383–404.

—— (2003) 'The alchemists' search for the philosophers' stone: The status of registered social landlords under the Human Rights Act', 66(5), *Modern Law Review*: 700–25.

—— (2005) 'Rent arrears: the disproportionate effect of administrative delay', 69, *The Conveyancer*: 524–44.

Morison, J. and Livingstone, S. (1995) *Reshaping Public Power: Northern Ireland and the British Constitutional Crisis*, London: Sweet & Maxwell.

Mullen, T. (2001) 'Stock transfer' in D. Cowan and A. Marsh (eds) *Two Steps Forward: Housing Policy into the New Millenium*, Bristol: The Policy Press.

Mullins, D. and Niner, P. (1998) 'A prize of citizenship? Changing access to social housing' in A. Marsh and D. Mullins (eds) *Housing and Public Policy*, Buckingham: Open University Press.

Mullins, D. and Pawson, H. (2005) ' "The land that time forgot"; reforming access to social housing in England', 33(2), *Policy and Politics*: 205–30.

Mullins, D., Niner, P. and Riseborough, M. (1993) 'Large-Scale Voluntary Transfers', in P. Malpass and R. Means (eds), *Implementing Housing Policy*, Buckingham: Open University Press.

Murie, A. (1997) 'Linking housing changes to crime', 31(5), *Social Policy and Administration*: 22–36.

—— (1998) 'Secure and contented citizens? Home ownership in Britain' in A. Marsh and D. Mullins, *Housing and Public Policy*, Buckingham: Open University Press.

Murie, A. and Ferrari, E. (2003) *Reforming the Right to Buy in England*, Birmingham: CURS.

National Audit Office (NAO) (2003) *Improving Social Housing Through Transfer*, London: The Stationery Office.

National Statistics (2004) *Social Trends 34: A Portrait of British Society*, London: The Stationery Office.

National Statistics (2006) *Labour Market Trends*, Vol. 114(5), London: Office for National Statistics.

National Strategy for Neighbourhood Renewal (2000) *Report of Policy Action Team 8: Anti-social behaviour*, London: The Stationery Office.

Nelken, D. (1983) *The Limits of the Legal Process: A Study of Landlords, Law and Crime*, London: Academic Press.

Nicol, A. (1981) 'Outflanking protective legislation – shams and beyond', 44, *Modern Law Review*: 21–39.

Nixon, J., Smith, Y., Wishart, B. and Hunter, C. (1996) *Housing Cases in County Courts*, York: The Policy Press.

Office of the Deputy Prime Minister (ODPM) (2001) *Private Landlords Survey. English House Condition Survey 2001*, London: ODPM.

—— (2002a) *Allocation of Accommodation: Code of Guidance for Local Housing Authorities*, London: ODPM.

—— (2002b) *How to Choose Choice: Lessons from the First Year of the ODPM's Pilot Schemes*, London: ODPM.

—— (2002c) *Tenants Managing: An Evaluation of Tenant Management Organisations in England*, London: ODPM.

—— (2003a) *Sustainable Communities: Building for the Future*, London: ODPM

—— (2003b) *Exploitation of the Right to Buy Scheme by Companies*, London: ODPM.

—— (2003c) *Best Value in Housing and Homelessness Framework*, London: ODPM.

—— (2003d) Guide to Social Rent Reforms, London: ODPM.

—— (2004a) *The Right to Buy and Right to Acquire Schemes, and Voluntary Sales to Social Tenants*, London: ODPM.

—— (2004b) *Guidance on Arms Length Management of Local Authority Housing*, London: ODPM.

—— (2004c) 'Demotion Orders ODPM Factsheet No. 3', online. Available HTTP: www.together.gov.uk/article.asp?c=79&aid=3322#What%20are%20 demotion%20orders?.

—— (2004d) *Housing Transfer Manual: 2005 Programme*, London: ODPM.

—— (2005) *Right to Buy – The Use of Discretionary Powers on Repayment of Discount*, London: ODPM.

—— (2006a) *English House Condition Survey 2004 Headline Report, 2006*, London: ODPM.

—— (2006b) *Housing in England 2003–4*, London: ODPM.

O'Hagan, A. (1999) *Our Fathers*, London: Faber.

Oliver, D. (2000) 'The Human Rights Act and public law/private law divides', 4, *European Human Rights Law Review*: 343–55.

—— (2004) 'Functions of a public nature under the Human Rights Act', *Public Law*: 329–51.

Orbach, L. (1977) *Homes for Heroes: a Study of the Evolution of British Public Housing*, London: Seeley.

Oxley, M. and Smith, J. (1996) *Housing Policy and Rented Housing in Europe*, London: E & F.N. Spon.

Pahl, R. (1975) *Whose City?*, Harmondsworth: Penguin.

Paley, B. (1978) *Attitudes to Letting in 1976*, London: HMSO.

Papps, P. (1998) 'Anti-social behaviour strategies: individualistic or holistic?', 13(5), *Housing Studies*: 639–56.

Pascall, G. and Morley, R. (1996) 'Women and Homelessness: Proposals from the Department of the Environment. I. Lone Mothers; II. Domestic Violence', 18, *Journal of Social Welfare and Family Law*: 189–202, 327–40.

Pawlowski, M. (2002) 'Occupational rights in leasehold law: time for rationalisation', *The Conveyancer*: 550–9.

Pawson, H. and Fancy, C. (2003) *Maturing Assets: the Evolution of Stock Transfer Housing Associations*, Bristol: The Policy Press.

Pawson, H. and Kintrea, K. (2002) 'Part of the problem or part of the solution? Social housing allocation policies and social exclusion in Britain', 31(4), *Journal of Social Policy*: 643–67.

Pawson, H., Flint, J., Scott, S., Atkinson, R., Bannister, J., McKenzie, C. and Mills, C. (2005) *The Use of Possession Actions and Evictions by Social Landlords*, London: ODPM.

Pawson, H., Jones, C., Donohue, T., Netto, G. and Fancy, C. (2006) *Monitoring the Longer Term Impact of Choice-based Lettings*, London: DCLG.

Payne, The Hon. Mr Justice (1969) *Report of the Committee on the Enforcement of Judgment Debts*, Cmnd 3909, London: HMSO.

Prevatt, B. and Sergides, M. (2005) 'Repairs round-up 2005', *Legal Action*: 25–6, December.

Prime, T. (2005) 'Mortgage default, limitation and law reform', *The Conveyancer*: 566–79.

Radford, M. (1988) 'Competition rules: the Local Government Act 1988', 51(6) *Modern Law Review*: 747–67.

Rahilly, S. (2003) 'From the rent stop to a rent allowance: the government's plans to introduce choice and responsibility in housing benefit', 10(3), *Journal of Social Security Law*: 124–35.

Raynsford, N. (1986) 'The Housing (Homeless Persons) Act 1977' in N. Deakin (ed.) *Policy Change in Government*, London: RIPA.

Rhodes, D. (2006) *The Modern Private Rented Sector*, Coventry: CIH.

Rhodes, D. and Bevan, M. (2003) *Private Landlords and Buy to Let*, York: Centre for Housing Policy, University of York.

Richards, J. (1992) 'A Sense of Duty' in C. Grant (ed.) *Built to Last?*, London: Roof.

Robertson, D. (2006) 'Cultural expectations of home ownership: explaining changing legal definitions of flat "ownership" within Britain', 21(1), *Housing Studies*: 35.

Robson, P. and Poustie, M. (1996) *Homeless People and the Law*, London: Butterworths.

Robson, P. and Watchman, P. (1981) 'The homeless persons' obstacle race', *Journal of Social Welfare Law*: 1–15.

Rodgers, C. (1988) 'Making a meal out of the Rent Acts: board, attendance and the protected tenancy', 51(5), *Modern Law Review*: 642–51.

—— (1989) 'Shams, subtenancies and evasion of protective legislation', 53, *The Conveyancer*: 196–204.

Rose, M. (1986) *The Relief of Poverty 1834–1914*, Basingstoke: Macmillan.

Rugg, J., Rhodes, D. and Jones, A. (2002) 'Studying a niche market: UK students and the private rented sector', 17(2), *Housing Studies*: 289–303.

Saunders, P. (1990) *A Nation of Home Owners*, London: Unwin Hyman.

Scanlon, K. and Whitehead, C. (2005) *The Profile and Intentions of Buy-to-let Investors*, London: CML.

Secretary of State for the Home Department (1998) *Fairer, Faster and Firmer- A Modern Approach to Immigration and Asylum*, London: The Stationery Office.

Shelter (1994) Homelessness in the 1990s – Local Authority Practice, London: Shelter.

Siebrits, J. (2005) 'An overview of the national housing and mortgage markets in the UK', *CML Housing Finance*: 1–17. Online. Available HTTP: www.cml.org.uk/cml/ filegrab/pdfpubhf01-2005.pdf.pdf?ref=3261.

Smith, P. (2003) 'Disrepair and unfitness revisited', *The Conveyancer*: 112–25.

Smith, R., Stirling, T., Papps, P., Evans, A. and Rowlands, R. (2001) *The Lettings Lottery*, London: Shelter.

Stedman-Jones, G. (1976) *Outcast London: A Study in the Relationship between Classes in Victorian Society*, Harmondsworth: Penguin.

Stephens, M., Whitehead, C. and Munro, M. (2005) *Lessons from the Past, Challenges for the Future for Housing Policy: An Evaluation of English Housing Policy 1975–2000*, London: ODPM.

Stewart, A. (1996) *Rethinking Housing Law*, London: Sweet & Maxwell.

Stewart, J. (2002) *Building a Crisis: Housing Under-Supply in Britain*, London: House Builders Federation.

Stirling, T. (1994) 'Blast from the Past', *Roof*: 12, September/October.

Stirling, T. and Smith, R. (2003) 'A matter of choice? Policy divergence in access to social housing post-devolution', 18(2), *Housing Studies*: 145–58.

Sylvester, C. (2005) 'Demotion or suspension? Tackling anti-social behaviour through the possession process', 9(1), *Landlord and Tenant Review*: 2–6.

Torgerson, U. (1987) 'Housing: the wobbly pillar of the welfare state' in B. Turner, J. Kemeny and L. Lundqvist (eds) *Between State and Market: Housing in the Post-industrial Era*, Stockholm: Almqvist & Wiksell International.

UK Government (1999) *A Better Quality of Life: a Strategy for Sustainable Development for the UK*, Cm 4345, London: The Stationery Office.

Vincent-Jones, P. (2001) 'From housing management to the management of housing' in D. Cowan and A. Marsh (eds), *Two Steps Forward: Housing Policy into the New Millenium*, Bristol: The Policy Press.

Waite, A. (1981) 'Dodging the Rent Acts', 131, *New Law Journal*: 460–2.

Walker, B. (1998) 'Incentives, choice and control' in A. Marsh and D. Mullins (eds) *Housing and Public Policy*, Buckingham: Open University Press.

Walker, R. (2001) 'How to abolish public housing: implications and lessons from public management reform', 16(5), *Housing Studies*: 675–96.

Watchman, P. (1985) 'Fair rents and market security', 49, *The Conveyancer* 199–216.

Watson, S. and Austerberry, H. (1986) *Housing and Homelessness: A Feminist Perspective*, London: Routledge and Kegan Paul.

Weir, J. (1975) 'Landlords Exploit Rent Act Loopholes', *Roof*: 11–14, October.

Whitehead, L. (1998a) 'The impact of consumerism on the home owner' in D. Cowan (ed.) *Housing: Participation and Exclusion*, Aldershot: Ashgate.

—— (1998b) 'The home-owner: citizen or consumer' in S. Bright and J. Dewar (eds) *Land Law: Themes and Perspectives*, Oxford: Oxford University Press.

Widdison, R. (1982) 'Plugging Loopholes in the Rent Act', *Roof*: 29–31, March/April.

Wilcox, S. (2002) 'Housing benefit and social security' in D. Hughes and S. Lowe (eds) *The Private Rented Sector in a New Century: Revival or False Dawn*, Bristol: The Policy Press.

—— (2005) UK *Housing Review 2005/2006*, Coventry/London: CIH/CML.

Wilkie, M., Luxton, P., Morgan, J. and Cole, G. (2006) *Landlord and Tenant Law*, Basingstoke: Palgrave Macmillan.

Wohl, A. (1977) *The Eternal Slum: Housing and Social Policy in Victorian London*, London: Edward Arnold.

Wood, P. (1991) *Poverty and the Workhouse in Victorian Britain*, Stroud: Alan Sutton.

Zuckerman, A. (1980) 'Formality and the family – reform or status quo', 96, *Law Quarterly Review*: 248–80.

Index